1000

JUDAISM AND CHRISTIAN BEGINNINGS

◆

SAMUEL SANDMEL

NEW YORK

OXFORD UNIVERSITY PRESS

1978

Library of Congress Cataloging in Publication Data
Sandmel, Samuel.
Judaism and Christian beginnings.
Bibliography: p.
Includes index.
1. Judaism—History—Post-exilic period, 586 B. C.-
210 A. D.   2. Christianity—Origin.   3. Bible. N. T.—
Criticism, interpretation, etc.   I. Title.
BM176.S26   296'.09   77-77609
ISBN 0-19-502281-5
ISBN 0-19-502282-3

Second printing, 1980

Printed in the United States of America

In Esteem and Gratitude
To my Cherished Colleague,
Ben Zion Wacholder
Scholar and Friend

PREFACE

What I hope is unique in this book is the range of literatures and religious ideas it covers. There are a reasonable number of reliable books available on Palestinian Judaism. There are fewer on hellenistic Judaism (hellenistic being the term for Greek culture after Alexander the Great and until A.D. 200). There are countless books available on the New Testament and early Christianity. The effort here is to present the relationships of these great streams of materials in a single book.

A lover of scholarship must in our days wonder if the explosion of learning has not yielded a superabundance. So great a flow has there been of books and essays that no one can keep up with it, as the honest scholar admits. The superabundance in part is marked both by an immense quantity of repetitive writings on the same general subject, and also by articles, some enlightening, but some confused and confusing, on minor points, marked by special theories ingeniously designed to solve the unsolvable. This book, in bringing together the literatures of many diverse manifestations of Judaism, some of which are admirably presented in other texts, seeks objectively to present for the general reader a coordinated exposition of a richly complex development.

Objectivity is an ideal. No one truly attains it. One strives toward it, buoyed by extravagant hopes and discouraged by a recognition of personal shortcomings. But religiously committed Jews and Christians are no less capable of dealing objectively with historical material than are secular scholars. This book has no special, subjective purpose. It was written solely to enlighten the reader, and inform the open-minded.

A "popular" book is an oversimplified, over-brief survey designed for him who runs as he reads. This is not a popular book. It is a non-technical one, respecting the intelligence of the reader by confronting him with major matters and their attendant arrays of problems. Abstruse ideas are not shunned; I trust that they receive adequate and clear explanation. I feel that I owe the reader an accurate understanding of some of the genuine historical problems, yet I have felt no sense of obligation to solve those which I consider unsolvable.

I have written for a readership which is essentially without technical training in ancient Hebrew or Greek and without extensive experience in literature inescapably necessary to the task of this book, but, unhappily, not universally known, or even known about. From my classroom experience I know too that there are students tolerably well informed on Palestinian Judaism who are not acquainted with hellenistic Judaism or Christianity, and students informed in New Testament and the Dead Sea Scrolls but not in the Rabbinic literature. There is no ready cure in our time for the demands of specialization which tend to restrict broad study. Hence, only one who has had the privilege of not years, but decades of study can partially escape from a preoccupation with only a single area of the several here dealt with. Even such a person cannot achieve fullest mastery in all this variety. If I were to set forth a claim of some tolerable mastery, it would be in Bible (Old Testament), in hellenistic Judaism, and in New Testament. I am experienced in Rabbinic literature, but am by no means an unqualified expert; I have studied and taught the Apocrypha and the Dead Sea Scrolls, but make no claim of special eminence. The full mastery of all these literatures, and of the scholarly writings about them, are

beyond what one man can achieve in the normal span
of a single life. I have dared to hope that where expertise
has eluded me, responsible competency has not.

But why all this in one book? Because the materials are
interrelated, and in many ways illuminate each other;
aspects seen in isolation can lack an important ingredi-
ent, perspective.

I have had to face an abundance of unsolvable literary
problems, primarily those of proportion, entailing issues
of inclusion and omission. I have deliberately repeated
myself in the Notes, especially those to the Gospels. The
adage is surely true that a young scholar is impelled to
teach more than he knows, but an old one is content to
teach less. I have written a book of moderate size about
Herod; here I allocate to him only a few paragraphs; I
have written a book and several essays on Philo of Alexandria; here I treat him in relatively few pages. I cannot
boast that the proportions here are right, but they have
been weighed and studied.

There are other problems—lesser ones—that can rob
an author of fullest comfort. For example, how shall one
spell Hebrew words in our English alphabet? The minor
winter festival, the "Feast of Lights," can be encountered
as Hanukkah, Hanukka, Chanukah, or Hanukkah—and
even other ways. Depending on whose system of transliteration we adopt, any of the ways of spelling the word is
right. My bent has been toward simplicity; those who
know Hebrew and Greek do not need extravagantly precise ways of transliteration, and the excess of pedantry—
how preposterous the partially learned can be!—surely
should be avoided. I have striven for some consistency,
but confess to having deliberately ruptured it in the case
of words that have achieved a certain currency; it would
be silly to make such words conform to consistency and
thus make them unrecognizable.

An over-all problem remains to be acknowledged with
some concern. It is a manifestation of the usual basic

difficulties surrounding any historical topic: the incompleteness of the sources, and valid anxieties about sources we have. Very often in this account of the rise of Synagogue Judaism and Christianity we first encounter an institution, Jewish or Christian, already rather well developed, and are in the dark about the origin, however much that origin interests us. Striking personalities, like Ezra, Hillel, Jesus, and Paul, often appear in the sources already established in eminence, yet the course of their rise is never revealed, nor can we entirely grasp the whole man. Moreover, some of the inherited documents themselves reveal ancient curiosities about such origins or such people, and go on to provide accounts which are simultaneously fascinating and whimsical.

The Letter of Aristeas,[1] dealing with the first known translation of the Bible into Greek, is perhaps a well-known example of such an intriguing yet questionable source. In Alexandria, during the reign of Ptolemy Philadelphus (283-247 B.C.) the noted royal librarian, Demetrios of Phaleron, informed the monarch that the royal library lacked only one treasure, the Bible of the Jews. Ptolemy authorized Demetrios to procure it. Demetrios invited seventy-two priests, as conversant with Greek as with Hebrew, to come from Jerusalem to Alexandria and there prepare a translation. The priests held a platonic symposium with the monarch, and then proceeded to their chore. So well did they do their work that the resultant Greek version is fully as reliable as the original Hebrew.

A modern historian finds some inescapable difficulties. The Letter of Aristeas so lauds the translation by the seventy-two (for which the Greek word for seventy, Septuagint, became usual) that he comments that faulty translations already in use can now disappear. We do not know for certain what those faulty translations might have been, but the bare mention of them suggests that, despite our having The Letter of Aristeas, we still do not know what the *origin* of the Greek version of the Bible was. Moreover, one can wonder whether the generous royal invitation and the impressive symposium reflect accurate history or only harmless legend. Was the high commendation of the Jewish sacred book a disinterested advocacy by a zealous librarian, or was it a bit of ancient Jewish advocacy, akin to propaganda? If propaganda, by whom and for whom? Was ancient propaganda free of distortion of the facts? and did such possible distortion, if it existed, ever trespass into untruth?

I have deliberately chosen The Letter of Aristeas as an example of frequent problems we shall encounter for the reason that I know of no one whose personal religious commitment hangs on the question of its truth or untruth. But comparable problems arise respecting sources which are still sacred, either to Jews or Christians, or both.

Yet much more important than the admitted difficulties themselves which we will encounter is the end result, which gives scholarship its purpose: That despite the problems, we can grasp the meanings of the institutions and the significance of eminent men even when we cannot always discover their origins. Historians and their readers should be ready to confess ignorance when necessary; we must retain constant alertness to the differences between what is known and what is not yet known. True, we remain in the dark about the origins of the Septuagint, but nevertheless we have come to know a great deal about it once it arose.

In the wealth of what we *do* know about Judaism and Christian beginnings, there is much I have omitted from this work. Some omissions may be regrettable oversight; most, though, as I have said, are deliberate in the effort to keep this volume manageable.

Greatly contributing to the success of this effort is the precise and artistically competent editing by Caroline Taylor of Oxford University Press, and to the capable indexing by Rabbi Benjamin Lefkowitz, who, in an emergency of time, selflessly placed the needs of this book above his own. The reader cannot fail to recognize the skill brought to these important tasks. Only I can truly value the devotion involved.

I am indebted to my close friend Dr. Geza Vermes of Oxford University for various kindnesses respecting the Dead Sea Scrolls. I must once again record my gratitude to my secretary, Mrs. Sam November, who transformed an illegible handwritten manuscript into her usual impeccable typescript.

SAMUEL SANDMEL
Cincinnati, Ohio

CONTENTS

ABBREVIATIONS

Acts	Acts of the Apostles	Heb.	Hebrews
Amos	Amos	Hos.	Hosea
Bar.	Baruch	Isa.	Isaiah
1 Chr.	I Chronicles	Jas.	James
2 Chr.	II Chronicles	Jdt.	Judith
Col.	Colossians	Jer.	Jeremiah
1 Cor.	I Corinthians	Jn.	John
2 Cor.	II Corinthians	1 Jn.	I John
Dan.	Daniel	2 Jn.	II John
Dan. &	Daniel, Bel, and	3 Jn.	III John
Bel.	the Snake	Job	Job
Dan. &	Daniel and	Joel	Joel
Su.	Susanna	Jonah	Jonah
Deut.	Deuteronomy	Josh.	Joshua
Eccles.	Ecclesiastes	Jude	Jude
Ecclus.	Ecclesiasticus or	Judg.	Judges
	the Wisdom of	1 Kgs.	I Kings
	Jesus, Son of	2 Kgs.	II Kings
	Sirah	Lam.	Lamentations
Eph.	Ephesians	Let. Jer.	A Letter of
1 Esd.	I Esdras		Jeremiah
2 Esd.	II Esdras	Lev.	Leviticus
Esther	Esther	Lk.	Luke
Exod.	Exodus	1 Macc.	I Maccabees
Ezek.	Ezekiel	Mal.	Malachi
Ezra	Ezra	Mic.	Micah
Gal.	Galatians	Mk.	Mark
Gen.	Genesis	Mt.	Matthew
Hab.	Habakkuk	Nahum	Nahum
Hag.	Haggai	Neh.	Nehemiah

Num.	Numbers	1 Tim.	I Timothy
Obad.	Obadiah	2 Tim.	II Timothy
1 Pet.	I Peter	Ti.	Titus
2 Pet.	II Peter	Tob.	Tobit
Phil.	Philippians	Wis.	Wisdom of Solomon
Philem.	Philemon	Zech.	Zechariah
Pr. M.	The Prayer of	Zeph.	Zephaniah
	Manasseh	Ant.	The Antiquities of
Prov.	Proverbs		the Jews of
Ps(s).	Psalms		Flavius Josephus
Rest of	The Rest of the	b.	ben or bar, "son"
Est.	Chapters of the	J.E.	Jewish Encyclo-
	Book of Esther		pedia
Rev.	Revelation of John	I. B.	Interpreter's Bible
Rom.	Romans	I. D. B.	Interpreter's Dic-
Ruth	Ruth		tionary of the
1 Sam.	I Samuel		Bible
2 Sam.	II Samuel	Moore	George Foot Moore,
S. of S.	Song of Solomon		*Judaism*
S. of	Song of the Three	R.	Rabbi
Three		War	The Jewish War of
1 Th.	I Thessalonians		Flavius Josephus
2 Th.	II Thessalonians		

A NOTE ON

TRANSLITERATION

Those not knowing Hebrew might be alert to two endings of Hebrew: —ōt/ōth and —āh/ā. The festival of Booths can be Sukko*t* or Sukko*th*. I usually use the "ōt." The legal book can be either Mishnah or Mishna; I use the latter. (The "h" at the end of a Hebrew word came to be unpronounced.) There are two "t's" in Hebrew; once they were different in sound, but they are no longer so; I do not distinguish between them. There are two gutteral "ch's"; I use "h" for the "het," and "ch" for the "chaf." The two sounds for "k," a distinction also no longer observed, will be represented, respectively, by "k" and "q." I do not distinguish between the "d" and "g" with and without the dagesh, but I do between "p" and "b" with or without the dagesh (a Hebraist will understand this; a non-Hebraist can and should ignore it).

Two Hebrew consonants besides the "h" (in Biblical and Rabbinic Hebrew) and "h" (in Rabbinic) lost their sound: The letter *ayin* is represented by the symbol ' and the aleph by the '. But often I omit both, especially in terms that are repeated (for example, I use '*amida* on its first occurrence, but *amida* thereafter).

As to Greek, e represents an epsilon, ē an eta. The chi is represented by "ch," and the xi by an "x."

JUDAISM AND
CHRISTIAN BEGINNINGS

INTRODUCTION

There is a special fascination in the study of Judaism and Early Christianity, both for themselves and even more so for what they came to mean to western civilization.

There had been world empires—the Egyptian, the Assyrian, the Babylonian, the Persian—before Alexander the Great. The Egyptian had moved east and northeast from Africa into Asia; the Assyrian, the Babylonian, and the Persian had moved westward from the east, the Persians even daring to cross from Asia into Europe, there to be repulsed. The conquest by Alexander the Great (356-23) was eastward, from Europe into Asia as far as India, incidentally wresting Judea and then Egypt away from Persia.

Alexander's conquest not only injected Europe into the intercontinental scene, but his conquest differed from that by the Asian and African powers in one notable particular. The previous conquerors had established their units of governance, but had transplanted little of their culture to the subjected lands; by contrast, Alexander and his successors planted Greek colonies throughout the conquered domains. The Greek language and culture spread throughout those areas. In turn the Romans conquered much of what had been within the domains of Alexander and his successors. By these two conquests, the hegemony of Europe over the east was established, and it endured until the rise of Islam in the seventh century, when Christendom then lost North Africa, some of the Balkan peninsula, and some of Spain, but remained the religion of Europe.

The Greeks and Romans, both people and lands, came to be conquered by Christianity, a religion born in tiny Judea. The Christian conquest was not marked by startling military engagements or decisive battles. It was, rather, a slow, pervasive, often painful conquest.

3

Christianity was a Judaism both in its origin and in its basic contours. If it had not happened that the name Christianity became attached to this religion, its essential Jewish nature would not require pointing out. The Judaism of the age of early Christianity was not the religion of the Hebrew Scriptures, but rather the Judaism of an age in which Scripture was already ancient, already a legacy from the bygone past. It was a Judaism into which new institutions and new ideas had come into being.

Diverse historic phenomena had entered in to fashion the Judaism into which Christianity was born. Had there not been the Greek conquest and colonization of Judea, all might have been different. Had there not been a widespread migration of Judeans—the word is ordinarily shortened into "Jews"—into Alexander's territorial conquests, such as Asia Minor, the Balkan and Italian peninsulas, Egypt, and North Africa, all might have been different. The Greek civilization and the Jewish encountered each other both in Judea and outside it. In Judea this Greek culture, though transplanted, was ultimately deliberately rejected. Outside Judea it subtly penetrated into Jewish circles and by some Jews was accepted and even welcomed; aspects of Greek culture, especially its philosophy, were harmonized by Jewish minds of learning and perception with the inherited profundities of Judaism. Minds less learned here and there fashioned what we might arrogantly describe as coarse syncretisms ("blends") of the two, verging on superstition. But what is important beyond any specific details is that as a direct result of Alexander's conquest, Jews, both those in Judea and those outside it, fashioned systems of thought and regimens of practice that transcended the biblical religion of tiny Judea. The eastern Mediterranean world had already been host to a variety of movements, quasi-philosophical or quasi-religious, that had come out of the east; Judaism was one more such eastern religion which entered into the west. It had so entered some two and a half or three centuries before Christianity, which arose in Roman times, and also moved into the west from the east.

This Judaism which, we have said, was not the Judaism of the Hebrew Scriptures is the substance of the concern of this book. A grasp of this Judaism, both in its Judean manifestations and in those which arose in parts of the Grecian world, is the prelude to a grasp of early Christianity and Christianity's ultimate growth and development.

To distinguish this Judaism from that of the Hebrew Bible and of the Temple in Jerusalem, the term "Synagogue Judaism" is here used. (Why this term rather than some others is explained on pp. 13-16.) Earliest Christianity is a direct outgrowth of Synagogue Judaism.

The circumstance that Synagogue Judaism, in the form of Christianity, ultimately became the religion of Europe, is surely one of the most spectacular developments in the recorded events of the past. That the ideas, notions, and practices of relatively few people, and of surely insignificant aspects of the world, were to come to color, dominate, and determine the standards and criteria, sometimes nobly, at times ignobly, of the march of western history is surely of overwhelming importance to anyone concerned with what has happened, or may happen to men. In our time there are those who believe, in all earnestness, that the world has now gone beyond the once dominant Christian tradition and largely turned its back on it. Perhaps this is correct; I think it is an exaggeration. But all the more is it worthwhile to understand what it was and how it arose.

The concern in this book is to describe the formation and consolidation of this unique Synagogue Judaism, both the Jewish and the Christian. The story of the later development, the final chapter, is. very brief, for a full description of that momentous set of occurrences is a task for another time and another hand. Here we deal essentially with what this complex Jewish civilization came to be, rather than with what happened when once it achieved its crystallized form.

PART · 1

· 1 ·

THE ROLE
OF THE BIBLE

The emergence in a civilization of a sacred book results inevitably in consequences that arise with the passing of time: Later generations accord the sacred book a unique authority that implies its eternal wisdom and binding force, and therefore the later generations turn to it for guidance for their own times. The more times change, through the inner economic and social developments or through conquest by foreign powers followed by an occupation of the conquered territories, the more patent is the disparity between the setting described in the holy books and that of the latter generations. But as the centuries roll on, the sense of authority of the sacred books grows in significance.

The view arose among Jews, for example, that surely Moses did not write for his time alone, nor did David, nor Amos, nor Isaiah. Surely they wrote for all ages.

Some passages in ancient books have immutable application for every age, this expressed in fullest clarity: Honor your father and mother; do not steal; do not murder. But other passages pose acute problems. For example, the laws in Leviticus which demand the offering of a variety of animal sacrifices at the Jerusalem Temple became a problem when the Temple was destroyed and this legislation no longer truly viable. Is a proper fidelity to the laws discharged if the intent behind the laws is retained even when the laws themselves are impossible of fulfillment?

Again, do not the words of Amos (about 750 B.C.), rebuking his people for their social unconcern, apply to every age in which social unconcern arises? When Isaiah rebukes the

9

arrogant King of Assyria of 725 B.C. (as occurs in 10.5-15), cannot that rebuke seem to apply to an arrogant Seleucid king or a Roman emperor? Does "Assyrian" mean in a limited sense the monarch of 725, or can "Assyrian" mean almost any arrogant monarch of any time?

Was the hope in Isaiah 11.1-9—that there would emerge a "shoot of the stock of Jesse," on whom the spirit of God would rest, so that he would judge not by what his eyes would see or his ears hear, but in righteousness and justice—limited to one single person of one single age? Or could that hope be recapitulated more than once, and be related to someone of a quite different age?

The Bible seemed to apply to all ages, whether clearly as in the case of the laws against theft and murder, or in the no longer feasible laws of sacrifice, or in the rebuke by Amos, or in the hope expressed in Isaiah. As the Bible was read and studied, fertile minds discerned from clear passages a direct application, or inferred applications from less clear ones, or ingeniously drew applications by investing passages with meaning or nuances not truly in the text. On the one hand, then, the Bible led irresistibly to the intuitive or studied application of the ancient message to later times; on the other, those later ages, confronted by the anxieties or enigmas of living, could turn to the Bible with the hope and intention of finding there a word of comfort or a resolution of what, without the Bible, could seem beyond understanding.

In the age with which we are concerned, the Tanâch, that is, the Old Testament, had already come to be both the book which demanded study for general knowledge and the book to look things up in for answers to specific questions. This double function of the Tanach lies behind all the literature we deal with: Apocrypha, Pseudepigrapha, Qumran, Philo, Josephus, Rabbinics, and New Testament.

As in our day there are poets and laborers, artists and farmers, fortunate rich men and the unhappy poor, whose personal concerns vary as men vary from each other, so in that period there were diverse people with diverse minds and diverse preoccupations. As a result, despite the common view that the Bible was the source of all knowledge and guidance, individuals and groups in using the Tanach followed the bent of their particular prepossessions. The man who dreaded the power of Rome sought assurance from Scripture that his travail would end; the man who wondered what new laws were needed for his time sought a basis in Scripture for a derivative new law. The particular interest of two such men could lead them to quite diverse parts of Scripture (as between the Prophets and the Mosaic laws), but we must never lose sight of the devotion to the Mosaic laws of the man whose bent was the Prophets, or the devotion of the legal-minded person to the Prophets. Four works we shall see in greater detail may illustrate this matter of a particular interest: The Antiquities of the Jews by Josephus uses the Bible in a historical bent, giving only relatively little attention to what we might call religion or theology. IV Ezra is preoccupied with the problems of God's justice, and of what is to happen at the end of time, this latter being revealed in a series of visions which utilize the language and content of Scripture in the exposition of what the future was to bring; neither past history nor the Laws of Moses enter directly into the purview of the book. The Wisdom of Solomon is a plea for the recognition of wisdom-revelation as a sure guide in avoiding the horrible trespass of idolatry and in the attainment of the rewards of well-being and immortality by the righteous; it provides a review of history to illustrate the part that wisdom had played in the Israelite past. The Wisdom of Solomon lacks the concern for the future found in IV Ezra, and expresses little direct attention to the Laws of Moses. The Rabbinic literature focuses almost entirely on the Laws of Moses, and exhibits little or no concern for the future and very little direct attention to "wisdom" as this is found in the Wisdom of Solomon.

Accordingly, though the Bible is the basis for all these works, the use of it varies in accordance with the prepossessions of the users. But not only is there variation in the manner of the use; in addition, the varying users can and do exhibit viewpoints, attitudes, and conclusions that reflect striking differences, some of which extend to irreconcilable antitheses. That the Bible is the common base does not at all mean that the inferences from it are inevitably common; quite the contrary.

Such differences or antitheses can be matters of substance; for example, what we might call the "doctrine of the Messiah" is not the same in IV Ezra and in Rabbinic literature. But an additional and important, subtle factor is the difference in emphasis. Even if the "doctrine of the Messiah" were identical in IV Ezra and Rabbinic literature, the observation is necessary that the doctrine is central in IV Ezra and relatively peripheral in Rabbinic literature.

To speak of Judaism in the age in which we deal is as difficult as it would be to speak of Americanism in the United States from 1930 to 1940. There was a depression in the 1930's, with debates as to whether the federal government or the states should meet the crises of unemployment and poverty. Various programs were adopted in Washington, some of which were declared unconstitutional by the Supreme Court; thereafter President Roosevelt made an unsuccessful effort to enlarge the Court so that the appointment of more Justices could provide a majority of liberals congenial to Roosevelt's programs. Roosevelt was a Democrat; the Democratic party during his terms in office included Northern urban liberals and radicals, and also Southern rural conservatives. The rise of Hitler in Europe and the outbreak of war resulted in a sharp division between "isolationists" and "interventionists." In the same period, labor unrest resulted in the rise of two opposing groups: the American Federation of Labor, which favored unions on the basis of the craft of workers (that is, carpenters or metalsmiths), and the Congress of Industrial Organizations, which favored industry-wide unions (for example, automobile unions, which would include both carpenters and metalsmiths).

A description of Americanism in that period would necessarily reflect a great diversity. Only if America were compared with Soviet Russia or Hitler's Germany would the perception arise that underlying the American diversity was a series of cohesive themes which significantly marked off America from both Russia and Germany. So too in ancient Judaism the admitted diversity paradoxically existed against a background of cohesive themes which marked Judaism off from paganism and pagan religion. The parties known as Sadducees and Pharisees had antithetical views on significant issues, but the antitheses arose from a common basis—namely, the divine origin of the Bible. The issues between

Pharisees and Sadducees were, accordingly, different from those between Jews and pagans.

The varieties in Judaism, and the lack of a single attitude toward some matters of consequence, have led to a complicated issue in the history of the scholarship on Judaism. A German scholar, Wilhelm Bousset, wrote a work whose translated title is "The Religion of Judaism in the New Testament Age." That portrait of Judaism, a disparaging one, had been composed with scant regard for Rabbinic religion and an almost total disuse of Rabbinic literature. It was therefore sharply criticized by a Jewish scholar, Felix Perles. Bousset wrote a reply in self-justification, arguing that Apocrypha and Pseudepigrapha (which he had used) reflected "popular piety," whereas Rabbinic literature reflected the learned and the elite. In an article in the *Harvard Theological Review* of 1921, an American, George Foot Moore, in "Christian Writers on Judaism," took Bousset to task for a variety of faults which Moore thought his book contained, but especially for the neglect of the Rabbinic literature. Moore made the point that Christians, not Jews, had preserved Apocrypha and Pseudepigrapha, and hence Bousset had used literature which Judaism had not perpetuated, and had avoided the literature Jews had preserved. To the religious content of the Rabbinic literature Moore gave the name "normative" Judaism. By implication the religious content of the Apocrypha and especially of the Pseudepigrapha was marginal or peripheral. Especially non-normative was the religious content of Graeco-Jewish writers such as Philo of Alexandria.

This supposition of the need to separate the strands of Judaism into normative and non-normative on the part of Moore was a reaction, or overreaction, to the scholarship of people like Bousset.

But still another facet of the matter needs to be considered. The scholarly inquiry on the part of Christian scholars into Judaism was motivated not so much by an interest in Judaism itself as in recovering the Jewish background of the birth and origin of Christianity. The ancient Christian writings presuppose the Jewish origins of Christianity and also set forth the conviction that Christianity was a religious entity superior to the Judaism into which Christianity was born. Accordingly, Christian scholars faced the need both to describe Judaism and also to present specifications of the ways in which Christianity was to be deemed superior to Judaism. It is understandable that partisans among Christian scholars approached this latter need by the device, often unconscious, of so interpreting, or misinterpreting Judaism, as to increase their contrast between a deficient Judaism and a perfect Christianity. Two main themes became rather standard in such scholarship. One theme, derived from the Gospels, was the presentation of Jesus as a Jew at odds with an ignoble Jewish environment. The second theme, derived from the Epistles of Paul, in which the great apostle stresses what to him were the inadequacies in the Mosaic Law as compared with Christian freedom from it, led such partisans to depict Judaism as a religion in which a single motif, fidelity to the Law, had created a debilitating entity, namely, Pharisaism, and Pharisaism's successor, Rabbinic Judaism. In his "Christian Writers on Judaism," Moore noted that the usual theme in early Christian literature was an emphasis on the continuity of Christianity with Judaism; the theme in many a modern partisan study has been that of discontinuity, with the contention that though Jesus and Paul had been Jews, the clue to understanding them is to recognize them as over and against the Judaism of their time. Jewish scholars tended to reply by idealizing the Pharisees even beyond the prudent yield of the documents. That is to say, the difficulties inherent in the modern study of ancient documents have been compounded by regrettable aspersions and defensive retorts.

Value judgments are inescapable in scholarship. The author owns up to an aversion to the apocalyptic writings; some themes in Philo are not to my personal taste. But if value judgments are inescapable, they are nevertheless susceptible of some restraint. Surely, a value judgment which precedes disciplined study is different from one which ensues from it. And surely a value judgment which arises from a modern prepossession ought not be recklessly superimposed on the ancient writings. A modern personal aversion to ancient apocalyptic writings ought not impede an effort to grasp the meaning and significance of those writings for the time in which they were written, and a distaste for some themes in Philo ought not obstruct a comprehension of what Philo was saying, and why.

The varieties of Judaism in the age with which we deal pose problems of balance and reliability in a modern exposition. Insufficient awareness of the *varieties* can lead to untenable generalizations. But it is *Judaism* of which there are varieties, and it is necessary to understand and emphasize this point. Pharisees and Sadducees quarreled within the framework of a common Judaism; those who wrote apocalypses and those ancients who came to frown on those apocalypses came out of a common Judaism. The methodological error which can arise is that of attributing total difference to what is in reality a restricted difference. In religion, divisiveness is often the product of only a limited concern, or a small number of concerns, while at the same time there abides an area of commonly held assumptions. Quarrels about the Jewish calendar, for example, centered on how to arrive at the proper date for observing a holy day, not on the question of the propriety of that holy day; quarrels about the procedure for lighting candles on the festival of Hanukkah centered on whether one should observe the eight nights of lighting by beginning with one candle and ascending to eight, or by beginning with eight and descending to one, but there was no quarrel about the substance of lighting candles. Quarrels about divorce focused on what were the legitimate grounds, not on whether or not divorce was admissible (though in Paul and in the Gospels the desire to make divorce inadmissible is attested; but even here the point of departure is the admissibility of divorce). There was then, despite internal differences, a broad and common Judaism.

I have deliberately chosen to play down such terms as normative and non-normative in relationship to Palestinian varieties of Judaism, simply because these terms, and the ideas they stand for, seem to me to obstruct understanding. Even while avoiding those terms, I have nevertheless consciously tried to reflect some sense of the varieties within Judaism. In speaking of Palestinian varieties, it is to prepare the way for a distinction, which affects the structure of this book, between Palestinian and Hellenistic Judaism. Even there, however, it is a *Judaism* which emerges in a Hellenistic form that in some ways is distinctive from the Palestinian.

I have used as the over-all term for my purposes Synagogue Judaism. Others have spoken of Pharisaic Judaism, or Rabbinic Judaism, or both. No term is completely satisfactory, for valid objections can be raised against all or any. Against Pharisaic-Rabbinic Judaism the objection can be raised, first, that much in the unfolding of Pharisaism is obscure, contradictory, and disputed in modern scholarship; second, it is difficult to the point of impossibility of so tracing the connections between Pharisaism and Rabbinic Judaism so as to know where the one ends (if it does) and the other begins.

By Synagogue Judaism I shall mean the array of developments and phenomena which are different in character, quality, and tone from the biblical religion as it centered in the Temple in Jerusalem, presided over by hereditary priests, under a high priest, and expressed primarily in the offering of animal sacrifices. Temple Judaism, then, was the established cult; Synagogue Judaism was what was thought and practiced outside that established cult. The established cult came to an end in 70 A.D. when the Romans destroyed the Temple. Synagogue Judaism, which arose long before 70, survived 70, and has survived to our day.

Manifestly, Synagogue Judaism was never monolithic. As I use the term, it encompasses the visions of the apocalyptists, the idiosyncrasies of the Qumran community, and the acute legal disputes of the various Rabbinic sages. The diversities within Synagogue Judaism included matters of theological differences, messianic entanglements, and divergencies respecting details of inferences about laws and practices. Granted these diversities, there is nevertheless a viable distinction between the cult of the Temple at Jerusalem and the Judaism outside and beyond that cult.

The Temple cult was operative (until destroyed) in the Temple compound, a restricted area of Jerusalem. Synagogue Judaism existed in Galilee, in Damascus, in Alexandria, in Rome, in Babylon. It encompassed, at one extreme, those who exercised a rigorous fidelity (as in the Academy of the Sage Shammai) and, at the other extreme, the marginal groups who blended together Judaism and paganism (as in the so-called cult of Sabazios). It included the moral precepts of the preserved tractate, The Chapters of the Fathers, and also the magical papyri recovered in the nineteenth century. It included the legalistic interpretations of an Akiba and the antithetical conclusions of a Paul.

To restate this in terms of history, after the Babylonian Exile (587-39 B.C.) a relatively tiny community came into being in Judea, about 534, along with those Judeans who remained in Babylonia. After Alexander the Great, Judeans spread throughout the then known civilization, in ever-increasing numbers. In the age of Jesus, the Jews outside Judea outnumbered those in Judea, the proportions being five to one, or even ten to one. Some have inferred that at that time Jews represented as much as one-tenth of the population of the Roman Empire.

The Bible was the adhesive that held the Jews together, that fed and nurtured their loyalty to the notion of being Jewish, and provided them with the basis from which they inferred their own understandings of what God and man and events meant. Without the Bible they would have surely disappeared, and quickly. With it, they preserved both their ethnic sense and their developed ways of living.

In Judaism the Bible was bequeathed in three divisions, the Torah (that is, the Five Books of Moses), the Prophets, and the [Holy] Writings. A sacred scripture ensues when writings already in circulation come to be collected, assessed for sanctity, and then elevated into Scripture. The three divisions are presumed to represent three chronological stages— that is, first the Torah, surely by 450 B.C., then the Prophets (and Psalms) by 100 B.C., and lastly the Writings, but no precise date can be given for the last, though the date of A.D. 90 and the place Jamnia are often suggested. For the process of collection and selection, Christians use the term "canonization," that is, the final determination of which writings are sacred and which not. There is no comparable Jewish term. Rabbinic sources discuss whether a particular writing should or should not be included in the Bible under the strange issue of whether or not a writing "defiles"[1] the hands; a book admissible to the Bible does, a book not admissible does not. But the precise import of "defile" is not readily to be explained.

It must be clear that a book admitted into the canon was older than the age of its admission; canon is the end of a process, which began with the writing, and at the time of the writing of a particular book it was not automatically "canonical." We know almost nothing of the process by which the canonical status was determined; we know only the end results. Jamnia and 90 are a convenient way of alluding to the completion of the canon of the Hebrew Bible. The Jewish Greek Bible contains some fourteen writings which did not become part of the Hebrew Bible. We know nothing at all of the process by which the Jewish Greek Bible came to canonization. The ancient Rabbis counted the books in the Hebrew Bible as twenty-four,[2] reckoning the twelve "minor" prophets as one, and the same with I and II Samuel, I and II Kings, I and II Chronicles, and Ezra-Nehemiah; a modern count would be thirty-nine.

If some books were included in the Bible, it follows logically that some were not; the Rabbinic term for the excluded works is "outside books." But as we shall see, the Jewish sages in effect rewrote the Bible,[3] in that what the Bible had come to mean, not what the Bible had actually meant, was their real concern. On the destruction of the Temple in 70, the regulations for Temple sacrifices were so interpreted as to mean comparable prayer-periods (without sacrifices) in the Synagogues. The penalty for an "eye for an eye" had come to mean an adequate monetary payment. Father Abraham, in leaving Ur, had migrated, as some had it, from contemporary idol-worship, or, as others had it, from atheistic astrology; Father Abraham was as much a contemporary Jew as he was the ancient progenitor of the people. The Bible of modern scholars, whether Jewish, Catholic, or Protestant, is the Bible in its original, in its pristine ancient meaning. The Bible of the Synagogue was very different. In the Synagogue the Bible was alive and contemporary. Did Synagogue Judaism find meanings in the Bible which modern scholars in good conscience need to say are not there? Of course it did! Indeed, our task in part is to see just what the understanding of the Bible in the Synagogue, and then in the Church, was. However much it may seem to us today that those whom we shall study strayed from the Bible, from their own perspective they did not stray even an inch.

· 2 ·

HISTORICAL
BACKGROUNDS
AND AN
HISTORICAL RÉSUMÉ

At what point do we begin? Surely in the latter part of the age of the *Tanách* ("the Bible[1]"), at what is ordinarily called the post-exilic period. The Babylonians had conquered Jerusalem in 597 B.C., and destroyed the Temple there in 587. They had exiled to Babylon the king, the court, and the upper classes. In 539, Cyrus the Persian had in turn conquered the Babylonians. He permitted the exiles to return to Judea, and many did so.

Ordinarily, the end of the exile is dated about 520. Traditionally,[2] its length is viewed as 70 years. About 517 or 516, through the spurring of the prophets Haggai and Zechariah, the returnees to Jerusalem rebuilt the Temple.

The ruler of Judea was then a governor, called in Persian a *peḥá*. How much self-government the returned Judeans were allowed is largely uncertain. Kingship was not restored, but apparently some comparable political office was held by one Zerubbabel,[3] regarded as a descendant of King David.[4] Alongside him, as part of a two-man rule, was the priest Joshua ben Jehozadak. (*Ben* is Hebrew for "son of"; the word is *bar* in Aramaic.) The relevant biblical texts about these men are most laconic. Moreover, Zerubbabel in some way fell into marked disfavor. In Zechariah 4 there intrudes into the context (as a consequence of a copyist's error of displacement) these rebuking words: "Say to Zerubbabel, 'Not by power or by might, but by My spirit,' says the Lord." We do not know what Zerubbabel did to call forth this rebuke. In Zechariah 6 there is evidence of some deliberate tampering with the text, for the passage seems to be describing the manner in which a "secular" person, together with the High Priest Joshua, would share the rule over Judea, with each wearing a crown and with the two of them exhibiting mutual harmony. The conclusion that the passage has been tampered with rests on the observation that two authoritative persons are clearly under discussion, but only one of them is named, yet vestiges abide in the passage of "*two* crowns" and of concord "between *them*."

Probably the solution occasionally offered for this problem is correct—namely, that Zerubbabel disappointed some unknown expectations, possibly of self-government, this to be attained by a revolt that failed, and he was then stricken out of Zechariah 6 by a disillusioned "editor." At any rate, the ruling authority seems to have fallen solely to the priest Joshua.

We lack for the post-exilic period the kind of consecutive historical account which the books of I and II Samuel and I and II Kings provide for the pre-exilic. The absence of a consecutive historical account is a lamentable impediment to our vision, for this period provides the background developments which were influential or even determinative in our topic. The surviving sources for narrative history (Ezra, Neh., 1 and 2 Chr.) provide many enigmas respecting the period of Persian domination (539-323). A chief puzzle, literary as well as historical, concerns both the books of Ezra and Nehemiah and also the men themselves. The literary problem is that imbedded in Nehemiah's first-person account of his accomplishments is the sudden intrusion of a third-person account about Ezra (Neh. chs. 8-9). The historical problem is this: Were the two men roughly contemporaries, with Ezra slightly preceding Nehemiah? Or are those modern scholars right who contend that Nehemiah actually preceded Ezra, Nehemiah returning to Jerusalem about 450 B.C. and Ezra about 390?

For our purposes, little is at stake in alluding to such problems, now well worn in the history of scholarship. The chief gain to us is to underscore how relatively little we know about the events of the post-exilic age until we come to the Maccabean period, which begins roughly about 168 B.C. That the Persian empire was conquered by Alexander the Great in 323 meant that Judea fell to the Greeks, but no surviving Jewish source provides any direct account of Alexander's conquest of Judea.

Passages in the Books of Ezra and Nehemiah disclose some of the vicissitudes in the Persian period which beset the Judean community, restored to its ancestral homeland, especially poverty and economic dislocations. These difficulties were increased through the hostilities between the Judeans and the Samaritans, and even though some aspects of these hostilities present enigmas, it seems reasonably clear that these two peoples espoused that kind of animosity possible only when communities have much in common and fall out over a restricted amount where they differ. From the Judean point of view (inherited from 2 Kgs. 17.24-41) the Samaritans were, like the Judeans, worshipers of Yahve, the Hebrew deity, but genealogically they were descended from Gentile peoples moved westward into the northern area by the Assyrians at the time the conquered ten tribes of Israel were moved eastward (about 722/21). The Judeans regarded the Samaritan worship as improper, for it was a mixture of Yahvism and the transplanted eastern religions. From the Samaritan viewpoint, on the other hand, they were as fully accredited as the Judeans themselves, and they were quite unwilling to accept a subordinate status. Whatever the origin, the bare fact of a mutual or Judean-Samaritan hostility persisted for centuries. Not only the Samaritans but other kindred peoples were both near at hand and also a source of constant discomfiture to the Judeans.

The post-exilic period, though its events are so little known to us, appears to have been an epoch of great literary activity. During this period books such as Psalms and Proverbs were compiled (that is, older literary legacies were assembled into younger collections) and were edited, and works such as Ruth, Jonah, and Ecclesiastes were composed.

I and II Chronicles were written in this age. In one sense Chronicles is a rewritten version of the substance of Samuel-Kings. It compressed some of the older material; it omitted much; it added to the Samuel-Kings account materials emphasizing the role of priests. Thus, the account of Solomon's dedication of the Temple in I Kings 8 makes no mention of the participation of priests; the account in Chronicles, on the other hand, relegates Solomon himself to a much smaller role than what is his in Kings, with the principal parts of the ceremony now attributed to priests. Chronicles, moreover, presents a picture of a highly organized ecclesiastical system, specifying the difference in levels among Priests and Levites, and the lower orders of workers such as musicians, hewers of wood, and drawers of water. The ordinary view of modern scholars is that in Chronicles the ecclesiastical organization which arose in the latter part of the post-exilic period was anachronistically read back into the times of David and Solomon, thereby giving the sanction of antiquity to the ecclesiastical system of the post-exilic period. This ecclesiastical organization (1 Chr. ch. 24) provided for twenty-four ma'ama-dôt ("stations"), priestly teams who took turns in serving in the Temple at Jerusalem.

The material in Chronicles, then, presupposes a Temple and an ecclesiastical organization already extant in the time of David and Solomon. But where was the ultimate sanction for the Temple and the well-organized priesthood, and what was the proof of its legitimacy? That sanction and proof were to be found within the Pentateuch.

Modern scholarship and religious tradition, normally quite apart from each other, indirectly approach a sort of agreement on the following matter: The passage in Nehemiah 8, centering on Ezra, describes an assembly of the populace in the wide gate area of Jerusalem. To those assembled Ezra read from what is described as "the book of the Torah of Moses." Jewish tradition utilized this passage as a basis for attributing to Ezra the great achievement of recalling to the people the ancient Torah of Moses which had "come to be forgotten." This attribution to Ezra, free of all doubt about the Mosaic authorship of the Pentateuch, could arise only from the observation that much of the Hebrew literature, such as Judges, Samuel, Kings, Proverbs, and most of the Psalms, lacks direct allusion to the Pentateuch; reasonably, then, Moses' book had come to be forgotten until the great Ezra had returned to Judea from Babylon to call it to mind.

As for modern scholarship, for well over a century and a half it was held that the Pentateuch as a totality dates from approximately the age of Ezra. More specifically, the ordinary scholarly view had supposed that older materials, identifiable as the J, E, and D "sources," had been preserved and gathered, and then incorporated, into a new encompassing document, the so-called Priestly (P) Code. This latter drew its nineteenth-century name from its dominant interest in the priesthood. The P Code, believed by scholars to have been written in the age of Ezra,[5] gave an account of the origin of the prevailing ecclesiastical system of that late age. But it asserted that in the Wilderness period a precursor to the Temple in the form of an elaborate portable sanctuary, the Tabernacle, had been built, and equipped with the paraphernalia enjoined by the Deity. Aaron, the brother of Moses, had been designated the first hereditary High Priest, and had been inducted into office (Lev. chs. 8-9). The priestly line was a family within the tribe of Levi, a tribe which had been so zealous in punishing the Israelites for their worship of the Golden Calf (Exod. 32.25-29) that it ceased to be a tribe like the others and became instead the body of ecclesiastical workers. The Priestly Code, and through it the Five Books of Moses, accounted for the origin and legitimacy of the ecclesiastical system arising in the Persian part of the post-exilic period.

The Priestly Code was also the last step, and, indeed, the decisive one, in the creation of the Pentateuch. Modern scholars attribute the preservation of the J and E codes to their utilization by the P author, for no trace of the J or E codes has survived separately. As to the D code, modern scholars speak of the "Deuteronomic history" (Deut., Josh., Judg., Sam., and Kgs.), a long chain of writings which lengthened through addition and extension over a period of centuries. The P "author," so it is often now held, detached the Book of Deuteronomy from the Deuteronomic writings and incorporated it into his compilation by moving the account of the

death of Moses from the end of Numbers (where it is alleged
to belong) to the end of Deuteronomy.

Whatever the elusive facts may be—namely, whether the
Pentateuch goes back to Moses, or emerged in the time of
Ezra (I personally incline to the modern scholarly view)—
it must be stated clearly, and beyond all misunderstanding,
that the most important event in biblical history is the Bible
itself, and, within the Bible, the writing of the Five Books of
Moses.

If the purpose of the composition of the Five Books was
primarily, or at least largely, to legitimize the Temple and
the Priesthood, its effect went quite beyond that one purpose.
Most important of all is that the sacred book, having once
emerged, was destined in time to rival in sanctity the holy
Temple itself. Moreover, since within the Pentateuch there
was the persistent theme that no Temple other than that at
Jerusalem was ever to be built, or if built, was ever to be
legitimate, the loyalty of Jews to the Temple was directly
strengthened by the Pentateuch. As Jews scattered throughout the Mediterranean world in increased numbers after the
conquest by Alexander the Great, they could neither trans-
port the Temple to the new places of settlement nor build a
temple there. What they could do, and did, was to take the
Book with them. The loyalty of the scattered to the Temple
abided; it was heightened and idealized by distance, and the
three pilgrim festivals (*Sūkkôt*, "booths" in early fall, *Pésaḥ*,
"passover" in early spring, and *Shāvúôt*, "weeks" in late
spring) drew countless worshippers to the holy city. But
since it is in the nature of men to wish for something near at
hand as well as for something remote, Scripture served as
the means for eliciting the ongoing Jewish loyalty. From the
vantage point of today we can see that Temple and Scripture
entered into a deep rivalry, though it is not at all to be asserted that this sense of rivalry was ever felt in the time with
which we deal. On the contrary, indeed, the sanctity of the
Temple was derived from the sacred Pentateuch.

If we try the impossible—namely, of giving a precise date
for the writing or at least for the completion of the Pentateuch—we should follow a loose scholarly consensus and
place it between 450 and 375 B.C. In the years subsequent to
its completion, the Pentateuch rose to authoritative emi-

nence; it was copied and it was circulated. How this occurred we do not know; we only know that it happened.

As we saw, the Letter of Aristeas described the translation of the Pentateuch into Greek to the year 250 B.C. Alexander had wrested Judea from the Persians between 334 and 323. That is, within seventy-five years after the Greeks first acquired Judea, Jews spread into the Greek world, drawn there by economic quests. They solved the problem of their abiding devotion to Scripture, and the reality of their having forgotten the ancestral Hebrew, by having Scripture rendered into the Greek language. Jews, whether in Athens or Alexandria, could now read Scripture and adulate it as holy, right where they lived and in their adopted language.

Similarly, within Palestine, however much nearer to Jerusalem Beersheba might be than Alexandria in Egypt, or Jaffa than Rome, a natural desire for something local existed, and Scripture served the purpose of satisfying a local impulse within Palestine quite as much as it did outside Palestine. It was Scripture, and only secondarily the Temple and its priesthood, which dominated the ordinary life of Jews.

That is, between 450-375 and 250 the Pentateuch acquired that sanctity and authority and relatively broad circulation which makes intelligible its translation into Greek. Though we do not have any knowledge about the rise of the Pentateuch to the eminence which we know it achieved, the circumstance that the Samaritans too adopted it as their own sacred book attests to the universal authority it attained.

Reverting again to Nehemiah 8, we are there told that when Ezra read aloud to the people from the book of the divine teaching of Moses, certain individuals "helped the people understand the teaching." Many interpreters believe that "helped understand" means translation. If this is right, then why was translation needed in Jerusalem? Because in the sixth pre-Christian century, the Judeans had begun to veer from Hebrew to Aramaic (a second cousin of Hebrew) as their spoken language. Perhaps there were pockets where Hebrew remained a spoken language; clearly Hebrew abided as a literary possession, as is discernible in the fluency of the Hebrew of the Priestly Code and of other writings from this same age.

The gap between a sacred book in Hebrew and a populace

no longer speaking it, but using Aramaic, needed to be bridged. Hence, translation into Aramaic was the first of several requisite steps that arose naturally to cement the bond between the sacred book and those who gloried in the possession of what they regarded as the revealed word of God. What we need to see most clearly is that as early as the age of Ezra there already existed both public reading from the sacred book, and also public explanation, probably including translation.

In earlier times, such as the occasion of Babylonian conquest in the sixth century, an alien nation was pitted against Judeans. After the Greek conquest it was both aliens and especially their mores and their habits that confronted the Judeans and that challenged the way of life enjoined on them by and in Scripture. The Assyrian conquest of 722, the Babylonian of 597-87, and the Persian of 539 were essentially nationalistic, with no premeditated impingement on the Judean religion. True, the Babylonians had felt impelled to destroy the Temple, but we see no evidence of any deliberate effort to undermine or influence the Judean religion as such. The Greeks, however, not only conquered Judea, but they also proceeded to colonize it, and to bring with them their language and their customs and institutions.

A new factor ensued in the decades after the Greek conquest—namely, the rise of a heightened fidelity to the Judean way of living. For there slowly arose the issue of the preservation of the Jewish religion against the inroads of the alien conqueror and settler. Two late biblical books, Esther and Daniel, each in a different way, illumine this significant distinction between an essentially nationalistic conflict, repeatedly experienced in the past, and the new, essentially religious conflict. Scripture, as we shall see through recurrent retrospect, had created (possibly re-created) in the Jewish mind a sense of historical continuity which made the religious perceptions of the present a cumulative legacy from the most distant past. Beginning with Abraham, there had long ago come into being the people specially designated by God as his own; with Moses there had been provided to that people the divine rules of religion which God's people were obliged to observe. Ancient by now as Sinai was deemed to be, the laws revealed there were in effect contemporaneous in that they still called for wholehearted observance. The inherited books such as Judges-Samuel-Kings were not viewed so much as an account of the political events of the past as they were an assessment of how religious fidelity or infidelity to God had marked the Judeans' ancestors, and from the records of fidelity and infidelity later Judeans drew their spur to their own fidelity, especially in view of the record of both dire punishments which past infidelity had caused, and also of the divine rescue which fidelity had occasioned. Accordingly, both Esther and Daniel, written in a later age, were set in the bygone past, Esther into the somewhat recent but vanished Persian period, and Daniel into the earlier Babylonian.

The Book of Esther was written about a situation outside Judea—the Jewish community of Persia was depicted as going through a crisis wherein its very life comes to be in jeopardy. The danger came from a certain Haman, a wicked man elevated to the role of prime minister by a perhaps well-intentioned but bumbling monarch, Ahasuerus. When the Jew Mordecai declined to bow down to the man Haman (since Jews would bow down only to God), Haman's wrath was kindled against all the Jews. These people, so Haman is depicted as saying to the king, "are scattered and dispersed in all the provinces of your empire. Their laws are different from those of every people, and they do not observe the royal laws" (Esther 4.8).

That the Book of Esther is fiction is of no importance, for even fiction grows out of life experience. Obscure and debated as the origin of the Book of Esther is, it correctly depicts the fundamental issue which Jews saw in their religion and corporate existence, namely, that they were a distinctive religious entity. The events in the Book of Esther focus not on the matter of Jewish versus Persian nationality, but on Judaism versus a coercion to paganism. If those scholars are right who interpret Esther as reflective of authentic Jewish experience in a dispersion Greek environment (skillfully narrated by the gifted author of Esther as occurring in Persia), then one begins to get an insight into the complex issues which culminated in the Maccabean revolt, a Jewish revulsion against contamination by Greek culture. In Esther an experience of the supposed Jewish past is being called on as a lesson applicable to the Jewish present.

As to Daniel, the political events which led ultimately to its writing are relatively simple and clear. After the death of Alexander in 323, his empire fell to his generals, with Judea being ruled by the Ptolemies of Egypt. In 198 B.C., the Seleucids, whose capital was Antioch, wrested Judea away from Ptolemies. In the period between 323 and 198, there had occurred a notable spread of Greek culture throughout the then civilized world. Semitic merchants—Phoenicians and Idumeans—became agents for business enterprises that flourished through the extensive international commerce. But Greeks colonized throughout the known world, and hence Judea too was host to cities, new or old, that were essentially Grecian. Greek culture thus spread in Judea, though in varying measures; some Judeans only adopted Greek words into their speech; others became bilingual; and some exchanged their Aramaic for Greek. In a sense, then, Judea itself became somewhat hellenized.

So long as Judea remained under the control of the Ptolemies, the general climate of relations between Judeans and their Greek overlords appears to have been peaceful; certainly the Letter of Aristeas reflects a high Jewish regard for the Egyptian Ptolemy Philadelphus: But after 198 B.C., matters changed; Judea now belonged to the Syrian Greeks, and the latter did not pursue the tolerance that apparently had marked the Ptolemies. Under the Ptolemaic rule, the Greek culture had penetrated in sufficient measure as to induce some Judeans to abandon observances enjoined in the Pentateuch. Indeed, some Judeans voluntarily succumbed completely to Grecian ways. But the Syrian Antiochus IV Epiphanes made the effort to coerce the Judeans away from their religion. In 168 Antiochus outraged Judeans by dedicating the Temple in Jerusalem to Zeus Olympius, spurring a revolt under the leadership of Judas the Maccabee, who was of a priestly family called the Hasmoneans. To rally support for the revolt, the Book of Daniel was composed.

In the book, we find ourselves in a supposedly Babylonian setting. The sacred vessels of the Temple, captured in 597, had been brought to Babylon, and there been placed in the treasury of a Babylonian temple. Certain young Judeans with scholastic aptitude were drafted to be instructed in the Babylonian language, under the expectation that after three years of training they could serve in the royal palace. Daniel was one of these; so too were three young men, Hananiah, Mishael, and Azariah. The four were given Babylonian names (at this time some Judeans had assumed Greek names!). Daniel was unwilling to defile himself by eating Gentile food or by drinking Gentile wine. The royal eunuchs were fearful that such an abstemious diet would physically weaken Daniel and the three. A test was arranged for ten days; at the end, the four Judeans looked better and fatter than did those who had eaten the forbidden food and drunk the forbidden wine (Dan. ch. 1). Next, King Nebuchadnezzar (like the Pharaoh of Joseph's time) dreamed a dream. No one in the court could interpret it. God, though, intervened to reveal to Daniel both the royal dream and also its meaning. The meaning was about what the future was to bring—namely, the rise of a series of conquering empires, the Babylonian, the Medean, the Persian, and the Greek, but these empires would be succeeded by an indestructible holy kingdom, Judea, which God would set up. Nebuchadnezzar thereupon acknowledged that Daniel's God was the God of Gods (Dan. ch. 2).

But Nebuchadnezzar then erected an image of himself to which all had to bow.[6] Daniel's friends, loyal to Judaism, declined to bow to the image. They were cast into a fiery furnace, the flames of which slew those who had cast the three into it, but they emerged unharmed, without even a sign of having been burned. Nebuchadnezzar then praised their religious fidelity, threatening to punish "any people, nation, or tongue who speaks against the God of the three" (ch. 3). Next, Nebuchadnezzar, for his presumptuousness, was driven mad by God, and restored to sanity only by becoming a worshipper of Him (ch. 4). Belshazzar, the last Babylonian king, was found wanting by God, and he was slain after seeing on the wall a hand, writing the names of three coins: "Mene, mene, tekel, upharsin" (ch. 5). When, under the Persian Darius, a plot against Daniel led to his being cast into a lion's den, Daniel was saved by an angel, so that Darius commanded all his subject people to revere Daniel's God (ch. 6).

This summary of the first half of Daniel bears out the contention that the Judean religion, not Judea the political entity, had emerged as the primary concern. Thus in the four "visions" comprising the second half of Daniel, even though they deal with what we might call political history, the dominant concern is the preservation of the Judean religion from defilement, and the assurance is given that, despite the onslaught of the foe, the Judeans who remained faithful to their religion will be vindicated.

The Hasmonean revolt against the Seleucidian Greeks, which arose in 168, was successful. The Temple was purified and rededicated (the latter celebrated by Ḥanukka, "dedication"). Political independence was achieved, and the Hasmoneans became leaders. They founded a dynasty, enduring from about 150 to 40 B.C., though they were not of the proper royal or priestly line.

Factors which need to be kept in some equilibrium respecting the period of the Hasmoneans are the throne, the Temple with its priesthood, and Scripture and its influences. In all these there were men involved, and inevitably there arose those factions that are natural to any society. The first Hasmonean rulers served as High Priests rather than kings, but it does not seem wrong to link Temple and throne together insofar as these were a primary concern of what we might call the upper classes, especially of Jerusalem. It is possible that the full influence of the priesthood flowered only in the Hasmonean age, however much earlier it began—indeed, possibly at the start of the post-exilic period.

Scripture and its adherents had their natural center in Jerusalem too, but whereas the Temple and throne were essentially within Jerusalem, Scripture and its derivative institutions—places of study and teachers of the Holy Writings— were spread both throughout the land and even throughout the world.

Besides these two natural factions, the upper-class residents of Jerusalem and the middle-class people outside it, the populace of Judea included small merchants, traders, craftsmen, and farmers, and they could be rallied in support of the internal factionalism. Moreover, there were Greek cities in Judea, and hence Greek influences near at hand. Once the Maccabean revolt broke out in 168, and a High Priest–king arose about 150, there began to develop ever more rapidly those preparatory tendencies which flowered in Synagogue Judaism.

The events from 160 B.C. to A.D. 200 can be here briefly outlined—a necessity if we are to achieve and retain a historical perspective. To much of this short outline we shall later return to add significant detail. In 160, Judas the Maccabean fell in battle, with leadership then falling to his brother Jonathan. In 152 internal uprisings in Antioch, the capital of Syria, brought one Alexander Balas to the Seleucidian throne; Alexander had been helped in his rise to power by the Hasmonean Jonathan, whom Alexander rewarded by appointment as the Jewish High Priest. Jonathan acquired a large measure of political power,[7] and was able to increase the borders of Judea.

Murdered in 143, Jonathan was succeeded as High Priest and political head (the latter without a clear title) by another brother, Simon. In 140 Simon was publicly proclaimed *ethnarch*, that is, "ruler of the people." In effect, he became king, though he was not so titled. Six years later Simon was murdered.

His son John Hyrcanus (134-104) consolidated Judea, and also expanded it to include Galilee in the north and the southern area[8] into which the Edomites (called Idumeans by the Greeks) had moved. John Hyrcanus forcibly converted the Idumeans to Judaism; he overran the Samaritans and destroyed their temple on Mount Gerizim. During his reign there arose to prominence a party, partly religious, partly political, called the Pharisees.

John Hyrcanus' son Aristobulus I reigned for only a year, being succeeded by John's brother, Alexander Jannaeus (103-76). Alexander Jannaeus violated some Judean sensibilities by marrying John's widow, Salome Alexandra, for a High Priest was prohibited by Mosaic law (Lev. 21.14) from marrying a woman who was not a virgin. Warfare with the neighboring Nabateans[9] led to internal upheavals, including an invasion, later repelled, by the Seleucidians. Alexander Jannaeus was the first of the Maccabean rulers to call himself "king."[10]

From 76-67 the throne was occupied by Jannaeus' widow, Salome Alexandra. During her reign the Pharisees, to whom Alexander had been hostile, gained some power, especially with the succession of Salome's elder son, Hyrcanus II, to the high priesthood. A younger son, Aristobulus, mustered support from the aristocratic party, called the Sadducees, as he sought to seize the throne. Succeeding, Aristobulus took the throne as Aristobulus II. Hyrcanus, whose chief adviser was one Antipater, a Jew of Idumean extraction, managed to obtain Nabatean assistance for an assault in 65 against Aristobulus, who was then in the fortified Temple compound. Rome had long had a significant presence in the eastern Mediterranean. Now the warring brothers each appealed to the Romans for help. The representative of the Roman general Pompey was partial to Aristobulus in 65, and the Nabateans thereupon abandoned Hyrcanus. Pompey came to Jerusalem in 63. Petitioners before him represented both Aristobulus and Hyrcanus, and also Jews who repudiated both brothers, asking instead that the rulership be entrusted to a proper High Priest, on the basis that the Hasmoneans, though priests, were not proper for the highest office. But Pompey determined to take Jerusalem for himself. Aided by partisans of Hyrcanus, he assaulted Aristobulus, who was still in control of the Temple. After bloody combat and massacres, Pompey took the Temple. He abstained, though, from ransacking it, and he allowed the priestly sacrificial cult, which had been suspended, to resume.

Judea now became a Roman possession, with its borders significantly reduced, and heavy Roman taxes were imposed. Hyrcanus, though no longer "king," was allowed to continue to serve as High Priest. When Alexander, a son of Aristobulus II, tried to seize power in Jerusalem, the Roman response was to remove all authority from Hyrcanus and to turn it over to the direct rule of the Roman governnor of Syria, Gabinius.

When Julius Caesar came to power in Rome, having been supported by Hyrcanus and Antipater, he permitted Hyrcanus to resume his position as High Priest, but made Antipater the governor of Judea. Antipater delegated authority over Jerusalem to one son, Phasael, and over Galilee to another, Herod. (He is called "Herod the Great" because sons and grandsons were at times also called Herod, though they had individual names.) Herod was able to win the admiration of the Roman authorities in Syria. When, in 44, Julius Caesar was murdered, the new Roman rulers again faced rival Jewish parties. Now Herod was able to win the confidence of the new Roman leaders, Mark Antony and Octavius Caesar. The Romans named him king of Judea in 40. The designation did not at all imply independence; hence, it is frequent to term his office as that of "client-king," for Herod ruled by the grace of Rome.

At that juncture, the Parthians, an eastern people, temporarily overran the Romans in Syria. They put on the Judean throne Antigonus, still another son of Aristobulus II. Herod, however, was able, with Roman help, to overcome Antigonus in 37, and to assume the throne the Romans had previously given him.

Herod reigned from 37 to 4 B.C. He held on to his Roman-sanctioned throne throughout the wars between Octavius (Augustus) Caesar and Mark Antony. He managed to please, or at least satisfy, his Roman overlords. He added territory to Judea. He used the wealth available to him for extensive building, including a temple to Augustus at Samaria. He turned into an important seaport the newly founded city of Caesarea (building an artificial harbor there). He built important fortresses at Machaeras and Masada. He repaired the Temple in Jerusalem, in effect rebuilding it, surrounding it with a complex of buildings, including fortresses, and a strong wall (of which the Wailing Wall is a relic) around the complex. Married to the Hasmonean Mariamne, Herod put her to death, and later he slew the children she had borne him, out of fear that they were plotting to supplant him. He maintained peace and order by relentless oppression.

At his death in 4 B.C., the Jews petitioned Octavius, now Augustus Caesar, to withhold authority from Herod's sons. Augustus, however, named Archelaus ruler over Judea, Antipas "tetrarch" over Galilee, and Philip tetrarch over north-

ern Trans-Jordan. In A.D. 6, on the complaint of Jewish dele-
gations, Archelaus was deposed. Antipas held on as tetrarch
until A.D. 39. Philip and his area fade from direct Jewish
concern.

After the deposition of Archelaus, Judea was ordinarily
ruled by Roman "procurators," from A.D. 6 to 66. The public
career of Jesus took place during the term of Pontius Pilate
as procurator, 26-36.

In A.D. 37, the Roman Emperor Caligula designated Herod
Agrippa (a grandson of Herod) king of Judea, temporarily
ending the direct Roman rule. Agrippa was in Rome when
named. En route to Judea his ship stopped at Alexandria;
there broke out vicious anti-Jewish riots, which the Roman
governor Flaccus was lethargic in stopping. A deputation of
Jews went to Rome to protest. Antipas of Galilee was deposed
in 39; Agrippa became king of the composite areas which his
grandfather Herod had ruled over. But Agrippa died in A.D.
44, and the rule of Judea now reverted to the procurators.

Uprisings against Rome and repressions were endless, with
more than one procurator inflaming the populace by acts of
blindness or vindictive cruelty. The designation, in the early
sixties, of Agrippa's son Agrippa II as king with limited authority did not appease the populace. Two "nationalist
groups," the Zealots and the Sicarii ("swordsmen"), sought
to drive the Romans from Judea. When the procurator Florus
(64-66) plundered the land and violated the Temple treasury, a bitter, open revolt against Rome broke out.

The Judeans were successful initially. But the tide began
to turn with the arrival in Judea of the general Vespasian in
68. A year later Vespasian was named Emperor of Rome, and
then his son Titus completed the task of putting down the rebellion. In August 70, Titus seized and destroyed the Temple
(his victory is commemorated in the Arch of Titus, still
standing in Rome). In 73, the Romans captured the last surviving Judean fortress, that at Masada, the event which
marks the end of the rebellion.

The destruction of the Temple ended the sacrificial cult
and the priestly system. The Judaism which survived was
the Synagogue Judaism, already reasonably well developed.
The transition from Temple religion to Synagogue Judaism

was marked, first, by an assembly of "Rabbis," held at Jamnia in A.D. 90, and, second, by the rise of a quasi-judicial, legislative body, the great "court of law." The presiding head, called *nasi* ("prince") or "patriarch," Gamaliel II, named by Rome, was descended from a great man of Herod's time, Hillel. By this time, too, advanced academies for the study of Scripture had arisen; from 90 on the Academy exerted decisive leadership in religious matters.

In the Greek Dispersion some traces are found of Jewish uprisings against the Roman Emperor Trajan in North Africa and Cyprus in 115. In Judea, the Emperor Hadrian (117-38) attempted to exterminate Judaism by creating a Roman city, Aelia Capitolina, on the site of Jerusalem, building a temple to Jupiter on the site of the Temple, and banning circumcision. He spurred a second revolt against Rome in 132, led by Simon[11] bar Kōzibá, known as bar Kōchbá ("son of the star"). As in 70, the revolt was initially successful. But Roman forces under Julius Severus succeeded in crushing the new revolt.

Judea was now left a shambles, and remained so for many decades. Jewish life went on more favorably in Babylon to the east and somewhat sporadically in the Graeco-Roman world to the west.[12] Some semblance of self-government was allowed in Judea.

Around 175-200 there was recorded a book, the Mishna, an assembly of the rules, habits, and procedures of Synagogue Judaism. In the same period Christians, having become a veritable movement and having spread throughout the known world, responded to inner challenges by elevating to the sanctity of "Bible" some of the collected Christian writings. That is, out of the welter of events—the Maccabean revolt, the Roman conquest, the age of Herod, the cruelties of procurators, repeated uprisings and two major rebellions—Synagogue Judaism and its offspring Christianity emerged. Both were, of course, shaped by events. Both, though, rose in significance far beyond the events themselves, and both rose to what one might call maturity at roughly the same time.

· 3 ·

THE

SOURCES

Much of the literature related to our topic is, unhappily, outside the ken of the usual American. Josephus' name is relatively well known; his writings were once, along with a Bible, an ordinary household possession. But in our time it is usually only the serious student who knows him by actual reading. There is a certain danger in the listing which follows of the surviving sources, for their abundance and unfamiliarity can unduly discourage the beginner.

A systematic arrangement of the sources is also somewhat difficult since the categories are so different. First we shall describe the sources that are essentially historical in the sense of events. For the earliest period, from 175 B.C. on, there are I and II Maccabees, books preserved in the Apocrypha.[1]

1

HISTORICAL

A. I MACCABEES

I Maccabees, which, by translation from the Hebrew, made its way into the Greek Bible, covers the events of the period from about 175 to 135 B.C. The bulk of the book (chs. 1-13) seems to have been written about 100; on the question of whether the last chapters, 14-16, really belong to the book, scholars are divided, some considering them a rather late ap-

pendix to the book. The summary here given is to convey to
the reader the book's thrust; this is not to suggest that the details need acute attention, and surely not memorization.

Chapter 1 briefly summarizes the conquest of the world by
Alexander the Great and gives a terse account of the division
of his empire among his generals on his death in 323. It
moves quickly across the period from 323 to 175, to the
"sinful root," Antiochus IV Epiphanes (reigned 175-64).
That king had inherited the throne established in Antioch in
Syria by Seleucus, one of the generals of Alexander the Great.
Antiochus' father had wrested Palestine from the rival
Graeco-Egyptian kingdom of the Ptolemies in 198, after the
battle of Paneas. In those days, so the account here tells us,
there arose lawless Judeans who wished an end to the separation between Jews and Gentiles. These Judeans proceeded,
with royal sanction, to live by Gentile ways; for example,
they built a gymnasium (the word means "a place for being
naked"), thereby outraging other Jews, and they underwent
surgery to remove the marks of circumcision. (Such Jews are
ordinarily termed "hellenizers," from the word *Hellas*, the
name in Greek for Greece; hellenizers were those who ac-
tively adapted themselves to Greek ways.)

When once Antiochus was secure on the throne he invaded Egypt, and there conducted a successful campaign and
plunder (169 B.C.). Rome, already a power in the East, then
threatened him with war if he tried to annex Egypt. Antiochus retreated. On his way home through Judea, he laid siege
to Jerusalem, plundered the Temple, wreaked much violence,
and then arrived in his capital, Antioch. Two years later he
sent a collector to Jerusalem to exact a huge tribute; the An-
tiochenes, aided by some Jews, plundered the city itself and
then turned it into their own fortress. Next, Antiochus decreed that all his subjects—residents of Syria, Palestine, Mes-
opotamia, Persia, and parts of Asia Minor—should relinquish
their religion. Many Jews acquiesced in the king's demand,
forsaking Judaism and adopting pagan ways. The climax
came in 167 when a pagan altar was erected where the Temple altar had stood, and pagan altars were raised throughout
the land. Copies of Scripture were confiscated and burnt or
torn to pieces. Those Jews who practiced circumcision were

executed on capture. Such is the background of the Hasmonean revolt as portrayed in I Maccabees 1.

Chapters 2-4 relate details of the successful revolt against
Antiochus, and the initial independence, under Judas the
Maccabee. The revolt began in a town named Modein, not
quite twenty miles from Jerusalem. There the king's officer
invited the residents to exhibit their apostasy from Judaism
by offering pagan sacrifices. When one Jew came forward to
comply, a certain Mattathias, a priest and the father of Judas
the Maccabee, killed both him and the king's officer and tore
down the pagan altar. Then pious Judeans who refused to
succumb to paganism gathered in the Judean wilderness
southeast of Jerusalem. These, on being attacked on a Sabbath and piously refusing to fight, suffered very many casualties and deaths. The news of that massacre moved Mattathias and his associates to decide to do battle even on the
Sabbath.

After that Mattathias was joined by people called Hasideans ("the faithful"). A guerilla army was formed. Some
Judeans who declined to ally themselves with the army were
struck down, while others managed to flee to the Gentiles.
The loyal guerillas destroyed pagan altars; uncircumcised
boys were circumcised

But Mattathias was now old. Before his death he designated his oldest son Simon as "counsellor," and his son Judas
as the military commander (ch. 2). Judas defeated in battle
the forces of Apollonius, the Syrian governor of Judea and
Samaria, and those of a higher general, Seron, by means of
clever military tactics. When the report came to King Antiochus, he determined to raise a larger, better paid army, and
went to his province of Persia to raise money, leaving a certain Lysias in charge. Lysias dispatched an army of 40,000
infantry and 7000 cavalry against Judea. Judas roused his
people against the foe, going through religious rites in preparation (ch. 3).

One of Lysias' generals, Gorgias, was defeated by Judas
through stratagem and boldness. A year later, Lysias himself
brought an even greater army, but Judas' smaller force defeated this army too. The desecrated Temple in Jerusalem
was rebuilt, purified, and rededicated (in 164 B.C.). It was

determined to observe the anniversary of the Ḥanukka ("re-dedication") by an annual festival lasting eight days (ch. 4).

In Chapter 5 we are told of the consolidation and expansion of the nation still at war. Chapter 6 tells of the death in 163 B.C. of Antiochus IV Epiphanes in Persia. A certain Philip was made regent, but Lysias brought Antiochus V Eupator to the throne. The fortress in Jerusalem was still in the hands of the Syrians; now Judas instituted an assault upon it. Lysias then led another attack against Judea. Despite the bravery of Judas' brother Eleazar, the foe seemed about to conquer. But Philip was now reported to be trying to seize power in Antioch; in view of the internal threats to his throne, Antiochus V made a fragile peace with the Judeans.

In 161 B.C., according to Chapter 7, a cousin of Antiochus, one Demetrius, usurped the throne of Antioch. A delegation of Judeans, led by a certain Alcimus, who wanted to be High Priest—there had been rivalries for that supposedly hereditary office—obtained military help from Demetrius, and a new onslaught by the Syrians on Judea ensued. Some Judeans—including Hasideans—welcomed Alcimus and his Syrian colleague Bacchides, only to have sixty of their number seized and slaughtered. Alcimus now gained control of Judea. Judas then gathered his forces against Alcimus and his Syrian supporters. The Syrian general Nicanor attempted to negotiate with Judas, who suspected Nicanor's good faith; a battle took place in which Nicanor fell and his army was defeated (ch. 8).

Judas now was able to negotiate a treaty with Rome, by then a strong force in Asia Minor. The treaty recognized the independence of Judea. But King Demetrius of Antioch (ch. 9) dispatched a force into Judea under Alcimus and Bacchides, Judas was killed in battle, and his guerilla army was scattered. Two brothers of Judas, Jonathan and Simon, carried on the war with Jonathan in command, and these defeated Bacchides.

In 152 Alexander I Epiphanes (known as Alexander Balas) threatened to take the throne of Antioch from Demetrius. Demetrius accorded Jonathan some limited authority in Jerusalem; but when Alcimus the High Priest died, Alexander Balas, to win Jonathan from Demetrius, designated Jonathan

High Priest. Demetrius thereupon made his own offer to Jonathan of a number of boons, especially exemption from taxes, in return for good relations. Jonathan declined, preferring to cast his lot with Alexander Balas. Thereafter Alexander Balas slew Demetrius in battle. Jonathan was named "general and governor" of Judea (150 B.C.). Three years later, Demetrius' son, also named Demetrius, challenged Alexander Balas, and he sent troops against Jonathan, but Jonathan defeated them (ch. 10).

In Chapter 11, Ptolemy VI Philometer of Egypt, father-in-law of Alexander Balas, embarked on a plot to seize his son-in-law's domains. He seized coastal towns in Judea and then marched against Antioch, having allied himself with the younger Demetrius. Ptolemy was able to take Antioch and put Alexander Balas to flight, but he died three days later. Next, Alexander Balas was killed in Arabia, and young Demetrius became king. At that point Jonathan determined to seize the fortress in Jerusalem as a sign of his full independence. With his ongoing seige as a lever, he wrested from Demetrius a confirmation of recognition as High Priest, and he was also granted possession of the fortress. Demetrius then faced inner revolt in Antioch, from which troops sent by Jonathan saved him. But next, another Antiochus, this one the son of Alexander Balas, challenged Demetrius for the throne, incidentally confirming Jonathan as High Priest. A complex plot arose: Jonathan was trapped in an ambush by troops of Demetrius, but he managed to rout them (ch. 11).

Jonathan then made alliances with the Romans and with the Spartans, with whom an even earlier alliance had been made (ch. 12.7). But now Demetrius sent new forces. In complex machinations, Jonathan was taken captive by forces under a certain Trypho. Simon, another brother, now rose to the forefront. He rallied the Judeans to his cause. His effort to effect the release of his brother Jonathan by paying ransom failed because Trypho broke his word: as Trypho pressed forward his invasion, he killed Jonathan. A heavy snow deterred Trypho from further military activities, and he left Judea. Trypho now seized and slew Demetrius' rival, Antiochus, son of Alexander Balas, and then turned to overcome Demetrius himself. The latter appealed to Simon for help, acknowledging Judean independence with Simon as High Priest. Simon won to his cause some Judean dissidents and he strengthened the independent country (ch. 12).

Demetrius then invaded Medea, but was defeated and captured. Simon renewed the treaty which Jonathan had made with Sparta and Rome. He spoke to the people of the great achievements of the Maccabean brothers. Simon's line was named by the people as their proper rulers (chs. 13-14).

The brother of Demetrius II, Antiochus VII, now challenged Trypho, and in doing so sought Simon's support. But, treacherously, Antiochus turned against Simon and invaded Judea (ch. 15). Simon's son, John Hyrcanus, became the military leader. In further complications, Simon was killed, treacherously, at Jericho, and John Hyrcanus became the High Priest (ch. 16).

The account, possibly tiresome as here abbreviated, is even more tiresome when not shortened, because of the tedious plots and counterplots and treacheries. As a writer of history the author must give a labored narrative about a dynasty that managed to establish itself. Poems do enter in at various points (2.7-12; 3.3-9) and a fine poem is dedicated to Simon (14.4-15), but the chief virtue in this book, from which literary virtues are alarmingly absent, is that of patriotism.

The account closes, as we have seen, with the accession to the throne of John Hyrcanus, whose reign as High Priest was from 134-104 B.C. The very last verses suggest that John Hyrcanus has already died. Hence, the book was apparently written some time after 104. A reasonable guess is about the year 100. Was the book written simply to present history? That is hardly the case. Its purpose, rather, is to glorify the Hasmoneans, in a vindication of their rise to the offices of High Priest and king. Why a vindication? Simply because the Hasmoneans were not by descent entitled to the high offices; true, they were priests, but not of the direct line of Zadok (1 Chr. 6.3-8) through which the hereditary office of High Priest was to be transmitted. There were Judeans who resented the Hasmonean usurpation of high offices not properly theirs. I Maccabees presents the case for the merit of the Hasmoneans, as if that merit could supplant questionable legitimacy. The community that wrote the Dead Sea Scrolls rejected the legitimacy of the Hasmoneans as High Priests. Presumably so did other Judeans. I Maccabees is a defense of the improper acquisition of the high priesthood (and royalty) by the Hasmonean family. It presents the family as the agency through which the God of Israel wrought wondrous deeds; hence, the book contends the family was legitimately entitled to the high offices it came to possess.

B. II MACCABEES

This book is not an account, as is I Maccabees, of a succession of personalities (Mattathias, Judas, Jonathan, and Simon). Rather, II Maccabees is confined to glorifying only Judas Maccabaeus; it does not narrate his defeat and death, and surely the omission is deliberate. II Maccabees is not a consecutive account of all the events that occurred, but rather an interpretation of the significance of some of them. It is more theological, more legendary than I Maccabees. Virtually all scholars regard II Maccabees as a composition in Greek, but I Maccabees was written in Hebrew, surviving though only in translation. II Maccabees utilizes an aspect of Greek historical writing, a concern for a personality, here Judas. (We use the more familiar Grecianized name Judas throughout, rather than its Hebrew original, Judah.)

II Maccabees has a preface we shall presently turn to, but it goes on to tell us that an account of the events "has been set forth by Jason of Cyrene in five volumes." It is the author's intent to so "condense [them] into a single book. . . . Because of the mass of material, we have aimed to please those who wish to read, to make it easy for those inclined to memorize, and to profit all readers. For us who have undertaken the toil of abbreviating, it is no light task, but calls for sweat and loss of sleep. . . . The one who recasts the narrative should be allowed to strive for brevity of expression and to forego exhaustive treatment."

II Maccabees, then, is a condensation (scholars allude it is as an "Epitome") of a longer work by Jason, written about 90-80 B.C., which, unhappily, has not survived.

The preface consists of two letters (1.1-9 and 1.10-2.18) sent from "the Jewish brothers in Jerusalem and Judea to their Jewish brothers in Egypt"; the second letter was sent, in addition, to a certain Aristobulus, described both as "a member of the anointed priestly family" and as "teacher of Ptolemy." This Aristobulus is not identified beyond a mere mention.[2] The allusion to "the anointed priestly family" raises the question of what function a priestly family might have served away from the Jerusalem Temple; the speculative answer sometimes given has to do with the so-called "Temple of Onias," the only instance we know of where Jews established a temple in the Dispersion.[3] The role of "teacher to Ptolemy" (probably Ptolemy VI Philometer, reigned 172-146/45) cannot be clarified beyond the bare words themselves.

The first of the two letters that begin the book gives a very brief review of the institution of Ḥanukka, urging Egyptian Jews to observe it as an important festival. The second letter repeats the urging, calling on biblical precedent to justify Hanukka, which, being new, lacked a Pentateuchal basis.

The main content of II Maccabees is a review of the achievements of only Judas, not that of his brothers. Yet the purpose in setting forth this is primarily to contend that not man's achievement, but God's salvation was discernible in the events depicted. All had been well during the reign of Onias III (ch. 3.1), and the Temple had then functioned most appropriately. But sin—the hellenization of Jerusalem under the High Priests Jason and Menelaus—had led to divine punishment, this in the wicked deed of Antiochus IV Epiphanes. Some atonement for past sin was achieved by the worthy martyrs (Eleazar, 6.18-31; a mother and seven sons, 7.1-42). Though they died at the hands of wicked men, they would find resurrection at the hands of the King of the universe (7.9-14). Now, through God's design, (his wrath having turned to mercy, 8.5) Judas was able to achieve his great military victories (8.1-15.36). But it was atonement from sin which led God to grant victories to Judas.

II Maccabees appears to be an effort to legitimize Ḥanukka as a proper sacred day. Resistance to the day may have been twofold: first, a general resistance to innovation, and second, a resistance to it because it glorified the prowess of the Hasmoneans, whose legitimacy was questioned. The appeal to the Jews of the Dispersion appears designed to enlist support for the Hasmoneans from abroad as a counter to the sporadic opposition within Judea.

In due course the Hasmoneans became quite respectable, as happens with the descendants of those who seize power. But the book comes from a time before that respectability was attained. Indeed, it seems reasonable to conclude that for some Judeans the Hasmonean dynasty never attained full respectability; in the Rabbinic literature the observance of Ḥanukka is commended, but without a single word about the Hasmoneans. The point of II Maccabees seems to be that it was the fidelity of the pious Jews which made Judas successful, not any special merit of the Hasmoneans.

C. JOSEPHUS

Our principal historical source for most of the period with which we deal, especially after John Hyrcanus, is the body of writings by Josephus. First we must summarize the career of the man himself. Josephus was born in Judea about A.D. 37 or 38. His Jewish name, Joseph ben Mattathias, was later Romanized into Josephus, and the Flavius, which was the imperial family name, added later. According to his own statements he was from a distinguished priestly family and a descendant of Hasmoneans on his mother's side. He boasted of his good general Jewish education and of his academic proficiency. At sixteen he had deliberately exposed himself to the schools of the Pharisees and Sadducees, and even the Essenes. We shall speak later in detail about these groups; here we only identify them. The Essenes were members of a movement that withdrew from communal Jewish life; modern scholars identify them with the Community of Qumran, more popularly called the "Dead Sea Scroll" community. The Sadducees were upper-class. The Pharisees might here be described as a middle-class urban group, that segment of society from which teachers and scholars ordinarily arise. Josephus spent some time in the Wilderness with an Essene teacher named Bannus. But thereafter he was mostly allied with Pharisees.

Josephus first emerged to some notice around 64, when he

was sent to Rome to plead for the release of some imprisoned priests who had been sent there by Felix, the Roman procurator of Judea (52-60). Through a Jewish actor of prominence (named Aliturus) Josephus was introduced to the Empress Poppea[4]; through her he obtained the release of the prisoners. During his stay in Rome, Josephus had opportunity to observe the wealth and power of the Romans.

Returning to Judea, Josephus discovered that the pot of rebellion against Rome was beginning to boil. He himself joined the "war party," though he did so, so he says, with some reluctance. When rebellion broke out openly in 66, the Judeans, initially successful, routed the army of Cestius Gallus, the Roman governor of Syria. Josephus now received a commission as governor and commander in chief of the Judean forces in Galilee; apparently he had had some military training. He held that post for some six months, but there arose enemies who accused him of treachery and even of treason; Galilean Jews were incited to uprisings against him, led by one John of Gischala. Josephus managed to contain these uprisings, and was also able to reverse a decision made in Jerusalem to remove him from office. Those six months in Galilee were filled with all manner of maneuver, killing, and disorders. In due course Josephus brought his troops to a city named Jotapata, where he held out against a Roman assault led by the general Vespasian for forty-seven days. When Jotapata fell, Josephus escaped, hiding in a cistern-cave with some forty of his soldiers. These died by their own hand in a succession of suicides determined by lot; the last two of the forty were Josephus and another soldier. Captured, Josephus was brought before Vespasian, whose good will he obtained by telling the general that prophetic powers enabled him to predict Vespasian's future elevation to the throne of Rome.[5] Vespasian then gave Josephus his freedom.

Subsequent aspects of Josephus' career have made him a villain in some Jewish estimates, for, justly or not, he is usually regarded as a turncoat.[6] He was brought from Judea to Alexandria in Egypt by Vespasian, but he returned to Judea as part of the retinue of Vespasian's son Titus, now the commander of Roman forces in Judea. Josephus' activities now further alienated the Judeans; and the Romans, in experi-

encing some setbacks, also suspected his integrity. But after
Titus' decisive victory in 70, Josephus was rewarded with an
estate in Judea, and then with high honors in Rome, to which
he moved. From 70 until his death he pursued a literary career, primarily in Rome under the patronage of a succession
of emperors. Possibly he died about 96; he fades from view
by 100; the latter year is given as the date of his death by the
Byzantine chronicler Photius. It is reported by the fourth-
century Christian historian Eusebius (*Ecclesiastical History*,
II, IX, 2) that a statue of Josephus was erected in Rome, a
curious matter in view of the Jewish opposition to human
statues.

Josephus has bequeathed a great quantity of writing, all
in Greek. His native tongue was Aramaic, and he needed assistance to produce his Greek writings. He wrote his first
book, The Jewish War, in Aramaic and had it translated
after it was complete. In the case of other writings, he apparently used translator-editors even while in the process of his
writing. Modern scholars have been readily able to detect
from the idiosyncrasies at least two principal, different literary assistants. That for Josephus' later major work an immense amount of research was entailed has led to the view
that Josephus had available to him a veritable staff of re-
searchers as well as literary stylists. He mentions a certain
Epaphroditus,[7] "a man devoted to every form of learning, but
specially interested in the experiences of history" as his patron, and possibly he received financial support from him; it
is also possible that he acquired some income from the sale of
his books.

Three direct motives impelled Josephus to begin to write.
One was his wish to vindicate himself from nasty (but possibly deserved) personal attacks made on him by a certain
fellow Jew, Justus the son of Pistus. Justus was a Galilean,
from the city of Tiberias. He was one of those who had agi-
tated for rebellion against Rome before 66, and he had personally directed assaults on Gentile cities. When Josephus
was put in authority in Galilee, Justus and his followers
were a double problem to Josephus; their rebellious activities
embarrassed him in terms of his own position as the designated Judean commander in chief and in terms of the re-

sponses that could be expected from the occupying Roman forces. To Galilean Jews, Josephus seemed pro-Roman. After the Roman crushing of the rebellion 66-70, Justus was able to ingratiate himself for a while with the Judean King Agrippa II, but after some ups and downs he finally lost his post as Agrippa's secretary. Justus thereupon wrote an account of the war against Rome, but, because it was unfavorable to Agrippa, he delayed publishing it. That account, which has not survived, included an assault on Josephus. Josephus, in his autobiography, The Life, defends himself against the accusations of treachery made by Justus. Accordingly, one motive of Josephus was a vindication of his integrity and his conduct.

A second motive was a product of his pro-Roman experiences. He had initially opposed the rebellion against Rome, joining in it reluctantly. But having later come to espouse the Roman cause, he felt the need to justify the Roman actions, this by ascribing the rebellion to the foolishness or the fanaticism of Judean leaders. (The Galilean guerillas who rose in rebellion he customarily describes as bandits.) In the preface of his first book, The Jewish War, he declares that the work was written to try to persuade peoples to the east of Judea that it was futile to rise up in arms against so powerful an empire as Rome. It is not unfair to allege that Josephus so slants his account in The Jewish War as to seem to be currying favor with the Romans.

The third motive stems from his genuine Jewish loyalties. Though there were Jews whose deeds he lamented, he did regard Jews as an aristocracy, a people of undoubted excellence, whose religion was without peer or rival. He was a defender of Judaism against calumnies we shall later review (pp. 267-77). Josephus was eloquent in his affirmative presentation of the virtues which unquestionably he discerned in Judaism and was loyal to.

The difficulty that arises out of the motives and other idiosyncrasies is that we cannot always take Josephus' accounts at face value. Also, the numbers he gives, about assemblies or army sizes or casualties, are invariably exaggerated. His role as an interpreter of Jews and Judaism to Romans involves him in a recurrent problem of conveying information intel-

ligibly, and we can charge him with glibness in his designation of Sadducees, Pharisees, and Essenes as philosophical
sects, using labels his Gentile readers would quickly grasp;
yet there is something misleading in equating· Jewish non-
philosophical religious sects with the Greek philosophical
schools.

Even more serious is a peculiar deficiency: Josephus gives
us relatively little information in detail about the inner religious life of Jews. What he does give is a review of biblical
religion and hasty characterizations of Sadducees, Pharisees,
and Essenes; what he does not give is any substantial information at all about the Synagogue, or Scribes, or Rabbis.
From his writings we would scarcely even suspect that they
existed. Hence precisely at the point that for the purposes of
this book we would want him, he fails us. Yet without him
we should be completely in the dark about the events which
are the background of Synagogue Judaism; thus Josephus is
our most important but rather imperfect source.

The Jewish War[8] often referred to in the Latin, *Bellum Ju-
daicum*, was completed around the year 80. It begins with
the period of Antiochus IV Epiphanes, the Seleucidian king
against whom the Maccabeans had rebelled in 168 B.C. It alludes at its end to events in A.D. 73. That is, it covers the
Maccabean period (168-37), the reign of Herod the Great
(37-4), that of Archelaus the son of Herod (4 B.C.-A.D. 6), the
Roman procurators (6-66), and the war against Rome (66-
73). Josephus was himself a participant in and an eyewitness
of the events just before the war and the war itself, or else he
had access to other participants. For the earlier events he had
sources such as I and II Maccabees, and a court biography of
Herod by Nicolaus of Damascus[9]; that is, he had access to
written documents.

His second and major work, called in Greek The Archaeology of the Jews but in Latin The Jewish Antiquities, was
completed around 93. Its twenty books give an account of
Jewish history from the creation of the world to A.D. 66;
that is, it repeats (from Book XII, Chapter IV to the end of
Book XX) material already covered in The Jewish War. Unhappily, there are serious differences and contradictions between the overlapping accounts.

At one point [Antiquities I (xv, 1), 240-41], Josephus quotes from a Greek writer, Alexander Cornelius of Miletus (his dates are often given 80-40 B.C.), alluded to as Polyhistor, "master of history." Alexander had compiled an anthology of writings about Jews. In our context, the mention of Alexander Polyhistor is a clue to Josephus' wider use of many sources. That is, Josephus wrote not only from his own recollections of the period of his activity, but by recourse to the writings of others. Some of the sources he uses and the names of their authors have survived in whole or in part, but some have not. For the review of biblical history, Josephus used the Bible. At some points the Bible he uses is not the Hebrew original or its Aramaic translation, but rather the Greek version; he uses for his accounts of Ezra and Esther materials found in the Greek Bible (1 Esd.) but absent from the Hebrew.

He inserts into his account of the biblical period a rather wide range of Greek writers, some a single time and others repeatedly, who had written about the Jews, especially about their ancient origin. Much of this material is a speculative blending of a wide variety of clues, or legends, about very ancient times; they serve Josephus as outside confirmation of biblical materials. Quite apart from the use of such material to set the patriarchs or Moses into the stream of ancient history is Josephus' embellishment of the biblical accounts and personalities without recourse to the citing of any sources. He presents details not found in the Bible; he alters some accounts slightly; he omits some biblical materials. The reader can learn this for himself by comparing the account, for example, of Abraham in Genesis and that in Antiquities. He will discover, among other alterations, that the Bible is laconic in its narrative (Gen. 12.10-20) of Abraham's journey to Egypt to escape the famine in Canaan; in Antiquities, Abraham, in going to Egypt, wished either to convert the Egyptian priests or to be converted by them; a native of Ur, where mathematics was born, Abraham knew mathematics and taught the Egyptian priests, and the Egyptians in turn taught mathematics to the Greeks. Some of the embellishments which Josephus presents, whether of narrative or of law, recur in the Rabbinic literature, which in written form dates from a century or so after Josephus; accordingly, Josephus helps verify the reasonable view that the material in the Rabbinic literature includes some which is much earlier than the date of its being set down in writing.

Mention was made above of The Life. That autobiography was apparently joined to Antiquities as an appendix. To the extent that this work of self-justification is credible, it provides information about the events in the Galilee at the beginning of the rebellion against Rome in 66. Still another work by Josephus, Against Apion, we shall speak about below (pp. 267-77).

D. GREEK AND ROMAN HISTORIANS

The testimony of Greek or Roman writers on Jewish matters was relatively small. Some of that testimony comes from writers who were historians, concerned usually not for Judea but for the broader area, known to them as Syria, of which from their perspective Judea was a part. Other Greek and Roman writers include poets and satirists as distinct from historians.

Of the Greek historians who enter into our concern we should first mention Polybius, whose uncertain dates are 202-130 B.C. His History, only part of which has survived, described the rise of Rome to world power, from about 220 to 146. In History (Book XXVI, Ch. 10) he treated Antiochus IV Epiphanes, providing a character sketch with some details about the king's caprices. "Epiphanes" means "made manifest," and as an epithet reflects the hellenistic notion of a king as "divine," so that Antiochus regarded himself a god "made manifest." It is from Polybius that we have inherited the well-known pun altering "Epiphanes" into "Epimanes," the latter meaning "insane."

Diodorus Siculus ("from Sicily"), who lived in the first century B.C., wrote a universal history, called The Historical Library. It began with the most ancient times and went through the Gallic Wars (58-51 B.C.) of Julius Caesar. Of its forty books, there have survived in complete form books 1-5 and 11-20; of the others only fragments have been preserved. Judea is mentioned only occasionally.

Strabo, whose dates are from about 64 B.C. to about A.D. 21, wrote many works. His Geography, in seventeen books, contains material of importance about Syria, especially his description (Book XVI, II, 28-46) of Palestine. He used sources that are lost and cannot be identified with certainty.

Plutarch (A.D. 46?-120) was an essayist, biographer, philosopher, priest, and city official. Of the many biographical essays he wrote in his Parallel Lives, fifty have survived; several relate to Jewish history, namely those about the eminent Romans Crassus, Pompey, Julius Caesar, Brutus, and Mark Antony.

Appian, an Alexandrian, wrote his History about A.D. 150. Not all its twenty-four books have survived. We have part of that segment on Syria and Parthia.

Cassius Dio (sometimes called Dio Cassius) was a native of Asia Minor, where he was born about 163. He became an eminent political figure in Rome, holding important offices. His Roman History, in eighty books, covered the period from earliest times down to his own day (to A.D. 229). Only some of the books have survived completely; some are partially preserved in excerpts inherited from late Byzantine chroniclers. He provides some materials about Judea, this in connection with Pompey.

Turning now to those who wrote in Latin, the first name is that of Cicero (106-43 B.C.). Cicero had suported Octavius (later called Augustus) Caesar against Mark Antony, but when Augustus and Antony became reconciled and formed a triumvirate along with one Marcus Lepidus, Cicero was at the head of the list of those executed as enemies of the state. Many of his speeches and letters have survived; some of these provide materials about Syria, especially for the period from 57-43 B.C.

Livy (64 B.C.-A.D. 17?) wrote an immense History, from Rome's founding up to 9 B.C. Of the 142 books in this work, only thirty-five have survived. Material related to Jewish history for the years 178-167 B.C. are contained in books 41-45.

Augustus Caesar (d. A.D. 14) wrote a review of the most significant events of his reign. It was to have been transcribed on brass tablets and set in front of his mausoleum. A copy, inscribed in Latin and Greek on the marble walls of a temple to Augustus in Ancyra (modern Ankara), has survived. So too have fragments, one in Greek and one in Latin, from two other temples.

Tacitus (A.D. 56?-120?) wrote two main historical works. His Annals, an account of the reigns of Tiberius, Caligula, Claudius, and Nero (covering A.D. 14-68), has not totally survived, but substantial portions have, and provide information about Syria and Palestine. His other work, Histories, covering the reigns of emperors from 69-96, has survived only in small part. In what has survived, in Book V, 1-13, Tacitus furnishes a short history of the Jews up to the time of Titus, that is, the Jewish rebellion against Rome in 66-70.

Suetonius, author of Lives of Twelve Emperors, appears to have lived from about A.D. 70 to 140. The twelve run from Julius Caesar through Domitian (who died in 96). Other works of this prolific writer, who was adept at purveying gossip, do not relate to Jewish history.

Last is a universal history written by Trogus Pompeius during the reign of Augustus. His history has not survived. A digest of it by a certain Justin, made in the second or third century (called an "Epitome") has been preserved. It gives information especially about Alexander the Great and the Seleucids.

This brief review possibly suggests how relatively little relating to Jewish history has survived from Greek and Roman historians.

For the sake of completeness, mention might also be made of passing aspersions of Jews in the works of such literary figures as Horace (65-8 B.C.); Seneca (4 B.C.-A.D. 65); Martial (A.D. 38?-135?); Juvenal (A.D. 60-140?); and others.[10] Horace and Seneca both deride the Sabbath, and Horace Jewish conversion efforts. Juvenal speaks contemptuously of the multitude of Jewish beggars. This thread of contempt will help explain the apologetic nature of Jewish writers such as Josephus; it is balanced by the Jewish contempt for pagan idolatry and emperor worship.

E. ARCHAEOLOGY

The history we know is somewhat amplified by the contribution of archaeology, especially by coins[11] and inscriptions.[12]

The relevant coinage includes both the Seleucidian, of various cities of the area, but especially the coins of the Judeans; coins, then as now, often provided the date of issue and the name of the issuer (or even his portrait). Perhaps a single example can illustrate the kind of information derived from coinage: Mention was made above (p. 40) of the effort, about 139 B.C., of Antiochus VII to win Simon the Maccabee as an ally against the usurper Trypho. The account in I Maccabees contains the statement (15.6) that Antiochus VII wrote to Simon, "I allow you to mint your own coinage for use in your country." Rather promptly, Antiochus lost his need of Simon's help; no coins, if any were minted, have survived. But Antiochus ended the autonomy of Judea under Simon's son John Hyrcanus, by conquering Jerusalem; in 132/ 31 B.C. Antiochus minted his own coins in Jerusalem. When some three years later John Hyrcanus was able to take advantage of Seleucidian inner upheavals and declare his independence, he struck his own coins, carrying the inscription in Hebrew, "Johanan [i.e. John] the High Priest and the community of the Jews." Such of those coins which have survived used for the Hebrew an ancient alphabet, sometimes called "Phoenician" and sometimes "Paleo-Hebrew"; that alphabet had begun to be replaced by the so-called "Syrian" or "square letter" alphabet used still today by the Jews.

Jewish coins lacked the representation of the human figure (prohibited in the Ten Commandments), but not floral or fruit designs, especially the cornucopia. The coins of Herod the Great bear Greek, not Hebrew, inscriptions. His son Archelaus did not inherit the title "king," but rather *ethnarch*, and his coins use that title. His brother, Herod Antipas, put on his Galilean coins his own title, *tetrarch*.

Herod Agrippa I, grandson of Herod the Great, and ruler from about 39-44, did put his portrait on coins, along with the words, "Great King Agrippa, friend of Caesar."

Copper coins of small value, issued under the Roman procurators from A.D. 6 to 66, usually carried the name Caesar, but abstained from a portrait. Bronze coins issued by Pontius Pilate (bearing the name of Tiberius Caesar) have been found.

When the war against Rome broke out in 66, the Jews

struck their own coins; one in bronze from the year 67 bears the legend, on one side, "second year," and on the other, "Freedom for Zion." After the Romans had destroyed Jerusalem and the Temple in 70, they also struck coins; on one side of a surviving bronze one is portrayed the head of the Emperor Vespasian and on the other a male Jew with hands tied behind his back and a seated Jewess weeping.

From the Bar Kochba rebellion of 132-35, there are coins which were originally Roman, Phoenician, or Syrian, but were overstruck to become Judean. The motifs from the rebellion of 66-70, palms, grapes, and vines and viny leaves, are repeated, but additional motifs are added—for example, four columns of the Temple, a Torah shrine, and two Torah scrolls on one side, with the reverse carrying the Hebrew for "Year two of the freedom of Israel." Bar Kōzibā's name Simon is found on still other coins. Yet another coin bears the name of "Eleazar the Priest," a man otherwise unknown to us.

As to epigraphy (that is, inscriptions) from the age with which we deal, those related to our topic are regrettably few in number. One inscription, in Aramaic, on an "ossuary" (an urn for the bones of the dead) reads: "Here were brought the bones of Uzziah, king of Judah. Do not open." Two Greek inscriptions have been found. One, in two versions, known as the "Balustrade Inscription," reads: "No alien is to enter within the balustrade and enclosure around the Temple. Anyone caught will be liable to the death penalty." (An allusion to this prohibition is found in Acts of the Apostles, 21.28-29.) Another stone inscription in Greek, from Jerusalem, is in honor of a certain Theodotus who was the head of a synagogue. The translation[13] is given as follows: "Theodotus, son of Vettenos, priest and head of the synagogue, son of a synagogue head, and grandson of a synagogue head, built the synagogue for the reading of the Law and the teaching of the commandments, as well as the lodging room and the chambers and the water pipes for lodging needy strangers. Its foundation stone was laid by his fathers, the elders, and Simonides." This inscription was found on a hill named Ophel, southwest of Jerusalem.

The yield of Greek non-literary papyri, principally from

THE SOURCES

Egypt, has been of immense quantity. The sands of Egypt
preserved this fragile leaf, cut from water reeds and pressed
into flat sheets, but the soil of Palestine did not enable the
papyri to endure. The Egyptian papyri have been collected,
translated, and explained.[14] The term "non-literary" has to
do with the nature of such papyri, for they are generally
brief private letters or petitions about taxes; that is, they are
not versions of literary works by authors of some consequence. They throw light on such matters as the daily life of
people or the workings of lower courts or government officials.

F. RABBINIC LITERATURE

The ancient Rabbinic literature, too, is a source for our knowledge of history, though it must be stressed that the historical
events appear in it indirectly, by mere allusion, or through
the perpetuation of some striking legends. Perhaps it would
be more proper here to speak in the plural of Rabbinic literatures, in order for us to begin with a clear view of the differences in their types. At this point we need speak only of
three types in a general way, for later we must address ourselves to more specifics than we need do at this stage.

One type is the Targúm, the "translation" of Scripture
from Hebrew into Aramaic. The Targum at times strays
from a literal rendering, and in so doing reflects the situation
of the time when the translation was made. A second type is
the Midrásh. As a term, midrash can be defined as "interpretation"; *The* Midrash is the collection of interpretations
of Scripture, arranged in the order of biblical books, chapters,
and verses, so that one can speak of *The* Midrash to Exodus
(for which, as we shall see, there is an additional special
name). A third type is exemplified by the Mishná ("teaching"); here the arrangement is on topics, such as Sabbath,
New Year, and the like, rather than on the biblical text as is
the case with the Midrash.

The Rabbinic literature is known among Jews as the Oral
Torah, in contradistinction to the Written, which is Scripture. Paradoxically, the Oral Torah came to be set down in
writing; for example, the Mishna was recorded around A.D.
175-200. This literature can, however, justly be known as

Oral in that it recalls the opinions of Sages and the events of the time long before its written form, these transmitted orally. As a repository of quite old oral traditions, some as early as about 200 B.C., and of events in the first and second centuries of the present era, the Rabbinic literature is a source of some knowledge of the historical events of the period with which we deal. This testimony to history is quite indirect and in manner coincidental, and far from full; one could not from the Rabbinic literature assemble materials that would enable one to write a sequential account of events. The chief utility of the Rabbinic literature, as we shall see, is in the realm of religious ideas and practices, of worship, and of pious observance, but not in that of history.

2

RELIGIOUS WRITINGS

The second category we turn to is those writings, essentially religious in their significance, with relatively less allusion to events than even the Rabbinic literature. These writings would include the so-called Apocrypha and Pseudepigrapha, which, from the perspective of Christianity, arose in the period between the youngest of the Old Testament writings, Daniel, and the New Testament writings, and hence are often called "intertestamental" by Christians.

A. APOCRYPHA AND PSEUDEPIGRAPHA

The Apocrypha (a term essentially Protestant) are the writings which made their way into the Greek Jewish Bible but not into the Hebrew.

The Pseudepigrapha are books from the intertestamental period which failed of inclusion in either the Hebrew or the Greek bibles. Some of these surviving books were assembled in the eighteenth century by a German scholar named Johann Fabricius. The word "pseudepigrapha" means "false titles," and was chosen because many of these books are ascribed, falsely, to biblical characters such as Enoch or Abraham. Since the Pseudepigrapha were assembled only in the modern age, there is not and cannot be a precise list of these books. Scholars later than Fabricius, in publishing their own collections, added books he did not include, and some of these added books are not in any sense "falsely titled." Therefore some modern scholars have suggested that the word "pseudepigrapha" be replaced by a substitute term such as "outside books," a phrase found in the Rabbinic literature for books that were not to be reckoned as within Scripture. (A confusion can exist in "Apocrypha," in that Roman Catholics have used this term to describe what Protestants have called Pseudepigrapha.) Later we shall look at some of these books. Here we should stress the diverse character of this literature and the fact that often its contribution to our understanding of the religion in its particulars is only indirect. From this abundance of diverse writings some generalizations are possible, but they are hazardous in the extreme. Two such generalizations can be set forth here. First, this literature provides information about the trends toward Synagogue Judaism which are somewhat older than the developments which flowered in Rabbinic literature. For example, a book known as Jubilees furnishes us with legends about the Patriarch Abraham which appear in more developed form in the Rabbinic literature. Second, a problem, possibly without solution, arises in that much of the Pseudepigrapha reflect a great concern for revealing what the future holds, this in the form of visions about the end of the world, while that sort of concern is relatively absent from the Rabbinic literature. Was pseudepigraphic literature simply forgotten by the rabbis? Or was it abandoned? The answer is elusive.

1. I Esdras

We have already looked at two books of the Apocrypha, I and II Maccabees. The Book of Esdras, also called I Esdras,[15] is of limited concern to us. In its content, it is a presentation of material found also in II Chronicles 35.1-36.23, the entire biblical book of Ezra, and Nehemiah 7.38-8.12; however, it ends abruptly, as if succeeding pages were lost. Why the presentation of the same material found in other books? The

answer is uncertain. It may be that it is a version of Ezra
and Nehemiah which did not undergo some scribal problems
that arise over those two books (originally they were one,
but in transcription and division into two books, parchment
pages were mixed up prior to being sewn together).

In I Esdras there is a passage, 3.1-5.6, without parallel in
the biblical books of Ezra and Nehemiah. Prior to this passage, there is in 2.16-30 a parallel version to Ezra 4.7-24,
wherein there had arisen opposition in Judea to the desire of
the exiles, newly returned from Babylon, to build the Temple, so that its reconstruction was delayed until the accession
of Darius I to the throne of Persia. The passage in I Esdras
3.1-5.6 explains why the king allowed the rebuilding to proceed. Darius gave a great banquet for all his nobles and then
went to sleep. Three young men of his bodyguard thereupon
embarked on a contest to determine which of the three was
the wisest. Each wrote a statement about what was the
strongest thing in the world. The statements were put under
Darius' pillow. One called wine the strongest thing; and the
second the king himself; the third was that though women
were the strongest, in reality truth was victor over all else.
On awakening, Darius read the three statements. He con-
vened all his nobles in the council chamber, so that each of
the three young men could explain his statement. First came
the young man who had chosen wine; he told how liquor
leads minds astray, and even leads to warfare. The second
exalted the power of the absolute king. The third young man
was the Jew Zerubbabel. Wittily he showed that women are
more powerful even than kings ("Many have perished, or
stumbled, or sinned, because of women"). But powerful as
women are, truth is even stronger ("Truth endures and is
forever strong, and lives to rule for ever and ever"). The decision in the contest went to truth. Those assembled proclaimed, "Great is truth, and it shall prevail." Darius offered
Zerubbabel a high position as his councillor, but Zerubbabel
declined, asking instead that Darius fulfill a vow he had
presumably made earlier to allow the Temple to be rebuilt,
and Darius complied.

This pleasant story, told in a witty way, is believed by
scholars to have been in circulation for a long time, as were

many comparable tales, and adopted in I Esdras so as to explain the leading role given to the Jew Zerubbabel. If in adapting the folktale something specifically Jewish was added, it is the equation of truth with God. (At a later time, other widespread folktales were retold by rabbis with similar nuances that made them Jewish.)

2. Tobit

The Book of Tobit is a tale reflecting a large measure of ancient folklore. The story line—one must avoid speaking of a plot—is complex. The hero Tobit was among the captives carried east to Nineveh at the time of the Assyrian conquest of the ten tribes of the northern kingdom in 722. (Those exiles constitute in other folktales the ten "lost" tribes, whose wondrous finding has taken various forms.)

Tobit, after a brief introduction, becomes a first-person account. Prior to his exile, Tobit had been singularly loyal to the requirements in the Mosaic laws, despite the disloyalty of his compatriots. In exile he maintained that loyalty, shunning prohibited foods, even after he was raised to be the royal purchaser of provisions. But his Jewish piety, manifest in his acts of charity to fellow Jews, got him into difficulties, so that he had to flee, leaving his property to be confiscated. His wife Anna and his son Tobias fled with him. But a change of dynasty[16] enabled him to return to Nineveh.

On the festival of Shavuot ("Pentecost"), Tobit sent Tobias out to invite to the joyous meal whatever poor Jews the son might find. Tobias returned with a report that he had found the unburied corpse of a Jew, which he had hidden. Tobit promptly went to the marketplace to remove the corpse; after sunset (when the festival had ended), he dug a grave and buried the body. Ritually defiled now by his contact with the corpse, Tobit slept out of doors near the wall of his house. His face was uncovered; hence, the droppings of sparrows on the wall fell on his eyes and blinded him. The physicians could not help him. For a while his nephew Ahikar supported him in his poverty, but then Ahikar was assigned a royal post far away. Tobit's wife Anna had to go to work. Once, on being paid, she was given the gift of a kid in addition to her wages, but Tobit was suspicious—he feared that she had stolen the kid. In his despair he prayed to God that his distress be ended by death.

At that same time a Jewess Sarah also prayed. Her prayer arose from her own peculiar distress: She had been given to a succession of seven husbands each of whom the evil demon Asmodeus had slain before the marriage could be consummated. In her distress, she (like Tobit) proclaimed an innocence of sin and a desire for death. God heard the two prayers. He determined to send the angel Raphael (the name means "God heals") to heal the two of them.

Long before, Tobit had left some money in trust in Medea with a certain Gabael. He now sent his son Tobias to recover the money, and at the same time counseled him to live uprightly by the commandments.

To Tobias Tobit handed the receipt given him for the money. Tobias needed a man to guide him to the place where Gabael livel. It was Raphael whom Tobias hired, though Raphael had identified himself as a man named Azarias, the son of a relative of Tobit's.

On the journey, Tobias was almost swallowed by a man-eating fish. He killed the fish and, at the direction of Azarias, removed its heart, liver, and gall. Presently Azarias told him that the heart and liver would protect a human from damage by a demon or evil spirit, while the gall could serve to cure a person whose eyes were covered by a white film.

Nearing the city of Ecbatana, Azarias proposed that Tobias marry Sarah, at whose father's home they were to stay. When Tobias protested that Sarah's previous husbands had died in the bridal chamber, Azarias told him that he could use the heart and liver to drive away the demon. Arriving, the marriage was proposed, the proposal accepted, and then the demon fled. Tobias was delayed by the hospitality of his father-in-law, so that Azarias went on without him to recover Tobit's money from Gabael. Meanwhile, Tobit was becoming anxious about the long time Tobias was away, and Anna was giving way to despair. Tobias now insisted on his need to leave for home, and he was sent away with a blessing.

Nearing Nineveh, Tobias and Azarias went ahead of Sarah, taking the gall of the fish with them. Arriving at Tobit's home, Tobias sprinkled the gall on his father's eyes.

When presently Tobit rubbed his eyes, the white film disappeared, and he could see again. Now the marriage of Tobias and Sarah was joyously marked by a great festivity in Nineveh.

When Tobit reminded Tobias to pay his guide Azarias, the latter revealed himself as Raphael, and, in chosen words, he gave sage counsel on prudent conduct. Raphael then ascended to God, and Tobit wrote an eloquent prayer in praise of God.

Then, when Tobit had become very old, he predicted to Tobias the events that would ensue in Jewish history. He advised Tobias to leave Nineveh, which was to be destroyed (and was, in 612), and to live piously. When Tobit and then Anna died, Tobias piously buried them. He left Nineveh to dwell in Ecbatana, and lived long enough to hear that Nineveh had been destroyed.

The account of Tobit is fiction, not history. The bare story outline does not convey the chief attraction in the story, which is the portrayal of Tobit's piety: His religious devotion to God, his acts of piety in pursuit of the welfare of his fellowmen, his staunch Jewish loyalties. Out of the portrait of this piety, one gets many glimpses into the manner in which biblical laws and exhortations served in later times as the basis of the admirable ways of the faithful.

Two aspects of further significance attach to Tobit. One has to do with the laws which Tobit obeys, in that these are specified in such a way as to include both the biblical, and also inferences from the biblical (especially in connection with the burial of the dead). Moreover, the overtones of religious belief and piety go quite a bit beyond the biblical. The second aspect is exemplified in the counsel given by Tobit to Tobias (4.5-19) and by Raphael to the two of them (12.6-13). The two passages reflect the significant motif of a wise person giving wise counsel. This motif of wisdom extends what was already common in Judaism through its presence in the Book of Proverbs.

Scholars are not united on the date and place of composition of Tobit. Perhaps a date of 200 B.C. is reasonable, since the book has no mention of the Maccabean revolt; the new but rising doctrine of resurrection (about which we will speak later) does not appear. The place of composition is disputed, but appears to have been outside Judea. One need not ascribe the book to the eastern lands, which is the assumed locale, for the book shows no first-hand knowledge, but only picks up clues from biblical books. Fragments of Tobit in Aramaic have been found among the Dead Sea Scrolls (in Cave 3), and a date even earlier than 200 for some possibly earlier version of the tale, often told and retold, is advocated by some.

The author of Tobit abstains from giving any information about how the Jews, supposedly in eastern lands, maintained their religion. They are loyal to the remote Temple in Jerusalem; if they were conceived of as having any local place of gathering, kindred to a synagogue, not a syllable of information is given us. The bond among the Jews is stressed, both in respect to marriage within the fold, to almsgiving for fellow Jews, and to abiding by dietary laws. A strong ethnic sense, then, pervades this book.

3. *Judith*

Judith is a patriotic book, with literary qualities of a high order and an ending that qualifies it as being among the best of all horror stories. Judith is fiction; the use by its author of Jewish history known from the Bible is marked by either freedom or recklessness about such matters as chronology.

The historical setting provided supposes that the Babylonian King Nebuchadnezzar had embarked on war against the Medes and their King Aphaxed. Nebuchadnezzar appealed to the nations in the west to help him, but they all refused; hence, after he conquered the Medes, he sent a general named Holofernes westward to punish those who had refused him help. Holofernes carried out a successful expedition, plundering Damascus and proceeding south along the coast of Palestine from the Phoenician cities of Tyre and Sidon to the Philistine cities of Ashdod and Ashkelon. Victorious, he demolished the sacred pagan shrines, compelling the people to worship Nebuchadnezzar as God. He came then to the borders of Judea. The Judeans armed themselves against the expected onslaught, preparing to resist it by holding the mountain passes. Our story focuses on a place named Bethulia, about which nothing is known.

Holofernes assembled peoples hostile to the Judeans to get information about that strange nation. A certain Ammonite leader named Achior gave Holofernes a résumé of Jewish history (using both biblical and post-biblical materials), warning Holofernes that if the Judeans were innocent of sin against God, Holofernes ought to desist from attacking them, for God would protect them. Furious at Achior, Holofernes had him bound and put within the vicinity of Bethulia. Judean defenders untied him and brought him to Bethulia, where he told what had happened between him and Holofernes.

Holofernes moved his immense force near to Bethulia so that its defenders could observe his power. A day later he deployed his cavalry, and, on the advice of the peoples hostile to the Judeans, chose to seize the springs so as to deprive Bethulia of its water supply, rather than attack directly. When the people of Bethulia began to suffer from thirst, they reproached their leaders for having determined so unwisely to resist Holofernes. The leader, one Uzziah, proposed that they wait five days, and if no help were to come, whether from God or man, the city would surrender.

In Bethulia lived a widow named Judith, a pious, beautiful, and wealthy woman, and of sterling reputation. She sent for the leaders, rebuking them for testing God in the matter of the decision to wait five days. She volunteered, in a plan she would not reveal, to be the instrument by which God would deliver His people.

Alone, Judith donned sackcloth and ashes and prayed to God for help. She then went to the house she used for Sabbaths and festivals and removed the sackcloth and her widow's garments. She bathed (whence came the water?), applied fragrant ointment, combed her hair, and put on a tiara and jewelry so as to be beautiful enough to entice any man who might see her. Accompanied by her maid, and carrying some food, she went out of the city.

An Assyrian patrol took her into custody. Identifying herself as fleeing from the Hebrews, she asked to be taken to Holofernes, whom she could show how to capture the area without losing a man. She was escorted to Holofernes by a hundred men, all of whom marveled at her beauty.

Holofernes received her in his tent warmly. Judith confirmed to him that the Judeans, if innocent of sin, could not be defeated. Now, however, they were preparing to violate God's law by eating what was forbidden—namely, food set aside as consecrated for the Temple. She proposed that she stay with Holofernes, but that every night she would go into the valley, there to learn if the Judeans had as yet sinned in the matter of the food. Delighted, Holofernes had food brought in on silver dishes, but Judith declined the food (lest she violate food laws), preferring to eat what she had carried out of the city.

Judith left the tent into which she had been put at midnight, to go out to the valley to pray. This happened three nights in succession. On the fourth night, Holofernes prepared a private banquet. He sent his eunuch to bring Judith to him, for it would be a disgrace for him not to have enjoyed her embrace. At the eunuch's visit, she donned her beautiful clothes, and her maid came with her, bringing soft fleeces for her to recline upon.

Filled with desire for her, Holofernes drank more wine than he had ever drunk before. The servants all withdrew, leaving the two alone. Holofernes was overcome by the wine. She picked up his sword, and, holding him by the hair, she struck at his neck twice, severing his head. She gave the head to her maid who was outside the tent, and the maid put the head into the bag in which they had carried the food. Judith and the maid then went out into the valley (as by now was their custom). She arrived at the gates of Bethulia and asked for admittance. The elders quickly gathered. She took the head of Holofernes from the bag and showed it to them. The people gratefully thanked God for bringing the enemy of His people into contempt.

Judith advised that the head of Holofernes be hung from the parapet; the Judean soldiers would then pass it on their way out of the city, as if to assault the foe, and be heartened. The outpost sentinels would rouse Assyrian officers, and these would go to Holofernes' tent. Then the Assyrians would flee in fright, and the Judeans could destroy them as they fled.

And that is how things happened. Amidst joyful dancing, Judith sang a song of triumph. They all went to Jerusalem, where Judith gave to the Temple the possessions taken from Holofernes.

Though many wished to marry Judith, she remained unmarried. She set her maid free. At her death at the age of 105, all Israel mourned her for seven days. Having no heirs, she distributed her property before her death in accordance with the Laws.

Scholars have varied greatly in the date to which they ascribe the Book of Judith, some believing it to be as early as the seventh century B.C., and some as late as the second century A.D. Most, though, ascribe it to the Hasmonean period, specifically to about 150 B.C. Such scholars view Nebuchadnezzar as a substitute for Antiochus IV Epiphanes, who had professed to deity.

The prayers and piety ascribed to Judith are reflections, similar to those in Tobit, of the age of the Tanach, reflecting additions to the biblical ordinances. Despite the erotic story line, Judith is portrayed as an ideally pious woman, as Tobit was an ideally pious man, both living noble lives in conformity with the biblical injunctions. The two stories are folktales in the sense that they are dedicated more to action than to thoughtful analysis. They both have an appealing literary quality, yet for our purposes it is their series of motifs of religious piety that should be our principal interest, these emerging out of the concrete situations that arise in the stories.

4. Additions to Daniel

In the Greek Bible there are some additions to the Book of Daniel, inserted into what in the Hebrew is after 3.23. One is a compound addition, in three parts. The first, The Prayer of Azariah (one of Daniel's three companions), is an eloquent plea to God, spoken as three companions walked amid the flames they had been cast into. It begins, as most Jewish prayers do, with the praise of God Who is just; next comes an admission of Israel's sin which led to their subjection to a wicked king; and last is an appeal for God's mercy, with a reminder of His past favors to Israel, culminating in a plea for deliverance by Him. Much of the prayer is a hearkening back to a vast variety of biblical verses.

There ensues directly the second part, a series of verses describing how the furnace fire was stoked high, but an angel descended into the furnace and reduced the fire to "a moist whistling wind." The third part relates that the three lads, now saved, sing "The Song of the Three Young Men," a hymn of thanksgiving virtually every line of which begins with the words, "Bless the Lord." Whereas the Prayer of Azariah seems to assume that the Temple has just been desecrated and is in disuse, The Song of the Three Young Men possibly alludes to its having been restored to use. The Song, like the Prayer, paraphrases many biblical verses.

The second addition, the Story of Susanna, appears in some ancient manuscripts as the first part of the Greek Daniel (in the text of Theodotion), but in other manuscripts (the usual Septuagint and the Vulgate), it is instead an appendix to Daniel. In this story, told to enhance the character of Daniel, he is presumably quite young, and already precocious in his wisdom. The story is that Susanna was the wife of a rich and eminent Jew of Babylon. Two elders, evil men, had both conceived a lustful passion for the beautiful woman, and had revealed this to each other. They hid themselves one day to watch her being bathed in the garden by her maid. When the maid had left, they emerged from their hiding place to demand that Susanna lie with them; if she refused, they would charge her with entertaining a young man. Susanna did refuse, and the next day the elders publicly accused her of adultery. She was condemned to death by the people assembled. Daniel declined to join in the condemnation, explaining that there had not been a proper interrogation to ascertain the facts. He was then designated to conduct an examination. He thereupon separated the two elders from each other. First to one and then to the other he put the question, Under what tree did Susanna commit adultery? One replied that it had been a mastic tree, and the other said an evergreen oak. In view of the discrepancy in their testimony, Susanna was acquitted, and the two wicked elders were punished by execution. The tale is sometimes called the world's oldest detective story, though in reality it is the ingenuity, shrewdness, and wisdom, of the trial lawyer which is here being praised.

The third addition to the Book of Daniel is called Bel and the Dragon. It comprises two short tales on the same theme, the silliness of idolatry. The first tale is about Bel, a Babylonian deity, on whose idol the Persian monarch Cyrus daily lavished a huge abundance of flour, sheep, and wine. Daniel, however, persisted in worshipping his own God. On the king's inquiry, Daniel explained that the idol in reality consumed none of the elaborate food. A test was arranged to determine whether or not the idol did consume the great amount of food. The priests of the idol had a secret passageway under a table in the temple, using it, and not the doors, to enter and eat the food set there, and then leave. But Daniel sprinkled ashes throughout the temple, with the king observing him. The temple was sealed up as usual. In the night the priests and their families entered through the passageway and consumed the food. The next day, when Cyrus and Daniel came to the temple, the seals were of course unbroken, but the food was gone. Daniel, though, invited the king to look at the footprints in the ashes, and the king recognized them as footprints of men, women, and children. When the priests were then seized, they showed the king their secret passageway. Cyrus put them to death, and allowed Daniel to destroy both the idol and the temple.

The second story, The Tale of the Dragon—really, a serpent—tells that Daniel, with Cyrus' permission, tested the divinity of the Dragon by feeding it cakes made of pitch, fat, and hair, boiled together. After the Dragon ate the cakes, he burst open! The Babylonians then conspired against the king, charging him with having become a Jew, and demanding that he hand Daniel over to them. Daniel (for a second time) was thrown into a den of seven lions whose daily food—two humans and two sheep—had been withheld from them so that they would now turn to eat up Daniel. But God spoke to the prophet Habakkuk, who had prepared a modest meal; Habakkuk was to take this meal to Daniel. An angel lifted Habakkuk by his hair and set him down in Babylonia over the lions' den. Daniel ate the meal, and the angel brought Habakkuk back to the prophet's own place. When, on the seventh day, the king came to the den, there was Daniel, still alive. King Cyrus acknowledged Daniel's God as the only one. The conspirators were then thrown into the den and devoured by the lions (who apparently had been without food).

These two less than exalted stories are of the genre of popular stories that reflect the scorn in which Jews held the worship of idols and the priests of the pagan religions. A partisan relish is, of course, reflected in them, and to that extent they have some value in our understanding of aspects of the mentality of the age.

5. *Letter of Jeremiah*

The same mentality is disclosed in the so-called Letter of Jeremiah (also called "The Epistle of Jeremy"). In ancient manuscripts it is found in diverse places, often directly after another Apocryphal work called Baruch (see pp. 69-70), the man who in the Book of Jeremiah was the prophet's secretary. The Letter purports to be what Jeremiah wrote to the Judeans exiled to Babylonia. The Letter predicts that exile would last "seven generations" (Jer. 29.10 sets the period, though, as seventy years[17]), after which God would bring the exiles back in peace. But in Babylon the exiles would see gods made of metal and wood, carried in processions, and they had to abstain from becoming like those foreigners. The idols would be elaborately adorned as people are, this out of the gold contributed by the people, but the priests kept the contributions for themselves, or gave some of it to harlots in brothels. Idols are subject to rust and corrosion; they need to be dusted; they cannot wield the weapons put into their hands. They are as useless as broken dishes. The temples need to have locks and bars to protect the idols—gods!—from plunder by robbers. Bats and swallows light on them, as do cats. They are without feeling or mobility; they need to be set firmly so as not to topple over. Idols are completely impotent, unable to save a man, or pity a widow, or befriend an orphan. A man who abstains from idols escapes reproach.

The Letter, a long expansion of a verse (Jer. 10.11), is by some thought of as having been composed somewhat earlier than the Maccabean period, but most scholars date it within the Maccabean age. Opinions are divided about the original language, but whether Hebrew, Aramaic, or Greek, it survives only in Greek. A tiny fragment (verses 43-44) in Greek is found among the Dead Sea writings, from Cave 7.[18] The Letter is somewhat repetitious, and far from cohesive. It is bound together by a refrain which asserts that idols "evidently are not gods" (as in verses 16, 23, 29, 40, 44, 52, 56,

65 and 69). One wonders if there would have been need for
such a composition, or for the additions to Daniel, if there
were not Jews who were being seduced into the cults which
worshipped idols.

6. Book of Baruch

Baruch seems to be a composite book. The first part (1.1-3.8)
is in prose; the second consists of two poems (3.9-4.4 and
4.5-5.9). An introduction tells us that Baruch, the secretary
of Jeremiah, wrote this book in Babylon, after the destruction
of Jerusalem (which had occurred in 587). He read the book
to the exiles, including King Jeconiah and the important
people. It was then sent to Jerusalem to be used in prayer
services there. Along with it were sent funds for sacrifices,
and the request to pray on behalf of Nebuchadnezzar, king
of Babylon, and his son Belshazzar. The prayer is in effect a
confession of sin on the part of the Jerusalem community
(1.15-2.5) and of the exiles (2.6-3.8).

The allusions to Nebuchadnezzar and "his son Belshazzar"
are simply wrong, for historically Belshazzar was the son of
Emperor Nabonidus, not Nebuchadnezzar. This is a clue to
the impossibility of accepting an origin of the letter in Babylon in 587. Rather, its origin is much later, but how late is
disputed, though the Maccabean period is often suggested.
Indeed, occasionally it is viewed as coming from the Roman
period, specifically after the Roman crushing of the rebellion
in 66-70. It is suggested that the first part of Baruch, in prose,
was written by Roman Jews, advising the Judeans to submit
to the conquerors and, indeed, to pray for them, in the hope
of healing the breach between the Romans and the Jews.
But this is uncertain.

The poem in 3.9-4.4 ascribes the exile as due to Israel's
neglect of wisdom. Wisdom is here identified with the divine
commandments, but these are not the explicit subject of the
poem. Rather, in the manner of passages such as Job 28 and
Proverbs 8, wisdom is portrayed as the elusive treasure that
the nations search for futilely. Israel, however, possesses wisdom which is "the book of the commandments of God, the
law that forever endures." Scholars speak of a "wisdom tradition," into which this passage and still others are fitted.

The second poem (4.5-5.9) offers comfort to Israel in the assurance that God, having justly punished Israel for its sins by exile, will in due time deliver his people from the enemy and lead them back to the homeland in joy. Jerusalem will witness both the punishment of her enemies and also the happy return from the east of those led away by the enemy.

It is almost impossible to know precisely when the two poems were written, or when they were fused with the prose section. Perhaps older poems were appended to the prose portion after the Roman destruction in A.D. 70. The poems themselves may come from the late Maccabean age, perhaps between 150 and 70 B.C.

7. *The Prayer of Manasseh*

The Prayer of Manasseh comes from the period between 200 and 50 B.C. It is a composition of sterling beauty and quality. The original language, whether Hebrew, Aramaic, or Greek, is uncertain; no Hebrew or Aramaic version has survived. Manasseh had ruled over the kingdom of Judah from about 687-643 or 642. He is described in II Kings 21.1-16 as a man of unique wickedness; his reign, however, was unusually long. The account of him in II Chronicles 33.11-13 seeks to explain how so evil a man could have been allowed to reign so long. It tells that Manasseh was taken prisoner by the Assyrians, but then he underwent sincere repentance, and was allowed to return to Jerusalem where he practiced the worship of God. This prayer appears in the Greek translation of Chronicles; it purports to be Manasseh's prayer of repentance, but it was written by an inspired author long after his time. Not only is the content an eloquent expression of contrition, but its form has unity. It begins with an invocation and words of praise to God (as do other, later prayers). Next comes a confession of sins, followed by a stirring plea for divine pardon. Finally comes a brief passage, "All the host of heaven sing your praise, and yours is the glory forever. Amen."

The composition, which has not survived in Hebrew or Aramaic, did not make its way into the later synagogue worship on the Day of Atonement. In content and form it would have fitted admirably.

8. Wisdom of Solomon

The Wisdom of Solomon is a work of extreme importance. It was not translated from the Hebrew, but was written in Greek. In other books in the so-called "wisdom tradition" there are brief lines in which a pithy statement contains some traditional insight, as might be exemplified in the English adage that "a stitch in time sometimes saves nine"; Proverbs contains many such lines. The Wisdom of Solomon, by contrast, is a matter not of lines, but of paragraphs in a connected, well-worked-out essay. It is therefore more profound, and more interesting, than any collection of proverbs could be. Its origin is the Greek Dispersion, quite possibly Alexandria in Egypt. (After Alexander the Great, Jews settled in very great numbers in the Grecian lands; this settlement is known by synonyms, "Dispersion" and "Diaspora," renderings of the Hebrew word gōlă.) In its frames of reference there is an acute awareness of an alien environment which attracted some Jews away from Judaism, this through the decline in the observance of the strict morals of the Five Books of Moses.

The book falls into three sections. The first, Chapters 1-5, is in essence a plea for righteous living, in accordance with the guidance which "wisdom" furnishes. A warning is issued to those who think that they may escape the notice, indeed, the scrutiny of God, and that their evil thoughts and deeds will go unobserved. A life of wickedness leads to death—that is, to eternal death, even though God had designed deathlessness for his creatures (ch. 1).

The wicked who die do so in part because they reason unsoundly. In this portion the author of Wisdom, in part, counters the sentiments, some found in Ecclesiastes,[19] a work attributed to Solomon, to the effect that life is short and sorrowful, and death is the end; we are born by mere chance, and once we are dead it is as though we never existed; we ought to enjoy ourselves without limit; there is no reason not to oppress the poor, or spare the widow, or treat the elderly with respect; the righteous man can be scorned, for if—the tone here becomes sarcastic—he is God's son, God will protect him. Such reasoning, the author of Wisdom tells us, is unsound, in that God created man, in his image, for immortality[20] (ch. 2).

If indeed the righteous seem to suffer, this is not the case, for the righteous, being immortal, are destined to receive great good. On the other hand, the wicked, as rebels against God, will be punished. The wives and children of the wicked are cursed; a barren woman and a eunuch, if righteous, will receive special gifts of God's favor (ch. 3). Childlessness, with virtue and immortality, is better than the numerous offspring of the wicked (4.1-6).

As if replying to those who contend that biblical passages (such as Prov. 3.16), which promise long life to the righteous, are wrong, our author alludes to Enoch of Genesis 5.24 as a righteous man who "walked with God, and was not, for God took him." Here, and later in the book, our author often abstains from mentioning the names of the biblical characters he speaks of. Enoch, he writes, was taken up to heaven[21] so that the evil of his age would not alter his understanding, or falsity pervert his mind. Yet Enoch, in having become perfected in a short time,[22] in effect fulfilled a great length of years. Enoch's wicked contemporaries did not understand that God was being good to Enoch in removing him from the environment of sin. The wicked do not understand that a final judgment, a day of reckoning, is to come. When it comes, the wicked will see the righteous man emerge in full assurance in the presence of the wicked who have afflicted him. This sight will induce amazement and remorse in the wicked, and move them to repentance. They will realize how futile and evanescent was the wealth they garnered out of their mistreatment of the righteous. The latter live forever, with God, in wondrous bliss (4.7-5.23).

The second section (6.1-9.18) is addressed to kings and judges. It warns that since their authority has come from God, they will have to answer to Him for their misdeeds. Therefore, they ought to learn wisdom, so as to abstain from trespassing (6.1-11).

Wisdom, so we are told here, is easily to be found by those who seek her,[23] and she readily appears to those who do. Wisdom begins in a person's earnest desire for instruction, and love of instruction leads to observing wisdom's laws (by which is meant the Mosaic Law), and the observance of the laws of wisdom leads to immortality, and immortality brings one near to God. The desire for wisdom, then, leads to participation in God's kingdom (6.12-20).

The author, speaking as if he is Solomon, proceeds to state (6.21-25) that he will now tell how he acquired wisdom. A mortal man, descended from Adam and born by the usual human process, Solomon was not different from other humans. Yet he prayed for understanding,[24] and in answer the spirit of wisdom came to him, and he cherished this above all else. He came to learn unerringly the structure of the world and the properties of the elements; he learned astronomy and the nature of wild beasts and of plants and roots. He learned both what is secret (that is, below the surface) and what is manifest (on the surface). He next presents the attributes of wisdom; he lists twenty-one[25] characteristics.[26] He sums these up by saying that wisdom, through her purity, pervades and penetrates all things. She is "a breath of the power of God . . . a pure emanation of the glory of the almighty . . . an image of His goodness." Though she is only one, she is capable of all things; though she is constantly the same, she renews all things, and in each generation passes into holy souls, making them into prophets of God. She extends from one end of the earth to the other, providing universal order (7.1-8.1).

Loving Wisdom (henceforth capitalized) Solomon desired her for his bride. By living and mating with Wisdom, he would achieve eminence among men. Through her he would gain immortality. He wondered, then, how to acquire her. He learned that he could do so only if God gave her to him, and he therefore prayed to God for this gift (8.2-21). This prayer for wisdom is the substance of Chapter 9. "What can a man learn about the counsel of God? Who has discerned what the Lord wills? The reasoning among men is worthless and human plans fail, this because a perishable body weighs the soul down. . . . Can one learn Your counsel unless You have given wisdom and sent Your holy spirit from on high?"

In the third section, the author turns to history to show how the power of Wisdom acted in the biblical history of Israel. The biblical characters are not named, possibly, as suggested, because anonymity added a sense of mystery and solemnity. Wisdom, not the biblical characters, is the heroine, and often the biblical material undergoes some embroidery or expansion. For example, Wisdom protected Adam when he was the only man: "She saved him from his transgression and gave him the power to rule all things." Cain departed from Wisdom in rage, and he died because he slew his brother in rage. The biblical characters treated in this way include Noah, Abraham, Lot, Jacob, Joseph, Moses, and the enslaved Israelites (ch. 10). Wisdom guided the Israelites in the Wilderness (11.1-4). When the Israelites thirsted in the Wilderness, Wisdom gave them water from the rock of flint, in contrast with the fate of the Egyptians, for whom water—that is, the River Nile—turned to blood (11.5-14). The Egyptians had gone astray when they worshipped serpents and animals of no account; they underwent the plagues (of frogs, flies, lice, and locusts); it could have been even worse, for Wisdom might have sent bears or lions or fiery creatures that belch forth smoke or flash damaging sparks from their eyes[27] (11.15-20). Yet though God can always punish with great power, in His mercy He prefers that men repent, so as to be freed from wickedness (11.21-12.2). God had dealt mercifully with the Canaanites, patiently providing a slow conquest so as to give them opportunity to repent, though He knew that they would not (12.3-24). The Egyptians were tormented by the very animals they worshipped, and by that punishment came to recognize the true God they had previously refused to know (12.23-27).

Men in their ignorance quite naturally turned to worship fire or wind or air or the stars or the ocean, assuming these to be gods. They were in a sense blameless in not moving from the greatness and beauty of created things to a perception of the Creator. Surely such men were earnestly seeking God, though they might not be excused in that they could have found God in their investigation of the world. But quite different is the case with men who fashion idols and call the work of their hands gods. How preposterous it is to beseech weak idols for the strength of health, or dead images for life (ch. 13)! Some seafarers put more trust in the wooden image on the prow of a ship than in the ship itself. An idol is accursed, and so is its maker. Idolatry began in the grief of a father for the untimely death of a child, and had an image made of him, and later that image came to be worshipped. Or else men at a great distance from a king made a near-at-hand image they could honor. An ambitious craftsman fashioned the royal image into something quite beautiful, and the multitudes were seduced by the beauty (14.1-21). But idolatry produced great evils, such as the killing of children in initiations, or the frenzies of the mystery religions. Marriages lost their sanctity, and society knew killings and murder and all kinds of personal pollutions, including sexual perversions (14.21-31).

The worshippers of the true God are deterred from sin, while the idolaters are driven to it. Israel's enemies worship the most loathsome of animals. The Egyptians were deservedly punished by such creatures. But God showed kindness to His people, exemplified in the quail (sent them in the Wilderness, Num. 11.4-32). When serpents briefly caused Israel suffering, this was only a warning, and healing came quickly (Num. 21.6-12), for God has power over life and death (15.1-16.14). The Egyptians were destroyed by hail from heaven; the Hebrews were fed by a rain of manna (16.15-28). The Egyptians suffered from the plague of darkness, while the Israelites experienced a great light, in the pillar of fire that led them in the Wilderness (17.1-18.4). The desire of the Egyptians to kill the first-born of the Israelites resulted in the death of Egyptian first-born children (18.5-19). When the Israelites underwent a plague in the Wilderness, Aaron (Num. 16.41-50) stopped the plague (18.20-25). Especially at the Red Sea, the Egyptians met a strange death, while the Israelites found an incredible route in the splitting of the Sea. Indeed, the Egyptians treated strangers even worse than did the wicked people of Sodom (Gen. 19.1-11). At the Red Sea, there took place a transformation of land animals into water creatures, and of water creatures into land animals, and fire resisted being quenched by water and, on the other hand, fire abstained from consuming the flesh of creatures (19.1-21).

A brief conclusion ends the book: "O Lord, You have exalted and glorified Your people in all ways, and have not neglected to help them at all times and in all places" (19.22).

While occasional scholars have the opinion that the first section, or even the first two, were first written in Hebrew or Aramaic, the prevailing view seems to be that the echoes of Hebrew or Aramaic are better viewed as reflecting an influence on a Greek writer in somewhat the same way that an American whose European origin is somewhat recent would echo the language of his forebears in his writing of English. No precise date can be assigned to the book, but many would date it about 50 B.C., so as to put it later than Ecclesiasticus, which we turn to next, and before the time of Philo of Alexandria (20 B.C.-A.D. 40), whose writings we shall see later (pp. 279-301).

We should especially notice three facets of the Book of Wisdom. One is the way in which Wisdom is heavily accentuated, and that it is here more thoroughly and specifically presented as equivalent to the divine laws of the Pentateuch than is suggested, but not made specific, in the Book of Proverbs. Second, the book in many passages reflects some knowledge of aspects of Greek philosophy, both in content and even in occasional phraseology. The author should not be described as well-versed in Greek philosophy, but he clearly caught at least significant overtones of it. The afterlife which he accepts (something denied in Ecclesiastes) is immortality, not resurrection; immortality is a Grecian idea of an afterlife, not a Semitic one. Third, as the author reviews biblical personalities and events, he does not adhere strictly to what is in the Bible; rather, he adds generous measures of embroidery. Some of the embroidery is unique to this book, but some of it is part of the general expansion which was becoming characteristic of the way in which the Tanach was being studied and meditated on. By the time that Wisdom was written, the Pentateuch had already achieved the highest sanctity; Wisdom in the third section illustrates the growing development of a conscious preoccupation with the Bible as the textbook of Jewish study and meditation.

9. Ecclesiasticus

Ecclesiasticus, also called "The Wisdom of Jesus[28] the son of Sirach," is in many ways unique among the Apocrypha.

First, it is the only book whose author is clear and unmistakable. Second, Chapter 50 speaks of a High Priest, Simon son of Onias, whose dates are known to be 219-196 B.C., so that the book was written toward the end of that interval, or shortly afterward, possibly about 180. Moreover, the Greek translation was the work of the author's grandson, as is disclosed in a prologue to the Greek version. The prologue speaks of "my grandfather Jesus," who, "after devoting himself to the study of the Law and the Prophets, was impelled to write a work of instruction and wisdom by which lovers of learning could make good progress in living in accordance with the Law." The grandson apologizes for passages imperfectly translated, since what has been expressed in Hebrew does not have exactly the same sense when rendered into another language. The grandson came to Egypt "in the thirty-eighth year of the reign of [Ptolemy VII] Euregetes [II Physcon]" (170-117 B.C.); that date would be 132 B.C. The translation was made sometime thereafter, out of the grandson's desire to publish the book for Jews living abroad.

By this testimony, Jesus son of Sirach wrote in Hebrew, not in Aramaic, which had become the spoken language. The Hebrew version has not survived in its totality; some fragments were found in a cave near Qumran in 1952. From the storehouse ("Genizah") of an old synagogue discovered in Cairo in 1896, five fragments of Ecclesiasticus which dated from the medieval period were recovered. These fragments amount to about two-thirds of the book. In addition to the Greek translation, there were versions in other languages, including Syriac and Aramaic. Ecclesiasticus is quoted a few times in Rabbinic literature.[29] Clearly, the book circulated broadly even in ancient times. That it was named Ecclesiasticus ("the church book") testifies to the admiration and respect accorded it.

Ecclesiasticus is not the kind of writing for which a faithful summary of the contents is useful. Like Proverbs, it is replete with sound wisdom; it provides a greater abundance of detailed advice than does the biblical book; but no pattern is discernible in the presentation; themes are presented, dropped, and returned to as if the author wrote short bits at various intervals, and then assembled them without truly correlating and coordinating them. Some scholars seem to feel that the book is, as it were, in two volumes, Chapters 1-23 and Chapters 24-51. (Presently we shall turn to a striking section, 44.1-50.24, which is a review of biblical history.) The portions of the book which provide counsel are sound, but rather less than exciting. The opening chapter, in praise of Wisdom, has some eloquence. But the repeated themes can seem to a modern reader extremely labored. Our author is in favor of piety to God, of obedience to parents; he endorses humility; he believes in divine rewards and punishments. While God is merciful, a man is foolish to suppose that mercy will always cancel punishment. One should practice self-control and curb his passions and lusts. There are duties to a friend, to a wife, to a servant, to one's animals, to children. There are duties to God, to the priests, to the poor. Society is full of all kinds of men and women, and one should be prudent in dealing with them. Jealousy of one's wife is wrong, as is subservience to her. The wiles of women must be resisted. Civil authorities have responsibilities to educate and discipline their people. Humility is admirable. Discretion, whether in estimating one's friends or in giving alms to the poor, is always useful. Idle talk gets one into trouble. Gossip does damage.

Wisdom is equated with fidelity to the revealed commandments. In Chapter 24 there are echoes of the personification of Wisdom as a woman, based on Proverbs 8.22-9.12. A passage, 26.1-4, in praise of the good wife, is touching; there ensues immediately (26.5-12) a section which describes an evil wife as worse than slander, a mob, or a false accusation. A good wife (26.13-18) should put weight on her husband's bones, be silent, and be modest.

One should never betray confidences or reveal secrets. Hypocrisy is to be condemned. One should be willing to lend money to a needy neighbor, but many borrowers are unreliable. Whoever loves his son should whip him often, so as to discipline him, and not spoil him. One should never exalt himself at a public banquet, and should beware of unduly exhibiting one's cleverness. One should not be deluded by dreams into pursuing the wind. The offerings of sacrifices at the Temple should be carried out acceptably.

Two chapters are of striking character. A prayer for the

preservation and elevation of Israel (35.1-17) is quite moving. The injunction is well presented that one should honor a physician (38.1-15), for he is the creation of God from whom healing comes.

The man learned in Scripture, the scribe, should be a craftsman in much the same way as artisans who use metals are craftsmen. God can fill such a scribe with the spirit of understanding, so that, by his sage counsel, the memory of him will not disappear (38.24-9.11). Throughout the book one sees either brief or lengthy reflections of the author's piety, of his being a God-intoxicated person. It is not only God the Creator of the glorious world, but God who is greater than all His creation who moves our author to occasional lyric outbursts of deep emotion.

The review of Israelite history (44.1-50.24) begins with the "praise of famous men, our fathers in their generations to whom God apportioned great honor and glory. . . . Some were rulers, some musicians and poets. . . . Some have left a name . . . some who have no memorial . . . were men of mercy. . . ." The first mentioned are Enoch, Noah, Abraham, Isaac, and Jacob. Joseph does not specifically appear. Moses and Aaron, and the wicked opponents of Moses, Dathan, Abiram, and Korah (Num. ch. 16) are allotted attention, as is Phinehas the son of Eleazar (Num. 25.10-13). Joshua and Caleb are named; there is allusion to the judges but their names are not given. The prophets Samuel and Nathan appear in connection with David, but Saul is not named. Many kings and prophets are mentioned. Nehemiah is named, but, curiously, Ezra is not, though the Bible couples them together. The brief mentions are just long enough for the author here or there to include slight expansions beyond the biblical accounts.

Our author now turns (50.1-21) to a figure from post-biblical times, Simon the High Priest, the son of Onias[30] II; this was Simon II, high priest from about 219 to 196 B.C. The passage in the inherited Greek version of Ecclesiasticus is significantly abbreviated from the recovered Hebrew. We must digress to backgrounds in order to understand this abbreviation: Onias III, the son of Simon II, is mentioned in II Maccabees 3-4; Onias III had turned against the Seleucidian Greeks before 175 B.C. and had sought the support of the

Egyptian Ptolemies. His brother Jason replaced him as High
Priest; Onias had fled to Egypt, building a rival to the sanctuary in Jerusalem, known as "the Temple of Onias."[31] The
sources give contradictory estimates of Onias III,[32] usually
in extreme disapproval of his temple, the building of which
was in defiance of a repeated motif in Deuteronomy that
only one sanctuary (that destined for Jerusalem) was to be
allowed. But because Onias and Jason were of the lofty
priestly family of Zadok, while the Hasmonean High Priests
derived from the less lofty priestly family of Jehoiarib,[33] it is
argued that the Greek version of 50.1-21 underwent editing
and omission to remove the glorification of the Zadokite
priests in the original Hebrew. It is further argued by scholars, as already mentioned, that the community of the Dead
Sea Scrolls abandoned their support of the Temple, this out
of loyalty to the Zadokite family, when the Zadokite priests
had been supplanted by the Hasmonean priests; the pro-
testers retired from public life to a monastic existence on the
west bank of the Dead Sea.[34] At any rate, the Greek version,
though much abbreviated[35] as compared with the Hebrew,
speaks in praise of Simon II, as one "who in his lifetime repaired and strengthened the Temple." The passage seems to
suggest that Simon II has died; it would have been written
at some time not long after 196. This clue to the date of our
book puts it between 196 and 168; it can scarcely be later
than 168 since no reflection of the Maccabean revolt appears.

The book closes with an autobiographical section (51.13-
30), in which our author describes his quest to acquire wisdom, and his desire to impart it to others. Jesus ben Sirach,
then, is a very important witness to the unfolding of inner
Jewish life in the period just before the Maccabean revolt of
168. He makes no mention of an afterlife, but appears,
rather, to believe that death is the end.

There is a certain tranquillity in the book, as if the author
was in no way even dimly aware that in just a few years the
turbulent events of the Maccabean revolt would take place.

10. IV Ezra

This book, known both as IV Ezra and II Esdras, may represent for our purposes a transition: we have been looking at

the Apocrypha; we shall shortly review some writings which never gained entrance into the Greek Bible. IV Ezra has survived in Latin and other translations, but only a few lines of a Greek version have been inherited. This book is part of the Apocrypha for some Protestants; for Roman Catholics it is not canonical, but is instead regarded as a sort of appendix to Scripture. Modern scholars are agreed that Chapters 1 and 2 and 15 and 16 are Christian additions to a book originally Jewish and written in Hebrew or Aramaic. Chapters 1 and 2 are often dated in A.D. 150, but 15 and 16 are possibly as late as A.D. 270.

The original chapters, 3-14, seem to come from the period after the Roman destruction of the Temple in A.D. 70; A.D. 100 is frequently given. The book is in part a lament over the disaster to Jerusalem, accompanied by a denunciation of Rome, spoken of as "Babylon." But the greatness of the book is its searching inquiry into the question of how a just God could have allowed great evils to befall Jerusalem. In structure we encounter a series of seven "revelations"[36] to one Sheatiel[37]/Salathiel, "also called Ezra." The purported setting is Babylon; the purported date is 557/556, thirty years after the destruction of the First Temple in 587. If thirty years is right, then the date of A.D. 100—thirty years after 70—is understandable.

The author, deeply troubled at the "desolation of Zion" and the prosperity of the "Babylonians," speaks to God. God had created Adam, whose sin in Eden led to the assignment of death for him and his descendants, who were the nations of the world without number. These nations had been destroyed by the flood. But the nations descended of Noah were even more wicked. God had chosen and loved Abraham, and revealed the future to him, and made an eternal covenant with him and his offspring; yet, through their wickedness, Abraham's descendants have been delivered into the hands of the enemy, the Babylonians. But were the Babylonians better than the Jews? Gentile nations abounded in wealth, despite the fact that they did not observe God's commandments.

A reply comes to Ezra from Uriel, an angel sent to him. If Ezra can understand the world, perhaps he can understand the ways of God! Can Ezra weigh fire, or give the dimensions

of a blast of wind, or bring back a day already past? Ezra
replies that no man can do this. Yet, as he says, it is better for
man not to have been born than to be born and suffer without
knowing why. The angel then speaks of war between the
forests and the sea, but fire destroyed the forests, and sand
impeded the sea. As land is assigned to the forest, and the sea
to its waves, so man is assigned to and can understand only
earthly things, but only He Who is above the heavens can
understand the heavens.

Ezra replies that his desire was only to understand matters
of everyday experience, namely, why Israel was put into the
hands of the foe, God's beloved people given over to godless
tribes, and the Torah no longer effective. The angel replies
that if Ezra lives long enough, he will see a new age dawn.
That cannot come, though, until the full harvest of evil has
been reaped. That evil was from the very beginning sown in
Adam's heart.

When Ezra asks precisely when the new age will come, the
answer is that first there must be born a predetermined number of righteous men; but the end of this age of wickedness is
near. Will it come in Ezra's lifetime? The angel does not answer the question. Instead, he speaks of the "signs" of terror
and falsity which must first come, when the sun will shine
at night and the moon in the day, and when blood will drip
from wood, stones will speak, and stars will fall; birds will
fly away from the disaster. But if Ezra will pray again, after
fasting and weeping, the angel will return to tell him even
greater things.

In the second vision (5.21-6.34), a series of figures of
speech are used to describe Israel as God's chosen people,
leading to the question, why has God allowed the nations to
oppress Israel instead of Himself punishing her for her transgressions? The angel replies that Ezra is unable to understand. But Ezra then asks, why, if he is deprived of understanding, was he born at all? If unborn, he would not have
had to witness the ordeal through which the people of Israel
had gone. The reply is that if man cannot understand earthly
things, he surely cannot understand God's justice or the goal
of love He has promised His people. To Ezra's next question
—when the new age dawns, what will happen to those alive

and to those already dead?—the reply is that all generations
of men would be treated in the same way. Then Ezra asks,
why has God created a succession of generations? Could He
not have instead created all men for the new age? The reply
is that the generations must follow each other in succession.
As a woman bears ten children in succession, not all at once,
so mother earth bears generations one after another. In early
times, when the earth was young, men were of greater
height[38]; as the earth grew old, height was reduced, as in
Ezra's generation; in the future men would be even smaller.
God had planned all the events that the generations of men
had gone through. The wicked present age (called the "age
of Esau"[39]) was ending, to be followed by the beginning of
the new age (called the "age of Jacob"). Ezra asks to be
shown the full array of signs a part of which he had been
shown the previous night. In reply he is told of many por-
tents and miracles and warfare that are to come. Whoever is
able to survive will be saved and will see God's salvation. At
that time evil will be totally blotted out, and deceit will give
way to truth. Finally, the angel, urging Ezra not to be
afraid, promises to reveal even greater things to him.

The third vision (6.35-9.25) portrays Ezra as reminding
God of the acts of Creation in Genesis 1. In this review, we
are told that on the fifth day there were created two monsters,
Behemoth and Leviathan, Behemoth having been given the
land and Leviathan the sea; these were being preserved to be
eaten by whomever God wishes, and whenever He wishes.
But if Creation had taken place solely on behalf of Israel,
why then does Israel not possess the world? In figures of
speech, the angel replies that the path to the new age is narrow and full of dangers, and Israel must follow that path.
The righteous in Israel will succeed in traversing the path, but
the wicked will not. When the signs already foretold would
come to pass, a heavenly city (Jerusalem) and a heavenly
land (Judea) would be disclosed, and the righteous would see
God's wonders. God's son, the Messiah,[40] would be revealed,
effecting rejoicing for many years.[41] Then the Messiah and
all humans would die. Thereafter a general resurrection
would take place, as would a general judgment; heaven and
hell would emerge. Only a few, the truly righteous, would

be saved. God, at the time of Creation, had already prepared heaven and hell. When a man dies, his spirit leaves him. If the man was wicked, his spirit wanders about, encountering seven torments; if the man was righteous, his spirit encounters seven kinds of comforting rest.

Ezra then asks if the righteous will be able at that future time to intercede and pray to God on behalf of unrighteous relatives. The answer is no. Such intercession is possible only before the great final day of judgment. Ezra laments that so much of humanity will end up in punishment, and he therefore appeals to God for mercy (in a touching prayer, 8.20-36). The reply ignores Ezra's petition for mercy; mankind is like the seeds a farmer sows, not all of which take root and grow. Ezra, though, should feel comforted, for his lot is with the righteous.

Yet Ezra now asks when the great events will take place. The answer is that when some of the signs already revealed come to pass, then the final day of judgment will come. But Ezra is to receive still another revelation.

The fourth vision (9.26-10.59) supposes that Ezra, lying on the grass in a flowery field, speaks to God, saying that wicked Israelites have perished, but the Torah given to them nevertheless abides. Ezra then sees a woman mourning and weeping. She explains that, long barren, she had borne a child who, nurtured with care, grew to the point of marriage, but died on entering his wedding chamber. She would continue to mourn until she died. Ezra rebuked her, for she was in mourning only for a son, while Zion was in mourning for countless offspring. In due course the woman could (or would) have another son; with the sanctuary devastated, the altar overturned, and the Temple destroyed, the woman should cease to lament her personal loss.

The woman abruptly becomes invisible, and Ezra sees, instead, a great city. Uriel then comes to him to explain the vision. The woman, he says, was Zion (the heavenly Jerusalem), which grieved for the destruction of the earthly city. (The heavenly Jerusalem was an assurance of the future revival of the earthly.)

The fifth vision (11.1-12.1) is about a dream in which there arises from the sea an eagle, with twelve wings and three heads, which came to rule the earth. In succession the wings and then the heads rose to rule. (The eagle is Rome; the wings and heads are successive rulers; the identification of the persons here is uncertain, or even impossible.) A lion then arose from a forest. To it a voice spoke for God, telling the lion that he was one of the four beasts[42] which remained (to rule), but he too would disappear, and the earth would be freed from the beast's violence and oppression. At Ezra's request, the meaning of the dream was given: The fourth beast, though endangered by struggles,[43] would survive. Eight wings (kings) would arise for brief reigns.[44] The lion was the Lord's anointed (the Messiah), an eternal being, descended from David, and preserved in heaven for the time of his arrival. This divine promise Ezra was to record in a book which he was to preserve in secret, though teaching its content to the wise who are able to keep secrets.[45] Ezra comes to the people now to assure them that, despite the destruction of the Temple, God has not forgotten them.

The sixth vision (13.1-58) tells of something like a man who came out of the sea and flew with the winds. Against him were gathered innumerable peoples from all over the world to make war against him. Yet he sent forth from his mouth a stream of fire and flaming breath which burnt up all those assembled; to the man there now gathered a peaceful multitude. This vision is then interpreted as the coming of the Messiah; after his conquest of the foe, he would rise to the top of Mount Zion, and destroy the foe. The peaceful multitude are the ten northern tribes.[46] They, and the non-exiled survivors, would be defended. The man (the Messiah) arose from the sea, this because the time when he would come is as obscure as is what is contained in the depths of the sea.

The seventh vision (14.1-48) tells of instructions to Ezra to preserve the legacy from Moses. Some of God's revelation to Moses was designed to be taught openly, but some of it included secrets of the unfolding future. In time Ezra would die; now, with nine parts of the twelve parts of the age over, Ezra must be prepared for the upheavals of the remaining three parts. Ezra replied that the sacred books (the Bible) have been burnt; he asked that the Holy Spirit be sent to him to enable him to rewrite these. Five secretaries-assistants were designated, and Ezra prepared the rewritings, some of which were to be made public and some kept secret. Of the total (ninety-four[47]), twenty-four were for everyone; the other seventy were to be reserved only for the wise. (The remainder of the book, 15.1-16.78, is, as mentioned, a very late appendix.)

The major themes, in retrospect, are the inquiry into God's justice for allowing Judea to be humiliated and the Temple destroyed; the cryptic, symbolic revelation of the future, with the advent of the Messiah, and the restoration of the sacred literature, both the public and the secret books.

A veritable host of writings has survived, some totally and some in fragmentary form, from the age with which we deal. They are at times identified with the "seventy books"[48] ostensibly prepared by Ezra for private circulation. The assembly of these books, as we have said, dates from about A.D. 1713, and was the work of the German scholar Johann Fabricius. The English compilation by R. H. Charles (published in 1913) included three[49] works not previously published in such collections, with their inclusion justified not because they were falsely titled but because they are related to the Judaism of the general period. So abundant are works from the age with which we deal that could conceivably be included in the category of non-canonical works that we cannot discuss them all, but must relegate most of them to Appendix I (see p. 487). Here we shall look at two works that seem more important than the others.

11. The Book of Enoch

The Book of Enoch was written in Hebrew and Aramaic. It was partly preserved in a translation into Greek; parts are preserved in Ethiopic (the language of Abyssinia) or in Latin. (Aramaic fragments have been recovered from Qumran Cave 4.)[50]

The book is of composite authorship, possibly coming from some time in the first pre-Christian century. A portion of it is believed to be in reality segments of a lost work, the Apocalypse of Noah.[51] The Book of Enoch is significant not only for itself, but also because it was well known to Jews[52] and Christians,[53] though about the fifth century A.D. it fell into disuse outside Abyssinia.

An introduction (chs. 1-5) purports to be the words of blessing of Enoch for the chosen and righteous, this for the time when the wicked and ungodly would be removed. God would descend from Mount Sinai with all his heavenly hosts to destroy the wicked.

The second section (chs. 6-36, of which chs. 6-11 may be from the Apocalypse of Noah) falls into three natural parts. In the first (chs. 6-11) we hear of fallen angels who came from heaven, two hundred strong, to take human women as wives (based on Gen. 6.1-4). Their giant offspring made vice flourish. When man appealed to God through archangels, in response He sent the angel Uriel to inform Noah of the impending flood, the angel Gabriel to impel the giants to fight and destroy each other, and the angel Michael to punish the fallen angels by having them witness the destruction of their offspring and to be buried in the earth until Judgment Day, this to come in seventy generations. Thereafter the "plant of righteousness" (based on Isa. 11.1-2) would inaugurate a new age of human longevity and prosperity and peace.

In the second part of this section (chs. 12-16), Enoch relates in the first person his mission to warn the wicked angels. They entreated him to ask God for their forgiveness. A vision came to him in which the request was refused. Then came a second vision, in the heavenly palace of the Almighty, where the refusal to forgive was confirmed.

In the third part (chs. 17-36) Enoch relates that, carried through earth and heaven, he was instructed in all the secrets of nature hidden from men. He went in all directions, even westward where the spirits of the dead, both the righteous and the wicked, await Judgment Day. He penetrated to the center of the earth, there to see both Judea and Jerusalem as prosperous and populous, and the place of punishment (Gehenna, the accursed "valley of Ben-Hinnom," based on 2 Kgs. 23.10; Josh. 15.8; and Jer. 19.2; 32.55). He went eastward to Paradise, where he saw the tree of knowledge from which Adam and Eve had eaten (Gen. ch. 3). There too he saw the gates out of which the stars come. In the north, south, and west, he saw the gates of the winds from these directions.

The third section, chs. 37-71, is called both the Book of Parables and, by some scholars, Similitudes, a synonym for parables. These parables (quite unlike Rabbinic or Gospel parables) are elaborate figures of speech. The first parable (chs. 37-44) narrates Enoch's trip to heaven, where the righteous would come after separation from the wicked. He is shown the divine throne before which are innumerable angels, and four archangels (Michael, Raphael, Gabriel, and Phanuel). The secrets of heaven, both of winds and storm and the courses of stars and planets, are disclosed to him. He sees where Wisdom dwells.

The second parable (chs. 45-57) deals with the Messiah, also called here the Son of Man and the Elect One (based on Dan. 7.31), who sits on a throne to judge mankind. He existed before the world was created, and abides forever in God's presence. He sits in judgment over men and angels. At the appointed time, the righteous dead will be resurrected and the wicked consigned to punishment. The flood of Noah's time is alluded to—possibly this is a misplaced portion of the Noah Apocalypse—and then comes a prediction of the overthrow of hostile nations and the return of the exiles to Judea.

The third parable (chs. 58-71) depicts the rewards of the righteous and the misery of the wicked in messianic times. Again there is an allusion to Noah's flood, possibly to suggest that God's judgment at that time anticipated His judgment which was to come through the Messiah. There are more secrets of heaven revealed; so too is a "new Jerusalem," where the holy saints are to dwell before God. More revelations ensue, as do some details about Enoch himself.

The fourth section (chs. 72-82) is called "the Revolutions of the Lights of Heaven." It is a treatise on astronomy (which Enoch invented, as he did writing and mathematics). Details of a solar calendar of 364 days, different from the solar-lunar calendar (see pp. 209-11) in what we might call ordinary Jewish usage, are given.

The fifth section (chs. 83-90) contains two visions. The

first (chs. 83-84) presents Enoch praying to avert the flood. The vision in Chapters 85-90 reviews biblical events from Adam to Enoch, and then, through symbols (oxen, sheep, birds of prey) traces history to the Maccabean age. (Much of this symbolic presentation is completely obscure). The wicked nations will be swallowed up at the coming of the "bull with great horns" (the Messiah). Evil angels and apostate Jews will be punished; surviving Gentiles will become converts. The righteous dead are to be resurrected, the Messiah is to appear.

The sixth section (chs. 91-105) first portrays Enoch predicting the punishment of the wicked and the resurrection of the righteous. Next comes a passage, largely obscure, which divides history into ten periods called "weeks." Enoch's age is the first week, Noah's the second, Abraham's the third, Moses' the fourth, the Temple's the fifth, and Elijah's the sixth. The seventh week is one of misfortune, and the eighth is the start of the Messianic age. In the ninth week, which lies ahead, the world will prepare for God's judgment. In the tenth week, after judgment, the old world will disappear and a new heaven will supplant the old. The final sections (chs. 106-8) are in effect, first, another section from the Noah apocalypse (chs. 106-7) and second, Chapter 108, which closes the book with a restatement of the punishment awaiting the wicked and rewards awaiting the righteous.

The Book of Enoch, transmitted from the Ethiopic, is painfully disordered, as indicated above. Yet even if it were not, it would scarcely make for enjoyable reading, for the very nature of the material is its own deterrent. The symbolism is so extreme, the partisanships to extravagant, and overstatement so abundant that students assigned the book to read have suggested that the mind of the author (or authors) was as disordered as the book itself.

Granted that this disorder is the case, Enoch is important especially for its clear statements about the Messiah and about resurrection. Background information for the use in the Gospels of the strange phrase "Son of Man" is more abundant here (though not clearer!) than even in the Book of Daniel, where the phrase is used in designation of the Messiah.

12. *Jubilees*

Jubilees, known also as "Little Genesis," has survived in an Ethiopic version, though quotations from it in various tongues are found in several Church Fathers. The Ethiopic text was found in 1844. The book was originally written in Aramaic or Hebrew; the Ethiopic seems to have been translated from a Greek translation.

The word "jubilee" is the Hebrew *yōvḗl;* it is the term for the last year in a cycle of fifty, crowning a succession of seven terms of seven years. The Hebrew word yovel means trumpet, possibly a very loud trumpet, heralding the significant year (Lev. 25.9-10). In the Jubilee year a Jew who had become enslaved to another Jew within the forty-nine years was released to freedom, and property sold to a Jew within the forty-nine years reverted to the original owner. Many historical puzzles surround the Jubilee year. Was it an ideal, or was it actually operative? If operative, were there some periods in which it fell into disuse, and others wherein it was revived? What was the relation of the solar calendar[54] in this book to the lunar-solar calendar of post-exilic biblical literature?

Our book is in a sense a review of biblical history, from Genesis 1.1 through Exodus 14.31. Its manner is to embroider the scriptural account by additions, and to enhance it by judicious omissions. Where Scripture is silent, as in the case of the wives of Jacob's twelve sons, the names are here supplied. The laconic biblical account of the birth of Abraham in Ur and his moving to Charran (Ḥarran) (Gen. 11.26-31) is greatly expanded with details that bear out the view that the patriarch left Ur in order to abandon the idolatry so rampant there.[55]

The format, quite beyond its reckoning time by Jubilees, is unique. The biblical author or authors of the Pentateuch, in ascribing the origin of Hebrew laws to the time of Moses and their beginning in Exodus 20, prompted later generations to speculate on the relationship of Abraham, Isaac, and Jacob of Genesis to the laws revealed only after their time.[56] It begins, accordingly, with a revelation to Moses by an "angel of the Presence [of God]" of the past and the future, and of a secret oral law to be entrusted only to great worthies (Enoch, Methusaleh, Noah, and Shem) and thereafter to Abraham, Isaac, Jacob, and Levi. These oral laws were written on heavenly tablets[57] at the time of Creation; that is, they were available to the Patriarchs in advance of the legislation that runs from Exodus 20 through the rest of Exodus, Leviticus, Numbers, and Deuteronomy. As a consequence of the existence of these heavenly laws at the time of Creation, biblical worthies such as Abraham, prior to Moses, observed such Mosaic sacred days as the New Year, new moons, and the three festivals, Booths, Passover, and Weeks.

Weeks (Shavuot) is especially significant in Jubilees. We should recall that this festival is dated by counting seven weeks from the "morrow after the Sabbath" which falls in Passover week.[58] Since the festival depends on a tabulation of days similar to the tabulation of years for the Jubilee, we can understand the special significance of the festival in the Book of Jubilees; it is there the most significant of the sacred days.

Yet it is not alone biblical injunctions which the Patriarchs observe. Extensions of Sabbath prohibitions are present. So too is the recitation of grace after meals (16.6; 45.5). What appears to be a clear but as yet undeveloped Passover Seder is also to be found (48.15; 49.5).

These materials are woven into a consecutive[59] account. The abundant additions at times simply satisfy curiosity for more detail than a laconic item in Scripture furnishes. More often there is something very pointed contained in the embellishment. The scorn of idolatry is a common motif of the Hasmonean age. A ministering angel teaches Abraham Hebrew (suggesting that his Aramaic-speaking descendants should learn the holy tongue!), which was Adam's language, but after the Tower of Babel had become forgotten.

Circumcision was ordained in the heavenly tablets, as was the covering of the genitals, a law the Gentiles (Greeks) violate (3.31). Only to Israel was the Sabbath given, for them to celebrate it as do the angels of heaven (2.30-31). Indeed, a rigid separation from Gentiles is enjoined. Eating, or fraternization, with Gentiles and intermarriage with them is rigorously prohibited (22.16-22; 30.7-10). Angels, good and bad, and demons abound in the book. A wicked angel, Mastema, is a frequent character. Only in one disputed passage (4.26) is there a mention that might allude to the Messiah. Another disputed passage (24.9) seems to reflect a belief in the afterlife; it is not clear whether it is resurrection or immortality; yet 23.26-31 seems to shun all sense of an afterlife.

The date of composition is possibly between 150 and 100 B.C. Several decades ago it was viewed as written either by an extreme Pharisee (see pp. 158-62) or by an Essene (see pp. 163-66). Because some fragments of Jubilees have been found in the Qumran caves, a Qumran authorship is now suggested from time to time, but this is unlikely.

G. The Dead Sea Scrolls

The Dead Sea Scrolls came to light in 1947-48, when dealers in antiquities in Jerusalem offered some of the manuscripts for sale, showing them to scholars associated with the Hebrew University and the American School of Oriental Research. They had been found by Bedouin Arabs in caves on the west bank of the northern part of the Dead Sea, in an area known as Qumran. In 1949 the cave from which they had come was investigated by archeologists, resulting in the discovery of hundreds of tiny fragments of writings, relics of what had presumably been a repository of some one hundred and fifty manuscripts. That cave has become known as Cave 1 (or Q1, the Q standing for Qumran). The area contains countless caves. As these were explored in the 1950s, it was found that some eleven of them contained fragments. Moreover, some eleven miles from Cave 1, at a place called Wadi Murabbat, two more caves with fragments were discovered. Other finds came to light at a place called Khirbat Mird. Khirbat means "ruin," the remains of what was once a settlement. Such a ruin was excavated in the Qumran area in 1951-56, a half-mile south of Cave 1. A complex was disclosed of what had once been a series of buildings; this complex has come to be called a monastery. Coins and pottery[60] fragments suggested that the monastery had been occupied principally between about 150 B.C. and A.D. 70. A room where manuscripts are believed to have been written, called a "scriptorium," was found, with relics of tables and even two inkwells. A "meeting hall" was identified. Another room had been a pantry, and in it were fragments of pottery plates, bowls, and cups. Secondary buildings too were found, as were the indications of the aqueducts for bringing in water and the cisterns for storing it. The total impression is that of a center of some thriving community. An event, possibly the rebellion against Rome which began in 66, prompted the hiding of the Scrolls in the many caves. Scholars who work in the Scrolls ordinarily identify the fragments by allusion to the caves in which they were found, for example, Q1, or Q4, or Q11.

One more word about discoveries. In 1963, the great fortress at Masada, some twenty-five miles south of Qumran, was excavated. Masada was built by Herod the Great. It was there, according to Josephus, that the last resistance to the Romans ended in A.D. 73, with the mass suicide of the defenders. One room at Masada yielded fragments of documents kindred to those of Qumran, as well as fragments of biblical passages. Perhaps some of the Qumran community came to Masada seeking refuge from the Romans.

The initial discovery of the Scrolls generated boundless excitement, both among scholars and archeologists, and, through newspaper accounts, the general public. There began rather quickly what scholars allude to as the Battle of the Scrolls. On the one hand, it was asserted that the Scrolls would necessitate a complete rewriting of Jewish and Christian history; on the other, the view was expressed that the Scrolls were not from the period 150 B.C. to A.D. 70, but medieval, and should be called "forgeries." Today there has emerged a consensus that authenticates the dates 150 B.C. to A.D. 70, though scholars dispute the interpretation of details.

In understanding the Scrolls, it is well to distinguish between biblical materials and the community documents. The biblical materials include a full, well-preserved copy of Isaiah, as well as a large portion of another copy of Isaiah. Fragments, often tiny, represent every biblical book except Esther. There are, moreover, fragments of some books of the Apocrypha and of the Pseudepigrapha, such as Enoch, mentioned above. These biblical materials serve us in two significant ways. One has to do with this question: How faithfully

has the Hebrew Bible been transmitted? The printed Hebrew
Bibles we use today were set in type from handwritten manuscripts. These manuscripts were written and transmitted
by Jews. Scribes who copied the manuscripts had a legacy of
notes about the text and conformed with them. Those who
concerned themselves with the reliable transmission of the
text are known as Masoretes; the word *masōrá* means "tradition, what is handed over." Therefore the Hebrew text preserved by Jews is called the Masoretic Text. Is the Masoretic
Text a faithful transcription of the long-lost original writings? Or did Masoretic activity commence at some given
point when varieties of texts were in circulation, and is the
Masoretic Text a single example of several "plural" types?
Why speak of plural types? Because ancient translations such
as the Septuagint display phenomena which suggest that for
the Septuagint a Hebrew text different from the Masoretic
was used. If there were, indeed, different types of Hebrew
texts, then just when did the Masoretic Text emerge? And is
the Masoretic Text a faithful transcription, or did it undergo
either accidental or deliberate alteration once it emerged?

The Qumran biblical materials tend to show two things.
First, the Masoretic Text of Isaiah is remarkably kindred to
some of those of Qumran, so that the relatively great antiquity of the Masoretic Text is confirmed. Second, there are
also Qumran materials reflecting a different Hebrew version,
which help to explain why certain passages in the Greek
diverge from the Masoretic; so too, some fragments corre-
spond to the Samaritan text. Hence, the older, simpler explanations of the ancestry of the inherited Masoretic Text
cannot be sustained. It seems we must conclude that the
Masoretic Text emerged from not one predecessor but from
more than one. It can be said, guardedly, that Qumran biblical fragments confirm the general reliability of the Masoretic
Text, but do not do so completely. Yet in no instance is there
any issue of theology or history at stake as between the Masoretic Text and Qumran materials in the Book of Isaiah.

The Qumran materials that are not biblical or apocryphal
are the creative compositions of the community, and expres-
sive of its viewpoints, its theology, and its manner of the use
of Scripture. From these materials we are able to come to

conclusions about this community, some fairly certain, some likely guesses, and some opinions both uncertain and disputed by scholars. The disputes arise mostly out of the poor preservation of the scrolls, for there are tears and holes in them, and in some the ink has completely faded. Moreover, there is much use of symbolic language, where we should have preferred clear, crisp prose, so that even where passages are legible the content is by no means so.

1. *Manual of Discipline.* The "Manual of Discipline"[61] is a title that some scholars have given to one of the Scrolls; others call it "The Community Rule." This writing occupies some eleven columns; in the translation into English by Geza Vermes it runs about thirteen printed pages, and is thus a document of some considerable length. In brief, the Community Rule sets forth the conditions for an individual's entrance into the organization, stressing the need of obedience to God, even for whatever time Satan may exercise dominion. The initiates are blessed by Priests, while Levites recite the record of the trespasses of the wicked (the Levites proceed to utter a curse on the initiates who are untrue to God or to the guidance by the council of the community.) There appears to be a "leader" who instructs the members of the community. Men have available to them both the spirit of truth and the spirit of falsehood. The righteous are ruled by the "Prince of Light," and the wicked by the "angel of darkness." God and the angel of truth are kindly to the righteous, but the wicked are beset by an abundance of plagues sent by destroying angels, and are destined for damnation until the appointed time of God's judgment.

The prospective member of the community, having informed the Council of his wish to "enter the covenant of God," takes an oath to observe all the commandments of the Torah in accordance with what has been revealed to the "sons of Zadok."[62] He takes the oath in the presence of the entire community. He separates himself from the wicked—that is, from those not in the community. Outsiders cannot partake of the pure meal prepared for the righteous, since they themselves have not been purified. Their ideas, and their food, are to be shunned.

One who enters the community is examined and re-examined by both the Priests and the lay members. The members are registered in a roll by rank, the latter fixed by their learning and good deeds. The re-examination is annual, and the ranks thereupon revised. The members of the community, if they rebuke one another, should do so in truth and charity, and as promptly as possible. A private rebuke should be tried before an open charge is made in public.

Meals, prayer, and discussion are to be held in common. At assemblies, each person sits in his assigned place, with the Priests seating themselves first, then the elders, then the people according to their rank. Interruption of a speaker is not allowed. A person of lower rank speaks after a person of higher. The permission of the Council is a prerequisite to speaking.

The admission of a candidate (this is partly a repetition) is debated by the entire community, but the decision to admit or exclude him is decided by the Council. On admission, he must wait a full year before being eligible for the sacred Meal, and even then must be examined respecting his spirit and his deeds. On approval, he hands over his possessions and funds to the treasurer for the time being. A second year must pass before he is eligible for the community's Drink. On passing re-examination, his possessions and funds now become merged with the community's, for he is now a full member.

Those admitted to membership, if they trespass, can be punished, whether by the reduction of food or by some other penalty. The improper utterance of the Divine Name is to result in expulsion. For lesser sins there are to be lesser penances; some lesser sins mentioned are falling asleep or spitting during an Assembly, or guffawing, or gesticulating with the left hand. Expulsion is the punishment for muttering against the authority of the community.

The Council consists of fifteen, three of whom are Priests. A member of the Council may be expelled from it for deliberate trespass; for inadvertent trespass, he may be suspended from it for two years. The Priests alone have jurisdiction in matters of justice and property.

There is also a Master, who is a teacher, an interpreter of

the rules, and a judge. He presides at the ceremonies of blessing God at dawn and dusk, and at new moons.

The writing closes with a long hymn, apparently reflecting
the responsibilities undertaken by the Master at his investi-
ture.

2. *The Damascus Document.* A second writing, called by
three names, the "Damascus Document," the "Damascus
Rule," and the "Zadokite Fragments," is only slightly
shorter. It was known prior to the discovery of the Dead Sea
Scrolls, for two incomplete copies of it were found in 1896-97
in the *genīzā* ("storeroom") of an old Cairo synagogue.[63] In
that storeroom there were placed worn-out manuscripts or
portions of them, it being against sensibilities to burn or destroy them. In three of the Qumran caves lengthy fragments
were discovered.

At the initial publication of the Cairo "Zadokite Fragments"[64] the work was considered to be a Sadducean document, or possibly that of an offshoot of the Sadducees, since
the Sadducees are often viewed by scholars as descendants of
Zadok (the Hebrew for Sadducee being derived from the
Zadok). The tendency today is to associate the document
with Qumran, and to regard the word Damascus as a cryptic
name for Qumran.[65] It is also held[66] that the Manual of Discipline relates to the rigidly organized and closed community
at Qumran,[67] while the Zadokite Fragments deal instead
with similar people settled throughout Judea.

The work is regarded as divided into an "Exhortation" or
"Admonition," spoken by a "Teacher," and a compendium of
community regulations. The Exhortation asserts that God in
the past, in punishing the unfaithful, always preserved a
remnant. For them he raised a "Teacher of Righteousness"
to guide them. This can be discerned by a review of history:
Mankind went astray before the age of Noah.[68] The sons of
Noah (that is, Ham and his descendants, Gen. 9.22-23) went
astray, but Abraham, Isaac, and Jacob did not. Jacob's sons
went astray in Egypt[69] and in the Wilderness, in that ten of
the twelve spies (Deut. 9.23-29) wickedly advised against
entering into the land of Canaan. So too in the time of the
kings.

Yet there was always a remnant faithful to the Covenant. These are exemplified in the praise of the fidelity of "Priests," "Levites," and "the sons of Zadok" (in Ezek. 44.15). The "Priests" are the penitents of Israel who left the land of Judah, and the Levites are those who went with them. The "sons of Zadok" are the chosen, called by name (as if a list were to ensue, but one does not).

Zadok himself had revealed the Torah,[70] which had been sealed up from the time of the death of Joshua. Yet—here the text seems confused—there arose new infidelity, with a resultant profanation of the Temple through sexual irregularities, for men arose who led Israel astray. God thereupon raised descendants of Aaron (that is, Priests) who were undeviatingly faithful to the Torah.[71] The faithful went out of the land of Judah to reside in the land of Damascus. These faithful abstain from entering the Temple, separating themselves from "the sons of the Pit."[72] As members of the new covenant in the land of Damascus, they are to observe the Sabbath, the festivals, and the Day of Atonement with precision as to the regulations.

The residents of the northern kingdom, of which Ephraim was the chief tribe, were apostates, deserving the punishment of the sword (inflicted by Assyria in 722 B.C.). The few faithful of the north managed to escape to Damascus.[73]

A subsequent passage condemns men who enter the community but fail in performing the requisite duties. Such people are to have no part in the community. Next an allusion is made to some of the community who deserted to the "scoffers." A period of forty years was to elapse between "the day of the gathering in of the Teacher" until "the end of all the men of war who deserted to the Liar." Those of the community who returned to the wicked ways of outsiders would be judged by the Council. Those who listened to the "Teacher of Righteousness" and remained faithful would rejoice and prevail over "all the sons of the earth."

So much for the Exhortation and its array of unclarities. The rules next provide for such matters as entrance into the community, after examination by the Guardian[74] and an oath to abide by the Torah of Moses with whole heart. The proper calendar[75] should be observed. A husband or a father

could cancel a woman's oath. No one should take the law into
his own hands. Priests are available for things that are lost
(stolen) or found. Trespasses against the Torah are to be reported to the Guardian; if the report comes from a single individual, the Guardian is to record the matter lest it be
repeated; if two witnesses report two different infidelities on
the part of the same man, the latter is to be excluded from
the pure Meal.[76] A death sentence cannot be passed on the
testimony of a witness too young for membership or by one
not God-fearing.

Ten judges, four of whom are to be of the tribe of Levi or
the family of Aaron, are to be elected for a definite period.
They are to be learned in the Book of Meditation[77] and in the
rules of the covenant community. They must be at least
twenty-five years old and no older than sixty.[78]

Purification must be by immersion in clean water and in
an amount sufficient to cover a man; it must be running
water. The Sabbath rules are given in full detail.

As in the Manual of Discipline, there is provision for the
formation of groups of at least ten men with a Priest over
them, unless the Priest is insufficiently learned,[79] and in that
case a Levite is the leader. Next come the rules for the Guardian, both the requirements for his office and the specification
of his authority. Rules are given for the assemblies of "all the
camps," and for the expenditure of funds for the orphans, the
needy, and such. These rules are to apply until the coming
of the Messiah "of Aaron and Israel."

The manuscript breaks off abruptly.

3. War Rule. The third scroll of some size is known by different scholarly titles, such as "The War of the Sons of Light
Against the Sons of Darkness," or else "The War Rule." The
manuscript is described by Geza Vermes[80] as consisting of
"nineteen badly mutilated columns." In briefest summary,
the document begins with a proclamation of warfare against
the "Kittim."[81] Then there ensues what seems to be a proposed
reorganization of the worship of the Temple, followed by
the necessary military accomplishments, to take a total of
forty years. Next come provisions for the utilization of trumpets, and for the standards (or flags). The military disposi-

tion of the front ranks is followed by instructions in turn for the infantry and then the cavalry. There are specifications about the horses (they must be stallions!) about the ages of the riders, and about the conduct of the military camps. The duties of Priests and Levites in the matter of exhortation and of trumpet signals are given, as are the prescriptions for the patriotic addresses and prayers, and victory songs.

The last portion predicts the victory of Israel over her foes, and gives instructions for the conduct of the battle, including the role of the High Priest, against the "Kittim," who are sure to be conquered.

In the case of the Manual of Discipline and the Damascus Rule, we are clearly within the domain of what appears to be reality; in the case of the War Rules we are not. It should be conceded, of course, that some real knowledge of the military procedures is discernible, with the result that the "Kittim" have some appearance of being Roman rather than Hellenistic troops. But one cannot truly know whether the War Rules reflect some true historical situation or some fantasy arising from a heat oppressed brain. Our author, who loathed the "Kittim"-Romans, undoubtedly did so with good reason. But the fantasies and the hatred so reflect what seems to be hallucination that one wonders if the manuscript might not have been written under the influence of drugs!

4. *The Hymns.* A collection, called by scholars either "Psalms" or "Hymns," runs to some eighteen columns. Many portions are very poorly preserved. Some modern scholars divide the scroll into as many as twenty-five separate poems. The poor preservation obstructs interpretive certainty, but it does seem that the poems are individual rather than corporate. If one uses the categories of types into which the canonical Psalter is divided by modern scholars, these poems are kindred to the type called "thanksgiving psalms." Most interpreters have a high regard for the quality of the poetry; if that quality does not approach that of the best of the Psalter, it does that of usual Psalms. While most of these psalms or hymns appear devoid of relationship to specific events or people, several of them (e.g., 1, 2, 7, 8, 9, 10, and 11) seem to allude to situations which, while indistinct, are

not simply broad and general. These allusions are to a person, possibly a Teacher who is the target of some enemies; the onslaughts of the enemies test the patience and fidelity of the Teacher. Some scholars have proceeded to suggest that this character is the "Teacher of Righteousness," though that specific title does not appear.

The hymns, so too it is suggested, may have been used by the community in its assemblies, whether for a sacred Meal or some less formal period of prayer.

5. *The Genesis Apocryphon.* The so-called "Genesis Apocryphon" has survived in such an extremely poor state of preservation that only small portions have been published. Although the content is quite different from the Book of Jubilees (see pp. 90-92), in a sense the manner is the same, namely, it is a retelling of the events of Genesis with the addition of legendary materials, exemplified in the way in which the matriarch Sarah is brought—forcibly abducted—into the Pharaoh's palace (based on Gen. 12.10-20), and retained there for two years but with her virtue left intact.

6. *Commentaries.* To several prophetic books there have survived interpretive fragments which seek to apply their ancient message to the new times and situations of the community. It is customary to allude to these as "Commentaries"; the term is not completely appropriate, but if it is understood that "commentary" does not imply what is meant today—that is, disciplined explanation—then the word can be used. The Qumran word is *pésher* ("application"). The pesher arises from identifying words in the ancient prophetic books with contemporary movements. For example, the Chaldeans of Habakkuk 1.6 are interpreted to be those called "Kittim," who are quick and valiant in war. The author of the commentary knew exactly whom he meant; scholars today infer—probably rightly—that "Kittim" means the Romans. The commentaries, in applying the ancient texts to their later times, do so in a manner cryptic enough to conceal from us certainty as to what was meant. Portions of Isaiah, Micah, Nahum, and Habakkuk, treated in this way, have been recovered.[82]

The scholarly desire to find the precise historical setting of the Dead Sea community has included the quest to identify certain persons and events. It seems clear that the community arose out of a deliberate abandonment of direct connection with or loyalty to the Temple in Jerusalem. A step so drastic is conceivable only if there was a disillusionment with the conduct of affairs at the Temple, and a maximum disapproval not of the Temple itself (for it had divine sanction), but of the personnel given authority over it. If emphasis on the family of Zadok is in effect a repudiation of the family of Jehoiarib, the former deemed legitimate and the latter not, then the Hasmonean high priesthood, descended from Jehoiarib, was the personification of the illegitimate.[83]

If there was an incident of some acute controversy connected with a particular High Priest, then perhaps the allusions to the "wicked priest" approach clarification and solution. It will be recalled (p. 31) that in 152 the Seleucidian Alexander Balas had designated the Hasmonean Jonathan as High Priest on the death of the High Priest Alcimus. But after some disorders in Antioch, Jonathan had been arrested, his brother Simon named High Priest in 143, and Jonathan executed while in prison in 142. A number of scholars (but by no means all of them) believe that the "wicked priest" is either Jonathan or Simon."[84]

The "Teacher of Righteousness" appears to be the leader of the community of dissidents who directly opposed the wicked priest and aroused a fierce enmity. The name-calling ("Scoffer," "Liar") is a reflection of the depth of the unpleasant involvements between that leader and the priestly establishment. The Teacher of Righteousness, if a single person, appears to have been the man who founded the community of dissidents after repudiating the Temple priesthood and perhaps other facets of the "establishment." But perhaps "Teacher of Righteousness" was the title for a succession of leaders, after the first Teacher of Righteousness had served out whatever term of office was his. A continued hostility between each new Teacher of Righteousness and each new High Priest was inevitable. There are scholars who try to solve matters in great detail.[85] Later, we shall discuss the probability that the Scroll community were the "Essenes."

H. The Rabbinic Literature as Religion

1. *Talmud: Mishná and Gemará.* We must begin here with
the definitions of some terms. The Talmud is a two-stage
compilation of the laws of Synaogue Judaism. The first
stage is the Mishná. It was compiled, primarily out of oral
materials, about A.D. 175. The definitive compiler, or the spur
for the compiler, was Rabbi Judah the *Nasí* ("Prince"), who
appears to have been born about A.D. 135. He came from a distinguished family, being a descendant, in the sixth generation, of the illustrious Hillel, an earlier contemporary of
Jesus; he was the political head of the Jews in Palestine
under the Romans, holding an office often spoken of as "the
Patriarchate" (see pp. 139-40). According to later tradition,[86]
Judah—usually alluded to simply as "Rabbi"—had before
him some thirteen earlier collections (whether oral or written, we do not know) of materials arising out of the schools
wherein the matters were discussed and taught.

The second stage is known as Gemará. Mishna, the first
stage, plus Gemara, the second, equal Talmud. The Gemara
has been transmitted in two versions which are called "recensions," one compiled among Babylonian Jews about A.D.
500 and the other by Palestinian Jews about 450. The latter
version is known both by the name of "the Palestinian" and
"the Jerusalem" Talmud. It is the Babylonian version which
became what we might term the standard Talmud, the one
studied in ordinary Jewish schools down to our day; the
Palestinian Talmud has been reserved, as it were, for the advanced student or the great scholar.

In biblical literature there is a variety of terms for law:
mitzváh ("commandment"); *mishpát* ("judicial precedent");
hōq ("decree"). The term mitzvah is used ordinarily as a
convenient way of alluding to any law which is biblical, in
the interest of distinguishing between a biblical law, explicit
in Scripture, and a derived law, recorded in the Rabbinic
writings. The term for a Rabbinic law is *halachá*. The word
means "walking," and by connotation it sets forth or guides
the faithful in their walking, and living, in consistency with
Scripture. The plural form of mitzvah is *mitzvót*;[87] that of
halacha is *halachót*.[88] A mitzvah, then, is a biblical law; a

halacha is a Rabbinic law. The Mishna is a compilation of halachot.

Because halachot were in part the result of the study of Scripture in diverse academies, there could be (and were) differences of judgment and opinion. That is, it is often the procedure for the Mishna to provide two (or more) opinions which are in direct contradiction. If we are curious as to which opinion should prevail, we might put our question in this form: "What is the acceptable halacha?" Accordingly, the term halacha in one sense means simply a Rabbinic legal prescription; but in another its thrust is that where the opinions of sages differ, the opinion which is regarded as prevailing emerges as *the* halacha on that matter.

At times, when the Mishna presents divergent or even contradictory opinions, it does not proceed from the contradictory opinions to a statement of what the accepted halacha[89] is to be; at other times, however, it does so. Where there is no statement about the accepted halacha, the matter would appear to be open and to suggest that it was a problem in need of resolution.

The halachot are, in theory, derived from Scripture. It is characteristic of the Mishna, however, to abstain from giving the biblical basis for the halachot it presents. The style of the Mishna is laconic in the extreme. A consequence of that laconic style is an occasional vagueness or, occasionally, complete obscurity.

The three factors—that often the halacha is left unspecified, that the scriptural basis is left uncited, and that the laconic style can breed obscurity—are the clues to the Gemara. What the Mishna lacks, the Gemara attempts to supply. The Gemara to a particular Mishna is a discussion of that Mishna; we shall presently by example see what kind of a discussion the Gemara presents.

Halacha, as already indicated, is a term used with reference to something legal. But the Bible, being narrative as well as containing legal sections, brought about the normal curiosities which biblical narratives could raise. Father Abraham was born in Ur, but left it. Why did he leave? The Bible is silent as to that, just as it is silent about his babyhood and his youth. In the synagogue study there was speculation about such questions, and imaginative teachers concocted answers: They said that Abraham left Ur to escape from the idolatry prevalent there. His own father had a shop where idols were sold, and once, when Abraham was left in charge, he chopped up all the idols but the largest, and put the axe into the hands of that idol. On his father's return he explained that the shop was a shambles because the large idol had destroyed the others. Such a tale is called a *haggadá*,[90] a "narrative."

The Gemara, in citing the legal opinion of a sage, might find reason to include a narrative about the occasion on which the Sage gave that opinion. That narrative is also a haggada. Or the Gemara, having mentioned a Sage, might proceed to exalt him by a series of anecdotes not apparently connected with the legal discussion being pursued; such narratives are also haggadot.

That is to say, it is possible to classify material as to its being haláchic, legal, or, to the contrary, haggádic, narrative or anecdotal.

Within the haggadic material, it is frequent that a Sage makes clear his point by an illustrative anecdote called *mashál* ("parable"). It is usual for such a parable to "compare"; that is, a certain somewhat unclear ethical, legal, or theological item is compared to something else, and that comparison lends clarity, or more vivid clarity, meaning, or application than mere abstractions might afford. A parable is often introduced by a question: "To what may this be compared?" Answer: "It is comparable to. . . ." Most often the parable involves a king, that is: "It is comparable to a king who. . . ." One of the best known parables illustrates the Rabbinic view of the full intertwining and inseparableness of body and soul, and is apparently a deliberate rejection of "dualism," the Greek tendency to separate one from the other. This parable on body and soul may be paraphrased as follows, "It is like a king who possessed a beautiful orchard. He appointed two guards over it, one lame and the other blind. He came to the orchard and discovered it denuded of fruit. The lame man claimed innocence; he could not move to the trees. The blind man claimed innocence; he could not see the fruit. But the king had his servants put the lame man on the blind man's shoulders, thus explaining how the fruit was stolen. The parable illustrates the inseparability of body and soul, for they are both involved, whether in acts of good or of evil. A mashal is normally rounded off by the citation of some passage from Scripture which seems to the citer to reinforce or to clinch the point.

Because parables in the Gospels often seem related in manner and even in content to Rabbinic parables, Gospel scholars have often had a special interest in the Rabbinic parables.

The Rabbinic parables are clear clues to the disposition of the Rabbinic mind toward concreteness, rather than to the abstractions such as marked Greek thought.

Next, in pursuit of definitions, there is a matter of the title used for a sage. The earliest Sages bear no title; for example, Hillel is never called Rabbi Hillel. A Sage mentioned in the Mishna is deemed a *tannā* ("teacher"); a Sage of the period after the Mishna is called an *amōrā* ("speaker"). In the Babylonian Talmud, a tanna is called *rabbī* ("my teacher"); an amora is called *rab* ("teacher," pronounced rav) in the Babylonian but rabbi in the Palestinian. For an apparently brief period, an eminent Sage was called abbā ("father"); see Matthew 23, 8-9. The age up to the compilation of Mishna is called "the tannaitic age," or else "the age of the *tannāim*" (plural of tanna); the subsequent age is called either "the amoraic age" or "the age of the *amōrāim*." The Talmud gives us almost nothing in the way of chronology by dates; but by telling us about Sages and who their disciples were, and who were the disciples of those disciples, it is possible to allocate personalities to the generations in which they lived. Hence, in the scholarship an allusion is made to the generation (first, third, and the like) of a Sage, rather than to a date. The Hebrew for Sages is *hachamīm*, the term by which the Talmud alludes to them. The earliest of the Sages are called "pairs," since tradition allocates two Sages to each early period. There is a sequence known of five "pairs," over a period of four "generations."

The compilation of halachot, the Mishna, is on the basis of topics; hence the Talmud is also *topical* (as distinct from a verse-by-verse explanation of, or commentary to, Scripture).

The largest units of assembled materials are each called a *Sēder*, "Order"; reasonable subdivisions within an Order are called in Hebrew *masséchet*, or in Aramaic *masechtā́*, meaning a "tractate." Thus, the second Order, Mo'ed, deals with the "set sacred days"; in this Order there are twelve tractates; for example, *Shabbát* ("Sabbath"); *Pesaḥim* ("Passover"); and *Yōmā́* ("The Day," that is, "The Day of Atonement").

The six orders[91] are these:

Zeraím	*"Seeds"*
Moéd	*"Set sacred days"*
Nashím	*"Women"*
Neziqín	*"Damages"*
Qodashín	*"Sacred things"*
Tohorót	*"Clean things"*

In Appendix II, there is a complete list of the tractates. There, too, the reader will find which of the tractates chances to lack a Gemara.

A modern student in a western country in approaching the Rabbinic literature will discover some extreme difficulties in understanding, quite beyond the usual difficulties inherent in the study of any literature written many centuries ago and thousands of miles away. These special difficulties arise from idiosyncrasies in the literature. The frequent terseness is at times punctuated by lengthy, seemingly irrelevant digressions. Again, much of the Rabbinic literature is in a sense an enormous casebook for lawyers; it contains the technicalities of the legal profession, and its bent is toward laconic phrases clear to lawyers but not to the ordinary layman.

The Mishna, to repeat, is markedly laconic, more so than other parts of Rabbinic literature. Ordinarily, as we have said, it abstains from giving the biblical basis on which the derived inferences are presumed to rest. Its compilers took it for granted that it was completely clear to its first readers and users, and unnecessary clarification simply labored the obvious, for, ordinarily, lawyers understand lawyers' talk. Here is a specimen of a Mishna passage:[92]

Two hold a garment. This one said, "I have found it." That one said, "I found it." This one said, "The whole of it is mine"; that one said, "The whole of it is mine." Each is to swear that not less than half is his, and they are to divide it. . . .

What is here presupposed? This much at least: That we are dealing with litigation in a law court; the oath to be taken implies that we indeed are in a court, but the text does not state this specifically. In this passage, we are not given the name of any Sage whose legal opinion is being reflected; such an instance is called a *stam* Mishna, meaning that it is either "anonymous,"[93] or else "general," in the sense that no dispute about it was transmitted.

Do any questions arise for a modern reader? At least three seem sure to emerge. First, under what circumstances could two different persons so simultaneously come upon an article as to be prepared to take an oath that he found it? Second, is not that oath, "not less than half is mine," peculiar? Third, does "they are to divide it" mean a literal division? Or does it mean a division of the money that a sale of the garment would yield?

Respecting the first question, suppose that one man spies a lost garment before another man does, but the second retrieves it before the first can get to it? Who is the finder? He who saw it or he who retrieved it? The Mishna does not answer; it ascribes equal rights to both. As to the oath, if it read, "All is mine," then the decision to divide would run counter to the end result, since neither he who saw it nor he who retrieved it is to receive the "all"; the oath prescribed here makes it possible for each taker of the oath to receive something commensurate with what he has sworn to. Moreover, the two oaths as prescribed avert the possibility of two solemn oaths so contradicting each other that falsehood could be attributed to one of the two. The prescribed oaths, then, are consistent with the decision about division. And, since cutting the garment into parts would destroy it, it is a matter of common sense that it is money derived from the sale of the garment that is to be shared.

Here is another Mishna: "If an egg is laid on a festival day (i.e. Tabernacles, Passover, or Pentecost), the School of

Hillel says it may not be eaten, the School of Shammai says it may be eaten. . . ." What questions can arise? First, is it the intent that the egg should never be eaten, or only that it may not be eaten on that festival day, but may be eaten another day? Second, why—on what basis—do we encounter views so directly antithetical to each other? Third, what is so important about an egg that sages and scholars should pay attention to it?

Respecting the third question, the answer is along the following lines: The basic premise behind the discussion is that Scripture provides specific guidance as to what is obligatory for the faithful man to do, and also not to do. If the faithful man can meet his obligation only when he knows *precisely* what is permitted and prohibited, he needs to be guided in situations not directly mentioned in Scripture. The egg itself is not important; for a man to know exactly what is permitted or prohibited on a sacred day is. This particular Mishna is the first item in a tractate known by two names. Out of a frequent practice to call a biblical book after the first word, or first significant word, in the book, this Rabbinic tractate is often called "Egg." But the tractate actually deals with laws related to the festivals; the Hebrew term for a festival is *Yōm Tōv* ("good day"). Hence, a second name, "Yom Tov," is often used in place of "Egg."

If we grant the assumption that in connection with a Yom Tov there are some activities permitted and some prohibited, then it is logical that even this question of the egg has a reasonable context. At stake is the following: labor which yielded income was prohibited on a Yom Tov; is picking up an egg from a hen's nest the kind of activity which yields someone some income? Or is it simply gathering a fortuitous egg, and in no way related to the question of productive income? It is this context which provided the contradictory opinions, for the School of Hillel viewed the question of the egg as related to productive income, while the School of Shammai viewed it as unrelated.

To repeat, Scripture makes no specific mention of the egg. Every tannaitic mishnaic conclusion was viewed in later amoraic times as requiring some specific connection with Scripture, either explicit or else demonstrable. The Gemara discussion of the Mishna about the egg seeks that connection.

It sets the discussion into a larger set of categories of acts prohibited on a festival in Scripture. Two such categories of acts are suggested: one, that picking up the egg is kindred to picking up fruit fallen from a tree, the other to finding in a saucer juice which has seeped out of some fruit. Is there labor involved in picking up a fallen apple? The Gemara reply is no. Yet it is, nevertheless, forbidden to pick up this apple on a festival. Why? Because a person picking up the apple may proceed, through forgetting that the day is sacred, to pluck an apple still on the tree, and such plucking is prohibited by the Scriptures since it is clearly labor. Or, one may proceed, through forgetting, to squeeze some fruit, and such squeezing is labor.

There is an important point here that needs clarification. It is this: in order to divert or prevent someone from committing an act that is clearly forbidden (that is, plucking fruit from a tree), a new prohibition is added respecting what is not clearly forbidden (that is, picking up a fallen piece of fruit). One protects the integrity of the explicitly forbidden act by extending the prohibition to what otherwise would not require prohibition. This extension of a prohibition is frequent in Rabbinic literature. Its technical name is *seyág la-tōráh*, "the fence around the Torah." We might define the "fence" as an extended prohibition whose function is to prevent the trespass of a clearly stated scriptural prohibition. Perhaps a modern example might clarify the situation. A mother entrusts her three-year-old boy to a baby-sitter so as to be free to go marketing. She says to the baby-sitter, "He may play in the front yard, but do not let him run out into the street." The mother departs. The baby-sitter, fearful that the boy might run out onto the street, prohibits him from playing in the front yard, allowing him only to play in the back yard. The baby-sitter has extended the prohibition; she has prohibited the front yard, lest the boy come to violate the injunction that he not go into the street. The "fence," then, is an extension, usually of a prohibition, designed to protect the integrity of the essential scriptural command.

A synonym for halacha, as far as the intent behind it was concerned, was the occasional *gezērá* ("decree"), a prohibition issued by a Sage of some standing and authority because in his view a set of prohibitions was urgently required because of some special circumstances; in such a situation the import of gezera is "emergency prohibition." On the other hand, changes of time and circumstance could bring it about that inherited prohibitions, presumably reasonable at the time of their origin, have become impediments to the welfare of the society. A *taqqaná* ("reform"), issued by a Sage of some standing and authority, is an edict of permissiveness canceling an inherited prohibition; its import is "emergency permission."

The Gemara, in effect, provides what the Mishna lacks: It gives a specification of the opinion which is to prevail as the halacha, and the biblical basis on which the halacha can be presumed to rest. The manner of the Gemara assumes that, at a time much later than the Mishna, there is an assembly of scholars who are engaged in probing the minds of the tannaim quoted in the Mishna. Before them there is a kind of narrator.[94] The narrator asks questions, such as "What is the intent of this Mishna?" or, if Rabbis X and Y are quoted in the Mishna in disagreement, the narrator asks, "What did Rabbi X have in mind, and what biblical verse can we assume he based his opinion on? And what did Rabbi Y have in mind, and what biblical verse can we assume he based his opinion on?" This narrator might be thought of as something like a lecturer in a modern law school. He has an audience listening to him, the audience of students. He will speak the jargon of the legal profession (as lawyers do today, with their array of Latin phrases). He will quote the names of the authorities he cites, he will allude to legal precedents, he will exhibit erudition and wit—and he will inform his students where matters stand at the given moment of his lecture, that is, whether the matters under discussion have already been finally settled or not.

The narrator is not hampered by rigid confinement to his post-Mishna age, or, indeed, to any age. He will cite Mishnaic passages other than the particular one he is discussing, or quote material from Sages of the Mishnaic age even if that material cited (called a *baraitá*, "an outside item") chanced not to be included in the Mishnaic assembly of Rabbi Judah the Prince. A rich collection of the non-Mishnaic has survived and is known as the *Tōseftā* ("supplement," that is, supplement to the Mishna). The narrator will also quote the debate of two Gemara contemporaries, or even set against each other two Gemara luminaries who lived remote from each other in time and place.

Our Gemara narrator utilizes his own manner of shorthand. The phrase *tnō rabbanān* (our Rabbis taught") introduces his citation of a passage found in the Mishna, while *tānya* ("it is taught") introduces one from the Tosefta. In connection with citing of Scripture, he may use *she-ne'emár* in the course of an argumentation in the sense of *because* it is said in Scripture; at times he supports his argument *from* Scripture as distinct from *basing* it on Scripture, and in that case uses the word *ka-katúv*, "*as is written* in Scripture." Again, he may reproduce the nub of a series of logical inferences, leading finally to his conclusion, and move from mere logic to Scripture itself by appending to his argument a biblical passage introduced by the formula, *haddá hu di-ketív*, "that is why there is in Scripture the verse. . . ." Our narrator uses the term *rami* ("he threw up against him") to introduce an allegation of illogic or contradiction. After citing a scriptural verse, his word *yalfinān* means "we infer from here." He may go on to suggest *le-rabót*, or *le-ma'ét*, that Scripture intends "to include" or, to the contrary, "to exclude." If to his mind the Mishnaic passage is vague or unclear, the phrase *mai qā-máshma' lān* ("what is the Mishna letting us hear") has the force of "What is the issue at stake?"

The point of burdening a reader with the above explanation of the narrator's shorthand is to make emphatic a significant conclusion: the Rabbinic literature is a literature of lawyers, lawyers thoroughly versed in Scripture and in law and laws. A tremendous quantity of information is presupposed in the Gemara, as would be the case with today's topnotch lawyers. Just as we non-lawyers are often baffled by the Latin jargon of modern lawyers, so too an ordinary person, thoroughly skilled in Hebrew, or having before him a literal translation of a Talmudic passage, can be completely mystified by what he is reading. Indeed, our narrator is so sure that we all know the Bible by heart that he will cite not the whole relevant passage but only a few words, supposing that we can spontaneously supply the full passage from memory; at times he even abstains from directly quoting the portion of the scriptural verse germane to his discussion!

To prove an argument by citing Scripture often entails either a little ingenuity or a lot. Let us take an example, this from the New Testament. In the Epistle to Timothy, which is attributed to Paul, there occurs the verse, "Take a little wine, it is good for your stomach." Prohibitionists had this verse thrown up to them by those who contended that Paul has here given a full sanction for the use of alcohol. But the Prohibitionists replied that Paul's sanction was severely restricted to the medicinal use of alcohol. And Shakespeare has taught us that "even the devil can quote Scripture for his own purposes."

In any community in which Scripture is quoted in support of some viewpoint, the possibility for "far out" inferences exists. In due course, it is likely that a distinction between what can be deemed proper or improper inferences can arise. Such was the case with the ancient Rabbis. Allusions, regrettably vague, speak of two types of interpreters as if they had once existed but had ceased to exist, and as if they were once approved, but were no longer sanctioned. They are *dorshé reshūmót* and *dorshé hamūrót*, meaning, respectively, "interpreters of matters sealed up" and "interpreters of matters of extreme difficulty." We are not certain who these interpreters were, or what their manner of interpretation was. The usual explanation is that they were "allegorizers." "Allegory" is a Greek term meaning "to say another thing"; that is, when a text, holy or authoritative, contains a passage which to a later generation seemed troubling, the passage was so interpreted as to eliminate the trouble. Philo of Alexandria (see pp. 282-84) reflects a Jewish tradition, borrowed from the Stoics in their study of Homer, of interpreting Scripture allegorically. For Philo the controversies between Sarah and Hagar in Genesis were troubling, for he was not willing to believe that Scripture would present the quarrels of two women: Philo turns to allegory: "It is not women that

are spoken of . . . it is minds—on the one hand the mind
which exercises itself in elementary studies [Hagar] and the
mind contending for the victorious prize of virtue [Sarah]."
Perhaps the two types of interpreters mentioned in Rabbinic
literature were also allegorists, kindred in method and spirit
to Philo. But such interpretation, being capricious and possibly unrestrained, apparently fell into disfavor and disuse.

To the great Sage Hillel (who with Shammai constituted
the last of the "pairs"; see p. 236) there is attributed a set of
seven *middōt* ("norms") by which Scripture could be legitimately interpreted.[95] They are as follows:

1. *Qal ve-hōmer.* This is a deduction. For example: If theft
is specifically forbidden in a law code, how much the more is
burglary forbidden, even if not mentioned? Or the reverse:
If all theft is specifically forbidden, surely the picking of
pockets is forbidden, even if unmentioned. The translation of
the term is "the simple and the more rigorous."[96]

2. *Gezerā shavā.* A deduction from "an equal decree." If
two biblical verses contain similar specific words, then the
similarity of the words creates an identity of intent.[97]

3. *Binyān ab mi-katūb ehād.* The application of a specific
regulation found in one biblical passage to another passage
where no specific is given, that is, the inference of a general
rule from some single biblical verse.[98]

4. *Binyān ab mi-shnē k'tubīm.* A general rule derived not
from a single verse, but from two verses.

5. *Qelál u-frāt, u-frát u-qelál.* The inference of a single
specific regulation where Scripture provides a general principle; and the obverse, the inference of a general principle
where Scripture provides only a specific rule.

6. *Ka-yótze bō mī-katub ahēr.* An inference in situation B
from a similar specific biblical regulation in situation A.

7. *Dabár ha-lāméd me-inyano.* A conclusion inferred from
a biblical *context,* as distinct from a clear and unmistakable
biblical *statement.*

A second Sage, Rabbi Ishmael ben[99] ("son of") Elisha, amplified this list into thirteen rules;[100] he flourished in the so-
called "third generation" of tannaim, about A.D. 70-130. A
third, Eliezer ben Jose of Galilee, a tanna of the fourth generation, expanded the work of his predecessors into a list of

thirty-two rules, applicable both to haggada as well as to halacha.

For the general reader or beginning student, these rules for interpretation can scarcely have an immediate impact and full meaning; if so, it is the significance of the rules rather than their specific content that has some relevance. That significance can be put in this way: the ancient Rabbis, aware that Scripture can be quoted capriciously or recklessly, sought to fashion some reasonable guidelines against irresponsibility or whim. As we shall see in our discussion of Pharisees and Sadducees, the latter in principle objected to and rejected all and any interpretation of Scripture, holding that only what the biblical text mentioned specifically was binding. The Pharisees, on the other hand, were convinced that Scripture can, and must, be interpreted. Yet the question became inevitable: Granted that interpretation was indeed necessary and desirable, were there any limits to it?

There is ample testimony in the ancient sources that the rules were essentially guidelines, and on occasion disregarded even by Ishmael and Eliezer, who had formulated them. In some scholarly literature of our time the Hebrew term middot is translated as "norms," a word which falls short of the implication of "rules."

Moreover, there were sages such as the highly important Rabbi Akiba (flourished in the first third of the second Christian century), who espoused a mode of interpretation that was in a sense somewhat independent of the norms. It was Rabbi Akiba's conviction that all the phenomena of Scripture, even conjunctions, adverbs, and ordinary grammatical phenomena, contained hints and clues to conclusions quite beyond what the middot could yield from the text.

From a standpoint a bit removed from that of norms, which suggest the mechanics of interpretation, there has been transmitted a list of four words which describe the content of interpretation. These are *p'shat, rémez, d'rūsh,* and *sōd.* The first letters have been formed into a typical Hebrew acronym. That word is PRDS, and by inserting vowels we end up with a real word, *Pardés.* Pardes (a cognate of the English word "paradise") is the term used by the Rabbis for the Garden of Eden.[101]

P'shat can be translated as "literal." The word means "simple." It is an interpretation which explains a passage but without deliberately adding any inference or overtone. Remez ("hint") and d'rush ("sought for") do add inferences and overtones. In a rémez, the wording of Scripture is regarded as providing clear hints or clues in the direction of the overtone and inference; in a d'rush, the interpreter *seeks* for a basis to add these, for d'rush implies that no clear clue is present. Sod means "secret." It describes the infrequently encountered passages which deal with the mysteries of Creation, or heaven, or God himself.

The term *sūgyá*, used in reference to the Talmud, defies ready translation by a single English word. It has come to be used for a consecutive, cohesive passage in the Gemara on a focused topic, such as the explanation of a mishna or of a part of a mishna. A sugya, as it were, is a relatively self-contained, connected discussion which in a modern book might be suggested by the term chapter. A sugya, then, has a beginning, a middle, and an end, as a cohesive, self-contained discussion should.

Yet the elements that can go into a sugya are multiple, and can include an inquiry into the intent of a mishna, a suggestion as to the possible biblical basis, followed by a counter-suggestion or even a debate, with the issue being raised as to the interpretive norm utilized; moreover, citations from the opinions of Sages could seem in order, or else precedents could be cited from words or deeds of the learned. By its very nature, a sugya can seem complicated to a modern reader, and its unifying thread elusive, and the apperceptive mass of assumptions not as readily available to him as they were to those who some fifteen centuries ago set down in the writing the sequence of materials presented.

But a larger difficulty can arise as a consequence of the shift in assumptions. For example, a Rabbinic assumption that travel is prohibited on the Sabbath led to a definition of how far one might walk on that day without trespassing into travel; the answer given was 2000 "ells," the "Sabbath walking-limit." Yet a situation could arise whereby some compelling reason urged that a distance beyond the 2000 ells be traversed. The way out of the dilemma was advocated in what we might term a "legal fiction," a device by which two "limits" could be intertwined. Thus, if I walk 1800 ells to call for my mother to escort her somewhere 1500 ells distant, I would be walking 3300 ells. But a "mixing," that is, an intertwining of the "limits," implied that I was not actually engaged in genuine travel, even though I exceeded 2000 ells. The term for "mixing" is 'ērŭb.

Here is another example of a legal fiction: It is prohibited to carry anything, even a handkerchief, on the Sabbath. Suppose one has a runny nose. If he ties the handkerchief around his wrist, it becomes an article of clothing; to be clothed on the Sabbath is permitted; hence, a handkerchief tied to a wrist is permitted, but a handkerchief in the pocket is not. The fiction involved is that the handkerchief is not truly an article of clothing; so to regard it, however, renders permissible and legal that which would not otherwise be permissible.

If a modern reader feels that the Sabbath limit is irrelevant to him, or the matter of a handkerchief so trivial as to be of no concern, then he can scarcely have that sympathy for the very substance of the Talmud which is the prelude to understanding it. We use the term "Philadelphia lawyer" for a person who goes in for modern hairsplitting. Cases today go from lower to higher courts, and finally to the Supreme Court, in which issues are handled, without regard to substance, on matters that are hairsplitting. From a different standpoint, a prominent gangster, Al Capone, was sentenced and sent to jail not for his gangster activities, but for deception respecting his income tax. Legal fictions exist in all legal systems.

The true clue to a sugya is, first of all, the assumption that the item of law under discussion actually came from God, as part of the "oral revelation." Therefore its obedience was mandatory and an understanding of the item was incumbent on any man of intelligence and curiosity. Hence, to understand the divine revelation and the manner in which a faithful adherent understood and complied with it was essential. To dismiss a Talmudic item as mere hair-splitting was to imply that God's revealed law could be of no consequence; hence, hairsplitting was a necessary obligation if God's revealed will was to be known and obeyed.

In order to understand Synagogue Judaism we must divest ourselves of each and every tendency to superimpose our modern prepossessions about relevancy, and about what seems important and what seems trivial. The ancient Rabbis were aware of the range of items from the trivial to the important, but they left us this injunction: "Be as concerned for the 'light' [the trivial] commandment as for the 'weighty.' "

Let us go back to the discussion in the Gemara of the issue of an egg laid on a festival day. It begins with a question posed by the narrator-lecturer: "What is the status of the hen which laid the egg?" In form, the question is put: "What is it we are discussing?" In reply, our narrator says, "If the hen in this case is one being fed for future eating [as distinct from a hen kept because of the eggs it lays], what is the reason of the School of Hillel which would prohibit its eating on the day? For the egg, though separated from the hen, is clearly to be regarded as an actual part of the hen. On the other hand, if the hen is one kept for the eggs it lays, what is the reason for the School of Shammai which would permit it, inasmuch as it is in the category of the 'unintended'?" (This category supposes that the owner did not *intend* or *prepare* before the festival something to be used on the festival. The Hebrew word for "unintended" is *mŭqzeh*.)

The questions raised may be restated in the following way: "If the School of Hillel regards the egg as part of the chicken which fortuitously became separated from it, and if the chicken could legally be slaughtered and eaten on the festival, then why not the egg? On the other hand, does the School of Shammai, which would allow the egg to be eaten, by implication reject totally the concept of 'intended'?"

The narrator continues: "Is this a valid question to be put to the view of the School of Shammai? Is it not possible that the School of Shammai in reality accepts the principle embodied in 'intention,' but regards the egg as in the category of the 'innovation'?" That is, it cannot have been either intended or unintended, for its being laid could not have been anticipated, and therefore it was not susceptible of being in the category of the intended. Now, if we assume that the School of Shammai embraces the principle of "intended," where does it stand with respect to "innovated"? One can consistently permit the eating of the egg if it is in the category of the "intended," but at the same time prohibit its eating if it is an "innovation," and without possibility of having been intended or not intended. (We should note the tendency here to find a larger category into which the festival egg might be put.)

Said Rabbi Naḥman: "The issue is indeed one in which the hen was kept for laying eggs. But it is a matter of obligatory consistency that he who accepts the principle of 'intended' (that is, the owner must have intended to eat the egg) must accept the principle of the 'innovation.'" (If he could not know that an egg was to be laid, he could not have intended to eat it.)

Rabbi Naḥman continues: "The School of Shammai conforms to the opinion of Rabbi Simeon [ben Yochai], but the School of Hillel to the opinion of Rabbi Judah [ben Ilai]." (What is this abrupt and laconic introduction of the names of two sages of the second generation? To the erudite the reason for the introduction is clear without exploration, namely, that it was well known that Rabbi Simeon argued totally against the category of muqzeh and that Rabbi Judah argued totally for it.[102])

Our narrator, however, raises an objection, for he doubts that Rabbi Naḥman has in mind the difference of opinion between Rabbi Simeon and Rabbi Judah. Rather, Rabbi Naḥman has in mind a difference of opinion between the School of Hillel and the School of Shammai.[103] (That debate centered around the clearing of a table after a Sabbath meal, and focused particularly on the removal of bones or of nutshells.) The School of Shammai permitted the clearing of bones and nutshells through removing them by hand; the School of Hillel prohibited the removal of bones and nutshells by hand, prescribing instead that the whole table-top be lifted up and the food debris shaken off. (The School of Hillel would have permitted the removal by hand only if the stuff to be removed had been deliberately "intended.") Rabbi Naḥman said, "The School of Shammai conforms to the view of Rabbi Simeon." (That is, Rabbi Simeon had rejected the whole category of "intended"; therefore, the issue of removing bones and nutshells could scarcely enter into the discussion.)

Moreover, respecting the Sabbath, there is a stam ("anony-mous") mishna (such a mishna is viewed as undisputed and authoritative) in agreement with Rabbi Simeon, which per-mits cutting up vegetables for cattle, or meat for a dog. (Such cutting up is not regarded as unnecessary work on the Sabbath, but rather a benefit to the animals). The School of Hillel conforms with that of Rabbi Simeon respecting the Sabbath. But there is another anonymous mishna about the festivals, and that mishna conforms with the view of Rabbi Judah; it prohibits cutting up firewood from a stack of build-ing lumber, or from a beam which gets broken (for in neither case was such wood "intended" for firewood). The School of Hillel conforms to the opinion of Rabbi Judah ben Ilai.

But now our narrator introduces a related but different element. Respecting anonymous mishnas, why, when Rabbi Judah the Prince compiled the Mishna, did he provide an anonymous mishna conforming with Rabbi Simeon about the Sabbath, while, in considering the festivals, he provided an anonymous mishna conforming with Rabbi Judah ben Ilai (Simeon's opponent)? The answer is as follows: "Respecting the Sabbath, the rules for which are rigorous, people must not treat the Sabbath lightly; therefore he taught the mishna anonymously in accordance with the lenient Rabbi Simeon. But the festival, being less rigorous than the Sabbath, might impel people to treat festival rules lightly, and hence he taught the mishna anonymously in conformity with the opinion of Rabbi Judah who was strict."

There is further discussion in the Gemara on the matter of the egg. Perhaps, though, enough of the sugya has been here reproduced to suggest the flavor of it. The necessary relevant apperceptive mass one must possess to follow a sugya is im-mense. It is assumed in the Gemara that we who try to fol-low the sugya know the distinction between "intended" and "innovation"; it is assumed that we understand the principle involved in an anonymous mishna; it is assumed that we will attribute to Rabbi Judah the Prince a deliberate purpose in his decision to present a mishna anonymously. Moreover, there is a thread of impeccable logic on the part of the nar-rator, and considerations of logic and of logical consistency are still demanded of the Sages whom he cites, even if they died long ago.

It should follow (and here we repeat) that trivial as an egg may be, the discussion uses the egg only as a point of departure for an inquiry into fundamentals. It is the array of fundamentals which is the concern of the Gemara (though the eating of the egg itself must be resolved).

Moreover, we have here a reflection of the working of the legal mind. The Jewish Sages were not capricious or arbitrary; they made serious and objective inquiries into the reasonable inferences to be drawn from the axiom that the scriptural laws were divine and eternal and, to be obeyed, needed to be clearly understood.

The common man was neither a lawyer nor a colleague in the respective schools of Hillel and Shammai. His concern was with the conclusion—that is, what the halacha was which he was to obey. The Gemara, a process, was outside his ken, as are the fine points of American law to the ordinary American layman.

2. *The Midrásh. Midrash*, in a broad sense, is the term used for what we might call "explanation or interpretation." But *The* Midrash is the term for a very large quantity of rabbinic materials arranged not on topics like the Mishna, but by the sequence of the biblical presentation; thus, there is a tractate of the Mishna called the Sabbath, but no Mishna to Exodus (or any other book); there is a Midrash to Exodus (and other books), but no Midrash on the Sabbath or similar topics. The Midrash, then, is by its nature intimately bound to the biblical text.

It is reasonable to expect to find, as we do, a reflection of a development from simple explanation to complex ones. Let us assume two related but different settings. One is the *bét ha-midrásh* ("the house of interpretation," that is, the school). The biblical passage is read by a class. Next it is translated into Aramaic. Then its meaning is clarified, verse by verse, or even word by word. The other setting is the *bét ha-knésset* ("the place of assembly," that is, the synagogue where on the Sabbath, and on Monday and Thursday, Scripture was read to a cross section of people, ranging from students through farmers and artisans). Again, translation would be the first step, but thereafter explanation would ensue. While in the school there would be an understandable discipline or

restraint, with the teacher confining himself to the lesson
with some rigidity, in the synagogue some imagination and
exhortation would inevitably enter in. Hence, midrash can
be restrained and disciplined, or imaginative and unrestrained. The custom prevalent in our day of a worship service *with a sermon* derives from the ancient synagogue practice, for the sermon, Jewish or Christian, is a lineal descendant
of the ancient synagogue practice of the explanation of Scripture. A sermon is more than a mere technical exposition of a
text, for at its best it reflects imagination and exhortation, in
the effort to make an ancient text meaningful to the faithful
of a later time.

The Midrash is the huge collection of recollections of how
Scripture was explained in both school and synagogue. It is
normal in the Midrash—though this is not universal—to recall the name of the Sage to whom an explanation is attributed.

a. Halachic Midrash—Midrash as a process is much older
than the age with which we deal.[104] As collections to specific
books, The Midrash is represented in its first appearance by
concentration not on Genesis, which notably lacks laws, but
on Exodus, Leviticus, Numbers and Deuteronomy, which
present abundant laws. Moreover, the earliest halachic midrashim reflect the early Sages whom we call tannaim (though
the actual collecting was probably done by later Sages called
amoraim).

The tannaitic, halachic Midrash to Exodus has the Aramaic title *Mechiltã* ("measure" or "container"). The biblical
material covered begins with Exodus 12, which is the first
legal section of that book; it extends through the explanation
of Exodus 23.19, but includes material on the Sabbath from
Exodus 31.12-17 and 35.1-3.

The Midrash to Leviticus is called *Sifrã* ("the book"). Its
name seems to have arisen because the instruction of the
young began with and concentrated on Leviticus,[105] and
hence Sifra merited being known as *the* book.

To Numbers and Deuteronomy, the Midrash is called *Sifrẽ*
("books"; sifre is the plural of sifra). That is, there is a single
composite collection to Numbers and Deuteronomy.[106]

b. Pesiqtã—There was a second stage of the Midrash

which was a bit more complex. That stage is alluded to as
the "homiletical," since it grew out of "homilies," that is,
full sermons as distinct from brief explanations. The Pesiqtá
de-Rab Kahana is a collection of rather complex homilies for
significant Sabbaths[107] and the festivals. *Pisqá* (Hebrew) and
pesiqtá (Aramaic) seem to mean "section," as in our sense of
the word chapter, that is, less than a book but more than a
paragraph. The opening pisqa is attributed to Rabbi Abba
bar Kahana; hence the name ascribed to this collection. Each
pisqa begins with an introduction (usually called a proëm,
"preface"), followed by an ingenious and complex set of biblical citations and their meanings.[108]

Another work of this second stage is known both by the
title *Tanhumá*, after Rabbi Tanhuma bar Abba, whose homily begins the collection, and also as *Yelammedénu* ("let him
teach us," that is, "let Rabbi ———— ———— teach us"), because of a frequently used type of introduction to a section.
Again a different homiletical work, compiled much later, is
Pesiqta Rabbatí ("the great pesiqta"). It is a collection of
homilies for special Sabbaths and the festivals.

c. Haggadic Midrash—A third stage (third in character,
rather than strictly in time) is the so-called Midrash Rabbá.
There is a Rabba to each book of the Pentateuch—for example, Genesis Rabba. Rabba means "great"; the first proëm
in Genesis Rabba is attributed to a Rabbi Oshaia Rabbah
("Joshua the Great"). It is undetermined whether the
"Rabba" in Midrash Rabba is meant to allude to this Sage,
or whether this fivefold collection was deemed particularly
"great" in itself. The Midrash Rabba is essentially haggadic.
The component books were compiled by a succession of Sages
in different eras, and they vary in manner from each other.
However, they came to be considered as if a single collection.

Some non-Pentateuchal books also bred expositions comparable to the Midrash Rabba, especially the Song of Songs,
Ruth, Lamentations, and Ecclesiastes.

In no sense should it be the view that the above listed
books even begin to exhaust the totality of midrashic works
which Judaism created and transmitted; they might be
viewed as a basic list. Compilation of midrashim continued
into late medieval European times. Some compilations were

known in only limited areas (such as Midrash ha-Gaddól—
the "great" Midrash to Genesis among Yemenite Jews), or
the *Yalqút Reubéni* ("Reuben's notebook"), a late collection
which is essentially mystical.[109]

Some awareness of the manner of The Midrash is essential,
but its presentation in translation is all too often ineffective,
especially when the interpretation derives from matters of
Hebrew grammar or spelling. An example may here be cited.
For example, a passage, in Deuteronomy (6.5) reads, "You
shall love the Lord your God with all your heart, with all
your soul, and with all your might." "You shall love" in Hebrew—recall that the biblical text was transmitted without
vowels, the latter having been devised only in medieval
times—is *v'hbt;* with the vowels, it would read *ve'áhabtá.*
Yet a Sage supplying a different set of vowels could trans-
form that same consonantal word into *ve'ihabbtá,* which
would mean "cause to love." The sense of the verse then would
be: "You shall cause the Lord your God to be loved. . . ."

The second example is derived from the consonantal word
bnk. The passage in which this occurs is Isaiah 54.13: "All
bnyk (*bánáyik,* "your sons") shall be taught of the Lord,
and great in peace shall be your banayik." The midrashic
passage[110] reads: Said Rabbi Elazar: "Rabbi Hanina said,
'The disciples of the Sages increase peace throughout the
world, as [is proved where] Scripture says, All banayik are
taught of the Lord and great of peace are banayik. Do not
read the word as banayik, your sons, but rather read it as
bōnáyik, your builders.' "

Substantial portions of the midrashic literature arise from
the innate nature of the biblical text and of the Hebrew, and
the translation into English of such passages is inevitably labored and artificial. Let any reader try to translate a play on
words from English into French and German, and the insight or ingenuity disappears in the ponderousness of translating.

In the examples which follow, the reader ought not unduly
concentrate on the process by which a midrashic expounder
reaches his conclusion, but rather on the conclusion itself.
The beginning of Genesis Rabba is as follows: "Rabbi Ho-
shaya Rabba opened [his homily by quoting Prov. 8.30], 'I

was an *āmōn*[111] unto him, and a plaything day after day.'
Amon (he says) means 'pedagogue'; amon means 'well-
dressed'; amon means 'well cared for.' " Yet there are those
who say that amon means "a powerful person." Amon means
"pedagogue?" Whence? (In reply,) Scripture (Num. 11.12)
speaks of "as an amon carries a baby." Amon means "well-
dressed?" Whence? (In reply,) Scripture (Lam. 4.5) speaks
of "Those who ate delicacies have perished in the streets,
those dressed[112] in purple have embraced ash heaps." Amon
means "well cared for?" Whence? Scripture (Esther 2.7)
speaks [of Mordecai who] cared well for Hadassah.[113] Amon
means "a powerful person"? Whence? Scripture (Nahum
3.8) speaks, "Are you better than *Nō Amōn?*"[114] for which
the Targum runs, "Are you better than powerful Alexandria
which lies in the delta?" But there is still another interpretation for amon: The Torah says, "I was the tool of the *uma-
nūtā* ('craftsmanship') of the Holy One, Blessed be He. In
ordinary procedure, a human king who builds a palace does
not do so from his own knowledge but from the knowledge of
an amon. And the amon does not build from his own knowledge, but rather he has the parchment scrolls and notebooks
[with plans], so as to know how he will make rooms and the
doorways. Similarly, the Holy One Blessed be He looked into
the Torah and created the world. The meaning of *b'rēshīt*,[115]
(God created), arises from the fact that *rēshīt* necessarily
means Torah, as is proved by the verse (Prov. 8.22), 'God
created me'[116] as the *rēshīt* ('first thing') of his work."

The preceding paragraph makes wondrous sense in the
original; I fear that even with the explanations supplied, it
makes little sense to the modern reader *as a process*. The
sense of the passage depends on something not stated at all,
namely, that so knowledgable of Scripture were the Sages
that they were impelled to find relationships and implicit
cross-references throughout the range of it. The explanation
of the import of "In the beginning" proceeds from the citation from Proverbs 8.30, focusing on amon. A series of proposals for the meaning of amon is followed by a series of
scriptural quotations, each in support of one of a wide range
of meanings. Then, at last, the homily that Rabbi Hoshayah
opened turns directly to the first words of Genesis 1.1.

By process we mean the step-by-step procedure as discernible in the translation given; the conclusion, though, can be separated from the process; the conclusion reveals an idea of some significance, namely, *that the Torah already existed at the time of Creation.* In ensuing chapters, in discussing the ideas of Synagogue Judaism, it will not be the usual procedure always to recapitulate the process, but only to supply the conclusion.

3. *Targŭm*. The word targŭm, we have said, means "translation." By *The* Targum one means the translation from Hebrew into Aramaic.

Three *targŭmĭm* (plural of targum) to the Pentateuch have been preserved. One is called the Palestinian Targum. Preserved for centuries only in fragments, it is by common consent the oldest; to this we shall return.

The second is known by different names. Jews have called it the Jerusalem Targum; they have also called it, through an error, the Targum of Jonathan ben Uzziel,[117] the traditional author of the targum to the Prophets. It has been preserved only in fragment. It seems to have a relationship to the Palestinian Targum, and hence it is here mentioned second, though in date it should come third. By accumulation over the centuries it was greatly expanded to include many midrashic materials.

The third, and for Jews most important, is the so-called Targum of Onkelos, which in written form comes from the second or third Christian century and is thus older than the Jerusalem Targum, which includes material that can be dated as late as the seventh Christian century. The Targum of Onkelos can be regarded as the more or less official Synagogue Targum; when printing began, Onkelos was normally printed alongside the Hebrew text. Onkelos is known in the Jewish tradition as Onkelos the Convert. He appears to be confused with another convert, Aquila,[118] though a tanna named Onkelos seems attested to. Targum Onkelos often so treats passages about God as to remove the anthropomorphisms ("God in human form") and anthropopothisms ("God with man's emotions") of the literal Hebrew text.

In 1956 the so-called Codex Neofiti I was found in the Vatican Library. It is a very large manuscript, intimately related to the Palestinian Targum, which, to repeat, had been known only in some fragmentary remains.

Onkelos is relatively free of midrashic embellishment; Pseudo-Jonathan and Neofiti reflect a great deal. Even more midrashic embellishments are found in what is called the "Fragmentary Targum."[119] These fragments are much more midrashic than translations.

To the Prophets[120] the Targum, as said, is attributed to Jonathan ben Uzziel. This translation is less literal than is Onkelos to the Pentateuch. Targum Jonathan is almost as much a midrashic paraphrase as a translation.

There is no Targum to Ezra, Nehemiah, and Daniel. To Esther there are three; the so-called "Second Targum" is a free midrashic composition.[121] Recently fragments of a Targum to Job were found in the Qumran caves.[122]

4. Other Works. Several other types of works need brief mention here for completeness. The Scroll of the Fast (*Megilát Taʿanit*) comes from the tannaitic age. It is a list of calendar dates, primarily Maccabean, on which fasting is prohibited because of favorable events which occurred.[123]

Sēder Olắm Rabbắ ("great order of the world") is a chronological work, running from Adam through the Herods and to the second Christian century. A later work (eighth Christian century) is *Seder Olam Zutắ* (the latter word means "small") deals with genealogies, including those of exilarchs (heads of the exiled community) of Babylonia in the late period.

Pirkē Abôt ("Chapters of the Fathers") is found, curiously enough, as a tractate in the Talmud Order of *Nezikin*, "Damages," where it clearly does not belong. Also known as "Ethics of the Fathers," it is a compilation of wise and prudent observations of the sages. *Abôt de-Rabbi Nathan* ("Fathers of R. Nathan") is an expansion of Pirke Abot, dating from the post-Talmudic age but citing many tannaim. Both works are important in the realm of religious ideas, and citation especially from the former will recur in our subsequent treatment of the doctrines.

One work has survived which was wrongly ascribed to

Philo of Alexandria; scholars allude to it as Pseudo-Philo.[124] The surviving version is a Latin translation made from the Greek; most scholars believe that the original language of the work was Hebrew. Pseudo-Philo recapitulates the biblical account found in the Pentateuch, and proceeds as far as the death of Saul in the time of David. The author both adds to and at points alters the biblical account. Apparently writing after the destruction of the Temple in A.D. 70, the author asserts that Israel is indestructible, for Israel was chosen as God's people at Creation, even before Israel came into being; at the same time he seems to regard Israel as having always been in existence. A clear belief in resurrection is affirmed. While the term "messiah" is found in the book, it lacks the overtones of the term found in the Pseudepigrapha and the New Testament, meaning no more than "ruler."

Lastly, mention should be made here of Graeco-Jewish writings and of the New Testament, which we shall consider in Part IV. Granted that this literature contains material relevant to Palestinian Judaism, there are problems so special about them that it is well to treat them separately.

PART · II

· 1 ·

THE

INSTITUTIONS

1

TEMPLE—PRIESTHOOD

The central institution of Jewish life, as prescribed in the Bible, was the Temple. The Bible contains instructions, allocated to the Wilderness[1] period in the age of Moses, for its future construction and its administration under *kōhanîm* ("priests"), descended from Moses' brother Aaron, the first High Priest, and its system of various animal sacrifices. The Temple was built in due course by King Solomon.[2] It was destroyed by the Babylonians in 587 B.C.

A new Temple was built after the Exile, about 516-515 B.C.[3] Jewish sources usually allude to it as *báyyit shēnî* ("second house," i.e. "temple"). Because Herod refurbished this Temple[4]—some say he completely rebuilt it—one encounters allusions to it as "the Temple of Herod."[5]

Respecting Herod's refurbishing or rebuilding, one should understand clearly that what Herod really did was to create a large compound, with the Temple in its midst. Not only was the compound walled in,[6] but in Maccabean times it included a fortress at the northwest corner of the area, called the Tower; this later Herod rebuilt and called it Antonia, in honor of Mark Antony. East of the Temple itself was a "court for women." The Temple itself was enlarged beyond the basic structure, through colonnades in which there were various rooms. The actual Temple was basically a two-room structure, the outer room and the inner "holy of holies"; to

the outer room there was a porch.[7] The precise data respecting the size and height are given in detail in both Josephus
and in the Mishna tractate Middôt ("measurements"); there
are, however, some disagreements in the data provided.

The compound[8] in one sense could be likened to a community center, encompassing a variety of chambers which were
like offices. The open space south of the Temple itself was
available to Gentiles, and, indeed, was known as the Court of
the Gentiles;[9] that is, there was a relatively unrestricted area.
There was another, smaller area which only Jewish men
could enter, and yet another restricted to priests. The inner
"holy of holies" of the Temple itself was restricted to the
High Priest, and even he was permitted entrance only on the
Day of Atonement.[10]

The accounts of the plundering of the Temple treasury (as
by the Roman general Licinius Crassus[11] about 60 B.C.) imply that there was some chamber or office which served as
the storage place of the moneys accumulated through gifts or
the tax of a half shekel, which every Jew, whether in Judea
or outside, was obliged to pay.[12]

Inevitably some administration of the compound, and a
police force, were necessary, this beyond the concern of the
priests[13] for the Temple rituals itself. A list of such officials,
devoid of data as to when they served, is provided in Mishna
Shekalim Chapter 5. It is to be inferred that a board of some
fifteen men, each with a designated responsibility, managed
the affairs. The rabbinic sources speak of a *segán* to the High
Priest; his office, about which many perplexities exist, might
be described, over-simply, as that of "executive assistant" to
the High Priest, charged with the responsibility of superin-
tending the operation of the Temple.

The Temple worship was essentially the offering of animal sacrifices. It is a frequent error, however, to state this as
if to suggest that prayer was excluded. Quite to the contrary.
Ritual prayers were part and parcel of the worship along
with the sacrificial system, and examples of these prayers
have been preserved, as in case, for example, the prayer of
the High Priest on the Day of Atonement: "O Divine Name,
I have trespassed, transgressed, and sinned before Thee—I
and my family. O Divine Name,[14] forgive the trespasses,

transgressions, and sins which I have committed, I and my family. . . ." The attendant priests replied, "Blessed be the name of his glory for ever and ever."

It might be useful to repeat and to emphasize as forcefully as possible that priesthood was hereditary. The office of High Priest went from father to eldest son (at least in principle), in continuation of the precedent ascribed in Scripture, whereby Elazar succeeded his father Aaron, and Phinehas succeeded Elazar. The term of a High Priest, again in principle, was for life; the Jewish sources contain no suggestion at all of appointments for a single year, as found in John 11.49; 18.18.

That there was in the priestly clan a family within which the office of High Priest was handed down implies some abundance of priests beyond the single august line. Even before the Rabbinic period, the general priestly clan was already quite numerous and complex. I Chronicles 23-26 describes the organization of the priests, conceived of as a clan within the tribe of Levi. While these chapters ascribe the priestly organization to the age of David, modern scholars believe that it came from and reflected the post-exilic period. The categories mentioned there might be described in the following way. The Levites, the tribe presumably descended from Levi, the son of Jacob, were the general ecclesiastical workers, with a status lower than that of the family of priests. The Levites included musicians (1 Chr. 25.1-8). The total clan of priests were divided into twenty-four entities (already mentioned) called stations; though the stations lived throughout the land, they were summoned, station by station, through a system of rotation, to work in the Temple. (In Luke 1.8, Zechariah is at the Temple when it is the turn of his station to serve there.)

Presumably, there were in Jerusalem priests—brothers, nephews, and their offspring—more intimately connected with the family of the High Priest than were the priests of the outlying stations. Little is directly known about such priests; perhaps the allusions to the "chief priests" in the Gospels should be interpreted as "leading members" not directly involved in the succession of the high priesthood. In general, the Rabbinic literature simply assumes the biblical categories without directly reflecting either the functions or the status of the broader categories of priests except in one respect, that of pedigree. Thus, whether a man of priestly ancestry directly functioned in the Temple or not, it was expected of him that he would abide by the biblical restrictions on priests. Such restrictions included the prohibition of marrying a widow or a divorced woman, and contamination by contact with a corpse beyond one of his immediate family. These restrictions abided even after the destruction of the Temple and the practical end of priestly activity there. (The restrictions are still maintained today among strictly observant Jews.) The priests have needed to abide in purity, so as to be able to resume their functions when, at the advent of the Messiah, the Temple would be rebuilt and the priestly functions re-instituted.

The Hebrew word for priest is *kohén;* in the form of Cohen, Cohn, Kagan, and the like it is the most frequent surname of Jews in our time, a reflection of the persistence of pedigree. After the destruction of the Temple, the distinction in pedigrees led to the emergence of three categories of people: Priests, Levites, and "Israelites," the last simply non-priests and the non-Levites. The son of a marriage of parents of two different categories belonged to the category of the father.

In Synagogue Judaism after A.D. 70, and up to our own day (except in Reform Judaism, which eliminated all recollection of the three categories), priests had, and have, special prerogatives. They are called to the lectern for the first blessings connected with reading the Torah (Gitin 5.8). They function in the pidyón ha-bén, "redemption of the [firstborn] son" of an Israelite. They deliver the priestly benediction in the Synagogue. In general, the tradition preserves the paradox that leadership, including legal and judicial, fell to the Sages and the academies, but there was also preserved a precedence in showing courtesies and amenities, first to the Priest, next to the Levite, and only thereafter to the Israelite.

2

SANHEDRIN

The Temple compound also served in the capacity of what we would call the statehouse, wherein, in modern terms, the legislative, judicial, and possibly the executive were located; however, during the Hasmonean dynasty and the reign of Herod the Great it is likely that the executive power was located in the royal palace.

It does not seem appropriate to distinguish too sharply between the legislative and the judiciary. Indeed, we lack full and consecutive[15] information, and such information as we have may well be inaccurate, for much of it, coming from the time of the redaction of the Mishna (175-200), may represent an idealization of past procedures rather than the realities.

The term most familiar to modern people, often mentioned in the New Testament, is Sanhedrin. In the perspective of the Mishna, the Sanhedrin dated back to the time of Moses. Numbers 11.10-24 depicts Moses as unable to carry alone the burden of teaching the people. The Deity thereupon instructs him to designate seventy elders to assist him. The seventy, plus Moses, constituted the seventy-one members of the ancient Great Sanhedrin; so Mishna Sanhedrin 1.6.

Other terms are known from the Apocrypha and Josephus. For example, the Greek word *gerousia* ("board of elders," for which the Latin is "senate") is spoken of in II Maccabees 11.27 and in Antiquities XII (3.3), 138, the latter mention coming in a letter from Antiochus IV Epiphanes to Ptolemy Philopator. In neither passage is there any information given beyond the mere mention.[16]

Another word used rather often by Josephus in addition to his use of Sanhedrin is *boulē*, apparently in the sense of a supreme council. Yet no specifications accompany the term; indeed, in one passage, War, V (4,2), 144, boule seems to mean the chamber[17] where the council met rather than the council itself.[18]

The case can be made, as it has been by scholars, that there existed an upper-class legislative-judicial assembly from 200 B.C. on. The evidence would seem to suggest, in conformity with Deuteronomy 17.8-12, that such a body was presided over by the High Priest. Perhaps the membership was first recruited from highly placed Sadducees but later modified to include Pharisees. But what does not emerge at all is whether this body was legislative as well as judicial.

It is clear, however, that when Herod the Great was called on the carpet about his conduct in Galilee (he had executed rebels without trial), he was brought before the Sanhedrin in Jerusalem. It was Hyrcanus II, the High Priest and client-king of the Romans, who summoned him. The Roman provincial governor demanded that Hyrcanus have the charges dismissed. Before the Sanhedrin, Herod conducted himself with unabashed arrogance. Hyrcanus then advised Herod to flee the country, and Herod did so. In this passage[19] Josephus leaps ahead of his account, telling us that when Herod became king, he slew "all those in the Sanhedrin"; the word "all" appears to be one of Josephus' many exaggerations. Later,[20] Josephus tells us that Herod, on assuming the throne, put to death forty-five prominent men, partisans of his arch-foe Antigonus, the nephew and rival of Hyrcanus; some scholars deduce that these forty-five were members of the Sanhedrin, but there is no direct evidence.

The king–High Priest, as we have seen, represented a single office under the Hasmoneans. Herod was able to claim the throne, but he lacked the family descent necessary to be High Priest. He appointed and deposed High Priests with some frequency.[21] Little is told us about the Sanhedrin in the time of Herod. If, however, the High Priest was its presiding officer and susceptible of removal, then surely the Sanhedrin was of little consequence under Herod's dictatorship. Indeed, when Josephus lists the High Priests from Herod to the time of Titus as numbering twenty-eight men,[22] he says not a word about the Sanhedrin.

The only sources of information about the Sanhedrin after Herod (who died in 4 B.C.) are the Gospels, which narrate that Jesus stood trial before this body, and Acts of the Apostles. A major concern for New Testament scholars has been the issue of how much of the Gospel and Acts presentations have been disadvantageously affected by the time and geographical distance between the events themselves and the written depiction of them. There are some points, relatively major, in which the role of the Sanhedrin in the trial of Jesus fails to conform to the procedures as set forth in the Mishna Sanhedrin. More significant than procedure, however, is the question of the extent of the authority granted by the Romans. The general tenor of the Gospel accounts supposes that the authority of the Sanhedrin was in some ways restricted; more specifically, its right to impose a death sentence was not deemed automatic, for its decision needed ratification by the Roman procurator. This limitation in authority is expressed explicitly in John 19.31-32; there "the Jews" remind Pilate that "it is not lawful for us to put any man to death," a passage much debated in New Testament scholarship. The view at one extreme is that it reflects an historical situation in which for some brief interval the authority of the Sanhedrin was indeed limited. At the other extreme is the view that the passage has no historical basis, but is a Christian effort to explain away the embarrassment that Romans had executed Jesus, this by implying that the Sanhedrin would itself have executed him if only it had had the authority; accordingly, the view is held that the Sanhedrin actually had relatively unlimited authority, and hence that the statement in John 19.32, apologetic in nature, is wrong.[23]

As to the depiction of the Sanhedrin in the Mishna tractate by that name, the relatively late date of the compilation of the Mishna has suggested to some scholars that the Mishna provides an idealized presentation, the accuracy of which is questionable, especially since after Jamnia in A.D. 90 the Sanhedrin as such ceased to exist.

The Mishna, as mentioned above, conceived of the Great Sanhedrin as originating with Moses, who himself constituted the final member, bringing its number to seventy-one. Smaller sanhedrins existed, each numbering twenty-three, apparently being local judicial bodies in those towns where the population was large enough to justify such a body.[24]

According to the Mishna, the Great Sanhedrin sat in a semi-circle, in three rows, with new appointees, when neces-

sary, assigned to the third row. Longevity determined which
row a member sat in, with a progression first from row three
to row two, and then to row one, this as vacancies occurred.
We are not informed about the duration of the term of membership; presumably it was for life, with vacancies arising
through death. If the material in the Mishna is historically
reliable, the fact nevertheless is that the Mishna abstains
from telling us a great deal that we should want to know,
such as the mechanism for appointment.[25]

The events of A.D. 70 ended whatever form of existence[26]
the Sanhedrin had had. In the reorganization of Judaism at
Jamnia, a new judicial body arose in replacement of the Sanhedrin. Confusingly, it is often alluded to as a sanhedrin, but
the more frequent term for it is *Bet Din*[27] ("Court of Law").
For an understanding of this particular matter, the larger
topic of the reorganization at Jamnia needs brief exposition.
When the Romans destroyed the Temple in A.D. 70, that act
brought to a virtual[28] end the biblical religion of sacrifices at
a Temple presided over by hereditary priests. Antecedently,
the synagogue was already in existence; after 70, it emerged
as the replacement of the Temple. The Rabbinic sources narrate that just prior to the Temple's destruction, an eminent
Sage, Rabbi Joḥanan ben Zakkai,[29] escaped from the disasters
in Jerusalem by the pretense of having died, with his disciples being permitted to carry his casket (and presumed
corpse) outside the beleaguered city. He was then taken to
Vespasian, the general; on his predicting to the general that
Vespasian would soon become Emperor of Rome, Joḥanan
received the right to the little town of Jamnia (in Hebrew,
Yavne). Joḥanan was able to transfer to Jamnia the Academy which he had headed in Jerusalem. This Academy at
Jamnia became the great hinge in the transition from Temple religion to Synagogue Judaism. The Romans imposed
only one restriction on the Academy, one respecting its
leader. The circumstances were these: The Rabbinic tradition ascribes the leadership in religious affairs to a family
dynasty traced to Hillel, an earlier contemporary of Jesus.
Hillel and his rival Shammai had each founded an Academy,
but the tradition conferred hegemony on Hillel and his lineal
descendants. Hillel was presumed to be a descendant of

David; in the time of Johanan ben Zakkai, Hillel's great grandson, Rabbi Gamaliel II, should have presided at Jamnia. It was this designation that the Romans vetoed, fearing that leadership by a supposed Davidic descendant would possibly induce insurrection. Hence Johanan was allowed to assume the leadership on a substitute basis. The title which, according to Rabbinic tradition, Gamaliel II would have borne was *nasi* ("prince"). That title became equivalent to what we would call "the head." Under the nasi there was the actual presiding chairman, the *Ab Bet Din* ("father of the Court"). It was this latter title that Johanan bore, but he never had the title of nasi.

But respecting the implication of the shift from "Sanhedrin" to "great court," the older Sanhedrin was a body of the elite, the wealthy, the aristocrats; its successor at Jamnia was a body of scholars. Tradition had ascribed to Hillel a group of eighty disciples; there were on hand at Jamnia accordingly, an adequate number of Sages to constitute the new Bet Din.

3

PATRIARCH

In time Gamaliel II was allowed to assume the title of nasi. The Greek word for his title is "patriarch." In a general sense, the patriarch was essentially the titular head of the community; the actual executive head was the Ab Bet Din.

What were the rights, privileges, and limited autonomy of the patriarch? These questions are fraught with uncertainties and confusions. He had power; but how much of it derived from Rome and how much from the consent of the Bet Din is uncertain. Gamaliel II appears to have served in a double capacity—as patriarch and also as head of the *Yeshība* ("Academy"). The Academy was either synonymous with the great Ben Din, or possibly a separate scholastic enterprise composed of the same people. Gamaliel II was, indeed, deposed for a time by his colleagues as head of the Yeshībá because they regarded him as arbitrary and tyrannical. He

could not be so deposed as patriarch; that office was hereditary (entailing a supposed descent from King David).[30] The
question raised by some scholars, as to whether the patriarch
was a religious or a political[31] office is irrelevant, for that distinction is modern.

The overlap between the Bet Din and the Academy because of the identity of personnel represents a transition of
tremendous consequence, amounting in effect to a turning
over of the legislative process to the Sages and scholars, much
as if our Senate and House of Representatives turned over
their legislative functions to the faculties of the American
law schools. The Yeshiba and its scholars became the legislators for the people.

4

COURTS

Mention is made in the Mishna Sanhedrin (ch. 1) of what
we might call "local courts." A local court consisted of three
judges, or, occasionally, five. We are not informed about the
manner of appointment or the terms of holding office. The
likelihood is that such courts represented an ancient practice,
arising out of the experience of the people. Gradations in
size—whether a village, a town, or a city—determined
whether or not there was an adequate population to justify
a court. One rule of thumb suggested that unless a municipality possessed ten unemployed men (batlāním), it was not
big enough for a court.

The jurisdiction of local courts appears to have been a matter of some uncertainty. Mishna Sanhedrin (ch. 1) appears
to ascribe petty or routine monetary matters to such courts,
but to reserve for a larger judicial body matters more recon-
dite or else those of greater consequence. In the case of crimes
punishable by death, a proper court had to consist of twenty-
three judges. The most important matters—the trial of a
tribe, a false prophet, or a High Priest—was to take place before the tribunal of seventy-one.

The number twenty-three for the local Sanhedrin was arrived at by joining two biblical verses,[32] each of which justified ten, thus totaling twenty, plus the arrangement normal in a local court of a minimum of three. If the court wished to acquit, it could do so by a majority of one; to condemn, a majority of two was required.[33] The dispute is recorded as to the requisite population of a municipality to justify the "lesser Sanhedrin"; one opinion called for a population of a hundred and twenty men, the other of two hundred and thirty.

But by what law or laws were cases decided? The ultimate basis unquestionably was Scripture; halacha as the inference from Scripture was clearly called upon. What is uncertain is whether prior to 70, halacha was the sporadic, spontaneous inference which a local court on its own made from Scripture, or whether halacha prior to 70 was a body of decisions, precedents, and injunctions already in circulation in some organized, systematic form. That is, two aspects appear to have characterized halacha. In part it was the experience of the courts in actual cases which had been adjudicated and concluded; in part it was the theoretical discussions of the Academies, emerging from speculations as to what the reasonable inferences would be, in the event a particular kind of case should some time arise. The quantity of allusions to actual past cases justifies attributing the halacha in part to historic experience; the ordinary Talmudic sugya suggests that halacha came to be the penetrating and ingenious imagining of cases that might arise but had as yet not done so.

The academies and the eminent Sages may not have been legislative de jure, but de facto they were. The Mishna, compiled by Judah the Patriarch about A.D. 175-200, in citing the Sages, scholars, and Rabbis and their opinions, cites them as authorities in law rather than as eminent jurists.

5

THE ACADEMY

An academy—yeshiba—was clearly a school of advanced studies. The origin is obscure, but academies appear to have arisen at least by the year 50 B.C. Presumably, disciples clustered around individual men of eminence such as Hillel and Shammai, and in turn those disciples reared disciples. A cluster of disciples became an academy, a college of scholars. That is, there existed quasi-founders of particular academies. A particular academy would follow a line of academic approach and disposition in passing on both the teachings and the spirit of the founder; the Academy of Hillel was "liberal," that of Shammai "conservative." The transmission of the words and the spirit came to be a matter of high significance, for the original teacher-founder was greatly revered, and the ability to cite his words and deeds provided the stability ordinarily associated with inherited values, free from possible caprice on the part of the unrestrained innovator. The authoritative legacy from the past is called *qabbalá* ("that which has been transmitted"). A striking anecdote illustrates the unique significance of qabbala. The great Sage Hillel too had had his teachers. It is related of him that, by birth a Babylonian, he has come to Palestine, already possessed of a good education, to study and compare what he had already learned from his teachers with what he was now to encounter. Unable to pay the entrance fee to the lectures given by two Sages, Shemaiah and Abtalion, he climbed onto a windowsill (or a skylight) to hear the lecture, but an overnight snow caused him almost to freeze to death. Later on, Hillel became involved in a discussion at a school in Nisibis on a point of law—whether or not the Passover sacrifice should be offered on a Sabbath. Hillel at first presented his viewpoint by citing and interpreting relevant biblical verses, but he failed to persuade his audience. Finally he alluded to the qabbala he had received from Shemaiah and Abtalion, and those present were promptly persuaded.[34]

But schools of higher education could exist only in a context in which there were lower, elementary schools. In a large sense, that unique institution, the synagogue, served in that capacity.

6

THE SYNAGOGUE

We know what the synagogue became: a place of prayer and of instruction. The word "synagogue" is Greek; it has become Jewish[35] by association rather than by any intrinsic meaning. At first the word seems to have had two somewhat different connotations. It could mean the act of assembly, so that one could, as it were, have a synagogue, a meeting, in one's home. In the course of time it came to mean the place of meeting, the edifice set aside for particular purposes. Even later the edifice became elaborate and was adorned with floor decorations such as mosaics.

When and where did the synagogue begin? The question is disputed by scholars, primarily because the clinching evidence is not to be found. In place of evidence, one must resort to reasoning. The reasonable answer is that the synagogue was the local institution, especially of Jewish communities remote from Jerusalem. More particularly, the Judeans exiled to Babylonia after 587 B.C. retained their identity; this suggests that they gathered in local assemblies for their common purposes. Perhaps one should look to the Babylonian exile in the sixth pre-Christian century as the place and time of the origin of the proto-synagogue. But only when Scripture, especially the Five Books of Moses, came into general circulation, perhaps about 300-250 B.C., could the synagogue have begun to emerge as what it later developed into. When the spontaneous center remote from Jerusalem possessed a sacred book that needed to be passed along to later generations, the synagogue began to assume its special character. People, purpose, and the sacred book combined to fashion this distinctive institution.

The Hebrew term for synagogue is *bēt ha-knésset* ("house of gathering"). That term was in origin neutral, meaning only a gathering, not necessarily a Jewish one.[36] An accompanying term, *bēt ha-midrásh* ("place of study") also had a neutral sense. In time, however, both terms acquired strictly Jewish connotations.

The Rabbinic tradition exhibits little interest in the origin of the synagogue or the place of study. In emphasizing the importance of qabbala, it speaks of "men of the great knésset,"[37] or "great synagogue." The context of this phrase in Chapters of the Fathers (ch. 1) is in the tracing of the transmission of qabbala:

Moses received (qibbēl) *the Torah at Sinai. He handed it over to Joshua and Joshua to the elders, and the elders to the prophets, and the prophets to the men of the "great knesset."*

The majority of modern critical scholars have expressed doubts that there ever was a model synagogue such as "great knesset." To them "great synagogue" has appeared to be an imaginative invention of a master model, on a large scale, to bridge what would otherwise be a gap between the biblical prophets and the later local *bet ha-knesset*.

If, then, there has existed no master model, nevertheless the three elements—people, purpose, and sacred book—combined to fashion that which responded to the felt need. The purpose of the synagogue was to enable ordinary Jews to live the religious life. The sacred writings constituted the textbook. The people were the students, and they were expected to carry out in their daily lives the lessons they learned in the synagogue.

Our knowledge of Jewish education in the Maccabean age is very limited. We know of teachers, of course, for whom the term was *soferím* ("scribes").[38] Apparently private schools existed even in Maccabean times. We do not know how the educational system functioned, but apparently there were two levels of instruction for children, the lower being the *bēt sēfer* ("place of the book"), and the bet ha-midrash, which was somewhat more advanced. Wherever there was a synagogue, there was also a school.

The notion of ubiquitous schools, at least for males (in that age before female liberation) rested on a unique quality of Synagogue Judaism: its practitioner needed to be literate, for an illiterate male could not know the content of sacred Scripture.

Perhaps the bet ha-midrash was the organized systematic school for the young; the bet ha-knesset was the assembly of adults for—to use a modern term—their "continuing education." The bet ha-knesset was where adults were reminded of the education they presumably once had had; on Mondays and Thursdays (market day for farmers) and on Saturday, Scripture was read and explained to those who gathered.

In due course the scriptural readings in the Synagogue worship became systematic: The Pentateuch was divided into sections, called *parashot* or else *sedarim* (the division into our inherited chapters in printed Bibles stems from medieval Christianity). In Palestine the systematic arrangement provided for completing the Pentateuch through weekly segments over a period of three years; modern Jewry utilizes a different arrangement, one developed in Babylonia, of completing the Pentateuch in a single year. Each *parashá* (the singular of parashot) tended to acquire a name based on the first significant word, exemplified in the phrase, "the parasha of *berēshit*" ("In the beginning," Gen. 1.1, or the parasha "Go thou," Gen. 12.1). The name of the parasha came to be attached to the Sabbath when it was read, exemplified in "the Sabbath of Bereshit," or "the Sabbath of 'Go thou.' "

Scripture was read from a continuous parchment scroll; the codex form—a stack of sheets sewn together on the same margin—did not arise in the Greek world until about the middle of the first Christian century. The scroll was stored in a "holy ark," a box-like container. It was ceremoniously removed when it was to be read, and ceremoniously returned when the reading was over. The scroll was wound on two wooden rollers; a cloth binder held the scroll together. In due course the holy ark became embellished, as did the cloth binder. The wooden rollers extended beyond the scroll itself; each roller was termed a "tree of life," for the Torah "is a tree of life to those who grasp it"[39] (Prov. 3.18).

The reading of Scripture in Palestine and Babylonia was

always the Hebrew text. Promptly a translation into Aramaic ensued. Thereafter, a teacher explained the passage. Such explanation, as I have said, entailed on the one hand clarification of the legal requirements, thus involving halacha. On the other hand, the narrative sections entailed expansion of the text. For example, Genesis 22 relates that at divine bidding Abraham took his son Isaac to a mountain named Moriah so as to offer him as a sacrifice. The biblical passage contains words and phrases that are suggestive. "God tested Abraham?" Why the "tested"? In order for God to have a basis for rewarding Abraham for his meeting the test. Was this the only test that Abraham was exposed to? Or was not his life a succession of tests? Was it not more like ten tests that Abraham endured, rather than one? And what did Abraham say to Sarah—the Bible is silent on this—when he left home early in the morning with Isaac? The reply is he told her that it was time to take Isaac to enroll him in a yeshiba, an academy. Which yeshiba? One founded by Abraham's two associates, Shem and Eber, mentioned in Genesis 14. The narrative tells that when Isaac lay bound on the altar, Abraham wept bitter tears; these settled into Isaac's eyes, and were the cause of the blindness which Isaac suffered in later life.

In our time, the biblical personages have come to seem so remote, or to be so lofty, or else so wicked—as in the case of the Pharaoh—as to seem almost anything but human. It was not so in the age with which we deal. To the people assembled in the synagogue, the biblical personages were close friends, even intimates, and they were gloriously human. Thus, when Abraham welcomed three visitors (Genesis 18), he bade Sarah to take fine flour and bake bread. Why the need to specify "take fine flour"? Simply because Abraham understood the mentality of women, who become stingy when unexpected guests arrive. Why in that chapter is no further mention made of the bread? Because it was not served, for while Sarah was kneading it, she became menstruous, and she and Abraham scrupulously observed the biblical injunctions of personal purity.

Moreover, the motives of biblical personalities, or of God himself, could be clarified by a telling anecdote, a pithy story that likened the Deity to a king, or some a biblical character to a merchant or farmer whose daily procedures were fully and clearly known to those who listened. From translation to amplifying the text, even to including a parable, was a natural transition, and thereby the explanation of Scripture in time became the full-length sermon.

To repeat, the synagogue was a school for adults. This aspect of the synagogue persists in Jewry even today; the German, the Italian, and the Yiddish terms for synagogue is "school" (*Schule, scuola, shul*).

But that the education in the synagogue dealt in matters of sanctity means that naturally and normally prayer became an inherent aspect of a gathering where Scripture was read. My own teacher, Erwin R. Goodenough, said repeatedly, "In Judaism it was but a half-step from study to worship." Initially such worship was sporadic; in due course a liturgy—"order of worship"—arose. Much is obscure about the development from the spontaneous to the fixed order.[40] Before the first pre-Christian century two aspects of a somewhat fixed liturgy seem to have become crystallized. One was a series of passages from the Book of Deuteronomy, introduced by the passage (6.1) called the *sh'ma* ("hear"): "Hear O Israel, the Lord Your God is one Lord."

The second fixed aspect, which is also apparently pre-Christian, is known by four names. This is a succession of benedictions, "blessings." Because it was the custom to recite these benedictions while standing, the sequence of prayers is known as the *amidā́* ("the standing"). Because it became the central segment of the liturgy when that was later expanded, it is known also as '*avōdā́* ("the worship"). It is also known as the *tefillā́* ("the prayer," that is, the prayer *par excellence*).

The blessings came to follow a pattern, indeed, a formula. The blessing usually began with the same words: "Blessed are you, O Lord our God . . ." The series of benedictions constituting the amida numbered eighteen (in Hebrew, *shmōné esréh*), the fourth name. The tradition ascribes the origin and sequence of the eighteen benedictions to men of the Great Synagogue;[41] yet a narrative relates that at Jamnia[42] under Rabbi Gamaliel II, Simeon ha-Pakuli arranged the benedictions in their appropriate order. Moreover, Gamaliel enjoined their daily recitation by males.[43] The accomplishment of Gamaliel II was apparently not the introduction of the benedictions, but the precise ordering of them in the worship.

Scholars are united in their belief that the eighteen benedictions are pre-Christian. Theories differ as to whether the eighteen were innovated all at a single instance or whether they grew to eighteen by accretion.[44]

The benedictions often come at the end of brief paragraphs.[45] The first of the eighteen, for example, now[46] reads:

Blessed are you, O Lord, our God and God of our fathers, the God great, powerful, and awesome, the God most high. You do deeds of lovingkindness and possess all that exists. You remember the pious deeds of the Fathers,[47] and bring a redeemer to their sons' sons, for His name's sake, in love;—[you are] a king who helps, saves, and protects. Blessed are you, O Lord, shield of Abraham.

The second paragraph reads:

You are eternally powerful,[48] O Lord. You are mighty to save. You sustain the living with lovingkindness. You make the dead live with great mercy. You support those who fall, heal the sick, free the fettered, and carry out the[49] faith to those who sleep in the dust. Who can be like you, master of powers, and who can resemble you, a king who brings death and makes alive, and makes salvation sprout? You are reliable in that you bring the dead to life. Blessed are You, O Lord, who brings the dead back to life.[50]

The third is very brief:

You are holy and your name is holy. Holy people praise you each day, selah.[51] Blessed are you, the holy God.[52]

The next prayers (four through six) speak of God's gift to men of understanding and knowledge; next, of His acceptance of man's repentance; and then of His gracious and abundant forgiveness.

Prayer seven speaks of affliction and misery, and the need of God's redemption. Prayer eight couples God's healing of the sick with His redemptive power. Prayer nine asks for a prosperous year of productive crops and work; prayer ten asks for the ingathering of all those exiled to the four corners of the earth. The eleventh speaks of orderly government and just courts under God, as if arising in a time of chaos or oppression.

The twelfth prayer reads:

For slanderers, let there be no hope. May all wickedness quickly perish. May all your enemies be cut off. May you speedily uproot the arrogant kingdom, and break it, crush it, and humble it speedily in our days. Blessed are you, O Lord, who breaks the enemies and humbles the arrogant.

This benediction presents a number of problems, both in its wording and how it fits with the others. In one view, it is the latest of the eighteen; in another, it is an added nineteenth benediction. A narrative (Berachot 28b-29a) tells that this prayer was composed orally at Jamnia at the instigation of Gamaliel II by a certain Samuel the Younger, but that a year later it had become forgotten and so had to be composed anew. At issue among scholars is the question, against whom is the prayer intended? The answers include a range of possibilities. One is that those denounced were informers, that is, Jews who gave Roman officials information about violators of the Roman prohibitions such as circumcision, this during the Hadrianic persecutions of A.D. 130-32. Others view those denounced as apostates (Hebrew *zēdīm*). The word slanderers is itself in all likelihood a medieval substitution for another term; the passage, Berachot 28b, uses the word *mīnīm* in some preserved Talmudic texts. At one early stage the denounced were the Sadducees; but probably medieval censorship of the Talmud[53] produced the alteration from minim to Sadducees. At one stage, very early, that target may have been "Nazarenes," a word possibly derived from Nazareth, the home of Jesus, and possibly meaning Christians.[54] The text of the twelfth benediction, then, has appeared in a variety of forms. About minim, two things are clear despite its obscurity. One is that they were Jews, insiders, whose views were deemed heretical (a heretic is always an insider). Second, their unorthodox views seem to have centered in a theory of two "forces," God representing goodness, and an equal force, the power of evil. It is, however, more likely that they envisaged a totally different set of two powers, with God Himself being viewed as so majestic as to be outside the world and out of contact with it because of its wickedness, and His having turned over the world to a second force or deputy (called in Christian gnosticism the "demiurge").

The thirteenth prayer, exactly the opposite in spirit, calls for the blessing of "the righteous, the pious, the elders . . . , the remnant of scholars, and worthy proselytes."[55]

The fourteenth and fifteenth are on behalf of the city of Jerusalem, and about the emergence of the Messianic redeemer, a descendant of David.

The sixteenth is a general prayer that men's prayers be acceptable. The seventeenth, regarded as one of the oldest of the eighteen, appears to have been originally a prayer for the acceptance of the sacrifices offered in the Temple,[56] but after 70 it became altered into a prayer for the future restoration of the Temple cult, at the advent of the Messiah.

The eighteenth is a long prayer of Thanksgiving for God's wonderful benefits and mercy, both in the past, and until current days.

The nineteenth—if number twelve is omitted as a late innovation, this would be number eighteen—is an eloquent prayer for peace.

Certainly the eighteen[57] (or nineteen) benedictions disclose alteration and development. Nevertheless, at the core they are pre-Christian in the time of their origin. From this core there eventuated an immense elaboration and extension of the synagogue liturgy.

When the reorganization of Judaism took place at Jamnia, it became the considered conclusion that prayer in the synagogue was a viable and acceptable substitute for the sacrificial system at the Temple. There had been sacrifices daily in the morning, afternoon, and evening; hence, the daily synagogue worship was also to be morning, afternoon, and evening. On the Sabbath morning, the daily sacrifice was supplemented with an additional offering; the Sabbath morning prayer period was supplemented with an additional sequence of prayers.

The synagogue was the place for corporate, communal prayer. For such worship, to distinguish it from private prayer, a minimum quorum of ten[58] males (the *minyắn,* "counting," or "quorum") was deemed essential. Yet home prayers—and private devotions—also were suggested or even demanded. In home devotions, one might perhaps distinguish between devotional acts deriving directly from Scripture and those only indirectly derived or else actually innovated. Of biblical derivation was the use of *tefilín* (literally, "prayers," called phylacteries in Matthew 23.5[59]). Two small leather boxes were utilized, in which there were recorded on parchment four brief passages[60] from the Pentateuch. The biblical verse of Deuteronomy 6.8, ["The divine words] shall be signs on your hands and frontlets between your eyes," apparently led to the practice. The one box was bound on the left arm by a leather thong wrapped around the arm downward, in seven turns, toward the hand, which could hold the excess part of the thong. This box, for the hand, was a single compartment; the second box, for the forehead, had four compartments, one for each brief biblical passage. The box lay on the forehead, being secured at the back of the head by a circular leather strap.[61] As one donned the tefilin, he recited appropriate biblical verses and non-biblical benedictions. Usage seems to have differed respecting the question of whether one donned the tefilin only for the brief period of morning prayer, or whether one wore them all day, wherever he wants. In time the tefilin tended to become primarily, but not exclusively, a home devotion (as it is preeminently today). (Perhaps it is somewhat inaccurate to classify the tefilin too strictly as a ceremonial for the home, since they were worn in the synagogue too; it has been, however, an individual, rather than a communal, ritual.)

On the doorpost of a house it was customary to nail a *mezūzắ.* The word, simply meaning "doorpost," came to be applied to a small box, made of wood or metal, in which a rectangular piece of parchment containing Deuteronomy

6.4-9 and 11.13-21 is set. The word *shaddái* ("Almighty")
was written on the obverse side of the parchment, and made
visible by an opening in the box. The biblical basis is Deuteronomy 6.8: "You shall write [the divine words] on the doorposts of your house and your gates."[62]

Of relatively great antiquity[63] is the thanksgiving prayer,
the *birkát ha-māzón* ("blessing for food"), after a home
meal. This prayer may be taken as a clue to veritable abundance of benedictions which accompanied the various daily
routines from one's rising to one's retiring. In due course, the
Sages in the academies tended to systematize and even prescribe the appropriate benedictions, but surely at some stage
these were sporadic and spontaneous, eventually becoming
routinized into characteristic formulas. The Tractate Berachot is replete with recollections of spontaneous prayers uttered by Sages.

The male was expected to comply with the biblical injunctions in Numbers 15.38-49 and Deuteronomy 22.12 to have
tzitzít, ("fringe") sewn onto their garments, with a blue
(some say violet) thread interwoven in the fringe. The purpose of the tzitzit was to be a reminder of divine injunctions
and of requisite holiness. The Rabbinic interpretation[64]
yielded a minor dispute; the Academy of Shammai supposed
that the tzitzit should consist of four white woolen threads
interwoven with four of blue, the Academy of Hillel two of
each. The fringes were sewn onto a sort of undergarment
called *arbá kanfót*, a square somewhat like a diaper, with
fringes joined to each corner. The *tallít* ("cloak") was originally an outer garment; the word came to be used as descrip-
tive of a shawl to be worn during prayer (the Yiddish pronunciation is *tállis*). Fringes are sewn at the corners of the
tallit.

The food laws were in part biblical, in that Scripture prohibits the eating of certain animals, fish, birds, and all crustaceans.[65] Rabbinic prohibitions were added, chiefly in a distinction not explicit in Scripture, between meats and dairy
products, wherein the halacha prohibited eating these two
kinds of foods at the same time.[66] This prohibition, termed by
the Rabbis as an "innovation," is based on the prohibition
found three times (Exod. 23.19; 34.26 and Deut. 14.26)

against "boiling a kid in its mother's milk.[67] Derivative from such prohibitions were a host of attendant prohibitions, relating to the proper pots and pans, to the contact with raw food by Gentiles, and to such matters as an egg with a drop of blood in it. Poultry was classified with meat, but fish was deemed neutral, edible with both meat and dairy meals.

The circumcision of a male baby on his eighth day was ideally the duty of the baby's father.[68] In due course an expert circumciser supplanted the father.

For women, the ritual bath after menstruation or childbirth was a biblical injunction (Lev. 15.19; 12.1-8). The bath took place in a *mikvé*,[69] a tank big enough to contain sufficient water to cover completely the body of a man of ordinary size.

It is not possible here to enter into the fullness of these matters. The general statement might be made as follows: There are biblical commandments which tell *what* must be done. Out of sporadic or spontaneous conformity, there arose guidance as to *how* to do what must be done. The halacha is preeminently the matter of how; in the course of discussions and prescriptions as to how, there were developed additional requirements of what. Thus, the home prayer and home rituals underwent minute examination and prescription in the unfolding of the halacha.

· 2 ·

THE
PARTIES

In the period from about 200 B.C. to A.D. 200 there emerged a number of groupings: Ḥasidīm ("the pious"), Sadducees, Pharisees, Essenes, Zealots, Sicarii ("swordsmen"). Some groups lasted for a considerable period of time, some only briefly. Our knowledge of them is far from complete, and fraught with many puzzles. In the case of the Pharisees, uncertainties combine with scholarly partisanship to obstruct understanding, as we shall see. As in our American society, where we have had Whigs, Democrats, Rotarians, and the American Legion, we need to understand that such groupings were not all of the same kind; moreover, as in our society, the Democrats have gone through transitions from the time of Jefferson until our day, coming to include George Wallace and George McGovern, so too a long-lasting group such as the Pharisees would have undergone notable alteration or transition.

I have used the word "grouping" here in an effort to escape a semantic problem which other terms seem to raise. Some writers have used terms such as sect or sectary, and others have objected to the use of these terms. The issue over the terms is essentially one of extent—that is, to what extent did a grouping have a vivid sense of its distinction from other groupings, and to what extent did it fashion some kind of inner organization to promote its purposes, and to what extent were its purposes clearly different from the purposes of other groupings?

The context in which to understand the groupings is the circumstance that the Jews constituted both what we would call a nation and what we would call a religious community. Intertwined as these were, there is nevertheless a certain distinction that can be discerned between a movement which out of patriotism challenged the rule by the Seleucidian Greeks and a movement which took a stand on the inner religious issues that arose quite naturally respecting the application of the Bible to the age which had adopted it as the guide to the rules of living.

A. ḤASIDIM

The Ḥasidim[1] are mentioned three times in the Books of Maccabees. In some English translations they are called Hasideans or Asideans. In the context of the rebellion against the Seleucidians, we are told that after some Maccabeans had been slain through abstaining from fighting on the Sabbath, and then determined to desist from such abstention, a company of "Asideans"[2] joined with the rebels. They are described as "mighty men of Israel," and "voluntarily devoted to the Law." When later the priest Alcimus persuaded the newly crowned king of the Seleucidians to install him as High Priest, declaring himself in opposition to Judas Maccabeus, the Ḥasidim supported him because he stemmed from the proper priestly background. Yet Alcimus soon put to death some sixty of the Ḥasidim (1 Macc. 7). In II Maccabees 14.6, Alcimus is portrayed as informing the king of the Seleucidians that the Ḥasidim, followers of Judas Maccabaeus, nourished warfare and sedition. Rabbinic sources speak of "ancient Ḥasidim" as martyrs and unselfish, long-suffering saints.[3] Places of honor at a Sukkot ceremony were allotted to them. The thirteenth of the Eighteen Benedictions (above, p. 150) alludes favorably to the *Tzaddikīm* ("the righteous") and then to the "Ḥasidim."

This amount of information is noticeably scanty. From it, however, a theory has arisen on the one hand that the Ḥasidim were the actual spearhead of the prolonged Maccabean resistance to the Seleucidians, and hence they were of foremost influence. On the other hand, some modern scholars have played down the importance of the Ḥasidim. Also, other theories have arisen which set the Ḥasidim in the role of antagonists to the hellenizers, those upper-class Jews who were responsive to Greek ways and adopted them. Such theories may be right, but they rest less on clear evidence than on the inference that if the hellenizers were impious, the pious must have been the Ḥasidim. Accordingly, the Ḥasidim, then, were at one extreme and the hellenizers at another.

B. SADDUCEES

The Sadducees are known to us essentially from their portrayal by their critics or opponents, including bitter ones. If any Sadducee ever wrote anything, not a line has come down to us.[4]

A relatively neutral source is a passage in Josephus.[5] He describes the Sadducees as deniers of "Fate";[6] they separate God completely from evil; they deny "the persistence of the soul after death"; they deny penalties in the underworld and also rewards in heaven. Josephus goes on to contrast the geniality of the Pharisees with the boorishness of the Sadducees. In another passage, Antiquities XVIII (1.3), 12, Josephus describes the Sadducees as rejecting the afterlife and any law not enjoined in Scripture. They are prone to dispute with the teachers of philosophy they seek out. Their viewpoint is shared by only a few, yet these few are men of highest eminence. Popular pressure at times pushes the Sadducees into the espousal of the Pharisaic way. Since written law requires interpretation, the Sadducees, even in bowing to that need, are in general more literal, and in questions of criminal law more rigorous, than the freer Pharisees.[7] So says Josephus.

The origin of the name Sadducees is unknown. It seems connected with Zadok, whom King David had designated High Priest (1 Kgs. 2.25); in Ezekiel 40-48 the "priests/sons of Zadok" are viewed as the proper line.[8] Perhaps since the word is related to *tzàddíq* ("righteous man"), the name was a derisive epithet, used in scorn by their opponents, in the sense of "the self-styled righteous."

The earliest historical notice of the Sadducees, if Josephus is to be trusted, is to be allocated to the reign of the Hasmonean John Hyrcanus (135-105). John Hyrcanus, he tells us, had at first been a disciple of the Pharisees. One of these, a certain

Eleazar ventured to suggest to the king that he lay down his office as High Priest because the king's mother had been a captive in the days of Antiochus Epiphanes. We know what the insinuation meant—that John Hyrcanus may have been the offspring of a rape and thus lacked the proper priestly lineage. The king resented the insinuation. That royal resentment increased when other Pharisees suggested to John Hyrcanus that Eleazar be only lightly punished for his offensive proposal. John Hyrcanus now shifted his partisanship from Pharisees to the Sadducees and he proceeded to persecute the Pharisees by abrogating laws which they had established, presumably with his consent.[9] That is, the Sadducees and Pharisees were rival groups, concerned for power in the court.

It is certain on the basis of the ancient sources that points of theology and religious law separated the two groupings, Sadducees and Pharisees, from each other. Modern scholars, however, have tended to emphasize what is reasonable enough, yet not found in those sources, namely, that the Sadducees represented a social segment, the Jerusalem upper classes, whose lives were intertwined with the priests and the nobility. It is also reasonable to suppose that, living in proximity to the Temple, the Sadducees were fully satisfied in their needs by the Temple rituals, so that they felt no compulsion toward that progressive adulation of Scripture which marked the Pharisees and the commoners in the synagogue. Respecting sacred Scripture, the Sadducees were, understandably enough, strict constructionists. Hence their rejection of the doctrine of an afterlife (explicit only in Daniel[10] and nowhere else in the Hebrew Bible) is readily intelligible.

The Gospels[11] bring Jesus into contact with the Sadducees, in similar versions of a passage[12] which could easily have been included in the Talmud. In Acts of the Apostles 23.8 the statement is made that the Sadducees disbelieved in angels and spirits. Angels are mentioned with some frequency in Scripture and it is therefore inconceivable that the Sadducees disbelieved in them. Perhaps the intention in Acts is to suggest that Sadducees disbelieved in the developed angelology, aspects of which appear in Daniel, and which later underwent great amplification.

One of the many individual points of controversy[13] between the Sadducees and Pharisees may be mentioned here; it was on the tabulation of the forty-nine days by which the date of the festival of Shavuot was to be determined. Leviticus 23.15-16 prescribes that the tabulation begin in Passover "on the day after the Sabbath." The Pharisees interpreted Sabbath here as the first day of Passover, whatever day of the week that was; Sadducees interpreted Sabbath literally as Saturday. For Sadducees Shavuot always fell on a Sunday; for Pharisees it could fall elsewhere during the week.[14] The importance of this particular controversy is its relationship to the sacred days; in religious differences within communities, calendar differences tend to assume a high significance because they are so noticeable.[15]

Josephus speaks repeatedly of the absence of a widespread popular support of the Sadducees. It is clear that they were already established when the Pharisees began to rise to ascendancy, but when the Temple was destroyed in 70 the focus of the Sadducees was lost, and they disappeared.[16] Clearly, the most important distinction between Saducees and Pharisees was on the issue of the legitimacy of the oral law, espoused by the Pharisees and rejected by the Sadducees. But a full understanding of the Sadducees is impeded by the relative paucity of information, and what limited information we have does not come from them.

C. PHARISEES

The problems in understanding the Pharisees are even more acute. Chief among these problems is this situation: Synagogue Judaism in a real sense arose from, or found its directing guidelines from, Pharisaism. Hence, preserved Judaism is in a sense a lineal descendant of Pharisaism. In the Gospels the Pharisees are villains, and from the Gospels there arises the circumstance that in ordinary English dictionaries the word Pharisee connotes a hypocrite, a misguided zealot for whom the externals of religion are of total consequence, and the internal convictions of little import. Since Christendom has so thoroughly disparaged the Pharisees, many modern Jewish scholars have felt impelled to defend them, feeling that to defend the Pharisees is in effect to defend Judaism from both ancient and also modern Christian slurs. Neither slurs nor defensive retorts promote academic understanding.

The origin of the Pharisees is as obscure as their name. The two suggestions for the latter, that the word means either "explainers," that is, explainers of Scripture, or "separators," that is, separators from evil or defilement, are the continuing suggestions. The first emergence of the Pharisees is obscure. It has been suggested that they derive from the Ḥasidim,[17] to whom there is ascribed also the origin of the Essenes, to whom we presently turn. The Essenes, so it is held, withdrew from public life in refusing to recognize the Maccabeans as legitimate priests (see above, pp. 41-42), but the Pharisees remained in the arena with the intention of promoting their ideas into the active life of the people. The first mention by Josephus of the Pharisees, like that of the Sadducees, is in the reign of John Hyrcanus. Under Alexander Jannaeus (104-78), against whom the populace seems to have rebelled, and as a result underwent wholesale slaughter,[18] the Pharisees seem to have been forcibly kept from any influence on the crown. On his deathbed (we here repeat), Alexander urged his wife to assign some of her authority to the Pharisees, so as to bring about a reconciliation between the crown and the people. Salome Alexandra (76-67) followed her husband's advice, giving the Pharisees a generous measure of authority. Josephus tells us that she restored practices which the Pharisees had introduced and which John Hyrcanus had abrogated, but he does not specify what these were. Relative tranquillity now existed, except that the Pharisees demanded that Salome Alexandra put to death the men who had persuaded Alexander Jannaeus to slaughter 800 of the Pharisees. The counter-slaughter welded together some opposition to the Pharisees, which somewhat later broke out in overt form. Josephus gives a less than coherent account of the matters. Yet it seems reasonably clear that unrest and violence were the order of the day, and that the seizure of power, and the capacity to use it cruelly, was an objective of both the Pharisees and the Sadducees of that time. The religious distinction, if remembered at all, was clearly secondary to the political.

The elder of the queen's two sons, Hyrcanus II, should have succeeded to the throne, as we have said. Instead, the younger, Aristobulus, took power even before his mother's death. The fraternal rivalries, the civil war, and then the intervention of the Romans in 63 are related by Josephus without specific mention of the Pharisees or Sadducees, though the partisans of Aristobulus seem to have been the nobility and those of Hyrcanus the masses. The adviser to the passive Hyrcanus was Antipater, the father of Herod the Great. In the course of the transitions by which the Hasmonean dynasty came to an end, and that of Herod began (it is to be recalled that he was designated king in 40 B.C. and took the throne in 37), both the Pharisees and Sadducees seem to have diminished in inner unity and in power. Herod's absolute rule apparently left little authority for either party. The support of the Pharisees for Hyrcanus and Antipater may have disposed Herod to certain acts of conciliation with them; on the other hand, the opponents of Herod had come from what we might call the Sadducean part of the populace. Yet little love was lost between Herod and the Pharisees, though he was concerned for the most part to avoid directly arousing popular opposition.[19] Moreover, he rebuilt the Temple. Conflict arose with the Pharisees when Antipater, Herod's son, plotted against his father.[20] When Herod was about to die, two leaders,[21] apparently Pharisees (though perhaps Essenes), stimulated young men to tear down some structures, pagan in character, which Herod had erected. No more is told us about the Pharisees as far as their history is concerned. The Gospels asperse them, but give no data that would help us understand their history.

The Rabbinic literature in several passages presents its own disparagement of Pharisees.[22] Seven categories of Pharisees are mentioned, with only the seventh laudable.[23] The "shoulder" Pharisee ostentatiously parades his good deeds. The "delaying" Pharisee lets a business associate wait a bit, so that he can take time to do a good deed. The "bruised" Pharisee, to keep from looking at a woman, injures himself by walking into a wall. The "pestle" Pharisee, with false humility, walks with his head down, like a pestle on a mortar. The "ever-reckoning" Pharisee asks what good deed he might do that would be reckoned as canceling out his neglects (as if there were no neglect at all). The "fearful" Pharisee is, like Job, in terror of God. Only the seventh, the Pharisee who, like Abraham, loves God, is admirable.

In addition to this passage two phrases are on record: one terms Pharisees "destroyers of the world"; the other, "Pharisaic plagues," seems to be applied to inadequate leaders (Sotah 3.4).

The assessment of these denigrations of the Pharisees varies among the scholars; an occasional view holds that it is the unlaudable Pharisees whom the Gospels scorn. But such an explanation is not consistent with what is in the Gospels, especially Matthew, where it is not hypocrites among the Pharisees who are decried, but rather all the Pharisees who are decried as hypocrites.

To add to the enigma of understanding the Pharisees, although it is frequent among scholars to characterize the Rabbinic literature as Pharisaic, yet the literature itself presents no such characterization. Rather, if any term is applicable, the literature arose from the ḥakamīm ("the Sages"). Perhaps at some point there was a subtle but perceptible shift from Pharisaism to the Sages. Just where the division point should be is elusive, and the abundant theories[24] of the scholars not too persuasive. Perhaps it is just as well not to stress unduly the significance of the early organized forms of Pharisaism, particularly its "brotherhoods," and to regard Pharisaism not so much as a continued movement, but rather as an impulse, or, at most, to infer that what had originally been an organized movement disappeared in time, but that the original impulse behind the movement endured. That impulse was the progressive shift of focus of attention from the Temple (which Scripture justified) to Scripture itself. Even before the Temple fell in 70, Scripture had gained a high ascendancy. Once the Temple fell, Scripture alone maintained its ascendancy. The oral law, which at first merely buttressed the ascendancy of Scripture, eventually came into its own loftiness. In the sense of a religious viewpoint, as distinct from a political party, the Pharisees were Scripture-centered, receptive to some change and development of legal requirements and also religious practices, be-

lievers in resurrection, and committed to the validity of the
Oral Torah. The Sadducees were literalists, "stand-patters";
the Pharisees were progressive, innovative, and amenable to
the reasonable adjustment of the legacy of the past to the
needs of the present.

The view which is espoused here requires no effort, such
as others have made, to allocate one time segment in the development of Judaism to Pharisaism and another to Rabbinism.[25] Human institutions do not conform to logical academic patterns and neat time divisions. Pharisaism itself, so
I believe, petered out, but its thrust persisted, and to some extent so did the name. But Rabbinic Judaism, deriving as it
did from Pharisaism, is what Pharisaism developed into, and
is by no means the same as Pharisaism, which was in part a
political impulse. Rabbinic Judaism, on the other hand, is the
result of the ascendancy of the non-political Academy, the result of the shift in authority from the ruling council (Sanhedrin or Bet Din) to the rule of the scholars, the Sages.

D. FOURTH PHILOSOPHY

When, after the death of Herod, Josephus lays the ground-
work for describing the uprisings that grew in intensity and
climaxed in the rebellion against Rome, he introduces those
who espoused what he calls "the fourth philosophy." Having
mentioned them, he proceeds in his account to describe Pharisees, Sadducees, and Essenes as three forms of philosophy,
this before actually describing the fourth. The latter group,
so he tells us, "agreed with the Pharisaic notion," but, attached to liberty, they held God to be their only ruler. They
were not afraid of death, nor able to be deterred by the
deaths of relatives and friends. Their leader was a certain
Judas the Galilean.

Perhaps when Archelaus was banished, and the series of
Roman procurators began to rule Judea in A.D. 6, the Pharisees relinquished to the "fourth philosophy" whatever political dispositions remained and became more essentially a
religious party. Perhaps, too, even that character became dis-
sipated, and both Pharisees and Sadducees began slowly to
disappear. But they did persist into the public career of Jesus

during the term of Pontius Pilate (A.D. 26-36) as procurator.

Perhaps the "fourth philosophy" and also the Zealots[26] are relics of the Maccabeans. But the inner life of the Jews was to become more and more dominated by the Academy and its Sages, not by the "fourth philosophy."

E. ESSENES

A sense of balance about the Essenes is difficult to achieve. On the one hand, Josephus lists them as if they are as significant as the Pharisees and the Sadducees. On the other, the Essenes fail of direct mention in either the Rabbinic literature[27] or the New Testament. The principal sources of information about them besides Josephus are Philo of Alexandria and Pliny.[28] Philo (20 B.C. to A.D. 40) speaks of them in a treatise called "That Every Good Man Is Free." That treatise is concerned with a thesis of Philo, namely, that *askesis*[29] ("practice") is, along with "learning" and "intuition," an appropriate way of progressing to God Himself. The Essenes exemplify askesis. Philo attributes to the Essenes a sanctity of the highest order; he ascribes to them a completely monastic life, devoid of all sex (and hence perpetuation only through recruitment).

A second passage from Philo is preserved in a quotation by Eusebius (fourth Christian century) in his *Preparation for the Gospel*.[30] The quotation is from Philo's work about the Jews, *Hypothetica*. The Essenes, numbering in the thousands, are found throughout the cities of Judea. Only the elderly belong. They own no private property. What they earn by work is turned over to a steward who spends money for food and other needs. They eat together, being inclined to frugal meals. They abstain from marriage. (Since Philo was an Alexandrian, one can wonder how much he truly knew about them, and how reliable is the information he gives.) Josephus confirms their abstention from marriage, though he mentions one faction of the Essenes who did marry.

Pliny (A.D. 23-79), in his encyclopedic work, *Natural History*,[31] completed in 77, gives a brief mention of the Essenes in the context of a geographical description of Judea, as he describes the area from Jericho and southward. He speaks of the Essenes as dwelling among the palm trees, in retreat from society; that is, he speaks of what we might call an Essene headquarters on the west bank of the Dead Sea.

Josephus both describes the Essenes and also provides a number of passing allusions to them. He says that the Essenes "live the same kind of life as do those whom the Greeks call Pythagoreans."[32] There also he likens them to "those Dacae[33] who are called 'city-dwellers.' " The identification of the Essenes with Pythagoreans has yielded an assortment of far-fetched theories on the part of those who forget that Josephus, in writing for Greek Gentiles, put things in terms that they would understand; accordingly, his identifying the Essenes with Pythagoreans may have no real substance, for he treats Sadducees and Pharisees too as if they were like Greek philosophical schools, and we know they were even more unlike them.

Was Essenism, as some assert, a completely and purely Jewish manifestation, or was it a blend of Jewish and Greek ideas? The disputes over these matters were acute until the discovery of the Dead Sea Scrolls; since then the supposed Greek elements in Essenism have been very much played down.

Another subject of controversy is the relationship between Essenes and early Christians. The range of opinions is wide, including conjectures that John the Baptist had been an Essene, or that Jesus too was among them, and extending to another extreme that denies all direct influence of the Essenes on the Christian movement, preferring to view the Essenes in this context as no more than one of the components of the total Judaism from which Christianity sprang.

A complicating factor is that Philo, in addition to his mention of Essenes, devotes a treatise[34] to a group called the Therapeutae. This Jewish monastic society was Egyptian, inhabiting the shore of an Egyptian lake. Certain similarities have led some scholars to couple Essenes and Therapeutae together;[35] perhaps more is lost than gained by such coupling.

In the mid-1850's, in the studies of early Christianity, a great deal was written about the Essenes, probably on this basis, that since the resurrection of Jesus is central to Christianity the movement could not have arisen from Sadducee-

ism, and since the Gospel denunciations of the Pharisees
made it seem likely that Jesus could not have arisen from
among them, the Essenes became the leading candidate. The
paucity of information about the Essenes stimulated a whole
rack of theories.[36]

When the Dead Sea Scrolls were found, an amazing quantity of articles, prudent and imprudent, were written, many
of them in complete ignorance of similar essays of a hundred
years earlier. Some scholars who had never read a line of
Philo used his works as if no critical issues were involved.
The problems which Josephus provides, such as some of his
inconsistencies, his tendentiousness, and his clear statement
that there were at least two varieties of Essenism[37] were often
ignored.

The discovery of the Dead Sea Scrolls led to a prompt identification of the Qumran community and the Essenes, and an
equally prompt set of denials. Now, in the 1970's, however,
most scholars have come to accept the identification. The archeological excavations at Qumran have contributed to an
understanding of the latter history of the sect, especially the
fate of the community settlement there (see pp. 92-93).

Perhaps the origin of the Essenes, like that of the Pharisees, is to be ascribed, with Josephus, to the Maccabean era,
and perhaps both the Essenes and the Pharisees stem from
the ancient Ḥasidim. The Pharisees, as we have said, par-
ticipated in the trials of community life, while the Essenes
withdrew from it; herein would be the sharp division. The
Essenes, especially those who settled at Qumran, developed
their rites and their organizational forms, described in the
Manual of Discipline, as would befit an isolated community.
Josephus[38] tells that at the age of sixteen (about A.D. 51), he
studied the three sects. In pursuing his study of the Essenes
he went into the wilderness and attached himself to an Essene named Bannus. Three years later, however, he returned
to Jerusalem and joined the Pharisees.

It appears to have been around 76 B.C. that the Essenes
founded their community at Qumran. Archeological evidence suggests that the Essenes temporarily abandoned Qumran around 36 B.C., and, returning to Jerusalem,[39] were able
to fashion some kind of *modus vivendi* with Herod, who,
anti-Maccabean, may well have welcomed them because

they too were anti-Maccabean. Perhaps under Herod, they were able to found little groups in a variety of cities and towns. They seem to have returned to Qumran toward the end of Herod's reign, but we do not know why.

What part the Essenes played in the rebellion against Rome is not known; they apparently underwent acute tortures in resisting the Romans.[40] The settlement at Qumran seems to have been burnt down during the 66-70 war. The Essenes fade completely from recorded history.

Both Philo and Josephus give us the figure of 4,000 as the membership.[41] One never knows whether such numbers are to be taken seriously or not. If we take them seriously, the Essenes were a relatively small group, and hence their influence, as evidenced by the attention of Josephus to them, was out of proportion to their numbers.

Other groupings are known, such as the "morning dippers," called the Haemerobaptists. Some eighty "heresies" were counted by Epiphanius; for our purposes it is sufficient that we have an awareness of the multiplicity of these groupings, and understand that local manifestations of infinite variety were characteristic of that age in Judea.

We must beware, however, of manufacturing more groupings than there were. Occasionally one reads about "Apocalyptic Judaism" as if it were a well-defined grouping from which the apocalyptic Pseudepigrapha arose. It is more sound to regard apocalypses as emerging from scattered individuals.

One reads in works by Professor Gershom Scholem about Jewish gnosticism. It has been observed that Scholem did a disservice in using the term "gnosticism" for what he describes, for the phenomenon, namely, the imaginative accounts of trips to heaven taken by individual Rabbinic Sages, could scarcely have been more different from what is usually meant by gnosticism. The records of such heavenly journeys are usually alluded to as *Hekalôt* ("Palaces"—that is, of God) literature.[42]

There remains for last a group which was not a group, the *ammê ha-áretz* ("people of the land"). We do not know who they were, but only that the Sages scorned them.[43] My own

guess has been that they were rural illiterates, ordinary peas-
ants, whose illiteracy impeded a scrupulous fidelity to the religious requirements. That they were "lower classes" seems
clear. That they were scorned is lamentable. They are listed
here only because here and there a scholar, eager to fit Jesus
into some grouping, leaps to the conclusion that it was to the
amme ha-aretz that Jesus belonged.[44]

· 3 ·

THE

DIVINE

A. GOD

The heritage from the Bible included a number of significant ideas concerning the Deity. God was not a physical being; He was intangible and invisible. He was the Creator and Ruler, indeed, the Judge of the World. He and He alone was truly God; the deities worshipped by peoples other than Israel were not God. Idols were powerless and futile; they were unworthy of worship; and indeed, to worship what was not God was a gross and sinful disrespect of Him.

Scripture contains an abundance of divine terms: Elohim, El, El Elyon, Shaddai. Insofar as God might be thought of as having a name, that name was Yahve. But so holy and awesome was He that His name Yahve itself had force and power, and it was unbecoming or even sinful for men to pronounce it, as was expressed in the words "You shall not take the name of Yahve your God in vain" (Exod. 20.7; Deut. 5.11). Only the High Priest might pronounce it, and only on one day in the year, that on the Day of Atonement.

God was, as it were, above and over the world. His dwelling was in heaven. At high moments, such as at Sinai, He had descended to reveal Himself. Accordingly, He was both in the world and also over and above it.[1] He had very early revealed Himself to the patriarchs; He had later revealed Himself to the prophets. To some of these prophets, such as Zechariah, He had disclosed His divine will and intention by sending an angel to bring His desires from the distance to earth. Apart from sending an angel, He could, and did, pour

His "holy" spirit onto selected men. In heaven there were a host of beings, subordinate to Him, who constituted His heavenly council. Among these was Satan who could with divine consent test a man such as Job; a lying spirit who could on occasion delude a presumptuous king or prophet.

Wilful disobedience of God could bring just punishment, whether prompt or deferred. Yet God was merciful and prone to forgive the trespasses of men, especially when men repented of their evil. God was the king *par excellence;* He was the father of all. He heard man's prayer, and could answer it, or be silent. He was to be revered; He was to be loved. Such, in great brevity, is the biblical legacy.

In Synagogue Judaism the biblical ideas about the nature of God were expounded and embellished, and the scriptural terms for the Deity defined—indirectly, in homily and parable.

A repeated theme in all the literature (Apocrypha, Pseudepigrapha, and Rabbinic) is the total uniqueness of Israel's God. The strictures against the worship of the pagan deities are ubiquitous and unrelenting. Yet how had man come to grasp the uniqueness of God? The reply, ranging throughout the literature, was that the patriarch Abraham was the first man to grasp that uniqueness. Precocious, Abraham had grasped this truth when he was a year old, or else three, or else forty-eight. Born and reared in Ur of the Chaldees, Abraham had been exposed to astrology,[2] for which the Chaldeans were famous. When in time Abraham left Ur, he did so to leave idolatry and astrology.

How was it that Abraham had come to the recognition of the one true God? He had observed a dwelling that was lighted, and reasoned that the house must have a master; so, too, the world must have a master. Abraham's achievement was that he was the first of all men to come to the recognition of the existence of God, and he had transmitted his momentous discovery to his descendants.[3]

What could one say about this God? In a variety of ways and in many figures of speech, Jewish thought stressed His sole sovereignty, His sole omnipotence. But just as men have personality traits, so did God. Genesis 1.1 reads: "In the beginning *Elohim* created the heaven and the earth." Genesis

2.4 reads, "On the day that *Yahve Elohim* had made heaven and earth." Why Elohim in the 1.1 and Yahve Elohim in 2.4? In answer, Elohim signifies God as the strict judge,[4] and Yahve God as the judge who is merciful.[5] To have created man and treated him with pure justice would have amounted to subjecting all men to condemnation, for no man is perfect; to have created him only in the light of mercy would have amounted to exempting man from moral responsibility. Therefore, man was created in the light of both justice and mercy, as the union of the two names in Genesis 2.4 proves. Yet to speak of God as just and as merciful is to speak in terms of the characteristics men ascribe to Him, (the "attributes"); it falls short of describing Him ontologically ("as He actually is"). Paradoxically, God was deemed remote to the point of dwelling above the heavens (which numbered seven), but was viewed nevertheless as able to be near to man in His compassionate demands of them. A variety of terms arose as ways of alluding to God, out of the impulse on the one hand to seek to characterize Him and yet, on the other, to abstain from an excess of familiarity. One might speak of Him as "Heaven."[6] Or one might instead speak of Him as the *Gevūrā* ("the Power," that is, the *true* power), or as *Ha-Shēm* ("the Name"). Because He thoroughly fills the world, so that no place is bereft of His presence, He can be called *Ha-Maqôm* ("The Place"). He was clearly the *ribbônô shel olâm* ("master of the universe"), a term frequently found in prayers addressed to Him.[7] Longer phrases, too, appear: "The Holy One, blessed is He"; or "He who spoke and the world was created."

All these expressions reflect two principal ideas: namely, that God was both the Creator of the World, that is, He had brought it into its first being; and He was also its Ruler, that is, He has directed and still directs it.[8] Creation was perfect; it was free of superfluities, and even the spider or the viper has a legitimate place in it. The daily routine of sunrise and sunset or other phenomena of what we call nature—for which there is no usual Rabbinic term, for the idea of nature was not part of their thinking—did not exhaust His creative insight or His benevolent rule. At the time of Creation He had created "miracles" which would be available to Him to use when later occasion would warrant. Since the miracles were at hand from the beginning, they were not (as we often think today) interruptions of, or interventions into, the flow of natural events; to the contrary, it was God's goodness that provided, on the given occasions, the unique help that cannot come from man. The age of Synagogue Judaism did not experience great divine interventions[9] such as the wondrous deliverance from Egypt, for recent men were less worthy than their early ancestors had been; but the future held out the prospect for a deliverance as great, or even greater, than the past deliverances.

While the literature stresses God as the Creator, and embellishes the account in Genesis 1 of the specific creative deeds, there is in the literature an expressed aversion to speculation about what it was that might have existed before Creation. Ecclesiasticus 3.21-23 had warned against inquiry into what was beyond one's understanding, or investigation into what is hidden; this passage is quoted (in Hagiga 13a and elsewhere), for there was evidence that men could go astray into false notions, if they raised such questions. The *Ma'aséh Beréshît* ("The Work of Creation") was speculation suitable only for the great Sages,[10] as was its counterpart, *Ma'aséh Merkavá* ("The Work of the [Divine] Chariot" on which God's throne was carried[11]). Public discourses on these two topics were restricted, or even prohibited.[12]

B. ANGELS

In Daniel, angels emerge with names—for example, Gabriel and Michael. Much earlier, Isaiah 6 had spoken of "seraphim." A number of biblical passages[13] mention celestial underlings of God, part of an array of heavenly beings so clearly subordinate to God that they in no way compromise His unity or uniqueness; they did God's errands. The rise of names for angels seems to have been accompanied by the assignment of specific types of errands or functions to specific angels. Raphael, who figures in Tobit, is, as his name means, the "divine healer." In Genesis 18 three "men" appear to Abraham; in Rabbinic elaboration they are Raphael, who was sent to heal Abraham who underwent circumcision in

Genesis 17; Gabriel, who was to overturn Sodom; and Michael, who in Genesis 18 informs Sarah that she will have a child.[14]

In due course a very elaborate angelology was developed, with assignments, as it were, to such functions as regulating the stars, the calendar, and rain or snow, much as if the workings of a highly organized human royal government were transferred into an even more highly organized heavenly government. Certainly the various kinds of writing—Pseudepigrapha on the one hand and Rabbinic literature on the other—abstain from system and from consistency, presenting a combination of folk beliefs in the elaboration of scriptural passages, but also exhibiting some restraints. Thus, in the visit of the three angels to Abraham (Gen. ch. 18) they only *seem* to eat the elegant repast which has been prepared for them; it is clearly asserted that angels neither eat nor drink. Angels lack the solid bodies which men have, but are instead either fiery, when in heaven, or else vaporous, when on earth.

If it is correct that in general in Judaism angels served to bridge the gap between a God deemed remote and men on earth, and if in this way angels could be useful, there was also a sense of a danger in that angels could seem to supplant God. The awareness of this danger is discerned in passages in Rabbinic literature which stress the deeds of God Himself.[15] The view is found that Israel is led by God Himself, and only the foreign nations by angels.

Two angels, Metatron and Sandalfon, whose names are not mentioned in Scripture, and who can be assumed to have emerged to prominence some time after Gabriel and Michael came to importance, figure with some frequency in the various types of writings. Metatron (who became very significant in literature of the medieval European period) varies from a role in which he has authority in this world to one in which he is the revealer of divine secrets, in a way kindred to the biblical Enoch. Sandalfon is at times regarded as the brother of Metatron; at other times he appears, as it were, as the personal servant and bodyguard of God.

The literature speaks also of "destroying angels," those who execute the punishments that have been divinely decreed. A repeated theme in the literature seems to attempt to shield the Deity from being the direct source of evil, and hence divine punishment comes through destroying angels rather than from God Himself. This motif is found in connection with the destruction of Sodom in Genesis 19, in the form of comments that angels rather than God did the work of destruction. But that view too had its danger—the possibility of so emphasizing that evil did not come directly from God as to conclude that a power other than and distinct from God could have sway almost equal to or in replacement of Him. The enigmatic mīnim spoken of above (p. 150) may have carried the shielding of the Deity from being the source of evil to the point of envisaging "two powers," God and Evil. While Rabbinic thought did tolerate a passing separation of God from Evil, it could not acquiesce in any view which compromised God's full and complete sovereignty. It is conceivable that the trespass of the minim, as viewed by their orthodox opponents, was their elevation of the power of evil to an equality with God.

C. SATAN

Genesis 6.1-4 speaks of the origin of the human corruption which led to the flood as the result of the mating of "sons of God" with beautiful human women. The Rabbis developed from this passage a view of "fallen angels" whose domain had changed from heaven to earth. The trespass of the "sons of God" was their uncontrolled sexual lust. In ways obscure beyond tracing, Satan changes from his biblical role of a legitimate member of the heavenly council, as in Job 1; the newer view is that Satan had led some rebellion in heaven, as a consequence of which God cast him to earth, where he took power. That view, dominant in New Testament passages, is sporadic in the Rabbinic literature. In a sense fallen angels and Satan become interchangeable.

Satan[16] had his own underlings, the demons. These were at times reckoned in fantastic numbers. They lurked everywhere to do damage to men. In time Satan moved his permanent abode from earth to the underworld, but he and his demons could rise from there. The popular mind naturally needed to develop means of resistance to demons, this through prayer, incantations, and amulets, often attested to in the haggadic materials, but only infrequently in the halachic.

D. HOLY SPIRIT

Clearly, man needed some communication from God to remind him that it was God and not the forces of evil who were truly sovereign. That communication, in clear, intelligible language, had existed in the days of the scriptural prophets, who had spoken divine words because God had poured His "holy" spirit on them, enabling them to prophesy. The expression "Holy Spirit" is relatively frequent in Scripture; it is relatively infrequent in Rabbinic literature, and, indeed, when used it is often in connection with explaining some aspect of Scripture. The idea underlying Holy Spirit is found more often in the Rabbinic literature than the phrase itself, for the idea came to be expressed in other ways. The most frequent use of Holy Spirit is in connection with the ancient prophets.

But prophecy was always dangerous, for there could arise men who were deluded. Deuteronomy 18.14-22 speaks of this peril, and in Jeremiah there is frequent allusion to false prophets. Hence prophecy could be the reverse of blessing. In a sense much of the Pseudepigrapha can be regarded as in a category similar to prophecy, for these writings usually contained revelations and predictions concerning God's future punishment of both wicked nations and men, whether Israel or the Gentiles. Were the pseudepigraphic books to be regarded as "true"? The indirect answer, as given by the Rabbis, was to consider only those prophetic books as legitimate which by their time were relatively ancient. After Haggai, Zechariah, and Malachi,[17] who were the last of the prophets, prophecy had ceased; the age of Ezra witnessed the termination of prophecy. Therefore no prophetic books later than what was deemed the age of Ezra could be accredited. (Outside the circle of the Rabbinic Sages the view that prophecy had ended simply did not exist.) By and large, then, when the Rabbis speak of Holy Spirit, it is in connection with what had taken place in the past, and very seldom in the present.

The New Testament writings, particularly Luke-Acts, mention the Holy Spirit, and are absorbed in its continued availability with a frequency that is in marked contrast to its infrequency among the Rabbis.

E. BAT QOL

Communication from the Deity in intelligible words was deemed to continue through the occasional voice from heaven called *bat qōl* ("daughter [!] of a voice," "reverberation"). (If a religion based on revelation relegates revelation exclusively to the past, then, as it were, God ceases to be a force in the present. The bat qol then, provided for current revelation.) The bat qol had a quality different from the usual[18] voice.

Though occasional Rabbinic passages equate the bat qol with the Holy Spirit, mostly the two are differentiated. The Holy Spirit impelled a prophet to speak; the bat qol was normally a brief utterance, a single sentence, not specifically addressed to one man. Often it spoke to comment on an academic dispute, or on the character of a martyr. It was a bat qol which announced publicly that halachic decisions should follow the Academy of Hillel, not that of Shammai, though both reflected the living God.[19]

F. SHECHINA

Quite apart from the bat qol was the *shechīnā* (often found as shekina). It is a word difficult to translate. Perhaps "divine presence" is as good a way as any, if we understand this in the sense of a feeling that can pervade men. It is perhaps clarified by the sentence, "When two sit and study Torah, the shechina rests on them." Against the background in which, on the one hand, God dwelled in heaven and annually entered into the sanctuary, and, on the other, He permeated the whole world, shechina is the way of expressing the special sense that some men felt of the nearness of God to them. Unlike the bat qol, the shechina never speaks; it is, rather, that mysterious presence which men are able to feel.

It has been long noted that the Synagogue interpretation recast Scripture so as to depart from a literalism that seemed gross. The Targum usually renders by circumlocution Hebrew passages which attribute to God either human form (anthropomorphism) or human emotion (anthropopathism). It is wrong to ascribe these avoidances as reflecting some lowered sense of God; to the contrary, they reflect a heightened belief in and awareness of God.

Yet man had something representing God to rely on quite other than and, in a sense, greater than angels or bat qol: Scripture itself.

· 4 ·

MANKIND,
ISRAEL,
AND TORAH

Torah is revelation, from God to man. Certain self-evident and universal observations about man influence the content of Torah: Men are born, live for a time, propagate, and die. They get hungry and thirsty; they require shelter from adverse weather; they help each other, but also they steal, they fight, they kill.

The religious questions about man are not in the realm of what is it that man does, but, rather, why does he do what he does? Moreover, what are the consequences of his deeds? Especially, what are the consequences of his evil deeds? And what can be the deterrents to his doing evil deeds, in order for him to avoid consequences which are deemed inescapable? In general terms, deterrents can be of two different kinds: the immediate and external, and the deferred and internal. Respecting the immediate and external, he who steals and is caught is soon punished by the human governing power. The internal deterrent, on the other hand, is the conviction that some concealed deeds are inherently wrong, and whether the doer is caught or not is irrelevant. He who acts against such a conviction (and escapes notice or being caught) lives either with a guilty conscience, which can deeply disturb him, or else he can fear that punishment can in due time come to him from the source (for example, God) from which his convictions have stemmed.

Moreover, it is universal among men to notice the distinction between one's body on the one hand, and, on the other, the non-physical aspects of his being (his ability to think or to remember). In a living person, blood flows in the veins and the lungs inhale and exhale breath; in a dead person, the blood ceases to flow and the lungs to function. At death the body decays. There is, accordingly, a distinction between the body with its flesh and bones and the non-physical part of a man. The inheritance from the ancient Jewish and Greek worlds of ways of viewing this distinction has given rise to two terms, monism and dualism, and an understanding of these terms is essential. Such an understanding does not focus as much on the difference between the body and the non-physical as on the matter of the relationship between them. On two points there are differences between the Jewish and the Greek views. First, the Jewish view, derived from biblical passages, held that body and soul were one; it did not regard the body and the non-physical as a merely temporary union of separate entities; in the biblical and Jewish view it was spirit (or blood) which made the difference between a living and a dead organism. In the dominant biblical view, which regarded death as the complete end, the non-physical part of man (let us use loosely the word "soul") was deemed to perish at the same time that the body perished. In the Greek view, on the other hand, the soul was regarded as having been in existence prior to its joining with a body; it remained joined until death; then the non-physical soul departed, as it were, and went on its own way, whatever that way was. When the doctrine of resurrection came into Jewish thought, possibly around 200 B.C., the supposition that accompanied it was that both the body and the soul perished, but were destined in time both to be revived. The distinction between resurrection (the Jewish view) and immortality (the Greek) can be put in this way—that in resurrection the body and the soul both die, but in immortality the body alone dies, while the soul survives.

Second, in the Greek view there is an assumption, of great consequence, that the soul is by its very nature good and worthy, while the body is by its very nature evil and unworthy. This qualitative estimate is not ordinarily to be found in intertestamental or Rabbinic views. In general, such Jewish religious thought did not asperse the functions of the body, whether the ingestion or digestion of food or the sex organs; the Greek view on the other hand ascribed to the body the desires, demands, and lusts which made a man do wicked things.

That body and soul are one and always joined together yields the term monism; that they are separable, and separate, the term dualism. Hence, we meet the frequent statement that the Jewish thought is monist, and the Greek dualist. An essential distinction we shall see later, as between the Greek Jew Philo and Palestinian thought, is that Philo is essentially dualist and the Palestinian monist. Yet it is important, even at the cost of some repetition, to notice that even in Palestinian monist thought the inevitable observation of the distinction between body and soul occurs. The Rabbinic parable (see p. 105) about a king who employed two guards, one blind and one lame, to protect his orchard of fig trees emphasizes the monism in Rabbinic thought.[1]

All men, Jews and Gentiles alike, exhibited universal human characteristics. This, indeed, is no more than could be expected, for all mankind is descended from the common ancestor, Adam,[2] the ancestor, indeed, of the good as well as of the wicked.[3]

What was it that determined whether a person would be wicked or not? Synagogue Judaism without deviation attributed to man the capacity to choose the way he would go. The choice lay before him in a context of Torah, of Laws which he knew, but his need to exercise a choice arose out of the presence in man of two "impulses," the one to do good, the other to do evil.[4] Though the presence of a good yétzer ("impulse") in man is mentioned in the Synagogue writings, it receives little attention from the Rabbis; the evil yetzer, on the other hand, receives an abundance.[5] Undoubtedly this is the case because the ordinary observation of men and their deeds discloses to the observer how abundant are the evil men in this world, and how few are the good.

There is a general consistency in the many comments in the literature about the evil yetzer, yet there is also some variation to be found. For the most part, the evil yetzer is viewed as an inner force within man, tempting him to act against his knowledge and conscience. The good man is able to conquer the impulse to evil,[6] and is thereby a "hero." But in other passages the evil yetzer is sometimes viewed as an almost personified force,[7] being much more than a mere disposition and, indeed, a strong incitement to hot temper or anger or wicked desires. The evil yetzer leads to the most evil of all trespasses, idolatry.[8]

Every man, even the non-Jew, is precious to God, for the Gentile also is a descendant of Adam, and thus is able to declare that for his sake, too, the world was created. Whoever kills a man is regarded as if he had destroyed the entire population of the world, and whoever saves a man from death is regarded as if he had saved the entire population.

But how is the non-Jew, not possessing the Torah, to know right from wrong, so as to be enabled to make a choice for righteousness? The answer, arising from Scripture, distinguishes between a limited set of obligations incumbent universally on men and the unlimited obligations incumbent on the Jews. On the Gentile there are incumbent the seven "laws of Noah" (Gen. 9.3-4). These laws, so it was held, had originally been revealed to Adam, though at that time they numbered only six.[9] They were the prohibitions of idolatry, blaspheming the name of God, cursing judges, murder, sexual misdeeds, and robbery. Noah was given a seventh prohibition; in the context of permission to eat the flesh of animals, a prohibition was specified against eating flesh with the blood still in it. Thus, a Gentile had a limited number of laws, and it was presumed that he knew them; the sources do not specify how he knew. Presumably the seven laws were transmitted orally from Noah to succeeding generations. It is observed in the Rabbinic literature that there are righteous men among the Gentiles; their observance of the limited set of seven laws qualifies them for divine reward.[10]

Scripture, in its unfolding account, tells that the law of circumcision was enjoined on Abraham (Gen. ch. 17), and that on Jacob was enjoined the prohibition against eating the "sinew that shrinks" (Gen. 32.33). Thus there was a growth in number of the laws from the early patriarchs to the high point in the revelation to Moses at Sinai, resulting in an encompassing totality, including both the Written laws and the Oral.

But, parenthetically, a question can arise (as it should for the conscientious reader of Scripture). What was the relationship of the patriarchs, who lived before Moses, to those laws which awaited the time of Moses for their promulgation? Synagogue interpretation, as early as the Book of Jubilees (see pp. 90-91) did not hesitate to ascribe to the encompassing laws of Moses an antiquity much earlier than the time of Moses. A verse (Gen. 26.5) speaks of Abraham as having hearkened to God's voice and as having observed the divine "charges, commandments, statutes, and torahs"; it was clearly to be inferred from this verse, with torah in the plural, that Abraham had observed the two Torahs revealed at Sinai, the written and the oral, even in advance of that great event. The conclusion, with its sanction in a biblical verse, is common to the Apocrypha, Pseudepigrapha, the New Testament, and Philo, as well as to the Rabbinic literature, that Father Abraham was not only the ancestor of the Jews, but was, as it were, the first Jew. He was therefore conceived of as personally embodying, in perfection, that fullness of piety which his later descendants viewed as commendable or obligatory.[11]

That is to say, the expectations from pious Jews were greater than from the pious Gentile, the difference being the multiplicity of commandments incumbent on the Jew as contrasted with the seven laws of Noah. What distinguished the Jews from the Gentiles was the encompassing revelation at Sinai of both the written and the oral Torahs.

The term Torah creates some confusion for the modern, over-logical student. It can mean the Ten Commandments; it can mean the Five Books of Moses; it can mean the totality of Scripture; it can mean, in a general way, the gracious act of revelation at Sinai, as if beyond both the Ten Commandments and the Five Books. The passage (which begins the Chapters of the Fathers), "Moses received the Torah at Sinai," means something more than merely the Ten Commandments or even the Pentateuch. Torah, so we might say, takes on the force of the very fullest inheritance of God's gracious revelation. The inheritance and the possession of Torah, then, marked the difference between the Israel of God and the nations of the world.

Inevitably, the Sinai experience, so central in the biblical account of the Wilderness period, underwent a multiplicity of embellishments in Rabbinic thought. Why was the Torah given in the Wilderness, a no-man's-land? If given in the land of Israel, Gentiles might have seemed disbarred from it.[12] If given in some other land, that nation might improperly claim it as an exclusive possession. Given in the Wilderness, the Torah was freely available to all the world. Indeed, God offered it to a variety of peoples, first in four languages, but when representatives of those peoples learned about its prohibitions of murder, adultery, and robbery, they declined the gift.[13] The nations of the world numbered seventy;[14] the revelation at Sinai was heard in all the seventy languages of the world at once.[15] Israel alone was willing to accept the gift.[16] A total silence, on the part of birds and heavenly beings, marked the high moment of the *mattán Toráh* ("the gift of Torah"). The word mattan recurs in the literature with great frequency, for the Torah came to Israel as God's gracious gift to them.

This notion of gracious gift was blended with the Scriptural account of God's choice of Israel to be His people, the divine election beginning with the calling of Abraham. Thus the people Israel and the Torah constituted a blended entity; without Israel the Torah had no significance, and without the Torah Israel had no uniqueness.

Modern scholarship views the growth of the canon of Scripture as having come in three stages (see pp. 17-18): first the Five Books of Moses, then the Prophets, and last the Hagiographa. While Synagogue Judaism, which bequeathed Scripture in these divisions, was aware of these three parts, it exhibited no awareness of a chronological growth in the canon. Moreover, all three divisions were of *equal* sanctity, though the Five Books were *primus inter pares*. There was also an unbroken unity in the content of the three divisions. Where difference, bordering on contradiction, seemed to lie on the surface, the ingenuity of the Sages was readily able to dissolve the contradictions and to obliterate all inconsistencies.

Inasmuch as in the Christian legacy, particularly from Paul, there is a viewpoint which ascribes both secondary status and only transient significance to the laws in the Pentateuch (see pp. 311-12), it is desirable to emphasize here that this viewpoint is completely absent from all the other Jewish literatures. Rather, the Torah, as a mattan, was both eternal and glorious, a gift unequaled in value, and one in which the recipient reveled. Passages in the Psalms and Proverbs had already set the stage for the encompassing view, that the Torah elicits what precious gifts ordinarily elicit, joy combined with gratitude. God the giver was not a foe whom one needed to fear; to the contrary, His gift of Torah expressed and symbolized His love, and in turn the gift called forth man's love of God. The commandments in the Torah were in no way a harassment; rather, they were the guideposts which directed a man into his fulfillment of his desire for sanctity and piety[18] (as in Prov. 6.23): "The commandment is a lamp, the Torah a light"[19] . Accordingly, the gift of the Torah was never viewed as other than a full blessing, for it was the manifestation of God's unique and total love for His people.

The Torah had been uniquely given to Israel. There were, unhappily, those in the Jewish community who perversely misinterpreted it.[20] And as Christianity developed in the Greek Dispersion, it utilized the Greek translation for many of its proof-texts.[21] After the de facto separation of Christianity, and its retention of Scripture,[22] it was no longer realistic to speak of Written Torah as Israel's exclusive possession. What remained as exclusively Israel's was the Oral Torah. There are on record sentiments which prohibit setting down the Oral Torah in writing,[23] as if such abstention would forefend against a usurpation of the Oral Torah by the Christians as they had usurped the Written. The Oral Torah, then, was exclusively Israel's, and thereby the *total* Torah belonged exclusively to Israel alone. While it is true that the Sages were at all times conscious of the difference between the Written and the Oral Torah, the difference between the two was not in the realm of authority or sanctity or divine origin, but only in the question of fact, of where in the inheritance such-and-such an item was to be found.

Mention was made above of the bat qol (p. 175), which had declared that the conflicting opinions of the academies of Hillel and Shammai were both "words of the living God," both being Torah. To the modern logical mind there can seem to be a total difference between God Himself and the Torah which He had divinely revealed, but to the Rabbinic mind such a difference could not be total. Rather, the Torah was the continuing presence of God among His people; the Torah, indeed, was the *living*[24] God. God's revelation, ancient as it was in the light of the centuries since Abraham and Moses, still abided with His people into the present. The figures of speech for Torah are abundant: a healing medicine, freedom, refreshing wine, water, golden vessels, delicate wool;[25] their significance is that they reflect man's everyday experience, for through the Torah God entered into that experience. The Torah, then, was both the ready bridge between man and God, and, in essence, it was God as He functions in this world.

Inasmuch as Torah was a body of materials, Written and Oral, these were susceptible of study. *Talmūd Torāh* ("study of the Torah") was commended in an infinite variety of ways. It ought to be man's constant preoccupation, the object of his meditation day and night. Study of the Torah was the most meritorious of all good deeds.

Moreover, the study of Torah needed to be done for its own sake, not for eminence or for the distinction of being called learned. One should not use the study of Torah for any ulterior purpose.[26] If a man has studied Torah, let him not boast of it, for it was for that purpose that man was created.[27] Indeed, though the Torah needed to be studied for its own sake, it was nevertheless sanctioned that one study it even for an ulterior purpose, because such study for an ulterior end led directly to study for its own sake.[28]

Yet any study of the sacred which did not result in a sanctified way of living was deemed futile. The sequel to study needed to be *ma'asīm tōvīm* ("praiseworthy deeds"). It is the "doing" of the Torah, not its study, which is the true principle.[29] He who "did" the Torah was in effect transcending the requirements themselves, and he was so attuned to God that he was acting as God acts; he was upright as God is, and he was merciful as God is. Indeed, God Himself was portrayed as studying and teaching Torah[30] in a heavenly Academy.[31]

Man, then, through study of the Torah, which was here on earth, lived in closest proximity to God in heaven. The genius of the mitzvot and the halacha is their bill of particulars, the statement of exactly what a person must do and exactly what he is divinely prohibited from doing. Accordingly, man could know what a sin was and what a good deed was.[32] Hence, Torah was both man's inspiration and also his living mentor.

· 5 ·

RIGHTEOUSNESS
AND SIN,
AND THEIR SEQUELS

That a tendency to sin was universal in man, the result of his evil yetzer, implied that the avoidance of sin arose both from his good yetzer and from his acquired knowledge of Torah. The evil yetzer had no power over the Torah, nor over him who had immersed himself in sacred study. The biblical commandments were tabulated as 613.[1] Of these, 248 were affirmative, injunctions telling what one must do. The remaining 365 were prohibitions, injunctions telling what one must not do. A sin was a deviation from one of the 613 requirements.

Scripture had presented the two manners in which sin could be committed: the inadvertent[2] and the deliberate[3]; it had specified the means of atonement for the inadvertent sin, and had declared that the deliberate amounted to an affront to God, and was unforgivable. In Scripture the punishment for deliberate sin was left in God's hands; that kind of sinner "would be cut off from the midst" of his people by God. Synagogue Judaism maintained the distinctions between the inadvertent and the deliberate. For inadvertent sin, it added to Scripture by prescribing the ready forms of atonement, as we shall see.

Obedience to the Torah, full and unreserved, was expected, especially from the learned.[4] The figure of speech that is used for obedience is '*ōl ha-tōrā́h*[5] ("the yoke of the Torah"). In no sense was the yoke conceived of as an intolerable burden;

rather, the figure of speech had to do with the fullness in which obedience was to be expected. The term "yoke" is also utilized as a figure for obedience to a government or, in the form of "yoke of the world," as the need to meet one's day-to-day obligations.

Deliberate sin is the rebellious casting off of the yoke of subjection to the one God. Rebellious sin was exemplified in any concession to, or acceptance of, idolatry, or in anything that smacked of idolatry. In due course of time two other trespasses were adjoined to idolatry as rebellion against God, namely, sexual irregularities and homicide.[6] In a related sense, a kōfér ba-iqqär ("a denier of the principle") was a person whose basic denial of God led directly to his rejection of God's commandments.

Scripture had provided the observation that no man can be completely free of some trespass (Eccles. 7.20). Not only did Scripture and the Rabbis ascribe trespasses to Abraham, Moses, and David, but it became standard for even the most illustrious of the Sages to concede that they too had sinned. Yet sin, if not deliberate, was forgivable. But there was the danger: one sin could readily lead to another[7] (as one good deed could lead to another); moreover, there was the additional danger that one sinner could cause others to sin.[8] Hence, though manifestly some commandments were "light" and others "heavy," the injunction to avoid all sin meant that one needed to be as punctilious about the light as about the heavy.[9]

And Scripture had provided varieties of penalties and punishments for trespasses.[10] It had also given assurance of the rewards for righteousness.[11] In our modern secular age, we expect no reward from our government for our abiding by its laws; we do, however, expect punishment if we are convicted of crimes. The ancient Rabbis discussed in detail the punishments that were to follow conviction in the court for specific misdeeds. But quite beyond what society might do in the case of an overt crime or misdemeanor, God, the true Judge, could provide punishment for trespasses (ordinary matters, not basic rebellion), which were not hidden from Him as they were from fellow men. Indeed, all sins, both overt and covert, were recorded in a heavenly account book,[12] in which there was a ledger sheet for every man. The scriptural views of heaven, where God sat on a throne surrounded by His angels, led quite naturally to envisaging the heavenly scene not only as royal but also as judicial (as in Dan. 7.9-10), with all the elements present in heaven that marked a human court.[13] There the Deity issued His judicial decisions respecting both nations and individuals.

Two related yet different judicial arrangements were conceived of, the recurring annual judgment and the future Great Judgment. For the individual the annual period of judgment would determine his fate in the ensuing year.[14] The New Year was the day of judgment on men. But there was something beyond the annual judgment. We all observe that wicked men and nations appear to escape punishment from the annual court. Hence, justice demands their ultimate punishment. That punishment is reserved for the Great Judgment Day. The wicked man, or the wicked nation, surviving this year unscathed, was inevitably destined to stand judgment in some remote future. At that future time the evils which dominate the here and now would be corrected, and then a new age would replace this miserable one. This notion of two ages is implicit in Scripture in passages which speak of "the end of days" (Isa. 2.2; 4.1; Amos 9.13-15). The present age lies in between the past and the future; hence the past needed to be assessed in the light of the infelicities of the present and of the hopes for the future. In Daniel 2 and 7 there is a picture of four world empires which is a review of the past. More elaborately still, another opinion views the progression of the events of the past as encompassing seven periods, in a sense corresponding to the seven days of creation in Genesis 1; this present age is the sixth of the seven periods. An abundance of speculations about the past, accompanied by mathematical calculations, are recorded in the Pseudepigraphic literature. These differ from each other in details.[15] What they share in common is that the past was prologue to the present, as the present is to the future; in the literature there is the common expectation of a transition from the present age to the future. The present is always an age of tribulation; the present travail is a necessary preparation for the great reversal from tribulation to tranquility destined some day to come. When that reversal does come, it would mark the *qētz* ("the End") of this miserable age. The End would be marked by the coming of the Messiah. The tribulations of this age were "pangs[16] of the Messiah." It was natural for those who resorted to mathematical computations with respect to the five periods of the past also to indulge in mathematical computations so as to determine precisely when the present sixth age would terminate. To these matters we will return in speaking of the Messiah (pp. 202-7).

The Rabbinic term for the present age is "this world"; the term for the wondrous future is "the World To Come." The two terms are, by their very nature, bound up with notions of time, for it was the passing of time which would usher in the "world to come." Yet two factors entered in to dissolve time as the distinguishing characteristic between the two worlds. One factor—beyond precise documentation—would appear to have arisen out of disillusionment with recorded determinations of the date of the End, for such computations had been too precise for comfort and, tragically, had been refuted by the failure of the End to arrive. The particulars described in the Pseudepigraphic literature about the End and the new age are most vivid, and what is found in the Rabbinic literature is quite pallid in comparison. Indeed, the "calculators of the Ends"—note the plural!—are scorned and denounced by the Rabbis in a number of passages.[17] In effect, then, the conception of the World To Come as related to time was weakened and dissolved, simply because the passing of decades and centuries had not provided that wondrous age.

A second factor in dissolving the bondage to time was the rise and spread of a belief in personal resurrection. What happened to a man who died in the present, so long before time would some day usher in the new age? The need, or the desire, to furnish an answer led to a consequence (here a bit over-simplified)—namely, the view that the World To Come was not a matter of the future, but rather it already existed and was entered into by the individual at his death. By death one could go now, as it were, from this world into the World To Come.

The Garden of Eden, the heavenly Paradise of the righteous, is the usual name of the World to Come as present reality.

Hell is the place for the wicked. At times Rabbinic thought seems to regard Eden as the permanent, eternal World To Come; at times Eden itself is only temporary, as if it too is to be followed by the Great Judgment.

One needs to thread his way gingerly through these matters, for full uniformity in thought is notably lacking in the sources. Thus, if a man was to be deemed so righteous as to be eligible for admission to the heavenly Eden, was that admission as a result of a court trial and a favorable verdict? Or, if Eden was only a temporary period, was it to be followed, or at least climaxed, by a court trial which, if the verdict were favorable, was to lead to resurrection? The relevant materials, arising as they did from many hearts and many minds, are fraught with variation, inconsistency, and contradiction. Nevertheless, a sort of dominant pattern is discernible: he who in this life is righteous receives at the time of his death his reward for his righteousness; he who is wicked receives his punishment.

A man might have as his motive for his righteousness an expectation of receiving a reward for it, or at least of avoiding the punishment due for being sinful. The Rabbis deal rather abundantly with rewards and punishments. In the history of religions, righteousness for its own sake is recurrently commended by better minds as loftier than righteousness which expects reward; so, too, the Rabbis. Antigonos of Soko[18] said, "Do not be like slaves who serve their master in order to receive a reward, but like those who serve without expectation of reward."[19]

Yet one can suspect that even such minds never completely escape from the notions of reward and punishment. In Rabbinic thought, an accumulation of good deeds becomes a repository, a treasury of accumulated merit; this motif is found not only in Rabbinic literature, but also in most of the intertestamental literature;[20] it is present too in the Gospels.[21] A Rabbinic narrative portrays the royal convert, Monobaz of Adiebene, justifying to his relatives his distribution of his wealth, inherited from his fathers, to the poor at the time of a famine. Monobaz contrasts the treasures laid up by his fathers on earth with those treasures he had laid up in heaven.[22]

The abundance of commandments were the invitations to,

and the device by which, an increased quantity of merits could be accumulated.[23] Accordingly, in a context in which the right thing to do was specified in Scripture, and these specifications refined in the halacha, it became a matter of concern to do the right thing *in the right manner*. Much of the difference of opinion recorded in the Rabbinic literature respecting halacha focuses on *how* to observe, with the need for observance commonly admitted by the disputants. That the candles for the right days of Hanukka should be lighted is held in common by Hillel and Shammai, though Hillel prescribed beginning with one candle and increasing nightly to eight, and Shammai prescribed beginning with eight and decreasing nightly to one. The modern person ordinarily is less concerned about how to do something as he is about what to do. Not so the developing Synagogue Judaism; for it the how was no less divinely ordained than the what. To be punctilious about the manner was virtually equal to the deed itself; the deed was the clue to commendable obedience, but the manner was the clue to commendable piety. Piety brought reward, especially in the World To Come.

· 6 ·

THE REALMS
OF TORAH

Our modern world makes a sharp distinction between the demands of religion and the domain of secular law. This is not the case with Scripture or with Synagogue Judaism. Scripture deals with such matters as laws of inheritance, acquisition of property, torts, and distinctions between theft and burglary and between manslaughter and murder. Hence, the Rabbinic literature too deals with the entire range of human experience. True, they distinguished analytically between the sacred and the "common,"[1] as, for example, between the Sabbath and the other days of the week, but in reality such a distinction is a difference in degree rather than in kind. The sacred and the secular were both of serious concern. The rules for compensation when someone injures someone else[2] are as much a part of Rabbinic concerns as are the regulations for the sacred days. It is impossible to present here the total range of these mundane concerns; it must suffice simply to declare that their range is infinite. A Yiddish expression, *Alles shteht in Talmud* ("The Talmud contains *everything*") is not an inaccurate summary. We shall necessarily bypass topics such as real estate, gleanings in the fields, the offering of bird sacrifices, and the signs of leprosy, simply for lack of space. To repeat, we must not read our modern distinctions between sacred and secular into the ancient Judaism.

Turning first to marriage, there was a ritual ceremony for a wedding called *kiddushin* ("sanctities"). Basically, marriage was viewed as a solemn business arrangement between groom and bride and their families. A clue to understanding the Rabbinic attitude to the business part is the notice that the Jewish world was essentially the man's; in a strictly legal sense, all the rights lay with him, and the woman, in a strict sense, had almost none. Especially was this the case with divorce; Scripture (Deut. 24.1) had made provision whereby a man could divorce his wife, writing a "bill of divorcement," but made no provision for a wife to divorce a husband. Hence, not only did the woman need protection, but the marriage had to be more than merely the business arrangements.

Marriage was enthusiastically approved,[3] and singleness condemned. An abundance of passages lauds the advantages of marriage, and notes the disadvantages which an unmarried man[4] labors under. Moreover, the earliest commandment in Genesis is "Be fruitful and multiply" (Gen. 1.28); it was not only the first, but the greatest of all the commandments.

There is in no ancient document any allusion to what we today know as fornication,[5] a term that arose in European law. In modern terms, by adultery there is meant illicit sexual intercourse by a married person; by fornication there is meant illicit sexual intercourse by an unmarried person.[6] The inattention to fornication in the Rabbinic literature may be due to one of two reasons. Possibly it seemed too unimportant to legislate about. (Our legacy from medieval romantic love, or from the Victorian Age, with marriage being deferred until well beyond the time of puberty, has bred a modern rebellion against the standards of society and has created an excessive preoccupation with sex.) Or possibly early marriage made unnecessary the sowing of wild oats. According to the Rabbis, a man ought to be married by the age of eighteen;[7] to be unmarried at twenty was regarded as a curse.[8] To remain single was discouraged. A widower was urged to remarry, though he ought to wait until three festivals have passed (unless there were tiny children whose need for a mother made it unreasonable to wait). A widow or divorcee needed to wait ninety days before remarriage, to discover whether or not she was pregnant, for if she was, the paternity of the child could be clarified by waiting. There is in the literature an abundance of sound advice, such as not marrying for money; there are also injunctions that smack of

superstition, such as abstaining from a union with a woman
similar in height or in complexion.[9]

There were two steps to the process of marrying, first
ērusīn and then *nissuīn*.[10] Erusin was a betrothal, an engagement, a sort of preliminary wedding, not consummated by
sexual relations, but dissolvable only through a divorce; thus,
parents of a girl who had not yet reached puberty could
contract for the marriage through erusin, and, when puberty
came, the marriage concluded by nissuin or its synonym,
kiddushīn. The normal interval was a year[11] Marriages were
ordinarily arranged by the parents, the father being obliged
to arrange for a mate for his child.[12]

While a marriage might take place as do modern common-
law marriages (in which the couple live together without a
formal ceremony), the wife in such a marriage was bereft of
full protection. The formalities of regular marriage included
the need to protect the woman financially, since the right of
divorce lay exclusively with the man. A dispute between the
School of Hillel and of Shammai underscores the onesided-
ness of the right to divorce; the dispute was over the issue of
whether the grounds for a man to divorce his wife could be
trivial, such as poor cooking (Hillel), or weightier, such as
sexual dereliction (Shammai). The opinion of Rabbi Akiba
was that the finding of a more beautiful woman was an adequate ground.[13] There is in Rabbinic sources no echo of the
prohibition of divorce recorded in the Gospels (Mt. 5.32;
19.1-9; Mk. 10.1-12; Lk. 16.18) and in I Corinthians 7.10-
11.

The marriage terms as arranged included money and
property. Scripture provides for a groom to give his bride a
gift (Exod. 22.16-17). In Exodus 22.16-17 the word *mōhar*
appears: it is the term for the sum of money paid in penalty
to the father of a girl whom a man seduces. Later the mohar
seems to have become the groom's financial settlement on
the bride. She, from her side, needed a gift from her father;
nedūnyā ("dowry") was the aggregate of money and possessions which a bride brought with her to the marriage.
The financial arrangements were recorded in writing, and
the document was called a *ketūbā* (plural ketubōt).[14] In the
ketuba, the groom, stipulating his financial gifts, agrees to

honor and support the bride. His gift is hers in payment for her virginity. He will provide food, clothing, and sexual intercourse. The bride too must have specified the amount of the dowry. The groom in return makes assurance that he, and his heirs, will live up to the terms of the ketuba, in effect giving the bride a lien on his property while alive, or on his estate after his death.[15] The essence of the ketuba was its financial protection of the bride, which placed an obligation on the groom in the event of divorce; the protection acted, of course, as a deterrent to capricious divorce.

The ketuba appears to have originated as a formal requirement through the influence of Simeon ben Shetaḥ, a Sage of the age of Alexander Jannaeus, and, by tradition (Berachot 48a) a brother of the queen Salome Alexandra, but the ketuba was apparently even older in origin. A passage, Tobit 7.3-15, depicts Tobit as writing out a marriage contract between his son Tobias and his bride Sarah, as if such a contract were required in the Mosaic law.

Divorce was simultaneously easy for the man and also greatly discouraged. Marriages, of course, do not always work out well, and the Rabbis give us repeated lists of the unseemly characteristics of women, such as their stinginess, propensity for gossip, bad temper, and the like. (I know of no such comparable lists about men!) But divorce was considered a calamity,[16] and sanctioned only as the last resort. The term for divorce is gerush (literally, "banishment"), but it is usually used in the plural, gerushin; There is no Talmudic tractate under this name. What there is is a tractate named Gitin, "writs of divorce," singular get. A divorce, as distinct from a separation, needed to be accompanied by a get, as seems implicit in Deuteronomy 24.1, which speaks of such a written document. The essence of a get[17] was a phrase it needed to contain, "You are free to any man." That is to say, a get was an authorization by a husband that his wife was now free to remarry. After a procedure of careful inquiry and scrutiny by experts in the matters, the get is delivered to the wife in such a way as to preclude any doubt about its validity. The purpose of this extreme care was to safeguard a wife who was too young to understand, or who was insane, or who was a captive. Moreover, when a husband had a get executed, he became liable for the financial obligations stated in the ketuba that might have remained unpaid.

There were some circumstances in which a woman might initiate a divorce, this by the mechanism of persuading a court to compel her husband to give her a divorce. Such grounds were impotence,[18] or abstention by the husband from sexual acts with her,[19] or his acquiring a loathsome disease, or his being in a stench-laden business.[20]

Once a couple was divorced, each party was free to marry. Indeed, except in certain cases, they could (and should!) remarry each other.[21]

Granted that divorce in a strict sense was the prerogative solely of the husband, the procedures for the get were such as to restrain or even virtually eliminate capricious divorce.

Scripture had spoken of a man's seminal discharge or a woman's menstruation[22] and childbirth as ritually defiling.[23] Defilement was transferred by contact; hence sex relations during a woman's menstruation was prohibited. Rabbinic definitions about sex relations arose quite naturally; many of these are found in the tractate Nidda ("the menstrous woman") which is found not in the Order Women (the third of the six "Orders") but in the sixth Order, Tohorot ("cleannesses"). Behind the many definitions of defilement lay the conviction that sex relations were holy. They could, of course, be defiled, but in themselves they were in no way defiling. Nor were the digestive functions deemed to be unseemly, for they too entailed the need for the recitation of ritual blessings.

The birth of a male child entailed the requirement, which is biblical (Gen. 17.10-14; 21.4; Lev. 12.3), of circumcision (see above, pp. 180-81). Rabbinic passages extol the rite as one of great joy and festivity.[24] Its high importance is indicated in that the Romans, in the age of Hadrian (reigned A.D. 117-38) and the Bar Kochba rebellion in 132, prohibited it.[25] Rabbinic halacha made it obligatory on a father to have his son circumcised.[26] It was to be performed on the child's eighth day, even on a Sabbath.[27] Precision respecting details of the ceremony are provided, including the procedure in the occasional situation of a baby born "circumcised."[28] The ac-

tual cutting was done by a medically informed *mōhēl*[29] ("circumciser").

Scripture (Deut. 21.15-17) had provided that the first
male child should receive a double portion (twice as much as
his brothers) of his father's inheritance; it had also specified
(Exod. 13.20; 22.28) that the first-born not only of man but
also of domestic animals needed to be consecrated to the
Deity, for the first-born "belonged" to Him. Definition of the
twofold matters quite beyond what Scripture enjoined naturally ensued;[30] thus, as we have mentioned, a non-priest
could "redeem" and retain his first-born son at the age of
one month by a payment to a priest of five pieces of money.[31]

The father, so it was assumed, was the wage earner, the
mother responsible for the home. It was she who prepared the
food; he, though, was responsible for its being ritually
proper. The food laws went quite beyond the mere question
of what food sources were permitted or prohibited. Modern
Jews, if at all observant, ordinarily concentrate primarily on
the prohibition of pork, crustaceans, or fish without scales;
equally in force, though, are proper modes of slaughter and
the requisite salting of meat or fowl to draw out the blood,
the consumption of the latter being prohibited in Scripture.
But meat in ancient times was beyond the usual man's pock-
etbook, and the principal items of diet were grains and fruits.
The range of food regulations extended even to these. Grains
and fruits were, in a general sense, available for eating only
if a set of appropriate "tithes"[32] had first been taken. The
yield of a fruit tree was permitted only in the fifth year after
the planting of a tree. Contact with food in its preparation by
a non-Jew made the food prohibited[33]; in part such prohibitions rested on the suspicion of unconscious, coincidental contamination, as in the making of cheese, and in part on the
belief that non-Jews were prone to such cruelties as hacking
off a limb from a living animal for food. Hence non-Jews
must not touch food which Jews were to eat.

Meat, if from a proper animal, required that the animal
be slaughtered appropriately;[34] the meat of an animal which
had died otherwise was prohibited. The hands needed to be
washed not only before eating, but before any sacred act.[35]

There is no direct information provided in the literature

as to how the housewife became aware or deeply knowledgeable about the regulations. The presumption is that the husband, having learned these in the school or the synagogue, conveyed them to the wife, and the wife to the daughter. Girls did not attend the schools; some did attain literacy in Scripture, but there are recorded aversions to any formal instruction of women in the halacha.[36] Yet a body of lore about proper food would reasonably have accumulated, and a daughter would learn it from her mother and transmit it to her own daughter.[37] At any rate, the housewife was expected to conduct the home in the light of the laws.

Home prayers and home observances, especially of the home aspect of the festivals, added their dimension to the need for a knowledge of proper procedures. To what extent the festival observances enjoined in Scripture as occasions of pilgrimage to the Temple became synagogue and home observances prior to the destruction of the Temple cannot be ascertained with certainty. A Jew living a great distance away, as in Asia Minor for example, would have found the cost of making three annual pilgrimages prohibitive; if he lived in Rome the interval of seven weeks between Passover and Weeks was short enough to pose its own difficulty and inconvenience. Hence it is reasonable to infer that observance in the synagogue and the home predated the destruction in 70; it is reasonable, on the other hand, to infer that after the destruction the liturgical aspects of both synagogue and home increased in elaborateness. Such home elaboration was especially the case with Booths, where each family was expected to fashion its own booth, adjoined to its house. From the bare scriptural injunction (Lev. 23.42) there arose the detailed specifications provided by the Rabbis whereby the observance of Booths would be valid.

The most significant shift, as far as the home was concerned, was the Passover. The biblical injunction to observe the Passover by the sacrifice at the Temple of a lamb or a kid (Deut. 16.1-8) was accompanied by the injunction that not only must leavened bread not be eaten during the festival week, but all leaven must be removed from the house (Exod. 12.15, 19; 13.7). To the preparations for the Passover based on Scripture there were naturally added the definitions and prescriptions for the home by which the scriptural intent could be accomplished; the ceremony of the sacrifice of the lamb or kid at the Temple became altered into the sacred meal known as the *séder* ("order," that is, the order of the prayers before and after the meal). The seder is described in Mishna Pesaḥím ch. 10 in those essentials that are still preserved by Jews today.

Moreover, the Sabbath and the complete rest enjoined by Scripture posed housekeeping problems, for while preparation of the food in advance was no issue, the serving of meals on the Sabbath posed a variety of difficulties, including the express prohibition against fire in the house, even for cooking or heating. The protection of the regulations[38] for the Sabbath included what we might call "a Friday afternoon deadline," a time by which all preparations needed to be completed, and also a Saturday night deadline, to provide certainty that the Sabbath was truly ended.

All this is to say that the home was a center of religious living and ritual, where both *mitzvá* ("approved deed") and *'avērá* ("trespass") lurked. If there existed anxiety about trespass, that was completely obscured by the sense that the commandments were God's gracious gift which one joyfully carried out. To repeat, obedience to God was a privilege, never an unwelcome burden.

As has been said, much of traditional Judaism as practiced by observant Jews still today was fully shaped in the ancient Rabbinic era. Two well-known Jewish matters, though, are not that ancient. *Bar mitzva* ("son of the commandment"), the occasion at which a thirteen-year-old boy publicly moves from boyhood to (theoretic) adulthood in a synagogue ceremony, arose only in medieval times, and is not attested to prior to the fourteenth century.[39] Second, a prayer known as the *Kaddísh* ("sanctification") is relatively ancient.[40] However, its use by a mourner both for a period immediately after a death in the family, and on the anniversary of such a death, represents a medieval development whereby an older prayer once unrelated to mourning came in time to be used for mourning.

The home was not only the place of living; it was preeminently the place where the Torah was practiced.

· 7 ·

DEATH-AFTER-LIFE
—MESSIAH

Scripture not only provides narratives of the past in the Pentateuch, the "Early Prophets," and Chronicles, Ezra, and Nehemiah. It also provides through the literary prophets a concern with the future, both of impending events, such as the Assyrian invasion, but also a perspective on the remote future, which in Isaiah 2.2 and Micah 4.1 is called "the end of days." In at least this sense, the Rabbinic mind was concerned with time: creation had taken place; in the present there were nations and men; there was a future[1] destined to unfold.

But past nations and individuals had come into being, and passed away, and other nations and other individuals had come into being, and some were still on the scene! What was the future of God's nation Israel? What was the fate of the individual, past or present? Such questions led to a variety of expressions in the Rabbinic literature.

As to the individual, Scripture is for the most part silent; there the usual view is that death is the complete end. Burial in the earth supposed that *sheól* was the underground place to which the dead came; sheol was the eternal abiding place of the dead, and there nothing at all happened. But in the age with which we deal sheol was not thought of as eternal, but only as a passing stage, for in due time the dead would, or could be, resurrected. Mishna Sanhedrin 10.1 begins with the words: "All Israelites have a share in the World To Come."

Yet even with some future awaiting the individual, nevertheless his death was something which his family would mourn. There were deemed to be four requisite periods of mourning. The first three days were to be marked by lament and weeping. For seven[2] days (these three and the next four days) the mourner did not leave his home. During the first thirty days, he was to wear somber clothes and abstain from personal adornment. During the first year[3] he was to abstain from pleasures and amusements.

The Talmud records the custom for the neighbors to provide the first meal after the funeral.[4] For the funeral, the body needed to be cleansed. It was then placed on a bier or a bed. The funeral was normally at home, but could be, if the eminence of the man warranted, in the synagogue.[5] A eulogy was delivered, though one ought not exaggerate the praises of the deceased.[6] A procession to the place of burial included trumpets or flute players, or both, and professional mourners.[7]

Burial in the ground, or in a cave, not cremation,[8] was the chief mode. In the case of the poor, it was an act of highest charity to help defray the costs. Burial was incumbent on the very day of death, if at all possible.[9] Such hasty burial prevented disgrace to the body. Burial was a means by which atonement was wrought for sins, since the decay of the body was painful to it. Embalming was rare. The corpse, after washing,[10] was wrapped in white clothes. The use of a coffin was infrequent.[11] After burial, those in the procession formed a double row through which the bereaved passed.[12]

What had happened to the soul of the departed? God had created for the wicked a place, Gehenna,[13] "hell," on the sixth day of creation.[14] It was so large as to be without measurement (Pesahim 94 a) and divided into seven compartments (Sotah 19 b). There was a fire there, which, indeed, replenished the sun at every sunset.[15] From this unquenchable fire there were heated the warm springs of Tiberias.[16] Despite the fire, hell is dark.[17]

While occasional mention is made in the Jewish literature of the ruler of hell, in none of the Jewish sources of the age with which we deal is that ruler spoken of as Satan or the devil; such elaboration is later and essentially Christian. A passage (Shabbat 104 a) mentions a "prince of Gehenna," but promptly proceeds to personify Gehenna itself as capable of speaking (as occurs also in Abodah Zara 17 a).

The righteous were to go to paradise, yet a man could be

uncertain, as is reported of Rabbi Johanan ben Zakkai, whether he was to go to paradise or to hell (Berachot 28a). One Rabbinic view allocates to every man a prospective share in both heaven and hell; at death, for the righteous, the share in hell is converted into a second share in paradise, and for the wicked the share in paradise converted into a second share in hell (Hagiga 15a). A stay in hell for moderate sinners purified them after twelve months, but the very wicked who both sinned and caused others to sin remained there forever—indeed, even after hell would itself pass away.[18] Such views, and others that could be cited, are random and less than integrated and unified. The general opinion that certain evil deeds led a man at death directly to hell, and worthy deeds directly to paradise, seems clear. But exactly how fully pervasive the opinion was is far from certain. It is clear, however, that both paradise and hell were not usually conceived of as being eternal, but rather only as places of sojourn between death and the future Great Judgment. It is to be noted that in the Rabbinic literature the view of hell is relatively undeveloped, but that of paradise, the heavenly Eden, very much elaborated. There were nine mortals—the names of these nine vary—who visited paradise while they were still alive.[19] There were various chambers in paradise, including one for pious women. In paradise at some future time there would be a banquet, the Messianic feast, where the meat of the Leviathan would be served, as would wine preserved in its grapes since the days of creation.[20] On the other hand, the Sage Rab[21] declared that "in paradise there is no eating, or drinking, or copulation; no business, no envy, no hatred, no ambition. Rather, the righteous sit wearing their crowns [of good deeds and knowledge of the Torah] and derive joy from the brightness of the Shechina."[22]

The Jewish ideas of the Messiah came to have a certain basic central focus; the details, though, are less than consistent, for reasons that will presently appear.

First is the need to notice the overt biblical expressions. The word Messiah means "the person anointed"; anointment by a prophet, such as Samuel, was the act or rite by which a commoner was raised to royalty, as had happened in the case

of Saul and David (1 Sam. 10.1; 16.13). That a prophet did
the anointing meant that the king was in effect designated by
God, and hence the expression "the Lord's anointed" (1 Sam.
16.6). Nothing of futurity inheres in such anointments; they
were incidents of the past.

The account of the monarchy in I and II Kings contains repeated incidents in which prophets warn kings of their down-
fall, or else they inform usurpers that they will come to the
throne. In the north, the dynasty of David had been supplanted by Jeroboam ben Nebat and his in turn by that of
Baasha, and, then that of Zimri, who after seven days was
killed, with the throne then going to the Omri and his dynasty. In the south, however, the dynasty of David was able
to persist, surviving even after the Assyrians had destroyed
the northern kingdom in 722, but itself ending at the hands
of the Babylonians in the sequels to the conquest of 597, the
destruction of the Temple in 587, and the subsequent Exile to
Babylon. From the Exile to the Hasmoneans there was no
king.

Passages in Jeremiah[23] speak of the future restoration of
the dynasty of David through a descendant of his, this at an
unspecified future time. Similarly Ezekiel 34.20-31 contains
the promise of such a restoration, under a shepherd called
"my servant David." So too in Psalms 89.3-4, 20-37 there is
an assurance of the eternity of David's dynasty.

Probably from the exilic period during or just after the
Babylonian Exile comes the ending appended to the Book of
Amos (9.11-12), which promises a rebuilding of the eminence of ancient times of the "fallen booth of David." Clearly
this passage appears to deal with some future day. This future becomes viewed as ideal in Isaiah 11; through a descendant of David, universal peace will ensue, and a great national revival will take place through the redemption of the
scattered of Israel from the foreign lands.[24] Thus, in the period when there was no king and no national existence, Jews
were counseled to await in the future a revival of their national existence under the eternal dynasty of David.

The descendant who was to reign in the future is called
both *tzémah* ("plant") and *hōtér* ("a shoot," part of a plant),
that is to say, some single individual. In the early restored

Judean community shortly after the Babylonian Exile, Zerubbabel appears to be such an individual (Hag. 2.20-23),
and in the Book of Zechariah 3.8 allusion again is made to
the tzemah, presumably Zerubbabel. But, as noted earlier (p.
20), something went astray with Zerubbabel, as if that which
seemed a present possibility now needed deferment to the
future.

At times David seems only the symbolic name of the future king, but at times it seems as if David himself is to be
the individual.[25] But let it here suffice that a restoration, into
perpetuity, of the Davidic dynasty became broadly hoped for
and expected, and passages in Scripture which have no direct
connection with this idea were so interpreted, and were so
rendered in the Targum.[26]

Accordingly, in sharp contrast to the present array of dislocations, or dependency, these the results of incursions of
neighboring people, or of Roman conquerors, the hopes and
wishes centered in the expectant advent of a divinely appointed individual through whom relief would come. Diverse single strands added their own complicating contribution. The future Davidic king could attain independence only
through the defeat of the national foes; Joel 4.1-21 (3.1-21 in
Christian versions) promised a day of Great Judgment on the
nations by the Deity. Malachi 3.19-24 (4.1 in Christian versions) repeats the theme of the Great Judgment, but adds
that the Deity "will send to you Elijah the prophet before
the coming of the great and awesome day of the Lord."
There was added to the exhortations the conviction of the
return of Elijah before the actual Day of Great Judgment.
Elijah had not died, but had ascended to heaven in a pillar
of fire (2 Kgs. 2.11). Inevitably he became the center of
countless legends,[27] but he always retained his role as the
forerunner of the Messiah. The Messiah came to be connected with the future Great Judgment, so that Elijah became the forerunner of both the Messiah and also the Great
Judgment.

In this compressed tracing of the idea of the Messiah, precisely where the Hasmonean experience fits is difficult to
assess. In neither I Maccabees nor II Maccabees is there any
passage which directly links these successful warriors with
messianic achievements. I Maccabees 2.57 speaks, almost in

the language of the citations from Scripture given above, about the eternity of the throne of David; 4.46 speaks of concealing the stones of the sacred altar[28] until a prophet would come to teach about them; 14.41 tells of the confirmation of Simon as prince and High Priest until the true prophet would arise.[29]

The Hasmoneans fulfilled some but not all the expectations hoped for in the future; the Judean independence, so long as it lasted, represented the realization of one hope. But it did not last. Moreover, in the time that it endured, it scarcely represented the glorious age of the lion lying down with the lamb. A passage, I Maccabees 14.12, boasts that in the reign of Simon each man sat under his own vine and fig tree, with none to make him afraid (cited from Mic. 4.4), but then Simon was assassinated, along with two sons, by his son-in-law. Simon's successor, John Hyrcanus—to whom Josephus[30] relates the gift of God's prophecy—shifted his allegiance from the Pharisees to the Sadducees; Josephus comments that it was from the Pharisees that there arose the hatred which John Hyrcanus and his sons met with from the multitude. If a subsidiary purpose in the writing of I Maccabees was to defend the legitimacy of the Hasmonean royalty, and of II Maccabees the legitimacy of the Hasmonean high priesthood, such defense would automatically preclude identifying the Hasmonean age with the Messianic. In the succeeding age, the repressive reign of the unstable but effective Herod would likewise have obstructed identifying the age of Herod with the wondrous age to come. The theme from Scripture of a "shoot from the stock of Jesse," meaning that the Messiah would be a descendant from David, can reasonably be interpreted not only as an emphasis on the seed of David as the legitimate background of the Messiah, but as the specific rejection of both Hasmoneans and Herodians.[31]

The multiple hints or ideas that constituted Jewish messianic thought may also have been affected by the emergence of messianic claimants. Jesus of Nazareth was clearly not the last man in Jewish experience for whom or by whom the claim of being the Messiah was advanced. A century after him there was Simon bar Kōzibá (see p. 35). Before him there is no clear evidence about claimants. The fervent ex-

pectations found in the Book of Enoch (see pp. 86-89), especially Chapters 85-90, or in the Sibylline Books[32] did not, so
far as can be known, eventuate in the emergence of any
messianic claimant. The view is at times expressed that a
certain Ezekias (the Greek form of Hezekiah), a Galilean
whom Herod, then governor of Galilee, had beheaded without a trial[33] in 49 B.C., was such a claimant, but Josephus,
from whom our information is derived, records no such item.
Scanty as is the information of claimants earlier than Jesus,
there are unmistakable literary predictions of the Messiah
from the century and a half before his time. Did such mes-
siahs emerge? We cannot be sure. If such predictions might
not have eventuated in the emergence of a messianic claimant, such non-emergence could well have been a disappointment to some. But the emergence of messianic impostors[34]
was inevitably a frustration quite beyond ordinary human
disappointment. That was so because of the belief of a connection between the Messiah and God. Even in passages
where the Messiah is only a man, he is nevertheless selected
and designated by God. In some Rabbinic thought the divine designation of who the Messiah would be had been
determined at the time of Creation,[35] and had awaited merely
the arrival of the scheduled moment for this advance determination to take place. In some passages, especially in Apocalyptic literature,[36] the view is expressed that not alone the
name but the Messiah himself was created before the Creation. The "pre-existence" of the Messiah himself, however,
seems absent from the Tannaitic literature.[37]

When messianic hopes were dashed, there naturally arose
a variety of different explanations. Thus, some Christian literature discloses a paradox of anxiety about the failure of
the hopes to materialize, and also a revision of basic ideas,
for the purposes of diminishing the disappointment.[38] In the
Jewish Apocalyptic and the Rabbinic literature, the hopes of
a future Messiah seem constant. Yet a sharp distinction is
valid as between the Apocalyptic and the Rabbinic in that
the doctrine of the Messiah becomes almost peripheral in the
Rabbinic literature, for eschatology is of only the most minor
of concerns to the Rabbis. A passage, difficult to interpret,
quotes a certain Hillel[39] (not the great Hillel) that "Israel
has no Messiah; they consumed him in the days of Heze-

kiah."[40] The passage occurs in a context of a series of statements by various sages in embellishment of aspects of messianic thought, especially about the mystery of the name of the future Messiah. Possibly Hillel's intent might be paraphrased in these words: "There will not be a Messiah in the future, for we have already had our Messiah in Hezekiah." The meaning of "they consumed [ate] him" is quite obscure. It seems clear in the context of the passage that the belief itself in the Messiah is in no way repudiated.[41]

Jewish messianic thought, though ultimately a fairly unified series of related ideas, nevertheless resembles a patchwork quilt. The recorded utterances of individuals should be regarded as reflections of something kindred to poetic license. Against such a background, the views of a Paul, arising before messianic thought achieved its relative stability, are in a sense characteristic of such individualistic utterances. In Paul's view, the Messiah was pre-existent; a heavenly being, the Messiah became the man Jesus for the period of Jesus' earthly career. Unique to Paul, as compared with the abundance of utterances about the Messiah in Apocalyptic and Rabbinic literature, is his interpretation of the career of Jesus as related to sin and atonement. Nevertheless, Paul's views too derive from the messianic speculations of the age.

In the period there are dim echoes of a Messiah "the son of Joseph"[42] as well as "the son of David." The "son of Joseph" seems to reflect a hope for the revival of the northern kingdom, often spoken of as Joseph, but more often identified with Joseph's son Ephraim. That northern kingdom, consisting of ten tribes, exiled eastward by the Assyrians, had become "lost." Perhaps the Messiah ben Joseph is related to the "finding" (and in-gathering) of the "lost ten tribes," but the views in the post-Talmudic literature about him do not contain this latter motif.

It will be recalled (see p. 99) that the Qumran documents speak of a Messiah of the stock of Aaron, as well as a Davidic Messiah. This is apparently a hope for the restoration of the proper Zadokite high priesthood, improperly usurped by the Hasmoneans.

The Rabbinic statements about the Messiah are abundant. Yet the time of his advent is significantly avoided. That he would come is taken for granted; precisely when he would come is a topic that appears to be taboo. Only the general conditions for his coming are set forth: upheavals and disorders and Roman imperial arrogance are the prelude, the necessary pangs. First, though, Elijah must return. And only thereafter does the Messiah come.

What was the basic content of the expectations? Foremost, that the Messiah would restore Judean independence through destroying the power of Rome. He would crush all enemies so that Israel would emerge as God's unique, elect nation. He would assume the throne of Israel as the son of David or designate the proper king, also a son of David. He would gather in the dispersed of Israel, miraculously bringing them back to the Holy Land (as in Isa. 43.5-7). He would usher in the Great Judgment, thereby inaugurating a new age, the World to Come. The wicked who had in the old age escaped punishment, and the righteous who had been denied reward, would be resurrected and dealt with appropriately (or else both would be made to stand judgment, with the vindicated righteous thereupon being resurrected). The new age would be unlike this age of hunger, war, and misery; it would be a glorious age of universal peace and prosperity.

Prayers for the resurrection, for the reign of the Davidic dynasty, and for the in-gathering of the dispersed were incorporated, as we saw (p. 150) in the Eighteen Benedictions. The sacred days of the calendar, too, also came to have a relationship to the Messiah, especially the Festival of Sukkot. Messianic thought or overtone came to permeate much of Jewish practice or observance, but without overbalancing that which it entered into.

· 8 ·

THE CALENDAR

The Festival Days and the Sabbath

1

CALENDAR: YEARS AND MONTHS

The legacy from Scripture respecting the calendar includes certain differences that necessarily required resolution. On one level, Scripture speaks of the months by number, but also by name.[1] Respecting the names that are mentioned, there are vestiges of two different sets of names, the older being Phoenician names and the younger Babylonian.[2] These appear to have been a development: first, the use of Phoenician names, then the use of numbered months, and then of the Babylonian names. The different usages represent different calendars. All three possibly, and the latter two certainly, were lunar-solar, that is, the duration of a month was determined by the moon, the duration of a year by the sun.

A calendar of sacred days is found in Leviticus 23; it gives precise dates for the sacred days in terms of specified days in numbered months. One festival, though, Weeks, as we have said (p. 91), is not prescribed by a day of a month, but by the "counting of sheafs," beginning in Passover on the "morrow after the Sabbath"; this unusual kind of dating has been interpreted as a relic of a calendar that was strictly solar, with the divisions in the year being seasons in the modern sense, that is, intervals between the equinoxes and the solstices.[3] The Book of Jubilees and the Qumran community appear to have used such a solar calendar, rather than the lunar-solar calendar of Leviticus 23. The calendar, then, was more than merely a measurement of time; it was intimately bound up with religious observances which centered on basic religious ideas.

For all that Scripture tells, there is much left untold, and Synagogue Judaism felt the need to fill in details and to dissolve uncertainties. A clue to understanding the task it assumed is to notice the basic problem in a lunar-solar calendar. First, the duration of time between one new moon and the next is roughly twenty-nine days, or, again roughly, twelve lunar months equal 354 days. A solar year is 365¼ days. The difference is 11¼ days. Hence, adjustment was required so as to bring it about that the difference of 11¼ days did not by accumulation result, as it were, in bringing June in January. In our modern secular calendar of 365 days, we observe a "leap year" every fourth year, adding a February 29, to avert ultimately having June in January. A Jewish leap year is more complex; it entails adding not a single day such as February 29, but a whole month seven times in a cycle of nineteen years. The added month is called the "Second Adar"; in the numbering system Adar was the twelfth month.[4]

The second basic issue is that though the period astronomically from new moon to new moon is 29¼ days, as far as the visible new moon is concerned, the appearance of the new month, after the "dark of the moon," can come on either the thirtieth or thirty-first day. Precise mathematical calculation today can inform us just when the new moon will be visible; the Jewish practice, though, was not to calculate mathematically when the new moon would be visible, but to "proclaim" the new month after the new moon was actually seen. A month of twenty-nine days (ending at the thirtieth day) was called "lacking"; a month of thirty days (ending at the thirty-first day) was called "full." Since actually seeing the new moon, rather than utilizing astronomical or mathematical tables, was the prevailing mode, an official "observatory" was utilized, first under the Sanhedrin, and then after A.D. 90 under the Great Bet Din.[5] The "proclamation" of the new moon was then disseminated to the populace. Accordingly the populace could observe the proper time for the sacred days, when once it knew exactly when the new month had begun.

But actual observation, entailing the testimony of witnesses, can be fallible, and result in chaotic observance respecting the date. A controversy in this regard (with few details given) is recorded: The patriarch Gamaliel II ordered the eminent Sage, Joshua ben Hananiah, to appear before him on the date which Joshua had settled on for the Day of Atonement.[6] For Joshua to comply with the patriarch's order meant that he would have to violate the regulations commonly agreed on for the Day of Atonement. Gamaliel had apparently accepted invalid testimony about the new moon.[7] Yet Joshua was compelled to bow to authority and comply.

To inform the populace that a "new moon" had been proclaimed, the device of lighting a succession of bonfires on hills was used. But in the time of Judah the Prince (in the latter half of the second Christian century), Samaritans mischievously and maliciously lit signal fires at the wrong time.[8] So instead of setting fire signals, messengers were sent out. Since astronomically the visible new moon comes on one of two awaited days, it became customary for those at a great distance, especially the communities of Babylonia, to observe both of the days, in effect adding a second day to the first; in the ensuing days the exact date, though past, was learned and the dating adjusted to the acquired certainty. (The Babylonian Jewish community, through the Sage Samuel, described in Berachot 58b as an astronomer who knew the heavens as well as the streets of his city, developed mathematical astronomical tables.) But Diaspora Jews, to be sure of inclusively observing the proper dates, added an additional day to the new moon, the New Year, Booths, Passover, and Pentecost. In Palestine the added day was limited to the New Year. (American Reform Jews have ceased to observe the added days; in modern Israel the added day of the New Year abides, but the other added days do not.)

But far beyond the bare question of the principles of establishing the calendar was the need to fill in those details which Scripture had not itself provided: Exactly when does the Sabbath begin, and exactly when does it end? On a fast day, how much food may be consumed by the slightly ill or the faint before the fast is violated? Does one remove all trace of leaven from his home for Passover in advance of Passover, or only after Passover has begun? If in advance, how

much in advance? The content of much of the Rabbinic literature is devoted to the elimination of uncertainties and
vaguenesses; the end result was the fullest specification by
the Rabbis of *what* should be done, and *how*, in fullest obedience to the divine requirement to observe the sacred occasions
exactly when they were supposed to occur.

2

THE SABBATH

The Sabbath was, despite its weekly nature, the most important of all the sacred days, except for the Day of Atonement.
Mandated in Scripture, which tells also that God Himself observed it (Gen. 2.2), the Sabbath regulations were more rigorous than those enjoined for the festival occasions; one
might cook on the festivals, but not on the Sabbath. The Sabbath was a recollection of God's gracious creation of the
world. It was to be observed with rejoicing[9]—the laws were
never designed to be blue laws! To protect its integrity of its
beginning at sundown on Friday—Jewish days run from
sunset to sunset—the preparation on Friday of foods for the
Sabbath was essential. The hours of late Friday afternoon
were inappropriate for those chores which could not clearly
be concluded well before sunset. The woman of the house lit
candles to welcome the sacred day. The Sabbath meal began
with a *kiddūsh*[10] ("sanctification"), a ritual in which wine
was drunk, and bread,[11] broken and dipped in salt, was eaten.
At the end of the Sabbath—when stars appear—comes the
ceremony of *havdalā*[12] ("separation," i.e. of the holiness of
the Sabbath from the ordinariness of the other days) in
which wine is drunk, fragrant spices are smelled, and a lamp
(or candle) is lighted.

The three festivals were enjoined in Scripture as pilgrim
festivals, with the expectation that the faithful would attend
the Temple at Jerusalem for observance. As we have said
(p. 24), even prior to the destruction of the Temple, for
those who lived at a great distance from Jerusalem this could

be prohibitively costly, or for residents of Rome difficult to make in so little time. After 70, the observances came to be home and synagogal.

3

PASSOVER

Leviticus 23.5-6 echo a distinction, which had once prevailed but in time became indistinct, between Pésaḥ ("Passover") and *Ḥag Ha-Matzōt* ("The feast of unleavened bread"). In origin Pesaḥ was probably pastoral, and Unleavened Bread agricultural. The separate occasions became united, but we do not know exactly when. Possibly the distinction between Passover on Nisan 14, and Matzot, beginning on Nisan 15 and lasting for seven days, endured so long as the Temple abided.

There is a scriptural injunction that, along with the sacrifice of the lamb in commemoration of the release from enslavement in Egypt, "You shall tell your son in days to come what God has wrought [for one's fathers] in his exodus from Egypt."[13] From the injunction "tell your son" there arose the home Passover celebration, a sacred meal, preceded and followed by recitations, and the use of symbols, which carry out the injunction. The recitation of the events furnishes the name *The* Haggadá for these prayers and the symbols; we might translate *The* Haggada as the "greatest narrative." The segments of the recitation came to follow a set "order," and hence the occasion is called sēder. The Mishna Pesaḥim, as we have said (p. 199), sets forth the required procedures in virtually the form perpetuated until this day.[14] The seder begins with a kiddúsh over the wine as does the Sabbath dinner; in the course of the seder service, three additional cups of wine are drunk.[15] The usual symbols present are the matzot, three cakes of which are prepared in a napkin for ceremonial use;[16] parsley (or some other green), and a bowl of salt water are provided.[17] Some bitter herb, horseradish or bitter watercress, are used to represent the bitterness inflicted by the Egyptians (Exod. 1.14). A mixture of chopped nuts and apple, called *ḥaróset*, represented the clay out of which the Hebrews had made bricks. A roasted bone represented the paschal lamb; a roasted egg represented the voluntary animal sacrifice which one might have wished to offer during Passover. (In later times, a large cup of wine, prepared for Elijah, and symbolizing messianic hopes,[18] was set on the festive table.)

The recitation included the practice of a son's putting to the father four questions, these being why the seder night is different from all other nights: Thus, why is the dipping twice, once of parsley in the salt water, and then in the bitter herbs? Why is the meat required to be a roast, whereas on other nights it may be stewed or cooked?[19] The father replies to the questions, citing biblical verses, particularly Deuteronomy 26.5 and succeeding verses.[20] It was expected that each person recite the biblical verses which mention the Passover symbols: The paschal lamb (Exod. 12.27); unleavened bread (Exod. 12.39); and bitterness (Exod. 1.14). A passage (Pesaḥim 5.5) makes the demand that "in every generation a man must regard himself as if he himself came out of Egypt."

The drinking of wine could be unlimited, beyond the four cups (though drinking between the required third and fourth cups was barred). The danger could exist that an excess of wine could make the religious recitation become distorted into drunkenness by the close of the meal. Hence, a piece of matzo is eaten to signify that the eating and drinking are ended. It is called *afikŏmen*.[21]

The service after the meal is the usual grace, followed by the recitation of Psalms 113-18, called the Hallel ("praise") and often alluded to as the "Egyptian[22] Hallel."

In the ensuing centuries, the Haggada was greatly expanded and prolonged.[23]

4

SUKKOT

The festival begins on Tishre 15, that is, two weeks after Rosh Hashanah. A harvest festival (possibly the ancestor of the American Thanksgiving), it has a variety of names in the Bible.[24] The symbols for the festival are these: "On the first day, take the fruit of an eminent tree, branches of palms, boughs of leafy trees, and brook willows, and rejoice before the Lord for seven days." The Sadducees and the Pharisees were divided as to whether the fruit and the branches were to be used for the building of a structure at one's home, or, instead, to be utilized quite apart from such a structure. The Pharisees insisted that these symbols must be carried in a sacred procession. The fruit came to be an *etróg* ("citron"), a cousin of the lemon. The foliage came to be used in a *lulắv* ("wreath"), with the myrtle and willow leaves attached to the bottom of the palm branch by weaving pliable palm leaves around the stems of the myrtle and the willow. In the public worship Psalm 118 was recited,[25] and at its beginning and end the lulav was elevated and shaken. The use of the lulav and etrog extended throughout the several days of the festival.

There is a recollection in Mishna Sukkot 4.9 of a Temple ritual, a water libation, entailing the pouring of water taken from the "pool of Siloam" from one jar to another. It was apparently symbolic of rain, the important prayer for which was recited on the last day of Sukkot. The libation was accompanied by the "rejoicing at the *bét hā-shōēbá* ("the place for drawing water"[26]) while flutes were played. Sukkot 5.1 comments that one who has not witnessed this rejoicing has never seen joy. Hymns of praise were sung to instrumental accompaniment on the first night, with the Temple "court of the women" illuminated and observers' galleries erected (a separate one being provided for women). The festivity, song and dance, lasted until dawn. At dawn a procession made its way to the eastern gate of the compound, and turned to face the Temple, which was west of them. They said, "At this place our fathers 'stood with their backs to the Temple and their faces looking eastward and they prostrated themselves eastward to the sun' (Ezek. 8.1 b), but, as for us, our eyes are unto the Lord."[27] With the destruction of the Temple, these ceremonies ended, but aspects appropriate to the synagogue (for example, the use of etrog and lulav) abided.

The seventh day is called Hōshaná Rabbá ("the great

hosanna"[28]). This name is younger than was the practice of a
procession about the steps of the altar before the Temple,
with the repetition of Psalm 118.25, "Save now, O Lord;
cause us now to prosper."[29] In the synagogue, it was commemorated in processions (*hakkafōt*, "circular walks")
around the *almēmar* ("desk"), in the center of the synagogue, where the prayers were read.

Scripture had prescribed the festival for a period of seven
days (Lev. 23.33-36). Yet verse 36 speaks of an *'atzéret* ("assembly") on the eighth day; an additional injunction (vv.
39-43) speaks in verse 39 of the first and eighth days each as
entailing a "Sabbath." There is, accordingly, a surface un-
clarity in Scripture as to the duration of the festival, whether
for seven or eight days; a number of explanations have been
offered.[30] In Rabbinic times the atzeret became incorporated
as the eighth day of Sukkot, and is called Sheminí Atzéret
("eighth day of solemn assembly").

When additional days were added to the festivals, a ninth
day was added to Sukkot, called in the Talmud[31] simply the
"second day of Shemini Atzeret." In very much later times
this ninth day came to be called *simhát toráh*, "the rejoicing
in the Torah," a term unknown in the Talmud.

The injunctions for Sukkot in Leviticus 23.41-43 prescribe
that all natives to Israel are to dwell in the sūkkā̌ for seven
days because the Israelites had dwelled in sukkot when God
had brought them out of Egypt. No such narrative exists.
However, Exodus 12.37 speaks of the Exodus journey from
Raamses to Sukkot, and 13.20 of the journey from Sukkot
to the edge of the Wilderness. The Leviticus passage not only
alters the place name into a term for booths, but, even more
significantly, transforms a thanksgiving festival into an observance of a historic occasion. Comparably, all Jewish sacred
days except Yom Kippur came to be viewed as commemora-
tions of historical events.

The home sukka was a rude building made of foliage.
Mishna Sukkot 1 and 2 provide in detail the building specifications as to size and roofing and inner supports, and the requisite rules for eating and sleeping in the sukka, and what to
do if by chance rain falls (for rain ought not fall during
Sukkot).[32]

5

SHAVUOT

There is no Mishna tractate on Shavuot ("Weeks"). The biblical name Weeks (Exod. 34.22; Deut. 16.10; 2 Chron. 8.13) does not appear in the Talmud, nor does its biblical synonym, *Bikkurím* ("first fruits," Num. 28.26). It is spoken of in Mishnaic passages[33] as an atzeret, for it was conceived of as "closing" the Passover, as we see presently. First, we notice that an injunction in Deuteronomy 16.10 calls for this festival to come "seven weeks from the time when you first put the sickle to the standing grain," as if the festival depended not on a fixed calendar date, but on the state of the crops. Second, there is a prescription found in Leviticus 23.9-21 which brings Shavuot into relation with Passover in quite a complicated way. The injunction involves a "wave[34] offering," the daily bringing of flour from an *ómer*, a "sheaf" of barley, in this case the first fruits of the harvest.[35] The omer offering was to have been brought first on the "morrow after the sabbath" in Passover week. From that date of bringing the omer seven weeks[36] were to be counted (that is, equaling forty-nine days), and on the fiftieth day was the festival of Shavuot. In this sense, Weeks can be spoken of as the "closing" of Passover. Greek Jews and Christians called it Pentecost, meaning fifty.

We have already mentioned (p. 158) the dispute between the Pharisees and the Boethusians (a Sadducean family), with the Pharisees interpreting "sabbath" as the first day of Passover, and the Boethusians,[37] consistent with the literalism of the Sadducees, interpreting "sabbath" as the Sabbath during Passover.[38] Was there more to this dispute than the mere matter of one date? Scholars have believed this to be the case.[39] It is to be observed that the view of the Pharisees takes a rather extreme liberty in interpreting "sabbath" as other than the Sabbath. Why? Possibly, or probably, because what was at stake was the use of marginal groups of Jews of a calendar quite out of accord with that found in Leviticus 23. Such a deviant calendar is found in Jubilees and the Dead

Sea Scrolls; it may well have been used even more widely. Accordingly, the Pharisees were concerned not so much about a single date as to counter a broad set of practices by marginal groups uncongenial to them.

Shavuot in time came to have its own historic association, not found in Scripture; it came to be viewed as the anniversary of the occasion at Sinai when the Ten Commandments were given.[40] The historicizing of the festival in this way appears to have had the particular aim of diverting it from the grain harvest festival that it had been. Unlike Passover, with its seder and the home obligation of removing the last traces of anything leavened, or Sukkot with its home observance within the leafy structure, Weeks is not marked by any special or notable observance. The absence of a Mishna tractate may be due to the supposition that the tractate *Betzá* (the "egg," see p. 109), which was about all three of the festivals, was sufficient.

Once the dating of Weeks was established through interpreting "sabbath" as the first day of Passover,[41] it could and did become fixed in the lunar-solar calendar, this as the sixth day of Sivan.[42]

As to the forty-nine days of "counting the omer," in the Bible omer means both a field sheaf of grain and also a dry measure, the equivalent, roughly, of two dry quarts. Rabbinic interpretation (Menahot 68b) veered away from sheaf to the dry measure, with the result that reaped grain was deemed the appropriate form of the "wave offering." In such later times, the period of the counting of the omer became marked by restrictions, such as prohibitions against marriage and haircutting, though precisely why is unknown. For the thirty-third day (in Hebrew 33 is *lg*, expanded into the word *lag*), these restrictions are abandoned.[43]

6

ḤANUKKA AND PURIM

Two festivals are minor, in the sense that the ordinary restrictions, such as the prohibition of labor, do not apply.

Pūrim, known also as the "Feast of Esther" comes on the fourteenth day of Adar. While the basis for the observance is scriptural (Esther 9.27-28), that passage does not contain specific injunctions about the observance, and it does not mention sacrifices at the Temple. Rather, the day was to be marked by "feasting and joy and the exchange of gifts" (Esther 9.22-23). An injunction in Esther 9.18-19 describes a difference in the date observance; people living in villages or unwalled towns kept the day on the fourteenth, but those in fortified cities on the fifteenth. There is a Talmudic tractate, called Megilla ("scroll," that is, the "Scroll of Esther") which clarifies the regulations of the public reading of the Scroll of Esther.[44]

Inasmuch as the Apocrypha, in which I and II Maccabees are found, were not part of the Hebrew Bible, there is from the viewpoint of the Rabbis, no scriptural basis for the second of the minor festivals, Ḥanūkkā ("dedication"[45]). In I Maccabees 4.59 and II Maccabees 10.6-8 there are mentions of eight-day observances (patterned after Sukkot). There is no single Talmudic tractate about Ḥanūkkā, but various mentions and prescriptions for observance are found throughout the literature.[46] The Talmudic basis for the observance is a legend that tells the following: When the Hasmoneans recovered possession of the Temple from the Syrian Greeks, they wished to restore it to purity, and to rekindle the perpetual light, but there was available only one tiny vial of uncontaminated oil. Miraculously, though, this tiny vial burned for eight days. The next year the anniversary of this miracle of the vial was observed,[47] and thereafter the observance became standard. Hanukka begins on the twenty-fifth day of Kislev. The major observance is the kindling of a lamp in the home, each of the eight nights.[48] The Rabbinic observance, to repeat, rests not on the Hasmonean military achievements— these are not recounted at all—but strictly on the miracle of the vial of oil.

There are scattered allusions to some other minor festivals[49] which ultimately fell into disuse.

7

THE NEW YEAR

Rósh Ha-Shaná ("beginning of the year"), the New Year Day, served, and serves, in a variety of ways. Though not enjoined in Scripture as a pilgrim occasion, as are Passover, Tabernacles, and Pentecost, it is nevertheless a festival. Since it falls on the first day of Tishre it is also a New Moon observance. It is also intimately connected with the penitential system; the period from the New Year through the day before the Day of Atonement (from Tishre 1 through Tishre 9) is known as "The Ten Days of Repentance." Moreover, the New Year had implications for such secular matters as the dating of legal documents, as we shall see. The diversity of conceptions that center in the New Year can create problems in comprehension.

It can come as a surprise that the biblical data about the New Year are relatively scant. Moreover there is evidence of the reflection in the biblical material of diverse calendars, and hence diverse ways of setting the date for the New Year. In brief, originally the New Year appears to have come in connection with a totally solar calendar on the occasion of the spring equinox (in our calendar, March 21 or 22). After the transition in the biblical period to a solar-lunar calendar, the New Year was shifted away from the spring, and set as the first day of the seventh month, Tishre. If it is somewhat illogical for New Year's day to come in the seventh month, the explanation may well be that the shift from the spring equinox was designed to disconnect the day from all facets of the worship of the sun, such as is known to have occurred on equinoctial days.

Yet even before the shift in dating, the New Year was apparently conceived of as the annual day of God's judgment; though this is not specifically stated in Scripture. The clearest biblical statement about the New Year is the brief passage in Leviticus 23.23-24; it sets the date as the first day of the

seventh month, and terms it a "sabbatical [day], of Memorial and *Terū'ā* ('trumpet sound'?), a day of Solemn
Assembly." In Numbers 29.1, the same content appears,
though the wording is altered. Numbers 29.2-6 proceeds to
the details of the obligatory sacrifice and its accompanying
requirements of a grain offering. The two passages (Lev.
23.23-24 and Num. 29.1-6) are the sole clear commandments
but, curiously, neither uses the phrase "New Year Day."
Psalm 81, especially verse 3, "Sound the trumpet on the new
moon, on the full moon for the day of our festival," was
brought into relationship and became conceived of, as it is
today, as a psalm for the New Year.

The tendency in Scripture to associate sacred days with
past historical occasions fails to occur there respecting the
New Year. Rabbinic thought made good this lack, conceiving
of the New Year as the anniversary of Creation.[50] Yet in the
sense that each new year recreates the years gone by, there
is also a sense in which the New Year Day implies an act
kindred to creation; that is, as at Creation God determined
what was to operate in the future, so on the New Year Day
He determines what is to operate in the coming year. In
Rabbinic thought, the New Year Day is the Day of Judgment, quite as much as it is the anniversary of Creation.
Since God is the Judge, presiding in His heavenly court,
courtroom figures of speech increasingly embellish the New
Year. There are, indeed, four days of divine Judgment: on
Passover the fate of agricultural yield is decided; on Pentecost, that of fruit trees; on Tabernacles, rain; on the New
Year Day[51] "all mankind passes before [God] like young
lambs."[52] The notion that all mankind undergoes individual
judgment supposed that the heavenly account-book, in which
each human's deeds during the preceding year have been recorded, is consulted, and on the basis of the past record God
makes his decision for the year to come. (The heavenly book
is mentioned in Exod. 32.32; Dan. 12.1; and elsewhere.)
God, as Psalms 33.15 declares, understands all the deeds of
men, for He has fashioned alike the hearts of all men.

On the basis of the record of the past year, clearly some
men were wicked beyond forgiveness and some righteous beyond condemnation. In between these extremes are those

who might merit either forgiveness or condemnation. While on the New Year God indeed determines the fate of all men, it is not until the Day of Atonement that His decision becomes sealed and final. Hence, those in the middle category have the intervening Ten Days of Repentance in which to appeal to God to cancel or reverse whatever individual adverse judgment He has arrived at on the New Year.[53]

The repentance should commence on the New Year in association with its character as the Day of the Trumpet-Blast. In the synagogue liturgy, a threefold prayer arose in connection with the ceremony of the trumpet. A *shōfár* ("ram's horn") rather than a metal instrument was, and is, used. The first prayer, *malchūyót* ("sovereignty"), extols God as the sole sovereign of the world. The second, *zichronót* ("remembrances"), implores God to recollect His past beneficences and the worthy deeds of the patriarchs. The third, *shōfarót* (plural of shōfár) expresses compliance with God's will. In due course, the testing of Abraham (Gen. 22.1-19) became associated with the New Year in that Abraham, on being told to desist from his obedient intention to sacrifice Isaac, saw a ram caught in a thicket by his horns; the shofar of the New Year calls to mind the ram's horn and hence Abraham's unreserved obedience.

As to the musical notes to be sounded on the shofar, much about this is obscure. A passage (Mishna Rosh Hashana 4.9) speaks of three types of sounds, *tekī'á*, *shebarím*, and *terū'á*, apparently entailing blasts of different length or of form. As these blasts later developed, the tekia was a single, long note, shebarim a series of three sets of tonic-dominant,[54] and terua a quickly repeated set of nine (or tonic sounds numbering twelve), but ending on the dominant. If the New Year fell on a Sabbath, the shofar was not blown (this being deferred to the next day), lest the man who was to blow it might improperly carry it, and such carrying was a Sabbath violation. (In later times, the shofar liturgy became expanded and more elaborate.)

As mentioned, the New Year Day served in a secular way for the dating of documents. It is this function that the opening Mishna of Rosh Hashna has in mind in speaking of the "New Year for kings." The Seleucidian calendar had been adopted, as is evident in connection with the dates that are found in I Maccabees. To understand the New Year for kings, in our terms, let us suppose that Nisan 1 fell on March 25 and that a new king had ascended the throne on February 5. That king's first regnal year was reckoned from February 5 to March 25; on March 25 he entered his second regnal year. Since legal documents bore the number of the regnal year, the "New Year for kings" was the dividing point between regnal years, however much less than a full year the first regnal year might have been. The new Nisan 1 also served as the month in which to take into account the travel plans for the three pilgrimage festivals, the first of which, Passover, falls on Nisan 14; the point appears to have been to elicit an alertness to the importance of the three pilgrimage festivals. Another New Year was Elul 1, on which occasion the tithe ("tenth") of animals was to be reckoned; that is, it was the date on which it was fixed how many animals one possessed, since a tenth of them was to be given to the Temple. (Two eminent Sages preferred Tishre 1 for the animal tithes.)

Tishre 1 served as the New Year for reckoning the date of the *shmittā* ("sabbatical year"); every seventh year planting was prohibited, and accrued debts canceled (Exod. 23.10-11; Lev. 25.2-7; Deut. 15.1-6). It served also for reckoning the Jubilee year (Lev. 25.8-28), which was to be proclaimed by a trumpet-blast on the Day of Atonement.[55] Tishre 1 served also as the agricultural New Year, respecting the tithing of produce, and the determination of the three-year period during which fruit of a new tree is not to be eaten. Yet when once a tree was old enough for its fruit to be eaten and its tithe to be given, a New Year for trees (as distinct from vegetables) was needed. The Academy of Shammai preferred Shebat 1, the Academy of Hillel Shebat 15.[56]

Yet Tishre 1 as the anniversary of Creation and Day of Judgment emerged as the most significant and lasting characteristic of the New Year.

· 9 ·

PENITENCE

AND FAST-DAYS

The fast-day[1] preeminent over all the others was Yóm Kippúr, the Day of Atonement.[2] It is enjoined in Scripture (Lev. 16.16, 19; 23.26-32; Ezek. 45.18-20) as a day of penitence, but not specifically as a fast. The words in Leviticus 23.26 and 32, "you shall afflict yourselves," led to the interpretation that they meant a fast. An elaborate ritual for the Temple, including the use of two goats, as "scapegoats," is enjoined. The Mishna Yōmá ("The Day," that is, the Day of Atonement) and the Midrash Sifra recapitulate and amplify the Temple requirements found in Scripture.

Yom Kippur was never enjoined as an occasion of pilgrimage to the Temple, as were the festivals, yet the proximity of Yom Kippur to Booths (Yom Kippur coming on Tishre 10 and Booths beginning on Tishre 15), meant that quite likely it attracted pilgrims who were coming for Booths.

Yom Kippur is called in Leviticus 23.32 a "sabbath of sabbaths." The natural meaning of the phrase implied the preeminent sanctity of the day; the consequence was a series of expanded requirements and prohibitions beyond the rather general prescriptions of Scripture.[3] Mishna Yoma 8.1 lists as prohibitions on the Day of Atonement eating, drinking, bathing, and marital sex relations. The precise amount of food or drink the consumption of which would constitute a trespass against the commandment to fast is specified: a mouthful of water, or a solid the size of a large pitted date (Yoma 8.2), provided, though, that these were consumed in forgetfulness and not deliberately. Children were exempted from fasting, but they were expected to prepare for their full fasting at maturity by partial fasting before maturity. A pregnant woman or a sick person craving nourishment could be given some food (Yoma 8.5).

The Rabbinic view of the day is best expressed in this quotation from Yoma 8.9: "He who thinks that he may [deliberately] sin and repent over and over achieves no atonement. He who thinks that he may deliberately sin and that the Day will bring him atonement, does not achieve atonement by means of the Day. The Day of Atonement brings no atonement for trespasses against one's fellow man unless one has first made an acceptable reconciliation with his fellow man. R. Eleazar ben Azariah inferred from [the scriptural passage, Lev. 16.39] 'From all your sin you will be cleansed before the Lord,' that the Day effects atonement for trespasses against God, but trespasses against a fellow man require an acceptable reconciliation with his fellow man."[4]

The Synagogue worship in the course of time became complex and full, entailing an evening sundown worship service and an unbroken dawn-to-dusk series of services conjoined to each other. In the transition from the Temple to the Synagogue worship there was one subtle alteration: in the Temple observance the ritual of atonement was performed by a priest on behalf of the corporate people, but in the synagogue worship the congregation, and each individual in the congregation, made his own atonement for himself.

Both the Hebrew language of the Bible and the modified Hebrew of the Rabbis lack a clear distinction which can be made in English between sin and guilt, a distinction significant for our understanding. To some extent sin and guilt can be separated in that a sin is an improper act or action, while guilt, strictly speaking, is the penalty that should be imposed because of the improper deed. The prayers on Yom Kippur center quite as much on guilt (though the word is not prominent) as on sins themselves; the prayers in reality become efforts to shed guilt. The Yom Kippur worship includes both the confession by the individual of the sins he has committed and also his prayer for divine forgiveness, in effect a prayer that his guilt be removed.

The courtroom imagery pervades the worship. God, of course, is the Judge. The trial of each individual is depicted

as having opened on the New Year; on Yom Kippur the verdict—the penalty for guilt—is deemed to have been finally
confirmed and a divine seal put upon the Judge's verdict. The
destiny of every man—who is to die, who to live; who is to
become rich, who poor—is accordingly, finally determined
on the Day of Atonement. As we said (p. 221), the judgment
was deemed to have been tentatively settled for each man on
the New Year Day.[5] The total period from the New Year
through the eve of Atonement are the Ten Days of Penitence.
On Yom Kippur God affirms, that is, "seals," the judgment
arrived at on the New Year, but He can set aside this judgment when it is one of punishment, especially of dire punishment, if the individual will undergo earnest and thorough
repentance for the previous year's trespasses. The confession
of sins, genuine remorse for misdeeds, and the high resolve to
avoid trespass in the future are the means by which the individual makes his personal atonement. In the Rabbinic view,
man sins; man atones; God, if he wishes, forgives. There is
a traditional phrase that runs as follows: Repentance, prayer,
and righteousness can nullify an unfavorable divine decree.

The view that the destiny of each man is predetermined
by God is only superficially similar to the Greek view of
fate. Fate was a blind force which dictated what was to
happen to men and gods alike, and what was fated could not
be altered. It is different too from the view known as pre-
destination, which, in a sense, is kindred to fate except that it
is God who fixes the unalterable fate. The Jewish view—we
might call it providence[6]—never concluded that a totally unalterable future lay ahead, for such a view contradicted God's
omnipotence and mercy. Nor did the view that God fixed a
man's destiny eliminate either man's free will or his moral
responsibility; if, philosophically, a doctrine of providence
and a doctrine of free will and moral responsibility seem contradictory (as, when carried to extremes, they are), Jewish
thought never so extended either doctrine so as to preclude
the other. The dictum of Rabbi Akiba is in effect an affirmation of the two contradictory sentiments: "All is subject to
providence, yet man possesses free will."[7] Unless God's proposed destiny for a man is subject to alteration, prayer to
God to institute such alternation is nonsensical. Basic to the

Ten Days of Penitence in general, and to the Day of Atonement in particular, was the conviction that man could choose what his actions could be (and was morally responsible) and, in having in the past sinned and acquired guilt, he could in the present appeal to God for mercy[8] in the future.

Biblical fast days lamenting the catastrophe of the Babylonian conquest included four days which were observed during the period of the Babylonian exile, and then abandoned.[9] After the destruction of the Temple in 70, these four fast days were revived. They were Tammuz 17,[10] Tishre 3,[11] Ab 9,[12] and Tebet 10.[13] The Ab 9 fast became a fast-day second in eminence only to Yom Kippur.[14] While labor on that day was not universally prohibited, there were local areas where it was, and eminent Sages advocated it.[15]

It is recorded in Esther 4.3 and 16 that still another fast-day, one in which Esther herself took part, had become desirable. Adar 13, the day before Purim, gained some broad currency as "The Fast of Esther."

In Rabbinic times quite an abundance of fast-days, and imaginative anniversaries they were presumed to commemorate, arose.[16] In later times even more fast-days came to be added, especially in local areas and situations, and periods of quasi-mourning, less than true fasts, arose (such as the first nine days of Ab). But the universal public fasts were ordinarily those specified above.

If a fast-day (except Yom Kippur) fell on a Sabbath, it was deferred until Sunday. Private fasts, imposed by a person upon himself, are recorded, but were not viewed with favor, and, in the case of scholars, were discouraged.[17] The purpose of fasting was to appeal to God. It was likened to the offering of one's own blood and fat on the altar of the Temple (Berachot 17b).

· 10 ·

PROSELYTIZING

In the Rabbinic literature Father Abraham is often depicted as the master missionary. Words and phrases from the biblical account are in the Midrash made ingeniously consistent with this theme: Abraham converted men, Sarah women.[1] This haggadic view of Abraham as the missionary could scarcely have arisen had there not existed some disposition in at least some segments of Jewry that looked favorably either on an active quest for proselytes or, at least on the reception into the faith of those who on their own sought conversion.

Biblical passages provided a clear sanction for converting outsiders. The visions in Isaiah 2.2-4 and Micah 4.1-3 spoke of the peoples of the world flowing to the "mountain of the house of the Lord," there to learn God's way, "For out of Zion comes revealed teaching and the word of the Lord from Jerusalem." A comparable passage, Zechariah 8.20-23, ends with these words: "In those days ten men from the nations speaking every language will take hold of the garment of a Jew, saying, 'Let us go with you, for we have heard that God is with you.'" Mention is made in Isaiah 56.3 of the "son of the *nochri* ("foreigner") who has joined himself to the Lord"; such a person is not to think that God has kept him apart from His people. In Jonah 1.16, the Gentile sailors, after the calming of the storm, "revered the Lord thoroughly and offered sacrifices to him and made vows"; what sort of vows taken is not specified, but clearly the author is portraying the sailors as having become worshippers of Jonah's God.

Intermarriage with Canaanites is expressly forbidden in Deuteronomy 7.3, and extended beyond Canaanites in Ezra 9.1-2; 10.10-11 and Nehemiah 10.31. In I Kings 11.1-13,

Solomon violated divine injunctions and married an abundance of alien women who "turned his heart away towards other gods." Clearly Scripture looked askance at intermarriage. Yet a Moses and a Samson were among those who had seemed to marry out of the faith. The Rabbinic explanation of such instances was quite simple; their brides had antecedently become converts to Judaism!

The words of Ruth to Naomi (Ruth 2.16-17) were crystal clear: "Where you go, I will go; your people is my people, and your God is my God. . . ." In the Midrash to Ruth, Naomi instructs Ruth in the obligations involved in conversion, and Ruth complies with them.

There is nothing in Judaism comparable to the "Great Commission" which closes the Gospel According to Matthew: "Therefore go and make disciples of all nations. . . ." There is no direct surviving evidence of Jewish missionaries such as the Christian missionaries mentioned in the Epistles of Paul and Acts of the Apostles. It is perhaps correct to characterize Judaism, in contrast to Christianity, as relatively non-proselytizing. Yet, as the Rabbinic view of Abraham demonstrates, there was at least a recurrent, at least sporadic, thrust toward it.

Indeed, the royal heads of Adiabene (in what is now Armenia) had become converted to Judaism, and apparently so had many of their subjects. Josephus[2] gives a rather long account of the matter. A Jewish merchant, Ananias, taught the king's wives to worship God in the Jewish manner, and thereby won the favorable attention of the crown prince Izates. The mother of Izates, Helena, had, quite separately, been brought to Judaism by another Jew. When Izates learned of Helena's conversion, he was eager to become circumcised. Helena tried to dissuade him, for this act could lead to the disaffection of many of their subjects who would not tolerate having a foreigner, a Jew, rule over them. Ananias agreed with Helena; moreover, God would forgive Izates if he abstained from the rite through the fear of his subjects. Izates did not become circumcised at that time. Yet later, another Jew, an Eleazar from Galilee, found Izates reading the Law of Moses, and Eleazar urged him to observe the laws, rather than merely reading them. Izates thereupon became circumcised. When Izates, and later his children, were threatened by dangers, God protected them.

Several considerations of significance were involved in the conversion of Gentiles to Judaism (some of these considerations applying also to conversion to Christianity). Physical proximity and contact were, of course, a pre-condition. Judea, as we have said, was dotted with Grecian cities, and hence both Greeks and also non-Greeks from various areas of the Grecian world were to be found in Judea. Outside Judea there were innumerable Jewish communities, some small, some very large, throughout the then known world. Judaism, whether in Judea or outside, constituted a *politeia*, an entity with its own inner government and organization, so that conversion to Judaism included reception into the Jewish political entity, a body more or less foreign respecting other peoples. In the array of the many religions in the Greek world, this "political" aspect of Judaism was unique. Moreover, there existed no exact counterpart to the Bible, a sacred library which declared that the one God, Who alone merited worship and Who demanded the exclusive worship of Him, had revealed the divine laws by which the faithful were to live. Hence, Judaism was not simply one more cult with a set of religious ideas which could be incorporated into the blendings of the multiple religions of the age; rather, it was, in its own eyes, the one true religion, which, on acceptance, needed to supplant the practices or loyalties which a would-be convert had antecedently been committed to. The Bible had to become the Bible of the convert.

From the perspective of a Gentile in the Greek world, Judaism partook of the character of both a religion and a philosophy. The synagogue, with its instructional system, and its worship in which Scripture was explained, was kindred to a philosophical school, with the explanation of Scripture (the sermon) kindred to a philosophical discourse. The ethical precepts were kindred to the virtues lauded in the various philosophical schools.

Foremost of all, the claims made on behalf of Judaism presented an assurance of certainty as contrasted with the uncertainties of both the religions and the philosophical systems, and the precise prescriptions of the rules of conduct as contrasted with the vagueness of the philosophical ethical precepts. Moreover, Jews such as Philo of Alexandria, as we shall see, contended that that which was worthy in the Gentile environment, such as the legacy from Plato, was contained within Judaism, and, indeed, that Plato had derived his wisdom from Moses. For Philo, Abraham was the model of the convert who abandoned his pagan legacy, in his case astrology, and became a worshipper of the true God.

The steps by which a Gentile became a convert, after some exposure and knowledge, came to include two major rites.[3] One was baptism (immersion in water) and the other, circumcision, from which women were of course exempt.

The origin of proselyte baptism is unknown. Scripture prescribes ritual bathing for purification from uncleanness.[4] Possibly proselyte baptism is by analogy a cleansing of oneself from antecedent defilement. Yet the Rabbinic literature gives no explanation of the meaning of the requirement. The baptism follows the circumcision, and occurs when healing has taken place.[5]

Since adult circumcision was painful, it was conceivably a deterrent to a would-be male convert. Perhaps the relatively greater number of women converts is explainable by the lack of the need for circumcision. The demands of Paul for conversion did not include circumcision, and conceivably the success of the Christian missionary enterprise profited enormously from the absence of this requirement.

Older scholarly literature speaks of "semi-proselytes," Gentiles, especially women, who seem to have attended synagogue worship and even adopted aspects of Jewish practice. It is to be questioned[6] that the term semi-proselyte is appropriate; one was either a convert or not, and there is little to be gained from using the term for what we might describe as "interested but undecided outsiders."

The Rabbis use the word *gēr* for a convert. It is a biblical word, there meaning a foreigner who has moved to the Holy Land on a permanent basis; the temporary sojourner was a *tōshāb*. In passages in Scripture the ger was fully responsible for the requirements, religious and civil, of the Torah: "You

shall have one system of justice, the ger and the native born
being alike. . . ." (Lev. 24.22). Ordinarily the Rabbis append the word *tzédek* ("righteousness") in speaking of an
acceptable, admired convert.[7]

Attitudes are inevitably affected by historical circumstances. The Jewish writings exhibit both a warm receptivity
to would-be converts, on the one hand, and, on the other
hand, a reluctance that almost smacks of rejection. During
the so-called Hadrianic persecutions at the time of the Bar
Kochba rebellion (about A.D. 132), there were converts to
Judaism who escaped the Roman cruelties by becoming informers,[8] disclosing to Roman authorities the violators of the
Roman prohibition of circumcision. Earlier, in the prosperous days of the Maccabeans, there were in all likelihood ambitious foreign settlers who wished to rise in the social world
of the court and who converted for that purpose. There were
also those Gentiles whose direct motive was to be acceptable
as the husband or wife of a Jewish spouse. If the motive of a
convert was social eminence or social acceptance, it could
seem less than pure. A distrust of the motives of some
would-be converts, or else a dismal experience with the converted, gave rise to a reluctance to seek them out, or to receive them when they came on their own.

The Talmudic passage (Yebamot 47a-b) which beyond
all others became more or less a norm for subsequent times
reads as follows:

*When, at the present, a man comes to convert, he is to be
asked, "What reason do you have for converting? Do you not
know that now Israel is persecuted and oppressed, hated,
harassed, and afflicted?" If he replies, "I know, and I am unworthy [of acceptance]," he is immediately accepted and he
is instructed in some of the less important and some of the
more important commandments. . . . He is also told the
punishment for trespassing the commandments. Also, he is
told, "You must know that prior to now, if you ate the fat [of
forbidden animals], you were not liable to the punishment of
excision.[9] If now you were to profane the Sabbath, you would
be punished by being stoned." At the same time as he is informed about the punishment for violations, he is also in-*

*formed about the rewards for fulfilling the commandments:
"Be informed that the world to come exists only for the
righteous; in the present, Israel does not acquire either great
prosperity or great suffering."*[10] *The dialogue is not to be extended, nor is it to go into an excess of details. If he is still
willing to accept [the implication of conversion], he is forth-
with to be circumcised. If in the circumcision the cutting is
not as complete as it should be, he is circumcised a second
time. As soon as he is healed, it is arranged for him to be baptized, with two Sages present to acquaint him with some less
important and more important commandments. On emerging
from his baptism he is considered an Israelite in every way.
In the case of a woman, there are to be women present who
have her sit in water up to her neck while two Sages stand
outside and instruct her in some minor and major commandments.*

The favorable receptivity to proselytes is often expressed
in legends which attribute to eminent Sages a descent from
proselytes, or in anecdotes which exhibit a welcome to them.
The best known of such anecdotes contrasts Hillel and Shammai. A would-be proselyte approached Shammai, offering to
convert if he could be taught the Torah in a jiffy (literally,
while standing on one foot). Shammai drove him off. He
then approached Hillel, who accepted him as a convert, saying "Do not do to others what you would not have them do to
you. That is the essence of Torah. All the rest is explanation
of it. Go, learn it" (Shabbat 31 a).

A passage (Ruth Rabbah II) contains an injunction based
on the triple use of Naomi's words of Orpah and Ruth: "Go
back, my daughter" (Ruth 1.5, 11, 12). A would-be convert
should be deterred three times. If thereafter he still persists,
he is to be accepted. In the same source Rabbi Isaac is quoted
to the effect that the left hand should repel the would-be convert, but the right hand should bring him near.

There has come down from the period a Christian work
known as the Didache ("Teaching"), called in Christian
sources "The Teaching of the Twelve Apostles." The first six
of its twenty chapters, alluded to as "The Two Ways," are
usually regarded by modern scholars as Jewish in origin.

The content is moral, in the form of instruction to would-be converts. The exact date of the work is not readily to be determined.[11] The Didache is at times alluded to as a manual for Jewish missionaries, but perhaps the phrase claims a bit too much.

Apostasy—the abandonment of a religion—is by definition distinct from heresy—the holding of views by insiders which co-religionists consider wrong. However, the two tend to be regarded as almost similar, even though a heretic has not necessarily abandoned the religion he had adhered to.

In the pre-Maccabean period, apparently apostasy in upper class circles was reasonably well known.[12] In Rabbinic times apostates are mentioned only passingly. The "denier" of the divine origin of Scripture was clearly no longer a believing Jew, but it did not necessarily mean that he had embraced a different religion. A nephew of Philo of Alexandria, Tiberius Julius Alexander, became an apostate and rose high in Roman circles; he was named the procurator of Judea in A.D. 46, and later became the prefect of his native Alexandria in Egypt. He also became the prefect of the army of Titus which put down the Judean rebellion in 70.[13] On the other hand, the Sage Elisha ben Abuya, who became a "denier" as a result of his entry into esoteric philosophy, retained the affection and loyalty of his student Rabbi Meir, and appears never to have joined another religion; heretic, not apostate, is the appropriate word for Elisha. It is rather surprising how infrequently apostasy is mentioned in the Rabbinic literature.

For what is presently to follow there is little confirming evidence, and rests on logic, rather than on ancient sources or documents. That Christianity succeeded in ultimately becoming the dominant religion in the Roman world is to be explained by factors such as the following: Its way had been prepared by a Jewish missionary impulse, so that it did not have to begin from scratch. It demanded of converts neither circumcision nor the observance of the regimen of mitzvot and halacha. It called on the same Scripture, which Jews did, in support of its contentions, and it set itself forth as the True Israel of God.

To what extent Jews in the Graeco-Roman world apsota-sized to Christianity is unknown. In Paul's time there was, by his own testimony, little such Jewish apostasy. Yet the hypothesis may be tenable that after 70 and after the up-risings of Jews in the Greek world about 112, and the Bar Kochba rebellion in 132, such apostasy became frequent. To a great extent hellenistic Jewry, which we will describe later, appears to have undergone dissolution and ultimate disap-pearance. Clearly it lacked survival force. Whether it disap-peared by apostasy to paganism or to Christianity is un-known, but it is the latter which seems the more likely, for the step from Judaism to Christianity was not as long as the step from Judaism to paganism.

From the Greek world there have survived texts which are usually called "magical" and which appear to reflect a com-bination of Jewish and pagan elements. Whether the users of these texts were Jews or Gentiles, or a mixture of marginal Jews and Gentiles, is uncertain. Not enough is known about them to determine whether or not they reflected missionary impulses. Fascinating as such matters are, they can here only be mentioned in the interest of completeness.[14]

· 11 ·

THE EMINENT SAGES

Religions are carried by people. Our survey of Rabbinic Judaism would be incomplete without brief sketches of some of the men of eminence who figure in the Rabbinic Literature. About such figures legends arose, and clearly some of the material to be presented is scarcely historically accurate and reliable; that, however, is not a matter of legitimate concern, for the goal here is to reflect the role of these men as the tradition viewed them, and the legends are as useful for that purpose as would be historical reliability, with which modern desideratum the ancient sources were not at all concerned.

The "chain" of Sages is presented in Chapters of the Fathers: Moses received the Torah on Mount Sinai, and handed it over to Joshua, and Joshua to the Elders, and the Elders to the Prophets, and the Prophets to the men of the Great Assembly.[1] The latter "said three things: 'Be deliberate in judgment; raise up many disciples; build a fence around the Torah.' " Simeon the Just[2] "was one of the last survivors of the Great Assembly"; his disciple was Antigonos of Soko. That is, the Sages are viewed as reflecting an unbroken continuity.

Now the text turns to *zūgŏt*, a succession of "pairs" of Sages (Jose ben Joezer of Zeredah and Jose ben Johanan of Jerusalem; next Joshua ben Peraḥya and Nittai of Arbelos; then Judah ben Tabbai and Simeon ben Shēlah; thereafter Shemaiah and Abtalion). Each pair "received the tradition" from their predecessors. After Shemaiah and Abtalion there came Hillel and Shammai, the last of the "pairs."

HILLEL

Of all the almost countless Sages mentioned in Rabbinic literature, Hillel is surely preeminent, in that his life, career, and teachings made him the model to be emulated. By birth a Babylonian, he was very poor. He "went up"[3] to Judea at the age of forty, during the reign of Herod (37-4 B.C.) for the express purpose of study.[4] It is presupposed that there already existed an Academy presided over by Shemaiah and Abtalion, who were, respectively, president and vice president of the Sanhedrin. Repeating here, admission to the Academy was dependent on the payment of a fee; Hillel lacked the funds, for his odd jobs brought barely enough income for his immediate needs. Unable to pay to enter the lecture hall, he climbed onto a "skylight" where he could hear but not see. At night—it was the winter solstice—a heavy snowfall covered him. In the morning Shemaiah remarked to Abtalion, "This room is always light, but today it is dark." Looking up, they perceived the body of a man. Some men ascended and found Hillel covered by three cubits of snow. They took him down, bathed and anointed him, and put him near the fire. They said of Hillel that he was worthy of having the Sabbath profaned on his behalf (Yoma 35b).

Hillel loved his fellow man as deeply as he loved the Torah, and he loved all literature of wisdom as much as he loved the Torah, neglecting no field of study. He used many foreign tongues and all areas of learning in order to magnify the Torah and exalt it (Soferim VII), and so inducted his students (Sukka 28a).

He had gone up to Judea to study lest what he had learned in Babylonia be out of accord with the conclusions of the great Sanhedrin in Jerusalem.[5] He was already learned in Scripture and halacha. He rose to eminence when he resolved a dispute occasioned by Passover falling on a Sabbath. (In a development obscure to us, the directorship of the Sanhedrin had passed from Shemaiah and Abtalion to certain Sages known as "sons of Bathyra"—an identification that remains enigmatic.) We saw above the account of Hillel and these sages (p. 142).

In popular acclaim Hillel was likened to the biblical Ezra, who had returned from Babylonia to restore the forgotten Torah (Sukkot 20a, based on Neh. ch. 8). It was, though, Hillel's love of his fellow man, and his irenic manner which elicited the great admiration for him. The sages said, "A man should always be gentle like Hillel, not irascible like Shammai." Two men agreed that if one of them succeeded in angering Hillel, the other was to pay him four hundred *zuzim;* if he failed, he was to give the money to the other. On a Friday afternoon, as Hillel was washing his hair, preparing for the Sabbath, the man asked at the door of Hillel's house if he could see Hillel. Hillel put on a robe and went to the man. "I have a question: why do the Babylonians have round heads?" Hillel replied, "They lack skillful midwives." A bit later, the man returned, and again Hillel put on his robe. The question this time was, "Why are the eyes of the [Syrian] Palmyrenes [who lived by a desert oasis] bleary?" Hillel replied, "Because they live where it is sandy." A third time the man interrupted Hillel's preparations for the Sabbath: "Why do Africans have broad feet?" He replied, "Because they live near wet marshes." The man said, "I have many more questions." Hillel said, "Ask them." The man said, "Because of you I have lost four hundred zuzim." Hillel said, "It would be better that you lose still another four hundred zuzim than that I lose my temper."

A heathen asked Shammai, "How many Torahs have you?" Shammai replied, "Two, the Written Torah and the Oral Torah." The heathen said, "I have confidence in the Written Torah. Convert me, but teach me only the Written Torah." Shammai angrily repulsed the man. He then went to Hillel, who accepted him, and began the instruction with the first four letters of the Hebrew alphabet (*áleph, bēt, gímmel, dállet*). At the second session, Hillel taught the letters in reverse order, and the man protested that that was not how he had been taught the previous day. Hillel said, "If you relied on me [about the sequence of the letters], you should also rely on me about the Oral Torah."[6]

Another heathen asked Shammai to convert him in order that he might be designated High Priest. Shammai drove him away. He went to Hillel, who accepted him, but told him he must study the art of government [as contained in Scripture]. The man encountered the biblical passage relating to the high priesthood that "the stranger who comes near shall be put to death" (Num. 1.51). He asked Hillel, "Would this passage apply to King David too?" Hillel said yes. The man thereupon reasoned that if a born Israelite could be ineligible for the high priesthood, how much more so would be a proselyte ineligible.

Later, heathens whom Hillel had accepted met together, concluding that Shammai's irascibility drove them "out of the world," but Hillel's gentleness had brought them under the wings of the Shechina.[7]

His sympathy for his fellow men was illustrated in the matter of charity to the impoverished. He taught that a man once rich who had fallen on evil days should be helped even in what for other poor people would seem luxuries, such as a horse to ride on (Ketubōt 67b). Again, a man should bathe his body to cleanse it; as the statues of pagan kings are washed, man, created in God's image, should also wash (Lev. Rabba 34.3).

The statements attributed to him in Chapters of the Fathers stress peace among men. ("Love peace and pursue it, love all fellow men, thereby bringing them near to the Torah.") "To seek to aggrandize one's name [that is, one's standing] is to lose it. Whoever does not constantly increase his knowledge decreases it. Whoever does not seek for wisdom cheapens his life, while to make unworthy use of one's learning is to waste one's gift." Respecting a sense of balance, he taught, "If I am not concerned for myself, who will be? Yet if I am concerned only for myself, what do I amount to?" As to when to respond to opportunity and challenge, he said, "If not now, then when?"

He was opposed to the "loner" who declined to partake in public endeavors. Because humans are unpredictable, he taught, "Do not trust in yourself until your death. Do not pass judgment on someone else until you yourself are in the same situation. The time to study is now, for if one defers study in the hopes of leisure, he may never have such leisure. A dull man cannot be alert to sin, nor an ignorant person pious. An insecure person is not apt to be a good student, nor an ill-tempered man a good teacher. Excessive preoccupation with business affairs is an impediment to wisdom. The more flesh [out of excess of food through wealth], the more worms [after death]. The more money one has, the more is his anxiety. The more Torah, the more life; the more understanding, the more counsel [one receives], the more understanding; the more righteousness, the more peace."

As to the contempt in which some hold their fellow men, he said, "Where there are no [real] men, you try to be a [real] man." Also, "Whoever acquires a [deserved] good name has enriched himself; whoever acquires knowledge of the Torah attains eternal life." His own pride, so he said, was his humility, and his humility was his pride.

He believed in divine retribution.[8] He had a deep feeling of God's presence. He spoke of God as saying to Israel, "If you come to My house [the Temple], I come to your house" (Sukkot 53 b).

In the realm of halacha, his fame rested not only on the seven norms he had drawn up (see p. 124) but also on another matter, which to our minds may seem very complex. Scriptural law (Deut. 15.1) supposed that at the sabbatical year all debts antecedently contracted would be canceled. A consequence was the broad disinclination to lend money—every society, especially the modern age, requires ways of financing—just prior to the sabbatical year. (Imagine our society if banks decided not to lend.) To Hillel the welfare of society[9] clearly was in jeopardy. The solution of the problem was to remove the fear on the part of possible lenders of the non-payment of debts owed to them. Hillel devised a legal form (the Hebraized word is *prosbul*, the Greek word probably being *prosboulē*) which exempted a given loan from cancelation.[10] In effect a biblical commandment was being annulled, and only a Sage as eminent as Hillel would have dared take such a step. Yet this action was justified on the basis of a biblical verse (Deut. 15.9), which enjoined against base thoughts, the indisposition to lend money being here viewed as base.

The Academy (*Bet Hillel*, "house of Hillel") over which Hillel presided was said to number either eighty disciples, or else eighty pairs of disciples.[11] A similar Academy was presided over by Shammai. The attitudes to Shammai in the literature include unlimited respect for his gifts of mind and his attainments, but Shammai is portrayed as personally irascible. He was as a halachist something of a strict constructionist and inelastic, while by contrast Hillel was elastic and concerned that the welfare of human beings not be harmed by excessively rigorous demands. In a sense, then, Hillel was liberal, and Shammai the opposite. So too were their respective academies. The Talmud records some three hundred and sixteen controversies[12] in interpretation between the schools; in some fifty-five instances, the Shammaites were more lenient than the Hillelites, but in the other two hundred and sixty-one, the Hillelites were more lenient. The views of the Hillelites became normative, and incorporated in the Mishna as the prevailing view in virtually every case.[13] The disputes were not always conducted amicably. But it is related that at Jamnia, where the disputes, and the decisions, were under review, a heavenly voice spoke. "The opinions of both academies are the voice of the living God; the halacha, however, is to follow the Academy of Hillel."[14] It is to be noted that the "voice of the living God" was deemed to apply to the rejected Shammaites.

Quite peculiarly, the generations between Hillel, whom we might date as around 20-10 B.C., and Rabbi Johanan ben Zakkai (A.D. 60-95) are passed over in silence in Chapters of the Fathers, Johanan being regarded as if a direct disciple of Hillel. The line from Hillel himself would appear to have been as follows:

Simeon I,[15] Hillel's son	(about A.D. 10-30)
Gamaliel I[16]	(about 30-50)
Simeon II	50-70
Gamaliel II	(about 80-110)
Simeon ben Gamaliel II	110-140
Judah the Prince	175-220

It is manifest that much is awry in this list, as it contains chronologically broken continuity, and therefore historical

problems. This is the case if one's concern is limited to the
Rabbinic literature alone; in the case of Gamaliel I there
arise some problems from Acts of the Apostles. There (5.34-
39) a Gamaliel, a Pharisee and a member of the Sanhedrin,
is depicted as speaking tolerantly respecting the Jewish
Christians; and in 22.3 Paul is depicted as saying that he
"was brought up at the feet of Gamaliel," as if once Gamaliel's student.[17] Was this Gamaliel the same as Gamaliel I?
Did he have an Academy? These historical problems are beyond solution, though many have tried in ingenious ways to
solve them. Ordinarily, scholars avoid the pitfalls of precise
chronology by speaking instead of "generations of tannaim,"
as we have said.

Gamaliel I, in legend the president of the Sanhedrin in his
time, is the first Sage to whom the honorary title *Rabbán*
("our rabbi") was applied. "Rabban" became customary epithet for the subsequent descendants of Hillel. Gamaliel, of
whom little is known, is not accorded by the tradition the distinction of being singled out for praise as a disciple of Hillel,
as are Jonathan ben Uzziel and Johanan ben Zakkai. The
latter two emerge to special notice with the ongoing Academy of Hillel. Not much is known of Jonathan[18] ben Uzziel
beyond the statement that he was Hillel's most distinguished
student (Sukkot 28 a; Baba Batra 134 a).

RABBI JOHANAN BEN ZAKKAI

The career of Johanan ben Zakkai spans at least the decade
before the destruction of the Temple in 70 and more than two
decades after it. He above all other Sages guided the formal
transition from Temple Judaism to Synagogue Judaism. Respecting the period before 70, there are recollections in the
literature of the leadership he apparently shared with others,
such as Simeon ben Gamaliel I. (Questions of chronology
have arisen, for Simeon I would seem to have been of a generation or so earlier than Johanan. Simeon was involved in
disputes with Sadducees, Menahot 65 a; Tosefta Para
III.8.) Apparently Johanan's life was divided into three periods,[19] one in which he was a businessman, second a student,
and third a teacher. So agreeable was his reputation as a

Sage, and as a successor to Hillel, that it is told that Hillel foresaw that Joḥanan, his youngest student, would emerge as the "father of wisdom, and father of generations to come."[20] The statement ascribed to him (Chapters of the Fathers II.8) is this: "If you have learned much Torah, do not vaunt yourself for it, for it was to this end that you were created."

The tradition attributes to him as a teacher a number of excellent students.[21] He used to speak of their virtues: Rabbi Eliezer ben Hyrcanus is a "plastered cistern which never loses a drop [of learning]." As to Rabbi Joshua ben Ḥananiah—"Blessed is the mother who bore him." Rabbi Jose the Priest—"A saintly man." Rabbi Simeon ben Nathaniel "is fearful of sin." Rabbi Eleazar ben Arak is "a spring that never ceases to flow." Eleazar ben Arak would, on a scale, have "outweighed all the Sages of Israel."

It is related there that Joḥanan asked the five disciples what good acquisition a man should cherish the most. Rabbi Eliezer replied, "A generous eye"; Joshua, "a good companion"; Jose, "a good neighbor"; Simeon, "the sight of the future"; Eleazar, "a good heart." Joḥanan said, "I prefer the words of Eleazar, for in his words the others are all included."

When the rebellion against Rome broke out, Joḥanan (as related above, p. 138) received permission to move his school from Jerusalem to Jamnia, a coastal town. What then took place was no less than the total reformulation of Judaism, with the consequence that Synagogue Judaism acquired what it needed in order to endure, as even to this day. Joḥanan ben Zakkai, in this sense, was the "father of generations to come."

The Sanhedrin, as we have said, became replaced at Jamnia by the Great Bet Din. Gamaliel II was presumably entitled to head the Great Bet Din, as a descendant of Hillel; apparently he had earlier headed the Sanhedrin. We have noted that for some period of time the Romans barred Gamaliel II from being head of the Great Bet Din, and to all intents and purposes Joḥanan ben Zakkai was the true leader.

Joḥanan and some disciples heard at Jamnia about the destruction of the Temple in Jerusalem. God, Joḥanan said, quoting Hosea 6.6, desired "mercy, not animal sacrifice." He and his students went through rites of mourning for the Temple as for the dead. But under Johanan's leadership, Jamnia took the place of Jerusalem as the center of Jewish life.[22] Indeed, the Academy which Johanan established at Jamnia became almost interchangeable with the Bet Din.

The tradition makes of Johanan a master teacher, one who reared an unusually large group of distinguished disciples. It was said of him (Sukkot 28a) that he never spoke an idle word. He could not walk four yards without pondering about the Torah. He was always the first to enter the Academy, and the last to leave it. His knowledge was vast and encompassing, but he was aware of the difference between learning and piety. ("Whoever possesses both scholarship and freedom from sin is like an artist with his tools in his hands.") His interpretation of Scripture was illuminating, and often more than simply literal, for there is ascribed to him some openness to the esoteric speculations about Creation and the "divine chariot."[23]

It was his leadership, then, that provided the reconstruction of Judean life after the events of 70. At Jamnia, in the judgment of modern scholars, there began the collection, and written recording, of the Oral traditions, both halachic and haggadic. Johanan apparently moved before his death to a village named Berúr Háyil. Visited by his students as he lay on his deathbed, they found that he was weeping. They said, "Light of Israel, pillar of the Temple, powerful hammer,[24] why do you weep?" His reply was that a man being led for judgment before a human king could hope to appease him, but a man led before God does not know whether he will go to heaven or to hell. (Johanan's great accomplishments had not brought him to immodesty or arrogance.) The disciples asked him to bless them. He said, "May you revere God as much as you revere humans." It is recorded that just before his death he said, "Prepare a throne for Hezekiah."[25]

The full tradition renders an adverse judgment on Rabbi Eleazar ben Arak, whom in Jerusalem Johanan had regarded as his most brilliant disciple. Eleazar is viewed as arrogant and conceited as he was brilliant. He declined to accompany the Sages who had gone to Jamnia; his wife persuaded him

that the Sages should come to him, rather than he go to them.
Because he was apart from the Sages, his mental capacities
disappeared.[26]

GAMALIEL II

This Sage, as we have said, was at first barred from leadership at Jamnia by the Romans, who feared that the eminence
of his family extraction from Hillel might promote political
troubles. When Johanan ben Zakkai had secured the gift of
Jamnia from Vespasian, he had asked for and received am-
nesty for the descendants of Hillel.[27]

Gamaliel II was by no means the greatest of the scholars
of his day, but he bore the title of nasi, and was recognized as
such by the Roman authorities; his position was officially
confirmed by the Roman governor in Syria.[28]

Whether Gamaliel II used his authority for self-aggran-
dizement, or merely to establish a necessary degree of unity,
is difficult to determine. A series of differences arose between
him and Rabbi Joshua ben Hananiah. The latter was a
highly respected but impoverished man, a disciple of Johanan ben Zakkai who had helped the latter in his escape
from besieged Jerusalem. Rabbi Joshua was of high importance in the transition to Synagogue Judaism in that he opposed excessive mourning over the Temple; he also expressed
opposition to excessive asceticism, mis-timed piety, and hypocrisy.[29] When differences of opinions over some halachic
matters arose between Gamaliel and Joshua, Gamaliel used
his high office to humiliate Joshua. One such incident related
to the calendar (see pp. 210-11). Though there were Sages
who believed Gamaliel to have erred on the calendar matter,
they raised the issue that if decisions of the Great Bet Din
which Gamaliel presided over were subject to review, then
all court decisions could possibly prompt demands for review;
hence they thought that Joshua ought to submit to Gamaliel
even if Gamaliel were wrong. Accordingly, Joshua went before Gamaliel on the day which Joshua had calculated was
the Day of Atonement. Gamaliel received him with the
words that "Joshua was both his master and disciple, master
in wisdom and disciple in having obeyed" (Rosh Hashana

2.8-9). This humiliation was private. But Gamaliel was deemed to be arbitrary,[30] and an occasion[31] thereafter arose when the Sages deposed him as head of the Great Bet Din. That took place as the result of a public humiliation of Joshua ben Ḥananiah, over a matter in which Joshua was reported to have had an opinion respecting evening prayer which contradicted Gamaliel's. After Gamaliel was deposed, it seemed inappropriate to raise Joshua to the office, for to do that would unduly embarrass Gamaliel, since Joshua was involved in the matter. The high position was, instead, offered to Rabbi Eleazar ben Azariah. The latter consulted his wife; she counseled against acceptance, for he too might be deposed, but Eleazar thought it well to accept the honor, however temporary it might be.[32] Eleazar abolished the strict entrance requirements to the lectures at the Academy, with the result that enrollment rose, according to one report by four hundred, according to another by seven hundred.

Gamaliel, after being deposed, did not petulantly shun his associates, and in due course he was raised again to the presidency of the Great Bet Din, though now he shared the office with Eleazar. Gamaliel's restoration came about as a result of his visit to Joshua ben Ḥananiah to apologize for the humiliations.[33] Appeased, Joshua took the lead in the restoration of Gamaliel.[34]

About the year 95, Gamaliel, Eleazar, Joshua, and Akiba ben Joseph made a journey to Rome, to the Emperor Domitian. That monarch is recorded in both Jewish and Christian sources as a persecutor, especially of converts; it is difficult to determine whether it was Judaism or Christianity that those converts had embraced.[35] Apparently the visit by the Sages to Rome was to avert some intention on the part of Domitian to restrict or ban the practice of Judaism; however Domitian died in 96, and what was feared did not come about.

RABBI AKIBA BEN JOSEPH

A disciple of Rabbi Eliezer ben Hyrkanos, Rabbi Akiba (about 50-132) was a Sage of greatest consequence who died a martyr's death. About him there arose a great abundance of legends. It is told that until the age of forty, he was unlet-

tered,[36] and hated the learned, but then determined to study
under those he had hated. His wife was reputed to be the
daughter of a man of wealth, Kalba Sabua, whose shepherd
Akiba was (but actually his wife was the daughter of a poor
man, who sold her beautiful hair to help finance his belated
education). Away for twelve years at the Academy, Akiba
on his return home overheard a neighbor complaining about
his long absence. Loyally, Akiba's wife replied that she would
be content were he to stay away another twelve years;
promptly Akiba, without crossing the threshold, went back
to the Academy. After twelve more years, he came home,
this time followed by 24,000 disciples, to whom he said that
for his accomplishments, and theirs, his noble wife deserved
the true credit.[37]

His contribution to the unfolding of Synagogue Judaism
included his decisive opinions about which books deserved a
place in the Bible, and which not; he defended most ardently
the canonization of the Song of Songs and Esther.[38] He it was
who influenced Aquila to provide a Greek translation of the
Bible (see p. 126), deemed a necessity for the reason that
Christians were citing the Septuagint in furtherance of their
claims; by implication Akiba was disowning the Septuagint.

To Akiba is credited the initial effort to systematize the developing halacha. Precisely what he did is not clear, but presumably he began the arduous task of collecting individual
halachot and arranging them under some topical rubrics,
and also arranging the accumulated midrashic interpretations with the sequence of biblical books and verses (Sanhedrin 86a). Yet quite beyond such systematization, there existed a problem which might be put in this way: that the
increase in halachot had tended to loosen the sense of a direct
tie between the Rabbinic laws and the text of Scripture itself.
Perhaps the disappearance after 70 of the Sadducees with
their strong insistence on Scripture promoted the attenuation
of a bond between Scripture and post-scriptural halachot. At
any rate, to Akiba there is attributed a manner of interpreting the Bible in such a way that the bond between Scripture
and the derived laws was emphasized. It was said of Akiba
(*Pesiqta*, Para 39 b) that he was able to discover in Scripture
what Moses himself had not known. Akiba held to the prin-

ciple that there were no superfluous words or even letters in
Scripture; everything in Scripture called for or suggested the
need for interpretation.

On the one hand, the approach of Akiba dissolved whatever remaining pure literalism might have abided, for Akiba
opened the way to the legitimacy of a non-literal interpretation. On the other hand, the approach of Akiba in effect
paved the way for the Rabbinic views and opinions to reach
an authority in a sense equal to that of Scripture itself. The
methods of Akiba made it possible to harmonize two principles that seemed irreconcilable—the unchangeable character
of Scripture on the one hand and the inescapable need for
constant development in Judaism on the other.

Later generations ascribed to Akiba the intellectual means
by which to welcome the new and still retain a sense of discipline respecting the old. That sense of discipline is found in
the story of four Sages, including Akiba, who entered "paradise," a term that encompassed theological speculations about
God and Creation, the result of which could become personally disastrous. One of the four, Elisha ben Abuya, "entered
paradise"[39] and as a result "destroyed the plants," that is, he
held unorthodox or even heretical views.[40] It became the
practice to abstain from mentioning his name, and to allude
to him as *Ahér* ("the other"), this being a way of treating
him with disrespect. A second Sage, Ben Zoma,[41] is said to
have lost his mind, this after having achieved a reputation
for unusual brilliance. Ben Azzai, a man assiduous in his
study, is said to have died—a saintly death—as a result of entering paradise. The only one of the four who entered paradise and escaped unscathed was Akiba.

In 117, under the Emperor Trajan, the Jews of Egypt and
Cyrene (in what is now Libya) had risen in insurrection
against the Romans, as had the Jews of Cyprus; those insur-
rections were repressed after much slaughter on both sides.[42]
Very little beyond the bloodshed is known of the uprisings.
Apparently the spirit of insurrection spread to Judea, fester-
ing for some fifteen years. It was during the latter part of
Akiba's career that the rebellion against Rome, led by Simon
bar Kōzibá, erupted in Judea in 132 in the reign of Hadrian
(118-38). Little is known of Simon bar Kōzibá. The name

Kochba comes from non-Jewish sources; in the Jewish sources his name is bar Koziba. Perhaps Koziba is only an ordinary name; perhaps, since Simon had messianic pretensions which were never realized, bar Koziba means "son of deception."

Hadrian's suppression of the Bar Kochba revolt was accomplished with relentless cruelty, and Hadrian figures in Rabbinic literature as an arch villain. Having suppressed the rebellion in 135, he rebuilt Jerusalem, naming it Aelia Capitolina for himself, Hadrianus Aelius. Among the Jewish leaders who died a martyr's death was Akiba.[43] While some modern historians attribute to Akiba a most active support of Bar Kochba, most hold that Akiba was himself not a revolutionary.

The tradition speaks of "ten martyrs" of the time, but only six or seven names are preserved. The tradition speaks glowingly of one Ḥananiah ben Tradion. The Romans burned him at the stake. They wrapped him in a Torah scroll, and put sponges of water around him so as to prolong the torture. A soldier, in hope of a reward in the world to come, mercifully added fuel to the fire to hasten the death of Ḥananiah and end the suffering. Indeed, the soldier himself jumped onto the fire. As the Torah scroll burned, the letters jumped from the parchment and flew into the air (Aboda Zara 18a).

A second martyr was Judah ben Baba. The circumstances were these: the Romans had prohibited the ordaining of scholars; that is, the public proclamation of the competency of a student ordination had apparently derived from the ceremony of the public investment of a new designatee to the Sanhedrin, in recollection of the ancient transfer of authority from Moses to Joshua. In early Rabbinic times, a ceremony, semīkā ("laying on," that is, of the hands[44]) marked such elevation, but at a later time the form of ordination was merely to proclaim him "rabbi," and to invest him with the authority to give decisions in religious matters and to serve as a judge.[45] There were five disciples whom Akiba was to have ordained, but he had not gotten to it. The Romans had decreed death for both the ordainer and the ordainee, and the destruction of any city where such ordination took place. At a place in Galilee, Judah ordained five disciples—another account says seven—but then the Romans appeared on the scene. The disciples fled, but Judah died from the spears, numbering three hundred, which the Roman soldiers threw at him.

As a consequence of the Hadrianic persecutions, Galilee in general, and the city of Usha in particular, became the center for the academic tradition of the Sages, for Judea proper had been devastated as a result of the Bar Kochba rebellion far beyond the destruction wrought in 66-70. (With the ascent to the throne of Rome of Antoninus Pius, 138-61, the stern decrees against the practice and teaching of Judaism became relaxed.) Little is known of the assembly of Sages at Usha in Galilee beyond that there was such an assembly. A bit later Sepphoris in Galilee became an important center, and somewhat thereafter so did near-by Tiberias. The sources emphasize the poverty and insecurity of the times.

There appears to have arisen some rivalry among the Sages for hegemony. The leadership should have reasonably gone to Rabbi Simeon ben Gamaliel II, whom the Romans apparently were prepared to recognize. Simeon was surpassed in learning by the Sage Rabbi Meir. Rabbi Meir, with a Rabbi Nathan the Babylonian, sought to depose Simeon, but that effort failed.

To Rabbi Meir is attributed the setting of a form for the Synagogue sermon: The first part was to be halacha, the second haggada, and the third the use of anecdotes of the kind we associate with Aesop's fables. Rabbi Meir's wife, Beruriah, was regarded as a "woman of valor" (Prov. 31.31), equal to her husband in knowledge and wisdom. When their two children died, she broke the news to Meir by speaking of a valuable possession left in trust, and then reclaimed by the owner; it was God who had entrusted the children to them and had reclaimed them.

Meir was an intellectual *par excellence,* a master both of learning and dialectic. Countless proverbial expressions are attributed to him. His lasting contribution was the perpetuation of the work begun by Akiba of arranging the inherited halachic material by subject matter, thereby helping to pave the way for the formation of the Mishna.

A contemporary of Meir was Rabbi Simeon ben Yochai, a student of Akiba, ordained—some say re-ordained—by Judah

ben Baba. He apparently was part of a successful mission to
Rome;[46] legend tells that he exorcised a demon from the
daughter of the Roman emperor. Beyond all else, however,
his name was associated with mysticism, as a consequence of
which the medieval cabbalistic work, the Zohar, became popularly attributed to him.

JUDAH THE PRINCE

The son of Simeon ben Gamaliel II, Judah is known in the
tradition as Judah the Prince.[47] His dates are about 135-220.
He seems to have spent his youth at Usha; he had an array
of teachers. His studies included Greek.[48] In his home it was
Hebrew rather than Aramaic that was spoken. His wealth
was proverbial. No end of legends cluster about him, but it is
difficult to separate these from real history. How or when Judah succeeded his father Simeon to the office of Patriarch is
unknown.

No data have been inherited respecting the manner in
which Judah continued the work of Akiba and Meir in so
systematizing laws that the Mishna came into being. The
tradition, though, unanimously ascribes the Mishna to Judah (though some sentences were added by his son Gamaliel
III). Not only did Judah compile the extant halachot, but he
also felt free to omit or reject some.[49] Modern scholars seem
agreed that the Mishna as we have it today is not precisely
the same as that which Judah compiled. Indeed, there is division among modern scholars as to whether Judah's compilation was oral or written.[50] His eminence, though, is reflected
in his being known in the tradition simply as Rabbi, as we
have said.

Such, then, are a few of the countless personalities of the
tannaitic literature whom the tradition respects. One notices
that there is no glossing over lamentable pride or arrogance,
or over quarrels, petty or weighty, that gives a sense of authentic humanity to these Sages. They were most human,
both in their frailties and in their accomplishments.

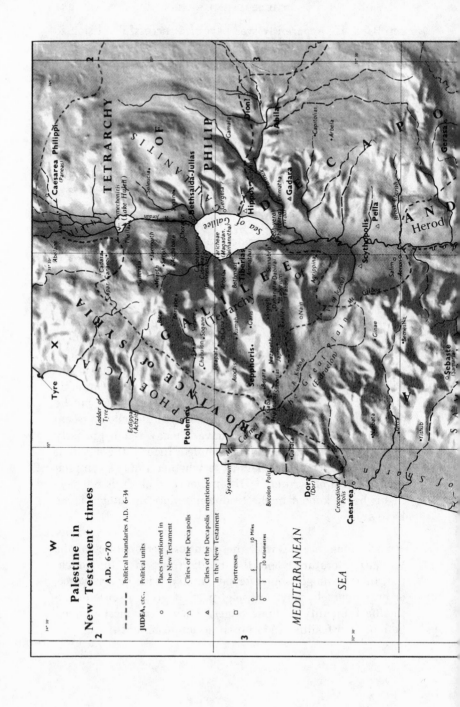

W

Palestine in
New Testament times

2   A.D. 6-70

- - - - -   Political boundaries A.D. 6-34

JUDEA, etc..   Political units

o   Places mentioned in
the New Testament

△   Cities of the Decapolis

▲   Cities of the Decapolis mentioned
in the New Testament

3   □   Fortresses

0   5   10 Miles

0   5   10 Kilometres

MEDITERRANEAN

SEA

Tyre

Ladder of
Tyre

Ecdippa
(Achzib)

Ptolemais

PHOENICIA

PROVINCE   of   SYRIA

Caesarea Philippi
(Paneas)

TETRARCHY

OF

GAULANITIS

PHILIP

Semechonitis
(Lake Hulen)

Seleucia

Jordan

Bethsaida-Julias

Gamala

Abila

Capitolias

Arbela

GERASA

DECAPOLIS

Hippos

Gadara

Emmatha

Pella

AND

Herod

Scythopolis

Sea of Galilee

Tiberias

Magdala
(Magadan,
Dalmanutha)

GALILEE

(Tetrarchy

Sepphoris

Chabulon

Jotapata

Arbela

Cana

Nazareth

Nain

Mt of Jesus)

Ginae

Sebaste
(Samaria)

SAM

Mt Carmel

Gabala

Sycaminum

Bucolon Polis

Dora
(Dor)

Crocodilion
Polis

Caesarea

The   Great   Plain
(Esdraelon)

X

34° 30'

35°

35° 30'

32° 30'

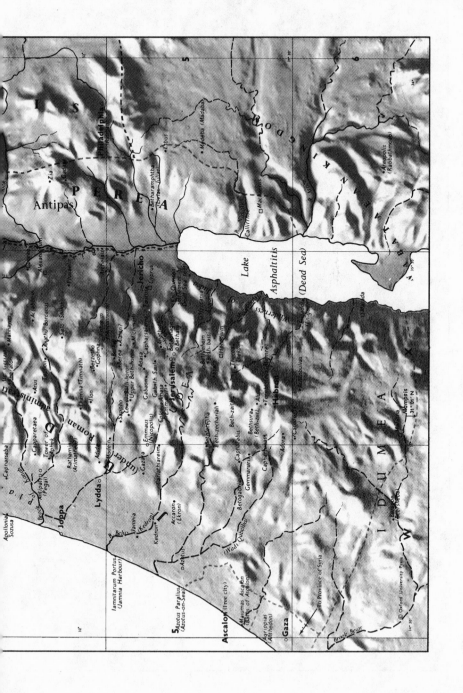

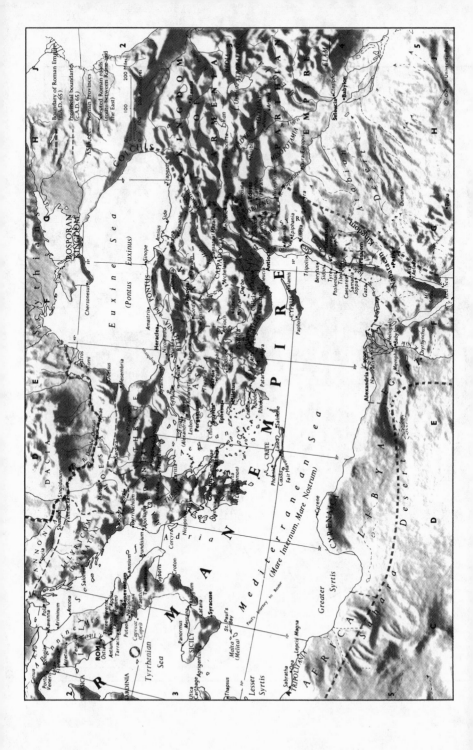

PART · III

HELLENISTIC JUDAISM

A. INTRODUCTION

To many, perhaps to most people, it comes as a great surprise to learn that there exists quite a vast Jewish literature that was written in Greek. It is even more surprising that in the first Christian century many, many more Jews lived in the Greek world than in Judea; indeed, there were more in the city of Alexandria, Egypt (the New York City of the time), than in the Holy Land. In ordinary elementary Christian education, this subject receives little attention; in elementary Jewish schools it is usually taught, wrongly, that the events of A.D. 70 created the dispersion of Jews into the Graeco-Roman world. The fact is that the Greek dispersion began with Alexander the Great about 325 B.C. The necessity for mentioning these matters is to point to a signal neglect of the Jewish hellenistic literature even by mature scholars. This field of study can be called the stepchild of both Jewish and Christian scholarship, for in addition to the sheer neglect is the accompanying phenomenon of an abuse of it.

An additional recurrent problem is the frequent failure of scholarly minds to meet. For example, on one level there is in the interpretive literature an honest confusion between geography and literature. Do we mean by Jewish hellenistic literature simply what was written in the Greek language? Or do we mean instead something geographic, that the literature was written outside Judea? (Here we shall mean Jewish literature in Greek, regardless of geography.)

There is a confusion also respecting the import of the term

"hellenization." When a Jew wrote about Judaism in the Greek language, it is reasonable to suppose that some measure of the Greek culture was in his ken and was reflected in what he wrote. To what extent would a Jew, loyal to Judaism and informed in it, welcome into his thought aspects of Greek culture? That culture included both the philosophy of Plato and the unrestrained frenzies of the Greek mystery religions; conceivably, a loyal, informed Jew could be receptive to Plato but would reject utterly the doctrines and practices of pagan religion.

Was it possible that Jews could live in a Greek city for many generations, know only the one language, Greek, and still be totally untouched by his environment? There are Jewish and Christian scholars who do believe that Jews and Christians could have been simultaneously completely at home in the Greek world and yet be fully insulated from it; such scholars are prone to limit hellenization to surface matters, like the use of the Greek language, and they go on to assert that the exclusive nature of both Christianity and Judaism inhibited any hellenization beneath the surface. Such scholars seem to misinterpret the crux of the matter—namely, that hellenization beneath the surface could be both extensive and intensive, but still it was a tenacious Judaism and Christianity being hellenized, this without any loss of identity or loss of essential characteristics. Properly understood, then, hellenization is the importation by loyal Jews or Christians of aspects of the Greek world into their continuing Judaism or Christianity. Hellenization is not the word to use for such Jews and Christians who gave up their identity and lost themselves in pagan society; for them the word is apostasy.

We shall see that there were, indeed, varying degrees of hellenization. As to language or geography, the reasonable possibility existed on the one hand for writings in Greek to emerge from Judea and, on the other, for Hebrew/Aramaic writings to emerge from Grecian soil.

B. THE SEPTUAGINT

The foremost example of Graeco-Jewish writing is the Greek version—indeed, versions—of the Bible. We have already encountered (p. x) the account of its translation in the Letter of Aristeas and the tradition recorded there that seventy-two priests, as fluent in Greek as in Hebrew, prepared the translation gives us the title the Septuagint. The translation presumably took place around 250 B.C., and encompassed at that time only the Five Books of Moses. It is a matter of utmost consequence, as we shall see, that Greek Jews gave to the Five Books the title of *nomos* ("law"), a word with a ring quite different from that of Torah ("divine teaching").

When the other parts of Scripture were translated into Greek is unknown. A reasonable terminal date is about 150 B.C. The various books exhibit in their translated form enough stylistic characteristics as to suggest that neither one man nor a collective team did the translating; rather, an abundance of separate individuals, whose identity is lost, did it. It is a common view among scholars that five different men translated the Books of Samuel and Kings. In some books the translation follows the Hebrew closely, but in others the translators allowed themselves generous measures of liberty. There is no dearth of matters of interest to scholars. For example, Jeremiah is about a seventh shorter in the translation than in the Hebrew, and the materials presented in common in both versions vary in the order of presentation. Presumably the translator of Jeremiah had before him a Hebrew version different from our inherited Hebrew version. What was it, and what happened to it? We do not know. Is the same the case with books other than Jeremiah?

The upshot is that modern scholars have varying views about the origin of the Septuagint, usually agreeing only to deny the historical reliability of the account in the Letter of Aristeas. One view, for example, holds that the Septuagint grew out of revisions of earlier translations; but other views regard the Septuagint as the primary translation, with the variations being later than the Septuagint itself.

Since any translation involves expressing with some clarity the ideas of one civilization in the vocabulary of another, there could at least in theory enter into a translation the characteristic ideas of the civilization in which the translation is prepared. By and large, though, scholars regard the Septuagint as free from any profound reflection of Greek philosophical ideas. Indeed, individual books are relatively slavish to the Hebrew, and free of any elegance, as if the translator knew the Hebrew from which he was translating better than he did the Greek into which he was rendering the text. Other books, however, are in quite good Greek.

Students of the Greek language distinguish certain periods, as we do with English. The Greek of the period before 300 B.C. is called "Classical"; the Greek from 300 B.C. to A.D. 500, Hellenistic; that from 550 to 1450, Byzantine; after 1450, Modern.

The Septuagint fits into the period of the Hellenistic, but a further breakdown is necessary. The distinction can be expressed in the words "Attic" (related to Athens) and "*koinē*" (common). Educated writers in the Hellenistic period often tried deliberately to absorb and imitate the manner of Athens of the Classical period—therefore the word Attic—somewhat as if an author today would try to write in the manner of the Elizabethan age. (Such imitations are called "atticistic.") Koine is the language of ordinary people, free of artificial polishing. Koine Greek was, on the one hand, the natural language of the age and, on the other it was the common, international language used by the Greeks and the various native peoples whom the Greeks had conquered. The Septuagint and the New Testament are in ordinary koine. Philo of Alexandria, however, wrote in imitation of the Attic. Some parts of the Gospel According to Luke are also in atticistic Greek.

Users of koine included those who paid some attention to grammar, and some who did not; hence, there are levels of koine. Some fifty thousand non-literary papyri—that is, ordinary business documents, as distinct from essays or books—have been published by modern scholars, and many of these documents exhibit in Greek the kind of misspellings and abuse of rules of grammar we often find in the English of unschooled Americans. The Revelation of John in the New Testament is normally judged to be quite poor Greek.

The Hebraisms which the translation of the Hebrew Bible would necessarily have entailed, blended with a common, unpolished Greek, seem to point to what we might call a "Semitized koine." Some generations ago scholars believed that there was an abundance of Hebraisms in the koine of the Septuagint and the New Testament; indeed, a century ago the view existed that New Testament Greek was a unique form of Greek, divinely designed for the Christian literature. Today it is a usual opinion that the Septuagint and the New Testament are in very ordinary koine.[1] The presence of Hebraisms in such Greek is broadly admitted, but it was demonstrated through the non-literary papyri that many phrases once deemed to be Hebraisms were actually not so at all, but characteristic of the language even of Greek pagans remote from contact with Jews or Christians.

As a document in koine, the Septuagint was intelligible throughout the Greek world of the time. We have said that very little of Greek philosophy is present in the Septuagint. From the other side, the question arises, to what extent do halachic and haggadic items appear in the Septuagint? The general answer is that such items are indeed present, but as compared with the Aramaic Targumim, they are relatively small in number.

A study of the manuscripts of the Septuagint—a quite complex matter—plus inherited information shows that the Septuagint has been transmitted in three forms, called recensions.[2] Today there are scholars who prefer to speak not of the Septuagint, but rather of "Septuagintal types," since they hold that *the* Septuagint itself cannot be ascertained.

C. OTHER GREEK TRANSLATIONS

The use of the Septuagint among Christians, and their basing their claims and theological doctrines on it, sometimes on passages where the Septuagint is markedly different from the Hebrew,[3] led the Rabbis to a virtual disowning of the Septuagint.[4]

Three translations into Greek besides the Septuagint were made. That by Aquila (see p. 126), which has survived only in fragments, was a most literal translation, designed apparently to provide a version which did not lend itself to the prooftexting for which Christians used the Septuagint. It is usual to ascribe the completion of Aquila's translation to A.D. 138.

The translation called Theodotion, surviving also only in fragments, is enigmatic. Its date is ascribed to the second

Christian century. Of Theodotion himself little is known.[5] Curiously, the Greek of the Book of Daniel quoted in the Revelation of John (and some Church Fathers) is that of Theodotion rather than of the Septuagint, and in some manuscripts of the Septuagint the Daniel of Theodotion is found in place of the Septuagintal Daniel. There is a view recurrently expressed that the version of Theodotion was at first an oral translation made earlier than the second century which came to be recorded by Theodotion in the second century.

Fragments of a translation ascribed to a Symmachus are also known. The date is given as the end of the second Christian century. Christian tradition identified Symmachus as an Ebionite. The Ebionites (whose name is in origin the Hebrew word for "the poor") seem to have been a Jewish-Christian sect. The inherited information about them is confused. They appear to have included some adherents who believed in the Messiahship of Jesus but not in his divinity, though other adherents did accept the divinity; they did not accept the writings of Paul, but regarded him as an apostate. From the perspective of the Church in general, the Ebionites were regarded as heretics.[6] The version of Symmachus is regarded as owing a debt to both Aquila and Theodotion. The style of Symmachus was florid and paraphrastic.

Fragments exist of still other translations,[7] but in quantity so small as to elude ready identification.[8]

D. DERIVATIVE WRITINGS

Yet transcending the innumerable issues respecting the Greek translations are the facts that the Bible was indeed translated into Greek and that the Greek translation was read and used in worship, both Jewish and then Christian. It was therefore inevitable that the Bible spurred interpretation, and also spawned derivative writings. In the Greek world these had a certain affinity to the general characteristics of Greek literature.

An anthology of such derivative writings in Greek was made by a Gentile known as Alexander of Miletus, whose dates are given usually as between 105 and 40 B.C. So much did he write in so many fields that he was called Polyhistor ("the historian of much"). He put together a book called "About the Jews," a collection of writings by various people. Alexander's book has not survived directly; Josephus, as we have said, makes use of it;[9] Clement[10] of Alexandria, a second-century Christian, and Eusebius,[11] a fourth-century Christian Church historian, quote from it. The authors whose work Alexander Polyhistor collected and excerpted included Samaritans as well as Jews.

1. Demetrius. The earliest author whom Alexander cites, a Demetrius[12] (probably an Alexandrian Jew of the third century B.C.), was a historian with a bent for chronology. One excerpt from Demetrius deals with Jacob; it assigns a date for the month and year of the birth of his children. A second item focuses on Zipporah, the Midianite wife of Moses; it appears to seek to exempt Moses from the trespass of marrying out of the faith, this by stressing that her father Jethro was a descendant of Abraham and his wife Keturah. A third item is an account of the sweetening of the bitter waters of Marah (Exod. 15.23). A fragment preserved in Clement of Alexandria (*Stromata* 1.21, 141) is an effort to establish a chronology of the period from 722 B.C. to Demetrius' own age. Josephus seems to have used the chronology of Demetrius.

2. Eupolemos. A work[13] by this author dealt essentially with the kings of Judea. Partly Eupolemos is concerned with chronology, partly with history, especially David and Solomon, and the latter's correspondence. The date of Eupolemos is often given as about 158 B.C.

3. Artapanus. This author is represented by the three excerpts.[14] He was half historian, half haggadist. Abraham's journey to Egypt (Gen. 12.10-20) included Abraham's instruction of Pharaoh in astrology. Joseph devised ways for the better cultivation of the soil in Egypt. Moses was the founder of all culture, the person whom the Greeks called Musaeus, the teacher of Orpheus. Moses even taught the Egyptian priests hieroglyphics, and taught them their worship of their gods—a strange ascription, but possibly a consequence of Artapanus' attributing all culture to the Hebrew forebears.

4. *Aristeas.* Not to be confused with the author of the Letter of Aristeas, this Aristeas provides some supplements[15] to the account of the biblical Job. The book he wrote was called "About the Jews."

5. *Cleodomus-Malchus.* This author,[16] with the Semitic name Malchus and the Greek name Cleodomus, seems intent on intermixing ancient Hebrew and ancient Greek materials. Three sons of Abraham joined with Hercules in the conquest of Libya and Antaeus. Hercules married Abraham's granddaughter, descended from the patriarch through a son, Epher (Gen. 25.3). Some scholars have believed that Cleodomus was a Samaritan, not a Jew.

6. *Pseudo-Eupolemos.* Two extracts ascribed to Eupolemos, seem to be Samaritan, and hence are denied to the Eupolemos mentioned above. This author[17] tells that Abraham had gone to Phoenicia on leaving Chaldea, and had taught the Phoenicians astronomy and military warfare. He had then gone to Egypt, where he taught the priests astrology and other things. While Eupolemos ascribes all knowledge to Moses, it is to Abraham that Pseudo-Eupolemos ascribes it.

7. *Philo the Poet.* This Philo is not to be confused with the later Philo of Alexandria. He is often identified as Philo "The Elder," the name Josephus uses for him.[18] Three small fragments of a poem, "On Jerusalem," are given in Eusebius.[19] One poem is on Abraham, the second on Joseph, and the third on the springs and water supply of Jerusalem. Philo uses the form of Greek epic poetry.

8. *Theodotus.* This poet was a Samaritan, who called Shechem (Sichem-Samaria) a holy city. His poem[20] is about the city. The name Sichem is given as derived from Sikimios, a son of the Greek god Hermes.

9. *Ezekiel.* Both Eusebius and Clement[21] allude to him as the poetic author of dramatic tragedies. Only one tragedy is di-

rectly known, "The Exodus." Several extracts[22] have survived. One contains a monologue by Moses at the time of his fiight to Midian, his marriage to Zipporah, and his narration to his father-in-law Jethro of a dream, interpreted by Jethro to mean that Moses would attain to some high position and have knowledge of all the past, present, and future. Another scene is that of the "burning bush," with the Deity not appearing on the stage, but with His voice being heard. Still another scene has God giving directions for the departure from Egypt and the Passover observance. In yet another, an Egyptian, having escaped from the events of the Red Sea, tells how the Hebrews passed through safely but the Egyptian forces were drowned. In the last excerpt, a Hebrew scout tells Moses about the springs of water of Exodus 15.27 and Numbers 33.9; he describes a figurative mighty bird (symbolic of a great king), followed by other birds.

Scholars have debated whether or not this drama was intended for actual production.

10. Aristobulus. Three fragments[23] have survived from this philosopher, apparently an Alexandrian. Scholars have offered a wide range of dates for him; perhaps 50-25 B.C. are reasonable. In one fragment he asserts that parts of the Pentateuch were translated into Greek well before the Septuagint of 250 B.C., and were available to Pythagoras, Socrates, and Plato to form the basis of their philosophy. He treats biblical materials as symbolic, rejecting the literalism of anthropomorphisms (the depicting of God in human form or human activity). There is in Aristobulus no clear allegory such as is abundant in Philo.

E. LITERATURE OF SOCIAL FRICTIONS

1. III Maccabees

This book is misnamed, for it has nothing directly to do with the events of the Maccabean revolt; the connection is a very thin one. It tells that the Egyptian king Ptolemy IV Philopator (222-204 B.C.), having defeated the Seleucidian Antiochus III The Great in 217, came to Jerusalem. He conceived the desire to enter the Temple. The Jews, unable to deter him by their pleas, prayed to God. God prevented Ptolemy's intention by striking and stunning him. When Ptolemy returned to Egypt, in vengeance he abolished the rights of the Jews of Alexandria and had the Jews of other parts of Egypt brought to Alexandria in chains, confining them, in their very great numbers, in a race course. He then made preparations for five hundred elephants to trample about in the race course. The appointed time was postponed by a day because the king slept too late. The next morning God caused him to forget, but later in the day Ptolemy remembered and set the execution for the morrow. At that time, as Ptolemy and his troops approached the race course, two angels terrorized and paralyzed Ptolemy and his troops, and the elephants turned about and trampled on Ptolemy's forces. Ptolemy thereupon liberated the Jews who were in chains, and at his expense the Jews celebrated their deliverance with feasting, determining to observe those days as festivals ever after. Ptolemy instructed the governors in all his provinces to protect the Jews. He gave the Jews permission to execute any Jews who became apostates.

Almost everything in III Maccabees is a puzzle: when was it written, how much, if any, is reliable history, or, if legend, is there some historical kernel behind it? Indeed, the basic question is, what is this rather juvenile book all about? That historical kernels could serve for semi-fictional writing can bring to mind both the Books of Esther and Daniel, but III Maccabees so specifically ascribes events to Alexandria that the usual procedure in fictional works of furnishing a remote setting (Babylon in Daniel, Persia in Esther) is strikingly missing—unless the author was far removed from Egypt. Scholars have struggled to find some historical event behind the book, and to ascribe a reasonable date (probably the first pre-Christian century) for its composition. The most that can be said with some probability is that the book is an attestation, greatly exaggerated, to some of the difficulties encountered by Jews in the Greek Dispersion. Their wish to receive royal sanction and protection for the right to live under Jewish law had its ups and downs, as is attested to in a variety of allusions in Josephus,[24] and the relations with pagans often marked by reciprocal hostilities or, as exemplified in

pogroms in Alexandria in A.D. 38-39, occasional extreme violence. Precisely how III Maccabees fits into such backgrounds is not at all clear. The wish for revenge on some
pagans has probably here stirred an unrestrained imagination to a fantastic narrative.

Yet the circumstance that Jews in the Greek world lived
under Jewish Law and, as a consequence, preserved some social separatisms, brought their religion under some suspicion
(as was the case later with Christianity), and Jews felt a
need for presenting an affirmative exposition of what Judaism was all about and what kind of people Jews were. The
general term for literature of this kind is "apologetics." The
chief characteristic of such apologetic literature is its defensiveness, namely, the necessity to refute unfair libels. In part
such disparagement of Jews (and, later, Christians) was a
matter of unthinking folk attitudes, or of merely passing
slurs by Greek or Roman writers; in part the disparagement
was expressed in focused essays.

2. *Josephus' Apologetics*

The Jewish response to the focused hostility took two main
forms. One was the writing of new essays; the other was the
interpolation of passages which spoke favorably of the Jews
into pagan works already in circulation. Basic to both types
of response was the attitude, almost invariably left unstated,
that aspects of the pagan legacy, particularly the writings of
Plato and Aristotle, were unreservedly admirable. The Jewish (and later Christian) apologists did not feel inclined to
spurn or attack this admirable aspect of the Greek civilization; rather, it became the task of Jewish apologetics to dem-
onstrate the congruency of the worthy aspect of the Greek
civilization with Judaism. A related motif was that some special virtue inhered in antiquity; Jewish writers therefore
stressed it; for example, in passages in the fragments from
Alexander Polyhistor mentioned above, and in the very title,
and opening exposition, of The Antiquities of the Jews of
Josephus. Indeed, quite apart from a special apologetic work
by Josephus called Against Apion, apologetic motifs appear
in virtually every chapter Josephus wrote.

A possible clue to the nature and tone of the Jewish apologetics can be inferred from a passage in *Against Apion*. In that text, Josephus has cited favorable statements about Jews from non-Greek writers, and he turns to cite such statements from Greek writers too. He tells that both the lowest classes of the Greeks and those with the highest reputations for wisdom admired whatever Jews they chanced to meet. The disciple of Aristotle, Clearchus, himself a peripatetic philosopher of the first rank, in his book on "Sleep," quoted his master Aristotle as having met in Syria a Jew "who was Greek not only in his language but even in his soul." This Jew had visited the same places as Aristotle and had held conversations with Aristotle and some other scholars to test their learning; intimate with many educated persons, he had imparted to Aristotle and the others some of his own learning. Moreover, Aristotle had gone on to speak of the wondrous endurance and sobriety exhibited by this Jew in his manner of life[25] (*Against Apion* I, 176-79).

Scholars have expressed contradictory judgments on the historical reliability of this encounter between Aristotle and the Jew. The case for its reliability rests on the statement in the passage that further information is available from Clearchus' book, for Josephus was quoting only as much as he thought necessary. Would Josephus tell a palpable falsehood which could easily be checked? Against the reliability is the opinion that this is a patent bit of apologetics, devoid of all historical worth; if, indeed, the incident could be found in Clearchus' book, it was one of an array of forgeries interpolated by Jews into pagan authors. Accordingly, very few modern scholars ascribe reliability to the encounter. For our purposes, what we should note is the device of apologetics here—namely, to ascribe commendation of Jews to no less an eminent person than Aristotle.

One more facet of Jewish defensiveness is to be noted. In Genesis and Exodus there are passages about Pharaohs and the Egyptians which hardly sat well with native Egyptians in Alexandria, who, on themselves becoming hellenized, encountered the Bible, probably from reports about it rather than from reading it. The events of the enslavement in Egypt, and the miraculous release, elicited counter contentions which made heroes of the Egyptians and objectionable

villains of the ancient Hebrews, with the particular contention that the Hebrews had not escaped from Egypt but had
deservedly been expelled.

Josephus begins Against Apion with the statement that
any reader of his Antiquities should have a clear understanding of how extremely ancient and pure of stock the Jews are,
their history embracing five thousand years. But some ma-
licious individuals have influenced others to disbelieve his
statements, and have contended that Jews are a young people, this on the basis that the best known Greek historians abstain from mentioning the Jews. Hence the treatise Against
Apion has as its purposes to show the falsehood and malevolence of these detractors, to correct the ignorance displayed
by some others, and to teach the antiquity of the Jews to all
those who want to know the truth.

Josephus proceeds to disparage the Greek historians. The
Greeks lack that antiquity possessed by the Egyptians, the
Babylonians (Chaldeans), and the Phoenicians, who have
left abundant and well-preserved official records. The Greeks,
on the other hand, experienced upheavals, and their records
are incomplete, and, moreover, in various epochs the view existed among them that the world had begun in those very
eras. Again, the Greeks learned the alphabet very late, and
with difficulty; even those who ascribed this learning to early
times conceded that it was borrowed from the Phoenicians
and from Cadmus.[26] The poetry of Homer, at first oral, was
not ancient; the first Greek historians were recent, coming
from the late period just before the rise of Persia (in the
sixth century B.C.). The first Greek philosophers admitted
borrowing from the Egyptians and the Chaldeans for their
scanty writings.

The Greeks kept poor records, and those that they did keep
are full of inconsistencies, for their historians were more concerned to exhibit their literary ability than to discover the
truth. The Jews, on the other hand, preserved their records
quite as well as did the Egyptians and the Babylonians, for
"no one, in the long ages that have passed, has dared to add,
remove, or alter a syllable."[27]

Josephus defends the reliability of his own writings on the
basis of having given or sold copies to men of eminence who

would not have kept silent had he distorted or omitted any of the data.

That the Greek historians had been silent about the Jews was explainable simply because of lack of contact, for the Judeans were an inland people, unlike the Egyptian or Phoenician coastal traders. But Egyptians, and the Phoenicians of Tyre, bitter enemies of the Judeans, did write about the Judeans. Among the Egyptians was Manetho.[28] Manetho had spoken of the Hyksos, a shepherd people who had been masters of Egypt for five hundred and eleven years. The Egyptians had revolted against the Hyksos. The Hyksos, defeated, ultimately made a treaty by which they were permitted to leave Egypt. They had traversed the desert and reached Syria, where, in the country called Judea, they had built a city which they had named Jerusalem. In sum, then, it can be proved from Manetho that the Judeans had come to Egypt from some other place, and had left Egypt almost a thousand years before the Trojan War.[29]

As to the Phoenician Tyrians, they had archives which record that the Temple of Solomon was built 143 years and eight months before the Tyrians founded Carthage. Letters exchanged between Solomon and Hiram of Tyre were still preserved in Tyre. Josephus quotes a Phoenician historian, Dius, who tells about some riddles which Solomon and Hiram had exchanged, with failure to solve them entailing the need to pay a sum of money agreed upon. Josephus then quotes a Menander of Ephesus who, in dealing with "barbarian" kings, also mentions the riddles of Solomon, king of Jerusalem. He adds a further paraphrase of Menander to prove the earlier statement that Solomon's Temple was built 143 years and eight months before the founding of Carthage.[30]

Josephus next cites Babylonian writers, especially the priest, Berosus, who had written on Chaldean astronomy and philosophy, and had mentioned the flood and the ark of Noah, the Babylonian conquest of Judea, the burning of the Temple, the Exile, and the restoration under Cyrus.[31]

He turns now to contend against those who will accept only the testimony of Greek writers. He alludes to a passage in a third-century writer which ascribes to Pythagoras (the famous philosopher of the sixth century B.C.), some custom-

ary appropriations of "the doctrines of the Judeans and Thra-
cians." Next he cites from the work of Theophrastus, the student of and successor to Aristotle, a passage which mentions
the oath of *corbán*,[32] a term limited to Jews (for the word is
Hebrew). He cites the historian Herodotus, who alludes to
circumcision among the Syrians of Palestine, and these, Josephus says, are only the Jews. Next, he takes a passage from
a historian named Choerilus to be an allusion to Jerusalem
and the Dead Sea. Thereafter he narrates Aristotle's encounter we saw above (see p. 268) with a Jew. He then quotes a
number of items from the historian Hecataeus of Abdera
(fourth to third pre-Christian century) on the migration of
Jews to Alexandria; his admiration for the Jewish fidelity to
their laws; the vast population of the Jews; a description of
Jerusalem and the Temple; and an account of a Jewish
archer. He quotes next a second-century B.C. writer, Aga-
tharchides, who wrote about the Sabbath. Then Josephus
chastises a writer named Hieronymus who, for some hostile
reason, ignored the Jews, though he could have written about
them. So much for the Greek historians.

Josephus next turns to literary calumniators. He mentions
first the many other nations which suffered calumniation
from various Greek writers. He then declares that the libels
against the Jews began with the Egyptians, who resented the
ancient domination of the Jewish ancestors (that is, Joseph)
over them, and the religious envy of the Egyptians, worshippers of animals, for the solemnity of Jewish theology. He reverts to Manetho, who had represented Jews as lepers who
had been banished from Egypt; he spends many pages in as-
sailing Manetho for errors, lies, and improbabilities. He defends Moses from Manetho's calumnies.

Next, Josephus assails Chaeremon, an author of approximately his own time, for using Manetho, charging that
Chaeremon made many silly errors. Josephus then turns to
Lysimachus, an Alexandrian of uncertain date, who surpasses all the others in his lies. Moses, according to Lysimachus, had instructed Jews to show good will to no one, to
adopt only the worst of counsel, and to overthrow any temples and altars they found. They maltreated people. They
built a town, Hierosyla ("temple-robbers"), the name of

which they had later changed to Jerusalem. Josephus calls Lysimachus an impudent liar.[33]

In *Against Apion II*, Josephus turns his attention to Apion, himself the author of a five-volume History of Egypt; it is unknown whether Apion wrote a separate work on the Jews. Apion was a first-century Alexandrian, and he headed the anti-Jewish deputation to Gaius Caligula to counter the Jewish deputation sent there to protest the pogrom of A.D. 38-39.

Josephus writes that he is uncertain whether to refute Apion or not, since Apion is a man of low character and a charlatan. But inasmuch as people find greater attraction in works such as Apion's than in serious books, Josephus proposes to inquire into three topics raised by Apion: The Exodus, Apion's attack on the Jews of Alexandria, and his attack on the Temple and the Jewish laws.

As to the Exodus, it appears that Apion, like Manetho, had alleged that the Hebrews had been expelled from Egypt[34] as lepers, and they included blind and lame people. But Apion, so Josephus says, was completely wrong in matters of chronology, as in other matters. Apion had alleged that Jews had suffered tumors of the groin, scalled "sabbs" in Egyptian, and from this word they had named the seventh day "Sabbath"; if they had suffered from such tumors, would they not have perished quickly in the march across the Wilderness? Moreover, Apion in one passage speaks of the march as taking six days, yet elsewhere allots forty days to Moses at Sinai! Apion lied in asserting that the Jews were Egyptians in origin. That was because Apion, though an Egyptian, pretended to be an Alexandrian (Greek), and he wanted to deny the Jews the privilege of being Alexandrians. Also, Apion scorned the section of Alexandria in which Jews resided—on the sea, toward the northeast of the city, in its finest residential section—but that area had come to them from the Macedonians.[35] Suppose Jews had lived in the cemetery area (on the southwest), what would Apion have said?

Josephus, after an initial statement about the rights granted to the Jews of Alexandria, from Alexander to Julius Caesar, defends the right of the Jews to be called Alexandrians. He reviews the privileges granted first by Alexander and then by the Ptolemies. He hearkens back to Jewish generals. He alludes to persecution of Jews by Ptolemy Physcon[36] and then by the wicked Cleopatra, the latter something of which Jews can be proud.

Josephus then defends the Jewish refusal to worship the Egyptian deities. Moreover, the disorders against Jews come not from Greeks or Macedonians, but from the mixture of these peoples with Egyptians. Such people do not truly possess the right to be called Alexandrians, a privilege specifically granted to Jews. Jews, duly paying honor to the emperors, were legally exempted from erecting statues to them.

In his third section, he mentions the charge[37] that Jews worshipped an ass-head[38] made of gold and on deposit in the Temple. If it were true, so he asks, would that be worse than the animals the Egyptians worshipped? There is, according to Josephus, ample testimony from such Gentiles as Antiochus Epiphanes (168 B.C.) and Titus (A.D. 70) that there never was a golden ass in the Temple.

Another calumny, out of the whole cloth, was that annually Jews kidnapped a Greek alien, fattened him up for a year, and then slew him[39] and ate him. Not only was Apion a liar, but why should it have been only Greeks, not Egyptians, whom Jews allegedly slew? The facts are quite otherwise, as any inquiry into the structure of the Temple and its way of functioning would make clear. Equally a lie was Apion's story about the supposed theft from the Temple of the golden ass-head by an Idumean disguised as Apollo.

Next Josephus deals with the allegation that Jews have an oath of hostility to Greeks. This is preposterous, Josephus says, for so great was the geographical distance between Judea and Greece that there was no occasion for hatred or envy. This oath was invented by Apion.

Apion's contention that the misfortunes (the conquest and occupation by aliens) in Judean history prove the worthlessness of Jews Josephus refutes by an allusion to the conquests of many other nations, especially the Egyptians, by invaders.

Apion had charged that Jews had not produced wondrous men, like Socrates, Zeno (the Stoic), Cleanthes (Zeno's successor), and—Apion! The refutation was to be found in the eminent men whom Josephus mentioned in Antiquities. Next, Josephus deals with Apion's allegations about the sacrifice of animals, the prohibition of pork, and circumcision.

But retribution overtook Apion; an ulcer led to the necessity of circumcision, and then gangrene set in, and he died in agony.

The second half of Against Apion II is an exposition by Josephus of the content of the Jewish laws. Moses was the most ancient of law-givers, whose achievements were magnificent, for he was both a military general and an educator. As a lawgiver, he created a theocracy, a system which put all sovereignty and authority in the hands of God. The wisest of the Greeks adopted views from Moses (including Pythagoras, Anaxagoras, Plato, and the Stoics). These philosophers addressed their wisdom to the few elite, Moses his to all Jews. He blended together both ethical precept and every-day practice, and made provision for all to know the Law, through deserting their occupations so as to assemble [on the Sabbath] and listen to the Law. Their unity of common religious belief and their uniformity in habits and customs have produced the inner harmony characteristic of Jews. Jews have not been inventors in crafts or literature because they were so stable as to need no such inventors.

The constitution devised by Moses has never needed alteration. It has not required improvement. This is demonstrated by a review Josephus gives which includes aspects of the Ten Commandments, the Temple and priesthood, marriage and sex laws—indeed he gives a rounded exposition of Judaism. He contrasts the practicality of Judaism with the impracticality attributed by statesmen to Plato. He lauds the law-abiding character of the Jews, and their obedience to the Laws even in the face of death.

Reluctantly, so Josephus says, he must criticize the Greek religion, with its gross and immoral ideas about gods, these caused by the neglect of religious standards by Greek legislators, and by the preposterous excesses tolerated in poets and artists. He adds some specific items in which he contrasts Greek and Jewish ways, leading to his conclusion: "Today among most nations violation of the laws has become constant; not so with us."

Josephus then proceeds to a brief recapitulation of what has come before, speaks eloquently about the Law, and ends with a dedication to his unknown patron Epaphroditus, whom he had mentioned at the very beginning.

Various stray mentions of the man Apion preserved outside Josephus present a somewhat clear portrait: Apion was
somewhere between a dilettante and a scholar, and both a
teacher of and a traveling lecturer on Homer. He was not
well received when he lectured in Rome. Later, settling in
Alexandria (of which he falsely pretended to have been a
native), he turned to demagoguery, with great success. The
disorders between the Jews and the pagans of Alexandria
came to a head about A.D. 38. Caligula had ordered that he
be worshipped as a god, and Flaccus, the Roman governor
in Alexandria, attempted to force this worship on the Jews.
On their refusal he proceeded to persecute them. The climax
of disorders between Jews and pagans was the visit to Alexandria of the king-designate of Judea, Agrippa I, the grandson of Herod; hostile demonstrations then arose, as did the
demand that statues of Caligula be placed in the synagogues.
To the latter demand Flaccus lent his support. He also issued an edict denying Jews the civil franchise they had possessed, and he encouraged the populace to plunder and murder, and allowed members of the Jewish *gerusia* ("council
of elders") to be tortured, some to death. Jews and pagans
sent deputations to Caligula, Philo being one of the Jewish
representatives, and Apion one of the pagan. Philo's accounts
(Against Flaccus and Legation to Gaius [Caligula]) reflect
the terror of the times, and the indifference and discourtesies
of Caligula. Later that year Flaccus was recalled to Rome,
and a year later executed. When Claudius[40] succeeded Caligula as emperor in A.D. 41, he set about restoring order in
Alexandria. He issued a decree that same year reaffirming
Jewish rights, and also imposing some limitations; he had
two pagan anti-Jewish agitators named Isidorus and Lampon
executed. Apion appears to have died about 48.

To what shall one attribute Apion's violent hatred of Jews
and Judaism? Much later the author of the so-called "Homilies of Clement,"[41] possibly a Jewish-Christian of gnostic
tendencies, ascribed that hatred to his pursuit of a woman
who successfully resisted him; the woman explained that her
chastity, and her contempt of the adulterous Greek gods,
were due to the influence of a Jew who had taught her to do
things pleasing to God. Hence, Apion came to hate the Jews.

That account sounds like legend. If so, then what can explain Apion's hostility? Perhaps the initial basis was ordinary social friction, found in many parts of the hellenistic world, where Jews lived under their own laws, abstained from emperor worship, and withheld themselves from social intercourse, such as eating with Gentiles or marrying them. Such friction could, in local situations, on sporadic occasions, erupt into some passing violence between Jews and Greeks. Yet a person of Greek origin did not have the same acute motivation to hatred of Jews that one of Egyptian origin would have had. In Genesis 12 Abraham becomes rich through the Pharaoh of Egypt. In the Joseph materials (Gen. chs. 37-50), Joseph the alien rises to the position of second in command in Egypt (and Egyptians in the first Christian century, like the Pharaoh who succeeded the one whom Joseph had benefited, could pretend not to have "known Joseph"). The plagues on the Egyptians, and the enrichment of the Hebrews at the time of the Exodus, could readily inflame an Egyptian, were he either to read the scriptural books or else learn orally about them. Perhaps this explains Apion and such predecessors of his as Manetho.

It is to be noted that in Against Apion Josephus does not hesitate to pour scorn on the Greeks, primarily for their parochialism. When Josephus wrote this work was in Rome, and it is likely that he was aware that Roman readers would enjoy his disparagement of the Greeks. It is noticeable that Josephus abstains from anti-Roman utterances, however often he will assail a particular Roman official.

In his exposition of Judaism in Against Apion II, 151-295, while contrasting Greek law and philosophy and Judaism, Josephus always gives a contrast between a good and a better, not between a bad and a good. But he carefully abstains from comparing Judaism with Roman law or philosophy; such a comparison would have been tactless in his situation. Josephus' echo of earlier Jewish views (which we have noted) that Plato and other worthy Greeks had derived their wisdom from Moses, contains by implication the conclusion that the wisdom of the Greeks was worthy and admirable. Obnoxious to Jews (and to Christians later) as was pagan religion, especially emperor worship; the Greek philosophy

—except for Epicurianism, which smacked of atheism—was quite congenial. Both Platonism, and its derivative, Stoicism, could seem completely congruent with Judaism.

F. RELIGIOUS WRITINGS

1. IV Maccabees

This eloquent writing is strongly influenced by Stoicism. It argues that the possession of piety (that is, a proper relation to God) results in the possession of the (Stoic) cardinal virtues: prudence, temperance, justice, bravery. The term here for piety is *eusebēs logismos*, which might be translated as "pious reason" or "religious reason." He who has such reason possesses the highest of the four virtues, prudence. Religious reason dominates the passions, such as gluttony and sexual desire, which obstruct temperance. It rules over malice, which can impede justice. It is sovereign over anger, pain, and fear, which can impede bravery (1.1-13).

This is proved, says our author, in the instances of Eleazar, from the Maccabean period, and of seven brothers and their mother.[42] The author digresses (1.13-3.18) to clarify his thesis, and then proceeds to give a brief review of the sufferings of the Jews under the Seleucidians, especially Antiochus Epiphanes (3.19-4.26). Drawing on II Maccabees 5.18-31, he turns now to the example of Eleazar (5.1-7.23). Antiochus had had brought before him a succession of Hebrews one by one, to force them to eat pork and meat dedicated to idols, on pain of death. Among these was the very old priest Eleazar. The latter spoke eloquently to Antiochus, first explaining the basis for avoiding improper food, and then asserting that he would not violate the Jewish laws, even if put to the torture, for he would never abandon self-control. To do so would be to reject the Laws, to shame philosophic reason, and to deny his honored priesthood and his knowledge of the (sacred) regulations.

Put to the torture, Eleazar collapsed to the ground but he kept his reason upright and unbent. When in pity some of the court proposed that they bring him proper food, which would be presented as if it were improper, and he could eat and thereby appease the king, Eleazar refused the offer. He was put on the pyre, but even at the point of death, he was true to reason, through the Law. Hence, religious reason is master of the passions. True believers, like Eleazar, and the fathers Abraham, Isaac, and Jacob, believed that they do not die respecting God, but live for Him.

The author turns from the old man Eleazar to the seven youths brought in before the king in the presence of their honored mother (8.1-18.24). The king spoke to them, advising them against following the example of the old man and to eat the meat instead. The instruments of torture were brought in. With no faintness of heart, the youths spoke to the tyrant with a single voice, rejecting his cajoling words. One by one, according to age, the oldest first, the brothers were put to torture and died. When it was the turn of the seventh brother, the mother was brought forward. She spoke to him, in Hebrew, to encourage him. He, however, asked to speak to the king (as if he was prepared to eat the meat), but he denounced the tyrant, threw himself on the burning braziers, and died. Inasmuch as the seven brothers despised suffering to the point of death, it is clear that religious reason rules over the passions.

The mother endured the agonies of each of her children. Yet for her sons she preferred piety to safety. This demonstrates that women too can exhibit mastery over the passions. The mother died by throwing herself on the fire, this in order to escape being touched by the pagans.

The author then addresses an appeal to the seed of Abraham to obey the Law, for religious reason is master over the passions and over both internal and external pain. He quotes words of the mother in a section on piety (18.6-19); some scholars regard this as an addition from a later hand. A conclusion assures the reader that the martyred dead achieved immortality.

Stoic ideas provide the frames of reference and even the content of IV Maccabees. To live by Stoic ideals was to live an unreservedly admirable life; to live by the Torah was in effect to live that admirable Stoic life. The assumption in the book is that the reader knows how admirable the Stoic life could be; the guidance that the reader needs is to recognize the identity of life under the Torah with the ideal Stoic life.

The commendation of the Torah is expressed not in its own terms, but rather respecting the identity of Torah and Stoicism.

The view of martyrdom here contains a significant difference when compared with the Ten Martyrs of the Hadrianic persecution (see above, p. 249). There the martyrs underwent the acute pain which their fidelity enabled them to endure; here the martyrs are portrayed as completely immune to the pain. What the book does not tell is precisely how such immunity can be achieved; such prescription, among other guidance, we will find in the writings of Philo, which we will presently turn to.

Where and when IV Maccabees was written is unknown, as is its occasion. A wide range of views exists among scholars, a clear token of the absence of unmistakable indications. Perhaps some incident somewhere, like the pogroms we know took place in Alexandria, spurred the writing of the book, to encourage a community of the writer's time by citing the precedent of martyrdom in the Maccabean age. The suggestion has been made that it was an address prepared for a memorial occasion, to comfort the survivors by saluting the martyrs of the local community. A date between 50 B.C. and A.D. 50 is reasonable, but not at all certain.

Curiously, IV Maccabees came to be attributed to Josephus, and it has been printed in editions of the works of Josephus as if by him.

2. *Wisdom of Solomon*

We have already looked at Wisdom of Solomon in connection with the Apocrypha (pp. 71-76). We need briefly to recall some of its motifs: its assertions of the unequaled quality of Judaism, its scorn of idolatry, its commendation of fidelity to the ancestral religion. We noted the rationalism which explained away aspects of Judaism that seemed to need defense against aspersion by intellectuals, this with the use of Platonic and Stoic motifs. We saw, too, that afterlife is presented not as resurrection, but as immortality.

3. *Philo*
a. The Man. To what point would a Jew, characterized by complete and unreserved loyalty to and pride in Judaism,

borrow significant motifs from the best thought of the Greek world? At what point does an understanding of Judaism, and an exposition of such an understanding, culminate in something that is as much Greek as it is Jewish, or, indeed, something in reality Grecian rather than Jewish? In Philo, the Greek philosophic tradition is absorbed to the maximum; on the other hand, Philo was as loyal to Judaism as any personality in the age with which we deal, and, indeed, as any personality in subsequent times. Was the Greek element in Philo, the presence of which is admitted on all sides, little more than a veneer? Or does the Judaism in Philo represent so thorough a shift as to lead to the conclusion that his Judaism represents something noticeably and significantly different from Rabbinic Judaism?

About Philo the man we know only a little. His exact dates are unknown. As we have said, he was part of the deputation to the Emperor Gaius Caligula in A.D. 40. He describes himself in his account of the visit as by then an old man. On the supposition that he was sixty in 40, he would have been born about 25-20 B.C. That would mean that his lifetime spanned those of Hillel, Herod the Great, and Jesus. It overlapped that of Paul. The events in Judea, such as the deposing of Herod's son Archelaus in A.D. 6 and the succession of Roman procurators ("governors") there, go unmentioned in his writings. His brother was the *alabarch* of the Jewish community in his native Alexandria; the exact meaning of that word, probably indicating the supreme office in the Jewish community, is obscure, regrettably. The inference, though, is that Philo came from a prominent family. A host of passages in his writings reveal his knowledge of how the wealthy lived, so that to conclude that he, or his family, was wealthy is reasonable. This is also borne out by the quality of his broad and exact knowledge of Greek literature, especially Plato; he was thoroughly schooled in Greek writings, and completely at home in them; he cites by name no less than fifty-three of fifty-four Greek writers; a poor man could scarcely have become so learned.

The exact nature of his Jewish education is less certain. He knew the Pentateuch with such a familiarity that it seems as if he had, whether deliberately or by coincidence, mem-

orized it. Though his writings concentrate on the Pentateuch, and the quotations from Scripture cluster primarily
from on it, he quotes from almost every book.[43] He alludes to
teachers, but not in such a way as to indicate clearly what
they taught him. His Bible was Greek, what we may call a
version of the Septuagint. The Pentateuch, it is to be recalled, had been translated into Greek in 250 B.C.; by Philo's
time there had arisen a body of scriptural interpretation, and
some of this he may have learned from his teachers. Was he
instructed in Hebrew? It is a moot issue. On the one hand,
he reflects a knowledge of some Hebrew in the explanations
he gives of the meanings of the names of biblical personalities, sometimes correctly and sometimes fancifully. Possibly,
though, this Hebrew knowledge was not his own, but a recorded body of data on which he drew, as will become clearer
a bit later. On the other hand, at no point at all does he revert
to the Hebrew original of Scripture, as modern rabbis do
from the English translation. The chief impression is that he
is so thoroughly content with the Greek as a faithful, inspired Bible that he is completely indifferent to the Hebrew
original.

His interpretation of Scripture contains what in Rabbinic
literature we would call halacha and haggada. Was it the
actual Judean interpretation that he knew, or only a hellenistic analogue of it? Was he completely, or at least mostly,
unaware of the content of Judean interpretation, as if a thoroughly separate hellenistic interpretation existed? Scholars
differ on this matter.

b. His Writings. Philo wrote voluminously. Some of what
he wrote has not survived. The Greek originals of some works
perished but have been transmitted in translation into the
Armenian. The surviving writings encompass thirteen volumes in the edition known as the Loeb Classical Library.

Modern scholars divide the surviving writings into four
categories. The first category is a set of miscellaneous essays.
Two are historical. Against Flaccus tells about the pogroms
in Alexandria in 38, relating the misdeeds and inactions of
Flaccus, the Roman governor, and the punishment which
came upon him, removal, banishment, and execution, for his
trespasses. The Legation to Gaius (Caligula) tells of the ex-

periences of a delegation of Jews, of which delegation Philo was a member, sent to Rome to protest against Flaccus. The delegation encountered mostly derision and indifference. Caligula was assassinated in 41. The treatise at its ending seems to expect to proceed to a so-called "palinode," but this has not survived. Presumably the palinode repeated the motif in Flaccus that God visits divine punishment on those who injure the Jews. The treatise That Every Good Man Is Free, in this same category of writings, is notable in that it mentions the Essenes (as does a portion of another work by Philo preserved by the fourth-century church historian, Eusebius). Concerning the Contemplative Life is a treatise describing an Egyptian Jewish monastic community, similar but only somewhat so, to the Qumran community.[44]

The second category includes Questions and Answers, one book of which is on Genesis, the other on Exodus. In form, Philo cites a biblical passage, asking what it means, and then proceeds to give that meaning. The content of Questions and Answers we shall deal with below.[45]

The third category is called The Allegory of the Law. It is an extensive series of essays. Each essay begins with a quotation of a biblical passage. The content of each of these essays is strongly influenced by the biblical passage. The essays, though, are on topics suggested by the passages.[46]

The fourth category is called The Exposition of the Law. These essays are on topics, but lack the biblical quotations which begin the essays in the third category. Though not essentially different in basic content from the essays in the third category, the essays in the fourth seem to presuppose little or no knowledge of the Bible. They appear to be addressed to an audience different from that to which category three is addressed. The third category, The Allegory, clearly is for pious Jews, and seems intended to enhance or deepen their piety. The Exposition, however, is significantly explanatory; some have thought it was written for Gentiles.[47]

c. Philo's Judaism. Philo makes unlimited use of allegory. Allegory was a device used regarding a revered ancient book; by allegory, that which was ancient could become contemporaneous by assuming that the text had a meaning quite other from what it was actually saying. The device was used by the

Stoics in their interpretation of Homer. Perhaps if we were to concoct our own example from ancient Grecian lore, allegory as a device can become clear. Antecedent to the events narrated in the Iliad was the set of traditions which told about the reason for the Achaean assault on Troy. Helen had left her husband Menelaus to run off with the Trojan Prince Paris. Menelaus had then prompted his brother Agamemnon to stir up the Achaeans to attack Troy so as to capture it and return Helen to Menelaus. To a Stoic these matters would seem either trivial or excessively sexual, or both. If, though, one used allegory, one might say that Helen represented education; Menelaus represented the slow, dull student. Paris represented the brilliant, quick student, who runs off with education. But the student who is brilliant and quick is often erratic. Agamemnon represents the teacher who is a strict disciplinarian; he restrains the brilliant student from erratic conclusions.

The above, our own concoction, reflects the very kind of thing the Stoics did with Homer. It also reflects what Philo did with Scripture. The biblical characters, Adam, Noah, Abraham—and countless more—represent types of human beings. Philo arrives at the particular type a biblical character represents by seeing him in his biblical context (that is, whether he is a villain or a hero) and by the supposed meaning of his name in the original Hebrew. Abram is two Hebrew words, *ab* meaning father, and *ram* meaning lofty; when Abraham was still Abram, he was an astrologer whose eyes ranged the lofty heavens. When Abram left Ur, he departed from astrology. Because he learned to abandon the untruth of astrology, he is, allegorically, the type of person who progresses by learning. The supposed Hebrew words in "Abram" poses no problem to one who knows that language, but the supposed Hebrew of "Abraham" does, for the word is presumed to mean "father" (*ab*), "chosen" (*brr?*) of "sound" (*hmm*) and connotes the divine choice of Abraham to whom God spoke audibly. This is a most strained use of Hebrew! Some of Philo's etymologies seem to be quite good Hebrew, some not; for example, Noah is good Hebrew for "rest, tranquillity"; the biblical Noah is the type of person who achieves inner tranquillity. The good etymologies suggest that some Hebrew knowledge was indeed available, the bad ones that that knowledge was scanty. But Philo may have had a list of Hebrew names and their supposed meanings, such as we know of from later times, and he may himself not have known Hebrew.

The use of allegory to make universal human types out of biblical characters leads to the telling statement that they are delineated and defined in terms of Philo's heritage from the Greek world. He interprets the patriarchs in terms of Aristotle's delineation of three types of persons, one who attains perfection by being taught (Abraham), a second who attains it by practice (Jacob), a third who attains it by intuition (Isaac).[48]

But a person who attains to perfection, as did Abraham, necessarily goes through a number of stages of learning. Thus, there is Abram in Ur, Abram in Ḥarran, Abram in Canaan. Such stages are universal in men, in that all of us are at some stage of our lives in Ur (error), but migrate to Ḥarran (introspection) and traverse the land of Canaan (the vices of adolescence). That is to say, the allegory provides us both with types of men and also with phases of human personality, or, more precisely, with aspects of the human traits of men. The Greek tradition speaks of five senses (sight, hearing, smell, taste, and touch) and four passions (anger, lust, hunger, and joy); the five kings who rebelled against the four eastern kings (Gen. ch. 14) are, allegorically, the five senses and the four passions.

But allegory is not an end, but only a means; it is the device by which Philo makes Scripture yield a host of philosophical items culled primarily from Plato and the Stoics. Since Philo pays most of his attention to Genesis and a good bit to Exodus, it is primarily from those books that he makes his philosophic inferences. Philo does not provide us with an orderly arrangement of his philosophy into a system; modern scholars—for example, Harry A. Wolfson (*Philo: Foundations of Religious Philosophy in Judaism, Christianity, and Islam*, 2 vols., 1947)—undertake to do this. Presently we will provide a summary of Philo's philosophy in a more or less orderly way.

But previous to such an effort is the urgent need to grasp

the significant setting of the philosophical ideas within Philo's total thought. That setting is his striking contention that Scripture reveals the experience of all men, including you and me. We too have senses and passions, and traverse the vices of adolescence. The experience of an Abraham, accordingly, is your experience and mine. Philo at one point states this very graphically; in speaking of the migration of Abraham from Ur, he says a journey that some man made a long time ago is completely meaningless unless it is a journey that we too can make.

The allegorical meaning of Scripture is, in effect, the spiritual journey of every man. The journey begins here where we are in the world which initially we understand by the perception of our senses; we live within "the world of perception." The goal of our journey is to move beyond this world into the better world, the world of thought, what Plato called "the world of concept."

A concept is a deduction which our higher mind can extract from sense perceptions. In the case of a dog, his eyes can perceive a bone, and his animal mind can spur him to walk to the bone; a dog, though, cannot discourse about food in general terms, for a dog lacks a higher mind. On the other hand, a man may be accused and convicted of a number of legal trespasses and be sentenced by a court to various penalties, whether fines or imprisonment. These experiences are all in the world of perception. If, out of these experiences, a man inquires into what justice is (that is, moving from individual instances into the general, abstract question) then his higher mind moves from perception into concept. A concept, then, is an idea, an abstraction that is far beyond the raw material which the senses can encounter and send on to the mind, for it to do with what it can; a concept is something lofty, something ideal.

Or one can reverse the process, that is, one can move from concept to perception. If I make a table, I make it out of wood with my hands and my eyes; yet I begin with an idea of a table and move to making a physical table. That ideal table is not a physical, material table; the table I build, though, is a material one. This material table can be broken into pieces, or it may burn up if the house catches on fire. A physical, material table is subject to decay, corruption, or destruction; the ideal table of the mind is not subject to destruction. A table which is perceptible is destructible because every thing in the world of perception is destructible. The idea, or concept, of a table is indestructible, because whatever is in the world of concept is free of taint and is indestructible. The concept of justice is free of taint; just as a table can turn out to be badly made, so a human court can blemish what pure justice ought to be.

The world of concept (*kosmos noëtikos*) is the goal of our journey because whoever arrives into that world, having left his perceptible world behind him, now lives in the realm of the purity of ideas.

The Bible tells us how to journey to the goal. Philo's allegory is his explanation, utilizing philosophy, of how we can accomplish the desired achievement; his essays are his exhortation to us to make the journey. So abundant is the philosophy in Philo that some interpreters, such as Wolfson, conceive of him essentially as a philosopher. Other interpreters, noting the decisive role of the mind in Philo's essays, prefer to regard him essentially as a psychologist. The exhortations in Philo do not conceal the preacher in him. Philo is all three: philosopher, psychologist, preacher.

How do we make the journey?[49] By following correct understanding. There are two stories of the creation of man in Genesis, crucial to our correct understanding of our own nature. In the Genesis 1, God "creates" man. This man is the "idea," not the physical being. The man of Genesis 2, whom God "makes" out of dust of the earth, and breathes spirit into, is a physical being like you and me. The dust of the earth is the clue to the physical, material part of man; the spirit breathed into him represents the non-material side. The assumption in Philo is that anything that is material is necessarily bad; anything immaterial is good. The senses and the passions reside in the material part of man, in his body. The senses are not trustworthy, for we often see incorrectly, or hear incorrectly; the passions lead us into foolish actions which can destroy us. The body, then, is by axiom bad. The immaterial side of man (spirit, soul) is good. A constant

struggle goes on in a man as to whether his body will dominate him, or whether his soul or spirit will.

To the somewhat synonymous terms spirit and soul we
must add another third synonym, mind. It has two aspects.
The lower mind collects the perceptions of the senses; the
higher mind extracts concepts from the senses. Adam, allegorically, is an ordinary mind, being neither deficient nor
gifted. Eve is the perception of the senses. Without the mind,
the senses do not function; without the senses, the mind has
nothing with which to work. Mind and sense perception,
hence, are joined together.

But in Eden, the serpent, allegorically, pleasure, intruded.
When mind and sense become bent on pleasure (that is, the
satisfaction of the body) they lose Eden. Allegorically, Eden
is virtue as a concept, an idea; four rivers flowed out of
Eden, these being the four Stoic cardinal virtues (prudence,
justice, temperance, and bravery). The four cardinal virtues
belong to the perceptible world, for we all have seen, known,
or heard of just or brave men. Virtue as an idea is in the
world of concept.

Man, having lost virtue, as Adam lost Eden, would have
been completely lost were it not that man has a characteristic
quality which distinguishes him from the animal, hope.[50]

Hope, in turn, leads to repentance (the allegorical meaning of Enoch,[51] Gen. 5.21-24). Repentance leads to tranquillity (the allegorical meaning of Noah, Gen. 6.1-9.28).
Scripture speaks of Noah as "righteous in his generation";
the latter words mean that measured by his own time, Noah
was righteous, but he was much less so than were the eminent men of later ages, such as the patriarchs, whose righteousness exceeded that of Noah. Inner tranquillity—we
might say "peace of mind"—is not the ultimate stage in
man's advancement, but is, rather, the third of the three
preparatory stages. If a man has moved from hope, through
repentance, and into inner tranquillity, he is then ready to
move further on the journey, on what Philo calls the "royal
highway." Progression on the royal road comes about
through the native gifts with which God has endowed a particular man. Such gifts are to be found in three qualities, in
three human capacities. They are, first, the ability to learn,

exemplified in Scripture by Abraham; second, in intuition, exemplified by Isaac; and third, in the actual practice of virtue, exemplified by Jacob. The patriarchs of history are, on the one hand, the historic men who achieved perfection, and in whom one of these three capacities was predominant, though each possessed aspects of all three. On the other hand, depending on our own endowments, there exist in us the attributes of Abraham, Isaac, and Jacob, for we too may be gifted with the capacities to learn, to possess intuition, and to practice.

What was it that Abraham learned (and that we too can learn)? He migrated from error, the basic error of astrology. Born in Ur, he had been reared in the custom of letting his eyes range the heavens to see the stars. The primary error in astrology was its dependence on one of the senses, that of sight, but the senses are not reliable; hence, the method of astrology was wrong. Second, astrology attributed to the stars the control of the future,[52] thereby ascribing to created things (Gen. 1.14-19) the qualities of the Creator. In effect, astrology was atheism. It was from such error that Abraham had migrated.

He came to Ḥarran[53] (Gen. 11.31). The word in Hebrew means "holes," orifices, such as are found in the body. Allegorically, Ḥarran means introspection, a turning inward. Such turning inward characterized Abraham, for it was a correct method, distinct from the incorrect method of letting the eyes range the heaven. By means of introspection, Abraham discovered within himself a *logos*, and, reasoning by analogy, concluded that there must be a Divine *Logos* in the universe. There is no single English term that renders the Greek word logos suitably, and even if there were such a term, it would scarcely contain its multiple denotations. It is conventional in translations of The Gospel According to John 1.1 to translate logos as "Word"; this translation can mislead, for logos does not mean word with a small "w." Rather, logos has meanings such as the following: the ability to reason; the conclusions attained by reasoning; the logical results derivative from reasoning. Logos is related to the higher mind; perhaps it might be defined as what occurs when the higher mind is busy functioning, and perhaps it can be summarized in the clumsy term "functioning reason." Logos belongs not within the world of perception, but in the world of concept.

But what is the Divine Logos? Perhaps to say that it is the functioning reason of God is correct, but surely saying this amounts to very little. The idea of the Divine Logos can perhaps be grasped by momentarily turning completely away from the term, in favor of trying to understand what Philo teaches about God.

First of all, God for Philo is transcendent, and, in effect, He is over, above, and even outside the universe. The term for God, borrowed from Plato, is the Greek *To On*, which means "that which exists"; another Platonic term is *To Ontos On*, which might be translated "that which alone truly exists."

God is not only conceived of as virtually outside the universe, but also as without *direct* contract with it, past or present. The bridge between the remote God and the world wherein man dwells is the Logos. Logos is that aspect of God which in the past and in the present is directly in contact with the universe.[54] In the past, the Logos, not To On, created the universe: in the present, the Logos, not To On, directs and controls the universe. In other words, God, in relationship to the universe below Him, appears in that universe not in His totality, but only in His Logos.

However gifted men may be, their use of functioning reason cannot take them as far as To On, for God in his essence is beyond man's grasp, even by man's reason. The highest that man can go, as he strives upward to God, is to the Logos. The Divine Logos, then, is the aspect of God which, as it were, descends to man, and it is the aspect of God which is the acme to which man can rise.

From the standpoint of man, a creature both of senses and of mind, there are differences in individuals in the depth of their possible understanding of God. The least gifted of men can recognize that the world has been created, for men are daily reminded of being creatures—for example, in eating and sleeping. The Greek word *Theos* (the Septuagint translation of the Hebrew Elohim, meaning "God") alludes to the fact that God created the world. This capacity to have created the world is only an aspect of God, for To On is more than merely that which was involved in creation. A person of limited capacities can be aware of the fact of Creation, for it is discernible to the senses. The word that Philo uses for that aspect of God which was involved in Creation is *dynamis* ("power").

Minds that are better than the lowest can perceive, through the senses, that the universe is ruled, for the sun rises always in the east and sets in the west, and the seasons follow each other with regularity. The Greek word *Kyrios* ("owner, ruler") appears in the Septuagint as the rendering of the Hebrew Yahve (which Rabbinic Jews pronounced *Adōnŏi*). Kyrios is the discernible power of God, which guides and rules the universe (but To On is more than just the capacity to rule). A mind better than the lowest can perceive God as ruler.

A mind gifted beyond these two can free itself from the senses, and, if functioning correctly, rise up to the Logos. The Logos, we recall, is within the world of concept, not in the world of perception (as is the case with the recognition of *Theos* and *Kyrios*). To repeat, the Divine Logos is the upward limit to which even the best mind can attain, as it is the lower limit to which To On descends. The Divine Logos is the *knowable* aspect of God; God Himself in his *plerōma* ("fullness") is unknowable.

Reverting now to Abraham, he abandoned the error of astrology and, having turned inward, came to the momentous discovery of the truth about God, having encountered God's Logos. He reached the highest rung that man can reach.

But there were additional things that Abraham in his progression managed to learn. These additional matters are the content, allegorized, of the chapters in Genesis about Abraham. For example, how did he respond to senses and passions? Like all of us, Abraham faced the issue of whether senses and passions would rule his mind, or whether his mind would rule his senses and passions. Gen. 14 presents this experience of Abraham (and of you and me). To repeat, it is related there that five kings of the area of Sodom and Gomorrah had rebelled against the four eastern kings, and had captured Abraham's nephew Lot.[55] Abraham then took up arms and defeated the eastern kings. In Philo's allegory, the battle is not of five against four, but rather of one against nine, that is, the mind in battle with the five senses and four passions. In the case of Abraham, his higher mind triumphed; his mind regimented his senses and passions. He did not destroy them, for to do so is in essence to distort man as God has created him; were lust destroyed, procreation would cease and race suicide would ensue. Rather, Abraham established "democracy" in his soul. Democracy[56] is the state of affairs when all portions of a kingdom are held in proper relation and function. Democracy arises when the king is a philosopher, and hence a proper king. Examples of an improper king are, at one extreme, the tyrant whose personal wishes distort democracy, or the mollycoddle whose incompetency prompts a comparable distortion. Abraham was a philosopher-king.[57] To this last we shall need to return; here it can suffice for the moment that the progressing Abraham learned to control his senses and passions.

Still another experience is derived from the matter of Hagar (Gen. 16; 21.9-21). In the biblical account Sarah was childless. She proposed to Abraham that he mate with her Egyptian slave Hagar, in order for Abraham to have a son and heir. Abraham assented. Promptly, though, Hagar became impudent to Sarah. When Sarah protested, Abraham gave Sarah the right to deal as she chose with Hagar. Sarah dealt harshly with Hagar, who fled into the desert. There an angel found her and told her to return and be submissive to Sarah; so Genesis 16. But later Hagar bore Ishmael and then Sarah bore Isaac. In Genesis 21.9-21, we read that Ishmael led Isaac into some dereliction. Now Sarah demanded that Abraham expel both Hagar and Ishmael. Abraham was troubled, but the Deity appeared to him to endorse Sarah's demand.

The matter of Hagar is turned by allegory into an experience of the progressing Abraham. Hagar, Philo says, was Egyptian by race but Hebrew in her conduct. Egypt means the body; Hebrew conduct is a matter of the mind. Hagar is to be found at the border between the world of perception and the world of concept. Allegorically, she represents the "encyclical studies," the ancient equivalent of what we would call a liberal arts education; when Abraham mated with Hagar, he embarked on such study. (It is Philo's conviction that a good education is a prerequisite to attaining perfection.) The treatise in which this matter is explained is called On Mating for the Sake of Erudition. In our terms it is a discussion of the assets of the liberal arts education, but also of its limitations. The encyclical studies among the Stoics were the *forerunners* to philosophy, and encompass grammar, geometry, astronomy, rhetoric, music, and other branches of learning. So, too, Philo treats the matter: Sarah is philosophy; before the progressing mind can mate with Sarah, he must first mate with Hagar. To mate with Hagar results in the begetting of Ishmael, allegorically the sophist (Ishmael is an archer whose arrows hit the target, but not the bull's eye). Only after one first begets sophistry can he move on to the begetting of Isaac through Sarah. (This last sentence seems clumsy, but it is deliberately so for a reason presently to emerge.) Isaac, as the child of Sarah, is spiritual joy.

Sarah, allegorically, is represented by the synonyms true philosophy and ideal virtue.[58] By true philosophy Philo means Judaism. He has a mixture of both admiration and contempt for Greek philosophy, being especially contemptuous of the abundance of philosophical lectures daily available, as he says, in Alexandria. The oppression of Hagar by Sarah is the requisite discipline by which philosophy refines the encyclical studies. If in the biblical account both the jealous Sarah and the compliant Abraham seem to raise problems in seemliness, Philo's allegory completely eliminates such unseemliness. Philo concludes the treatise with these words: "Hence, when you hear of Hagar as ill-treated by Sarah, do not consider this as one of the usual manner of female jealousy. The matter is not about women, but about minds, one of which is instructed in the preliminary learning, but the other is contesting for the palm of virtue."

Again, Genesis 18 yields an allegory which represents a very high point in the progression of Abraham. When he is seated at the portal of his tent at noon, God appears to him; he raises his eyes and sees three angelic men. He runs to welcome them hospitably, gives instructions to Sarah for the baking of bread, and himself goes to his flocks for an appropriate animal.

In the unfolding of the chapter there are two interpretive difficulties. The three men are at times alluded to in the singular, but also in the plural; and in the very first verse, one wonders about the relationship of God and the three visitors, namely, are they one and the same, or are they different?[59] In Philo's allegory, there are two important lessons we have already seen, and here repeat. The three visitors are, respectively, Theos, the creative power; Kyrios, the ruling power; and the Logos. Some men, of limited minds, discern God only from the results of creation; somewhat better minds discern Him from his rulership; the best minds perceive Him in the Logos. For the best minds, the triple vision is in reality a single vision, that of a unity which transcends every other form of unity.

The three entered Abraham's household, for it was a well-ordered household. Similarly, the allegorical Abraham had a well-ordered spiritual household. Into such a well-ordered spiritual household God enters.

The last example of Abraham's progress to be given here involves Philo in a rather bold image. He describes it as a mystery not suited for everyone, and, enigmatically, that it was taught him by Jeremiah. The complex allegory may perhaps be best understood by some introductory words: No man can beget his own happiness; rather, God begets happiness out of a man's virtue; it is virtue which bestows happiness on a man. In the allegory, Abraham is the man who has progressed and become the Sage; since no man can beget his own happiness, Abraham is not the father of happiness, Isaac. Rather, God is the father. Sarah, virtue, is the mother. An ideal virtue, Sarah belongs within the world of concept, free, then, of contact with the world of perceptions. Sarah is, in Philo's words, a virgin, having been restored to virginity. The virgin Sarah conceives and bears Isaac, happiness, which Sarah then bestows upon Abraham. (The virgin birth of Isaac is an allegorical, not a literal one.)

This small sampling should illustrate Philo's treatment of Abraham. He comments that the attainments of Isaac and Jacob come to the same wondrous result (as would be illustrated by assembling the Philonic materials which, though ample, are not as abundant on Isaac and Jacob as on Abraham).

We must now return to Abraham as a philosopher-king. The philosopher-king is a ruler who is able to free his higher mind from the impediments of sense and passion. Such a higher mind rises into the world of concepts where it encounters ideal law. Once the higher mind absorbs ideal law, it enables the philosopher-king on reverting to the world of perception to issue particular, written laws which are imitations of, or substitutes for, ideal law, but consistent with it. Thus, the laws decreed by a philosopher-king are truly legal, even though blemishes inhere in all written laws. The term which Philo uses for ideal law is Stoic: "the unwritten law of nature." A philosopher-king whose decrees are truly legal is, in Stoic terms, a *nomos empychos koi logikos,* a "law embodied in a man and made vocal." The patriarchs Abraham, Isaac, and Jacob were all laws embodied in men.

What does this all mean? We begin with the curiosity that Greek Jews gave to the Pentateuch the name Nomos, the Law. On the one hand, Greek Jews faced the broad and general problem that inevitably the Jewish legal system underwent comparison with the pagan legal systems. Alexandrian Jews lived in the center of three concentric circles of law: the inner circle, Jewish law; around it, the local hellenistic law; and around the latter, the over-arching Roman law. In virtually all legal systems there are items that are similar or identical, such as the distinction between theft and burglary or between manslaughter and murder. Inevitably, the similarities or identities led to the question, in what way is Jewish law unique? Or this question: "What, if any, is the special quality of the Jewish law?"

On the other hand, Genesis is almost exclusively narrative; how does it fit within the Nomos? The answer which Philo gives is that Genesis is indeed a legal book, for it is the Unwritten Law of Nature. The patriarchs, as historical men, lived by the Law of Nature;[60] the patriarchs were natural law embodied in these men. If you or I wish to live the highest form of life, we would need to live in accordance with the Unwritten Law of Nature. We can achieve this in one of two ways. One way is to possess the native gifts of an Abraham, Isaac, or Jacob. If we possess *orthos logos* ("impeccably correct reason"), as they did, then we too can abandon Ur, regiment our senses and passions, mate with Hagar, let God enter us, and attain to spiritual happiness.

But suppose our gifts are less than those of the patriarchs? God in mercy has provided a second way. That way is for us to observe the laws of Moses, for these laws are simply the record of what Abraham, Isaac, and Jacob did. If we observe the laws of Moses, we are living like Abraham, Isaac, and Jacob.

If our personal gifts are meager, our living like Abraham, Isaac, and Jacob is only coincidental. If, though, our gifts are such that we can move from the literal laws into the allegory of the laws, we can live like them deliberately. Like the narratives, the laws too are subject to allegory. Pork is prohibited, not because it is bad (it is the sweetest of all meats!), but to teach self-control. Circumcision, allegorically, means pruning passion from the body. Passover, allegorically, is the passing of the soul out of domination by the body.

The name which Philo associates the literal laws with is Aaron; he associates the allegorical with Moses. Moses, the author of the Laws, is, allegorically, the Logos, pure thought; Aaron, allegorically, is "uttered thought," that is, speech (which is never quite equal to pure thought).

While the Laws of Moses, since they are written, belong within the realm of the perceptible world, these Laws are the best possible imitation of the Law of Nature. The proof is that when kingship changes in an Athens, laws are repealed or new laws introduced, but the Laws of Moses are immutable. Again, if one moves from Athens to Sparta, the law changes, but the Laws of Moses are everywhere the same. Hence the Laws of Moses are the best legal system available to men.

The journey along the royal road from the world of perception to the world of concepts is the journey to salvation, namely, the rising out of corporeality, rising out of this world, and attaining to communion with God in the form of the Logos, and then to the deathlessness represented by the term immortality. The Laws make this possible for all men.

Philo, accordingly, transmutes Judaism into a religion of salvation and communion with God. Philo both explains how all this works, and shapes his tractates so to persuade his readers to put it all into practice.

We have seen in passing aspects of the philosophy in Philo. We shall here look at this in terms of topics, but rather briefly, for an exposition in all its details is beyond the scope of this volume. An arrangement of Philo's philosophy in topic form is modern, for Philo himself abstains from providing what one might call a system. The principal work in the last decades on Philo's philosophy is that of Harry A. Wolfson, mentioned above. A problem which Wolfson has to contend with in his effort to provide a system is, on the one hand, the absence of that fullness of exposition which Philo himself might have supplied had he elected to furnish it. On the other hand, Wolfson, in order to do fullest justice to Philo, feels the necessity to suggest the way in which Philo fits in both with what came before him and what came after; these matters, however, are not always readily at hand. Wolfson tries to handle this matter of incompleteness by what he calls the "hypothetico-deductive method," namely, to provide through inference that completeness which is lacking from Philo. There have been scholars of philosophy who have challenged this method on the ground that it goes beyond the evidence. For our purposes it must suffice to say that any presentation of Philo's thought in a topical, systematic way is fraught with insuperable difficulties. Nevertheless we must try.

For Philo, God in His essence is beyond man's knowledge and beyond man's grasp, even through reason, simply because philosophically God is by axiom so completely other than man as to be immune from man's intellectual grasp. Accordingly, affirmative statements cannot be made about God, for such statements by implication limit God; by assumption God is unlimited. One cannot say, God is just. Statements about God can be made only in negative terms; one can say that God is not unjust. To adopt such a negative way of speaking about God avoids the pitfall of seeming to limit God, but still permits men to discourse about Him.

Man can know about God only partially; man cannot comprehend the pleroma of God. Man's reason cannot ascend to the fullness of God, but only to that aspect of God which is available to man's reason, namely, to God's Logos.

Philo gives no definition of Logos, though he makes many enlightening statements. If man were to distinguish between what God is, on the one hand, and what God does, or has done, on the other hand, then he can indeed know the action of God. It is essentially the Logos which is, as it were, the actions of God. It was not God who created the world, but it was the Logos. The Logos, then, is the term for God's actions knowable to man. More precisely, Logos is the term for God's actions as man can reason about them; there are activities of God discernible to the senses, such as creation and rulership; but Logos is the answer to that aspect of God's actions which are beyond perception by the senses.

It was part of God's action that He had revealed Himself to man. A thorough-going rationalist, Philo turns the biblical accounts of revelation (as in Gen. ch. 12, to Abraham, and in Exod. ch. 3, to Moses) into thoroughly rational manifestations. That is to say, Philo alters the biblical account from historical events entailing revelations into the non-historical results involving man's rational process.[61] It is not so much that God revealed Himself as that gifted men, pursuing orthos logos, have been able to rise to the best possible awareness of Him. Such men can ascend as high as the Logos, but no higher.

The antecedents of Philo's Logos are both Grecian and Jewish. From the Greek world, especially the Stoic, comes the notion of Logos as the universal knowledge which all thoughtful men can participate in. From the Jewish past comes the notion of revealed wisdom, Ḥokmā (pronounced chochma). In Proverbs the question is raised about the source of Wisdom; does it perhaps come from learning or else from man's experience? The obvious answer is no, for we all know of learned men who are fools and of older people who, despite decades of human experience, remain bereft of Wisdom. Now we repeat some matters treated earlier: The source of Wisdom is God; this is illustrated in the narratives about Solomon (1 Kgs. 3.3-12), who asked God neither for wealth nor for long life, but for an understanding mind. God was so pleased that Solomon had not asked for wealth, long life, or the death of his enemies, that He responded to Solomon by giving him Wisdom. Wisdom, then, is a gift from God. In Proverbs, Wisdom becomes equated with Torah, revelation. Indeed, the presence of Proverbs within Scripture attests to the identity of Wisdom and Torah, since they have both been revealed by God. Wisdom was already available to God at the time of Creation, for God had created Wisdom at the beginning of His work (Prov. 8.22-31).[62] Moreover, in Proverbs, Wisdom is presented as personified: Wisdom calls to man (8.1); Wisdom builds a house (9.1). Wisdom, then, is an entity, about which one can speak as if Wisdom were a person.

In the time after Proverbs, the notion of Wisdom as an entity became transformed from personification, that is, from speaking about Wisdom figuratively as if it were a person, into a view of Wisdom as a hypostasis ("actual being").

Philo's Logos derives from an earlier encounter of Jewish and Greek ideas, wherein the content of similar terms and ideas resulted in a blending of them. Torah equaled *Ḥokmā* which equaled *Sophia* ("Wisdom") which equaled *Logos* ("rationality"). The Divine Logos was a synthesis of these earlier ideas, and were brought together into an amalgam.

In Philo there is a notable development beyond Proverbs; there Wisdom was present, and used by God at Creation, whereas in Philo, Logos was the creator. Logos is also to be viewed as the "pattern" of creation. Philo uses additional figures: Logos is God's "first-born son"; Logos is God's "image" or "shadow"; Logos is God's ambassador to man, and man's suppliant or advocate to God. At times Logos and Wisdom are one and the same; at other times Wisdom is the "mother of Logos."

An unsolvable problem respecting Logos in Philo is the following: Did Philo view the Logos as a genuine reality? Or, rather, was Logos to him only a philosophical construct, but not a genuine reality? Philo makes no statements as clear-cut as that in John 1.1, where unmistakably Logos is far beyond a mere construct.

For Philo, the existence of God is demonstrable by means

of reason as distinct from simply accepting the biblical assertions. As we saw above, Abraham had reasoned by analogy that as there was a logos within him, so must there be a
Logos in the world. But Abraham also reasoned from effect
back to cause, that if there is a ship, there must have been a
ship-builder, and as a ship has a steersman, so does the world.

Prophets are those especially gifted persons within whom
divine reason enters to replace human reason. The experience of prophecy comes when there occurs ecstasy—literally,
"standing" outside; ecstasy means that the soul has come to
stand outside the body. The scriptural prophets are the assembly of God's "family," whom God addresses by name.

Man, as a mixture of immaterial spirit and of material
flesh, is innately neither good nor evil; his being the one or
the other is the consequence of control, whether the immaterial mind, which is good, controls the senses and passions,
or whether the senses and passions control the mind.

The Jews to Philo are Israel,[63] those who, with the mind,
not the physical eyes, "see" God. Such "sight" is the highest
kind of "seeing." The Jews constitute the *ekklesia* ("assembly") or *synagogē* ("congregation") of God and are a *politeia* ("commonwealth") which is to be ruled by the constitution created by Moses. The kinship of Jews is not that
of blood (that is, not ethnic), but that of fidelity to God.

A Gentile who abandons polytheism,[64] recognizing and
worshipping the one God,[65] is equal to born Jews, and superior to those who are born Jews but not by virtue and observance. The born Jews are to love proselytes as themselves.

With respect to the Messiah, Philo provides some views of
the future based on Deuteronomy 30.3-5, and hence he presents those aspects of what in the Rabbis is the messianic age,
as the Deuteronomic passage would suggest.[66] Of the Messiah as a person Philo says not one clear word, though some
scholars infer the personal Messiah from one passage.[67] Philo
does not use the word Messiah at all. Indeed, there is no vivid
eschatology in Philo, despite the eschatology abundant in the
scriptural prophets. His opinion that if a new start of things
were to occur, every nation would throw away its ancestral
ways and turn to honor the Laws, follows on Philo's contention that the Greek translation of the Pentateuch is as reli-

able as the Hebrew (Philo says "Chaldean"). Hence, this passage (Moses II, 44) is scarcely eschatological or messianic. Indeed, it is quite in order to conclude that there is precious little messianism in the Judean sense in Philo.

What following did Philo have? We do not know. His repeated scorn of "literalists" suggests that he was hardly the darling of the entire community. Indeed, in some circles he could well have been quite unpopular, not only because he was an intellectual who wrote, or spoke, over the heads of ordinary people, but also because he made the Laws of Moses a means, rather than an end. True, he defended the need for Jews to observe the literal laws, against certain "spiritual" people who believe that their adherence to the allegorical significance of the laws exempted them from literal observance.[68] He had enough of a following that his writings were preserved.

Philo goes unmentioned in Rabbinic literature.[69] He mentions none of the Rabbinic Sages of his or earlier times.

In what way was the loyal Jew Philo hellenized? That his language was Greek, his Scripture Greek, his knowledge of Greek philosophy abundant scarcely touches the heart of the matter, for these matters are essentially secondary. Rather, Philo is hellenized in the following ways: he is a dualist, not a monist; his Judaism has become a religion whereby man abandons this perceptible world and enters into the world of concept and achieves immortality; the commandments, a set of means, not ends in themselves, are the vehicle for moving into communion with God; Philo has conceived of his Judaism as if it were the one true Mystery religion (in the context of his unreserved denunciation of the Greek Mysteries as false).

Some motifs are common to Philo and the Rabbis in the interpretation of Scripture; that Noah was righteous only in comparison to his own time is found in both. There is no reason to deny the possibility of communication between Judea and Alexandria as a result of which the common character of such items can be explained. On the other hand, Scripture itself could have yielded parallel but unrelated, derived conclusions. One might note that haggadic narratives, frequent in the Rabbis, never appear in Philo, nor does he present even one parable of the kind abundant in the Rabbinic literature and in the Gospels According to Mark, Matthew, and Luke.

Philo was scarcely insulated from contact with Judaism in Judea, and we know he visited there once. His words on the Essenes, however, reflect his own philosophy rather than the facts about the Essenes, and are to be taken with a grain of salt.

Almost no echo of Philo is to be found in pagan literature. In later Christian literature, such as Clement of Alexandria (150-220?) and Origen (185-255?) there are generous echoes. Christians preserved his writings, surely because they saw an affinity in their developed views and those he had written about. Scholars have noted that there are a good many passages in the Epistles of Paul which echo notions in Philo; though an occasional scholar has thought that Paul might have read Philo, scholars overwhelmingly reject this. The Logos prologue to the Gospel According to John and occasional passages in Hebrews are often linked with Philo; it is more prudent to link these with a general amalgam of combined Jewish and Greek syntheses rather than with Philo himself. Indeed, Philo is best viewed as representing a relatively self-contained Jewish hellenism, not totally severed from Palestinian Judaism, but distinctively different from it. It is from such Jewish hellenism that Philo, Paul, The Gospel According to John, and Hebrews arise.

When Christianity moved outside Judea into the Greek world, Jewish hellinism expedited the transition from Palestinian Jewish Christianity into Dispersion Gentile Christianity.[70]

PART · IV

EARLY
CHRISTIANITY

• 1 •

INTRODUCTION

Christianity, in a paradoxical way, arose from and has many affinities with Synagogue Judaism. Not only was Jesus a Jew, but a figure such as he could not have arisen in any other tradition or culture but Judaism. He is to be approached and understood historically only in a Jewish context. So too Paul. We shall see four phenomena: Christianity perpetuated some central aspects of Judaism unchanged; it altered some of what it inherited; it rejected large portions of its legacy; it created its own materials and embellished these creations. It was born in Aramaic-speaking Judea, and was at first a Jewish movement, making it possible for one to speak of Judean Jewish Christians. Then it spread beyond Judea, welcoming Gentiles into its midst, and in a relatively short time it became essentially a Gentile movement. Oral traditions recorded in Christian writings hearken back to Judea and the Jewish setting, but no Aramaic documents of that time have been preserved, if any were written. The literature of early Christianity is in Greek, and was composed outside Judea.

A host of problems, both literary and historical, are listed in the usual handbooks to the New Testament about Jesus, Paul, and early Christianity; some of these must be touched upon. But the purpose here is to set forth the sense in which Christianity is both related to Judaism and significantly different from it.

An acute problem arises from the circumstance that Christianity, in setting forth its claims, also sets forth criticisms of Judaism and of Jews. Indeed, the Christian writings which enter into our purview, namely the Epistles of Paul, the Gospels, and Acts of the Apostles, contain passages and elements that can be described as hostile to Jews and Judaism, and some of these are exceedingly hostile. As a consequence, attitudes of Christians toward Judaism throughout the ages have been in part influenced or shaped by the hostility and the attitude of Jews toward Christianity offer a response only to the anti-Jewish matters.

Did "the Jews" really do the awful things ascribed to them in some passages? Or has a historical kernel been altered and then raised to an exaggeration beyond credibility? Can we, whether we are Christians or Jews, or neither, understand the documents, and dispassionately assess both the special, affirmative Christian claims, and also the reasons behind some excesses of anti-Jewish character? In short, can our motive be primarily that of learning to understand? Perhaps comprehension will always be impeded by bias. But an effort at least can be made.

To begin with, it comes as a bit of startling information to many students that we have inherited absolutely no written sources of information about Jesus from his own time. If any Jew or Gentile wrote about Jesus during Jesus' lifetime, that writing has failed to survive to our own.[1]

The Gospels and other New Testament writings are the most significant literary materials about Jesus.[2] As to the Gospels, those which made their way into the New Testament number four. A Christian conviction that the message in all four is essentially the same can explain the way in which these writings are known, namely, as *The* Gospel, followed by the phrase "According to . . ." In the sequence in which the Gospels appear in the New Testament, they are According to Matthew, According to Mark, According to Luke, and According to John.

The historical questions—when and where was Jesus born, and how long was his career and what kind of career was it—depend on the literary sources. Yet the Gospels represent not the first stage of Christian writings, but rather a second stage. Their content, of course, deals with the first stage, but as documents they are preceded in time by the Epistles of Paul; there is universal agreement among scholars about this. That is why we shall look at Paul in some detail before we look at the Gospel accounts about Jesus.

We begin with the barest of statements about Jesus. He was a Jew of the Galilee. He may have been born about 4 B.C. He had a career of indeterminate length in Galilee. He gathered followers, traditionally numbering twelve. He was a leader; he was a teacher; reports tell of his miraculous cures of the sick. He was deemed to be the Messiah.

He journeyed to Jerusalem, whether once (as in Matthew, Mark, and Luke) or more often (as in John). There difficulties arose, with Jewish authorities and then with the Romans, this during the term of Pontius Pilate as "governor" of Judea (26-36). Jesus was executed about A.D. 29 or 30. His followers believed that he had been resurrected. They came to view his Messiahship not in the normal Jewish way of a single climactic event, but rather as divisible into two aspects—first, his initial coming, which was preparatory and had already taken place, for he had ascended to heaven; and next, he was soon to return in his "Second Coming." This Second Coming would be the climax to all history, and usher in the events of the Great Judgment. The idea of the Second Coming is of crucial significance in New Testament writings.

We need to think now of two diverse directions in which this basic data about Jesus resulted in New Testament writings. One direction was the telling, retelling, and embellishment of stories and anecdotes about Jesus; it was a process that eventuated in the canonical Gospels. The other direction was that of meditation about him, about *what* he was, and about the significance of his career. This second direction leads to Paul, his career, and his writings, and those later derived from Paul. The justification of speaking of two directions is that the material which constitutes the substance of the canonical Gospels is notably absent from the surviving letters of Paul, whether deliberately so or by the mere accident of what the letters chanced to include. To point to these two directions is not to suggest that they are necessarily in conflict with each other, but rather to understand the literary materials which we shall review.

· 2 ·

PAUL

Scholars have had to face a problem preliminary to any inquiry into Paul. Material in Acts of the Apostles about Paul seems out of character with the data about him which his Epistles contain. Here we shall deal essentially only with the Epistles. Next, while the Epistles provide a clear and even rounded reflection of Paul's theological doctrines, they provide rather incomplete information about Paul the person. We do not know his father's name, or his mother's, or very much about his youth, or details about his life before he came into the new movement. Was he a Greek Jew, deeply influenced by the Greek world, or was he essentially no different from an ordinary Judean?

But the further question is this, how typical was Paul of either Palestinian Judaism,[1] or hellenistic Judaism, or both? While a particular man often transcends his environment— as I believe Abraham Lincoln and Paul both did—to know the frontier background of Lincoln enables us to grasp the man much better than we would if we knew nothing about it. In the case of Paul, his doctrine seems so unique, and so extreme, that data about him could help make him less the enigma that so often he is. For example, the important word apostle can imply no more than an emissary, someone who has been sent, but it might have instead significant overtones of personal supernatural illumination far beyond the bare meaning of merely a traveling agent. The approach here can be expressed in two conjoined sentences: Paul was a person of such individual uniqueness that he could have readily been either close to Palestinian Judaism, or, instead, a hellenistic Jew. But if one is compelled to choose, then Paul is more intelligible as a hellenistic Jew than as a Palestinian.

In the 1830's, some acute questions were raised from the circumstance that Paul's letters, and, indeed, all the New Testament, were composed in Greek.[2] Data in the Epistles of Paul and in Acts ascribe Paul's activities to the period roughly of 40-55. If the death of Jesus took place in 29 or 30 (within the term of Pontius Pilate, A.D. 26-36, as "procurator" of Judea), how could Christianity have become so at home in the Greek world so quickly as by the year 40? A recurrent answer, given in the early nineteenth century (and since), has been that hellenized Judaism, exemplified by Philo, facilitated this startlingly rapid hellenization of Christianity. A different answer came in 1830 from F. C. Baur—namely, that there had not been at all any rapid hellenization of Christianity, but rather, that the bulk of Christian writings come from the second Christian century. As to Paul, Baur considered only four of his Epistles (Romans, I and II Corinthians, and Galatians) authentically his.

Since Baur's time, scholars have debated as to which of the thirteen or fourteen Epistles are really by Paul. In answer, three Epistles (I and II Timothy and Titus), called "the Pastorals" since they deal with the pastoral care of congregations, have come to be viewed by Christian scholars as reflecting a church environment so settled as to be necessarily late and distinct from the unsettled early times reflected in Galatians and the two Corinthian letters. The Pastorals are broadly viewed as not by Paul, but they bore his name because of the authority that it had come to have. Also, Ephesians seems to have been derived from views in Paul, but Ephesians is so theologically developed that it too is often denied to Paul.[3] Colossians is often but not as uniformly denied to Paul as is Ephesians. The relationship between I and II Thessalonians has raised problems, the solution of which has often been to suggest that II Thessalonians is not by Paul. As to Hebrews,[4] Roman Catholic scholars until about twenty-odd years ago defended the Pauline authorship which Protestant scholars almost uniformly denied, but now a good many Catholic scholars too deny Paul's authorship of Hebrews. In sum, then, the Epistles normally attributed to Paul are Romans; I and II Corinthians; Galatians; Philippians; Philemon, and I Thessalonians.

The chronological sequence in which the Epistles were written is difficult to ascertain.[5] These Epistles, except for Romans, were written to churches which Paul had either founded or had visited. The Epistles are either his responses to questions that have come to him—though whether by word of mouth or by letter is uncertain—or else they are comments which he is impelled to make because of reports that have come to him. The destinations of the letters are all to places outside Judea. If Paul ever wrote to a church in Judea no such a letter, nor even a rumor of one, has come down to us.

A few more preliminary remarks are in order. "Christ" is the translation into Greek of the Hebrew word "Messiah"; its distinctive meaning in Paul will emerge as we proceed.

Paul's special achievement was bringing the Christian message to Gentiles. Christianity was originally a Judaism. Its cornerstone was Scripture. Were the mitzvot of the Pentateuch, and the halacha, incumbent on Gentile converts to the new movement? Early Christians were quite divided on this matter; Paul's stand was that the Laws and the halacha were not incumbent, and, indeed, were an impediment, outmoded and canceled. The activities and views of Paul involved him in controversies with other Christians and in Christian challenges to his authority. Was he truly entitled to carry the Christian message? Was his version of the Christian message proper and reliable?

When Paul came into Christianity there were still alive and flourishing among his predecessors those who had followed Jesus before his death and whose belief in his resurrection had provided the impulse for the continuation of the movement. Some of these predecessors were still in Jerusalem. From Jerusalem there had journeyed forth, before Paul, emissaries of the new movement. No authentic, separate literature has survived from Paul's contemporaries or predecessors, if any was written. Some passages in his letters appear to be liturgical elements he inherited from predecessors. He tells in Galatians of being in Jerusalem with Christians there. Possibly the Gospels retain authentic recollections of Christianity in Judea before Paul. But we have very little secure data by which to describe to what stage the new movement had come when Paul came into it. We are dependent primarily on conjectures, not on surviving literary materials, or on inferences mostly from his Epistles.

A passage, II Peter 3.15-16, which is regarded as the latest book in the New Testament, in alluding to Paul, speaks of his Epistles as "hard to understand." The person inexperienced in reading Paul will surely agree with this ancient Christian judgment. For the modern person the difficulty is all the greater, for the Epistles arose in a world greatly distant in thought patterns from ours. The following may help a person in reading Paul. His arguments are ordinarily drawn from Scripture; unless we too know Scripture, his allusions can be lost and the force of his argument dissolved. Yet to complicate matters, the ordinary modern reader, on looking up the scriptural passages which Paul cites or paraphrases, will not usually find in them the meaning Paul ascribes to them. Though he does not explicitly tell us (as Philo does) that he is ascribing a non-literal meaning to such passages, he seems to assume that we will know that this is the case. He ordinarily ascribes a "spiritual" meaning, with the result that scriptural items have a connotation that can be surprising. Often this connotation is made to have relationship with the Christ; the rock which Moses struck in the Wilderness (Num. 20.7-11) becomes in I Corinthians 10.4 the supernatural rock which was the Christ. The manna of the Wilderness (Exod. 16.4-35) becomes in I Corinthians 10.3 "spiritual food." Often when Paul uses the word "spiritual" he means what we would mean by supernatural; accordingly, there can be spiritual men, those who through the Holy Spirit become supernatural. In Paul that which is "natural" is perishable; that which is "spiritual" is supernatural and imperishable.

Especially hard to understand, particularly by Jews, is Paul's attitude to the Laws in the Five Books of Moses. For him the Laws are in a sense devoid of supernatural origin (though he wavers about this). He sets in contrast the Laws in Scripture and the "Holy Spirit," to the disadvantage of the Laws. The goal of religion, he argues again and again, is not attainable through observing the Laws; it is attainable, rather, through one's receiving the Holy Spirit within him.

At times Paul uses the phrase Holy Spirit, but at other times simply "the spirit"; he also speaks of the spirit of Christ, and at times he uses the word Christ as if it means holy spirit. It is seldom that he uses the word Christ to mean the man Jesus; rather, he means that divine aspect of God which became the man Jesus. Accordingly, the contrast he often provides is not simply that of the Laws on the one hand and the Holy Spirit on the other, but rather between the Laws and the Christ. Despite his attitude to the Laws, his citation or paraphrase of Scripture reflects the unlimited authority which Scripture had for him, for in his own lights he was a loyal Jew. But it must be said plainly that his effortless use of Scripture does not promote clarity to the modern reader.

It has long been noted that Paul can start on one train of thought, be diverted from it, and not return to the original train. Equally disconcerting is what in a sense we might call his "stream of consciousness" manner. Paul dictated his letters; his mention, for example, of Abraham's old age and weakness brings it about that a few paragraphs later he picks up the word weakness and applies it to himself. In literary manner he deals abundantly with contrary matters: weakness and strength; courage and cowardice; the letter and the spirit. Also, he can string together an abundance of synonyms or synonymous phrases.

It is necessary for clarity to try to define a key phrase of Paul's: "justification by faith," a phrase meditated on and embellished in later Christianity. The term "justify" comes from the law court; it means "to declare just," "to acquit," that is, to acquit rather than to find guilty. In Paul's use, though, there is a greater subtlety. A person, definitely guilty *in the past* of sin or crime, can be "justified," that is, transformed into innocent, through the erasure, as it were, of the admitted trespass. "Justified," then, does not imply that a person was free of guilt, but rather that a guilty person has become freed of his guilt. In other words, "to justify" does not mean to assert that there had been no trespass, but rather to contend that guilt for admitted trespass has been wiped out.

As to "faith," Paul does not mean *what* a person believes, but rather a person's complete and unreserved reliance on

God, to which God responds by justifying the person. God "acquits" the person not through that person's having earned or merited God's favor; not at all. Rather, God provides a free gift, "grace," to the person who relies on Him completely. One cannot earn the wiping out of admitted trespasses; but God's grace can wipe them out for the person "of faith."

For a man to try to earn God's grace or favor is futile; it cannot be earned. For a person to suppose that he can earn God's favor means he is relying on himself, and, if so, he is thereby not relying on God. The Synagogue mitzvah system (which Paul speaks of as "works of the Law") is precisely that reliance by man on himself which Paul considers utterly and totally wrong and ineffective. It follows, then, that Jews are unable to *earn* God's favor; therefore they are not better off, despite their inheritance of Scripture, than are Gentiles who have no such inheritance. It is to Gentiles, to repeat, that Paul feels himself appointed. He offers them not obedience to the Laws of Moses, but the opportunity of receiving the Holy Spirit.

Perhaps this introduction can make the reading of the Epistles easier. But the difficulties will not all disappear, for we deal, lamentably, with one side of an at least two-sided correspondence, and there are bound to be gaps in our knowledge and in our understanding of matters that chance to be only alluded to and not fully presented.

When Paul had been in Thessalonica he had preached with great eloquence and vividness that the Second Coming was to take place in the near future. But apparently between the time of Paul's first visit and the time of the writing of the First Epistle to the Thessalonians there had been those in the church who had died. Paul had to address that disturbing matter. Paul writes that God would bring these dead to Him along with Jesus, who had also died. That is, when the Second Coming would take place, those still alive at that time would not precede the dead; rather, the Lord Himself would descend from heaven, fully in command, with an archangel's voice and a trumpet of God. Then those dead who were in Christ[6] would rise first, and afterward the living would be snatched away in the clouds to meet the Lord in the air

(4.13-18). As to when this event would take place, the Thessalonians ought to have known already that the End would come without precise schedule, that is, like a thief in the night; it would come as sudden destruction on those who thought themselves secure, as suddenly as birth pangs come to a pregnant woman. The believer therefore needed to be alert for the unknown time when it would come.[7]

In II Thessalonians, Paul cautions against excessive credulity about the Second Coming. Apparently some other leaders insisted that it was soon to take place and said too definitely when that would be. Before the End there must first be "apostasy," and then the revelation of "the man of lawlessness, the son of destruction, who raises himself over everything, so that he seats himself in the Temple of God, showing himself to be divine."[8] But in due course this wicked man, and his followers, will be destroyed. The Epistle goes on to counsel the avoidance of contact with any "brother" who acts in a disorderly way. And if any one in the community does not want to work, the community should not support him.

At one time Paul was imprisoned.[9] From prison he wrote his Epistle to the Philippians, an essentially cheerful letter, apparently in thanks for a gift or gifts sent to him. Paul speaks of the progress made in spreading the Christian word ("preaching the Christ"); regrettably, this spreading is occurring through some men of low character, marked by envy and strife.[10] Paul urges the Philippians to stand fast in unity with him against his opponents; these latter are not identified.

He proceeds to encourage them to humility, in imitation of Christ Jesus. Paul quotes what appears to be an older hymn which declares that the Christ

who existed in the form of God did not consider equality with God something to be seized, but rather emptied[11] himself, taking the form of a slave and coming into the likeness of men, so that, now as man, he humbled himself, becoming obedient even until death, death on the cross.

The allusion in "something to be seized" is usually taken to be Satan, who was once a member of the divine council (as in Job ch. 1), but who in rebellion tried to seize the powers or the throne of God; God had thereupon cast Satan from heaven to earth, and Satan had become the master of the earth. The hymn, then, celebrates the contrast between the arrogant Satan who grasped for power and the humble Christ Jesus: the Christ had come to earth as the lowly man Jesus and had in obedience to God submitted to death on the cross. God had therefore "raised him to the highest and given to him the name that is above every name, that in the name of Jesus every knee should bend, whether of those in heaven, on earth or below the earth, and that every tongue should acknowledge that Jesus Christ is Lord for the glory of God the father."

But Paul also advises the Philippians to "look out for the dogs, look out for the evil workers, look out for the mutilators [of the flesh]." The warning is against opponents of Paul. These opponents contend that circumcision is obligatory on converts to the new movement. Paul considers circumcision unnecessary. Speaking of "spiritual circumcision," he contends that the "truly circumcised" are those who do sacred service in the spirit of God, not those who are circumcised "in the flesh." If there were any basis for confidence in the flesh, Paul certainly possessed his own. He was "circumcised on the eighth day"; he was "by extraction an Israelite, of the tribe of Benjamin, a Hebrew of Hebrews." Respecting the Law, he was "a Pharisee; respecting zeal, a persecutor of the church, respecting righteousness in the Law, blameless." But he goes on to give a contrast between righteousness arising from obedience to scriptural Law and a higher righteousness arising from faith.

Whereas in Philippians the contrast between scriptural Law and faith is coincidental, in Galatians the contrast comes into sharp focus. The background for this eloquent letter is clearly stated in the Epistle: Paul had founded this church,[12] and had done so on the premise that scriptural mitzvot would not there be observed; now word has come to him that certain visitors have persuaded the Galatians to change and to become observers. At issue for a very angry Paul is both the principle of the necessity of observing the scriptural Law and also that of his own personal status and authority.

The opening words disclose his angry defense of his person: "Paul, an Apostle not from men nor through men but through Jesus Christ and God the father. . . ." After routine but brief greetings, he says: "I wonder how quickly you have shifted from me who called you. . . . If I, or an angel from heaven, preaches to you something different from what I had preached to you, let him be cursed."

The message which he had brought the Galatians was not of human origin. Paul had not received it from men, nor been taught it by men; it had come to him as a revelation of Jesus Christ. To prove this, he turns to data about himself: When he had still been within Judaism, he had "persecuted" the church of God and "laid waste" to it. His progress in Judaism had been greater than that of many of his same age and background, for he had been more zealous for the paternal traditions than they. But God had set him apart while still in his mother's womb, and had called him in divine grace to reveal his Son in him in order that Paul might declare the good news to the Gentiles. On being called, Paul had not conferred with any man. He had not gone to Jerusalem to those who were "Apostles before him." Rather, he had gone to Arabia, and thereafter to Damascus. Three years later he had gone to Jerusalem for fifteen days, to visit Cephas;[13] apart from Cephas, the only other Apostle he had seen was "James,[14] the brother of the Lord."

Paul had then gone into parts of Syria and further north into Cilicia, and was still unknown personally in Judea, though there it was reported that the former persecutor was now preaching the faith, to the delight of those in Judea. Fourteen years elapsed before he had gone to Jerusalem. He had gone in accordance with a revelation (that is, God, not man, had sent him there). In Jerusalem he had set forth "the gospel which he was preaching to Gentiles," privately, to the leaders, for he feared that they might impede him. As a mark of Paul's independence of the leaders, Titus had not been compelled to be circumcised, though he was a Gentile.[15] Some "false brothers" in Jerusalem had challenged Paul, but Paul had not bowed to them. The leaders in Jerusalem had nothing new to impart to Paul; when they grasped that Paul had been entrusted (by God) to preach to the uncircumcised, as Peter had been to the circumcised, the "pillars" (leaders) approved of what Paul and his other companion were doing, provided that they would keep the poor of Judea in mind. All, then, presumably had been settled and agreed on during that visit about Gentiles not observing the commandments.

But later on there was an incident in Antioch; Cephas and Paul were both there, eating with the Gentiles. But when some men, sent out from Jerusalem by James, the brother of Jesus, arrived, Cephas had ceased to eat with the Gentiles, out of fear of the circumcised visitors. For this cessation, Paul had condemned Cephas to his face. Moreover, other Jews in Antioch had also ceased to eat with Gentiles. Paul had said to Cephas, in the presence of the people: "If you, a Jew, live as do Gentiles, why are you compelling Gentiles to live like Jews?"

Moreover, Jews like Paul recognized that a man is justified not through the mitzvot of the Law, but rather through their faith in Christ Jesus. Paul had long ago abandoned (literally, "died to") the Law. If righteousness could have come through the Law, then (logically) Christ had died in vain.

Paul as the father, the founder, of the Galatian church, was like Abraham, who had believed in God and this had been "accounted to Abraham as righteousness" (Gen. 15.6). People who relied on faith were indeed the sons of Abraham, for Scripture had declared earlier (Gen. 12.3) that through Abraham the (Gentile) nations would be blessed. On the other hand, those who relied on "works of the Law" were under a curse (as proved by Deut. 27.26).

But no one can achieve righteousness through the Law. "The righteous person will live through faith" (Hab. 2.4); the Law, however, has no direct connection with faith. Christ had redeemed "us" from the Law—which was a curse—by himself becoming that curse (through his crucifixion), proved by the passage (Deut. 21.23), "cursed is any man hanged on wood." The Christ event had happened in order that Abraham's blessing should come to Gentiles, so that they should receive that promise (in Gen. 12.3) through faith.

The line of reasoning, if put in other words, is the following: A promise, involving a blessing, had been made to Abraham. The blessing was promised to Abraham's descendants.

But who were his descendants? While the natural answer would be the Jews, Paul's answer is, instead, that they are the Gentile Christians. Paul's proof is that a valid "covenant" cannot be set aside, nor can it undergo additions. The verse (Gen. 12.3) which speaks of promises to Abraham mentions his seed, in the singular. That seed, being singular, cannot be the Jews (a plural), but must, instead, be the Christ. That promise about the seed was a covenant of the time of Abraham that could not be set aside or added to. Now, the Law of Moses came onto the scene 430[16] years later than Abraham. The Law of Moses could not set aside the earlier covenant of the time of Abraham.

The Law was valid only for the period of time until the "seed [the Christ] would come to whom the promise had been made." Moreover, the Law had been ordained by angels[17] in the hand of a mediator (Moses). Where there is only one party concerned, there is no need of a mediator,[18] and God is one; neither a mediator nor that which was mediated were needed. (That is, the Laws were of a relatively lowly origin and Moses was not truly needed.)

We need to keep in mind that for Paul Scripture is unreservedly sacred, and that the Mosaic Laws are in Scripture. Therefore Paul needs to find a harmony between the ongoing sanctity of Scripture, which he accepts, and the Mosaic Laws, which he has turned his back on. He does this in relationship to factors of time. Scripture had at one stage incorporated everything under sin (that is, under the Law), but for only a limited period, this in order to look forward to the time when the promise would be fulfilled to those believing in Jesus Christ. Until this ultimate time of faith, Jews were under the Law; during that period, the Law was a tutor. Now that the time of the Christ has come, people have outgrown the tutor and are no longer under him. "You are all sons of God through faith in Christ Jesus." The Law is irrelevant now. "There is no longer Jew or Gentile, slave or freeman, male or female: you are all one in Christ. If you are of Christ, then you are really Abraham's seed, heirs in accordance with the promise."

The word "heirs" now prompts him to repeat the idea of the tutor, but in different terms. When an heir is a baby, he

is no different from a slave, for he is under the charge of
overseers and household stewards until the time designated
by the father.

So even we, when babes, were enslaved, under the "ele-
ments" of the world.[19] *When the full period had elapsed, God*
sent out his Son, born of a woman, born under the Law, so
that He might ransom those under the Law, in order that we
might receive the status[20] *of sons. Inasmuch as you are sons,*
God sent the spirit of his Son into your hearts, and it cries
out, "Abba, Father." You are no longer slaves, but sons. Dur-
ing your time of enslavement, you were slaves to beings not
divine by nature.

But if the Galatians revert to observing the Law, they are
turning back to the weak and poor "elements." They are un-
necessarily observing days, and months, and seasons, and
years, that is, the sacred days, as in Leviticus 23.

Paul proceeds to attack those willing to be under the Law,
asking them if they really know the Law. It is narrated in
the Law that Abraham had two sons, one out of a slave (that
is, Hagar) and one out of a free woman (that is, Sarah). The
son out of the slave was born under ordinary circumstances;
the other was born through a promise. Paul says that this is
allegory. The women represent two covenants.[21] The one
covenant, that of Hagar, is from Mount Sinai, the mountain
in Arabia; Hagar brings forth children to slavery. Sinai is
like the present Jerusalem, which with her children is in
slavery to the Law. But there is a Jerusalem "above," and
that lofty Jerusalem is free, and is the true mother.[22] He goes
on: "We [Christians] like Isaac, are children of the promise
[Sarah]. Just as the one born of the flesh [that is, the Jews]
long ago persecuted the one born according to the spirit [the
Christians] so now also." (Paul seems to derive this by a
very free interpretation of Gen. 21.9.) Scripture had enjoined that the slave and her son (the Jews) be driven out
(Gen. 21.12-13), since the son of the slave should not be an
heir together with the son of the free woman (Christians).

He asserts, "If you become circumcised [as the Law en-
joins], Christ is no profit to you. He who undergoes circum-

cision, moreover, is thereby obligated to observe the entire Law. If you try to observe the Law, you are separated from Christ, and have fallen away from his grace.[23] We who do not observe the Law await, through the spirit, the hope of righteousness by faith. In Christ Jesus, neither circumcision, nor uncircumcision, is of any value. The true value is love working through faith."

Paul's attitude toward the Law is exactly the reverse of the views in all other surviving Jewish writings. We do not know precisely how and why Paul came to this reversal of attitudes; it is clear, though, that he came to it with unreserved conviction.

At no point does Paul propose lawlessness; to the contrary. It might be put this way, that he saw no prospect of man's achieving through obedience to the Law the ethical goal in them; that ethical goal, though, was achievable through faith and the spirit. The ethical goal was no less precious to Paul than to other Jews.

Passingly, in Galatians, Paul raises the issue of his personal authority and the validity of what he taught. I and II Corinthians are reflections of the rise of this double issue to a central concern. Paul's defense of himself and his doctrines arose because in Corinth both were challenged.

It is standard in modern scholarship to view II Corinthians as a composite of fragments of possibly as many as three different letters. Indeed, it is held that II Corinthians 6.14-7.1 is a fragment of a letter earlier than I Corinthians; II Corinthians 10.1-13.10 is a fragment later than I Corinthians. The fourth and latest fragments are viewed as II Corinthians 1.1-6.13, 7.2-9.15, and 13.11-13.

The nub of II Corinthians 6.14-7.1 reflects counsel to Christians not to be inappropriately yoked (married) to unbelievers, asking what there can be in common between righteousness and lawlessness, between Christ and Beliar? What is not clear is the context for this passage.

I Corinthians reveals that Paul has been disturbed by reports from Corinth of dissensions and parties. These parties are listed as "Paul's"; "Apollos' "; "Cephas' "; "Christ's."

The "party of Paul" presumably held viewpoints and ideas such as we have already seen. The party of Cephas would presumably be that of "judaizers," advocates of observing the mitzvot. Apollos is identified in Acts 18.24-28 as a Jew of Alexandria, and possibly the "party of" Apollos was extremely partisan to allegory, as was Philo, and possibly espoused a contrast beyond that of Paul's between "flesh" and spirit, and possibly was unconcerned about the literal traditions taught about Jesus. Possibly the "party of Christ" was even more extreme.

As to the party that bore his name, Paul asks, Was it Paul who was crucified on their behalf? Were they baptized in Paul's name?[24] His own followers ought not to have formed a separate party and thus contributed to the divisiveness. In preaching in Corinth, Paul had not relied on human wisdom, but rather on a demonstration of spirit and power. He had revealed God's wisdom in a hidden mystery which God had foreordained (before Creation) for the glory (of believers). Not a single ruler of the world (such as Roman officials) had known this divine secret, for otherwise they would not have crucified the Lord. To know the depths of the spirit of God requires that one have the divine spirit (like Paul), and not the spirit of this world.

He scolds the Corinthians. They vaunt themselves over Apostles, but should not do so, for Apostles have endured ordeals of hunger, thirst, ill-clothing, and homelessness. He is sending Timothy to them to remind them of what Paul, their founder, had taught them; he himself would also come at some time. Did the Corinthians wish him to come with a rod (to punish), or with love and gentleness of spirit?

Paul tells that he is shocked at a sexual irregularity, unknown even among pagans, but tolerated in Corinth— namely, that between a man and his father's wife. Were Paul present, he would compel them to hand that man over to Satan for destruction. When, previously, Paul had instructed the Church not to associate with those who commit sexual irregularities, he had not meant people outside the Church, but rather the irregular within it. Paul informs the Corinthians that it is well for man not to touch a woman. Yet to forefend against sexual irregularity, each man should have his own wife, and each woman her husband, and they should render (the sexual gratification) due. They should not deprive each other, except by common consent, and this only for a restricted time, using that period for prayer. The unmarried ought to remain unmarried, like Paul himself. If they lack control, they should marry, for it is better to marry than to be aflame.

Paul then cites "the Lord": A married couple should not separate. If they separate, the wife must either remain unmarried or become reconciled to her husband. A Christian married to a non-Christian should not leave his or her mate. If, however, the non-Christian leaves his or her mate, that is admissible. (The term "Christian" arose after Paul's time; it does not appear in any Epistles and I use it to avoid cumbersome alternate expressions.)

As to food, specifically food offered to idols, such food does not truly defile the eater. Since, though, the sight of a Christian eating such food can offend another Christian, it is better to abstain from it.

Paul turns then—with some abruptness—to defend his being an Apostle. "Am I not an Apostle? Have I not seen Jesus our Lord? Are you not my work in the Lord?" If other (communities) do not regard him as Apostle, certainly the Corinthians should regard him as one. The Corinthians can judge from Paul's conduct whether he is truly an Apostle or not: He had abstained from marriage, though the brothers of the Lord, and Cephas, had not. He had worked for his food, though he could have expected the Church to care for him.[25] He had abstained from benefiting in any human way from his office as an Apostle. Free as he was, he had made himself a slave in order to win adherents. Respecting Jews, he acted as a Jew; to those under law, as if he were under law, to those not under law, as if he were without law. He had become all things to all people, that by all kinds of means he might save some. He cites an example from Scripture[26] to warn the Corinthians that their having become Christians would not automatically save them.

Paul urges the Corinthians to hold fast to the traditions he had handed over to them. Men should pray with head uncovered, but women with head covered.[27]

It was reported to Paul that when the Corinthians assembled, they did not really come to "eat the Lord's meal."[28] Some had eaten their meal before coming; others came hungry, and some came drunk. Paul reminds them that he had received (instruction) from the Lord[29] which he had in turn handed over to the Corinthians: On the night when the Lord was handed over,[30] after[31] the eating, he had broken a loaf and raised a cup, identifying the loaf as his body and the cup as "the new covenant in my blood. Do this as often as you drink for remembrance of me." Whoever eats the loaf or drinks the cup unworthily will be guilty of profaning the body and blood of the Lord. A man should be mindful of what he is doing, lest he eat and drink improperly, thereby not discerning the body (of the Lord). For this reason many among the Corinthians are weak and sickly and many have died. When the Corinthians come together to eat, they should wait for each other; the hungry person ought to eat at home.

Paul feels impelled to speak of the variety of gifts which people possess, gifts that all come from the same spirit of God. One person has the "word of wisdom," another "the word of knowledge"; one has faith, another the ability to heal; one can do powerful works; another can prophesy; one can discern (differences among) spirits; one can make ecstatic utterances, another interpret such utterances.

But all these gifts emanate from one and the same spirit. Hence, the Church ought to be unified, as a body is unified, despite the differences in eyes and ears and the limbs. The Church is the body of Christ: "If one member suffers, all other members suffer with it." The parts of this Church body are "first, Apostles; second, prophets; third, teachers; then doers of powerful work, healers, helpers, directors, and the competent in ecstatic utterance."[32]

The clashes that take place among those possessing these different gifts need to be eliminated. But how? By the use of love. I Corinthians 13.1-7 is a hymn to love; though in prose, it is genuinely poetic.

Paul rebukes some in the Church who doubt resurrection.[33] He alludes, first, to what he had preached to them: Christ had died, according to the Scriptures, had been buried, and had been raised on the third day, according to the Scriptures.[34] Christ then had appeared "to Cephas and then to the Twelve. After that he appeared to more than five hundred people, most of whom are still alive, but some have died." He had then appeared to James and to all the Apostles.[35] Last of all, he had appeared to Paul.[36] He speaks of himself as the least of the Apostles, indeed not deserving to be called one, because he had persecuted the Church. Yet on coming into the movement, he had labored more than all of the Apostles and therefore the Corinthians should join in his belief in resurrection.

But those who accept resurrection are prone to ask questions, for example, "In what kind of body will the resurrected come?" In answer, God gives every plant a body that he chooses, and bodies vary, as among men, animals, birds, and fish. So, too, there are heavenly bodies and also earthly ones; and there are different kinds of glory, as in the case of the sun, or the moon, or the stars. The resurrected body is raised in its own kind of glory, as a spiritual body.[37]

In II Corinthians 10.1-13.14, Paul speaks again of his personal authority. If he seems to boast too much about the authority God gave him, he will nevertheless not be put to shame. Nor should the Corinthians be persuaded by those rivals of Paul who belittle him, charging that he writes weighty and tough letters, but that in person he is weak and his speech amounts to nothing. He does not boast beyond measure, but only in accordance with what God has given, and God's gifts to him include the Corinthians! Paul had been the first to come to them preaching the good news; they were within the measure of what God had allotted to him.

Having founded them ("betrothed them to Christ"), he is now afraid they are being seduced away from the purity and chastity due the Christ, as Eve had been by the serpent. When someone comes and preaches (a message about) Jesus different from what Paul has preached, they, foolishly, receive it readily. But Paul does not consider himself in any way inferior to these outstanding[38] Apostles. He had preached the gospel to them without its costing them anything. He had "robbed" other churches in accepting their provisions in order to serve the Corinthians. He would continue not to be a burden, in order to refute those who boasted that they worked as he did. These boasters were false apostles, lying workers, masquerading as Apostles of Christ. This was not to be wondered at, for Satan masquerades as an angel of light, and Satan's servants know how to masquerade.

Were (his detractors) Hebrews? He too was one. Were they Israelites?[39] He too was one. Descendants of Abraham? So was he. Are they servants of Christ? Speaking as if a madman,[40] Paul is a far better servant, more outstanding in the work that has been done, more often imprisoned, much more often subject to beatings, more often exposed to death. Five times he had received the thirty-nine lashes imposed by Jews (as a court sentence, Deut. 25.3). Three times he had been beaten with staffs; once he had been stoned.[41] Three times he had been shipwrecked, adrift at sea a day and a night. He had traveled constantly, undergoing dangers from rivers and highwaymen, dangers from fellow Jews and from Gentiles, dangers in the city, dangers in the wilderness, dangers at sea, and dangers from spurious Christians. He had undergone labor and toil, frequent sleeplessness, frequent hunger and thirst and fasting, the cold and nakedness. It had happened that the governor of Damascus under King Aretas[42] had stationed guards around the city to seize him; Paul had escaped by being lowered in a wicker basket through a window.

Paul can boast also of visions and revelations of the Lord. He, a man in Christ, fourteen years earlier was caught up to the third heaven—whether in the body or out of it, he did not know; only God knows. There, in paradise, he had heard things not to be told, things a man ought not utter. But, alas, he had been given a thorn[43] in his flesh, this a messenger from Satan to prevent him from being too much exalted in his own eyes. Three times he had entreated the Lord to rid him of the pain, but He had said, "My grace is enough for you; [My] power is being perfected in your weakness." Paul therefore was content to endure weaknesses, insults, necessities, persecutions, and calamities; for whenever he was weak, that was when he was strong.

The Corinthians may have erroneously believed that it was to them that Paul was defending himself. No, it was to God; he would not spare those whom he had warned already, once when there and once by letter.

There was a lapse of time—how much we do not know—during which there were some developments, regrettably unclear, which changed the tone of Paul's relationship from anger and rebuke to that of reconciliation and relief, as in II Corinthians 1.1-6; 6.11; 7.2-9.15. He had deliberately shunned returning to Corinth, so Paul writes, in order to spare them. He had written a painful letter (probably, but not certainly, that found in part in II Corinthians 10.1-13.14), to let the Corinthians know his love for them!

Paul proceeds to expound the "new covenant" of which God had made him the agent. The old, the written covenant (the Laws of Moses) kills; the new covenant, "the spirit," is life-giving. The old covenant had come with such radiance that the Israelites could not look constantly at the face of Moses. The radiance of the old covenant has come to an end; the radiance of the new excels it. Moses (as is related in Exod. 34.33-35) had worn a veil, for even now whenever Moses is read, a veil lives over the hearts of Jews.[44] But Christians, not veiled, behold the glory of the Lord and are transformed into his image, to a (higher) glory. If Paul's teaching seemed veiled, it was veiled only to those who were perishing, whose minds the God of this age had blinded.

Paul was only a human. He was perplexed as to where to go, but not without available roads to travel. He was persecuted, but not completely abandoned. He was thrown to the ground, but not destroyed. He always bore in his body the death of Jesus, in order that the life of Jesus might also be manifest in his body. Death was a constant for him; life was a constant for the Corinthians.

Paul alludes to allegations against him, including the charge that he is out of his mind. If out of his mind, it is on behalf of God. If sound in mind, it is on behalf of the Corinthians. The love of Christ alone is determinative; the purely human (as implied in soundness or unsoundness of mind) can mean nothing. The purely human is of no consequence, not even in the case of the Christ as a human; the latter is no longer of concern.[45] A man in union with the Christ is a new creation. Through the Christ, God had reconciled[46] Paul to him, and had put on Paul the burden of reconciling other men to God. Paul, accordingly, was an ambassador in the role of Christ. As men had become righteous through Christ, now they could become righteous through Paul.

At this point in our exposition, we need to grasp clearly the issue in the controversies in the Galatians and Corinthians. To the question, did the adherents of, or proselytes to, the new movement need to observe the Jewish laws imbedded in the Pentateuch, Paul not only said no; it is clear that he also contended that the observance was an obstacle to the attainment of righteousness. Paul regarded what he taught as unique, compared with other Christian teachers. In the Church there were not only those who rejected Paul's preachment as misguided and wrong, but also those who went on to deny his credentials as an Apostle. It is likely that those Apostles whom Paul calls impostors and liars called him similar names; it seems reasonable that the rivals of Paul carried with them credentials written for them by the leaders in Jerusalem. When Paul, in Galatians, asserts that he is an Apostle from and through God, he is in effect conceding that he lacks such written credentials. But he believed that he did not need them.

The Epistle to the Romans is Paul's effort to provide a rather full-bodied exposition of his unique stand. It is an *apologia*, a statement almost defensive in character of his highly personal version of Christianity, addressed to a church which he had neither founded nor ever visited.

Romans 16 is widely viewed as a later addition[47] to the Epistle (or two additions, vv. 1-3 being one and vv. 4-13 a second). Manuscript evidence points to the circumstance that the words *in Rome* (1.7) "were absent, if not from an early recension of the Epistle, at least from a number of early copies. . . ."[48] The possibility has commended itself to some scholars that this Epistle, or at least a form of it, was not specifically directed to Rome but rather was designed as a circular letter, to tell many a church just what Paul's preachment was. Most scholars, though, believe the letter was for Rome. In it Paul gives a calm and reasoned presentation of much he had written in anger to the Galatians, and we need not reflect the repetition in full.

Paul seems to be at pains to persuade and win "judaizers,"

rather than merely to level attacks on them. Whereas in Galatians he emphasizes in the first sentence that he is an Apostle from God and not man, here he is more restrained. He writes that he owes an obligation to declare "my version of the Gospel to you in Rome. . . ."

That message entailed the conviction that God's wrath was being revealed from heaven against all human impiety and unrighteousness. People should have known what can be known of God, for God Himself had revealed that; God's invisible qualities have been clearly discernible, at least in man's perception of the results of creation. Therefore, not to have known God is inexcusable. The wicked, obviously having known God, did not glorify or thank Him; rather, they engaged in futile pursuit of their own logic, so that their stupid minds became even less enlightened. Such people became foolish and exchanged the glorious, incorruptible God for images of corruptible men and of birds and reptiles. God let them wallow in the defilement of their bodies; women and men both became homosexuals, and their minds became all the more debased, filled with all forms of wickedness. When the Great Judgment would come, God would reward the righteous with eternal life, and punish the wicked with wrath and fury, in each case the Jew first and then the Gentile (1.18-32).

As to the standard by which men would be assessed, Gentiles, being outside the Law, would be punished by a standard which was not the Mosaic law, but Jews would be punished by that Law. Gentiles have a law[49] in their hearts. The Jews, having the (written) Law, are wicked and in defiance of the Law, their trespasses going beyond hypocrisy into sheer blasphemy.[50] Circumcision is a benefit only if one truly observes the Law; an uncircumcised person who is righteous is to be regarded as if circumcised. A man is not a Jew by outward appearances, nor is true circumcision outward. The true Jew is a Jew inwardly, and the true circumcision is that of the heart, not that required in a written Law (2.1-29).

"What superiority does a Jew have? What is the benefit of circumcision?" (He does not directly answer this second question.) His answer to the first question is, Very much in every way. To Jews were entrusted the sacred words (of

Scripture). If some Jews were faithless, that does not affect the faithfulness of God.

But Jews, despite the advantage of having had the sacred words entrusted to them, are not at all in a better position than anyone else, for all men, Jews and Gentiles, are under sin.[51] Now, however, all men have been made righteous as a free gift by God's grace through the redemption by Christ Jesus, whom God made an expiation, through faith, by his blood. God had thus shown forbearance for sins previously committed; now, too, he makes righteous anyone who has faith in Jesus.

To boast of being Jewish is futile, for a man is not justified by the deeds required in the Law; he is justified by faith without regard to the requirements in the Law. God is not the God of Jews alone, but of Gentiles, too.

But does this mean that Paul is abolishing the Law? Not at all! He upholds the Law. One should look at the instance of Abraham. Genesis 15.6 declares that Abraham believed in God, and it was counted for him as righteousness; as yet Abraham had not been circumcised (for that comes in ch. 17). First had come his righteousness; later, circumcision was added as a sign or a seal. Abraham was the father of the faithful uncircumcised and faithful circumcised!

The promise[52] to Abraham did not come through the Laws, but came, rather, through the righteousness of faith. If who these heirs are is determined by the observance of Laws, then faith becomes empty, and the divine promise is voided. The Law (ultimately) produces wrath (for trespasses); where there is no law there is no violation.[53] Accordingly, it is faith which is decisive. Since the promise to Abraham rested on faith (rather than on the Law), Abraham is the father[54] both of observers of the Law and of non-observers who share in his faith. The passage, "This was reckoned for him as righteousness," applies not only to Abraham, but to Paul too, and also to those who believe in God who raised Jesus the Lord from the dead, after Jesus had been put to death for the sins of the believers and was resurrected for their justification (ch. 4).

Paul speaks of one man (meaning Adam, as in 1 Cor. 15.21-49) through whom sin and death had entered the world. Sin had existed before the time of Moses and his law,

but sin is not really counted when there is no law. Death and
sin, indeed, had reigned from Adam to Moses, even over
those who had not sinned in the way that Adam had. But the
grace of God, and the free gift of the one man Jesus Christ,
had affected many, many more people. A single trespass (on
the part of Adam) had brought condemnation on mankind;
the free gift (of God) had brought justification through
Christ after many trespasses of mankind. Adam's disobedience (of God) in the Garden of Eden (Gen. ch. 4) had
brought condemnation for many; Christ's obedience (of
God) had made many righteous.

When, after Abraham's time, Law entered in through
Moses (on the one hand), Law increased trespass; (on the
other hand) through the increase of sin, God's grace became
even more abundant. As (at one time) sin, leading to death,
could reign (supreme), now grace, leading to eternal life,
could reign through the Lord Jesus Christ.

Paul digresses to knock down a straw man, namely, a contention that to remain in sin is a means of increasing divine
grace.[55] He says, "Not at all."

But, as if fearful that he has too clearly identified the Law
and sin, and possibly thereby offended, Paul denies emphatically that the Law is indeed sin. Rather, Paul says that he
would not have known what sin was were it not for the Law.
The prohibition of covetousness in the Law (Exod. 20.17;
Deut. 5.21) brought him both to a knowledge of covetousness
and also to all manners of personal covetousness. Had there
been no Law, there would have been no sin, and sin would in
effect have been dead; when the commandments (of Moses)
came into being, sin came to life again. Paul had thereupon
"died," since the commandment whose purpose was life had
instead brought him to "death." In the very commandments,
sin had found encouragement by which to seduce Paul and
thereby to "kill" him. But the Law was nevertheless holy,
and the commandments were holy, just and good.

It was not the Law that brought in death; rather, through
the holy and good Law sin had come about, and thereupon
men became even more sinful, this, to repeat, through the
Law itself. How could this be? The Law, Paul asserts, is
"spiritual"; Paul, the would-be observer, is "fleshly," sold to

sin. As a result of the latter, Paul does not control his actions. He does not do what he wants to do; he does what he hates. That is, the Law itself is good, but man is not. Yet it is not Paul himself who is actually the doer or the non-doer of the Law, but rather sin that dwells in him. On the one hand, within himself he delights in God's Law, but, on the other hand, he observes in the parts of his body a "different law," at war with the "law of his mind," which makes him captive to the law of sin dwelling in the parts of his body. In his (resultant) misery, he gives thanks to God through Christ Jesus for deliverance from his body of "death."

If anxiety—namely, the fear of ultimate punishment at the hands of God for trespasses in the past—exists, Paul gives an elaborate assurance for believers that all is now well, and will be well in the future. Those who are in Christ are exempted from the punishment which normally ensues on condemnation. God had provided such exemption, unattainable under the Law, by sending His Son in the likeness of sinful flesh (that is, in the form of a man), and had passed condemnatory judgment on the sin in the flesh, this for the purpose of having the righteous intent in the Law carried out by those who walk in the spirit.

If the spirit of Christ is in someone, then his body is "dead" but his spirit is alive. Through the spirit of Christ, God gives life to mortal bodies. Those led by God's spirit are sons of God, joint heirs with Christ.

God works for good in everything for those who love Him and for those who have been called in accordance with His purpose. (That purpose was for) those whom He already knew to be fore-ordained[56] for conformity with the image of His son. Those whom God had fore-ordained, He had then summoned, and those whom He had summoned, He had justified, and those whom He had justified, He had also glorified.

But the Jews constituted a problem for Paul, in that they of all people, by his reckoning, should have been believers, but were not. Paul speaks in deep sorrow, wishing that he himself would be accursed and be cut off from Christ on behalf of his fellow Jews. He goes on to detail the advantages of Jews in the bygone past; indeed, Jesus himself was a Jew. But "not all of Israel are indeed Israelites." There is a distinction within Israel, so that God was concerned to save not all of Israel but only a portion, a remnant.

Jews have, indeed, a zeal for God. But they seek to establish their own righteousness (by observing the mitzvot) because they have not known the righteousness of God, or that Christ is the objective (*telos*) of the Law. What Jews should have done, instead of futilely trying to observe the Law, was to come inwardly to faith in Christ, and to profess this faith publicly, and then be saved.[57]

The Jews had had the opportunity to hear the Gospel, for it had been preached to them,[58] but they had not listened. Does this mean that God has rejected His people? Not at all! Indeed, Paul himself was a Jew! A portion of Israel, a "remnant,"[59] God had chosen by grace, but the rest of Israel was dulled so as not to see or hear.[60]

If, through Israel's trespass and its decline, riches had come to Gentiles, how much more would these riches be if the fullness of Israel were to come to believers!

Paul uses two figures of speech to clarify the relationship of Israel to the new movement. The first hearkens back to the ancient grain offering, a cake of which was to be presented to God. The cake itself was sacred; that lump of dough from which the cake was taken was therefore entirely sacred.[61] The cake was the patriarchs of Israel; the lump of dough was their descendants. Without developing the figure, Paul turns to another, that of an olive tree which has both its natural branches and also branches engrafted on it.[62] The olive tree is the patriarchs. Some of its branches (that is, the Jews) were broken off; Gentile believers, a branch from a wild olive tree, were grafted onto the tree in their place, to share in the fertility of the tree. However, the Gentiles needed to remember that it is not the branches which sustain the roots, but the roots which sustain the branches. Hence, Gentiles should in humility understand that as God had not spared the natural branches, so He could abstain from sparing the Gentiles, should unbelief arise among them. The natural branches, if they did not persist in unbelief, could in time be re-engrafted onto the tree.

Gentiles should understand a mystery: a dullness has come upon a part of Israel. This dullness would last until the time when the full number of Gentiles would come to salvation. Thereafter all Israel would be saved.[63] On the one hand, the Jews are enemies of the Gospel; on the other, through the patriarchs, they are the chosen, the beloved of God. God does not revoke his gifts and his call. He had called Gentiles who had been disobedient; in His mercy He could at some future time turn to disobedient Israel.

Paul turns now to advise believers about their conduct. They should be conformed not to "this age," but to a "new mind" (that is, the age to come). Paul commends humility; he commends the recognition of different capacities among the believers.[64] Love should be genuine; Christians should love and honor each other, rejoice in hope, endure under tribulation, persevere in prayer. They should contribute to the needy of the holy poor. They should bless, not curse, those who persecute them. They should leave vengeance to God.[65] They should give food and drink to the enemy.[66]

Paul speaks now of the Roman government. Every person should subject himself to the governing authorities, for no authority exists except from God, and the present authorities were instituted by God. Whoever resists the authorities resists what God has instituted, and will stand judgment. Believers should pay taxes, or tribute, and should respect and honor the civil authorities, for they are ministers of God.

As for fellow men, all the commandments are summed up in "You shall love your neighbor as yourself."[67]

Salvation (the Second Coming) is now nearer than it once was; the night is well along and day has come near. The gratification of the flesh in orgies and drunkenness, loose conduct, strife and jealousy, should give way to "donning" the Lord Jesus Christ.

He goes on to say that while he is aware of the virtues of the recipients of this letter, he has nevertheless dared to write to them as if to remind them of certain matters, for as a minister of Christ to the Gentiles, he is concerned that the offering of the Gentiles (to God) be acceptable. In the past he has constantly gone to new places, not building on the foundation of some other man; he intends to go to Spain, but will see the Roman Christians en route there.[68] Now, however, he is about to take to Jerusalem the contributions for the "saints." He speaks of his hope to be delivered from unbelievers in Judea, and to be approved by the saints in Jerusalem, so as to be able to come in joy to those to whom he writes.[69]

To tie threads together, we might give the following brief summary of Paul. By "Apostle" he meant, at least in his own case, one who held a supernatural office, the result of divine designation. He was aware that his doctrine was in aspects unique, and he gloried in that uniqueness.

His accomplishment was that, more than anyone else, he transformed the new movement from one essentially Jewish into a Gentile movement free of all obligation to the scriptural laws.

We do not know how broad and deep Paul's personal influence was in his own time, nor do we know just when or how his written Epistles became a direct influence on the new movement (as in time they surely did).

Though the developing Church was shaped by him, it did not accept him in all things on his own terms. Some of the modifications of him we will see. What it definitely accepted, as related to Judaism, was the nullification of the binding force of the demands of the Laws.

It should be clear that Paul in the Epistles said little about the human career of Jesus; that matter has almost never been the topic of his concern.

The Christ for Paul might be understood, in our words, not Paul's, as a means of Paul's "solving" the problem of God's transcendence. Paul means by "Christ" something kindred to what Philo meant by "Logos," namely, the immanent aspect of the transcendent God. For Paul, God was too elevated, too exalted Himself to be directly available to man; the Christ is the facet of God which was attainable by man, as is the Logos in Philo.

Yet there is an important distinction between the conceptions of Philo and Paul. In Philo, the Logos is a philosophic concept, an abstraction, a possibly unreal device suitable only for discourse, but in Paul the Christ is fully a reality. In

Philo, the Logos is an abstraction unrelated to time and place; in Paul the Logos is an *event*, that is, the Logos became Jesus at a time and place in history. Philo's abstract Logos could scarcely have become incarnate. Paul's sense of the incarnation is possible only because his Christ could, and in his view, did, historically become incarnate in Jesus. The Christ for Paul, then, was a divine entity, lower than God, that became Jesus in very recent history. In Paul's view, the Christ had always existed, and always would; the interval in which the Christ became the man Jesus was limited to the span of the human career of Jesus. But that interval was for Paul the crucial event in all the history of man.

There are at least two other significant differences between Philo and Paul, both relating to the Laws of Moses. For Philo the Laws were eternally valid; for Paul they had been valid only for the period from Moses to Paul himself, and now they were abolished. Philo would never have assented to a view that nullified the Mosaic laws.

Nor would Philo have agreed that man was unable to observe the Laws, and therefore unable to effect his own salvation. That is, not only is man in Philo not helpless, as Paul contends, but, to the contrary, man can and should move forward on the strength of his innate capacities.

The goal of religion, though stated in different manners in Philo and Paul, is essentially the same, that of salvation from bondage to this world and of movement into life in the spirit. While both contend that the world needs escaping from, Philo provides no direct counterpart to Paul's view of the omnipresence of controlling sin under which man is caught, nor does Philo, rationalist that he is, reflect the view of the presence of Satan in man's flesh. In Philo, Judaism is a religion of salvation by which man saves himself, while in Paul, Judaism is a religion of salvation in which man is saved by divine grace.

Paul's similarity to the Rabbis is primarily found in his sharing in their sense that Scripture is sacred, that it is susceptible of interpretation, and that, properly understood, it guides the life of the worthy. One reads occasionally that Paul argues like the Rabbis for a purpose different from them. The phrase "like the Rabbis" can be misleading; Paul argues from Scripture, and so do the Rabbis, but in no sense is his manner of arguing *like* theirs, nor his intent similar to theirs.

The origin of Paul's denigration of the Laws of Moses is, as we have said, unknown. There are some remote similarities to such pre-exilic prophets as Amos and Jeremiah, for whom the revealed word of God was the essential and the rituals dispensable. But we do not know the precise and direct influences which led Paul to his views on the Laws. Perhaps there were no influences, and perhaps his views resulted from his own intuition.

Paul was acquainted, or even familiar, with the content of the Pharisaism of his time and some passing reflections of it are found in his letters; yet it seems more reasonable to conclude that his own personal background was not Judean Pharisaism, but a Jewish Diaspora milieu into which hellenistic ideas had deeply penetrated. Jews such as Paul could absorb aspects of hellenism without any sense of the loss of personal loyalty to Judaism. Paul, of course, understood the difference between his inherited Judaism and his new convictions. He considered the latter, though, to be the true and sure version of Judaism.

· 3 ·

THE GOSPELS

Though the setting of the Gospels is the Aramaic-speaking community of Judea (and Galilee), the Gospels were written in the Gentile, Graeco-Roman world. At some stage between the events themselves and the composition of those Gospels as found in the New Testament, translation of materials about Jesus took place. It is in theory possible that one or more complete Gospels was originally written in Aramaic and that such a Gospel or Gospels was as a totality translated; indeed, Christian tradition tells that Matthew was first written in "Hebrew." Modern scholars, however, believe that, as complete documents, the Gospels were written in Greek, and were not translated from complete Aramaic documents.

While the Greek Gospels could have been written in Judea, it is more likely that they were written outside it. When modern scholars have tried to determine precisely where the Gospels were written, they have had to move from stray clues into reasonable hypotheses, this simply because none of the Gospels tells where it was written. For the most part, the scholars allocate Matthew to Antioch in Syria, Mark and Luke to Rome, and John to Ephesus in Asia Minor. An occasional scholar has suggested that John was written in Judea, but this view has met with more resistance than agreement. That the language of composition was Greek and the places of composition outside Judea suggest some distance in time and in geography between the events and the time of the writing of the Gospels.

As to when the Gospels were written, the answers given by scholars rest on deductions, not on any certainty. The deductions begin with an antecedent question: Are the four Gospels fully independent accounts, not related to each other as literary documents? Or is there reason for supposing that some literary relationship or literary dependency existed? An ancient view that survived into the nineteenth century was that Mark was an abridgement of Matthew. Its implication was that Mark was not an independent work, but, instead, derived from Matthew. When the scholarly inquiry into the Gospel questions began to flourish in the 1830's, it was noted that, on the one hand, Matthew, Mark, and Luke are largely similar in structure, and that they overlap very considerably in their content, while, on the other hand, John differs significantly in structure and extensively in content from the other three. Prior to rigorous modern study, an assumption existed that the differences in the Gospels were of little concern and had led to a composite study of the four, this through printing them in four parallel columns; such a printing arrangement was called a "harmony." Printing in parallel columns could be done quite readily with Matthew, Mark, and Luke, but John's distinctiveness posed problems. When rigorous study arose, the parallel column arrangement for Matthew, Mark, and Luke proved particularly convenient for the student, for his eye could quickly take in the similarities and differences. For these three Gospels, the collective name Synoptic ("seen together") has arisen. As scholars probed the possible relationship of these three Gospels to each other, the probing came to be called "the Synoptic problem."

As to the inherited opinion that Mark was later than and an abridgement of Matthew, there arose in 1835 a view that completely reversed things, proposing that Mark was the earliest Gospel and was written in Greek and that Matthew was a later expansion of it. That is, Matthew was not only dependent on Mark, but whatever date was arrived at for Mark implied that Matthew came some time later. Matthew, derived from the Greek Mark, was also written in Greek. Moreover, scholars came to believe that Luke also was dependent on Mark. Next, notice was taken of a matter of some importance: Matthew and Luke are both longer than Mark, with the greater length of Matthew and Luke primarily occasioned by their presentation in common of materials absent from Mark. These materials depict Jesus as teaching; Mark deals essentially with Jesus as acting. The teaching material, though it is largely common in content, is presented by Matthew in rather tightly knit, consecutive sections; in Luke this same material is found to be scattered throughout. The question was raised: Did Matthew derive this teaching material from Luke? Or did Luke derive it from Matthew? Or did both Luke and Matthew derive it from some common source, a source now lost? To most scholars, the feeling that Matthew and Luke had drawn on a now-lost common source seemed the most persuasive answer. The German word for source is *Quelle;* the letter Q became the scholarly symbol for the hypothetical source for the material common to Matthew and Luke (and absent from Mark).

Matthew, then, had composed his Gospel out of Mark and Q, and so had Luke (though both Matthew and Luke had a minor amount of material peculiar to each). That Mark and Q were sources used by Matthew and Luke, called the "two source hypothesis," came to dominate Gospel scholarship in the latter half of the nineteenth century.

The sequence of the Synoptic Gospels appears to scholars to have been Mark, then Matthew, and then Luke. Passages such as Mark 13 seem to reflect the destruction of the Temple in Jerusalem in 70. Most scholars consider Mark to come from shortly after 70, Matthew 80-90, and Luke 85-95. True, an occasional scholar ascribes Mark to a date such as 51 (as was done by Adolf von Harnack); others have suggested that a lost, earlier "edition" of Mark, rather than the inherited version, served as the source for Matthew and Luke, and that the canonical Mark comes from A.D. 135-50. But the main lines of scholarship have abided by the dates I have given.

John is normally allocated to about A.D. 100. While some scholars have felt that John is in some way related to the Synoptic Gospels, most scholars view it as coming from outside the chain that ties Mark, Matthew, and Luke to each other. The suggestions mentioned above that Mark and Luke come from Rome, Matthew from Antioch, and John from Ephesus arise from clues in statements found in Church tradition and from deductions made from the particular Gospels.

Assuming that the main lines of the literary problem have

been here adequately dealt with, the next issue is that of history—more precisely, how reliable are the historical data
presented in the Gospels: completely, mostly, partially, or
not at all? A wide range of viewpoints is found among the
scholars. Some stress the reliability of the transmission to the
later age of the material from Jesus and his Judean setting,
while at the other extreme others stress the passing of time
and the geographic distance between Jesus and the writing of
the Gospels and are skeptical about the reliability of the
transmission. The consensus among scholars is that the Gospels both contain materials authentically reflecting Jesus and
also materials which reflect the period after his time. Some
scholars express this view in saying that the Gospels reflect
as much the "Church" of the age of the Gospels as they do
Jesus himself.

That impulse in Christian scholarship (primarily Protestant) which has been called "the recovery of the historical
Jesus" has been a variety of efforts over a period of a century
and a half to try to separate material in the Gospels deemed
to go back to Jesus from the materials reflecting later times.
Among such efforts has been "form criticism." Borrowed
from the study of folklore in general, form criticism as applied to the Gospels has rested, first, on the premise that the
traditions about Jesus resembled folk traditions found in
other cultures, and that the transmission and the growth of
those traditions followed the usual folklore patterns; if one
were to classify individual Gospel items or paragraphs with
respect to their external form, it could be possible to trace
the progressive growth of an item. That is, one could begin
with an item as it is found in a Gospel, and, in theory, strip
it of the layers of growth so as to get back to the supposed
pristine or original form. Accordingly, though the Gospels as
they have been inherited reflect the Church at the age when
the Gospels were written, through form criticism one could
move back from that age to the earliest aspects of the life and
career of Jesus. New Testament form criticism might be ascribed as arising in the late 1910's.

A half-century later there arose a related discipline, "redaction criticism," namely, the inquiry as to how the authors of
the four Gospels put to use, each in his Gospel, those items

which through form criticism had been traced back to the presumed pristine aspect.

Throughout the scholarship from the 1830's until our time, there has dominated the theme of the "recovery" of the Jesus of history. The resultant convictions range from the view that only a limited quantity of material is historically authentic respecting Jesus to the view that virtually nothing is historically authentic about him.

One more observation is in order. By and large, the "recovery of the historical Jesus" has rested on the premise that the Jesus of history, a Jesus viewed in purely human terms, could be isolated, and a unique man, unique in a purely human way, described. What was the uniqueness? To be sure, Jesus was a Galilean Jew of the first century, and in a sense allied with Judaism, yet by virtue of his uniqueness (if this could be ascertained) he must have been significantly different from his fellow Jews. Out of the quest for a uniqueness in Jesus in purely human terms there arose a range of views. Some scholars described him as a social reformer, kindred to the pre-exilic prophets, who rebelled against the Jewish establishment. Others have seen him as a Jew whose personal obedience to God exceeded and transcended that of his fellow Jews. Still others saw him a Zealot whom Christian tradition had transformed into a "pacific Christ."

Such matters, important and fascinating as they are, are not in the purview of the present concern. Our topic is very limited, namely, the Jewishness of the Gospels. Here we must acknowledge the paradox that the geographical setting in the Gospels is Galilee and Judea, approximately in A.D. 29-30, when the Temple was still standing, but that the Gospels, the result of growth and development, are products of the Grecian world from A.D. 70 and thereafter, when the Temple was no longer standing. In the period between 70 and 100, the dates when the Gospels were presumably written, there took place the reorganization of Judaism at Jamnia in 90 and the maturation of the academies. But the Rabbinic literature was recorded in writing almost a century later, between 175-200. Can we use the Rabbinic literature to describe the exact contours of Judaism in 29-30? Alas, there intrudes between the recording of the Mishna about 175-200 and a look back-

ward to 29-30 the events of the end of the Temple in 70, and
of Jamnia in 90, and other developments; it is not possible to
know from the Rabbinic literature precisely what Judaism
was in 29-30. To try to be too specific is to resort to caprice.

But the issues are even more complex. Whatever it is that
the Gospels present about Judaism, their intent is not to give
an exposition of Judaism, not to echo the Rabbinic literature,
but rather to give an exposition of Jesus. True, Jesus was a
Jew. True, there are Jewish presuppositions in virtually
every paragraph of the Gospels. Yet it is a Jesus at variance
with, or over and against, Judaism and Jews that constitutes
not all, but a great deal of the warp and woof of the Gospels.
Just as serious, perhaps, is the array of Jewish matters that
completely fail of mention in the Gospel writings—the New
Year and the Day of Atonement, for example; hence the
statement that the Gospels are expositions of Jesus, not of
Judaism. Incompleteness, plus a portrayal of Jesus as over
and against Judaism and Jews, are constant problems. The
issue has been raised by Christian as well as Jewish scholars
as to whether the criticisms, aspersions, and denigrations of
Judaism and Jews are sound and fair, or not; the issue can
be raised also whether or not the specific criticism of Judaism and Jews can apply with quite equal force to Christianity and Christians. Are the Christian documents partisan
to the point of some possible unreliability? (My own opinion
is that Paul and his Epistles influence all three Gospels, but
indirectly.)

We said, after our brief summary of Jesus above (pp.
306-7), that Paul reflects one direction taken, a preoccupation
with the divinity of the Christ Jesus. The Gospels represent
a somewhat different direction; they are accounts of the human career of the Jesus. (Yet there is the supposition throughout the four canonical Gospels that Jesus was more than a
man.)

But because the Gospels are about the man Jesus, who was
a Jew, there is present in the Gospels an array of materials
which in content and form resemble materials in the Rabbinic literature. The synagogues are constantly present, as is
scriptural interpretation.

It has not seemed to me that the Gospels were written to

present an unknown Jesus to total strangers. Rather, the Gospels use and array material already familiar to Christians; the purpose of Gospels is for such known material to be properly, indeed, correctly, understood. Granted that the contents of the Gospels was important, the crux for the writer of a particular Gospel was his wish to present the contents in a manner consistent with his particular viewpoint. Similar as Mark, Matthew, and Luke are, we should note that Mark lacks both a birth narrative and a narrative about resurrection appearance; these are present in Matthew and Luke, though in quite different ways. All the three portray first a period in Galilee, then a journey to Jerusalem, and thereafter the events in Jerusalem. The route to Jerusalem in Mark and in Matthew entails having Jesus cross the Jordan eastward at the start of his journey, and then cross westward at Jericho; in Luke, on the other hand, the journey is due south from Galilee to Jerusalem. The point is that though the structure of the three is rather the same, and the content quite similar, the three nevertheless have striking differences, even in the common structure and contents.

But let it be clear that the Christian writings reflect only a tiny portion of what was developing in Christendom.

· 4 ·

THE GOSPEL
ACCORDING TO
MARK

Mark is short enough to be read in an hour or so, but rapid reading can entail the missing of important subtleties. In Greek, Mark is a plain piece of writing, not an elegant one, suggesting an unlearned but quite intelligent mind.

Mark has a clear structure. It begins with the appearance of one John the Baptist, who is identified as Elijah, the forerunner of the Messiah.[1] Jesus is baptized by John so that he is able to resist the temptations of Satan. Jesus was from Galilee; it was there that his public career began and brought him fame and followers. That career consisted of the exorcism of demons, the healing of the sick, conflicts with Jews, and the rearing of disciples. Then he went to Jerusalem, with his journey being portrayed. He arrived in Jerusalem to the acclaim of crowds, taught in the Temple compound, but alienated Jewish leaders through his teachings and his deeds, especially the cleansing of the Temple. A "plot" arose against him. One of his disciples, Judas Iscariot, "betrayed" him for money. Jesus, abandoned and denied by his disciples, was "examined" on the eve of the first day of the Feast of the Unleavened Bread. The next morning a consultation of the leaders was held, as a result of which he was brought before the Roman procurator Pontius Pilate. The latter, though deeming Jesus innocent, yielded to Jewish hostility and condemned him to death, this by crucifixion carried out by Roman soldiers. He was buried in a tomb. On the third day, women followers came to the tomb, found it empty, and were told that Jesus had been resurrected. The women fled in fright.

So much for the bare outline. More significant are some motifs and themes that are repeated. For example, prior to Jesus' arrival in Jerusalem, he three times predicts to his disciples that he will there be put to death and then be resurrected (8.31; 9.30-32; 10.32-34). How can we understand this motif? The suggestion has been made that when Christian missionaries spoke about the divine nature of Jesus, they were challenged: why had the divine Jesus let himself be put to death? The response in Mark is that the death of Jesus was neither a surprise nor a defeat.

Another motif is that Jesus, on working a miraculous cure, enjoined secrecy on the persons benefited. Why? This motif seems to answer the challenge from pagans as to why the divine Jesus needed to be taught and preached about. Why was Jesus not known without the need of missionaries to preach and spread the word about him? The answer in Mark is that Jesus was a mysterious figure and the missionaries were informed about secrets connected with him and were enjoined to reveal what in Jesus' own lifetime had been secret.

A third motif is the result of a need to explain something embarrassing, that Jesus had been crucified by the Romans. Why should Gentiles in the Roman Empire respond affirmatively to someone whom the Romans themselves had executed? The answer in Mark is that although the Romans had indeed carried out the execution of Jesus, it was the Jews who were truly responsible. The Jews had been blind about and hostile to Jesus and it was their malevolence that had brought about the death of Jesus. The motif of blind hostility takes related forms, such as controversies over healings and over who and what Jesus was and the assertion very early in the Gospel (3.6) of a consultation on the part of "Pharisees and the Herodians" about destroying Jesus. The "passion narrative"—passion means suffering—is so written as to exculpate the Roman procurator Pontius Pilate and to assign the blame to the Jews. The "parable of the wicked tenants" (12.1-12) is not truly a parable, that is, it is not a usual didactic anecdote, but is, rather, a symbolic story. The owner of a vineyard let it out to tenants and went to another country. When it was time to collect his part of the produce from the tenants, he sent a servant. The tenants beat that servant, and then another servant whom the owner had sent. A third servant the tenants killed, and so with still other servants. The owner then sent his beloved son, thinking that the tenants would respect him, but they killed him. The owner of the vineyard, accordingly, was going to come and destroy the tenants and give the vineyard to others. In this parable, the owner is God, the tenants are the Jews, the servants are the prophets, the son is Jesus, and the vineyard is God's favor. No place exists in the parable for the Romans. In Mark's account, the Jews, hearing the parable from Jesus, perceive that it is told against them.

The controversies between Jesus and others rotate around two main themes. One theme is the Sabbath, and, more precisely, whether the Sabbath regulations are or are not excessively rigid. Another theme is that the opponents, since they witness the cures or exorcisms done by Jesus, can scarcely deny the reality of them; instead, they cause controversy as to the source of the supernatural power which Jesus has displayed. The opponents charge that Jesus has received this power from Satan.

At the synagogue in Capernaum on a Sabbath (1.21-28) Jesus heals a man with an unclean spirit. Those in attendance note that "he taught as one who had [supernatural] authority, not as the scribes." His cures brought him fame throughout Galilee. On returning to Capernaum, he heals a paralytic through saying, "My son, your sins are forgiven." Scribes present wonder if this is blasphemy, for only God can forgive sins. Jesus thereupon asserts that he (the Son of man) has "authority on earth to forgive sins" (2.1-12). Scribes and Pharisees see that he and disciples sit at table with tax collectors and sinners—tax collectors were notoriously crooked. To their criticism Jesus says, "I came not to call the righteous but sinners."

A controversy over fasting (2.18-22) is followed by a Sabbath controversy. Disciples of Jesus pluck ears of grain on the Sabbath. Jesus defends this through citing an incident (1 Sam. 21.1-7) in which David, through necessity, ate sacred bread which only priests were to eat: "The Sabbath was made for man, not man for the Sabbath."[2] It is the next Sabbath healing, that of a man with a withered hand, which is described as bringing about the wish of the "Pharisees and the Herodians" to destroy Jesus.

The blindness of the Jews is reflected in the view ascribed to friends of Jesus that he is insane (3.19b-21). Scribes from Jerusalem allege that it is through his being possessed by Satan (Beelzebul) that he is able to cast out demons. Jesus refutes them by showing the absurdity of alleging that he casts out Satan through the power of Satan. The allegation against him is really against the Holy Spirit,[3] and this is unforgivable blasphemy.

Jesus is portrayed (3.31-35) as rejecting his family (his mother and brothers). The true family of Jesus is whoever does the will of God.

By contrast, the Gentiles (5.1-20) acclaim his marvelous exorcisms. Despite two spectacular cures (5.21-43), Jesus is rejected by the Jews in the synagogue at Nazareth, through their blindness as to what he is: "A prophet is not without honor except in his own country, and among his own kin, and in his own house." Disbelief brings it about that "he could do no mighty work there. . . ."

There is a dispute with Pharisees and with scribes, the latter from Jerusalem, over washing of the hands, this being not a biblical commandment but a halacha: in the passage it is called a "tradition of the elders." Jesus is portrayed as alleging that Jews allow a *human* tradition to nullify a biblical command. The example is that of an oath to offer a sacrifice, *corban*, with this oath adhered to even at the cost of abstaining from helping one's parents. The commandment to respect parents is biblical; the supposed inviolable oath is halachic; that is, the halacha is allowed to cancel the mitzva. (One notes that the passage by implication rejects the Rabbinic view that a halacha is divine in origin, being part of the Oral Torah.) The washing of the hands does not explicitly remain a concern in the incident. It is supplanted by an assertion that "whatever enters a man from outside cannot defile[4] him." Jesus then declared all foods clean.[5]

Jesus heals the daughter of a Gentile woman in Phoenicia[6] (7.24-30).

Whereas, in the matter of foods, Jesus is depicted as permitting what Scripture forbids, in the matter of divorce (10.1-12), Jesus prohibits what Scripture permits (Deut. 24.1).

When Jesus enters Jerusalem (11.1-10) he is welcomed by the crowds. His "cleansing of the Temple" (11.15-19) prompts the chief priests and scribes to seek a way to destroy him; they fear the crowds. He readily parries their question to him about his authority (11.24-33). The parable of the wicked tenants (12.1-12), mentioned above, repeats the authorities' fear of the crowd. He also parries the effort of Pharisees and Herodians to entrap him respecting tribute to Caesar (12.13-17). He confounds the Sadducees on resurrection (12.18-27). His answer to one of the scribes about the greatest of the commandments concludes with the words, "After that no one dared to ask him any question." He denounces the scribes as hypocrites (12.37b-40), and, in contrast, praises a widow for her tiny but sacrificial gift (12.41-44).

He reveals to his disciples what the future will bring (ch. 13).[7] The temple will be destroyed, wars and earthquakes (13.5-8) will precede the End, and there will be persecution and strife, followed by tribulations (13.9-19), and then the "Son of man" will return, coming in the clouds (13.24-27). While these events will take place within that generation, only God knew at precisely what hour it will come (13.28-37).

Mark speaks again of the anxiety of the chief priests and scribes about stirring up the crowds by seizing Jesus. We are told that the time is "two days before the Passover and the Feast of Unleavened Bread" (14.1-2). Judas Iscariot goes to the chief priests to betray Jesus and they give him money. What is elusive is exactly what the betrayal consists of. It appears to be to point out a Jesus unknown to them; Judas does this with a kiss (14.44-46). But it seems previously that Jesus is perfectly well known through the events and the encounters narrated.

Curiously, we are told (14.12) that it is now "the first day of Unleavened Bread." At the "Last Supper," the Passover is eaten in an upper room, and during the meal, Jesus predicts his betrayal by one of the twelve. He institutes the eating of bread, symbolizing his body, and the drinking of wine, his blood.[8] The Last Supper in Mark is not to be regarded as a Passover seder; the expected elements of a seder are not present.

While Jesus prays in the company of three disciples (who fall asleep), he knows that his betrayer is at hand (14.26-42). Judas comes "with a crowd with swords and clubs, from the chief priests, and the scribes, and the elders." He kisses Jesus; they lay hands on him and seize him. A bystander draws a sword and cuts off the ear of the slave of the High Priest. Jesus protests that "day after day I was with you in the Temple teaching. But let the Scriptures be fulfilled" (14.43-52). Led to the High Priest, where other leaders are assembled, "the chief priests and the whole Sanhedrin sought testimony against Jesus to put him to death." False witnesses arise, but they give conflicting evidence. In reply to the question of the High Priest, Jesus answers that he is the Christ. The High Priest asserts that this is blasphemy. They all "condemned him as deserving death." (This is in the evening.) As soon as it is morning, a consultation is held by the "chief priests, with the elders and scribes, and the whole Sanhedrin." They lead Jesus to Pilate (14.53-15.1).

The chief priests accuse Jesus of many things. Jesus answers one question of Pilate's evasively: "Are you the king of the Jews?" "You have said so." He makes no further answers (15.2-5).

Though Pilate is prepared to release Jesus, since on the festival he used to release a prisoner,[9] the chief priests stir up the crowd to have him release a certain Barabbas, "among the rebels in prison who had committed murder in the insurrection."[10] Pilate knows of no evil that Jesus has been guilty of, but "wishing to satisfy the crowd, released for them Barabbas; and after having scourged Jesus, he delivered him to be crucified" (15.2-15). The Roman soldiers mock Jesus (15.16-20).

When Jesus is crucified, "those who pass by deride him. 'Save yourself and come down from the cross.' " So, too, the chief priests and scribes mock him (15.21-32). At the death of Jesus, a Roman centurion—a Gentile!—recognizes Jesus: "Truly this man was the Son of God."

Pilate verifies from the centurion that Jesus is dead. A Joseph of Arimathea receives the body from Pilate and lays it in a tomb with a stone rolled against it. When, on the third day, Mary Magdalene and Mary, the mother of Joses—the women are previously unmentioned—come to the tomb to anoint the body of Jesus, the stone has been rolled away, and a young man in the tomb tells them that Jesus had risen from the dead. They flee "in fear and trembling."

There are confusions, or problems, in the passion account. When was it, *before* the Passover or *on* the Passover? The fear by the chief priest of the crowd is followed by deeds that seem to show no such fear. The crowds, at first so partisan to Jesus, seem abruptly to become hostile to him.

As to Passover, it strains credulity that the Sanhedrin would meet and act that day.[11] The procedure for trials as set forth in Mishna Sanhedrin are strikingly absent here. Granted that the date of the compilation of the Mishna is almost a century and a half later, and its provisions possibly not in force in the time of Jesus, we are given so laconic an account that it is not reasonable to accept it in the form presented as historically reliable. What is presented is not the record of a trial, but an exceedingly brief impression of judicial bias.

The range of Jewish matters presented in Mark is so narrow that one could not reconstruct any rounded presentation of Judaism from it. We are not given priestly procedures in the Temple, synagogue liturgy, or home observances. The main Jewish convictions—ideas, doctrines, viewpoints—are virtually totally absent. Jesus is presented as opposed by people in the synagogues, Pharisees, Herodians, scribes, elders, Sadducees, the High Priest, the Sanhedrin.

But the disciples—these are Jewish—are presented in an even worse light. Though Mark in some early passages, when the disciples are summoned, presents them in an affirmative way, the over-all characterization is negative. They do not understand what Jesus is; they do not understand his predictions of his death and resurrection, or even what resurrection is; two of them vie for leadership; Jesus needs to rebuke Peter ("Get thee behind me, Satan"). The predictions of Jesus that the disciples will abandon him, and that Peter will deny him, come true. The disciples do not witness the crucifixion; it is women, not disciples, who find the tomb where Jesus is buried empty, and even these women seem not to understand what they have seen.[12]

Whatever the full range of the purpose of Mark, the denigration of Jews, especially the Jewish disciples, is a leading motif. So extreme is this denigration that it appears to suggest a disconnection between Christianity and the Judaism in which it was born.

The negative portrayal of the Jews etches all the more sharply the Gospel's affirmations about Jesus: his healing of the sick, exorcism of demons, and capacity to forgive sins. The intent of the Gospel According to Mark is to present the affirmations; the denigration of Jews and their Judaism is related to the main intent, but is not that main intent.

· 5 ·

THE GOSPEL
ACCORDING TO
MATTHEW

How shall one explain the paradox that Mark presents a Jewish Jesus in a Jewish setting, yet consistently portrays an over and againstness between Jesus and his Jewish setting and the Jewish people? Perhaps the answer might be that Mark, writing his Gospel for a community that is composed primarily of Gentiles, is saying to them, "Though we are a Gentile community, we are fully 'authentic.' It is true that our movement began in Judaism in Judea. Yet there existed there only blindness and a hostility, throughout the Jewish community. The Jewish disciples too were opaque and ultimately disloyal. Only the Roman centurion, a Gentile, saw clearly what Jesus was. Our movement became a Gentile movement. It is we who are the authentic believers."

If this suggestion is in any way right, it both explains the chief motifs in Mark and it also suggests a dissatisfaction which Matthew may well have felt, namely, that Mark had gone much too far in suggesting an almost total separation of the new movement from Jews and from Judaism.

In Matthew, quite beyond Mark, there are explicitly clear reflections of controversies between Christians and Jews, these living in the same vicinity. The direct reflections in Matthew have to do with the belief in the resurrection of Jesus. Matthew 27.62-66 adds to Mark's account that the chief priests and the Pharisees asked Pilate that the tomb in which Jesus was buried be guarded to prevent the disciples from coming and stealing the body of Jesus. One of the bases of Christian contentions that Jesus had been resurrected was the emptiness of the tomb when the women came to prepare the body of Jesus; in the Christian-Jewish controversies, Jews seem to have denied the persuasiveness of the tomb's being empty, alleging the body had been stolen. Matthew counters this Jewish denial by stressing that guards were posted to prevent the stealing of the body. Indeed, a few lines later (28.11-15) Matthew tells that Jews bribed the guards to lie and say that while they were asleep the disciples had come and stolen the body; he ends the passage with the words, "This report is found among the Jews to this day." Matthew, accordingly, is reflecting an active, ongoing controversy, one of contention and countercontention, with Jews in his vicinity. (There seem to be few Jews in the vicinity of Mark.)

What might other contentions and countercontentions have been? Jews in Matthew's vicinity might well have charged that Christians, through neglect, or even actual Pauline nullification, of the Laws of Moses, were a lawless people. Jews might also have contended that Christians were poorly versed,[1] or even unversed, in Scripture. The Gospel According to Matthew appears to be countering allegations of this kind. As to Christians being poorly versed in Scripture, a comparison of Mark and Matthew discloses that where Mark merely alludes to Scripture, Matthew quotes it directly; indeed, one of the notable differences between Matthew and Mark is the great frequency with which Matthew quotes scriptural passages.

As to the allegation of lawlessness, Matthew's response is to portray Jesus as a lawgiver surpassing Moses, and to present Jesus as inaugurating a law more rigorous than that of Moses. Consistent with the theme of Jesus the lawgiver, Matthew's birth narrative draws on themes from the Book of Exodus about Moses. As Moses as a babe almost died at the hands of the wicked Pharaoh, so Jesus at the hands of wicked Herod. Matthew, alone of the Gospels, tells that Joseph, the father of Jesus, fled with Jesus and his mother to Egypt, so that, in fulfillment of prophecy (Hos. 11.1), Jesus, like Moses, could be summoned out of Egypt.

That is, Matthew alters considerably the attitude found in Mark of a total unrelatedness of Jesus and the Jews. The Jewish leaders, including the Pharisees, are treated in a quite different way from Mark. In Mark they are wrong both in doctrine and in personal integrity; in Matthew they are guilty of a lack of personal integrity, but they are conceded to be proper interpreters who need to be listened to: "The scribes and the Pharisees sit on the seat of Moses; do what they tell you, but do not do what they do, for they themselves do not live up to their demands" (23.2-3). In the birth narrative,[2] it is the chief priests and scribes who advise Herod that the Messiah is to be born in Bethlehem; that is, Matthew approvingly ascribes authenticity to their words to Herod.

Matthew occasionally modifies the depiction of the disciples from what Mark presents. They are not opaque, they are not so disloyal;[3] indeed, whereas in Mark Peter is the prime example of opaqueness and disloyalty, in Matthew he is portrayed as the direct successor to Jesus: "You are Peter ("rock") and on this rock I will build my church." Where in Mark Jesus is depicted as exhibiting deep human emotions, it is Matthew's tendency to soften these, as if fearful of making Jesus too human.

But, above all, Matthew exhibits a most precise and organized mind. His Gospel is most systematic. He opens with a genealogy[4] and proceeds to a birth narrative. The birth narrative, with its reminders of Moses, is followed by five blocks of teaching material, kindred in number to the Five Books of Moses. The first of the five is the Sermon on the Mount, arranged in a highly systematic way; much of the same material is found in Luke but is there in scattered form, while here it is compact and tightly knit.

Jesus sees the crowds and ascends a mountain and teaches his disciples (5.1-2). There comes first ten[5] "beatitudes," verses which, except for the tenth, all begin with the word "blessed."[6] They are, except for the sixth, quite similar in thought to aspects of Jewish piety.

1. "Blessed are the poor in spirit;[7] the kingdom of heaven is theirs" (5.3).

2. "Blessed are the mourners; they shall be comforted"[8] (5.4).

3. "Blessed are the humble; they shall inherit the earth" (5.5).

4. "Blessed are those who hunger and thirst for righteousness;[9] they shall be satisfied" (5.6).

5. "Blessed are the merciful; they shall obtain mercy" (5.7).

6. "Blessed are the pure in heart;[10] they shall see God"[11] (5.8).

7. "Blessed are the peacemakers;[12] they shall be called sons[13] of God" (5.9).

8-9. "Blessed are those who are persecuted because of righteousness; theirs is the kingdom of heaven" (5.10); "Blessed are you when men curse and persecute you and speak all kinds of evil against you, falsely,[14] on my account"[15] (5.11).

10. "Rejoice and be glad; your reward in heaven will be great. Men similarly persecuted the prophets before you"[16] (5.12).

The eighth, ninth, and tenth sentences seem to envisage an age much later than that of Jesus, one in which Christians undergo persecution. That disorders including violence arose in various local areas between Jews and Jewish Christians seems unmistakable. The disorders appear to have been sporadic, local, and spontaneous. Romans, on the other hand, appear to have devised and carried out officially enjoined disorders against Christians,[17] usually because Christians abstained, as did Jews, from emperor worship, and hence were suspect as to their loyalty and obedience.

Matthew expands two items found in Mark in other contexts. Mark 9.50, "Salt is good . . ." becomes (5.13) *"You are* the salt of the earth." Mark 4.21, "A lamp is not put under a bushel," becomes (5.14), *"You are* the light of the world. A city built on a hill cannot be hidden. Men do not light a lamp and put it under a bushel. . . . Let your light shine before men so that they can see your good deeds and ascribe glory to your Father in heaven." (Matthew, accordingly, alters brief, vague statements found in Mark into the direct encouragement of future Christians.)

There come now striking sentences about the Law (5.17-20): "Do not think that I have come to abolish the Law and the Prophets; I have not come to abolish them but rather to

fill them in." The words, "Do not think," raise the question
of what people might have been wrong in their thinking. At
one extreme is the scholarly explanation that Jesus accepted
biblical Law in principal, but, in making moral commandments more important than ritual ones, he was wrongly interpreted as negating the ritual, and he here corrects that
misunderstanding. At the other extreme is the view that
Matthew is here opposing the viewpoint of Paul, or of Paul's
extreme disciples, and is portraying Jesus as denying the
nullification of the Law.

The words "to fill them in" are often translated "to fulfill,"
and they are equated with a frequent Rabbinic phrase, *le-
qayyém*. There is a subtle but important difference. "To fulfill" in Rabbinic thought has the sense of "to conform"—
that is, if someone faithfully observes a biblical law, he is
conforming with the requirement and thereby "fulfilling" it.
Here, though, the sense is that Jesus has come to "fill in,"
that is, to bring the incomplete to completion; the contrast is
between the denial of the abolishment of the Law and the
affirmation of the intent to bring the Law to its full completeness.

The next verse (5.18) begins with the Hebrew word *amen*,
usually translated "truly." Until heaven and earth pass
away, not a "jot" or a "tittle" (of the Law) will vanish, until
the totality will all be fulfilled. A "jot" is the smallest of the
letters of the Hebrew alphabet (the *yōd*); the "tittle" is a
tiny stroke which is part of the form of many of the letters
of the Hebrew alphabet.

Anyone who loosens[18] the least significant of the commandments, and teaches this to others, is to be regarded as
the lowest member of the Church, while one who observes
the least significant of the commandments and teaches so to
others, is to be regarded as great in the Church. (In this passage the term for Church is "kingdom of heaven.")

This emphatic validation of "law" is promptly followed
by the words, "Unless your righteousness surpasses that of
the scribes and the Pharisees, you will never enter the kingdom of heaven"; the latter words apparently here mean the
future kingdom, rather than the Church. This demand for a
higher righteousness is followed by seven contrasts wherein

Jesus is portrayed as setting requirements which go beyond those quoted from the Mosaic Law. Each of the seven is introduced by "You have heard . . . but I say to you. . . ."

The first contrast (5.21-26) attributed to "men of old," rather than directly to Scripture, extends "You shall not kill" (Exod. 20.13; Deut. 5.17), a deed, into a prohibition against deadly anger.

The second (5.27-30) is between adultery (Exod. 20.14) as a deed and the looking at a woman lustfully.[19]

The third is between the Mosaic permission of divorce (Deut. 24.1) and a prohibition of it. Such a prohibition is in Mark 10.11-12, where it is total; here the prohibition has an exception; if the ground is unchastity, divorce is possible. (Many scholars ascribe to Jesus himself a prohibition of divorce, but this exception in Matthew is viewed as representing the Church at a time after Jesus, when difficult cases needed decision.)[20]

The fourth (5.33-37) is between swearing falsely, derived from Leviticus 19.12, and the new injunction not to swear[21] at all (based on Isa. 66.1 and Ps. 48.2). One should simply say yes or no; anything more (in the form of an oath) comes from Satan. (The view seems to be that the taking of an oath will not make a congenital liar truthful.)

The fifth (5.38-42) deals with retaliation. Instead of an eye for an eye or a tooth for a tooth, Jesus is portrayed as advocating nonresistance to evil: "If some one strikes you on the right cheek, turn the other one to him too." (There is nothing in Jewish writings that advocates nonresistance.)

The sixth is between the sentiment "Love your neighbor and hate your enemy" and the injunction to love one's enemies and to pray for one's persecutors. ("Love your neighbor" is found in Leviticus 19.18; there is no biblical or Rabbinic passage which directly enjoins the hatred of one's enemy.) God deals generously with both the just and the unjust; if one loves those who love him, this is doing no better than tax collectors. "You should be perfect as your Father in heaven is perfect."

The next contrast (6.1-18), departing from the form of the preceding six, is addressed to true piety, as distinct from the eternal show, here attributed to "hypocrites." Piety directed

solely to drawing human approval fails to win reward from
God (6.1). Almsgiving should not attract the attention of
men nor be designed to elicit their praise (6.2-4). Prayer
should be unobserved and private, rather than ostentatious
as among hypocritical Jews, or babbling as among Gentiles
(6.5-8). The proper prayer is:

> Our Father, who is in heaven,
>   Sanctified be Your name.
> May Your kingdom come,
>   May Your will be done
>   On earth as in heaven.
>   Give us today our daily[22] bread
> Forgive our debts
>   As we too have forgiven our debtors.[23]
> And do not lead us into temptation,
>   But deliver us from Satan.[24]

(The prayer could readily have appeared without change in
Rabbinic literature.) There is appended an injunction (6.14-
15) on the forgiveness of sins, seemingly derived from Mark
11.25.

Next (6.16-18) comes instruction on proper fasting,
namely, to avoid the lugubrious ways of the "hypocrites."
The proper use of possessions then follows (6.19-24), contrasting treasures on earth with those that can await one in
heaven. One notices in the above (and in what ensues) Matthew's fondness for sets of threes, here charity, prayer, and
fasting.

Next come words on anxiety (6.25-34), these presented as
the assurance that God will provide for the faithful, for He
knows all men's needs. Prior to one's concern for his physical
necessities is his obligation to seek God's kingdom and to
attain the righteousness He requires. Injunctions against
judging others then follow[25] (7.1-5).

A single, puzzling verse (7.6) enjoins against giving what
is holy to dogs or throwing pearls before swine. Perhaps the
meaning is to direct religious teaching only to those worth
receiving it.

Assurance is given that prayer is answered; God answers
prayer as a father responds to the requests of his children
(7.7-11).

The "golden rule" follows (7.12): Whatever you wish men to do to you, do to them. This is the Law and the Prophets.[26]

There now ensue a succession of warnings (7.13-23). One is to beware of false prophets (7.15-20), apparently Christian teachers of an age later than that of Jesus who teach doctrines uncongenial to other Christians, as seems clear from the assertion (7.21-23) that not all Christians (those who say "Lord, Lord") truly do the will of God, and some such ignoble Christians will be repudiated. The section closes with a parable, contrasting a wise man who has built a house able to withstand floods and storms and a foolish one whose house collapses. The wise man hears and executes the words of Jesus, while the foolish man hears but does not execute. A final word ends this discourse: "When Jesus ended these sayings, the people were astonished. . . ." Such a statement ends each of the five blocks of discourse[27] (7.28).

The Sermon on the Mount is the clue to the significance of the entire Gospel. Mark is essentially a negative writing, in the sense that Mark instructs Christians about what to avoid, not about what to do. The opposite is the case with Matthew. He provides affirmative instructions which tell the faithful what they are to do in a range of situations, whether prayer, the giving of alms, or the dealing with fellow human beings. The Sermon on the Mount provides guidance; that is, it gives the answer to the implied question, "What is the proper Christian life?"

Matthew's portrayal of Jesus as a new Moses who did not come to abolish the Law and the Prophets is not to be viewed as designed to validate, or revalidate, the Laws of Moses, or to establish, or re-establish, prophetic authority. The intent is to give a prelude to a brand new law, the Christian law, obedience to which is to effect a righteousness which is to surpass that of scribes and Pharisees. Hence, it is not the Mosaic Law or the Hebrew Prophets here being commended, but rather Matthew's version of Christianity. But a problem arises, in that any reasonable man can recognize the circumstance that abstention from all deadly anger is indeed more exalted than abstention merely from killing. But can abstention from hatred, or from lustful thoughts, be legislated? The Sermon on the Mount is simultaneously unreservedly lofty and, as legislation, unreservedly impractical. Christians have struggled with this situation. It has been suggested, for example, that the mandate in the Sermon is "interim ethics," a demand not on all Christians of all times, but only for the limited interval between the First Coming of Jesus and the Second Coming expected to take place in the near future. Another suggestion has sought to harmonize the affirmed legalism of the Sermon on the Mount and Paul's nullification of the Laws by proposing that in essence the Sermon on the Mount and Paul's nullification are identical in intent and meaning, despite their being couched in quite different ways. (One suspects that in such harmonization Matthew is improperly read into Paul, and Paul into Matthew.)

In essence, then, the Sermon on the Mount is a remarkably elevated charter for a religious community that sees itself as a new entity.

Matthew does not treat each and every facet of a man's life from waking to sleeping in the five blocks of discourse, as does the much larger body of Rabbinic literature. The acute debates of the tannaim on details of the halacha are not reflected in Matthew; at most there are passing nuances of the use of Scripture and of argumentation that can dimly be related to the manner of the Jewish Sages. Matthew does not arise from a Christian equivalent of a Rabbinic Academy, with Sages debating on subtleties. Matthew's concern is not the *details* of halacha for the Church, but rather the general norms.

Perhaps it is significant that in his rewriting of Mark 12.28-34, Matthew 22.35-40 omits Mark 12.29, the citation of the Shma, "Hear O Israel the Lord our God the Lord is One." If, as is likely, the omission is deliberate, it is because the Shma had become the "watchword of Judaism," and for that reason Matthew avoids it.

Matthew 22.1-4 presents a parable about a king who, angry at guests who were invited to a marriage feast but who do not come, sends an army to destroy and burn their city. If this allusion to the destruction of the city is to the destruction of Jerusalem and the Temple in 70, as scholars believe, we not only must date Matthew after that time, but in addition have some confidence in a scholarly view that Matthew (and later Christians) viewed the disaster which the Jews experienced in 70 as due to their rejection of Jesus. The Jews not only merited the disaster, but it justified Christian claims.

There have been Jewish scholars who have cited from Matthew out of context, especially the words in 15.24, spoken to the Gentile woman: "I was sent only to the lost sheep of the house of Israel," and have concluded that these words represent the authentic Jews of history. But it is not sound to cite selectively in this way. The words need to be balanced by 28.19-30, where the Risen Christ instructs the disciples to "Go and teach all nations, baptizing them in the name of the Father, Son, and Holy Ghost." The usual Christian contention is that the message of salvation was offered to the Jews first and only when they were unresponsive was it offered to the Gentiles. That same contention is presented here, in two distinct parts of the Gospel, but the first of the parts ought not be separated from the second.

In his version of the passion narrative, Matthew increases the responsibility of the Jews for the death of Jesus beyond what is in Mark, and decreases the role of the Romans through his handling of Pilate. Matthew adds to Mark a message to Pilate from his wife, to have nothing to do with Jesus, a just man, for she has had a dream about him. When Pilate is unable to persuade the Jewish mob that he should release Jesus, he washes his hands as a symbol and says, "I am innocent of the blood of this just person." The text then states that "*all the people* said 'His blood be on us and on our children.'" This ascription of guilt for the death of Jesus on *all the people* has troubled Christians, for in subsequent ages it was applied even to those unborn; a frequent Christian view is that the correct meaning of the passage limits the guilt to only those Jews who were present. This, however, is a quite modern, quite recent view.

Matthew 23 is an unhappy display of religious invective, charging the Pharisees with hypocrisy, superficiality, ostentation, avarice, distorted perspectives, and the murder of the Prophets. In the midst of this unreserved denunciation—devoid of any semblance of charity or love—Christians are forbidden to call any man Rabbi or Father (the latter a respectful way of speaking of a teacher as a spiritual father). It is, of course, not to be ruled out that there were Jews who were hypocrites and guilty of the misdeeds here mentioned; one wonders if Christianity produced any hypocrites or guilty people. This chapter is from Matthew, not from Jesus.

A paradox is to be found in Matthew in that words of Jesus (and of John the Baptist) speak of the imminent End of the age. When Jesus sends out the twelve, forbidding them to go to Gentiles or Samaritans, and sending them "only to the lost sheep of the house of Israel," he says that they are to proclaim that "the kingdom of God is at hand"; but the twelve "will not have time to go to all the cities of Israel before the Son of Man will come." Yet along with such expressions of the nearness of the End, there appears a motif which is quite at variance, namely, that the great climax of history is not a matter of the near or remote future, but rather took place at the First Coming. This view can be expressed in the following way, that that which at first seemed destined for the future has already taken place in the past. In a number of passages, "kingdom of God" is a synonym for the Church, and the phrase in such usage lacks all sense of future time. The view in Matthew is that Jesus, in the past, founded a Church destined always to endure, and to that end it required standards and even laws and regulations. This is found in its most explicit form in Matthew 18, especially 18.15-22, a passage which is addressed to the Church's governing itself.

A frequent view suggests that Matthew was a Jew. Perhaps so. However, there is a recurrent pro-Gentile bias in Matthew that seems inconsistent with Matthew's having been Jewish. There have also been those who, from Matthew's frequent use of Scripture and his assertion that not a jot or tittle would depart from the Law, infer he was a Rabbi. One needs to note, however, that that array of concerns presented in the Six Orders of the Mishna are only minimally present in the Gospel. Certain matters of common circulation, including some of the parables, are found in Matthew and in the Rabbinic literature, but these are invariably popular motifs and parables. Matthew, whether by birth a Jew or a Gentile, was a Christian; it is Christian Law, not the Torah and not the halacha that he is commending. In his Gospel, Christianity is portrayed as a separate, a new religion.

· 6 ·

THE GOSPEL
ACCORDING TO
LUKE

The most skillful of the Gospel writers, Luke was a gifted literary artist. He availed himself of the artist's need of freedom. It is believed by almost all scholars that he used, and reworked, Mark; a minority believe that he also used and reworked Matthew, omitting, altering, and also creating. In his treatment of Judaism and of Jews, he is significantly different from Mark and Matthew, for in his view there was never any conflict between Christians and Judaism; when antagonism arose, it was that Jews were over and against Christians and Christianity, these unremittingly loyal to Judaism. Indeed, for Luke, Christianity is the true Judaism, the unbroken legatee of the Judaism in the past.[1] Luke is concerned that not only Christians should understand this, but also that the Romans, especially Roman officials, should understand this too. In the Gospel, and in its second part, Acts of the Apostles, both of which he wrote, Luke is concerned to equate Christian incidents with Roman events and the names of Roman officials. It has long been thought by scholars that it was Luke's purpose to contend that Christians and Christianity merited the privileges which Roman emperors and governors had extended to Jews.

The directly hostile tones of Mark and Matthew about Jews are rare in Luke; he is ordinarily genteel and indirect. His nativity story is one of beauty, of quiet peace, about admirable people, devout and unfailing in their Jewish obligations. (Matthew's account is about the violent Herod and his killing of innocent babes.) Luke begins with the conception of John the Baptist, whose mother Elizabeth and priestly father Zechariah are very old. Elizabeth is a relative of Mary. In the sixth month of Elizabeth's pregnancy, the aged Gabriel tells Mary she is to conceive Jesus through the Holy Spirit. (In Matthew, it is Joseph whom an angel informs.) Mary, now pregnant, goes to Judea to visit Elizabeth; when Mary, entering the home, greets Elizabeth, the babe in Elizabeth's womb leaps for joy. When John is born he is circumcised, in fidelity to Judaism.

Because a census is to take place, Joseph goes to his home in Bethlehem, taking Mary with him. There Jesus is born in a manger—there is no room in the inn. Jesus is circumcised on the eighth day. The family goes to the Temple for the rites of purification after childbirth (Lev. 12.2-8). There a pious old man named Simeon, picking up the babe Jesus, declares that he himself is now ready for death, having lived long enough to see the Messiah. An old prophetess, Anna, tells people that through the child the redemption of Jerusalem is to come.

The family faithfully goes to the Temple every year at Passover. When they do this when Jesus is twelve, they leave him behind by mistake on leaving for home. They return to the Temple to find him discussing matters with teachers of the Law who are amazed at his understanding and at the answers he gives to questions. He tells his parents that they should have known that he was in his Father's house; they did not understand the saying, but Mary kept everything in her heart.

Luke next gives a precise Roman date—the fifteenth year of the reign of Tiberius Caesar, Pontius Pilate being governor of Judea[2]—for the beginning of John's public career.

In Luke's handling of material in Mark, he often makes changes that are as effective as they are subtle. That Jesus was baptized by John bothered Matthew, for baptism is for forgiveness of sins, so that Matthew rewrites the passage to have John say that it would be more appropriate for Jesus to baptize him, rather than he Jesus. Luke's way is to put the baptism of Jesus in a subordinate clause. In the cleansing of the Temple (Lk. 19.45-48), Luke adds that Jesus "was teaching daily in the Temple," as if to imply that the cleansing was of little importance or note. Luke omits material found in Mark and Matthew. He omits the "feeding of the four thousand." His omission of the "walking on the water" is probably because the narrative in Matthew 14.22-33 and Mark 6.45-52 disparages the disciples; Luke shuns such disparagement. He omits the cursing of the fig tree (Mk. 11.12-14, 20-25; Mt. 21.18-21). He condenses to a single mention the falling asleep of the disciples when Jesus prays, which in Mark and Matthew is mentioned three times (Lk. 22.45-46; Mk. 14.32-42; Mt. 26.34-46); moreover, the rebuke is greatly softened in Luke's version.

Luke also shifts material.[3] He gives a genealogy of Jesus after the baptism (3.23-28); Matthew had begun with it. Matthew's genealogy runs from Abraham forward to Joseph; Luke's runs back from Joseph, but to Adam[4] rather than Abraham. He gives the age of Jesus as thirty;[5] Mark and Matthew are silent. After the genealogy comes the temptation (Lk. 4.1-13). Luke's ending is artistic: "When the devil had ended every temptation, he departed from [Jesus] until an opportune time." That opportune time is found in Luke 22.3: "Then Satan entered Judas Iscariot."

After the temptation, Jesus returns to Galilee; "he taught in all their synagogues, being glorified by all." Luke moves to this point (4.16-30) the "rejection at Nazareth" which comes much later in Mark's account (6.1-6) and in Matthew's (13.54-58). In Luke the rejection is virtually at the beginning of the career of Jesus. That is, Luke not only shifts material, but he freely expands, as he does the incident here: Jesus reads from Isaiah, applies the verse to himself, and proceeds to cite from the careers of Elijah and Elisha acts of benefit to Gentiles. Those in the synagogue become angered and make an attempt to kill him.

This Gentile "bias" influences the route in Luke that Jesus follows from Galilee to Jerusalem. Mark and Matthew have Jesus cross the Jordan from west to east at Galilee, and cross westward at Jericho, thereby avoiding the area of the Samaritans, whom Jews regarded as Gentiles. The route in Luke (9.51ff) is due south, through the Samaritan area. The

Samaritans do not receive Jesus because his destination is Jerusalem. The parable of the Good Samaritan (10.29-37) contrasts a callous priest and a Levite who did not succor a man who had been mugged and was half-dead with a Samaritan who did. It is told in 17.11-19 that after Jesus heals ten lepers, only one of the ten shows gratitude, and that one is a Samaritan.

There are a number of parables found only in Luke. That of the rich man Lazarus has two parts. In the first part, both have died. Lazarus, the poor man, is received in heaven, into Abraham's bosom, while the rich man goes to flame-filled Hades (which seems near by, separated by a chasm). The rich man wishes Lazarus to dip the end of his finger in water and from this the rich man will cool his tongue. Abraham replies that the rich man received good things within his lifetime, Lazarus evil things; hence, their fates are now reversed, and nothing can be done. To this there is added a second part, the rich man's request that Lazarus be sent back to earth to warn the brothers of the rich man, lest they also come to the place of torment. Abraham replies that they (the Jews) have the Law and the Prophets and should listen to them. The rich man replies, "If some one comes to them from the dead, they will repent." Abraham says, "If they do not listen to Moses and the Prophets, they will not be convinced if someone should rise from the dead [like Jesus]."

The parable of the prodigal son (15.11-32) illustrates the joy of the father (God) at the repentance of a sinner. To this is added that the elder brother (the Jews) was angry at the joyous reception of the repentant sinner.

Luke (16.16-18) alters the statement in Matthew 5.17-18 into, "It is easier for heaven and earth to pass away than for one dot of the law to become void, thereby omitting "Do not think that I come to abolish the Law and the Prophets. . . . I have come to fill them in."

In Matthew the impression is that the Christian message, the Gospel, is a rupture, a direct break with the past, as, for example, in the seven contracts, each beginning, "You have heard it said, but I say to you. . . ." Not so in Luke; rather, Law develops into Gospel smoothly, without any break.

In Mark and Matthew, at the arrest of Jesus, the ear of a

slave of the high priest is cut off—in Mark by a bystander, in Matthew by a follower of Jesus. In Luke it is added that Jesus' followers wished to wield their swords; when the ear of the slave is cut off, Jesus touches the ear and heals the man. He says, "No more of this." (The motif is again the fidelity of Jesus; he did not resist or challenge the Jewish authorities.)

In Mark and Matthew Jesus is condemned by the Sanhedrin before he is taken to Pilate.[6] Not so in Luke. The loyalty of Jesus is expressed through the repetition of the motif of Jesus' frequent teaching in the Temple; for example, Luke adds to the beginning of the controversy over authority that Jesus was teaching the people in the Temple and preaching the Gospel (Lk. 20.1-8; Mk. 11.27-33; Mt. 21.23-27). The sequel to the encounter with the Sadducees over resurrection is that scribes react by praising Jesus for speaking well (20.27-40; Mk. 12.18-27; Mt. 22.23-33).

Luke has no evening hearing before the High Priest such as is found in Mark 14.55-63 and Matthew 29.59-68. The Sanhedrin enter the scene only the next morning, and meet in the Temple, rather than in the home of the High Priest. Luke omits Mark 14.55-61, and Matthew 26.59-62, that witnesses reported that Jesus has the intention (so Mark) or the ability (so Matthew) to destroy the Temple. The Sanhedrin in Luke never condemns Jesus, nor does the High Priest ever allege blasphemy. The charges made to Pilate are that Jesus "is perverting the nation, and forbidding us to give tribute to Caesar, and saying that he himself is Christ a king." Pilate, after a single question, "Are you the King of the Jews?" to which Jesus answers, "You have said so," says "I find no crime in this man." Learning that Jesus is a Galilean, and that Herod Antipas, tetrarch of Galilee, is in Jerusalem, Pilate sends Jesus to Antipas. Though Antipas questions Jesus at length, Jesus makes no answer. Antipas returns Jesus to Pilate, but without any condemnation. Pilate thereupon informs the chief priests, "the rulers," and the people that neither he nor Antipas had found Jesus guilty of the charges. He proposed to chastise Jesus and to release him. The response was the demand that he release Barabbas instead. Pilate again tried to persuade them that Jesus be released, but they shouted "Crucify him." Again Pilate proposed chastisement, and again they demanded that Jesus be crucified. So Pilate gave in to their demand. (That is, Jesus was never condemned to death by any proper authority but was, in effect, lynched.) Some manuscripts of Luke have Jesus say, on being crucified, "Father, forgive them, for they do not know what they are doing."[7]

In Mark and Matthew the Roman centurion says, "Truly, this man was the Son of God." In Luke (23.47) his words are, "Certainly this man was innocent."

In both Mark and Matthew, the disciples have scattered and fled; in Mark and Matthew, Jesus predicts that the disciples will fall away (Mk. 14.27; Mt. 26.31), and they do. Not only does Luke omit the prediction, in 23.49 he writes that "all his acquaintances and the women who had followed him from Galilee stood at a distance and saw [the crucifixion]."

The women who are to come to the tomb rest on the Sabbath "according to the commandment" (23.56). They find in the empty tomb not a young man dressed in white (Mk. 16.5) nor an angel (Mt. 28.2), but two men. Luke does not suggest a Galilee appearance (24.6) as do Mark (16.7) and Matthew (28.7).[8]

The resurrection appearances in Luke (24.13-35) take place at Emmaus, near Jerusalem, and in Jerusalem. Mark and Matthew lack accounts of what happens to the disciples after they scatter in fear. Luke makes good this lack in his account of the resurrection appearances to the Apostles, first to two of them with whom he walks and explains the Scriptures that apply to him, and with whom he eats, breaking bread and giving it to them, and then vanishing. The two go on to Jerusalem and there join the others, a total of eleven. Then Jesus stands among the eleven, explaining how Scripture was bound to be fulfilled in his death and resurrection. Repentance leading to forgiveness of sin was to be preached to all the nations in the world. Jesus would send the Apostles the Holy Spirit. They were to stay in Jerusalem until they would be armed with the power from above. (These words foreshadow the second of Luke's works, Acts of the Apostles.) The disciples are in great joy in Jerusalem, and they continually attend the Temple, blessing God. Though Luke stresses the great hostility of the Jewish leadership, and even the mobs, to Jesus, the account in Acts presupposes that, despite the crucifixion, there has been no decisive separation between Christians and Jews. Not only was Christianity never guilty of any infidelity to Judaism, it was indeed, in Luke's view, the true and proper Judaism. To use a phrase from later Christian history, Christianity is the true Israel, the legitimate legatee of the promises and favor of God as set forth in the Scriptures (which as yet were only the Old Testament). The true Israel was Gentile; the infant Jesus was, in the words of the prophet Simeon, a light for revelation to the Gentiles. In the "rejection in Nazareth," just as Elijah and Elisha had been sent to Gentiles, so Jesus had been sent to Gentiles. Samaritans—non-Jews—figure favorably in Luke's Gospel; there is no reflection in Luke of the passage in Matthew 10.5, "Do not go among the Gentiles and into no town of the Samaritans." There is nothing in Luke like the passage in Matthew 15.24, "I was sent only to the lost sheep of the house of Israel." Luke completely omits the incident told in Mark and Matthew of the Cyro-Phoenician woman to whom Jesus only reluctantly responded affirmatively.

It has been noted that more frequently than Mark and Matthew, Luke uses as the title for Jesus the word "Lord." Though the matter is disputed, it is a reasonable conclusion that in Luke's use of the term he has in mind to present Christianity as comparable to other religions of the Roman Empire; these were dedicated to some supernatural figure who was the "Lord" of the cult. It is true that in Luke's mind "Lord" means much more than a comparable equivalent to a central figure in other cults, and Luke means to stress the unique divinity of Jesus. His use of the word, however, in some respects does parallel its use in other cults.

Luke in his own unique way, with his freedom and literary artistry, gives full testimony to the existence of a vivid Christian midrash.

· 7 ·

THE GOSPEL
ACCORDING TO
JOHN

We said above that John differs from Matthew, Mark, and Luke in structure and content; it differs even more in tone and in feeling. It also differs substantially in its way of presenting the issues between Judaism and the new movement.

Incidents, abundant in the Synoptic Gospels, are in John only a rare handful. John presents not a single parable, not a single exorcism, not a single pithy saying. Rather, the substance which makes John so long is what are called "discourses" spoken by Jesus. These discourses arise out of incidents in which there is a repeated pattern: First there is a misunderstanding, followed by its correction, and then an embroidery on the correction. It is normally a Jew or else "the Jews" who misunderstand and require the correction. In such misunderstanding there is an occasional hearkening back to the kinds of conflict-incidents found in the Synoptic Gospels. There the conflicts are over primarily what Jesus does, while here they are primarily on what Jesus is. To say this in another way, the Synoptics present, as it were, a record of the conflicts in Galilee and Judea within the career of Jesus, in this or that synagogue, in connection with healings on the Sabbath. In John the issues, though presented about the past, are in reality those of "to this day." In John Jesus is the spokesman for the view of later Christians about Jesus in conflicts with later Jews.

The controversies here are not essentially those of Galilee

or Judea. Rather, the world of scribes and Pharisees is here altered to a setting somewhere in the Graeco-Roman world, though precisely where is not to be ascertained. The atmosphere is what we might call a popular kind of Philonism. Though the words "literal" and "allegorical" are not used, the contrast is present in that "the Jews" misunderstand because they are literalists; the correction of their misunderstanding entails the equivalent of "allegory" (not at all the specific allegory of Philo!), called "spiritual." Thus, there is literal rebirth versus the spiritual, or else literal bread versus the spiritual. Though the phrases "world of perception" and "world of concept" found in Philo are not used here, reflections of the distinction are present. In Philo, the world of perception is one of error and delusion, while the world of concept is that of truth and "reality." In John, "this world" is that of darkness, sin, and death; the "spiritual world" is that of truth, light, righteousness, and escape from death.

In John the opportunity is present, both now and in the future, for man, through mystically identifying with Jesus, to rise out of the world of delusion into the "real" world, the spiritual world of the Christ. In the Synoptics, Jesus is the teacher *par excellence* of the past; in John, Jesus is the divine being with whom the pious can unite in mystic communion today and tomorrow. The Jesus of John is presented more as if already resurrected than as the figure for whom resurrection is destined to occur later. The conflicts with the Jews arise from their belonging to "this world," not the spiritual world of the Christ. John deals constantly with subtle nuances and overtones. Because of these the Gospel is not a simple, straightforward historical account, nor is it easy for a modern person to follow.

Already in Matthew's account of the resurrection appearance to the disciples, it is stated that among these "some doubted." Such doubt on the part of Christians is even more frequent in John; Jews once "Christian" are among the doubters, but there are others too. The doubts within the community of believers seem to have been of two quite different characters. One kind of doubt resulted in rejecting entirely the Christian contentions and leaving the Church. But a second kind of doubt is in essence a disagreement with the views of other Christians, such as John, about Jesus. By the time John was written, Christian views had become multiple and diversified. One issue, already encountered in the Corinthian Epistles (p. 324), was particularly divisive, namely, whether Jesus had been truly human; if so, he had the bodily functions of men and was subject to the usual human frailties and infirmities. The same issue is found in this Gospel, within the Christian community.

The bitterest conflicts in John are not with Pharisees or scribes but with "the Jews." Scribes and Pharisees probably were not in the neighborhood of the author, or else of no consequence at the late time (about A.D. 100) when he was writing. It is "the Jews" who are presented as the opponents of Jesus. Who is meant by "the Jews"? Is it a term simply used to replace such Synoptic phrases as "scribes, Pharisees, and chief priests?" Is it meant to include *all* the Jews, wherever they are? Does it mean only the Jewish leaders? Does it mean different things in different passages? All those views have been offered by scholars.

Again, a matter in the Synoptic Gospels appears to have troubled John. There the Jerusalem experience of Jesus is presented as enduring for only a week, after a career in Galilee of only a few months. If the total career of Jesus was indeed so short, then how could one reasonably charge the Jews with total blindness, for their retort could have been to the effect that Jesus was not around long enough to be known, let alone rejected. In John, unlike the Synoptics, Jesus is in Jerusalem several times,[1] and his total career is a matter of years, not a few months.

Second, the account of the arrest, trial, and execution, all on the first day of Passover, as in the Synoptics, is one which is historically unlikely, and which conceivably might have aroused strenuous objections from Jews in John's vicinity. These events are presented in John as occurring on the day before Passover. The difference between the Synoptics and John in dating the trial and crucifixion has elicited a large body of explanatory literature, with attendant theories about special sources of information which John might have been presumed to have had, and various ways of harmonizing the discordant dating are on record. The simplest explanation has not to my knowledge been offered—namely, that John meets the Jewish objections of his own time by feeling free to allocate the events to the day before Passover, despite their allocation by the other three Gospels to Passover.

No exposition of John which is to take account of the abundance of nuances and overtones can be presented in less than a full and long volume. Our brief presentation, necessarily selective, revolves about two matters, one, the role of the Jews in John, and two, by far the most significant aspect of the Gospel, the matter of mystic communion with the Christ.

John has no birth narrative such as Matthew and Luke provide. Rather, he begins with a prologue. The first sentence reads: "In the beginning was the Logos, and the Logos was with God, and the Logos was *divine*." (Most translations read, "and the Logos was *God*.") From the very beginning of time, the Logos was with God. The Logos had created everything that came into being. Through the Logos came (true) life, and this (true) life illuminated men. The light shines on in the darkness (the delusions of life in this world), but the darkness has not overcome the light (1.1-5).

Much has been written about these words, and the possible currents of thought, Jewish and pagan, which influenced the inherently complex thought patterns. Some view the sentence as a poem, and, indeed, as a poem borrowed from an earlier source and here incorporated by John. That source is called "gnostic."[2] But there exists no gnostic hymn-poem like the prologue, and to suppose that a non-extant hymn was borrowed by John strains belief. The explanation of the prologue can be much simpler. The Graeco-Jewish world knew the term Logos[3] and what it implied. John is here speaking in that Graeco-Jewish milieu. He is speaking in the light of Jewish opposition, as if he is saying to such Jews, "You do not understand Jesus. You do, though, understand what Logos implies. If you wish to understand Jesus, then you must grasp the relationship between Logos and Jesus. The Logos (1.14) became the real man Jesus, and he dwelt on earth." That is, John uses neither the motif of the virgin birth, nor genealogies, nor even baptism (as do the Synoptics) to suggest the divine character of Jesus. Rather, he speaks in a way his Graeco-Jewish audience can understand if it wishes to.

The assertion that the Logos and Jesus were one and the same is interrupted by mention of John the Baptist, emphasizing his subordinance[4] to Jesus. The passage then goes on to say that the Logos, now man, had come "to his own" (that is, the Jews), but they did not receive him. Those who did receive him were able to become children of God, as if fathered by God Himself rather than by human fathers. The Logos-man came to dwell in the world; the believers saw his glory there, that is, the glory of God's only Son. From their encounter with God's Son, the believers have received the fullest[5] measure of grace, and that grace continues. (Grace, we recall, is a free gift; what a man *earns* by his piety in the way of divine favor is not grace.) The Law—obedience to which supposes that man *earns* divine favor—came through Moses; (divine) grace came through Jesus Christ (the first mention, 1.17, of Jesus by name). The continuation is, "No one has ever seen God, but God's only Son."[6]

John the Baptist tells a deputation of "the Jews" plainly that he is not the Messiah; that he is not Elijah;[7] that he is not "the prophet" (possibly an allusion to Deut. 18.15). He is, rather, what is "predicted" in Isaiah 40.3, "the voice crying in the Wilderness," for the purpose of revealing to Israel someone unknown who is greater than he. (The point here is to stress the inferiority of John to Jesus; the disciples of John were a movement still in existence, as in Acts 19.3.) The next day, when John sees Jesus coming to him, John makes known what has before been unknown, namely, that Jesus is the greater one looked forward to. This is expressed in the words, "See, here is the lamb[8] of God who takes away the sin of the world."

There comes next the gathering of disciples. When Nathanael, "an Israelite without guile,"[9] comes to Jesus, Jesus (supernaturally) knows him, having seen him under a fig tree. He tells Nathanael that he will have even better basis for his faith later on, for "You[10] will see God's angels ascending and descending on the 'Son of Man.'"

Next, through a series of seven signs,[11] John presents the public career of Jesus. Within the presentation of the signs other materials appear; these include hearkenings back to John the Baptist, controversies with "the Jews," and misunderstandings which lead to discourses. The narration is not crisp and straightforward; rather, a matter can seem to be ended and to lead into a sequel, but abruptly some afterthought refers back to the item presumed to have been completed. Characters appear as needed, and then seem to disappear, without being accounted for, if not needed. Repetitiousness is recurrent.

The first sign comes at Cana in Galilee (2.1-12). At a marriage feast, Jesus turns water into wine. (The "wine" is probably intended to allude to what in the Synoptics is the blood[12] of Jesus.) The scene promptly shifts to Jerusalem at Passover, and now the "cleansing of the Temple" is narrated (2.13-22). In the Synoptic Gospels this occurs later, within the "passion" narrative (Mk. 11.15-19; Mt. 21.12-13; Lk. 19.45-48), where it prompts the antagonism which leads to the arrest of Jesus. Here, coming very early, it provides an opportunity for John to contrast the Temple and "the temple which is the body of Jesus."

Jesus tells an important Pharisee, Nicodemus,[13] that he requires rebirth. Nicodemus misunderstands, saying that a man cannot re-enter his mother's womb. The reply of Jesus is that rebirth is spiritual, the result of baptism. Jesus had ascended to heaven—an allusion to the sequel to the resurrection, presented as if the resurrection and the ascension have already taken place—and has now returned to earth to teach about heavenly things. God has sent Jesus to earth because He loves the world and wishes to provide eternal life for those who believed in Him. (John, though he often uses ideas and terms that are gnostic-like, differs from the gnostics in a crucial matter: The gnostics regard this world as a hated place, the object of divine scorn; John stresses the opposite, God's love for the world.) Whoever believes in Jesus escapes condemnation; whoever does not is already condemned (3.1-21).

Jesus, returning to Galilee, passes through Samaria (4.1-42). At Jacob's well he asks a Samaritan[14] woman for a drink of water. This leads to a contrast between ordinary water and "spiritual" water, which is Jesus. Neither the Samaritan temple on Mount Gerezin nor the Temple in Jerusalem will endure (for a spiritual "temple," that is, Jesus, will replace them). He identifies himself to her as the Messiah. The woman goes into the city and reports this to Samaritan men, who now come to Jesus. [There now intervenes a brief item in which his disciples ask Jesus to eat; he replies that his "food" is to do the will of God who had sent him (into the world). He urges the disciples to proceed promptly to missionary activity.] The account then reverts to the Samaritans, many of whom acknowledge Jesus as the Messiah, "the savior of the world."

The second of the seven signs (4.43-54), occurring in Galilee, is brief; it is the healing, from a great distance, of the sick son of a nobleman.

The third sign (5.1-16) occurs in Jerusalem during a festival, on a Sabbath day. Jesus heals a man who has been paralyzed for thirty-eight years. A controversy (5.9a-16) then ensues between the man and "the Jews," since the man, on being healed, has carried away the bed-mat on which he lay, and such carrying violates the Sabbath. John comments that it was for violations of the Sabbath that "the Jews" used to persecute Jesus.[15]

Jesus replies to the charges of Sabbath violation in the words, "My Father is still working, and I am working." (The supposition is that Jews hold that God, once He had completed Creation, had totally ceased from work. To the contrary, a passage, Hagiga 12b, which speaks of God as renewing daily the acts of Creation, was adopted into the synagogue liturgy.)[16] The words ascribed to Jesus are part of the Christian rejection of Mosaic Law, including the Sabbath restrictions. "The Jews" now want to kill him for violating the Sabbath and also for making himself equal to God. The reply to this latter is a discourse (5.19-37) which sets forth the relationship of the Son (Jesus) to the Father (God). Jesus denies he is equal to God; rather, it is through him that God has been revealed, and an even greater revelation (his resurrection) will ensue. The Father, though, has entrusted judgment over men to the Son. To dishonor the Son is to dishonor God. The Jews, though they read Scripture, misread it; Scripture, if correctly read, has a meaning relating to Jesus: "If you believed Moses, you would believe me, for he wrote of me."

The fourth sign (6.1-15)[17] is the feeding of the five thousand (Mk. 6.33-44; Mt. 14.13-21, 15.32-39; Lk. 9.10-17). This sign leads people to try to force Jesus to become their king, but Jesus withdraws from them. (The Gospels emphasize the lack of any political activity on the part of Jesus.)

The fifth sign (6.16-21) is the walking on the water (Mk. 6.45-52; Mt. 12.22-34). The account here is different in that Jesus gets into the boat and is immediately brought to the other side of the lake. There Jesus is left alone by his disciples, but many people gather about him, at the place near Capernaum of the feeding of the five thousand where they had eaten bread. Jesus tells them that they seek him because they had eaten his bread and were filled, not because of any miraculous signs. (That is, they had not understood the import of the miraculous bread.) He tells them that they should labor for food that produces eternal life, which comes through him, rather than for food that perishes. They still do not understand, and they allude to the manna given their fathers in the Wilderness, this by Moses. Jesus replies that Moses had not given them "bread from heaven"; it is rather God who gives "bread from heaven," namely, Jesus: "I am the bread of life. Whoever comes to me will not hunger; whoever believes in me will not thirst." He goes on to charge these hearers with not having believed, despite what they have seen.

"The Jews" then murmur: How can Jesus come from heaven, since he is the son of Joseph, and they know his father and mother? He rebukes them, saying that their fathers, subsequent to eating the manna, had [in time] died; whoever ate Jesus, the "bread from heaven," would live forever. That "bread" was his "flesh."

"The Jews" dispute as to how Jesus gives his flesh to be eaten. He tells them that unless they eat his flesh and drink his blood,[18] they cannot "live." Many of his disciples consider what Jesus has said to be a "hard saying" which they cannot accept. He charges them with not understanding the higher realm which is his true home. Suppose they were to see him ascend to heaven whence he had come? Do they not understand that his spirit gives eternal life? The comment then comes that Jesus has known from the first which of the disciples would not believe him[19] and who it was who would betray him. Only those would come to him whom God has determined (6.51-65).

Thereafter many cease to be his disciples. Jesus asks the Twelve (mentioned here for the first time in this Gospel) if they too will leave him. Simon Peter assures him that they regard him as the Holy One of God.[20] Jesus replies that one of them is the devil; it is Judas[21] he is speaking of (6.66-71).

After these things,[22] Jesus remains in Galilee, avoiding Judea, "because the Jews sought to kill him" (7.16-18). The festival of Sukkot is near; the brothers of Jesus urge him to go (to the Temple) so that he may display himself publicly to the world. The brothers have not believed in him. Jesus replies that his "time has not yet come"; his brothers should go (to the Temple), since they are not hated. The brothers go to the Temple.

But then Jesus also goes to Judea, but secretly, so that "the Jews," seeking him, do not find him. While some Jews there speak of him as a good man, others charge that he is leading people astray. But no one speaks openly about him, for fear of "the Jews."[23]

Jesus goes up to the Temple and teaches (as if he has not gone there secretly!). "The Jews" marvel at his teaching, for he has never studied. Jesus replies that his teaching is God's, not his own. Though Moses has given "the Jews" the Law, none of them keep it.[24] Why do they seek to kill him, since killing is prohibited in the Law? They reply that he is possessed by the devil; they ask, "Who is trying to kill you?" (The intent here is to convict "the Jews" of lies and hypocrisy, since it has been said earlier, in 5.18 and 7.2, that they have tried to kill him, as the reader of the Gospel would recall.) As to the observance of the Laws, Jews practice circumcision on the Sabbath (Lev. 12.3).[25] If the Sabbath laws can be broken for circumcision (which wounds the body), why are "the Jews" angry at Jesus for making a man's entire body well on the Sabbath?

Some of the people, Jerusalemites, now recognize Jesus as the man whom (the people) had wished to kill. They wonder that Jesus speaks openly. Can it be that the authorities really know that he is the Messiah? The Messiah ought to be unknown, yet they know from whence (the Galilee) Jesus comes. To this, Jesus replies that they do not know from whence (heaven) he truly has come. He has not come on his own, but has been sent (by God).

They now wish to seize him, but his "hour" has not yet come. Some of the people believe in him. The Pharisees and chief priests send Temple police to arrest him; Jesus tells them that (since his "hour" has not come) he will be with them a little longer, and then go to Him who had sent him, and there "the Jews" cannot go. "The Jews," misunderstanding about where he will go, wonder if he is going to the Dispersion to teach the Greeks.

On the last day of the (eight-day) festival, Jesus arises and proclaims "If any one thirsts, let him come to me and drink."[26] The "drink" is the Holy Spirit which is not to be given to the faithful until after Jesus will have been glorified.[27]

There comes presently (8.12-59) the most extreme in the controversies in John between Jesus and "the Jews." The setting (8.20) is "the treasury" of the Temple (but exactly what this means is unclear). Jesus now speaks again: "I am the light of the world. Whoever follows me will not walk in darkness, but will have the light of life." (The meaning is dwelt upon later, 9.5-41.) The Pharisees declare that the testimony of Jesus about himself is not true. Jesus retorts that in the Law of Moses the testimony of two witnesses is deemed true (Deut. 17.6; 19.15); the two who ought to be believed are Jesus and the Father who sent him. They ask, "Where is your father?" Jesus replies, "If you knew me, you would know my Father too." Jesus further asserts, "He who sent me is true, and I tell the world that I have heard from Him." "The Jews" do not understand that he is speaking of God. But now many believe in him.[28]

Now Jesus addresses some Jews who (up till now) had believed in him. "If you continue in my word, you are indeed my disciples. You will know the truth, and the truth will make you free." Misunderstanding, they reply that as descendants of Abraham, they have never been in slavery. He replies, "Whoever sins is a slave to sin. The slave does not remain in the house forever, but the Son does. Hence, if the Son sets you free, you will be truly free. You are indeed sons

of Abraham, yet you [sinfully] seek to kill me. . . . I speak
of what I have seen with my Father, but you do what you
have heard from your father." They reply, "Abraham is our
father." Jesus contradicts them, "If Abraham were your father, you would do what he did. You do what your father
did." They reply that they are children of God. Jesus retorts
that they are "children of the devil, a murderer and
liar. . . ."

They retort with contempt that Jesus is "a Samaritan, possessed by a demon." Jesus denies that he has a demon:
"Truly, truly, if anyone keeps my word, he will never die."
They respond, "Abraham died; so did the Prophets. Are you
greater than Abraham?"

Jesus says, "Your father Abraham rejoiced to see my day"
—that is, the Eternal Christ was known to Abraham. "The
Jews" reply, "You are not yet fifty years old! How could you
have seen Abraham?" He answers, "Before Abraham was, I
am." They now pick up stones to throw at him, but Jesus
hides and then leaves the Temple.

The sixth sign is the healing of a man blind from birth.
The disciples ask Jesus whose sin[29] was it, the man's parents'
or his own, that he was born blind? Jesus replies that he is the
light of the world, for so long as he is in the world. With clay
mixed with his spittle,[30] he touches the eyes of the blind man
and tells him to go to wash in the pool of Siloam.[31] The man
does so, and returns with his sight restored. He tells his
neighbors and the bystanders that Jesus has cured him. As
if in an afterthought, John now says that this has occurred
on a Sabbath. The Pharisees say that Jesus cannot be from
God, for he has violated the Sabbath. "The Jews" do not believe that the man was really blind and gained his sight. The
parents of the man confirm this, but, fearing "the Jews," suggest that the man is of age and should speak for himself; it
had already been determined that anyone who contended
that Jesus was the Messiah was to be put out of the synagogue.[32] The Pharisees then tell the man that God had healed
him, not Jesus the sinner. He replies that Jesus had indeed
healed him. The summary of the preceding comes now:
Jesus says, "I have come into the world that those who are
blind may see, and those who see may become blind." The

Pharisees ask him if they are blind. He answers, "If you were blind, you would be free of guilt; because you say that you see, you bear guilt" (9.1-41).

A discourse on the shepherd and his sheep follows.[33] The first part[34] contends that the sheep know the true shepherd from the false one who comes into the sheepfold but not through its door. Jesus affirms that he is the "door." He is, indeed, the "good shepherd," who gives his life for the sheep: "There are other sheep [Gentiles] who must be brought into the fold; there will be one flock and one shepherd. . . . I lay down my life. . . . No one takes it from me." (That is, his death is voluntary; such a contention became frequent in the second Christian century. Alongside it the view persisted that "the Jews" had killed him.)

Jesus is in the Temple on Ḥanukka. "The Jews" ask him to say plainly whether or not he is the Messiah. He replies that he has already told them, but they have not believed him. His "sheep" know him and will have eternal life, for God gave the sheep to Jesus. He says: "I and the Father are one."[35] "The Jews" want to stone him for his blasphemy, in that he is making himself God. Jesus replies that if the judges (Ps. 82.6) can be called "sons of God" without blasphemy, in what way is it blasphemy for him to be called the Son of God?

There is another effort to arrest him, but he escapes to the area beyond the Jordan where John the Baptist had been active. There many believe in him (10.22-42).

The seventh sign is the raising from the dead of a man named Lazarus (11.1-46). In the account it is assumed that the reader knows of antecedent friendly relations between Lazarus and Jesus; a sentence identifies a sister by an act which occurs only later in the Gospel. This sister, Mary, and another, Martha, send word to Jesus that Lazarus is sick. Unhurried, Jesus decides that he will go to the home of the sisters, at Bethany, near Jerusalem. The disciples remind him that "the Jews" have sought to stone him. Jesus replies that so long as "daylight" lasts, he can proceed in safety.[36] Jesus now knows (miraculously) that Lazarus has died. This is expressed in terms that Lazarus has fallen asleep, and

Jesus will go to waken him. The disciples misunderstand, taking "asleep" literally. Jesus then tells them plainly that Lazarus is dead. He adds that it is better that he was not present before Lazarus had died,[37] so that what will ensue will increase the faith of the disciples. The disciple, Thomas[38] Didymus ("the twin") says, "Let us go also [with Jesus] and die with him."

At the time of arrival at Bethany, Lazarus has been buried for four days and many have visited Martha and Mary to console them. Martha goes to meet Jesus. He assures her that her brother will rise. Martha misunderstands, thinking that this is the general resurrection destined for the remote future. Jesus replies, "I am the resurrection and the life. He who believes in me, even if he die, will live. Whoever believes in me will never die." Martha expresses her belief in Jesus.

At the grave, Jesus asks that the stone be taken away. Martha replies that there will be a stench, since Lazarus has been dead for four days. (The point is to emphasize the real death of Lazarus.) Jesus prays to God, and then summons Lazarus to come forth from the grave. Lazarus does so, bound in the burial clothes (which would impede his walking). Jesus tells those about him to unbind Lazarus, so that he can walk. Many of "the Jews" now believe in Jesus, but others of them, not believing, go to the Pharisees to tell them what Jesus had done. The Pharisees and chief priests now consult with each other. If they leave Jesus alone, all the people will believe in him, with the result that the Romans will "destroy our holy place [the Temple] and our nation." (One needs to note the implication of Roman hostility to a messianic claimant, because of the political implication.) The High Priest Caiaphas[39] says that it is better for one man to die than for the whole nation to perish. It is added that Caiaphas now prophesies that Jesus will die for both the nation and also for "children of God scattered abroad [beyond Judea]." From that day on, "they" take counsel on how to put Jesus to death (11.1-53). (In the Synoptic Gospels, as mentioned, it is the cleansing of the Temple which is viewed as prompting "the plot" against Jesus; in John, the cleansing has come very early, 2.13-22, and it is, instead, the raising

of Lazarus which prompts "the plot." The resurrection of
Lazarus is the greatest of the seven signs; it also foreshad-
ows the greater sign, the resurrection of Jesus himself.)

Passover is near at hand, and many go to the Temple before the festival, to purify themselves (Lev. 7.21; 2 Chron.
30.17-18). At the Temple people wonder if Jesus will appear,
for the chief priests and Pharisees have issued orders to arrest him on sight (11.54-57).

Six[40] days before Passover, at Bethany, at the home of
Mary, Martha, and Lazarus, Mary anoints the feet of Jesus
and wipes them with her hair. Judas Iscariot hypocritically
objects to this use of expensive ointment, the cost of which
might have gone to the poor. Jesus replies that Mary is alert
to the day of his burial;[41] besides, they will always have the
poor but not always have Jesus (12.1-8). (This account
seems derived from Mk. 14.3-9; Mt. 26.6-13. Here it takes
place before Jesus enters Jerusalem for the Passion; there it
takes place after; here the woman is Mary, there she is unnamed; here it is at the home of the women, there at the
home of Simon the leper; here the ointment is put on the feet,
there it is poured over the head of Jesus. See also Lk. 7.36-
50.) The chief priests now determine to put Lazarus to death
(12.9-11). (However, no sequel is provided; Lazarus, like
other characters in John, disappears when once the account
no longer needs him.)

A spontaneous demonstration takes place at Jesus' entry
into Jerusalem, to the chagrin of the Pharisees. Some
Greeks[42] are at the Temple. They ask Philip, and through
him Andrew, to see Jesus. The request of the Greeks prompts
Jesus to say that, at last, his "hour" has come: "Whoever
loves his life will lose it; whoever hates life in this world will
keep it in the eternal life. Whoever wishes to serve me should
follow me; where I am, there will my servant be. . . ." But
he is troubled. Should he ask to be saved from this "hour"?
A heavenly voice calls out, "I have glorified [your name]
and will glorify it again." The people hear the voice, some
thinking it thunder, and others the voice of angels. The
voice, Jesus tells them, has come for their sake, not his. It is
time for judgment on the world; its prince (the devil) will
be cast out. When he (Jesus) will have been "lifted up" from

the earth, he will draw all men to him; in saying this he knows how he will die (that is, by being "lifted up" onto the cross). The people reply that they have heard that the Messiah is eternal; what did his words (v. 23) about the "Son of man" being lifted up mean? And who was this "Son of man"? Jesus says—scarcely in direct reply—that they will for a while have the "light" with them, and they should believe in the "light" while there is still time, in order to become "sons of light." Jesus now leaves them and "hides" from them (12.20-36). ("Hides" is probably meant symbolically.) But despite the seven signs, "the Jews" have not believed in him. Some of the Jewish authorities have believed in Jesus, but they fear to do so publicly lest they be put out of the synagogues.[43]

The "passion narrative" (Jn. 13.1-19.42) occupies almost a third of this Gospel, whereas in the Synoptics it is roughly an eighth of each. This extension in space in John is accounted for by three long discourses, 13.31-14.31; 15.1-16.33; and 17.1-26. The three discourses defy easy summary because of John's free rather than logical manner; moreover, they repeat some themes touched on before. But some items are new; for example, "I give you [disciples] a new commandment that you love each other, as I have loved you. . . ." (13.34-35). Jesus says, "I am the way, and the truth, and the life. No one comes to the Father but through me. . . ." Philip asks to see the Father; Jesus replies, "Whoever has seen me has seen the Father. . . . I am in the Father and the Father in me." Again, "Whoever believes in me will do the works that I do."

Now a new idea is introduced (14.16) and developed a bit later (14.26). At stake is this matter, that Jesus will reascend to heaven; how then will teaching and guidance be continued on earth? The answer is that these will come from the Spirit of Truth, conceived of as a "paraclete,"[44] a Greek word used in the sense of a lawyer who advises, defends, or intercedes for a client. The world will neither see nor know this paraclete, but the disciples will. To the question,[45] how Jesus will reveal himself to the disciples and not to the world, in answer the "paraclete" is now specifically identified as the Holy Spirit (14.1-31).

The second discourse begins with three themes addressed to the disciples: First, "I am the true vine, and my Father is the vinedresser. . . . Abide in me, and I [will abide in you]. . . . I am the vine, you are the branches." Second, "Continue in my love. . . . No man has greater love than of laying down his life for his friends. . . ." Third, "If the world hates you, you know it hated me before you. . . . If they persecuted me, they will persecute you. . . ." (15.1-27). The discourse continues with the prediction of persecution and expulsion from the synagogues (16.1-33).

The third farewell discourse begins with a prayer by Jesus, since his "hour" has come, that God may glorify him (17.1-5). He prays for both the Church of the day and that of the future, especially for its unity (17.6-26).

The farewell discourses over, Jesus comes into a garden, unnamed here but identifiable with Gethsemane; John lacks the agony and the falling asleep of the disciples (Mk. 14.37-42; Mt. 26.40-45; Lk. 22.42-46). Now Judas comes with a cohort of soldiers (600 men) and Temple police (this is unique to John). Jesus knows all that is to happen: he asks, "Whom are you seeking?" "Jesus of Nazareth." "I am he." [This is unique to John; the betraying kiss (Mk. 14.44-46; Mt. 27.48-50; Lk. 22.48) does not appear in John.] Then Simon Peter cuts off the ear of Malchus, the slave of the High Priest. (In the Synoptics the slave is unnamed; there a bystander, but not Peter, cuts off the ear; in Luke, Jesus touches the ear and heals it.) Jesus will now drink the "cup" his Father has given him (18.1-11).

The hearing before the High Priest is different from the Synoptics (18.12-27). Here Jesus is led to Annas, described only here as the father-in-law of Caiaphas, the High Priest that year.[46]

The High Priest questions Jesus about his disciples and his teaching. Jesus says, "I have spoken openly to the world. I have taught always in synagogues[47] and the Temple, where all Jews assemble. I have said nothing in secret.[48] Those who have heard me know what I have said. Ask them." One of the police strikes Jesus, rebuking him for the (discourteous) way he has answered the High Priest. Jesus says, "If I have spoken something wrong, tell me what it is. If I have spoken

what is right, why do you strike me?" (Instead of replying)
Annas sends Jesus in bonds to Caiaphas. Very early in the
morning Jesus is led to the Roman praetorium ("barracks");
those (Jews) who lead him there remain outside, lest through
entering they be defiled and be barred from eating the Passover. Pilate goes out to them, asking, "What accusation are
you making?" He goes on to say, "Judge him by your law."
They reply, "It is not legal for us to put anyone to death."
(There has been a great debate[49] over whether or not the
Romans permitted Jewish authorities to execute someone.[50]
John seems to be implying that "the Jews," would have
killed Jesus if they had been allowed to; hence, though it is
the Romans who crucify him, it is "the Jews" who are responsible.)

The questioning by Pilate is more extended than in the
Synoptics. Pilate finally now tells "the Jews" that he has
found no crime in Jesus. "The Jews" have the custom[51] that
Pilate releases one prisoner at Passover. (This custom is unknown outside the Gospels.) Pilate now asks if he should release the King of the Jews. They all cry out, "Not this man,
but Barabbas."

Pilate now scourges Jesus (19.1-7); his soldiers mock him
and hit him. Again Pilate tells the crowd that he finds no
crime in Jesus. To the crowd he exhibits Jesus ("Behold the
man!"), dressed in the mocking crown of thorns and a purple
robe which the soldiers have put on him. When the chief
priests and police see him, they cry out, "Crucify him." Pilate replies, "You crucify him. I find no crime in him." Pilate delivers Jesus to (the soldiers) to be crucified.

Jesus carries his own cross. [Simon of Cyrene (Mk. 15.21;
27.32; Lk. 23.26) is here unmentioned. The pathos is increased if Jesus carries his own cross.] Pilate writes, for the
crossbar, "Jesus of Nazareth, The King of the Jews."[52] Unlike
the Synoptics, John tells that this titulus is read by many
Jews, being written in Hebrew, Greek, and Latin. The chief
priests ask that the titulus run, not "The King of the Jews,"
but rather, "This man said, I am King of the Jews." (That is,
they wish a titulus to be even more sarcastic.) But Pilate is
content with what he has written and will not change it.

The soldiers divide the garments of Jesus into four parts,

one for each soldier. The tunic is without a seam;[53] they do not divide this, but cast lots for it.

In Mark 15.40-41, women look on from afar. Here the (unnamed) mother of Jesus, her sister, Mary the wife of Clopas, and Mary Magdalene, stand by the cross. Jesus sees his mother, and the "beloved disciple" near her. To her he says, "Mother, behold your son"; to the beloved disciple he says, "Behold your mother." Thereafter the disciple takes her to his own house. (Only John has the mother of Jesus at the cross. Perhaps the suggestion is right that "mother" allegorically means the Church, and the disciple the faithful Christian. There seems to be no solution for the problem of why John abstains from giving Mary's name.)

Jesus at last says, "It is ended"; then he dies.

"The Jews," to prevent the bodies (Jesus and the two crucified with him) from remaining on the cross into the Sabbath, which is to begin at sundown, are described as wishing to hasten the deaths, this by breaking the legs of the three. The Roman soldiers do this to the two, but not to Jesus because he is already dead.[54] A soldier stabs him with a spear, and blood and water come out. (This is unique to John. The intent is probably to insist, against the Gnostics who considered Jesus merely an apparition, on the true humanity of Jesus.)

John describes Joseph of Arimathea, as the Synoptics do not, as a disciple of Jesus. Joseph asks Pilate for the body of Jesus; John alone describes this request as made "secretly, because of fear of the Jews."[55] Joseph comes and takes the body. Nicodemus (see 3.1-15) now provides the myrrh and aloes to be used for the embalming. Joseph and Nicodemus bind the body of Jesus in linen cloths with the spices, "as is the burial custom of the Jews." (That two eminent and pious Jews buried Jesus seems to be a refutation of allegations, recorded in Mt. 27.62-66; 28.11-15, that the disciples had stolen Jesus' body; by giving the details of the burial, John seems to be contending against disbelief and scorn.)

In John, Mary Magdalene alone comes to the tomb. The stone (which in the Synoptics needed to be moved away from the entrance) has here already been moved. John here does not narrate that Mary enters into the tomb. Instead, she runs to Simon Peter and to the other (the beloved) disciple, saying, "They have taken the Lord[56] out of the tomb and we" —note the unexpected *we*—"do not know where they have laid him." The other disciple outruns Peter to the tomb, stoops and looks in, and sees the burial cloths, but does not enter. Then Peter comes and enters the tomb. He sees both the burial cloths and also the napkin, which had been on the head of Jesus, now rolled up. The second disciple now enters the tomb; he sees and believes. John adds that as yet the disciples have not known the scriptural prediction that Jesus is to rise from the dead. (The passage suggests that only after the resurrection did the disciples come to understand what Jesus had been telling them.[57]) The two return to their homes.

Mary Magdalene is now back at the tomb (20.11). She sees two men in white. They ask why she is weeping. She answers that "they" have taken the body of her Lord and "I do not know where they have laid him." She then turns around and sees Jesus standing there, but does not know that it is he, thinking that he is the gardener. Jesus calls Mary by name.[58] She turns and addresses him in Hebrew as *rabboni*.[59] (John tells that it means "teacher.") Jesus tells her not to hold[60] on to him since he has not yet ascended to heaven. (The intent here is that Mary not impede the ascension. In some traditions outside John, in Luke for example, the ascension takes place after the day of the resurrection, not, as here, on that very day.) Jesus tells her to go to the brothers (the disciples) and to tell them he is ascending to "my Father and your Father, and to my God and your God." She goes to the disciples and tells them. That same day at evening, the disciples are in a room to which the doors are shut, in fear of "the Jews." Jesus comes into the room (without the doors being opened), stands in their midst, and says, "Peace be with you." He shows them his hands and his side (explained a bit later, 20.25, as the marks of the nails of the crucifixion and the soldiers' spear thrust.)[61] The disciples become joyous. Jesus repeats, "Peace be with you." He adds, "As the Father sent me, so I send you." He then breathes on them, and says, "Receive the Holy Spirit. When you will forgive any sins, they are forgiven; when you will not, they will persist."

There ensues an episode found only in John. The disciple Thomas has not been with the gathered disciples when Jesus has come. When they tell him that they have seen the Lord, he says, "Unless I will see the print of nails in his hands, and place my finger in the nail marks, and put my hand in his side, I will not believe." Eight days later, Thomas is with the disciples and again the doors are shut. Jesus appears. To Thomas he says, "Put your finger here and see my hands. Put your hand on my side. Cease from being without faith, and believe!" Thomas replies, "My Lord and my God!" Jesus says to him, "Blessed are those who have not seen, but yet believe."

John tells that Jesus did many other signs in the presence of his disciples not recorded in this book. (It is believed by many scholars that here the Gospel has ended.)

An appendix, chapter 21, ensues. Whether the appendix is by the author of chapters 1-20, or by someone else, is debatable. It has a number of purposes: to provide a resurrection appearance in Galilee (as do Mark and Matthew), to restore Peter, after his denials of Jesus, to leadership of the disciples, and to tell what happens to the "beloved disciple."

The Galilean appearance to the disciples takes place at what is called both the Sea of Galilee and, here, the Sea of Tiberias.[62] Jesus gives them bread and fish. This is the third time Jesus has appeared after the resurrection (21.1-14). Three times Jesus says to Peter, "Do you love me more than these [others do]?" Peter answers each time, "Yes, Lord. You know I love you." Jesus says, "Feed my lambs. . . . Feed my sheep." (The threefold denial by Peter is balanced here by the threefold assertion of love.) The next sentences seem to prophesy Peter's future martyrdom (21.1-19).

Peter now asks Jesus what the beloved disciple is to do. Jesus replies that it is not of concern to Peter whether this man is to tarry (on earth) until the remote End. But the disciples spread the word among believers that this disciple is not to die, even though Jesus has not said that (21.20-23).

Then follows a sentence (21.24) that the "beloved disciple" has written "these things" and his testimony is true. Finally (21.25), there are many other things which Jesus did; the world could not contain the books that presented everything.

There is an important distinction respecting "identification" to be noticed in the presentation of Jesus in the Synoptics and John. The Christian reader of the Synoptics can readily revere and unreservedly admire Jesus, but the fullest identification with him is elusive, for the reader himself can no more work his exorcisms and healings than could the disciples who are portrayed in the Synoptics as unable to do what Jesus has done; in this sense, there is a limit to the extent of personal identification with Jesus in the Synoptics. In John, the identification with Jesus is by contrast unreserved; it does not rest on the capacity, or lack of it, to do miraculous works, but rather on the mystic union in terms of spiritual water, or spiritual bread, or resurrection, all of which Jesus represents and in which those who go through spiritual rebirth can fully share. Moreover, the brief passage, 1.16-18, provides the perspective that the identification with Jesus is in effect identification with God: The Law was given through Moses, but quite beyond Moses, God's only Son has made God known. To be united with Jesus is in effect to be united with God.

John appears to be contending against three different groupings. One is the movement of the disciples of John the Baptist, which continued into the period when the Gospel was written. The author John is concerned that the role of John the Baptist not be overstressed, or John the Baptist himself unduly elevated or his movement unduly admired. In the Synoptics, John the Baptist is brought into close relationship with Jesus, but the author here explicitly denies what the Synoptics affirm, that Jesus is Elijah (1.21). He is willing to say that John the Baptist gave testimony that a Jesus was to come, but, against the Synoptics, especially Luke, John the Baptist is portrayed as himself not knowing Jesus in advance (1.30-31).

A second grouping is the Gnostics, as we have seen above.

The third grouping is "the Jews." The Pharisees as opponents appear in 7.32-50; 8.13-26; 9.13-16, and 11.45-47; but in 7.32-36, 8.13-26, and 9.13-23, the term "Pharisees," though used, rather promptly gives way to the term "the Jews." The latter term occurs in John approximately seventy times (the exact count varies slightly because of variations in the manuscripts). Some of the occurrences are matters of simple differentiation, as between Jews and Samaritans in chapter 4, or between Jews and Gentiles, as in parts of chapters 18-19. There are some passages, such as 11.49-50, in which "the Jews" seem to mean the priests and members of the Sanhedrin. But for the most part, "the Jews" is John's general term for the foes of Jesus. Indeed, though in John, both in particular passages, such as 18.20, and elsewhere in general, the Jewishness of Jesus is explicitly or implicitly affirmed, the antagonism depicted seems to dissociate Jesus from being Jewish; in 8.17 he is depicted as speaking of *your* Law, rather than *our* Law or *the* Law.

It is the judgment of many, indeed, most Christian scholars, that John, writing at a time of acute controversy between Jews and Christians, ascribes to the lifetime and career of Jesus the controversies of his own later time. That Jesus heals on the Sabbath outrages his opponents in the Synoptics; what Jesus is claimed to be outrages them in John. That is, the opponents of Jesus in John are scorned and hated for denying that Jesus is the divine Son of God. (Some scholars express this difference by saying that in John the controversies are "christological.")

The depth of the controversy is increased by two items. One is that there have been in John's area Jews who were believers at one time and had then ceased to be; these former Christians are addressed in 8.31-32 and the sequel, but we are not told what has weaned them away from the new movement. The second item is reflected in the charge that Jews put pressure on fellow Jews not to become Christians openly (9.22; 12.42; 16.2). Though it was denied (p. 149, n. 54) that there is direct connection between the Twelfth of the Eighteen Benedictions of the Synagogue and the expulsion of Christians from the Synagogue found in John, that is in no way to deny the reliability of the contention that Jews put pressures on fellow Jews not to become open Christians and that local synagogues expelled them. This pressure and scattered expulsion reflect undoubted historical situations.

The Jewish denial of the divine nature of Jesus has as its background a cultural atmosphere in which Jews and Christians shared in a desire for the spiritual life which John sets forth from the Christian side, both wishing to live in the world of spiritual water, and spiritual bread, and escape from death. The issue was that Christians affirmed that these benefits came from the Christ, and Jews denied that this was so. Jews as fervently as Christians wished to live by the Divine Logos, but they could not identify the Logos with Jesus.

In John, the issue of the nature of the belief in Jesus is an either-or; one either believes completely in the divinity of Jesus and is thereby a Christian, or else, by disbelief or only partial belief, one is an outsider to Christianity. There is, in John's view, only one way to God, and that is through the Christ. Any other way is futile, or wrong, or both.

· 8 ·

JESUS AND
JUDAISM

No one would deny that an Amos or an Isaiah was other than a Hebrew, or see in their denunciations of their Hebrew contemporaries anything other than the ultimate in concern for the religion shared in by the Prophets and those whom they denounced. The same could be the case with Jesus; that he criticized or denounced some or all fellow Jews need not imply anything other than an ultimate concern arising out of loyalty.

In the growth and development of the new movement, the successive Gospel portrayals alter Jesus from a loyal insider into a critical outsider. Jesus becomes increasingly depicted as over and against his fellow Jews; he is progressively portrayed as representing something new and unprecedented, which marks him off from his fellow Jews. Whether what is new and unprecedented arose historically in the lifetime and career of Jesus, or arose only later but was ascribed to his lifetime and career, cannot be objectively determined. On the one hand, it is beyond refutation that at least some of what is deemed new and unprecedented arose only after the lifetime of Jesus. On the other hand, is it credible that Jesus neither said nor did anything that in some way or other marked him off from his fellow Jews? That hardly seems possible. But precisely what this was is scarcely to be determined.

There are those who make the following set of contentions: The Jesus of history was a messianic claimant whom the Romans, correctly or incorrectly, regarded as a political rebel, and for that reason they executed him. Then among his followers the view arose that Jesus had been resurrected;

393

from the belief in the resurrection, rather than from anything that Jesus had said or done, there emerged the historical development of the new movement. Later, when the Gospels came to be written, they ascribed to the career of Jesus major developments that occurred after his career.

Surely this is in part right, but is it the whole story? Granted that the Romans executed Jesus as a political rebel, was he indeed one? There is no clear and unmistakable evidence, but only a scattering of clues, such as the titulus on the cross with its mention of kingship, or the passage, Acts 1, about the restoration of the kingship to Israel. In the absence of direct and unmistakable evidence, the case that Jesus was a political rebel, a loyal guerilla, rests on logical inferences: Just as a messianic claimant such as bar Kōzibá was a political rebel, so Jesus must also have been. The line of reasoning often proceeds to assert that a would-be Messiah who was not an activist rebel would seem unreal. The contention that the Jesus of history was a political rebel was made in the eighteenth century by a German Deist, Samuel Hermann Reimarus; it reappears with some frequency. The most recent major instance of such a contention was made in the 1960's by S. G. F. Brandon, in *Jesus and the Zealots*, including the assertion that the Gospels deliberately disguise this role through the artificial portrayal of a "Pacific Christ," so depicted as to conceal the reality that Jesus was a political figure. I personally subscribe to the view that Jesus was indeed a political rebel, but I cannot accept much of Brandon's argumentation; my espousal of the view rests on only logical inference and not on clear and demonstrable evidence.

The earliest disciples were Jews; earliest Christianity was a Judaism. To repeat (see p. 340), a frequent view in New Testament scholarship for over a century has been that the Gospels reflect legends and theological ideas of the developing Church of the time well after the career of Jesus. The major thrust of nineteenth-century Protestant Gospel scholarship was the effort to "recover the Jesus of history," that is, to try to sift from the Gospels whatever could be deemed to be authentically related to Jesus himself. A review of that scholarship was written by Albert Schweitzer, *The Quest of the Historical Jesus.*[1] (There exist a good many books and articles on "the quest.") For the most part, it has been the conclusion of liberal or radical scholars that the quest has failed, for it has not seemed objectively possible to separate in the Gospels what is authentically about Jesus from what is the reflection of the later Church.

In the quest, there were utilized, besides a rigorous study of the Gospels, whatever materials could be assembled from both Jewish and pagan sources.[2] Thus, Jesus is mentioned in Josephus. A passage, Antiquities, XVIII (5.2), 116-19, speaks of the death of John the Baptist at the hands of Herod Antipas, as do the Synoptic Gospels. Josephus tells also [ibid. XX (9.1), 200] of the condemnation by the Sanhedrin of James, the brother of Jesus, at the instance of the High Priest Annas. As to Jesus himself, there are three passages which mention him. One passage[3] [Antiquities XVIII (3.3), 63-64] has been studied and restudied, for from the sixteenth century on, scholars have doubted its authenticity as written, since it is marked by Christian convictions that are out of accord with what a Jew such as Josephus would have written. The passage suggests that Jesus was more than a man; it states that "he was the Messiah"; it affirms that Jesus was indeed resurrected. Most modern scholars regard the passage as completely a Christian interpolation into Josephus; others view it as a passage not interpolated but rather as an authentic core significantly rewritten and expanded by some Christians.

The second passage is found not in the inherited Greek text of Josephus, but in a version of The Jewish War that had been translated into old Russian; this version is often called "the Slavonic Josephus." Immediately after II (9.3) 174, there is found a passage which expands the one in Antiquities[4] by alluding to a number of traditions in the Gospels, but with some noticeable changes. Thus, the Slavonic passage tells that after Jesus had worked cures and assembled a following, the Jews wanted him to destroy the Romans and Pilate and become their king. The Jewish leaders and the High Priest, however, were fearful that the Jews lacked the power to defeat the Romans, so they informed Pilate about Jesus; Pilate's soldiers then killed many of the "multitude."

When Pilate then examined Jesus, he found him innocent of crime and rebellion; moreover, Jesus had healed the wife of Pilate when she was sick and dying. Pilate released Jesus, who returned to his usual works, gathering even more followers. The scribes then gave Pilate thirty talents[5] to kill Jesus; he gave them permission to seize him and crucify him.

To be paired with this passage is the third, also in the Slavonic version of the Jewish War, at V (5.2), 195, in a context in which Josephus speaks of warnings posted in Greek and Latin barring non-Jews from entering the sacred precincts. The Slavonic Josephus speaks of an inscription, reading "Jesus, a king who did not reign, was crucified by the Jews because he foretold the destruction of the city and the desolation of the temple."

While an occasional scholar[6] has regarded the two passages, and some others, in the Slavonic Josephus as having a core of authenticity, most scholars emphatically deny any authenticity to them.

Again, in the search for sources about Jesus, especially the Jewish sources, scholars have often turned to the mentions of Jesus in the Talmud. These mentions are relatively few. One such is a *baraita* (Sanhedrin 43a): "Jesus was hanged on Passover eve. For forty days a herald had proclaimed 'He is to be stoned for practicing sorcery, leading Israel astray, and seducing them to apostasy.' No one came to his defense. He was hanged[7] on Passover eve." (The context of the passage is the discussion of the requirement that witnesses are to be sought in favor of a man convicted of blasphemy who can testify for the man's acquittal.)

There follows the *baraita* a comment by a Sage named Ulla (end of the third Christian century), which in effect wonders why defending witnesses should have been sought; he gives his reply—that Jesus was "near to the kingship."

There are still other passages, but of no significance beyond the unfriendliness.[8] Some of the disparagement of Jesus appears through associating him with Balaam (Num. 22.1-24.25), a character whom the Rabbinic tradition has no fondness for. (Less clear is the possibility that a Rabbinic scorn for a certain Ben Stada in reality means Jesus.)

The net effect of the Talmudic statements is to attribute to Jesus wonder-working and cures, as in the Gospels, but to ascribe these to evil sorcery rather than to benign supernaturalism. (The direct accusation of being possessed by the devil does not appear.) His birth is viewed as quite natural. That which is meant by "christology"—that is, the divine role of Jesus—is not denied in the Talmud for the simple reason that it does not appear at all. Knowledge is reflected about the "Gospel" (Gk. *euangelion*, Heb. *ēvangēlion*, made into a pun meaning "wicked scroll"), but without any specification of the content. In sum, the contribution of Rabbinic literature to knowledge about the figure of Jesus is scant, and even that material is of no value for Jesus himself, as independent testimony to him, but is derived from hearsay about what is in the Gospels.

A Jewish work, *Toldôt Yĕshu* ("the account of Jesus"), of uncertain origin but probably medieval in its written form, is denigration of Jesus to the point of vilification, in response to Christian vilification of Jews. Old material, even from early pagan[9] attacks on Christianity, appears, in particular that Jesus was the illegitimate son of a Roman soldier, Panthera. Often Toldot Yeshu uses a Gospel item, but so twists it as to turn it from praise to contempt. This unhappy work is the Jewish side of reciprocal extreme Jewish-Christian animosity.

Accordingly, though Jesus was a Jew, there are no Jewish sources of any value about him.

In the medieval Jewish philosophers there are occasional mentions of Jesus or Christianity, or both, that are in a different spirit, indeed, a relatively generous[10] one, depending largely on external events, namely, the absence of direct persecution.

In the early nineteenth century, when modern critical scholarship on the Gospels began to flourish, political and social conditions prompted Jews to study early Christianity with the same freedom which Christian scholars claimed for themselves. As a result, there has come into being quite a vast quantity of writings by Jews on Jesus.[11] Some of the writings by Jews have been an effort, as it were, to reclaim the Jesus of history for Judaism.[12]

Neither the Christian nor the Jewish scholarship which aims to "recover" the Jesus of history has ever succeeded, for even books which achieve some eminence fail ultimately of persuasion. The writings by modern Jews, however, much as they may respect and even admire Jesus, do not ascribe special divinity to him. When Christians of our time write about a purely human Jesus, they are extracting him from a literature which depicts him as divine. Yet a purely human Jesus was not at all the center of the convictions of the earliest Christians.

Modern Christian scholars often regard "the Jesus of history" as beyond recovery. Yet even Christian scholars who hold such a view ordinarily have each his own unexpressed image of Jesus to which he feels able to relate. Thus, the assertion that the Jesus of history is beyond recovery does not at all mean that for holders of this view Jesus simply disappears. To the contrary.

Precisely what kind of a person Jesus was—a teacher, a leader, a wonder-worker, a prophet, a social reformer, a political rebel—cannot be ascertained. But that Jesus was a Jew, a son of the Synagogue, is beyond doubt.

· 9 ·

ACTS OF THE
APOSTLES

Luke, as we have said, wrote a two-volume work—Volume One, the Gospel about Jesus, and Volume Two, the Church after the time of Jesus. In the Gospel there is the repeated motif that the new movement is ultimately to become Gentile, but throughout the Gospel and up to Acts 1.1-11.18 the setting is primarily Judea. Then Gentiles come into the movement; from Acts 11.19 to 28.31 the setting is primarily the Graeco-Roman world. That is, the two-volume work relates how the new movement was born within Judea, but became a Gentile movement outside it. That which impels the motion and transplanting is the Holy Spirit, and Acts is in a sense an account of what the Holy Spirit accomplishes. The motifs found in the Gospel continue into Acts, namely, that the new movement is fully faithful to its parent Judaism; the new movement was, indeed, the unbroken continuity of the ancient Judaism, and it was "the Jews" who had gone astray.

Acts picks up where the Gospel has ended, telling that after Jesus has given commandments to the Apostles through the Holy Spirit, he has appeared to them during a period of forty days. They are to remain in Jerusalem until the Holy Spirit will come to them. They ask Jesus if he will now restore the kingdom to Israel; his reply is that they need not know the times, but rather they should wait for the Holy Spirit. Then Jesus ascends to heaven; two angels assure the Apostles (here called "men of Galilee") that they will see Jesus return in the same way they have seen him go into heaven.

Judas Iscariot dies;[1] it is necessary now to elect a successor

399

to bring the number of Apostles back to twelve. Of the many disciples, two men are nominated and one, Mathias, is elected by lot (ch. 1).

On Pentecost in Jerusalem the Holy Spirit descends on the many adherents of the new movement. There are present Jews from many countries. The adherents, though Galileans, speak miraculously in all the languages of these many countries, to the amazement of some, and the scorn of others, who allege drunkenness.[2] Peter now makes a speech, denying the drunkenness, and asserting, with scriptural quotations, that the Holy Spirit has prompted the prophetic speech just heard. He speaks, further, of Jesus, whom his hearers had had crucified by lawless men. All Israel ought to recognize that God has made Jesus Lord and Messiah; the auditors should "Repent and be Baptized, and receive the Holy Spirit" (ch. 2). (This speech, and others to come, are regarded by scholars as written by Luke; Greek historians ordinarily wrote speeches which the characters they tell about were imagined as giving.)

At the Temple, Peter and the Apostle John heal a lame man. Peter then addresses the people, this in rebuke for their having had Jesus crucified, though they had done this in ignorance (ch. 3). Peter and John are arrested and the next day they are brought before the Sanhedrin. Peter again speaks about Jesus. The authorities, though not punishing Peter and John, order them to cease to speak about Jesus or teach in his name. Peter and John reply that they cannot cease (ch. 4).

The community lives by sharing its possessions. A certain Ananias keeps back from the Apostles money from the sale of a field. At Peter's rebuke Ananias falls down, dies, and is buried; Sapphira, his wife, also falls dead (5.1-10).

The Apostles do many signs and wonders, and accomplish healings and exorcisms. The Apostles are arrested, but an angel opens the prison doors for them. Arrested a second time, they are brought before the Sanhedrin. The High Priest reminds them of the order not to teach about Jesus. Peter replies that they must obey God, not men; it was God who had raised Jesus after "you killed him by hanging him on a tree."[3] The Sanhedrin is enraged. A Pharisee named Gamaliel[4] asks that the prisoners be led outside for a bit. He speaks, then, urging caution. He mentions that a certain Theudas,[5] claiming to be someone great and having gathered adherents, was killed and his followers scattered and the movement came to nothing. After him, Judas the Galilean, who arose at the time of the census (A.D. 6, Lk. 2.1), also perished. Accordingly, these prisoners now before them should be let alone; if what they do is of men, it will fail, but if it is of God, men cannot overthrow them, and the Sanhedrin might even be opposing God! The Sanhedrin, heeding Gamaliel, beat the Apostles and, ordering them again not to teach about Jesus, release them. But the Apostles continue teaching in the Temple and in private homes (5.11-42).

The disciples continue to grow in numbers. Now a dispute arises between those speaking Greek and those speaking Hebrew, over the distribution of food. The Twelve, assembling all the disciples, propose that seven men be designated to serve the tables ("handle the chores"), relieving the others for the praying and the service of the (Christian) message. Seven are chosen, and the Apostles lay their hands on them. [The laying on of the hands, as Moses did to Joshua (Num. 27.20,23), appears often in Acts. The Seven in Acts are never called deacons, an office mentioned elsewhere in the New Testament, though "serve" is a verb from the same Greek root as the noun.] The number of disciples increases, and a great many priests join the movement (6.1-7).

Among the Seven is a man named Stephen who works miracles and signs among the people. Some members of the "synagogue of the Freedmen,"[6] made up of Jews from the Greek areas,[7] enter into a dispute with Stephen. Unable to contend with the wisdom and Spirit which Stephen possesses, they prevail secretly on some people to charge Stephen with blasphemous statements against Moses and God. Stephen is brought before the Sanhedrin, where false witnesses say that Stephen continually speaks against the Temple and the Law, to the effect that Jesus will destroy the Temple and change the practices which Moses has handed down. In reply, Stephen speaks to the Sanhedrin. His long speech reviews biblical matters from Abraham through Solomon;[8] he then denounces those he is speaking to as persecutors and killers of the prophets who had predicted the coming of the Righteous One (Jesus), whom they had betrayed and murdered. They are enraged. Stephen, looking to heaven, sees the glory of God, with Jesus standing at His right hand. They rush at Stephen, cast him out of the city, and stone him. The witnesses (the false ones mentioned above?) take off their coats and put them at the feet of a young man named Saul.[9] Stephen prays, "Lord Jesus, accept my Spirit. . . . Lord, do not hold this sin against them."[10] He dies, with Saul approving the killing. A violent persecution arises in Jerusalem. The disciples scatter. (The spread of the movement outside Jerusalem and then the entrance of Gentiles is ascribed to this persecution, for refugees become missionaries.) The "Church,"[11] except for the Apostles,[12] spreads into Judea and Samaria. Saul devastates the church in Jerusalem, entering from house to house and sending the believers to prison (6.8-8.3). [No explanation is offered about the authority of Saul/Paul, nor is any word given about the unusual legal procedures. In the Epistles (Gal. 1.13,23; 1 Cor. 15.9; Phil. 3.6) allusion is made to Paul's persecution of the Church, but never in connection with Jerusalem; indeed, in Gal. 1.13-24 Paul seems to say that he had never been in Jerusalem prior to his "conversion" and even after it he remained unknown in Judea.]

Philip, one of the seven "deacons" (4.5), performs healings and exorcisms in his successful missionary work in Samaria. Even a magician named Simon[13] believes and is baptized. The Apostles in Jerusalem hear of Philip's successes (among these Gentiles). They send Peter and John there so that the many converts will receive the Holy Spirit. (Apparently there has been there no laying on of the hands, the rite which confers the Holy Spirit, as in Acts baptism alone seems not to do.) Simon now offers a bribe for the right also to convey the Holy Spirit to others, but this is indignantly refused. (The point is to emphasize the ethical integrity in the new movement.)

Philip, at an angel's direction, goes on the road toward Gaza. An Ethiopian eunuch who has made a pilgrimage to Jerusalem is on his way home, in his carriage. He is reading Isaiah 53 to himself, out loud. Philip meets him, gets into the carriage, and asks if he understands what he is reading. The eunuch replies that he needs a guide, to tell him whom the passage is speaking about. Philip explains that it is about the good news of Jesus; he then baptizes the eunuch. Philip then goes to Azotus (Heb. Áshdód) and the movement spreads further as he preaches the Gospel in the coastal area in the direction of Caesarea[14] (8.26-40).

The account reverts to Saul/Paul. He gets letters from the High Priest, addressed to the synagogues in Damascus, to extradite[15] from there any men or women belonging to what is here called for the first time "the Way."[16] On his nearing Damascus, a light from heaven flashes on him, and he falls to the ground. He hears a voice, "Saul, Saul, why are you persecuting me?" Saul asks, "Who are you, Lord?" "I am Jesus whom you are persecuting." Saul is enjoined to go on to Damascus where he will be told what to do. The men with Saul are speechless, for they hear the voice but see no one. Saul arises, temporarily sightless; he neither eats nor drinks. (There are two additional accounts, Acts 22.4-16 and 26.12-13, of the "road to Damascus," as the incident is known in Christian lore. There are minor discrepancies in the details in three accounts.[17] Paul in Gal. 1.13-17 speaks of his conversion, but makes no mention of this incident on the road.)

In Damascus there is a disciple named Ananias, who lays his hands on Saul so that Saul is filled with the Holy Spirit and he recovers his sight. (Ananias goes unmentioned, as does this incident, in Paul's Epistles. Indeed, Paul's assertions that he is an Apostle from God seems contradicted by the matter of Ananias' laying the hands on him. Some scholars handle the contradiction by ascribing to Paul an exaggeration of his independence from men; others take Paul at his word and regard the Ananias matter as pious legend.)

In the synagogues in Damascus Saul preaches about Jesus, and he confounds the Jews there. They determine to kill him, but he escapes when his disciples let him down over the city wall of Damascus in a basket. (Paul, 2 Cor. 11.32-33, briefly alludes to an escape from Damascus, in a basket lowered from a window in a wall. But in that account he is escaping from an official of the Nabatean king Aretas; there is no word there about a Jewish "plot.") Saul returns to Jerusalem, but the disciples suspiciously fear and shun him until Barnabas brings him to the Apostles, informing them of what has happened in Damascus. Now Saul preaches openly in Jerusalem. Greek-speaking Jews dispute with him, and try to kill him. The "brothers" therefore escort him to (the port of) Caesarea, and send him to Tarsus (9.1-30).

In Judea, Galilee,[18] and Samaria, the Church has peace, and now it prospers (9.32). Peter goes about Judea. A cure at Lydda of a paralytic brings converts. At Joppa, his prayers revive a woman disciple whose name is Tabitha ("doe") in Aramaic, Dorcas in Greek. At Caesarea, there is a Roman centurion, Cornelius, generous to Jews and pious in Jewish worship (but apparently not a full convert). A vision comes to Cornelius; an angel bids him to send messengers to Joppa for Peter to come to him. While these are on their way, Peter is hungry; in a trance, he sees a vision, a huge cloth or net full of creatures of all kinds. A voice says to him, "Rise, Peter, kill and eat." He replies, "Lord, I have never eaten anything profane or unclean." The voice says, "What God has cleansed you must not call profane."[19] This happens three times, and then the cloth is taken up to heaven.

Peter, perplexed by the vision, is told by the Spirit to accompany the three men (whom Cornelius has sent). At Caesarea, Cornelius, in the midst of his friends, falls down at Peter's feet and worships him, but Peter bids him rise since Peter, too, is only a man. Peter tells those assembled that they know that Jews hold it unlawful to visit, or associate, with anyone of another nation.[20] Yet God has shown Peter that he must not call any man[21] profane or unclean.

Cornelius repeats the account of his vision. Peter asserts that God has no favorites; in every nation, whoever reveres him and does the right is acceptable.[22] He then speaks of Jesus, his death and resurrection, and his appearance, not to the whole (Jewish) people, but only to those who ate and drank with him after his resurrection. As Peter is speaking, the Holy Spirit comes on to all who have been hearing about Jesus. There are present some circumcised (Jewish) believers;[23] these are astonished that the Holy Spirit is poured out on Gentiles.[24] Peter concludes that these Gentiles, having received the Holy Spirit, are now entitled to baptism (9.33-10.48). (The Jewish food laws have been nullified, and Peter has preached to Gentiles, and Gentiles have come into the movement.)

When Peter comes back to Jerusalem, he is criticized for going to Gentiles and eating with them. Peter recounts the vision (10.9-16) and the incident at the home of Cornelius, contending that God has given to the Gentiles the same gift of the Holy Spirit which He has given to Jews. Peter's critics are silenced. The Apostles and the brothers glorify God: "God has granted repentance for eternal life to the Gentiles" (11.1-18). (The entrance of Gentiles into the new movement is now fully legitimate.)

The scene now turns to Antioch (which is beyond the borders of Judea, and beyond Samaria and the Galilee; that is, it is fully outside the Jewish territory). In the scattering of the believers after the stoning of Stephen, some traveled as far as Phoenicia, Cyprus, and Antioch and there made converts. Certain Gentile converts from Cyprus and Cyrene have come to Antioch, there preaching to Greek Gentiles, converting a great number. The church at Jerusalem now sends Barnabas to Antioch (apparently to see what has been going on). Through Barnabas even more believers are added. Barnabas now goes to Tarsus to find Saul to bring him to Antioch. For a year Saul and Barnabas meet with the church in Antioch, where for the first time the disciples are called Christians (11.22-26). (In Acts the beginning mission to Gentiles is not attributed to Paul; in Paul's Epistles there is no mention of this particular time spent with Barnabas at Antioch.)

Prophets from Jerusalem, including one Agabus,[25] come to Antioch. Agabus predicts that there will be a world-wide famine.[26] This takes place in the days of Claudius (reigned 41-54; Luke often associates Christian events with Roman history). The disciples (in Antioch) determine to send relief to the brothers in Judea, sending it to the "elders"—that office is mentioned here for the first time—through Saul and Barnabas[27] (11.27-30). (The point is that the Gentile Christians undertake the responsibility to the Jerusalem church, for they are not a rupturous element.)

In Jerusalem, Herod Agrippa lays violent hands on some of the Christians. He kills the Apostle James, son of Zebedee (this is narrated in a single sentence.) Because this pleases the Jews, Agrippa also arrests Peter during a Passover. Peter is to be brought out to the people after the Passover (for public execution?). But an angel appears to Peter in his cell and leads him out of the jail (12.1-11).

Peter goes to the home of a Mary. The people there believe that it is not Peter, but his guardian angel.[28] Entering, Peter describes what has happened, asking them to tell "James and the brethren." (James is the brother of Jesus and the leader of the Jerusalem church, 15.13). Herod Agrippa, unable to find Peter, has the prison guards executed; Agrippa then goes to Caesarea, the seat of the Roman authorities, where he dies (A.D. 44) after the populace hails him as a god.[29] (Persecution of the faithful leads to divine punishment.) The Church grows. Barnabas and Saul return from their mission, and John Mark is with them (12.12-25).

At Antioch word comes through the Holy Spirit to prophets there that Barnabas and Saul are to go on a mission. They go to Cyprus and preach in the synagogues. They encounter a Jewish false prophet and magician named Barjesus ("son of Jesus"; later his name is given as Elymas). The (Roman) proconsul[30] Sergius Paulus (of whom nothing more is known) summons Barnabas and Saul to listen to their preachment; Elymas opposes them. Saul—now identified for the first time as Paul—miraculously blinds Elymas, and Sergius Paulus is converted (13.1-12). (This is the first conversion of a Roman official.)

Paul and his companions—John now leaves to return to Jerusalem[31]—journey (by sea) to Perga, in the Asian Minor region called Pamphylia, and then to Antioch, in near-by Pisidia.[32] At the synagogue, Paul presents a brief review of biblical events, ending up with a preachment about Jesus. Many are converted. Paul is invited for the next Sabbath to speak again; on that Sabbath the whole city turns out. Now the Jews, envious of the big crowd, contradict Paul and revile him. Paul and Barnabas reply that it was necessary that the word of God be spoken first to Jews; but since Jews are pushing them away, they are turning to Gentiles. The (Christian) word continues to spread. But the Jews stir up persecution so that Paul and Barnabas are driven out of the area. They go to Iconium (13.13-52).

Success at Iconium among Jews and Greeks prompts Jews to stir up the Gentiles against the missionaries. These missionaries flee to near-by Lystra and Derbe. At Lystra Paul heals a man who has been a cripple from birth. The people of that area, Lyconia, call Barnabas "Zeus" and Paul "Hermes." The priest of Zeus wishes now to offer sacrifices (to Barnabas), but Barnabas and Paul tell the people that they are only men, and that they have now brought witness to the Gentiles who previously had been allowed to walk in their own (sinful) ways. They restrain the people from offering sacrifices to them. Now, however, Jews come from Antioch and Iconium; they stone[33] Paul and drag him out of the city as dead. (Here the Jews from a distance intrude, even though the preaching is not in synagogues to Jews, but to Gentiles outside synagogues.) Paul, surviving the stoning, goes with Barnabas to Derbe, winning many disciples, and then to Iconium and Antioch, encouraging their converts there to abide courageously in the faith. They appoint elders in each church. They now return to Antioch in Syria, reporting how God has opened a door of faith to Gentiles.

To Antioch there come men from Jerusalem who assert that the Christians there must become circumcised. (Before, 10.10-16, the issue was the biblical food laws.) Paul, Barnabas, and some others are designated to go to the Apostles and elders in Jerusalem for counsel about the question. To churches on their journey[34] they report on the conversion of Gentiles, to the great joy of the brothers. At Jerusalem, however, believers of Pharisaic background demand both circumcision and also observance of the Law of Moses. After much debate, Peter, who is present, asserts that God had earlier chosen him for the mission to the Gentiles. (Paul makes that assertion about himself in Gal. 2.10, where he says that Peter had been entrusted with the mission to the Jews!) Peter speaks against "putting on [Christians] a yoke [the Law] which neither we nor our fathers have been able to bear. We believe we shall be saved through the grace of Lord Jesus. . . ." Now Barnabas and Paul relate the signs and miracles they have done among Gentiles.

Then James (the brother of Jesus, and the leader) gives

his judgment, that they, the leaders, should not trouble (impose circumcision and the Mosaic Law on) Gentiles. Rather, a letter should be written that Gentiles are to abstain from pollution of idols, from (sexual) unchastity, from what is strangled,[35] and from blood.[36] (The food laws abrogated in 10.10-14 are related to proper or improper animals, fowl, or beasts; here food offered to idols, a different category, is prohibited. The abolition of Mosaic Law is not to include the abolition of its demands for sexual chastity. "Blood" probably means murder, still another exception to the broader abolition of laws. The point in the retention of these prohibitions is to deny the implication that the abolition of the Mosaic Law implies ethical anarchy.) It is then added, as if to explain the reason for the exceptions, that in every city from early times people have preached about Moses, and he is read every Sabbath in the synagogues. (That is, the retention of these prohibitions is a concession to Jewish sensibility.) Now a letter embodying the judgment of James is composed, to be carried to Antioch by two men, Judas Barsabbas and Silas, along with Paul and Barnabas. (In Gal. 1.17 Paul asserts his independence of the leadership in Jerusalem; here he is silent, and he acquiesces in the decision that has been made. There is abundant scholarship, some of which harmonizes Acts 15 and Gal. 2, and some of which declares the two contradictory beyond harmonization, and proceeds to question the historicity of Acts 15.)

From 15.36 to the end of Acts, the attention focuses on Paul. Because Paul will not agree that John, who had earlier left him,[37] accompany him, a sharp dispute arises between Paul and Barnabas, and the two separate from each other. Barnabas and Mark sail to Cyprus, while Paul, now taking a man named Silas (15.39) with him, goes to visit the brothers where Paul had already been. He and Silas go through Syria and Cilicia. At Lystra there is a Christian named Timothy, son of a Jewish mother[38] and a Greek father; to placate Jews in that area, Paul circumcises Timothy. (In Gal. 2.25, Paul's companion Titus is not compelled to be circumcised. Scholars have debated about the difference and the inconsistency. Some view the circumcision of Timothy as unhistorical, the result of a motif repeated in Luke, the Jewish fidelity of eminent Christians; other scholars, insisting on the historicity, suggest that the two cases are quite different.) Arriving at Troas, in southwest Asia Minor, Paul in a vision sees a man from Macedonia who asks him to come there to help him. (That is, the movement now spreads from Asia into Europe.)

At this point there comes the first of four so-called "we passages" (16.10-17; 20.5-15; 21.1-18; 27.1-28.16), because they are written in the first person plural, as if parts of a travel or diary account. (Debates on the "we passages," whether they are authentic quotations from an earlier source or a literary fiction, have been sharp; the majority of scholars seem to accept their authenticity, but the minority includes some eminent professors.)

In Philippi, Paul (with his companions) exorcises a demon from a slave girl whose ability to divine the future had brought monetary gain to her owners. Brought by the owners before magistrates, the charge is made that Paul and his companions are Jews, disturbing the city and advocating customs illegal for Romans to accept or practice. The crowd beats them up, and they are put in jail. An earthquake at midnight shakes the foundations of the prisons, the doors are opened, and the fetters are loosened. The next day the magistrates decide to free the missionaries and the jailer reports this to Paul. But Paul replies, "They have [already] publicly beaten us, without a trial. We are Roman citizens, yet we have been thrown into prison. Instead of releasing us secretly, let them come [openly] and take us out." (It seems to be forgotten that they are no longer in jail!) The magistrates are now fearful (that they have improperly punished Roman citizens), so they come to apologize (16.11-40). (The purpose of this story is to set forth the contention that Paul is a Roman citizen, to prepare for the recurrence of the matter more significantly in Acts 22-23; many scholars deny that Jews, such as Paul, were full citizens.)[39]

In Thessalonica Paul argues over Scripture with Jews in the synagogue. Crowds, including Jews and the rabble, attack the home of a certain Jason, apparently Paul's host, and drag Jason before the city authorities, charging that the Christians violate the decrees of Caesar, through saying that there is another king, Jesus. Paul and Silas are sent away to Beroea, where the Jews are "more noble." But Jews come from Thessalonica and stir up the crowds in Beroea (17.1-

16). Paul now goes alone to Athens. (No mention of his being in Athens is found in the Epistles.)

Paul is greatly vexed that Athens is full of idols (17.16-34). He argues with the Jews in the synagogues and with Gentiles in the Agora. Epicureans and Stoics call him a babbler; others scorn him as someone preaching about foreign deities. He is brought[40] to the Areopagus ("the hill of Mars"), and asked to explain what he has been saying. Paul, after complimenting the men of Athens for being very religious, mentions that he has seen there an altar with the inscription "To an unknown God." He says, "What you worship as unknown, I [know and] proclaim to you. God does not live in shrines. He has allotted territories for all the nations, descended from the one man [Adam] so that they should seek God, feel after Him, and find Him. The [past] period of ignorance, God has overlooked; now He commands all men, everywhere, to repent, before He judges the world through a man [Jesus] whom he designated. He has given assurance of this to all men by raising [Jesus] from the dead." Some who hear him mock; others say they would like to listen to him again; but some become converted.[41] (Perhaps the point of the narrative is to give later Christians an example of how an early Christian dared to contend with philosophers. That Paul is not spectacularly successful is possibly meant to alert later Christians to the futility of trying to persuade philosophers. Contempt for philosophers is expressed, for example, in 1 Cor. 1.18-22. Christianity ultimately accepted and used Greek philosophy, but not until toward the middle of the second century.)

Paul now goes to Corinth. There he seeks out a Jew named Aquila and his wife, Priscilla; they had come from Italy when the Emperor Claudius had compelled Jews to leave Rome.[42] Paul goes to see them; they are tentmakers, as he is.[43] Paul argues in the synagogue every Sabbath, persuading Jews and Gentiles. Opposed and reviled by the Jews, he goes to the house of a Titius Justus, a worshipper of God,[44] who lives next door to the synagogue. The unnamed head of the synagogue becomes a convert. Encouraged by a vision of the Lord, Paul remains in Corinth a year and six months.

Jews now bring charges against Paul to the proconsul Gallio,[45] alleging that Paul is persuading men to worship God in

ways that violate the (Jewish) law. Gallio declines to inter-
vene in what he regards as an internal Jewish matter. (Romans see no differences between Judaism and Christianity.)
The crowd beats Sosthenes, the head of the synagogue, but
Gallio (contemptuously) ignores this (18.1-17). (The account here of Paul in Corinth is very brief, and gives no reflection of the acute issues there, described in I and II Corinthians.)

Paul now sails for Syria, taking Aquila and Priscilla with
him. At Cenchrae, the port of Corinth, Paul cuts his hair, for
he had made a vow.[46] (This passage is extraordinarily brief.
The intent seems to be to show Paul's fidelity to the Law.)
After a brief visit in Ephesus, Paul tells the believers that he
will return, if God wills. He goes on to Antioch and travels
about Asia Minor, encouraging the faith (18.18-23).

An Alexandrian Jew, Apollos, eloquent and well versed in
Scripture, has come to Ephesus (where apparently Aquila
and Priscilla have remained). Apollos preaches about Jesus
and knows about the baptisms by John the Baptist, but he
seems not to know about baptisms in the name of Jesus. (The
effort here seems to be to explain the "party of Apollos," 1
Cor. 1.12.) Priscilla and Aquila give him the correct information about baptism. Apollos goes on to Achaia (where
Corinth is). There Apollos refutes Jews, eloquently showing
by Scripture that the Christ is Jesus (18.24-28).

Meanwhile, Paul comes to Ephesus. He finds Christians
there who, not having been baptized in the name of Jesus,
have not received the Holy Spirit. They are now so baptized;
Paul lays his hands on them and they receive the Holy Spirit.
For three months he speaks in the synagogue, but meets disbelief and scorn; he moves on to a hall. In the next two years
God does miracles through Paul, both healings and exorcisms. Seven sons of a Jewish *high priest* (this is either an
error or a gross exaggeration) named Sceva try to do an
exorcism in the name of Jesus, but the evil spirit leaps on
them, and they flee, naked and wounded. Some of the magi-
cians of Ephesus now burn their books of magic, worth fifty
thousand pieces of silver. (The point is twofold, to show the
supernatural importance of the name of Jesus, and the superiority of Christian exorcism over all others.)

Paul now determines that, after going to Macedonia and

Achaia, he will go on to Rome. But in Ephesus a riot breaks out against "the Way," when a certain Demetrius speaks against the economic losses to him and other silversmiths because Paul has scorned the idols as not gods (19.21-41). Paul then goes to Greece; a plot by Jews forces him to change his travel plans. He and his companions come to Troas. There he resurrects a certain Eutychus who has died after falling from a third-story window. After more travel, he sails on, by-passing Ephesus because he is in haste to reach Jerusalem for Pentecost. (Again, Paul is faithful to Judaism). At a stop at Miletus, he summons to him the elders of the church at Ephesus. He tells them that he does not know what will happen to him in Jerusalem; but he has encountered the Holy Spirit wherever prison and affliction have awaited him. He knows, however, that all to whom he has preached will see him no more (20.1-36). When his ship stops at Tyre, the disciples there tell him, through the Spirit, not to go to Jerusalem. At Caesarea, the prophet Agabus (see 11.28) tells Paul, symbolically, that at Jerusalem the Jews will deliver him into the hands of Gentiles. Importuned not to go to Jerusalem, Paul says he is ready to go to prison or even to die for the name of Jesus (21.1-14). (Like Jesus, Paul knows that troubles will arise in Jerusalem, but nevertheless he goes there.)

At Jerusalem, James and the elders tell Paul that the false accusation will be made that he teaches the Jews who live among Gentiles to forsake Moses, to neglect circumcision, and not to observe the ancestral customs. There are in Jerusalem four men under a vow; Paul should purify himself along with them, so that all will know that Paul does indeed live in accordance with the Law. Paul does as they have suggested. (Christian scholars have noted the hypocrisy involved here.)[47] Paul, after the rites of purification are over, is recognized by Jews from Asia Minor.[48] He is seized and dragged out of the Temple, but he is saved by Roman soldiers from death at the hands of the mob. The tribune (captain) asks Paul if he is the Egyptian[49] Jew who had recently stirred up a revolt and led four thousand murderers out into the Wilderness. Paul replies, "I am a Jew, of Tarsus in Cilicia, a citizen of no mean city." Paul now asks for permission to speak, and he does so, in Hebrew (which probably means Aramaic). (Is this another example of Paul's Jewish fidelity? His "Bible" in the Epistles is never the Hebrew.) Paul begins by saying that he is a Jew, born at Tarsus, but raised in Jerusalem, at the feet of Gamaliel, educated in accordance with the strict way of the Law of the fathers, zealous for God, as are those to whom he is speaking. He alludes to the events of his persecution of the Way and his journey to Damascus; he speaks of a vision to him in the Temple of the Christ, enjoining him to leave Jerusalem and to go to the Gentiles.[50] (Nothing in the Epistles suggests at all that Paul was raised in Jerusalem or was a student of Gamaliel. Some Christian scholars have doubted the historical reliability of these items.[51])

The crowd now shouts its resentment and its wish to kill him. He is led by the Roman soldiers into the barracks and there tied up, preparatory to their scourging him. Paul protests that it is illegal to scourge a Roman citizen who has not yet been tried by a court. His protest is carried to the tribune of the soldiers, who asks Paul if he is indeed a Roman citizen; he replies, yes. The tribune says that he himself has bought his citizenship for a high price;[52] Paul replies that he was born a citizen. The tribune the next morning brings Paul before the Sanhedrin, this to learn what the charges against Paul are.

Before the Sanhedrin, the High Priest Ananias has Paul smitten on the mouth. Paul charges that this is illegal, and he denounces Ananias. Observing that the Sanhedrin consists of Sadducees and Pharisees, Paul says that he is a Pharisee, a son of Pharisees, and that he is being tried because of his belief in resurrection. Now the Pharisees and the Sadducees quarrel with each other.[53] Scribes of the Pharisees assert that they see no crime in Paul. So bitter is the acrimony between the Pharisees and the Sadducees that the tribune has the soldiers forcibly take Paul away, less he be torn to pieces. That night the Lord appears to Paul, assuring him that he will go on to Rome (which Paul, in 19.21, has intended to do).

The next morning, some forty Jews take a vow to taste no food until they have killed Paul. They propose to ambush him. A nephew of Paul—this is the sole mention anywhere of members of Paul's family—hears of the ambush plans and informs the Romans. The latter determine to send Paul to Caesarea, to the Roman governor Felix,[54] with a letter which says that Paul was accused before the Sanhedrin about matters relating to the Law, but not charged with anything deserving death or imprisonment.

Before Felix, the High Priest Ananias, through a spokesman, charges Paul with being an agitator among Jews throughout the world and a ringleader of the sect of the Nazarenes. (The implication is that Paul belongs to an insurrectionist sect.) It is added that Paul has tried to profane the Temple. The Jews present support these charges.

Paul, in his defense, asserts that during his stay in Jerusalem he has only worshipped, and has not been involved in any disputes, whether in the Temple, the synagogues, or elsewhere in the city. He admits to being a member of "the Way"; he worships God, and believes everything in the Law and in the Prophets, and, through these, in the resurrection and the great Judgment. He had come to Jerusalem to bring alms and offerings. But Jews from Asia—Paul now breaks off in the middle of the sentence—these ought to be present to set forth their accusation, or those present ought to say what crime was established before the Sanhedrin, beyond his belief in resurrection. It is about resurrection, he says, that he is on trial before Felix.

Felix determines to postpone matters (23.7-26) until the tribune can come to Caesarea (to present data). Meanwhile, Paul is to be kept in custody, but to have some freedom. Felix, we are told, has a somewhat accurate knowledge of "the Way."

Felix is married to a Jewess named Drusilla. (She was the sister of Herod Agrippa II. Felix had seduced her away from her first husband, the king of Emesa.)[55] Felix sends for Paul to hear him speak about faith in Christ Jesus, but when Paul speaks of justice, self-control, and future judgment, Felix (because of his well-known corruption) is alarmed, and sends Paul away. Also, he hopes for some bribery from Paul; he often sends for Paul, and speaks with him. When Felix is recalled[56] two years later to be succeeded by Porcius Festus, he leaves Paul in prison, this to please "the Jews."

When Festus, after arriving in Judea, visits Jerusalem, the

chief priests and leaders tell him about Paul and ask that Paul be sent to Jerusalem, for they intend to ambush him and kill him. Festus turns down the request. When Paul is brought before Festus, he denies any crime against Jewish or Roman law. He appeals to Caesar—that is, he asks to be tried in Rome in accordance with Roman law. Felix agrees that Paul should go to Caesar.

Herod Agrippa II and his wife Bernice come to Caesarea to visit Festus. Agrippa examines Paul in the presence of Festus. After Paul has spoken of his career, asserting his Jewish fidelity, Festus charges him with being mad. When Agrippa, Festus, and Bernice are alone, they agree that Paul has done nothing to deserve death or imprisonment. Agrippa says, "Had this man not appealed to Caesar, he could be set free" (21.15-26.32).

(The long, involved account of the arrest and the interrogations disclose the main themes: Paul is a most faithful Jew, innocent of all trespass. It is "the Jews" who cause him his acute difficulties. The Romans, by contrast, protect him. Neither Felix nor Festus, Roman officials, find any crime in him. Just as Herod Antipas had found no crime in Jesus, Lk. 23.6-15, so now Herod Agrippa II finds none in Paul. The doctrines of Paul, so distinctive in the Epistles, justification by faith and the annulment of the Mosaic Laws, are not reflected to the slightest, and the issue is presented instead as if it is only the belief in resurrection.)

The journey to Rome (27.1-28.16) entails many difficulties, with wind and violent storm,[57] and running aground on Malta. During the storm Paul sees an angel, and he assures the crew that though the ship will be lost, the crew will be saved (27.21-26). Ashore at Malta, a viper bites Paul, but, to the astonishment of the natives, he is unharmed. He then cures the father of the chief man of the island of fever and dysentery, praying and laying hands on him. He heals the rest of the people on the island who are diseased (28.3-10).

Three months later they set sail on a new ship, and, after some stops, arrive (28.11-13) at Puteoli, the port of Rome, on the bay of Naples. There are Christians there,[58] with whom Paul stays for seven days, and then goes on to Rome (28.14-16).

At Rome, Christians there come to meet Paul. He is allowed some freedom, staying alone but with a soldier to guard him. Paul calls together the Jews of Rome. He tells them that though he has done nothing against the (Jewish) people, or the customs of the fathers, he has been made a prisoner and turned over to the Romans. These had wanted to free him, but when the Jews had objected, he had appealed to Caesar. He has wanted to speak to the Jews at Rome, since it is because of the hope of Israel that he is a prisoner. They reply that they have had no letters from Judea about him, nor any other reports. They do want to hear his views, since his sect is everywhere spoken against. On the appointed day, the Jews come to his lodging in great numbers. He expounds matters to them all the day. Some are persuaded, some not. Paul then makes a statement, citing Isaiah 6.9-10, here meaning that the Jews will reject the Christian message, in order that God's salvation can be offered to the Gentiles, who will listen. He lives in his lodging for two years, teaching about the Lord Jesus Christ quite openly, with no one hindering him (28.17-31).

This is the point at which Acts ends, without any account of the outcome of the appeal to Caesar. Much speculation has therefore arisen. Did the author write before the matter was settled? What do the "two years" mean? Would not the author have mentioned an exoneration of Paul, if he knew of it? Or was Paul executed after two years, in conformity with 20.37-38, where, in a farewell address, Paul says that his associates would not again see his face? There are no persuasive answers to such questions. Later Christian tradition describes Paul as a martyr at Rome, but this is nowhere explicit in the New Testament.

Modern liberal and radical scholars have raised countless problems about Acts of the Apostles. Is its portrait of the expansion of Christianity a reflection of how the movement really spread? Or is it an ingenious schematic picture? Again, is the portrait of Paul in Acts reliable, in view of the conflicts with material in the Epistles, and the absence of Paul's distinctive doctrine of "justification by faith?" The range of views of scholars extends from affirming the reliability of Acts to the almost total denial of that reliability.

But Acts, even if reliable, raises problems about omissions.

It does not tell how Christianity came to Damascus or Rome; it completely abstains from mentioning Alexandria, which became a foremost Christian center. It gives little clear reflection of the varieties within Christendom such as do apocryphal ("non-canonical") Gospels; it is asserted by scholars that Acts glosses over the abundant and acute inner Christian differences and controversies.[59]

Granted that such problems respecting Acts are real, the fact remains that it is the only account that has come down about the Church in the age after Jesus. If it is completely set aside, then virtually nothing is left, and we would be as bereft of information about this period as we are, unhappily, about the period immediately following what Acts relates, for no account of that ensuing period has come down to us (if any such account were ever written).

Rather, the development of Christianity after the period covered by Acts is both fragmentary and uncertain. New Testament literature, such as the Gospels, the Epistle to the Hebrews, the Epistle of James, the Epistles of Peter and of John, cannot be given fixed historical dates, for there are no pegs on which to hang firm historical conclusions. By means of inference, educated guesses, and hypotheses, one can put together a subjective view of the unfolding of Christianity, but an objective reconstruction is not possible. We can know that it indeed spread and developed, but we cannot trace these matters.

· 10 ·

SYNAGOGUE JUDAISM
AND CHRISTIANITY

The New Testament writings not reviewed here reflect inner Christian concerns of a time after direct connection of Christianity with Jews and Judaism has largely receded or ended. Earlier, mention was made of four phenomena in early Christianity: motifs carried over from Judaism; motifs abandoned; motifs carried over but altered; and newly created motifs.

Early Christianity was more, at least in quantity, than the Epistles, the Gospels, and Acts of the Apostles. Much that undoubtedly was developing in early Christianity failed to be recorded. Hence, we lack the full historical account of the period that the literature reviewed covers.

A summary setting forth of the main similarities and the main differences between Judaism and Christianity can be useful. It is not to be doubted that Christianity historically arose not from the Temple, but from Synagogue Judaism. Christianity shares with Synagogue Judaism the conviction of the sanctity of Scripture, and that religious contentions are probable not by logic or philosophy, but by what is in the Bible. Such Christian citation is often literal, but more often it is not. As to the legitimate ways of citing Scripture, there exists nothing in the Christian legacy similar to the seven norms of interpretation ascribed to Hillel or the thirteen ascribed to Ishmael (see p. 236). The general mode of Christian scriptural interpretation is usually different in form as well as in content; Christian interpretation, it must be self-evident, is directed to Christian purposes.

In due course Christians elevated some circulating writings into Christian sacred Scripture, this about the years 150-75. They gave to these writings the name "New Covenant." In the sixteenth century "testament" and "covenant" were synonymous; "New Covenant" and "New Testament" meant the same thing. To the older collection Christians gave the name "Old Testament." In the Christian view, the Old Testament and the New are a single, continuous Bible. The occasional Christians who speak of the Old Testament as a "Jewish" book are deviating from the normal Christian view in which the Old Testament is invariably regarded as a Christian book.

Continuous as is the New Testament with the Old in the Christian view, nevertheless Christians viewed the New Testament as superseding the Old in essential ways. First, it is the Christians, not the Jews, who are regarded as the "people of God" and who are the legatees of the divine promises and concerns expressed in the Old Testament. Christians contended that they had supplanted the Jews; Jews, as the parent, found little occasion or need directly to deny Christian claims; there is no analogue in Jewish sacred writings, biblical or Rabbinic, to the expressed concerns found about Jews and Judaism in the Christian writings. Second, the Mosaic laws, both the general mitzvot and those centered in the occasions of the sacred calendar, are no longer obligatory on Christians. Thus the Jewish sacred days, and the vast array of Pentateuchal laws, are not preserved in Christianity. The New Year and the Day of Atonement are not carried over, for Christianity innovated its own atonement system. Passover is preserved, altered into Easter, and Pentecost, Shavuot, is given a new interpretation, part of historic Christian experience in Acts 2. Sukkot was not carried over. The Sabbath abided, but was shifted to Sunday; the essentials of the Sabbath mitzvot and halachot were abandoned. What was retained in the alteration was the emphasis on the Sabbath as the pre-eminent weekly day of prayer, along with the reading of Scripture. Judaism and Christianity diverged as to what arrangement should exist for the reading of Scripture, but held in common the belief that Scripture reading was to be central.

The great dividing point respecting external matters can be expressed in the following way: Synagogue Judaism affirmed the eternal binding force of the Mosaic Laws. Therefore, Synagogue Judaism proceeded to make whatever inferences seemed necessary for those Laws to be defined, clarified, protected, and extended. Christianity, denying the eternal binding force of those Laws, had no reason to produce a Mishna or a Gemara. One can lament that there has not been preserved the kind of full recommendation or obligation to daily, ordinary piety by Christians as is the case with Synagogue Judaism. We can, as it were, follow an ordinary Jew from sunrise to sunset, from Sabbath to Sabbath. Would that there were a comparable prescriptive Christian literature! Perhaps the extraordinary attention to the role of Jesus, combined with abandoning prescriptive mitzvot on principle, led to obscuring what was expected of the ordinary Christian in his day-to-day life. In time, Canon Law arose in Christendom, simply because every large institution requires some form or organizational structure and regulation. But Canon Law arose as a Christian response to necessity, as a resource to turn to when issues have arisen not out of the wish to provide a direct application of scriptural law to daily life, as are the Mishna and the Gemara. Only in medieval times did Christianity create a significant literature of personal devotion and piety for ordinary communicants.

Early Christianity developed its own officialdom. It shunned the title "rabbi" specifically. Slowly three major offices arose, the bishop ("overseer"), the elder (*presbyteros*, brought into English as priest), and the deacon. It is often unclear what these offices meant in early times, or how those who held them were selected. The view arose that all legitimate officials were designated in accordance with an unbroken chain of designation and appointment that ultimately went back to Jesus. This unbroken chain is called "Apostolic Succession," and derives primarily from Luke-Acts, wherein, out of countless disciples, Jesus designated twelve as Apostles, and these designated Apostles later designated others as Apostles. There is some similarity in the Jewish view of a chain of qabbala (see p. 236) and Christian Apostolic Succession, though there are also striking differences.

It is perhaps oversimplification, but nevertheless helpful to notice the distinctive difference in basic motifs between historic Judaism and historic Christianity. In Judaism, the recommended religious life is that in conformity with the inherited mitzvot and halachot; the emphasis has been on what man should *do* in obedience to God. In Christianity the step was taken from "faith," as set forth in Paul, there meaning a full and unreserved reliance on God, into faith meaning the content of belief. Because beliefs within the community of the Christians came to vary and to create acute difficulties, as a next step *proper* faith came to be a Christian concern and demand; what became important was what one believed respecting man's relationship and obedience to God.

Much of the Christian emphasis on proper belief centered, naturally, on the figure of Jesus. What one believed about him, both with respect to what he had done and, even more significantly, what he was, was the clue to "orthodoxy" or to "heresy." While the word "Christ" is, as said, a Greek translation of the Hebrew word "Messiah," and while some aspects of the views of Synagogue Judaism were carried into Christianity—for example, that Elijah must appear first— the chief impression ought to be that of acute difference. The Messiah in Judaism is not related to atonement, to saving mankind from sin, as is the Christ in Christianity. Again, for Jews the Messiah is yet to come (though some modernist Jews have rejected the belief in a "personal Messiah" and speak instead of a "messianic age" in the future); for Christians the Messiah came in the past and some day, in the future, his Second Coming is to take place. There is some similarity in the Jewish expectation of the first coming and the Christian of the Second, especially in that each is conceived of as the climax of history; there are, however, some differences.

Yet not only are there clear distinctions theologically between Judaism and Christianity, but also the common terms of religion, such as sin, righteousness, and atonement, though these are used in both traditions, mean quite different things.

It can reasonably be asked, in view of these acknowledged differences, in what way is Christianity, apart from its his-

toric origin, related to Synagogue Judaism? In reply, however differently Scripture has been viewed and interpreted
respectively by Jews and Christians, at the core of each religion is its central allegiance to a sacred book. Mohammed
perceptively spoke of both Jews and Christians as "people of
the book."

The question of whether, historically, Christians broke
with the Temple before its destruction in 70, or only thereafter came to view Jesus as their "temple not made with
hands" is difficult to answer. But it is clear that the Temple
was not an abiding force in Christianity. Neither was it an
abiding force in Judaism, though prayers for its restoration
continue in traditional Judaism (but such prayers are more
traditional piety than reflective of genuine desire for such a
restoration!).

Christians have shunned the word "synagogue," as they
have the title "rabbi." Yet a local church is in its way a Christian synagogue. It is not a place of animal sacrifice, but one
of prayer, instruction, and inspiration. So too is a Jewish
synagogue. A recurrent view (perhaps too simple) regards
the liturgy of church worship as directly derived from synagogue worship, though altered by the centrality of the figure
of Jesus in the Christian worship; it is perhaps more prudent
to think of parallel developments, with each institution having
gone its own way in prayer, rather than of some extensive
borrowing by Christians of the content of Jewish worship.

It seems right that the synagogue was much more a school
than the local church has been. But both were the gathering
place of the community, and education, as well as care of the
sick and of the poor, came to have a natural setting in both.

But most significant of all is the matter of God. Judaism
and Christianity share in a monotheism and they worship
the same God, and both describe Him as the God of Israel.
The Jewish views of God did not enter into the acute theological definitions and distinctions that came to be a necessity and the custom among Christians. Jews never developed
the view called "the Trinity," and ordinarily they seem quite
unable to grasp what it means. Jews have never elevated a
figure as Christians have done with Jesus. Recurrently it has
seemed to some scholars, both Christian and Jewish, that
some Christian views about Jesus amounted to either signifi-

cantly modifying or even rupturing monotheism; there are Christian scholars who assert that in segments of second-century Christianity Jesus was conceived of either as a second deity, slightly subordinate to God, or else made equal to and interchangeable with God. This was a route which Judaism never took. Clearly, then, there has been a distinction between Judaism and Christianity in its theological formulations of its views on God; whether these admitted differences are limited to formulation, or else extend into substance, is quite a tangled issue, beyond settling here. One can say, however, that at the heart of the matter of God there is a similarity that borders on identity respecting basic assumptions and even some basic convictions.

That Christians came to reach very great numbers and thereafter proceeded to delimit Jews in their freedoms, and then horribly to persecute them, is the supreme tragedy of the western world. That Jews persecuted early Christians is also a fact of history, but it was more in the form of spontaneous violence than of concerted, deliberate policy, enjoined on Jews by some authority as obligatory; there is no evidence at all for this latter. That Christians should have put on Jews the responsibility for the death of Jesus (as if he were not a Jew), and completely to have exculpated the Romans was monstrous. Moreover, the death of Jesus, in usual views, brought a benefit to mankind! For those Christians who wish it, the Christian writings reviewed in this book can provide a sacred sanction for a continued denigration of Jews and Judaism, and one fears that anti-Judaism, genteel or coarse, will inevitably mark such nominal Christians. But that, on the other hand, Christians include an abundance of men and women who have been able to rise above hate and persecution is also a fact of history.

Perhaps it is useful to notice that Christians even in early times were readily able to hate each other and later to persecute each other. The very nub of the historic animosity toward Jews is a product of the anomaly that Jesus was a Jew who became central in a set of religious ideas which other Jews did not accept but Gentiles did. Had Christianity not been born in Judaism, the anti-Jewish motifs in Christian literature, history, and theology would scarcely have arisen.

Is hostility to Jews and Judaism a basic, a permanent aspect of Christianity? Some Jews, and now occasional Christians, affirm this. But were not hatred and denigration and violence part of the accepted norms of the times, as witnessed by the inner Christian hatred and the denigration of fellow Christians at least as extreme as the Christian hatred of Jews? Is it not to be hoped that education and understanding and charity can combine to relegate this hostility to a sad chapter of the past, some day to be overcome and even forgotten? After Christianity came to permeate western civilization, there were recurrent occasions when it was notably untrue to itself (as were the Jewish High Priests to Judaism in the pre-Maccabean period). Organized Christianity spurred lust for power, dreadful wars, and repeated injustices, and stood in the way of science and social amelioration. Yet if one looks at both those untoward aspects that need lamenting and at the benefits conveyed, then surely, on balance, the benefits have outweighed the negatives.

It is only in western countries—for example, the United States, Britain, Canada, Holland, Denmark, and a few others—that Jews and Christians have begun to understand and to become able to assess what has divided Judaism and Christianity. It is only recently, a matter of decades, not yet of centuries, that there has begun a reversal of the hideous relations of the past. Since this reversal is so very recent, it is as yet only a beginning. How much remains to be done!

It ought to be self-evident that neither Judaism nor Christianity ended in the period covered in this book, and one hesitates to point out that each has a long history of development after this period. Why do so? Simply because there are Jews who are unaware of Christian unfoldings in the ages beyond its early beginnings, and Christians who are curiously unaware that Judaism did not end when Christianity came onto the scene, and also went through many unfoldings. Each religion continued on its own way, responding to historic events and cultural development, and each underwent vicissitudes and tensions and even bitter divisions. They have both developed, and changed, and often deepened. It has not always been well with them. Yet they have survived. And, despite episodes of shame, they both have much to be gratified by.

NOTES *

PREFACE

1. When the story reappears, it grows in dimension: The translators, working in isolation in separate chambers, emerged at the end of the day with exactly the same Greek wording for the day's chore!

PART I

CHAPTER 1

1. The Mishna passages relating to "defiling the hands" are in Yadaim 3.2, 5; and 4.5-6. It is there stated that at Jamnia, on the day when Gamaliel II was deposed and Eleazar ben Azariah appointed head of the Great Court, Song of Songs and Ecclesiastes were declared "canonical." The Gemara passage most often cited respecting canon is Baba Batra 14b-15a. There a *baraita*—an extra-Mishna item—is cited which deals with the proper sequence of the prophetic books. Next there comes an effort to set the chronological sequence of the prophets, non-literary as well as literary. Thereafter the sequence of the Hagiographa is set forth. In this latter context the question of the date of Job is raised, in relation to a possible chronological sequence of the Hagiographa. This leads to similar questions respecting Joshua, Samuel, the Psalter, and other works. To Joshua is attributed the authorship of the final passage in Deuteronomy which describes the death of Moses. That is, the passage is only indirectly related to canon and gives no direct information about the process by which it came about. There are scattered passages which reflect objections to the presence of certain books; thus, Ezekiel: Shabbat 13b; Menahot 45a-b; Hagiga 13a; Proverbs: Shabbat 30b; Song of Songs: Yadaim 3.5; Megillah 7a; Ecclesiastes: Yadaim 3.5; Eduyot 5.3; Shabbat 30a-b; and Esther: Megillah 7a; Sanhedrin 100a. Despite the expressed reservations, these books came into, or, better, were retained in, the canon. From the Yadaim passages and the affirmation of the presence of Song of Songs and Ecclesiastes at Jamnia there has arisen the view mentioned that canon was finally fixed at Jamnia in the year 90; Jamnia and 90 are a convenient way of alluding to canon, but it is scarcely right. A more prudent view would be that canon was the result of consensus, arrived at over a long period of time.

* There are deliberate repetitions in the notes, there for the convenience of the reader.

2. In Against Apion I.8 (sentences 38-39), Josephus gives the number as twenty-two.

3. This is brilliantly set forth in Geza Vermes, *Scripture and Tradition in Judaism*, 2nd ed., 1973.

CHAPTER 2

1. Tanach is the traditional Jewish designation for the Hebrew version of what Christians call Old Testament. An artificial word, it is an acronym of the consonants T, N, and K, which are the initials for the threefold division: T for *Tōrāh* ("revelation"), alluding to the Five Books of Moses; N for *Nevi'im* ("prophets"), and K—at times the consonant, as in this word is pronounced like the German or Scotch ch—for *Ketuvim* ("writings"), the heterogeneous collection which includes Psalms, Proverbs, and other books. The vowels were inserted to make the sequence of consonants pronounceable.

2. By "traditionally" here and elsewhere I mean a viewpoint or idea that arose many, many centuries ago, and has been bequeathed to our age. Some traditional notions are exalted and some are fatuous. Usually they are at best fraught with some difficulty and at worst often unreliable. The seventy years' duration of the Babylonian exile is based on Jer. 29.10, "When a full seventy years have passed . . . I will [bring] you back to this place."

3. The title given him is *peḥa* (Hag. 1.1; 2.2, and elsewhere).

4. That he was such a descendant is uncertain. The genealogical basis (1 Chron. 3.17-19) seems confused about his father. The Davidic ancestry is implied in Zech. 3.8; 6.9-15, especially v. 12; see also Isa. 4.2; 11.1; Jer. 23.5; 33.15. It is quite possible that anyone who emerged to high leadership was adulated as the "branch of David," whether descended from him literally or not.

5. Indeed, Spinoza, in his Theologico-Political Tractate, VIII-IX, suggested that Ezra, not Moses, was the actual author of the Pentateuch.

6. This episode seems to be a reflection of the action of Antiochus IV Epiphanes in erecting a statue of Zeus in the Temple in Jerusalem.

7. Neither he nor the other Maccabean High Priests truly possessed the genealogy that the Priestly writings, especially Chronicles, supposed that priests should have, namely, a descent from Aaron, the brother of Moses, through Zadok, the priest of the time of David. That Jonathan exercised political power was a source of some popular disapproval. Some scholars trace the origin of the Dead Sea community to a disapproving, voluntary withdrawal from the Jerusalem scene into the Wilderness.

8. Idumea was at this time the area west of the Dead Sea. In earlier times, the Edomite territory lay south of the Dead Sea, but the Edomites had been pushed out by the Nabateans (an Arabian people) who made the former Edomite territory the center from which they achieved notable conquests, as far north as Damascus.

9. See note 8.

10. Josephus, War I (3, 1), 70. The title was inscribed in Greek on coins containing both Hebrew and Greek words.

11. Coins were struck on behalf of "Simon, Prince of Israel." Possibly, too, animal sacrifices was resumed on the temple site for a short period.

12. See Part III, Introduction.

CHAPTER 3

1. Those works found in the Greek Jewish Bible, but not the Hebrew, are conveniently referred to as the Apocrypha.

2. An Aristobulus is known as a philosopher who flourished about 150 B.C. Two fragments of his writings are preserved in Eusebius, *Preparation for the Gospel*, VII.10 and XIII.12. Scholars are divided on whether the two are the same or different. On the philosopher, see below, p. 265.

3. See pp. 79-80 and note 31.

4. Josephus in Life III and Ant. XX (8-11), 195, terms her *theosebes* ("religious"). Some have inferred that she was a virtual convert to Judaism, but this goes beyond the evidence.

5. War III, 8, 1-9. A similar story, found in Rabbinic literature, names Rabbi Johanan ben Zakkai as the person who predicted Vespasian's elevation to Emperor (Gitin 56b; Lam. R. I, 5; Ab. R, N. IV). It is a common folktale.

6. In the 1930's, in the time of Chicago gangsterland, one of my teachers, a European who made occasional forays into American slang, customarily alluded to Josephus as "a pigeon-stool."

7. He mentions his patron four times: Ant. I (1, 2, 8; Life, #76 (verse 430); Against Apion I.1 and II.1. Epaphroditus is identified by St. John Thackeray (Loeb edition, vol. IV, pp. x-xi) as a "grammarian . . . who had been trained in Alexandria and spent the latter part of his life . . . in Rome, where he amassed a library of 30,000 books. . . ."

8. Two ways of giving references to Josephus are common. One way is that of noting a division into book, chapter, and paragraph, exemplified in Antiquities III, 2, 5; it means paragraph 5 of chapter 2 of Book III. More recently the habit has arisen of replacing chapter and paragraph numbers with the number of the sentences, exemplified in Antiquities II, 59-62. The Loeb edition (Greek on the left page and English on the right) does provide book and paragraph, but not nearly as prominently as the sentence numbers; the latter appear at the top of the pages. The arrangement of Book and sentence enables one to be more precise than does the Book, chapter, and paragraph arrangement. My own procedure is to provide Book, chapter, paragraph, and also sentence number, e.g., Ant. III (2, 5) 59-62.

9. This has survived separately only in fragment. See the excellent Ben Zion Wacholder, *Nicolaus of Damascus*.

10. See "Classical Writers and the Jews," JE, IV, pp. 107-9. M. Stern (ed.), *Greek and Latin Authors on Jews and Judaism*, I, 1974, replaces

the older Reinach; vol. II, which will complete the work, is eagerly awaited.

11. For an introduction to the coins see A. Reifenberg, *Israel's History in Coins from the Maccabees to the Roman Conquest*, London, 1953, or H. Hamburger, "Money, coins," in IDB, III, pp. 426-35.

12. The collection of J. B. Frey, *Corpus Inscriptionum Judaicarum Recueil des inscriptions juives qui vont du IIIe siècle avant Jésu-Christ au VIIe siècle de notre ère*, 2 vols., 1936-1952, has been criticized as defective. A second edition (New York, 1975), has additions, corrections, and updated bibliography in a "prolegomenon" by Baruch Lifshitz; see note 14. On the "balustrade inscription," see Howard C. Kee, *The Origins of Christianity*, p. 259, and compare War V (5, 1), 193-194; VI (2, 4), 124.

13. See G. Ernest Wright, *The Biblical Archeologist*, Vol. VIII, #1.

14. V. A. Tcherikover and A. Fuks, *Corpus Papyrorum Judaicarum*, 3 vols., 1957-1964. This has become the standard work.

15. Esdras is the Greek form of Ezra. In some reckoning, the biblical book of Ezra is called I Esdras, the book of Nehemiah is II Esdras, and the book here under consideration III Esdras. There is still another book we consider below (pp. 80-86) known both as II Esdras and IV Ezra.

16. The new dynast, in other folklore, designated a certain Ahikar to be the royal keeper of accounts. In our story, Ahikar is viewed as the nephew of Tobit. Many diverse tales from various cultures survived about Ahikar.

17. The duration of the exile seems conceived of in Ezek. 4.6 as forty years, and in Dan. 9.24 as 490 years, expressed as "seventy weeks of years."

18. On the method of referring to the Dead Sea writings, see below, p. 93.

19. See Eccles. 3.19-22; 4.2-3; 7.2-3; 9.2-12. The Wisdom of Solomon attributes to the wicked attitudes more evil than those found in Ecclesiastes.

20. The explicit doctrine of immortality is strikingly unique to Wisdom; in usual Jewish writings afterlife is resurrection.

21. In the period with which we deal the figure of Enoch was of high importance, for fertile minds speculated on what happened to him on his being brought up to heaven. See below, pp. 86-89, on the Book of Enoch.

22. Gen. 5.23 tells that Enoch lived 365 years. But his father Jared lived 962 years and his son Methusaleh 969 (Gen. 5.20, 27).

23. The usual view, to the contrary, is that wisdom is very elusive. The passage here seems derived from Prov. ch. 8, where wisdom is also a necessity for monarchs.

24. Solomon's prayer for wisdom is in 1 Kgs. 3.5-15.

25. Possibly he means to suggest that the twenty-one are the result of multiplying the sacred number seven by three.

26. The terminology he uses here reflects his use of Greek philosophy, especially Stoicism.

27. In 11.17 it is stated that God "created the world out of formless matter." This is an interpretation which "clarifies" Gen. 1.1, which, without interpretation, might have meant that God did his creation using matter already in existence (an idea found in Plato), or, the exact contrary, that God had created *ex nihilo*, "out of nothing."

28. "Jesus" is the Greek form of the Hebrew name Jeshua, and Jeshua is a form of the name Joshua as found in post-exilic biblical writings. There was an even earlier form of the name, Jehoshua, which became Joshua.

29. These are given in detail in M. Z. Segal, *Sefer Ben Sira Ha-Shalem* ("The Complete Book of Ben Sira"), Jerusalem, 1953, pp. 37-38. Echoes of the book in other Rabbinic passages, these lacking the specific mention of our book, are these assembled on pp. 41-43.

Both an Aramaic and a Hebrew collection of aphorisms of various origin exist under the title "The Alphabet of Ben Sira," these coming from medieval times; some of these aphorisms echo our book.

30. Onias is the Greek of *Ḥuniah*, a diminuative of Joḥanan. Simon is addressed in the second person, but not mentioned by name in 45.26.

31. Its destruction is related in Josephus, War VII (10, 2) 420-25.

32. 2 Macc. 4.43 speaks of Onias' murder, contradicting accounts of his resettling in Egypt.

33. This family is mentioned in 1 Chron. 9.10. Zadok was a priest of David (2 Sam. 15.24-37) whose descendants became the dominant priestly family (as seen in Ezek. chs. 40-48).

34. Confer Vermes, *The Dead Sea Scrolls in English*, 1962-68, pp. 61-64.

35. The Hebrew contains a Hallel ("Praise") poem, modeled after Ps. 136. Segal, in the Hebrew *Sefer Ben-Sira Ha-Shalem* (p. 152) believes that this "great Hallel" was used in the Temple worship until the time of the Maccabean high priesthood.

36. They are 3.1-5.30; 5.21-6.34; 6.35-9.25; 9.38-10.59; 11.1-12.51; 13.1-58; 14.1-48.

37. Shealtiel (Ezra 3.2) was the father of Zerubbabel; he lived at least a generation before Ezra.

38. This is an allusion to the "giants" of Gen. 6.4 and Num. 13.33.

39. The use of Esau and Jacob here is quite arbitrary. It reflects the freedom with which the Bible was interpreted to apply to current affairs.

40. The Latin version identifies the Messiah as Jesus. In ch. 7, verses 36-132 are regarded by many as a late addition; they are not found in the Latin Vulgate, but are present in other ancient translations, including two Latin versions.

41. The inherited texts of 7.28 give different numbers of years.

42. Based on Dan. ch. 7, with its vision of four beasts, that is, the kingdoms which had overcome Judea in the past.

43. This is possibly an allusion to the struggles for power in Rome on the death of Nero in A.D. 68.

44. If at one time in the writing of this book the allusions to the

wings and heads were clear (i.e. to the Roman rulers such as Vespasian, Titus, and Domitian), later re-writing has so blurred matters as to provide a grand enigma. The main thrust, that Rome would collapse, is clear; just whom the symbols allude to is hopelessly jumbled.

45. This is based on Dan. 7.13.

46. According to 2 Kgs. 17.1-6, these were exiled eastward, to become the "ten lost tribes." Developing tradition repeatedly spoke of the eventual "finding" of them. They are here symbolic of the dispersed Judeans of the Roman period.

47. The text is uncertain respecting "ninety-four" and "twenty-four," but not respecting "seventy." The normal Rabbinic tabulation of "canonical" books is twenty-four; we seem to have here a distinction between the twenty-four books, available to all, and seventy additional ones designed for secret or private circulation.

The figure twenty-four is arrived at by reckoning as follows: Pentateuch 5; Joshua 1; Judges 1; 1 and 2 Samuel 1; 1 and 2 Kings; Isaiah-Jeremiah-Ezekiel 3; the Twelve Minor Prophets 1; "Scrolls": Esther, Ruth, Ecclesiastes, Lamentations, Song of Songs 5; Ezra and Nehemiah 2; 1 and 2 Chronicles 1; Job, Psalms, Proverbs 3.

48. Rabbinic literature speaks of "outside books" with which these seventy are often identified.

49. They are the Mishnaic tractate *Pirke Abot* ("Chapters of the Fathers"); "Fragments of a Zadokite Work"—known also as the "Damascus Document" (on which see below, pp. 97-99); and "Ahikar," an Aramaic tale of a folk hero mentioned in the Book of Tobit. C. C. Torrey, in his *The Apocryphal Literature: A Short Introduction* (1945), omitted these three and included "Lives of the Prophets" and the "Testament of Job."

50. I have not seen the very recent *The Books of Enoch*, ed. by J. T. Milik, 1976.

51. The Noah portions are chs. 6-11; 54.1-55.2; ch. 60; 65.1-69.25; and chs. 106-7.

52. See "Enoch," JE, V, pp. 178-179. Another book is known both as "The Book of the Secrets of Enoch" and the "Slavonic Enoch" (because copies were found in Russia and Jugoslavia); it gives data on the Jewish notions of seven layers of heaven (with hell being the third layer!) and about the Messiah. It is viewed as by a Greek Jew. On the Hebrew work, often called 3 Enoch, see "Apocalyptic Literature," JE, I, pp. 676-78.

53. Enoch 1.9 appears to be quoted in the Epistle of Jude 14.

54. Jubilees, like Enoch, and some of the Dead Sea Scrolls, use the same solar calendar which is out of accord with the solar-lunar calendar; compare Jubilees 6.22-38 with Enoch chs. 72-82, and see p. 209.

55. Some of the embellishing expansions reappear in Josephus and in Rabbinic literature; some do not. Compare, respecting the Jubilees material on Abraham, my *Philo's Place in Judaism*, pp. 38-49.

56. This matter is a problem to the Rabbis, Philo, and Paul. Philo and Paul solve the problem quite differently from Jubilees and the Rabbis.

57. Jubilees is a polemical work against Greek ways. Nevertheless, the matter of heavenly tablets is derived from the Platonic and Stoic notions of ideal law (also called the "unwritten law of nature") of which written laws are imitations or substitutes. This conception, presented in thorough hellenization in Philo, is in Jubilees much less hellenized, yet it is still a borrowing from Greek patterns of thought.

58. Pharisees, Boethusians (see p. 209 and note 3), and Sadducees disputed over whether "Sabbath" here means Saturday (the Sadducean view) or the first, very sacred day of Passover (the Pharisaic view). For Sadducees Shavout fell always on Sunday. Jubilees conforms with the Sadducean procedure.

59. Comparable or identical embellishments in Rabbinic literature are single and separate in the sense of individual items which did not become shaped into a consecutive account, insofar as we know. The Genesis Apocryphon (see p. 101) is a consecutive account, regrettably imperfectly preserved and as yet only partially published (see Vermes, *The Dead Sea Scrolls in English*, 1968 rev., pp. 214-24).

60. Pottery has been a chief tool utilized by archeologists in fixing dates, this out of the classification of countless finds and knowledge about the relationships of pottery to historic periods.

61. The basic work comes from Cave 1. Caves 4 and 5 have yielded fragments of perhaps eleven different copies.

62. In late times there were two major priestly families, one of Zadok (see note 70) and the other of Jehoiarib. The Hasmoneans who became High Priests seem to have set forth their eligibility as descendants through Jehoiarib, and to have displaced their predecessors of the family of Zadok. In scripture (Ezekiel 40.46) the legitimate line is that of Zadok. Hence, saying "the sons of Zadok" is equivalent to saying "the proper priests." See also 2 Sam. 8.17 and 1 Chron. 6.3-8. Jehoiarib, also called Joarib, is mentioned as the Hasmonean forebear in 1 Macc. 2.1.

63. Its name was the Ibn Ezra Synagogue. The Genizah Damascus documents were published by Solomon Schechter, *Documents of Jewish Secretaries*, I: *Fragments of a Zadokite Work*, London, 1910. The most recent edition is Chaim Rabin, *The Zadokite Fragments*, Oxford, 1954.

64. Because the book speaks of the Covenant of the "Damascus" Community, it has been referred to by scholars by the initials CD, or CDC.

65. Some, though, take Damascus literally, or at least to mean the eastern wilderness controlled from Damascus. The enigma is as yet beyond solution.

66. By O. Betz, "Sadokite Fragments," IDB, IV, p. 932.

67. Qumran people are usually identified as Essenes. On this, see below, p. 165.

68. The "sons of the Gods" of Gen. 6.1. Later they were called "Heavenly Watchers," a term found in Dan. 4.13.

69. For this there is no biblical basis.

70. The item is not found in the Bible. Zadok (2 Sam. 8.17) was one of David's two priests. In the struggle for David's throne in David's last days, Zadok backed Solomon; the other priest, Abiathar, supported

Adonijah. Solomon removed Abiathar (1 Kgs. 2.26-27) and expelled him to Anathoth. (Jeremiah was from Anathoth, and may have been a descendant of Abiathar.)

The phrase "the priests, sons of Zadok" occurs in Ezek. 40.46; 43.19; 44.15; and 48.11, in the context of the one family among the Levites who abstained from going astray, and hence were alone to be allowed to minister at the altar of the restored temple.

71. There is quoted Num. 21.18, which mentions a *well* which *princes* dug and *nobles* turned the soil, using the staff as a tool. In our document, *well* is identified with Torah, *princes* with members of the community of the faithful, the *staff* with the "interpreter of the Torah," and the *nobles* are those who comply with the guidance of the interpreter. Such free application of biblical words is found again further on in the document.

72. "Pit" probably connotes "underworld," the abode of the wicked.

73. There ensues a review of history which is cryptic in that biblical words are used as symbols, e.g. *king* for congregation, *star* for interpreter of the law, and *head of asps* for the avenging chief of the kings of Greece.

74. Hebrew *me-baqqḗr*. The translation "Guardian" is Vermes's; others render it "overseer."

75. It is kindred to, or even identical with, the calendar of the Book Jubilees; see above, note 54.

76. We are nowhere given a description of the "pure Meal."

77. Probably the Bible.

78. The text proceeds to justify the upper age of sixty by quoting the Book of Jubilees 23.11.

79. It is to be recalled that priesthood was a matter of lineal descent, not of learning. For ritual matters, the biblical injunction requires a priest for purification, and a subsequent rule suggests that a Guardian is to be present to instruct an unlearned priest in what to do!

80. In *The Dead Sea Scrolls in English*, p. 122.

81. Ordinarily the "Kittim" of the Bible are people of a Mediterranean island, possibly Crete. In the Dead Sea Scrolls they are ordinarily taken to be the Romans, who took control over Judea in 63 B.C.

82. Other Qumran materials include liturgical prayers, a Commentary on Ps. 37, and a so-called "Copper Scroll," which is a list of some sixty or more places where the treasures of the Temple were presumably hidden.

83. See notes 62 and 70.

84. Other scholars allocate the events to the period 175-160 B.C., or to the reign of Alexander Janneus (103-76); however, these views seem to be receding in scholarly acceptance.

85. Géza Vermès does so (*The Dead Sea Scrolls in English*, pp. 58-65), but, with admirable candor, describes his effort as "bound to lead some distance into the realm of conjecture" (p. 58).

86. Recorded in Nedarim 41a.

87. Because there are varying ways of spelling Hebrew words in the English alphabet, *mitzvot* can be encountered as *mitzvoth* or else *mitzvos*.

The caution needs to be expressed that in East European Yiddish, the term mitzvah was changed in connotation from a biblical law to a synonym for a good deed or for what Boy Scouts call "a good turn." In dealing with mitzvah in Rabbinic literature, the pleasant Yiddish sense ought not intrude.

88. It is also found in such English spellings as halakot, halakhot, halakoth, and halachos.

89. That is, after citing the opinions of Rabbis X, Y, and Z, it can append the statement, "The halacha is according to Rabbi Y."

90. The word also appears spelled aggada. The narrative *par excellence* among Jews is that of the Exodus from Egypt; *the* Haggada is the assembled readings used in the Jewish home at the Passover *sĕder*.

91. The division into the six orders created some problems of the assignment of tractates. Some tractates are not logical for the particular order in which we find them; one tractate, The Chapters of the Fathers (see pp. 127; 236), is, curiously enough, the ninth of the ten tractates of the order Neziqín, "damages."

92. This is taken from Bābā Metzīā, "middle gate," the second tractate in the Order Damages; it is at the beginning of the tractate.

93. However, a passage, Sanhedrin 86a, cites a Sage, R. Joḥanan bar Nappaḥa (died 279) to the effect that a *stam* Mishnah reflects the eminent R. Meir (died about A.D. 160).

94. In the traditional Jewish way of study, it is usual to personify the Gemara. Thus, the student is trained to say, "The Gemara asks . . . ," or, "The Gemara asserts," or, "The Gemara answers." That is to say, it is supposed that a dialogue, still alive, is taking place.

95. These are reproduced in "Rules of Hillel, The Seven," JE, X, p. 511, and the sources (Tos. San. vii, etc.) there supplied.

96. Here is an example. Exod. 21.28-32 makes provision for the punishment by the death of the owner of an ox when the ox is known customarily to gore people; but such an owner can escape the death penalty by payment of a ransom. Hence, the passage, "eye for an eye, tooth for tooth" can also entail a ransom, that is, a monetary ransom, in place of the actual putting out of an eye or a tooth. That is, if in the case of a death by goring by an ox, a monetary payment is admissible, how much more is this the case when a man injures another man.

97. Num. 28.2 specifies that a sacrificial offering is to be made *in its proper season*. Num. 9.2 specifies that the Passover sacrifice must be offered *in its proper season*. Suppose Passover falls on a Sabbath? Then possibly its sacrifice should not be offered. But Num. 9.2, by the use of the identical phrase *in its proper season*. demands conformity with the general rule of Num. 28.2, so that the Passover sacrifice is offered on a Sabbath.

98. The bed or chair of a man with a discharge from his body (as in pus from a boil) is to be regarded as "unclean" (Lev. 15.4). Hence this verse may be regarded as containing a *general rule* on the transmission on uncleanness.

99. The Aramaic for "son of" is *bar*.

100. They are found as the introduction to the Midrash known as Sifra (see p. 122); they are there explained. The explanation is known as the "Baraita of Rabbi Ishmael." The "thirteen rules" ultimately made their way into the Synagogue prayerbook.

101. Pardes is also their word for speculations about God and Creation, as in Haggiga 14b.

102. The debate between R. Simeon and R. Judah is found in Shabbat 44b.

103. This is found in Shabbat 143a.

104. Indeed, in a sense Chronicles is a "midrash" on Samuel-Kings. See my "The Haggadah within Scripture," *Journal of Biblical Literature*, 80 (1961), pp. 105-22.

105. It is recorded in Yoma 27a and Levit. Rabba ch. 7 that R. Asi said, "Why does one begin the instruction of children with *torát kohanim* ("the law of the priests," that is, Leviticus) rather than with Genesis? Because the children are [still] pure and the sacrifices represent purity. [Hence,] let the pure begin their study with purity."

106. While this statement is adequate for the beginning student, it is much too simple for the advanced or the technical student. For the latter, there are a number of complexities. First, it appears that there arose two rival collections, one from the School of Akiba and another from his academic rival Ishmael. It is frequent to attribute the Sifra to the School of Akiba and the Mechilta to the School of Ishmael. From the School of Akiba there arose the Sifre to Deuteronomy, and a so-called Mechilta of Simeon ben Yochai. Again, there is evidence that there once existed a Mechilta of Ishmael to Leviticus. A beginning student needs some horizon on these matters, but is scarcely prepared for the issues involved.

107. Special Sabbaths would be the Sabbath between New Year and the Day of Atonement, known as "the Sabbath of repentance," and the Sabbath before Passover, known as "the great Sabbath."

108. The Pesiqta de Rab Kahana has had a strange and enigmatic history, having been reconstructed by the scholar Leopold Zunz (1794-1886) prior to the availability of actual manuscripts.

109. The articles "Midrash," "Midrash Haggada," "Midrash Halakah," and "Midrashim, Smaller" in JE, VIII, pp. 548-80, are a treasury of information, not significantly superseded. See also Herman L. Strack, *Introduction to the Talmud and Midrash* (Eng. translation), pp. 201-34. Much of this latter is merely a listing of Midrashic works, but without description.

110. Actually, this passage is at the end of the Talmudic tractate Berachot.

111. In Prov. ch. 8, "Wisdom" is personified and speaks. Modern scholars note that the *amon*, Hebrew for "artisan," is rendered as "little child" in the ancient translations, as if amon is an error, the parallel word being "plaything." That is, *artisan* is scarcely the idea one would expect in the passage; hence, the Rabbinic effort to explain the import of the word.

112. The word in Lam. 4.5, *amūnim*, is a plural, presumably of amon.

113. Her Hebrew name; Esther is her Persian name.

114. In Nahum 3.8, Nō Amon is clearly the name of a city.

115. Literally, *b'* means "in," and *reshit*, "beginning."

116. The "me" in the Proverbs passage is Wisdom. Wisdom and Torah are customarily identified.

117. This targum is known among scholars as *Pseudo*-Jonathan, to correct the error in ascribing it to Jonathan.

118. We are told about Aquila by Jerome (347-420), the great Christian scholar, in his commentary to Isaiah, at 7.14. Aquila, by legend, became a convert to Christianity, but he was excommunicated and then turned to Judaism. He translated the Bible into Greek about A.D. 130. His translation was very literal, and possibly had the purpose of undercutting Christian proof-texts based on the so-called Septuagint. The translation of Aquila was known only in part through extracts preserved in the six-column "Hexapla" of Origin (185-251?); in 1897 some fragments of Aquila were found in the Caira Geniza (see p. 77). See "Aquila," and "Onkelos the Convert," JE, II, pp. 34-38; IX, 405.

119. This title is found in the Vermes and Millar-revised Schuerer, *A History of the Jewish People in the Age of Jesus Christ*, I, p. 103.

120. In the Hebrew Bible, Joshua, Judges, 1 and 2 Samuel, and 1 and 2 Kings are termed "the earlier prophets"; Isaiah, Jeremiah, Ezekiel, and the twelve minor books are termed "the later prophets."

121. It is found in English in Bernard Grossfeld, *The Targum to the Five Megilloth*, New York, 1973, a collection of photographic reprints of translations of the targumim to Ruth, Lamentations, Ecclesiastes, Esther, and Song of Songs.

122. For more detail, see Bernard Grossfeld, *A Bibliography of Targum Literature*, Cincinnati–New York, 1972.

123. An English version of this Aramaic work is Solomon Zeitlin, *Megillat Taanit as a Source for Jewish Chronology and History in the Hellenistic and Roman Periods*, 1922.

124. The English translation is in M. R. James, *The Biblical Antiquities of Philo*, Prolegomenon by Louis H. Feldman, New York, 1971. Parts are found in the *Chronicle of Jerahmiel*, a Hebrew work of the Middle Ages.

PART II

CHAPTER 1

1. During the Wilderness, a portable sanctuary, at times called the "Tent of Meeting" or, more usually, the *mishkán* ("tabernacle") was constructed, as were its paraphernalia (Exod. 25.1-31.18; 35.1-46.38). The Wilderness paraphernalia were, at least in principle, to be moved into the forthcoming Temple. The sacrifices are detailed in Lev. chs. 1-7. The "ordination" of priests is found in Lev. ch. 8, and the installation of Aaron in Lev. ch. 9.

2. See 1 Kgs. 5.1-6.38; 2 Chron. 1.18-7.11.

3. See Hag. 1.1-15; Ezra chs. 3-5.

4. Ant. XVII (1-8), 380-425; War I (21, 1), 401.

5. So, for example, W. F. Stinespring, "Temple, Jerusalem," IDB, IV, p. 550, insists that Herod's is the "third" temple. This is probably right; nevertheless, Jewish sources persist in the term "second temple." If the theory of Julian Morgenstern, "Jerusalem—485 B.C.," *Hebrew Union College Annual*, XXVII-XXVIII, is right, Herod's temple would be number four, or even five.

6. The "wailing wall" in Jerusalem is part of the western wall around the compound, not the wall of the Temple.

7. The Hebrew terms are *ūlām,* porch or vestibule; *hēkāl,* the holy outer room; and *debir,* the holy of holies (for which the usual biblical term is *qódesh ha-qodoshim*).

8. Passages in the Gospels seem to blur the distinction between the compound and the Temple itself. The tables of the moneychangers were not in the Temple (Mt. 21.12-17; Mk. 11.11, 15-19; Lk. 19.45-48; Jn. 2.13-17), but outside it. The Gospels seem to conceive of the Temple as if kindred to a small Greek temple in some local area. Two Greek terms, *hieron,* apparently implying "holy compound," and *naos,* the Temple itself, are both translated "temple."

9. The inscription restricting Gentiles is on p. 54; see also Part I, ch. 2, note 12.

10. See Lev. ch. 16.

11. Ant. XIV (7.1), 105-109; War I (8.8), 179.

12. Mishna Shekalim deals with this topic.

13. Mishna Tamid ch. 1 provides information about the functions of the priests. See "Precedence," JE, X, pp. 180-181.

14. On "Name" as a form of speaking of God, see p. 170. The response of the attendant priests was to the pronunciation of the word "name"; it is derived from Ps. 89.53 and 72.19; see Israel Abrahams, *A Companion to the Authorized Daily Prayer Book,* revised ed. 1922, pp. li-lii.

15. For example, Herod the Great (37-34 B.C.) interfered both in the high priesthood and in the Sanhedrin.

16. In Acts 5.21 there is an allusion to the "sanhedrin and all the gerousia"; it is enigmatic, especially if its purport is to allude to two different bodies. It is likely to be no more than an inaccuracy arising from a simple careless use of supposed synonyms.

17. The Mishna speaks of "the chamber of hewn stone," as the traditional Jewish understanding of the phrase runs. Some scholars regard the Hebrew for "hewn stones" to be a hebraizing of the Greek word *xystos,* "colonnade."

18. Another term, *presbyterion,* apparently signifying a council of elders, is found in Lk. 22.66 and Acts 22.5.

19. Ant. XIV (9, 3-5), 163-184.

20. Ant. XV (1, 2), 5.

21. Ant. XV (2, 4), 21-22; (3, 1), 39; (3.3), 50-56; XVII (6, 4), 164.

22. Ant. XX (10, 5), 250.

23. The most significant essay denying the historical reliability of Jn. 19.31 is Heinrich Lietzmann, "Der Prozess Jesu," in *Sitzenberichte der Akademie der Wissenschaft* XIV (1931), pp. 310-22. Of the immense quantity of literature on the general topic, one might cite Paul Winter, *On the Trial of Jesus* (1960). My essay, "The Trial of Jesus: Reservations," *Judaism* (Winter 1971), asserts that the facts are beyond recovery; this assertion is challenged, objectively, by Gerard Sloyan, *Jesus on Trial* (1973), by far the best book for the student on the trial.

24. Sanhedrin 1.6.

25. The dearth of desirable information has inevitably led to a variety of conjectures. The best known of these has supposed that in the age of Jesus there were two different Sanhedrins, one concerned with political affairs and the other with religious, and that it was the political Sanhedrin which had sentenced Jesus to death; see Adolph Büchler, *Das Synedrion in Jerusalem und das grosse Beth-Din in der Quaderkammer des jerusalemischen Tempels* (1902). Büchler's view is espoused by some scholars and is reflected in Jacob Z. Lauterbach, "Sanhedrin," in JE, XII, pp. 41-46. But many scholars reject Büchler's theory; see S. Sandmel, *The First Christian Century in Judaism and Christianity*, pp. 77-78.

26. A laconic passage, Sota 9.11, reads: "When the Sanhedrin ceased to exist, singing ceased at [wedding] banquets."

27. Usually it is called the *"Great* Bet Din."

28. One says virtual because of stray bits of evidence of a brief continuation of sacrifices where the Temple has stood; see Alexander Guttmann, "The End of the Jewish Sacrificial Cult," *Hebrew Union College Annual*, V.

29. On Johanan, see Jacob Neusner, *First Century Judaism in Crisis*, 1974.

30. Gen. Rabbah 98.8.

31. Moore cites the statement of Origen (*Epistula ad Africanum*, ch. 14) that ascribed to the patriarch an authority no less than that of a king, even to impose, with Roman permission, a death sentence.

32. Num. 35.24 and 25.

33. The notion of a required majority for condemnation was derived from Exod. 23.2.

34. Jer. Pesahim 33a.

35. Among pagan writers the word occurred in its bare meaning. See Samuel Krauss, *Synagogale Altertümer*, 1922, p. 3.

36. The term "house of gathering of aliens" occurs in Baba Metziah 24a.

37. Modern writings render this phrase both as "men of the Great Assembly" and "men of the Great Synagogue."

38. A scribe was a teacher who was versed in Scripture. The title later became altered into rabbi. Rabbi as a technical title is later than the age of Hillel and Shammai (about 20 B.C.), neither of whom is even alluded to by that term. On the other hand. Johanan ben Zakkai (fl. 55-90) bears the title.

39. In much later times considerable embellishment through the work of artisans took place. In a modern synagogue, an ornate crown of silver is set on the top extensions of the "tree of life." The entire scroll is cov-

ered by a cloth, with elegant embroidery. A metal "breast-plate," usually silver, and reminiscent of that worn by the High Priest, hangs by a chain from the top of the rollers. The binding cloth (called in German *Wimpel*) was also beautified. In some eastern communities, such as Persia, the scroll was encased in a fitted wooden container, rather than covered by cloth. One can cite with approval an anonymous statement: "In the Temple, the High Priest had rich vestments; in the Synagogue they were transferred to the Torah Scroll."

40. Statements from the Rabbis warn against fixed prayer (Berachot 4.4) because it tends to become mechanical. Yet other statements advocated it as a desirable discipline, provided *kavanā* ("intention") prevents it from becoming mere rote.

41. Megillah 17b.

42. Berachot 33a.

43. Berachot 4.3. Others, though, were willing for a digest to suffice.

44. See Moore, I, p. 293.

45. The words "Our God, King of the World" are normal parts of most benedictions, but not of the "eighteen."

46. Evidence points clearly to alterations or else to local differences, but these are relatively minor.

47. Hence, the benediction is called *abōt*, "the fathers" (Rosh Hashana 4.5).

48. The Mishna calls this benediction *geburōt*, "powers" (Rosh Hashana 4.5).

49. Benedictions normally begin in the second person, but often shift to the third. In the Hebrew, the precise reading is *his* faith, not *the*.

50. On resurrection, see pp. 200-208.

51. "Praise you . . . selah" is a paraphrase of phrases in the Psalms.

52. The prayer is known as "the sanctification of the name," Rosh Hashana 4.5.

53. See "Censorship of Hebrew Books," JE, III, pp. 642-52.

54. It has become rather standard among Christian scholars to regard the prayer as against Christians, indeed, against all Christians everywhere. From this premise the derived opinion is frequent that the incident of the creation of the prayer at Jamnia marks the total expulsion of Christians from the synagogue, alluded to in the Gospel According to John several times; indeed, this incident is interpreted to be the occasion of the definitive break between Judaism and Christianity. Jewish scholars in general (see Israel Abrahams, *The Authorized Daily Prayer Book*, pp. lxiv-lxv) deny not that Christians were here or there expelled from synagogues, but that the creation of this prayer reflected a universal, mandatory expulsion; such a conclusion exceeds the evidence.

55. On proselytes, see pp. 228-34.

56. In Mishna Yoma 7.1, this prayer is called *'avōdā*, a term later extended to the full list of the eighteen.

57. In the Sabbath worship, the eighteen benedictions are reduced to seven.

58. A variety of scriptural passages justifies the number of ten. It be-

came customary for certain particular prayers to be reserved for the synagogue.

59. Since the word "phylacteries" means "guards" or "protectors," there are theories that their origin is in the superstition that their use made for safety. See "Phylacteries," JE, X, pp. 21-28.

60. Normally they have been Exod. 13.1-10; 11-16; Deut. 6.4-9 and 11.13-21.

61. On variations and embellishments, see "Phylacteries," 62. JE, X, pp. 21-28. The use is ancient; it is mentioned in Josephus, Ant. IV (8,13), 212-13.

62. JE, X, pp. 21-28. The use is ancient; it is mentioned in Josephus, Ant. IV (18,13), 212-13.

63. This is the view of Joseph Heineman, Ha-Tefilla bi-Tequfat Ha-Tannaim veha-Amoraim, 1964, pp. 73-74. He cites Jubilees 22.6 in support of the antiquity.

64. Menaḥot 41b.

65. Biblical prohibitions also include fruit of a tree during the first three years after its planting (Lev. 19.23-25) and new corn prior to the second day of Passover (Lev. 23.9-14). There were also prohibitions of vegetables planted in a vineyard (Deut. 22.9) or mixed plants in a single field (Lev. 19.19).

66. Hullin 108b; 115b; Pesahim 44b.

67. The ancient Rabbis knew no reason for this biblical prohibition. Archeology, namely through the Ras Shamra tablets, discovered in 1929, has proposed that boiling a kid in its mother's milk was a Canaanite practice. Some scholars, though, question the proposal.

68. In early post-Talmudic times, the ceremony was moved from the home to the synagogue, and it was embellished by the presence of a designated "godfather" (Heb. sandîk), who sat on a special "Elijah's chair." Later the ceremony was restored to the home. The occasion of a circumcision is joyous.

69. See "Mikweh," JE, VIII, p. 588. See also "Ablutions," JE, I, pp. 68-71, and "Niddah," JE, IX, p. 301. Ablutions were incumbent on men when there was a flux from the body.

CHAPTER 2

1. This ancient group should be kept clearly distinct from the modern Ḥasidim who emerged in the eighteenth century in eastern Europe.

2. This is the Greek form of Ḥasidim. In modern literature they are spoken of also as "Hasideans." The reference is 1 Macc. 2.41.

3. Sanhedrin 10b; Chapters of the Fathers, 5.4 and 13; Berachot 5.1; Sukkot 5.4.

4. Erwin R. Goodenough has suggested (By Light, Light: The Mystic Gospel of Hellenistic Judaism, 1935, pp. 78-80), an affinity between Philo of Alexandria (see pp. 279-301) and the Sadducees. Against this view is the summary article, Valentin Nikiprowetzky, "Note sur l'interpretation

littérale de la loi et sur l'angélologie chez Philon d'Alexandrie," in *Mélanges André Neher*, 1975.

5. War II (8, 14), 164-66.

6. Since Josephus writes for a Greek audience, Fate is probably his word in place of what is meant by divine providence. That is, the Sadducees believed in "free will," as the passage proceeds to affirm. Confer George Foot Moore, "Fate and Free Will in the Jewish Philosophers according to Josephus," *Harvard Theological Review*, XXII (1929), 371-89.

7. Ant. XX (9, 1), 199.

8. See Part I, Chapter 2, notes 62 and 70.

9. An account in the Talmud, Kiddushin 66a, ascribes a comparable confrontation between Alexander Jannaeus and the Pharisees. About John Hyrcanus, a Talmudic dictum advises against self-confidence about one's righteousness prior to one's death, for Johanan (i.e. John Hyrcanus) was a priest for eighty years but then became a Sadducee!

10. Daniel appears to have been written (or written in its present form) about 160 B.C. When it became "canonical" is uncertain, but posbily not until into the first Christian century. But for both Pharisees and Sadducees, the acid test would have been whether the Pentateuch contained the doctrine; the Pharisees "proved" resurrection on the basis of Exod. 15.1, Sanhedrin 90b.

11. Mk. 12.18-27; Matt. 22.23-33; Lk. 20.27-40.

12. Its nub is the derision the Sadducees resorted to in their denial of resurrection: Say a woman chanced to marry a succession of seven brothers; at resurrection time, to which of the seven was she to be the wife?

13. See "Sadducees," JE, X, pp. 630-33.

14. Menahot 65a; Megillat Taanit ch. 1.

15. Thus, until the Council of Nicaea in 325, Christians ordinarily observed Easter as the Sunday within the Jewish Passover week. From Nicaea there arose a formula freeing Christians from depending on the Jewish calendar, Easter being decreed for the first Sunday after the first full moon after the spring equinox. Since Passover occurs at the full moon, often Easter does fall in Passover week, yet from time to time it does not.

16. A Jewish sect called the Karaites arose in the eighth Christian century. The word means "Bible adherents." The Karaites rejected the accumulated halacha, reverting to Scripture itself. No organic connection is demonstrable between the Sadducees and the Karaites, though a few similarities are striking. Occasional scholars conjecture that the Sadducees did not disappear, but that "underground" Sadduceeism persisted and came into the open as Karaism.

17. Later literature alludes to these Ḥasidim as the *early* pious, implying that there was a later, but unknown, group of the pious.

18. Alexander Jannaeus put to death 800 Pharisees, but only after cutting the throats of their wives and children in their presence.

19. Ant. XV (10, 4), 365-66.

20. Ant. XVII (2, 4), 41-45.

21. Ant. XVII (6, 1), 151.

22. Sotah 22b; Jer. Berachot 14b and Sotah 20c.

23. The list of seven as given in Moore, II, pp. 193, differs slightly from that followed here, from "Pharisees," JE, IX, p. 565.

24. I earnestly wish that I could acquiesce in the view of my colleague Ellis Rivkin: his attribution to the Pharisees of an "interiorizing" of Judaism (in *The Shaping of Jewish History*), does not persuade me.

25. The view expressed here is related to that in Morton Smith, "Palestinian Judaism in the First Century," in Moshe Davis, ed., *Israel: Its Role in Civilization* (New York, 1956), and in Jacob Neusner, "Josephus' Pharisees," in *Ex Orbe Religionum Studia Geo. Widengren Oblata* (Leiden, 1972), I, pp. 224-44. Neusner writes (p. 243): "It therefore seems that the time has come to stop describing the Phariseees as the 'normative' sect of pre-70 Palestinian Judaism." I can concur with this view. But some themes are characteristic of both Pharisaism and of Rabbinism.

26. The Zealots arose in Galilee, during the reign of Herod. Josephus, who blames them for the ill-fated rebellion against Rome, which erupted in 66, consistently describes them as bandits. "Guerillas" would be a more appropriate term. From among the Zealots in the period of 66-73 there arose a more extreme, more desperate group, Sicarii ("swordsmen"). (Some, however, attribute a quite separate origin to the Sicarii.)

27. In some passages in Rabbinic literature, words somewhat similar to "Essenes," are indeed found: *hashayim* ("the silent"); *ḥasayá* ("healers"), and the like.

28. Later Christian sources mention them (Hypolitus, *Philosophumena* 9.4; Epiphanius, *Panarion*) but these are not to be regarded as principal. Morton Smith, "Josephus and Hypolitus," *Hebrew Union College Annual* (1958) supposes that both of these writers used a common source. Epiphanius (310?-403), in his account of some eighty heresies, views the Essenes as Samaritans. Hypolitus' dates are unknown; 220-60 is a guess.

29. In Philo's many works, askesis is symbolized in Scripture by Jacob, learning by Abraham, and intuition by Isaac; see pp. 283-84. The point is that Philo first sets forth some philosophical principles and then turns to the Essenes as a living community exemplified by askesis.

30. VIII, 11.

31. The reference is V, 17, 4.

32. Ant. XV (10, 4), 371, and XVIII (1, 5), 18-22; War II (8, 2-13), 119-159. The "marrying" Essenes are in War II (8, 13), 160-61.

33. The allusion is far from clear. See "Dacians," *Encyclopedia Britannica*. What is plain is that Josephus is likening the Essenes to presumably well-known Greeks.

34. Its name is On the Contemplative Life.

35. So, typically, William A. Farmer, "Essenes," IDB, II, pp. 143-44. He ascribes the differences to "socio-economic and climatic factors plus a period of separate historical development . . ." More germane, however, is that in Philo's writings, just as the Essenes supposedly exemplify the Jacob type of piety, "practice," the Therapeutae exemplify the Abraham

type, "learning"; On the Contemplative Life has many echoes of Philo's allegorical treatment of Abraham; see my, *Philo's Place in Judaism* (1956 and 1971), pp. 194-96, and note 389 on p. 193; "Much if not most of what Philo has to say about both the Essenes and also the Therapeutae is fanciful, and congruent rather with Philo's *Tendenz* than the facts."

36. In the magnificent Jewish Encyclopedia most of the articles on Pseudepigrapha were written by Kaufmann Kohler (who later became President of the Hebhew Union College). Kohler almost invariably ascribed the authorship of the pseudepigraphic writings to the Essenes. Yet William Farmer is right ("Essenes," IDB, II, p. 149) in terming Kohler's article "Essenes" in the Jewish Encyclopedia "the best pre-Qumran study of the Essenes."

37. See note 32, above.

38. In his Life, 10-12.

39. One of the gates to the Temple compound, in the south wall, was known as the "gate of the Essenes," War V (4, 2), 145. Possibly the Essenes settled in that vicinity.

40. War II (8, 10), 129.

41. That Every Good Man Is Free, 75; Ant. XVIII (1, 5), 20.

42. For fuller discussion, and references to the literature, see my *Philo's Place in Judaism* (1971 edition), pp. x-xv.

43. See Moore, II, pp. 157-60.

44. This conclusion is often supported by the citation of Jn. 7.15, which tells that Jesus was "untaught."

CHAPTER 3

1. A Rabbinic example runs: Just as ocean water can fill a seashore cave without diminishing the quantity of water in the ocean, so God can come into the sacred Tabernacle without diminishing the totality of His Godliness; Canticles Rabba to 3.10.

2. There were two aspects to astrology. It held that the stars and planets controlled the future; this view was totally obnoxious, for it ascribed to created heavenly luminaries the power of God the Creator. The second aspect was that the future could be read in the stars and planets; this was less obnoxious. Philo, who rejected the first, accepted the second.

The modern Yiddish phrase, equivalent to "congratulations," *Mazál tōv*, means literally, "favorable planet"; the astrological origin, however, is not at all reflected in this expression.

3. In Rom. 4.16 Paul speaks of Abraham as "the father of us all."

4. Exod. 7.1 reads: The Lord said to Moses, "Behold I have made you an elohim over Pharaoh."

5. This based on Exod. 34.6, "Yahve, Yahve, a God merciful and gracious. . . ."

6. This expression is found as early as I Macc. 3.50; 4.10,24,40; 12.15; 16.3. The familiar Gospel expression "kingdom of heaven" reflects this usage.

7. When one spoke *to* God, ribbônô shel olâm is frequent. When one spoke *of* Him, Heaven or Place is the ordinary expression.

8. A piquant narrative tells that a Roman ruler, a pagan skeptic, willing to concede that God had been the Creator, wanted to know what He has been doing since Creation. The Rabbinic answer was, deciding who shall marry whom. The Roman thought this a trivial occupation, one that he, a mere mortal, could perform. On his trying it, however, he reaped a huge harvest of the results of marital discord in the physical beatings his couplings had prompted.

9. Certain Sages, such as Ḥanina ben Dosa, were uniquely successful in private miracles, such as a healing prayer (Berachot 34b; compare Jn. 4.46-53); or the postponement of rain (Ta'anit 24b).

10. Some of the Pseudepigrapha, such as Enoch, do present reflections of kindred speculation, but is uncertain whether passages in Enoch are to be identical with the esoteric thoughts of the Rabbis, for we lack sufficient data by which to make a conclusive judgment.

11. The holy *ḥayyôt* ("creatures") who drew the chariot are much embellished.

12. Mishna Hagiga 2.1 permits such expounding only to a single auditor. It is related that four Sages entered into these mysteries; Simeon ben Azzai died, Simeon ben Zoma went mad, Elisha ben Abuya became a heretic, and only Akiba escaped unscathed; Hagiga 14b.

13. Gen. 6.2; Ps. 82; Job 1.6; 2.1 are only a few of such passages. One recalls too the expression "Lord of *hosts*."

14. Ordinarily an angel embarks on only a single chore; Baba Metziá 86b.

15. In Rabbinic homilies, as Moore notes (I, 407), angels are depicted as at times voicing objections to divine intentions, prompting God to express His justification of them. Thus it is made clear that God is wiser than the angels. The angels collectively constitute God's heavenly "family," corresponding to Israel, God's earthly family. See "Angelology," JE, I, pp. 583-97.

16. Satan is also known as Beelzebub, a name apparently altered in derision from the old Canaanite deity, *báal zebûl* ("the baal—god—of heaven"). Similar alteration changed the term "baal of *shamáyim*" ("heaven") into *shiqûtz* ("abomination") *shamén* ("makes desolate") as in Dan. 11.31; 12.11, alluded to in Mk. 13.14.

17. Modern scholars, of course, date Daniel as later than these three books, but Daniel purports to come from the age of the Babylonian Exile and was regarded as earlier.

18. At stake was not softness or loudness, but rather the timbre, exemplified in sounds like the chirping of a bird.

19. A narrative, Baba Metzia 59b, relates that a bat qol intervened in a dispute on a matter of halacha between R. Eliezer ben Azariah and R. Joshua ben Hananiah on the side of Eliezer. Joshua thereupon declared that one need not heed a bat qol in a human dispute, for it could not supersede the oral revelation at Sinai. God thereupon commented on Joshua's assertion, saying, "My children have bested Me."

CHAPTER 4

1. Lev. R. Va-Yiqra IV.5. Another passage, Gen. R. VIII, 1, notes that man is like an animal (he eats, propagates, defecates, and dies), but is also like the ministering angels (he stands erect, speaks, and possesses reason).

2. Creation began with Adam (though God in His omnipotence might have created many men) so that no one can vaunt his extraction over anyone else, especially since Adam was created in the image of God; Sifra, Qedoshim IV; Gen. R. xxiv.

3. God, at Creation, faced the dilemma that both the wicked and the righteous would arise from Noah. Hence, if He proceeded with Creation, He was in effect preparing the way for the wicked; if He did not, he was impeding the righteous. He therefore removed from His sight the future prospect of the wicked, and called on His mercy to be part of His creative deed.

Another view tells that, at Creation, He consulted the ministering angels, informing them of the future righteous, but He abstained from informing them of the future wicked, lest they disapprove of the creation of man. Still another view holds that the angels, on being consulted, were divided. "Love" (based on Ps. 85.10) urged that He proceed, but "Truth" that He not. God thereupon cast Truth to the earth (Dan. 8.12), leading the angels to declare that God despised the angel of Truth; Gen. R. viii, 4-5.

4. The good impulse is the *yếtzer ha-tốv*, the evil *yếtzer hā-rẵʻ*. The root meaning of *ytzr* is to create, make, or shape; hence yetzer is something created, shaped. That is, the two yetzers are innate in men. That there are the two yetzers is derived from an orthographic peculiarity in Gen. 2.7 (see Gen. R. xiv,4 and Berachot 9.5).

5. Provision is made in one passage for a class of men in between the righteous and the evil. In these, at times the good yetzer dominates, at times the evil; Berakot 61b. The inference is that the two yetzers struggle with each other to dominate a man.

6. Chapters of the Fathers, IV.1. E. E. Urbach (*The Sages: Their Concepts and Beliefs*, Heb. ed. 1969, p. 417, note 5*) cites Plato, The Laws, I, 626, which states that a man's victory over himself is the first and best of all victories.

7. It is first a passing lodger, then a house-guest, and then the owner; Gen. R. xxii, 6. The evil yetzer lodges in the 248 organs of the body (which are distinct from the 365 bones).

8. The Fathers of Rabbi Nathan (Version A), xvi, 32a; Shabbat 105b.

9. There is no direct biblical basis for the laws of Adam such as there is for the laws of Noah.

10. That is, they have a place "in the world to come"; on the latter, see pp. 201-2.

11. Abraham is, indeed, the exemplar of full piety. There remained, however, the residual question as to whether the norm was Abraham, or,

NOTES 445

instead, Moses. In general terms, and here repeating, the Palestinian literature regard Moses and Sinai as the norm, and in their interpretation have Abraham reach the norm. On the other hand, Philo (pp. 294-96) and Paul (pp. 317-20) make Abraham the norm and estimate Moses and Sinai in the light of Abraham.

12. Mechilta to Exod. 19.2.

13. Sifre to Deuteronomy 142b (ed. Friedmann).

14. This number is arrived at by adding up the peoples mentioned in Gen. ch. 10. In Rabbinic literature "seventy" is often the equivalent of "nations of the world." One recalls that the Greek version of the Bible is "Septuagint," meaning seventy.

15. Shabbat 88b. In other passages, the availability of the Torah in the seventy languages is ascribed to other occasions (Gen. R. xlix, 2; Tosefta Sota viii, 6). Compare Acts 2.6.

16. However, a curious passage speaks of even Israel's reluctance, which God overcame by raising Mount Sinai above the people and threatening to drop it on them, unless they accepted the Torah; Shabbat 88a.

17. See also Ps. 119.70, 97; Prov. 3.17-18; 29.18.

18. The commandments were given not to please God, but in order for man to purify himself through them; can it matter to God whether a beast is slain at the throat or the neck? See Gen. R. xliv, 1; Tanhuma B, Shemini 15b.

19. Compare Ps. 119.105.

20. Chapters of the Fathers, 3.12.

21. The most notable instance is Isa. 7.14, where the Greek reads "virgin" but the Hebrew "young woman."

22. A passage in the appendix to the Megillat Ta'anit calls for a fast on the anniversary of the translation of Scripture into Greek.

23. Temura 14b; compare Moore. II, p. 68, footnote 6; see "Oral Law," JE, IX, p. 426 and Claude G. Montefiore, *Rabbinic Anthology*, pp. 159-60, 430-31.

24. Sifre Deut., Va-ethanan, 74a: "When you study the Torah, let the commandments not seem old to you, but regard them as given *this* very day" (Exod. 19.1).

25. See Claude G. Montefiore, *Rabbinic Anthology*, sections 329, 332, 342-43, 351, 356, 383, 384.

26. "Do not make the Torah a spade with which to dig"; Chapters of the Fathers, 4.5.

27. Chapters of the Fathers, 2.8. Moreover, some worthy deeds yield fruit which comes in this world (as does interest on a bank deposit), with the capital surviving into the World to Come. These deeds include honoring of one's parents, good works of love, and peace-making. But the study of Torah equals all of these worthy deeds.

28. Pesahim 50b; Sanhedrin 105b.

29. Chapters of the Fathers, 1.17; 2.1.

30. Baba Metzia 85b-86a.

31. The process by which the conclusion was reached was the follow-

ing: First, one imagined what the ideal conduct for men should be; then, one portrayed God as Himself acting out the ideal; third, one inferred from God's actions what man's ought to be. In many such passages there occurs the Hebrew word, *ke-va-yachól* ("as if this were possible"); the import is this, that God, *as it were*, studied and taught Torah.

32. E. E. Urbach, *The Sages: Their Concepts and Beliefs*, p. 275.

CHAPTER 5

1. Makkot 23b.
2. Lev. 4.5; Num. 15.22-29.
3. Num. 15.30-31.
4. A passage Baba Metzia 33b, states that an inadvertent sin on the part of a Sage is equivalent to a deliberate sin; a sin by an unlearned man, even if deliberate, is equivalent to an inadvertent sin.
5. Chapters of the Fathers, 3.5. The expression "yoke of heaven" is also used; Berachot 2.2.
6. See Moore, I, p. 467.
7. Chapters of the Fathers, 4.2.
8. Jeroboam ben Nebat (1 Kgs. 11.26-14.21) is often cited as a "sinner" and "inciter to sin"; Chapters of the Fathers, 5.18 (based on 1 Kgs. 15.30).
9. Chapters of the Fathers, 2.1; Sifre Deut. Re'eh, 91a.
10. See, for example, Exod. 21.12-22.17 for trespass and the penalties.
11. For example, Deut. ch. 28.
12. Scripture speaks of a heavenly book (Exod. 32.32-33) in which God keeps the records of the living. The idea of a heavenly account book is found in Phil. 4.3 and a number of times in Revelation (3.5; 13.8; 17.8; 20.12,15, and elsewhere). It is also found in Enoch, 89.74; 90.20; and 28.29.
13. The last words of Dan. 9.10 are: "The court convenes, and the books are opened."
14. A much later prayer (*u-netáne tóqef*), dating from medieval times but still used, expands the notion found in Rosh Hashanah 2.2 of annual judgment, this by specifying how God scrutinizes the heavenly record, which reads itself, to determine who will survive, and who will die, how many pass away and how many are born, who will become rich and who poor, and the like. It culminates in the words: "But repentance, prayer, and righteousness can avert an unfavorable decree."
15. See "Eschatology," JE, V, p. 211, for the summary of and references to the welter of ways in which the various periods are conceived of.
16. Shabbat 118a; Pesahim 118a; Sanhedrin 98b; and elsewhere. Compare Mk. 13.7-31; Mt. 24.9-25; Lk. 21.20-24.
17. Sanhedrin 97b; Ketubot 111a; Shabbat 138b.
18. Chapters of the Fathers, 1, 3.
19. Perhaps it needs to be said in all candor that many Christian scholars before the publication of George Foot Moore's *Judaism* ordinarily scorned Rabbinic Judaism as a mechanical religion of rewards

and punishments. American and British New Testament scholars have largely abandoned this condescension; some German New Testament scholars, alas, have continued to repeat the adverse judgment, to the discomfort of some of the younger German scholars. Parenthetically, reward and punishment is an idea as characteristic of usual Christianity as of Judaism; reward and punishment, as Moore notes (II, p. 90, note 1), "are as freely employed by Jesus in the Gospels."

20. For example, 4 Ezra 7.77; the Syriac Baruch 24.1.

21. There a contrast is drawn between "treasures on earth: and "treasures in heaven," that is, between transient material possessions and eternal spiritual ones; Mt. 19.16-22; Mk. 10.17-22. Rewards for good conduct are in Mt. 6.1,6 and the parallels.

22. Baba Batra 11a: Treasures on earth can be seized by powerful men, but those in heaven are immune from seizure; treasures on earth bear no fruit, those in heaven do. Elsewhere (Peah 1.1), good deeds have a double yield, namely, capital that survives in the world to come, but fruit, that is interest on the capital, comes in this world.

23. Makkot 3.16: "The Holy One Blessed Be He desired to increase Israel's worthiness. Therefore he multiplied the amount of Torah and the quantity of commandments."

CHAPTER 6

1. Between *qôdesh* ("holy") and *hōl* ("common"); Hullin 26b.

2. Baba Kama 8.1; compensation for the damage done, i.e. payment for the loss of a limb; for the pain; for medical costs; for unemployment; and for attendant embarrassment.

3. A man without a wife is unthinkable, and a woman without a husband is unthinkable, and a marriage without the Shechina also unthinkable; Tosefta Berachot ch. 9; compare Berachot 12a.

4. Gen. R. to Gen. 2.8 ("It is not good that man be alone; I will make him an *ēzer ke-negdō*"). The literal meaning of these last words is "a helpmate to balance him"; by etymology, the second of these words comes from a root meaning of "opposite, against." Since the outcome of a marriage is uncertain, there are men whose fate is to acquire an "ezer," a helpmate, but others acquire a "ke-negdo," an antagonist. The advantages of man's being married are listed in frequent passages, as are the disadvantages in being unmarried.

5. See "Fornication," JE, V, p. 437, for a comparable statement.

6. The word fornication appears in English translations in and since the King James Version of 1611; there it means adultery, or else, in New Testament passages, "sexual irregularities."

7. Chapters of the Fathers, 5.21. In Sanhedrin 76a marriage at puberty—fourteen?—is advocated; marriage prior to puberty was discountenanced.

8. Kiddushin 29b.

9. Berachot 45b.

10. Confusion can result from the divergence in the scholars in trans-

lation; some use "betrothal" for erusin, and some for kiddushin. Properly, erusin was a first step; it is often considered analogous to our "engagement," and so served in medieval times; but erusin has many differences from what we mean by engagement.

11. Ketubot 5.2.

12. Kiddushin 2.1.

13. Gitin 9.10.

14. Hence the Talmudic tractate on the topic, Ketubot. Medieval Ketubot included beautifully ornamented documents, hand illuminated. The ketuba is still read at a traditional Jewish wedding, but usually left untranslated; some Reform Jewish ceremonies use a ketuba, modified by the omission of the traditional financial details. The standard work is L. M. Epstein, *Marriage Laws in the Bible and the Talmud*, 1922.

15. Gitin 48b; 55b.

16. It is declared that when a man divorces his wife, the altar of the Temple weaps tears; Gitin 90a.

17. In due course, the get became a complicated document, and only experts were deemed valid to execute such a document (Kiddushin 13a). Today it is normal that a usual Orthodox or Conservative rabbi will deem himself insufficiently expert to execute the document, and hence refer someone to an expert. Reform Jews ignore the get. In modern times, traditional Jews regard the get as the religious divorce, accompanying a civil divorce granted by the secular courts.

18. Nedarim 11.12.

19. Ketubot 5.16. The obligation to sex acts is mentioned in the ketuba.

20. Ketubot 7.9.

21. If a divorced woman married another man, and the second marriage terminated, she could not remarry her first husband (Deut. 24.1-5). The Rabbinic extensions of barriers to remarriage included instances in which the divorce had occurred because of the wife's adultery, or suspicion of fraud (Gitin 4.7, 11).

22. Lev. ch. 15.

23. Lev. ch. 12.

24. Shabbat 130a; Megillah 16b.

25. Since circumcision was practiced by non-Jewish peoples too, the Roman prohibition is explained as derived from Roman laws, and was not simply an anti-Jewish expression; see "Hadrian," JE, VI, p. 135.

26. Kiddushin 29a.

27. Shabbat 19.1. See Jn. 7.22.

28. Shabbat 137b. In this event, a drop of the baby's blood through a pin prick supplanted the actual cutting.

29. Baba Batra 21a; Shabbat 130b-33b. See Ant. XX (2, 4) 46 for the use of a physician in the circumcision of Izates, the royal convert.

30. The tractate Bekorot ("first births") deals with these matters, ch. 7 with the first-born of a priest and ch. 8 largely with the firstling of a non-priest.

31. Exod. 13.13; 34.20. The key passage is Num. 18.15. The amount is given in terms of the shekel in Scripture, but the *séla* in the tractate

Bekorot. The *pidyón ha-bén* ("redemption of the son") is still observed by traditional Jews. Let it be noted that such redemption is, of course, not incumbent on a father who is by descent a *kóhén* ("priest") since in principle he always belongs with the sacred servants.

32. The tithe is mentioned frequently in Scripture, especially Num. 18.21-26 and Deut. 14.22-29. The Rabbis discerned a discrepancy between these two passages, which had to be resolved. Num. 18.21-26 seems to prescribe that Levites are to receive a tenth of everything; Deut. 14.22-29 seems, instead, to envisage the tithe as related to the new crop, with the tithe to be brought to the Temple and there eaten. Out of the harmonizing of the passages there emerged three types of tithe. The "first tithe," of grain or fruit, was for the Levite. The "second tithe" was then taken to Jerusalem and eaten there. The third was the "tithe of the poor," that is, it was to be given to them.

33. Abodah Zara 35b, 38a. See also Abodah Zara 2.3-7.

34. By cutting the throat; Ḥullin 27a. Ḥullin 17b-18a prescribes what kind of knife may be used.

35. Ḥullin 106a. The purpose of the hand-washing was ritualistic, though the result hygienic. The passage in the Gospels (Mt. 15.1-20; Mk. 7.1-19) which, as it were, abolished hand-washing, had a definite unhygienic effect: In the Black Plagues, many more Christians died than Jews, leading some Christians to allege that Jews had poisoned the common wells. Note that in Mk. 7.3, the mandate is called a "tradition of the elders," and extends to "cups and pots and vessels of bronze."

36. Sotah 3.4. The context, though, is that of a woman suspected of adultery, and the statement relates to a woman's knowing these laws, and need not have extended beyond them. Such enthusiastic statements ought not be taken too literally.

37. While it is wrong in method to read modern times into the ancient, an observation from my own family might be enlightening. My parents were East Europeans, my father highly schooled in Rabbinic literature, and my mother literate but unschooled. Yet she knew the principal regulations and transmitted them to my sisters.

38. Exod. 16.29 ends with these words: "Let a man not go out of his place on the Sabbath." From this verse there were derived related prohibitions in the form of definitions about how far on the Sabbath one might walk from his home, and how far he might carry objects; but there was also created a means of legally getting around the inconvenience that a strict literal interpretation might occasion (see p. 117). The means alluded to was the *'erúb* ("mixture"): Within one's private dwelling or its courtyard, one could walk or carry things; often a single courtyard was surrounded by a number of houses; the latter courtyard could be deemed a "mixture" or combination of several private possessions. Comparably, if one was in urgent need to walk beyond the Sabbath limit of 2000 cubits (this regarded as the radius of a circle, and amounting in reality to 4000 cubits), he could move the center of his circle by placing Sabbath food on Friday on the new spot and thus extend the area permitted him.

Still another erub arose; it was permitted to cook food on a festival for needs of the festival, but not for times beyond it. But if a festival fell on a Friday, how could one prepare food for the Sabbath? The answer was in an erub for cooking; one began his preparations before the festival for both the festival and the Sabbath, and thereby one might on the festival complete the cooking for the Sabbath; Betza ch. 2.

39. See "Bar Mizwah," JE, II, pp. 509-510.

40. It is found cited in the post-Talmudic tractate Sōferim, ch. 19 ("scribes") which was set down in writing in the seventh or eighth Christian century. David de Solo Pool, *The Kaddish*, p. 80, believed that it was not likely to be earlier than the third century. Originally it was a public praise of God recited after a public discourse. It eventuated in several different types, by the addition or elimination of paragraphs, such as the "Orphan's Kaddish" (also known as the "Mourner's Kaddish"), the "Scholars' Kaddish," the "Congregational Kaddish" (sometimes the first half of this is used to introduce significant prayers such as the Eighteen Benedictions), and the "Private Kaddish."

CHAPTER 7

1. From a Greek word meaning "end" or "border" comes a term, eschatology. It is used respecting views on what is to happen at the end of time.

2. *Shiv'á*. The Yiddish phrase, "to sit shiva," means to sit at home for "seven" days; one in deep mourning sits on the floor or on a very low bench.

3. In medieval times, prayers to lessen the trials of the dead in hell arose. To pray for a beloved dead a full year implied full wickedness in the deceased; hence, the period of such propitiary prayers was charitably reduced to eleven months.

4. Baba Batra 16b. This "comforting meal" usually consisted of bread with eggs or lentils.

5. Megillah 28a.

6. Shabbat 105b; Berachot 62a.

7. Ketubot 46a; 48b.

8. Deliberate cremation is unmentioned, though there is mention (Oholot 2.2; Nidda 27b) of the ashes of those accidentally burnt to death.

9. Sanhedrin 6.4 and 46a-b. A tractate dated in the post-Talmudic era, Ebel Rabbati ("the big book of mourning"), assembles the regulations; the work is also known as Semahot ("joyous occasions"), a euphemistic name. It is found in many printed editions of the Talmud immediately after the fourth order, Nezikin. An English version appears in the faulty Rodkinson translation of the Talmud, in vol. 8. Apparently an older, smaller book, now lost, preceded the "big book."

10. See "Taharah," JE, XI, p. 668.

11. Moed Katan 8b; Berakot 3.1.

12. Ketubot 100a.

13. Gehenna is the Greek form of the Hebrew Gehinnom, which in

Scripture (Josh. 15.8; 2 Kigs 23.10; Jer. 2.23; 7.31-32; 19.6, 13-14) is the "valley of the son of Hinnom." There sacrifices were offered to the god Molech. An especially illuminating exposition of biblical antecedents respecting Sheol and of Greek views of Hades is in Moore, II, p. 287-93.

14. Sotah 22a; Gen. R. 9.9. But other passages allocate the creation of hell to the second day, or even prior to creation (Gen. R. 4; Pesahim 45a). The fire of Gen. 15.17 is identified as the fire of hell, Erubin 19a; one should compare Enoch 98.3 and 103.8 and Mt. 13.40-42, 49-50. Strictly speaking hell was below the earth, with the valley of Hinnom being the gate to it. In some other views additional gates were deemed to exist (Erubin 19a). Indeed in some passages the location of hell is set above the firmament of heaven (Ta'anit 32b; Sanhedrin 110b).

15. Baba Batra 84a; Hagiga 13b. The idea is found also in Enoch 17.4-6.

16. Shabbat 39a; compare Menahot 100a. The notion of a sulfurous odor is found in Enoch 67.6.

17. Yebamot 109b; Enoch 10.4; 72.2. Mt. 8.12; 22.13; and 25.30 speak of the "outer darkness."

18. Rosh Hashanah 17a; Baba Metzia 58b.

19. See "Paradise," JE, IX, p. 516. The list includes some very minor biblical characters. The third-century Sage, R. Joshua ben Levi, is often cited as among the fortunate few.

20. Baba Batra 74a-75a. Leviathan is the sea monster in Job 40.14. Legends embroidered the Leviathan in many ways. The banquet at times seems connected with the future advent of the Messiah, and at times not.

21. The name of this third-century Sage was Abba Areka. He founded the celebrated academy at Sura. Just as Judah the Prince is alluded to simply as Rabbi, so this Sage is called simply Rab, the ordinary title of a Babylonian Sage, rather than Rabbi.

22. Berachot 18a.

23. Jer. 23.5-6; 33.14-22.

24. It seems envisaged that the northern kingdom of Israel with its ten "lost tribes" will also be restored.

25. A passage, Jer. Berachot 5a, suggests this; compare Sanhedrin 98b. The view is found opposed in Ekah Rabbati to Lam. 1.16.

26. For example, the Targum to Isa. 42.1; 43.10; and elsewhere. As David was from Bethlehem, Bethlehem is the place from which the Messiah will arise.

27. It is likely that Elijah has received more attention in legendary narratives than any other biblical personality. Especially notable is the view of his appearance on earth in a vast variety of guises, or even disguises. Hence, the identification of John the Baptist in the Synoptic Gospels as Elijah, the forerunner of the Messiah Jesus, is integral to the legends. Needless to say, the Talmudic legends themselves underwent even more embellishment in medieval Jewish folklore. The abundant legends are summarized in Louis Ginzberg, *Legends of the Jews*, and in JE, V, 121-28.

28. This is mentioned in Middot 1.6.

29. Compare E. E. Urbach, *The Sages*, p. 594.

30. Ant. XIII (10, 7), 300; War I (2, 8), 69.

31. A pseudepigraphic work, the Psalms of Solomon (not to be confused with The Odes of Solomon), provides information about messianic expectations, especially in the seventeenth of its eighteen poems. In the second poem, verses 30-31, mention is made of the death in 48 B.C. of Pompey, who had ended Judean independence in 63. The author (VIII.18-26) is bitter against Hasmoneans and Sadducees. In ch. XVII the Messiah is conceived of as a man called by God to purify Jerusalem and then to reign over the nations of the world. The views are not expressed in a totally new way, but they are, instead, derived from passages in the Prophets and Psalms.

32. From the Greek world there was an accumulated legacy which grew over the centuries, attributed to a prophetess Sibyl (*Sibylla*), who flourished before 500 B.C. (as is known by the mention of her in a writer of that age, Heraclitus of Ephesus). The prophecies and proverbs, in increased quantity, circulated broadly. About A.D. 500 someone assembled the so-called Sibylline Oracles. Both Jewish (and later Christian) additions had penetrated the accumulated body of material. In what has come down as the third of fifteen books, the interests are essentially Jewish, and the author of the third book was certainly a Jew. The fifth book has many Jewish elements, and has undergone Christian interpolation. The Third Sibylline (book) is often ascribed to the period between about 170 and 140 B.C.; the Fifth comes from the reign of the Roman Emperor Hadrian (A.D. 117-138), who is mentioned, but apparently prior to the Bar Kochba rebellion which erupted in 132. In the Third Sibylline (verses 652-66) a passage depicts the Messiah, but purely in human terms.

33. See Josephus, Ant. XIV (9,2), 159.

34. Invariably Josephus described as brigands, or worse, any activists against Roman authority. Josephus speaks of a later time (the first half of the first Christian century) which witnessed the emergence of "deceivers and deluders . . . under the pretense of divine illumination" who prevailed on the populace "to act like madmen, going before them in the Wilderness," where God would show them "signs of liberty" [War (13, 4), 259; Ant. XX (8.6), 167-72]. He mentions a certain Theudas (about A.D. 44) who persuaded his followers of miraculous powers, Ant. XX (5.1), 97-99. The Romans beheaded Theudas. Acts 5.36-37 mentions two men whose claims ended with their death. One is Theudas; if he is the same Theudas as in Josephus, there is a discrepancy in chronology, for the Theudas of Acts is much earlier than 44. The other is Judas the Galilean who likewise perished; for him the date is ascribed of "the census," the census of Quirinius known from Josephus as taking place in A.D. 6.

Josephus also mentions two other "impostors," one an Egyptian and another not at all identified as to person, Ant. XX (8, 6, and 10), 169-72, 188; War II (13.5), 261-62. See Acts 21.38 in which the question is put to Paul, "Are you not the Egyptian who . . . led four thousand dagger men into the Wilderness?"

35. Seven things were created before the creation of the world: the Torah, repentance, paradise, hell, the Throne of Glory, the heavenly Temple, and the name of the Messiah (Pesahim 54a; Nedarim 39b, and elsewhere). The list varies in other passages both in number (sometimes only six, sometimes more than six) and in what is included.

36. For example Enoch 98.6, 4 Ezra 12.32; 13.26,52; 14.9; Syriac Baruch 29.3.

37. So, too, Moore II, p. 344.

38. The revised view is often called "realized eschatology," a phrase coined by C. H. Dodd, *The Parables of the Kingdom*. The import of the term is that it was the initial appearance of Jesus which marked the division between "this age" and "the age to come"; with Jesus' first appearance the "future" kingdom had already come in the past.

39. The passage is in Sanhedrin 98b; this Hillel is often taken to be a third century amora; see "Hillel ben Gamaliel III," JE, VI, p. 401.

40. Hezekiah (2 Kgs. 18.1-20.21) reigned over the kingdom of Judah for twenty-nine years, about 726-697. He is praised in 2 Kgs. 18.5, in that "he trusted in the Lord, and there was no king like him among the kings of Judah after him, or before him." In 712, the Assyrians seized some cities of Judah and exacted tribute; they camped before Jerusalem, but at night the angel of the Lord slew 185,000 soldiers in the Assyrian camp, and the Assyrians departed, thus lifting the siege. A somewhat different account is given in 2 Chron. 29.1-32.33, but it also praises Hezekiah without reservation. In the Talmud (Sanhedrin 94a) he is praised for having restored the study of the Torah; he was destined to be named the Messiah, but since King David himself had not attained this eminence, therefore Hezekiah could not, for he had not composed songs to the glory of God as David had. To Hezekiah there was attributed the redaction of the books of Isaiah, Proverbs, Songs of Songs, and Ecclesiastes (Baba Batra 15a).

41. The deathbed words of Johanan ben Zakkai were "Prepare a throne for Hezekiah, who is coming" (Berachot 28b). The suggestion has been made that Hillel's denial is directed at Christians respecting Jesus.

42. Succah 52b. The Messiah ben Joseph appears to have been killed prior to the emergence of the Messiah ben David. The obscurity here is very great. The Messiah ben Joseph is probably related to the hopes and expectations of the revival of the northern kingdom, the chief tribe of which was Ephraim, son of Joseph.

CHAPTER 8

1. The account of the dedication of Solomon's Temple, 1 Kgs. ch. 8, furnishes dates with both a Phoenician name and a number (e.g., "Ethanim which is the seventh month," I Kgs. 8.2).

2. They are, beginning with the spring month: 1) Nisán; 2) Iyyár; 3) Siván; 4) Tammúz; 5) Ab; 6) Elúl; 7) Tishré; 8) Ḥeshván; 9) Kislév; 10) Tebét; 11) Shebát; and 12) Adár.

3. Spring begins about March 21, when the sun, apparently moving northward on the eastern horizon at dawn, crosses the equator; spring is

the period from the "equinox" to the furthest point north the sun seems to move, a point it reaches about June 21; from the solstice ("the sun's stopping" its northward motion) until September 21 is summer. On September 21 the sun crosses the equator as it moves south; fall is the interval between September 21 and December 21. On the latter date, the sun ceases to move southward. Winter is a period from the solstice, December 21, to the spring equinox of March 21.

4. This is not the occasion for a completely detailed exposition of the Jewish calendar. Only broad essentials are here given. The adding of a leap year month is called '*ibbúr* ("intercalation").

5. The visible new moon is always in the west, briefly after sunset. Its thin sliver may appear horizontal, or nearly horizontal, and is the lower part of the moon. The new moon cannot be in the east, nor set as late as midnight, nor be illumined in its upper half. At the "observatory," various depictions of the moon were shown to those who appeared with the claim of having seen it, and their testimony could thereby be tested.

6. Rosh Hashana 2.8.

7. See note 5, above.

8. Rosh Hashana 2.2.

9. The Sabbath was figuratively the "queen" or the "bride." Her courtiers needed to robe themselves in finery appropriately to greet her (Baba Kama 32a-b).

10. Berachot 8.1; Pesaḥim 105a. Wine, according to Ps. 104.15, "gladdens the hearts of men."

11. Berachot 35a-b.

12. Berachot 8.5; Pesaḥim 104a.

13. Exod. 13.8. The rendering here is for its sense, and does not strictly in the latter portion adhere to the Hebrew.

14. Reform and Reconstructionist Jews have abbreviated or modified aspects of the seder, but retain the basic format.

15. The four cups are derived from four different Scriptural words for "rescued."

16. This is not specified in Pesaḥim 10.

17. The parsley symbolizes the plant hyssop, the salt water blood. In Exod. 12.22, hyssop was to be dipped in blood and the blood then put on the doorposts to identify a Hebrew home, so that the Deity would "pass over" it and put his plague only on Egyptian homes.

18. It was a popular belief that at seder, Elijah visited every home where a door was opened for him, and entered silently and invisibly to drink from his cup.

19. The text of Pesaḥim 10.4 varies in manuscript traditions. Some have the question, "Why do we eat only bitter herbs, but on other nights all kinds of vegetables?" The latter usually supplants the question of the roast versus stewing or cooking in the modern seder. Or, in memory of the practice in Roman times of reclining on couches at mealtime, the question can be, "Why do we recline on this night, and not on other nights?"

20. Deut. 26.5 reads "A wandering Aramaean was my father, and he

descended into Egypt. . . ." The Hebrew for wander has a root similar to one meaning destroy. The sense of the verse is made to mean: "An Aramaean [Laban; Gen. 31.2-5] sought to destroy my father [Jacob], who descended . . ."

21. The word is obscure. Some take it to be a Greek word (epikōmon), an after-meal song or even revelry. A passage (Pesaḥim 109b) which suggests that the service not be prolonged lest the children be bored led to the practice still observed of the father's breaking off a piece of matzoh at the start of the service, to hide it for the children to find and be rewarded by a gift. This piece of matzoh is called afikomen. Mishnah Pesaḥim does not mention afikomen in this sense.

22. From Ps. 114.1, "When Israel came out of Egypt." Comparable, Ps. 136 is alluded to as "the Great Hallel."

23. It became customary to read Song of Songs after the seder. The practice is not Talmudic.

24. Sukkot is the name in Lev. 23.24; Deut. 16.13,16; Zech. 14.16,18-19, and elsewhere. In Exod. 23.16 and 34.22, it is "the Feast of the Ingathering"; it is called simply "The Feast" in 1 Kgs. 8.2; Ezek. 45.23. Probably "Ingathering" was an ancient harvest festival which developed into Sukkot, the development including a calendar change from a solar dating ("at the cycle," or "outgoing of the year") into the dating in the solar lunar date of Tishre 15; probably in very ancient times the "Ingathering" preceded, and culminated in, the New Year. See note 27.

25. While the Gospel narratives allocate the entry of Jesus into Jerusalem at Passover, the use of palm branches strewn before him, and the use of Ps. 118.26 in Mt. 21.9 has suggested that, through confusion, an entry actually near or on Sukkot became altered into one near Passover. This, of course, is mere conjecture.

26. The phrase is obscure. "The place of water-drawing" is a guess.

27. Slightly different versions of the procedure are recorded. Possibly the ceremony is a folk recollection of ancient solar worship in a dawn ritual on the fall equinox. See note 24.

28. Hosanna means "Save now," as in Ps. 118.25.

29. Sukkot 4.5.

30. For example, that atzeret meant "closing," rather than "assembly." Compare Deut. 16.8.

31. Megilla 31a.

32. If it does, that is a sign of God's wrath (Ta'anit 1.1). One prays during Sukkot for rain *in its season;* rain within Sukkot was unseasonable.

33. Ḥagiga 2.4; compare Pesaḥim 42b.

34. It is also called a "heave" offering. The priest "waved" the offering towards the altar as if giving it to God, but then "waved" it away from the altar as if returning it to the person who had offered it.

35. The bringing of flour from the first sheaf made it permissible to use the rest of the barley.

36. Hence the name Weeks.

37. It is not known precisely who they were (Moore, I, p. 69). It is

inferred that they were a priestly family, arising in the time of Herod; as such, they were kindred to the Sadducees. Herod married the daughter of a priest, Simon the son of Boethus, but only after he had removed the then High Priest. Once Simon was High Priest, his daughter was now of a family with sufficient prestige for Herod to marry into. Ant. XV (9.3), 320-22.

38. Menahot 65a-b.

39. So Hans Lichtenstein, *Hebrew Union College Annual*, VIII-IX; Louis Finkelstein, *The Pharisees* I, pp. 113ff.

40. In Acts ch. 2, there is an account of a Pentecost event, namely, the Christians in Jerusalem received the gift of the holy spirit to their community.

41. A Jewish sect, the Karaites, which emerged in Persia in the eighth Christian century, followed the Bible and in principle (though not entirely in practice) rejected Rabbinic laws and traditions. It spread slowly, with inner divisions, and reached its zenith in the thirteenth century, numbering many adherents and producing eminent scholars and philosophers. It is extant today, but in very small numbers, primarily in Turkey and Israel. The Karaites have preserved the Sadducean-Boethusian dating of Weeks.

42. In American synagogues, especially but not exclusively among Reform Jews, Weeks is the occasion of "confirmation," marking the completion of an adolescent's completion of instruction in the religious school. Confirmation in this sense is quite dissimilar from Roman Catholic confirmation, which is one of the seven "sacraments." Jewish confirmation is not essentially sacramental.

43. Traditional Jews do not marry during the ómer period even today, except on the thirty-third day. That day (lag be-ómer) became in medieval times a festive day, especially in Rabbinic academies; the "scholars' festival" became an occasion of great merrymaking.

44. The tractate proceeds to specify regulations for the public reading of other scriptural books and for the purchase and sale of synagogue buildings.

45. It is mentioned in Jn. 10.22.

46. Especially in Shabbat 21b-23b.

47. Shabbat 21b. An apparent allusion is found in 2 Macc. 1.18.

48. A dispute existed between the Shammaites and the Hillelites (Shabbat 21b). The former advocated the kindling of eight lamps the first night, reducing the number by one on the subsequent nights. The view of the Hillelites (which prevailed) was to kindle one lamp the first night and to increase the lamps by one on the subsequent nights. Josephus, Ant. XII (7.7), 325, calls the festival *phōta* ("lights"), a name often encountered in current writings.

In actuality, the origin of Ḥanukka (as of Christmas) is to be traced back to a folk festival of lights at the period of the winter solstice.

49. On the fifteenth of Ab there was dancing in the vineyards, and the girls challenged the boys to choose their marriage partners. "Nicanor's day" commemorated a victory over the general sent by Antiochus Epi-

phanes to subdue the Hasmonean rebels (Megillat Taanit XII; Taanit 18b).

50. Rosh Hashana 11a. The view that Tishre 1 is the anniversary of Creation came to dominate over another view that Nisan 1 was the anniversary.

51. Rosh Hashana 1.2.

52. The figure is that of a shepherd bringing his sheep back from the pasture into the sheepfold through a gate; the returning sheep pass before the shepherd one by one.

53. Rosh Hashana 16b. The matter of the three categories is ascribed there to R. Johanan ben Zakkai.

54. In a musical scale the "do" is the tonic and "sol" the dominant.

55. The data respecting the Jubilee year are highly complex. Rabbinic authorities differed as to its being the forty-ninth year, and identical with the seventh of the sabbatical years, or the fiftieth year; in this latter case, there would have been two successive years of abstention from planting, with obvious resultant difficulties (Rosh Hashana 9a). Both the sabbatical year and the Jubilee could threaten the economic stability implied in the cancellation of debts; hence the *prosbŭl* of Hillel (p. 240). The Mishna *Shebi'it* ("seventh") deals with the sabbatical year, the first nine chapters with the laws respecting land, and the tenth with the cancellation of debts. The Palestinian Talmud has a Gemara to Shebiit, the Babylonian Talmud not, since the regulations applied primarily to the Holy Land, not to Dispersion.

56. The observance of Shebát 15 as a semi-holiday became a very widespread custom, this as distinct from a halachic requirement. It became in effect an "Arbor Day," and acquired increased significance in recent decades in connection with the reforestation by Jewish settlers in Palestine-Israel. The Hebrew numerals for fifteen can be read as a word, *tŭ*, and hence the day has come to be known as *Tŭ Be-Shebát*.

CHAPTER 9

1. A Jewish fast-day (unlike some Christian fasts) entails a total abstinence from food and drink from sundown through sundown.

2. Solemn as the Day of Atonement was, there was a sense in which it was also a festival. There was, moreover, a recollection of an earlier time when the Day of Atonement had been a day of rejoicing; Ta'anit IV.8.

3. In general, Sabbath prohibitions exceed in rigor the festival prohibitions; the Yom Kippur prohibitions, however, are much more rigorous than those for the Sabbath.

4. In some parts of Europe, Germany for example, there arose the practice in communities of fostering personal reconciliations before the Day of Atonement.

5. Rosh Hashana 1.2.

6. This word comes from the Latin, "to see in advance"; the Hebrew equivalent is *tzōfé* ("see"), that is, God sees.

7. Chapters of the Fathers, 3.15.

8. See Part II, ch. 8, note 53.

9. See Zech. 7.5 and 8.19.

10. The supposed anniversary of the Roman breach of the walls of Jerusalem; Ta'anit 28b.

11. The death of Gedaliah (2 Kgs. 25.25).

12. The supposed anniversary of the destruction of the Temple in both 587 B.C. and A.D. 70.

13. The beginning of Nebuchandnezzar's siege of Jerusalem (1 Kgs. 25.1; Jer. 3.4).

14. To the prohibitions usual on the Day of Atonement there was added the prohibition of study of the Written and Oral Torah (Taanit 30a), this to withhold from the day the delight that sacred study entailed.

15. Ta'anit 30b.

16. They are listed at the end of Megillat Taanit.

17. Ta'anit 11a.

CHAPTER 10

1. See my *Philo's Place in Judaism: A Study of Conceptions of Abraham in Jewish Literature*, p. 85.

2. Ant. XX. (2, 1-5), 17-56.

3. Prior to the destruction of the Temple, a third rite, the bringing of an offering there, was incumbent; Mekilta to Exod. 12.48; Keritot 9a.

4. See the various injunctions in Lev. ch. 15.

5. Yebamot 47a.

6. As Moore does, with justice, II, pp. 326-27.

7. The Maccabean king John Hyrcanus forced Idumeans to convert, and his successor did the same with the residents of northern Galilee and southern Lebanon. Such converts included those who later apostatized. Hence, there were converts who were not admirable, as compared with the ger tzedek.

8. In some texts, the twelfth of the Eighteen Benedictions is addressed against "informers." See p. 149 and Part II, ch. 1, note 54.

9. *Karēt* ("cutting off") is punishment from God, such as premature death, as distinct from punishment by human courts.

10. The allusion is probably to the depressed conditions after the Roman crushing of the Bar Kochba rebellion after A.D. 135.

11. See IDB., I, pp. 841-43, "Didache." Another work, often dated in the fourth Christian century, is "The Apostolic Constitutions." It either expands a work called Didascalia ("instruction"), or else the Didascalia is an abridgement of Apostolic Constitutions. There is evidence which leads to the theory of a Jewish original, or, at least, to the presence of pre-Christian prayers and benedictions; see, for this latter view, "Didascalia," JE IV, pp. 588-94.

12. See 1 Macc. 2.15; 2 Macc. 5.8,15.

13. War VI (4,3), 237; "Alexander, Tiberius Julius," JE, I, pp. 357-58.

14. A brief summary, now out of date, is to be found in Charles Guignebert, *The Jewish World in the Time of Jesus* (trans. by S. H. Hooke), London, 1939, "The Judaeo-Pagan Syncretism," pp. 238-52.

CHAPTER 11

1. See p. 144.

2. He cannot be precisely identified, since there were several early Simeons.

3. The mountainous character of much of Judea probably accounts for the Hebrew idiom in which to go to Judea is spoken of as "going up." From that ancient usage arises the modern term *aliya*, which connotes moving to and settling in the State of Israel.

4. Apparently at that time Babylonian Jewry lacked academies; these developed in number and eminence two centuries later.

5. Three questions in particular required clarification: the regulations respecting the leper, the eating of matzoh made from new grain, and the matter of sacrifices on festivals. The uncertainty rested on the lack at that time of settled "rules" for interpreting Scripture.

6. On another heathen proselyte, see p. 233.

7. Shabbat 30b-31a.

8. On seeing a skull floating in a river, he said, "You caused others to drown, and now you have drowned. Those that drowned you will themselves be drowned" (Chapters of the Fathers, II, 6).

9. The Rabbinic phrase is *tiqqŭn ōlắm*, "betterment of the world" (Gitin IV.3).

10. The prosbul document was attested to by witnesses or by judges of a court; Shebiit X.3-6.

11. Sukkot 28a; J. Ned. V 39b.

12. The rather caustic judgment is made that the disputes brought it about that the one Torah had become two! (Shabbat 15a).

13. Berachot 36b.

14. Jer. Berachot 3a bottom.

15. Virtually nothing is known of him; the tradition made him his father's successor as president of the Sanhedrin (Shabbat 15a).

16. In the Jewish tradition the name is pronounced Gamliél, in the Christian Gamáliel. Possibly the name was G'máliél.

17. The problems inner to the New Testament are stated in "Gamaliel," IDB, II, p. 351. One problem is the allusion, Acts 5.36-37, to Theudas as preceding Judas the Galilean; data in Josephus would put Theudas about A.D. 44 but Judas about A.D. 6. That Paul was a student of Gamaliel has been denied (Morton S. Enslin, "Paul and Gamaliel," *Journal of Religion*, 1927 [VII], pp. 360-75), primarily because Gamaliel goes unmentioned in Paul's Epistles and the attitude of Paul toward Torah and halacha is so completely at variance with attitudes in the Rabbinic Literature in general and those of Gamaliel I in particular.

18. A certain father, to punish his wayward children, bequeathed his property to Jonathan. The latter, however, retained only a third of this legacy, giving one third to the Temple, and one third to the disinherited children (Baba Batra 134a). To Jonathan ben Uzziel (p. 127) was attributed the authorship of the Targum to the Prophets.

19. They are given as forty each, a total of 120 years, the same age as

Moses. It is customary among Jews, in wishing someone long life, to phrase it, "May you live to 120."

20. Sukkot 28a; J. Ned. 39b; Rosh Hashana 30b.

21. Apparently the Academies of Hillel and Shammai, if still extant, were gradually supplanted by schools such as one led by Johanan. After 70 the academies of Hillel and Shammai disappear, though residual viewpoints from these Academies seem to have persisted.

22. This shift is exemplified in Rosh Hashana IV.1, which relates that in Jamnia, as once in Jerusalem alone, it was permitted to sound the Shofar when the New Year fell on a Sabbath. See also there, IV.3.

23. See p. 171.

24. That is, "forceful personality."

25. This is a cryptic allusion to the Messiah. See Part II, ch. 7, notes 40-41.

26. One needed to go to the place where the Torah is studied, not expect the Torah to come to a place to seek out a person (Shabbat 147b).

27. Gitin 56b.

28. Eduyot VII.7; Sanhedrin 11b.

29. He mentions "the plagues of the Pharisees," an unclear matter, usually interpreted to be self-mortification in repressing a normal sexuality (Sotah 3.4).

30. He put his own brother-in-law, Eliezer ben Hyrkanus, "in Coventry" (Baba Metziah 59b). Such a "ban" was social and academic, and did not entail being barred from religious practices or observances. It was much different from later Christian excommunication. See "Excommunication," JE, V, pp. 285-87.

31. The Talmudic sources allude to that occasion in a phrase which acquired special meaning, "on that day"; Berachot 28a.

32. It is told that Eleazar was then eighteen, and manifestly too youthful in appearance for the high position. Miraculously, overnight part of his hair turned white.

33. Gamaliel, arriving at Joshua's home, noticed that the walls were black, said, "I infer from the walls that you are a blacksmith." Joshua said, "Alas for a generation whose leader you are, for you know nothing of the struggles of the Sages to support themselves financially." Thereupon Gamaliel spoke his apology.

34. Berachot 27b-28a. A confused, mostly unintelligible story (Shabbat 116a-b) brings Gamaliel into contact with a *min*—the manuscripts vary, with one reading "philosopher—who is apparently a Christian. The latter's integrity was being tested. The passage appears to cite Mt. 5.17 with some correctness, but it also contains a supposed Matthean passage on inheritance which does not occur there or elsewhere in the Gospels.

35. See "Flavia Domitila," JE, V, pp. 406-7.

36. An *am ha'äretz* ("one of the people"), in this context signifying only an unlearned man.

37. Nedarim 50a.

38. Yadaim III.5.

39. Hagiga 14b.

40. See p. 171 and note 12, above. Modern scholars have sought ingeniously to identify these "heretical" views, but with minimum success, some opting for gnosticism, some for a Philonic dualism, some for Sadduceeism, some for Christianity. Legends arose uncomplimentary to Elisha, yet his disciple, the eminent R. Meir, retained a fidelity to and regard for him.

41. His name was Simeon ben Zoma; he is never alluded to as Rabbi.

42. The Roman historian Dio Cassius, LXVIII, 32, reports that the Jews of Cyprus killed 240,000 Greeks. The primary account of the insurrection of the Jews of Egypt is in Eusebius, *Ecclesiastical History*, IV.2.

43. Akiba died while reciting the Shma, "Hear O Israel, the Lord our God, the Lord is One" (Deut. 6.4). His flesh was flayed as he was reciting the verse, but he retained enough strength to utter the Hebrew *ēḥắd* ("One"). He had earlier taught that the love of God (Deut. 6.5) implied a willingness to die on behalf of God (Berachot 61b).

44. In early Christianity, the laying on of hands raised a commoner into being an Apostle, as in Acts 6.6 and 13.3; compare 1 Tim. 5.22; 2 Tim. 1.6.

45. Ketubot 112a; Sanhedrin 13a; 19a. At an even later time the Patriarch seemed to have had the sole authority to ordain.

46. Meilah 17b.

47. He is also called *Rabbénu* ("our master"; Yebamot 45a), or else "Rabbenu the Holy" (Pesahim 37b; Shabbat 156a).

48. Sotah 49b.

49. The Tosefta, we have said (pp. 111-12), is a compilation of tannaitic utterances not included in the Mishna by Judah. In addition to the Tosefta, there are individual tannaitic utterances (*baraitôt*) cited in the Gemara.

50. On these and other matters, "Mishna," JE, VIII, pp. 609-19, though somewhat antiquated, is still worth consulting.

PART III
HELLENISTIC JUDAISM

1. The great name respecting this conclusion is Adolf Deissmann, in *Bible Studies* (2 vols.), 1895 and 1897, and *Light from the Ancient East*, 1908.

2. One recension is to be traced to the Alexandrian Christian, Origen (fl. c. 185-254), who had settled in Caesarea in Judea and had learned Hebrew. To him is attributed a work in six columns. One column presented the Old Testament in Hebrew; a second presented it in Hebrew but written in the Greek alphabet. The other four columns presented four different Greek translations, the third of these being the Septuagint. (On the other translations, see below). The work is known as the Hexapla ("six columns"). Copyists of the Hexapla normally limited themselves

to the Septuagint column; the Hexapla has not survived, but portions of a translation of it into Syriac have. The "recension" of the Septuagint in Origen is called either Hexaplaric or, because Origen had settled in Caesarea, the "Palestinian."

It is known that a second recension of the Septuaginst—largely lost—was made by a bishop named Hesychius (died 311). The third recension, made by a certain Lucian (who died a martyr's death in 311), is called Lucianic; it circulated in Asia Minor. It is sometimes called "The Antiochian recension," connected with a comparison of the Hebrew and the Septuagint made before Lucian's time in Antioch, Syria.

3. The best known instance is Isa. 7.14. The Septuagint reads "virgin" and the verse is cited in Mt. 1.23 to prove the virgin birth of Jesus. The Hebrew word is 'almā, which ordinarily means "young woman." That is, the virgin birth could not be proved from the Hebrew text. It came to be alleged by Christians that Jews had altered the Hebrew from virgin to young woman. Actually the particular word, in the total context, is of no importance; nothing in the context suggests that "the virgin" remained a virgin." Moreover, the point of the total passage is that in the period of time in which a baby could be conceived and be born, and begin to run around, the coalition of the kingdoms of Syria and Israel against the Kingdom of Judah would come to naught. In all traditions, "prooftexting" ordinarily ignores the total context and instead plucks out a gratifying verse.

4. The day of the translation of the Bible into Greek was as calamitous as the day when the Golden Calf was made; Tractate Soferim 1.8-9. The oral character of the Rabbinic tradition was deliberate; if recorded, it might have been translated as the Bible was, and have become the property of hostile outsiders. With the haggada and halacha restricted to oral form, they remained the exclusive possession of Israel alone; J. Peah II, 17a.

5. He is viewed as a proselyte, sometimes to Judaism, sometimes to Christianity.

6. Such was the view of Irenaeus, *Against Heretics*, 1.262. For other references see "Ebionites," JE, V, p. 31.

7. Origen knew some of these.

8. The complex problems of the translations of the Bible are presented in the excellent book, Bleddyn J. Roberts, *The Old Testament Text and Versions: The Hebrew Text in Transmission and the History of the Ancient Versions*, 1955. So greatly has research proliferated that, recent as that book is, it is in some respects out of date. The bibliography in J. W. Wevers, "Septuagint," IDB, IV, p. 278, is a very fine selection.

9. See p. 49.

10. *Stromata* I, 21, 130.

11. In *Preparation for the Gospel*, Books VIII-IX.

12. In *Preparation for the Gospel*, IX, 17-39.

13. A single work is so variously alluded to that three supposedly different works have at times been ascribed to him. The quotations from Eupolemus are in Clement, *Stromata* 1.23.153, and Eusebius, *Preparation for the Gospel*, IX, 17 (usually denied to Eupolemus), and IX.30-34. A

work remarkable in its scholarship is the book by Ben Zion Wacholder, *Eupolemus: A Study of Judaeo-Greek Literature*, 1974.

14. In *Preparation for the Gospel*, IX, 18, 23, and 27.

15. In *Preparation for the Gospel*, IX, 25.

16. He is cited in *Preparation for the Gospel*, IX, 20 not directly from Alexander Polyhistor, but from Ant. I (15), 240-41. Apparently Cleodomus simply associated North African place names with similar-sounding biblical names.

17. Cited in *Preparation for the Gospel*, IX, 17 and 18.

18. Against Apion 1.23; Josephus seems to have taken him to be a Gentile.

19. *Preparation for the Gospel*, IX, 20, 24, and 37.

20. *Preparation for the Gospel*, IX, 22.

21. *Preparation for the Gospel*, IX, 28; Clement, *Stromata* 1.23.155.

22. *Preparation for the Gospel*, IX, 28; 29.4-17.

23. Two fragments are in Eusebius, *Preparation for the Gospel* VII.10 and XIII.12, and repeated in Clement *Stromata* I.22 and VI.3. The third is in Eusebius, *Ecclesiastical History*, VII.32.17. A summary is found in JE, II, pp. 97-98. See above, Part I, ch. 3, note 2.

24. See, for example, the appeal of the Jews of Ionia in Asia to Agrippa in the presence of Herod on the violation of their rights in Ant. XVI (2, 3-5), 27-65.

25. This account of Aristotle and a Jew is found also in Eusebius, *Preparation for the Gospel*, IX, 5, and is alluded to in Clement of Alexandria, *Stromata* I.15.70.

26. He was a Phoenician prince who founded the Greek city of Thebes while searching for his sister Europa whom Zeus had kidnapped. There are those who have associated the name Cadmus with the Semitic word for east (*Heb*. qédem) and Europa with west (Heb. *'éreb*, "evening," signifying west because that is where the sun is in the evening).

27. Against Apion I, 1-42. A good recent work worth consulting is J. N. Sevenster, *The Roots of Pagan Anti-Semitism in the Ancient World*, Leiden, 1975, Supplement XLI to *Novum Testamentum*.

28. He flourished around 270 B.C. He is known primarily from this passage in Josephus. He wrote a History of Egypt in three volumes.

29. Against Apion I, 73-105.

30. Against Apion I, 106-27.

31. Against Apion I, 128-60.

32. A gift which by an oath was destined for the sanctuary. Compare Mk. 7.9-13.

33. Against Apion I, 161-320.

34. According to Apion, Moses was by birth a native of Heliopolis ("city of the sun") and had erected open air places of worship, with sundial devices. Josephus denies that such devices appeared either in the Wilderness Tabernacle of Moses or in the Temple of Solomon. Moreover, if the place of birth of people as recent as Homer and Pythagoras was unknown, how could the birthplace of Moses, who lived so long ago, be known? The answer: Apion was a liar (II, 8-14).

35. Today we incline to view the Macedonians, including Alexander

the Great, as Greeks; in the ancient world a distinction was maintained between Greeks and Macedonians. In this section Josephus by implication contrasts the early Macedonians with the later Ptolemies.

36. Some confusions exist as Josephus reproduces (II, 53-55) the substance of 3 Macc. chs. 5-6.

37. Apion drew his material from two earlier anti-Jewish writers, Posidonius of Apamea (135-51 B.C.) and Apollonius Molon (± 50 B.C.).

38. The allegation of the worship of an ass was also made later against Christians (Tertullian, *Apology* 16).

39. Christians at various times in various places have made a similar allegation about Jews, usually that Jews kidnap and kill a Christian child, draining his blood for use at the Passover seder. See "Blood Accusation," JE, III, 260-67. The most recent celebrated instances was the Beilis case, 1911-13, in the Ukraine; the novel *The Fixer* by Bernard Malamud is based on that case. Beilis, it should be noted, was acquitted. In refuting Apion, Josephus preserved Apion's material for use by the Nazis.

40. In Ant. XIX (5, 2), 280-85, Josephus quotes the edict of Claudius, the tone of which is altogether favorable to the Jews of Alexandria. A papyrus, published in 1912, provides another document from Claudius (called a "rescript") which is at variance with the edict found in Josephus in a number of ways, and has led to acute scholarly differences. (The rescript is reproduced in V. A. Tcherikover, *Corpus Papyrorum Judaicarum*, I, pp. 48-92). The edict seems to confirm Jewish rights and citizenship; the rescript is clearly a limitation, especially of citizenship. See Victor Tcherikover, *Hellenistic Civilization and the Jews* (tr. S. Applebaum), 159, pp. 409-15.

41. Often alluded to as Pseudo-Clement. The author is unknown, but traditionally was wrongly believed to be Clement of Alexandria, about A.D. 150-220. The date of the Pseudo-Clementine writings is uncertain, but the late second or early third century is often suggested. The passage about Apion is in Homilies V, 2-26.

42. She is nameless here and in 2 Macc. In the Rabbinic versions she is known at times as Hannah, at times as Miriam.

43. The books he does not quote are Ruth, Esther, Ecclesiastes, Song of Songs, Lamentations, Ezekiel, and Daniel.

44. Some scholars deny these last two treatises to Philo; others regard the mention of the Essenes in Every Good Man as an interpolation. Additional surviving treatises, often ascribed to Philo—That The World is Incorruptible, Sampson, and Jonah—are usually believed not to be by Philo. On Pseudo-Philo, see p. 128.

45. The two survive not in Greek, but in an Armenian translation.

46. The essays in The Allegory of the Law are as follows: three books called Allegory of the Law; On the Cherubim; On the Sacrifice of Cain and Abel; That the Worse Destroys the Better; On the Posterity of Cain; On the Giants; That God is Immutable; On the Plantation of Noah; On Drunkenness; On Sobriety; On the Confusion of Tongues; On the Migration of Abraham; Who is Heir of Divine Things?; On Mating for the

Sake of Erudition; On Flight and Finding; On the Change of Names; and On Dreams (consisting of two essays).

47. My view is that the Exposition was written for Jews on the fringe of Judaism, to deter them from impending apostasy; Philo's own nephew, Tiberius Julius Alexander, became an apostate. The titles are On the Creation of the World; On Abraham; On Joseph; On Moses; On the Decalogue; On the Special Laws; and On the Virtues. Fragments of a work by Philo are preserved in Eusebius, *Preparation for the Gospel*, VIII, 6.1-9; 7.1-20 and 11.1-18; they are reproduced in the Loeb edition of Philo, vol. IX, pp. 414-43, preceded by an introduction, pp. 407-13. This work—its title varies from "About the Jews" to "Hypothetica"—seems more designed for outsiders than does the Exposition.

48. Aristotle had suggested intuition as a possible type, but then had denied it as impracticable.

49. The ensuing exposition arises most readily from On Abraham (not to be confused with the treatise On the Migration of Abraham). Abundant Philonic material supplementary to On Abraham is presented in my *Philo's Place in Judaism*, chap. III.

50. Philo derives this from Gen. 4.26. There Enos, the grandson of Adam, is spoken of in the Septuagint as one who "hoped to call on the name of God." Enos in Hebrew means man. Hence, hope is a quality only men have. (On this verse, see my "Genesis 4:26b," in *Hebrew Union College Annual*, Vol. XXXII, 1961.)

It might be added here that for Philo, Cain is the man who is fluent in speech but deficient in thought, while Abel is a man of worthy thought but deficient in fluency. The fluent man of poor thought always "kills" the thoughtful man who lacks fluency.

51. For Philo the meaning of Gen. 5.24 is that Enoch's past had been wiped out.

52. Philo, however, affirms that the future can be read in the stars.

53. Both the place and a brother of Abraham bear the same name in Hebrew; the spelling in the Septuagint differs, between the man Arran and the place Charran. The place name is found in English renderings as both Ḥaran and Ḥarran.

54. The notion of a universal wisdom, available to thinking men, is Stoic. Philo owes a debt respecting Logos to the Stoics, but, as we see below, he invests the term Logos with meanings and implications, derived from Judaism, far beyond the Stoics.

55. In the allegory, Lot means one who "inclines," that is, one who has not yet reached stability. In having settled in fertile, luxurious Sodom, Lot had inclined to pleasure, as we all do. But Lot is, curiously enough, the experience of Abraham who in the process of learning went through the temporary stage of inclining to pleasure.

56. One needs to forget modern definitions. What we call democracy, Philo would have called ochlocracy, "mob rule."

57. In the Septuagint Gen. 23.6, the Hittites so address Abraham as *basileus* ("king"); the Hebrew there reads *nasi'* ("prince").

58. We saw above (pp. 287-88) that Eden also represented ideal virtue.

59. Rabbinic interpretation distinguishes God from the three visitors, but Philo's interpretation does not.

60. The Book of Jubilees and Rabbinic literature assert that the patriarchs observed the Laws of Moses in advance of their appearance, since the Laws of Moses are regarded as the norm, and the patriarchs must be raised to the norm. In Philo, the Law of Nature is the norm, and the Laws of Moses need to be raised to it, as appears presently.

61. Philo frequently dissolves the historical events of the Bible into existential symbol, but, having done so, manages to restore history by making the patriarchs and Moses men who historically experienced the symbols. Thus, his Abraham is essentially any man who can progress by learning, yet Abraham is also the historical man who long ago achieved this progress.

62. See also Jer. 10.12; 51.15; Ps. 104.24; Wis. 9.1-2; 18.15.

63. Often Philo uses the man Israel and the nation Israel rather interchangeably. For Philo the Hebrews are "migrants" who abandon sense perception and go to objects of the mind.

64. Philo seems not to have demanded circumcision of a proselyte. The view is expressed that he conceives of as "semi-proselytes" certain people who have become Jews in effect, but have abstained from circumcision. Such people are by some identified the *phoboumenoi* ("fearers") or *sebomenoi* ("reverers") of God, the latter term found in Ant. XIV (7, 2), 110.

65. Philo views Abraham as if he were a proselyte, the exemplar for proselytes of Philo's time (On the Virtues, 219). Philo uses the term "epilyte" rather than "proselyte."

66. Deut. 30.2-5 promises that, if repentance occurs, God will gather His people from wherever they have been scattered and bring them to the Holy land, there to be more prosperous and numerous than their ancestors.

67. Rewards and Punishments, 165.

68. On the Migration of Abraham, 79-81.

69. The effort of Louis Finkelstein, "Is Philo Mentioned in Rabbinic Literature?" *Journal of Biblical Literature*, LIII (1934), 142-49, to find a mention of Philo there is ingenious but unconvincing.

70. The view of Harry A. Wolfson that Philo is little different from the Rabbis is to be rejected. The opposing view of Erwin R. Goodenough (e.g. *By Light, Light*) is basically sound, but blemished by frequent excesses. Goodenough's view of an "underground," non-normative Judaism (see my *The First Christian Century in Judaism and Christianity*, pp. 86-88) is probably not right, but even if right, is not properly to be inferred from Philo. Goodenough's multi-volume *Jewish Symbols in Greco-Roman Period*, a work of monumental scope, reflects his aim to "prove" the case that there was such an underground Judaism by means of discovering a mystic significance in these symbols, based not on surviving literary evidence but on an analysis that owes a great and primary debt to Jungian psychology.

PART IV
EARLY CHRISTIANITY

CHAPTER 1

1. Hans Conzelmann, *Jesus*, tr. J. Raymond Lord, 1973, p. 12, puts it: "The non-Christian source material is extremely scanty. It confirms the fact that there was never any doubt about the historicity of the person Jesus, but it yields nothing of concrete knowledge about him."

2. Two passages in Josephus mention Jesus. Ant. XX (9, 1), 200, speaks of the execution of James "the brother of Jesus called the Christ." The more significant passage, XVIII (3, 3), 63-64, is so Christian in tone as to have yielded three views: that the passage is authentic; that it is in total a Christian interpolation; that an authentic mention has been expanded by some Christian hand. See Part IV, Ch. 8, below, for more detail.

PAUL

CHAPTER 2

1. W. D. Davies, *Paul and Rabbinic Judaism*, attempts to explain Paul on the basis of Rabbinic literature. The book has been influential, but its views have also been challenged.

2. Only in the case of the Revelation of John is there a widely held view that a prior Aramaic work lies behind the book.

3. To deny that Paul wrote Ephesians is by no means to asperse Ephesians; it is simply to enter into the questions, freely and openly, as to who wrote it, and when.

4. The last verses (13.22-25) are similar to the close of Epistles genuinely by Paul, and though Hebrews lacks Paul's signature, it has been (and occasionally still is) ascribed to Paul.

5. The usual procedure tries to align the letters with the missionary journeys of Paul, usually taken to be three (Acts 13.1-14.28; 15.36-18.22; and 18.23-21.17), or from data in the salutations at the end of his letters. A sequence occasionally suggested is

1 Thessalonians
Galatians
2 Thessalonians (if genuine)
1 Corinthians
2 Corinthians (which is composite, containing portions of at least
    two, or even three, different letters)
Philippians

Romans
Philemon

6. The phrase "in Christ" here means simply a Christian. Elsewhere its overtone is that a man mystically unites with the "spirit" of Christ.

7. In 1 Thess. 2.14-15—and there only in all of Paul's Epistles— blame is put on Jews for the death of Jesus. So out of keeping is this passage with other materials in the Epistles that some scholars believe that it was expanded from a briefer statement, while others believe that the entire passage is an interpolation from after Paul's time.

8. The allusion is not clear.

9. The details of why, and even where, are lacking. Because Acts 27.1 depicts Paul as taken to Rome as a prisoner, older scholarship ascribed the prison Epistles to Rome. More recently the prison experience has been ascribed to Ephesus, based on 1 Cor. 15.32, which mentions that there Paul "fought with beasts."

10. These apostles are at the minimum rivals of Paul, or at the maximum personal enemies.

11. The Greek word for emptying is *kenosis*, and the word has become the title for the passage.

12. The region in Asia Minor was known as Galatia because Gauls (from France or Spain) had settled there. The effort to fit the founding of this church into Paul's journeys has yielded contradictory opinions, these known, respectively, as the "South Galatian hypothesis," and the "North Galatian hypothesis."

13. Cephas in Aramaic means rock; Peter in Greek means rock. Perhaps Cephas and Peter are the same person, known in the Gospel also as Simon bar Jona; perhaps they are not.

14. Curiously, this James, known also from Josephus Ant. XX (9.1), 200, fails of mention in the canonical Gospels, but is the leader of the Jerusalem church as in Acts ch. 15.

15. By contrast, it is related in Acts 16.3 that Timothy, with a Jewish mother and a Gentile father, did undergo circumcision at the hand of Paul.

16. The number is the presumed span of time from Abraham to Moses, possibly drawn from Exod. 12.40.

17. There is no antecedent Jewish source. One often cited is the Septuagint reading of Deut. 33.2; it has no relevancy at all.

18. The meaning is uncertain.

19. The meaning is not human masters, but the demons in control of the world.

20. The usual word here is "adoption"; however, it ruptures the figure of speech, which is that of a babe emerging from custody into the full rights of a son.

21. Earlier (3.15-17) Paul had set forth that the promise was a covenant, and that the Law apparently was not.

22. He cites, as if in proof, Isa. 54.1.

23. The contrast here and elsewhere is between earning righteousness by observing laws, and receiving it as grace, an unearned free gift.

24. He lists those whom he has baptized to show how few they were.

25. In support he cites Deut. 25.4, inferring that the muzzling of the ox is equivalent to not supplying food to an Apostle.

26. The example is the death of many Hebrews in the Wilderness. It cannot be determined whether Paul meant seriously that the Hebrews were connected with Christ, as it were, or whether in his desire to warn the Corinthians by the example drawn from the Wilderness, he ascribes to the Wilderness the experience of the Corinthians. What Paul says here is clear; his direct intent is less clear.

27. The significance of Paul's instructions are unclear. That long hair dishonors a man but is a glory to a woman seems to have some significance, but exactly what is elusive. That a woman ought "to have a sign of authority on her head because of the angels" makes some sense if here angels are understood as demons (as is the likely meaning of angels in Gal. 3.19).

28. The Lord's supper is a meal in common, also known as *agape* ("love feast").

29. The natural meaning is that Paul is speaking of a revelation. Some prefer to understand the phrase "received from the Lord" as meaning "received from church tradition." My own view is that Paul means revelation, not about the practice, but about its meaning.

30. Some translate "betrayed," in the sense of "hand over" in the light of Mk. 14.18-45 and its parallels. That Jesus was "handed over" to the Romans seems to me historical. The Gospel theme of betrayal, nowhere else even hinted at in Paul, seems to me a bit of polemics arising considerably after the time of Paul.

31. The wine and the loaf came before the meal in the Jewish home at the Sabbath. That the Christian rite is directly borrowed from Judaism is less than certain, for it was found in Mithraism too. Also, here the sequence is bread first and then wine; in 10.16 the sequence is implicitly wine first and then bread, though there Paul is not necessarily concerned with sequence and hence the verse need not apply. In some manuscripts of Lk. 22.17-20, wine appears twice, both before and after the loaf.

32. The traditional English phrase is "speaking in tongues."

33. It is likely that the denial was not specifically of the resurrection of Jesus, but of resurrection itself. Physical resurrection, congenial to the Semitic, eastern world, would have been uncongenial to the Greek mind. In light of the Pythagorean-Platonic tradition in philosophy or of popular religion, the Greek mind could have concluded that this life is a delusion and misfortune, and hence escape from it ("salvation") urgent. Physical resurrection hence would restore one to the very situation he desired to escape.

34. If Paul has in mind proof-texts, he does not here supply them.

35. These resurrection appearances are not mentioned in the Gospels or in Acts of the Apostles. This is curious. Also, there seems to be a distinction between "the Twelve" and "all the apostles."

36. Paul describes himself as "one born prematurely." Clearly he is denigrating himself, as the sequel shows, but the intent in the figure of speech is elusive.

37. The term "spiritual body" involves a surface contradiction which

Paul is acutely aware of, for if the body is spiritual, then it lacks that characteristic which defines it as a body, namely, its physical aspect.

38. The word is used sarcastically.

39. That he speaks both of Hebrews and Israelites is peculiar. Perhaps he does so for the purpose of emphasis. Indeed, "descendant of Abraham" is a third statement of the same thing.

40. He means this ironically.

41. The beating would be a Roman punishment, the stoning Jewish. Compare Acts 11.22-23 and 14.19, respectively.

42. This is the Nabataean king, Aretas IV.

43. Is the thorn an illness? Or an opponent? One does not know.

44. In Paul's use of the veil, he transfers the wearing of it from Moses to the Israelites, that is, the Jews of his time.

45. Possibly Paul means here that he is no longer concerned, as once he had been, about the human career of Jesus, the substance of the canonical Gospels. If this is the case, it is a clue to the surprising absence from the preserved Epistles of the bulk of the Gospel traditions.

46. The idea appears to be that man, because of sinfulness, had become alienated from God. The death of the Christ, bringing atonement from sin, ended that alienation, thus becoming reconciliation.

47. Presumably Paul is writing to a church which he does not know and which does not know him. The greetings in 16.4-25 fit better a situation of mutual acquaintance. There are on records denials also that ch. 15 is an authentic part of the Epistle.

48. James Moffatt, *Introduction to the Literature of the New Testament*, 1911, p. 141.

49. It seems likely that Paul is here alluding to the "unwritten Law of nature"; see above, pp. 294-95.

50. He cites Isa. 52.5: "The name of God is blasphemed among the nations."

51. Paul seems almost to ascribe to sin a power that makes it a demonic force, equivalent to Satan.

52. Gen. 12.3.

53. It is likely that here Paul has in mind not just the Mosaic Law, but any legal system.

54. He cites Gen. 17.10: "I have made you the father of many nations."

55. Possibly he is here replying to an allegation by his opponents that he encourages sin.

56. The basic contention appears to arise from the implicit premise that man cannot *earn* God's favor. Then on what basis does this or that man receive it? The reply: God foreordains people for it.

57. He here quotes Isa. 10.22; 1.9; 28.16; and 8.14-15.

58. He cites Isa. 52.7; 53.1; Ps. 19.14; Deut. 32.21; and Isa. 65.1-2.

59. He quotes 1 Kgs. 19.10, 18.

60. He paraphrases Isa. 29.10 and Ps. 69.22-23.

61. Paul's basis is Num. 15.19-20, from the Septuagint version.

62. The figure of the olive tree as symbolic of Israel is found in Jer. 11.16-17.

63. He cites Isa. 59.20-21; 27.9.

64. This is an echo of 1 Cor. 12.4-31.

65. Deut. 32.35.

66. He quotes Prov. 25.21-22.

67. Lev. 19.18. A comparable summary of the Torah is ascribed to Hillel (see p. 233).

68. Possibly the church at Rome arose through the gathering there of those already believers; hence, in writing to the Romans, Paul would not be building on another man's foundation. Paul here quotes Isa. 52.15.

69. The Epistle to Philemon is of human, not doctrinal, interest. Onesimus, a slave, had run away from his master Philemon and in time put into the prison with Paul, and Paul had converted him. Paul had also converted Philemon. The Epistle is Paul's personal appeal that Philemon let Onesimus return without being punished—indeed, perhaps Philemon will free him.

CHAPTER 4

1. Elijah has the same role in Jewish legend; he is able to appear in a variety of guises. See Part II, ch. 7, note 27.

2. The Rabbinic view unhesitatingly subordinates Sabbath observance to medical urgency: "Critical danger supplants the Sabbath." If there is a difference, the Rabbis would have sanctioned only healings that could not be deferred; the attitude ascribed to Jesus would sanction Sabbath cures even if there was no emergency.

The sentence "the Son of Man is lord even of the Sabbath" describes the encompassing nature of the authority ascribed to Jesus. Scholars debate whether this sentence authentically goes back to Jesus or reflects the later Church.

3. That is, it is by the Holy Spirit that Jesus works the exorcisms. To call the Holy Spirit Satan is unforgivable blasphemy.

4. The passage has some confusions respecting defilement. Improper foods, though prohibited, were not deemed to produce ritual defilement.

5. If Jesus had abrogated food laws, why the controversies over food in Galatians? Or is the abrogation of food laws here an anachronism, ascribing to the time of Jesus a development after his time?

6. As the episode is written, Jesus is portrayed first as saying something narrow and parochial, but at her humble words he cures the child.

7. The chapter is in tone, but not entirely so in content, like the apocalypses found in many Pseudepigrapha.

8. Wine and bread (in that order) are used in the *kiddūsh* ("sanctification") ushering in the Sabbath or a festival. See Part IV, ch. 2, note 31. If the kiddush is here intended, the symbolic meanings are Christian, these unknown in any Jewish literature.

9. The custom is not known outside the Gospels.

10. Nothing is known about this insurrection.

11. The suggestion is offered that Mark underwent addition and in-

terpolation. The original version ascribed the events to within the Feast of Unleavened Bread. But Mark's community encountered from Jews in the vicinity an articulate denial that the events—an evening trial, a morning consultation, the turning of Jesus over to Pilate, and the crucifixion of Jesus could have taken place on a sacred day. By the addition of verses such as 14.1-2 Mark tries to meet the Jewish objection. Reasonably, he should also have altered 14.12.

Another Jewish objection, Pilate's ascertaining that Jesus is indeed dead, is hinted at in 15.44-45. Jews who denied the resurrection of Jesus appear to have asserted that Jesus had not truly died; Mark 15.44-45 replies by affirming the real death.

On the Christian "proof" of the resurrection through the emptiness of the tomb, and the Jewish counterallegation, see below, on Matt. 27.62-66 and 28.11-15, pp. 352-53.

12. See the following passages: 4.35-41, the opaqueness on what Jesus is; 6.52, the misunderstanding about the loaves miraculously multiplied; 7.17-19, the misunderstanding about defilement; 8.16-21, the misunderstanding about the bread; 8.31-33, the first prediction of the passion; 9.10-11, opaqueness about resurrection and Elijah; 9.14-29, the inability to cure an epileptic boy; 9.30-32, the second prediction of the passion; 9.33-34, the desire to be the greatest; 10.13-16, obstructing children; 14.26-31, the prediction that the disciples will abandon Jesus and Peter deny him; 14.32-42, the infidelity in Gethsemane; 14.50, the foresaking of Jesus and then flight, 14.53-72, Peter's triple denial of Jesus.

The expression "Son of Man," about which countless essays have been written, is derived from Dan. 7.13, where there is a cryptic term for Messiah. The phrase appears to be used in Mark as a title, as if to suggest the role of Jesus. Why this phrase rather than the title Christ? Perhaps it is enigmatic, and consistent with the motifs of opaqueness. See my "Son of Man' " in Mark, *Two Living Traditions*, pp. 166-77.

CHAPTER 5

1. See this motif respecting Jesus in Jn. 7.15.

2. See below, pp. 363-64, on the different birth narrative in Luke. John, like Mark, lacks a birth narrative.

3. Compare, for example, Mk. 9.30-32 with Mt. 17.22-23; Mk. 10.35 with Mt. 20.20.

4. The genealogy is arranged in three sections, each with fourteen names.

5. Some count the beatitudes, as seven, by omitting the fifth, combining the eighth and ninth, and viewing the tenth as extraneous.

6. Blessed is a usual translation in the Septuagint of Heb. *'ashré*, "happy," Ps. 1.1; 32.1; 112.1.

7. "In spirit" is sometimes regarded as an addition.

8. See Isa. 61.2. The Messiah in Judaism was viewed as a comforter.

9. "For righteousness" is regarded as an addition.

10. The heart was viewed as the seat of thinking.

11. What the intent is here is difficult to determine. No Rabbinic statement is at all similar.

12. Ps. 34.14; Chapters of the Fathers, 1.2.

13. Probably the sense of "sons" is "precious"; see Deut. 32.6.

14. This word was possibly added by a later scribe.

15. Scholars have been puzzled by the similarity of 5.10 and 5.11, and especially the words "on my account." Possibly 5.11 is a variant of 5.10.

16. Reward in heaven is a typically Jewish idea. The persecution of the prophets is found in Amos 7.10-17 and in several passages in Jeremiah. It is to be noted, though, that in Christian writings, the theme is altered and put into the form that "the Jews" persecuted the prophets, as if the prophets were not Jews, but Christians; see 1 Th. 2.14-15. The killing of the prophets, in Christian polemics, was regarded as the prelude to the killing of Jesus.

17. Such Roman persecutions were those, for example, under Nero, in 64.

18. The Rabbinic terms for forbid and permit are respectively the words bind and loosen (*āsar* and *nātar*, the latter found in "causative" forms such as *hitīr*, ("he permitted," or *mūtar*, "it is permitted"). "Loosen" here is not used in the Rabbinic sense, but rather in the sense of carelessness about or nullification of the commandments.

19. In Rabbinic thought the actual deed is decisive; for the Rabbis, while a good intention can be the equivalent of a good deed, an evil intention is not at all the equivalent of an evil deed.

20. On Jewish divorce, see pp. 195-96. The matter of divorce is repeated in Mt. 19.9.

21. There were different types of oaths, as set forth in the tractate Nedarim.

22. The Greek word translated "daily" is of uncertain meaning; various suggestions (such as "necessary" or "for the future") are ancient proposals. Some modern scholars think that the word has the nuance of "supernatural."

23. The idea seems to be that God may forgive unmet obligations to Him, as men can cancel debts owed them; see Mt. 18.23-35. In Rabbinic literature, the root meaning of "obligation" implies a sinful trespass, or the resultant guilt.

24. Literally, either "from evil" or "from the evil one." The clause, "For Yours is the kingdom and the power and the glory forever, Amen" is commonly regarded as an addition, and is not found in significant ancient manuscripts.

25. Direct parallels are found in Rabbinic writings (the Chapters of the Fathers, 1.6; 2.5; and Sotah 1.7).

26. The "golden rule" is found widely among many peoples. Its being joined to the "Law and the Prophets" is ascribed to Hillel, too (see p. 233). Hillel's formulation is negative, that is, "Do not do to others what is hateful to you." Partisans quarrel as to whether the one formulation is superior to the other; it is a futile quarrel!

27. The other endings are 11.1; 13.53; 19.1a; and 26.12. Here Matthew

inserts the first discourse at what in Mark is 1.20; after this lengthy material, Matthew reverts to Mark's material at Mk. 1.22.

CHAPTER 6

1. See, for example, his additions to the matter of putting new wine in old skins. The natural meaning is that the new wine is Christianity and the old skins Judaism. Luke rejects this contrast and seeks to divert one from this natural meaning by adding, "No one after drinking old wine wants new, old wine is good"; some manuscripts read, "old wine is better"!

2. He mentions, too, Herod Antipas of Galilee, Herod Philip of Ituraea and Trachonitis, and Lysanius of Abilene; he mentions Annas and Caiaphas as High Priests, presumably making simultaneous two High Priests, one of whom succeeded the other. Luke writes in the manner of a historian.

3. After 9.50, Luke for a long while abandons the order of events in Mark and Matthew. Luke 9.51-18.14 is spoken of as "Luke's special section."

4. Perhaps the intent is to align Jesus with all mankind, rather than with Jews alone.

5. In Jn. 8.57, the age is set forth as "not yet fifty."

6. In connection with a parable on repentance (13.1-9), Luke has two allusions, one to eighteen people who died when a tower of Siloam fell on them, and another to some "Galileans whose blood Pilate had mixed with their sacrifices." Nothing is more known about these allusions. In view of the part played by Pilate in the execution of Jesus, also a Galilean, further information about these Galileans would have been most welcome.

7. This passage is absent from some ancient manuscripts of Luke.

8. Luke alters what in Mk. 16.7 and Mt. 28.7 is the implication of a future appearance of the resurrected Jesus in Galilee into a recollection of the past, that *when still in Galilee*, Jesus had told his followers of his coming death and resurrection.

CHAPTER 7

1. Whether five or six times depends on whether or not in ch. 6 it is in place, or belongs before ch. 5.

2. On aspects of the issue of gnosticism, see my *Philo's Place in Judaism*,[2] Introduction. The matter is highly complex and not readily to be simplified.

3. See above, pp. 288-90.

4. This inferiority of John the Baptist is touched on recurrently: 1.15, 24-27; 4.1; 5.36; and 10.41.

5. *Pleroma*, "fullness," may have been a Gnostic term, but is scarcely used in such a sense here.

6. There seems to be an allusion here to Exod. 33.20, "No one can see My face and live"; the implication is the superiority of Jesus over Moses. Num. 12.8, that Moses sees the Deity, is ignored here.

7. This contradicts Mk. 9.11-13 and Mt. 11.14 which affirm that he was Elijah.

8. "Lamb" has many general biblical associations (e.g. Isa. 53.7-12), but in the Hebrew Bible not this sense of taking sins away.

9. Some take this as an allusion to the guile of Jacob (Gen. 27.35), and the mention of angels in verse 51 as a further allusion to him (Gen. 28.12).

10. Though Jesus is portrayed as speaking to Nathanael, he speaks to him in the plural, "you." The Gospel is speaking to more than just Nathanael.

11. A "miracle" is less than a sign. A sign not only suspends nature as does a miracle, but it also signifies something beyond the event itself.

12. See Mk. 14.24 and the parallels.

13. In 7.50, Nicodemus seems to be a member of the Sanhedrin.

14. In speaking to the Samaritan woman, Jesus is depicted as telling her, "Salvation is from the Jews." This is not entirely consistent with the main lines of the thought in this Gospel, which usually denies such Jewish priority. Some scholars view the passage as surviving from a source which the author has used.

15. An additional phrase, "and wished to kill him," is found in some manuscripts, but appears to be an interpolation.

16. In the so-called yōtzér ("Creator") prayer.

17. Jn. ch. 5 is allocated to Jerusalem; in 6.1 he goes across the Sea of Galilee. How did he get from Jerusalem to Galilee? Scholars have proposed that ch. 6 became dislocated, and should precede ch. 5.

18. Mk. 14.22-25; Mt. 26.26-29; Lk. 22.17-19.

19. This seems to be addressed to later generations, as if in warning.

20. Some manuscripts read "the Christ, the Son of God."

21. Here Judas is called "Judas son of Simon Iscariot"; in 14.22 and Mk. 3.19 Iscariot in Judas' name, not his father's.

22. Possibly ch. 7, as mentioned in note 17, should follow ch. 5, with ch. 6 to precede ch. 5.

23. John presumably has forgotten that the people are all Jews. Some interpreters escape from the awkwardness here by interpreting "the Jews" as Jewish leaders.

24. See Rom. 3.23. The view here is a usual Christian one, namely, an attack on the Law on the basis that Jews do not truly observe it, or do not observe it completely.

25. See also Mishna Shabbat 18.5-19.5.

26. On the water-libation on Sukkot, see Mishna Sukkot 4.9 and above, p. 215. In Jn. 7.37 a biblical verse is supposedly quoted, but no such precise verse is found; perhaps Isa. 55.1 is intended.

27. In Acts of the Apostles, the Spirit is given at or immediately after baptism.

28. The incoherencies reflect those present in the Gospel passage.

29. This is a curious question, unless it implies that God punishes men in advance of their birth!

30. See Mk. 8.22-26.

31. See Isa. 8.6.

32. An explanation repeatedly found alludes to the expulsion of Christians from the synagogue, this through the Twelfth of the Eighteen Benedictions. The supposed direct connection between that benediction and this passage is to be rejected. See pp. 149-50.

33. Scholars believe that there are dislocations in ch. 10, and that the correct order of verses should be: 1) verses 19-29; 2) verses 1-18; 3) verses 30-42.

34. The word "parable" is found in some translations of verse 6; "figure of speech" is a better translation.

35. This passage has had a long history of interpretation. Its meaning is not to suggest the equality or identity of Jesus and God, but rather their being joined together in supernatural work.

36. Verses 11.9-10 are enigmatic; the meaning given here is possible, but not certain.

37. Had Jesus been with Lazarus, presumably Lazarus would have recovered from his illness.

38. Thomas figures in three other places, 14.5; 20.24-29; 21.2.

39. Lk. 3.2; Ant. XVIII (2.2-4.3), 29-95. It is stated in Jn. 11.49 that Caiaphas is the High Priest "for that year." Pagan priests served only annually; Caiaphas was High Priest from A.D. 18 to 36.

40. One recalls Mk. 14.1, "two days before the Passover." See Part IV, ch. 4, note 11.

41. The Greek of 12.7 is rather unclear.

42. Probably Greek Gentiles, not Greek Jews.

43. See above, note 32.

44. The word appears as *praqlit* in Rabbinic texts, usually in the sense of an effective intercessor. In 1 Jn. 2.1, Jesus is called a "paraclete to the Father."

45. This is asked by a disciple named Judas, hitherto unnamed; he is not Judas Iscariot.

46. On this error, see above, note 39.

47. See, for example, 6.59.

48. This may be addressed against Gnostics, some of whom asserted they had inherited secret doctrines from Jesus.

49. See Part I, ch. 2, note 23.

50. See Avoda Zara 8b; Pal. Sanhedrin I.1 (18a) and VII.2 (24b) in support of the lack of the right.

51. Mk. 15.6; Mt. 27.15; and Lk. 23.17 (missing from some manuscripts of Luke) ascribe the custom not to the Jews, but to Pilate.

52. Mk. 15.32; Mt. 27.37; Lk. 23.38 have slightly different wordings; none of them mention Nazareth.

53. It is known in Christian tradition as the "seamless robe."

54. See Exod. 12.46; Num. 9.12, which prohibit the breaking of the bones of the paschal lamb. Respecting the passage here, the view has

been expressed that the breaking of bones prevented physical resurrection.

55. This is part of the recurring motif in John that some Jews were impeded from becoming Christians because of fear of "the Jews."

56. The word "Lord" appears here, surprisingly.

57. But see Mk. 8.31; 9.31; 10.32-34, in which Jesus speaks of this to the disciples.

58. See 10.1.

59. The word, in this unusual form, is Aramaic, not Hebrew.

60. Some translations read "touch." It has been suggested that a similar Greek word, meaning "fear" (see Mt. 28.10) is the right word, but there is no such reading in any manuscript.

61. These wounds are not mentioned in the Synoptic Gospels. Neither they nor John mention nails in the feet. Some scholars consider the matter of the nails unhistorical, and derived from Ps. 22.16.

62. See 6.1.

CHAPTER 8

1. The German original had the title, From Reimarus to Wrede. Samuel Hermann Reimarus was the eighteenth-century Deist mentioned above, p. 394. William Wrede was a scholar who, at the end of the nineteenth century, in a book, *The Messianic Secret*, contended that Jesus in his own lifetime never claimed to be the Messiah; this claim arose only after the belief in his resurrection arose among his disciples. (I consider Wrede wrong in almost every major contention.)

2. A most useful compilation of materials and a study of them is F. F. Bruce, *Jesus and Christian Origins Outside the New Testament*, Grand Rapids, 1974.

3. It is known from the Flavius part of the name of Josephus as the "Testimonium Flavianum."

4. A translation of the passage in Slavonic Josephus is in Bruce, *op. cit.*, pp. 43-44.

5. A talent was of great value, worth about 3,000 shekels!

6. Especially Robert Eisler, *Iesous Basileus Ou Basileusas*, 2 vols., Heidelberg, 1928-29, abridged and translated as *The Messiah Jesus and John the Baptist*, London, 1931.

7. The execution, if by Jews, would have been by stoning. The hanging would have been after death, to exhibit the body, in order to deter other from such offenses.

8. See JE, VII, pp. 170-73; Samuel Krauss, *Das Leben Jesu nach jüdischen Quellen*, Berlin, 1902; R. Travers Herford, *Christianity in Talmud and Midrash*, London, 1903. A brief but adequate summary is in Bruce, *op. cit.*, pp. 54-65.

9. The chief such pagan foe was the second-century Celsus. His attack, *The True Word*, has perished, but an eight-volume assault on him by Origen (about 185-254), *Against Celsus*, preserved large portions.

10. The words of the eighteenth-century Jacob Emden of Amsterdam, *Resen Mat'eh*, p. 156 (quoted in *JE*, IV, p. 57) are as follows: "Chris-

tianity has been given as part of the Jewish religion by the apostles to the Gentile world. . . . There are, accordingly, many Christians of high qualities and excellent morals. . . . Would that Christians would all live in conformity with their precepts. . . ."

11. These have been surveyed from time to time. The best known is Gosta Lindeskog, *Die Jesusfrage im neuzeitlichen Judentum*, Uppsala, 1938. See also my *We Jews and Jesus*, New York, 1973.

12. See *We Jews and Jesus*, pp. 107-12.

CHAPTER 9

1. Here, he falls, splits open, and dies; in Mt. 27.3-10, he hangs himself.

2. Scholars have noted that Luke alters ecstatic speech, glossolalia (1 Cor. 12.10, 31; 14.5-6) into the ability to speak alien languages.

3. See Deut. 21.22. Scriptural passages influence an occasional allusion to the cross as a tree (as also in Acts 10.39).

4. This is presumably Gamaliel I, son of Simeon and grandson of Hillel (see pp. 241-42).

5. The Theudas known from Josephus arose some years later. See Part II, ch. 7, note 34. Perhaps Luke has his history confused.

6. Possibly former slaves, or else former war prisoners, after military service as mercenaries.

7. Cyrene, Alexandria, Cilicia, and Asia Minor.

8. The speech speaks in 7.56 of the Law as delivered by angels, an echo of Gal. 3.19.

9. This is Paul, as is later explained in 13.9. Nothing in the Epistles suggests at all that Paul had the Hebrew name Saul.

10. Reminiscent of the death of Jesus in Lk. 23.34.

11. Luke has, as in this word, subtly marked off the new movement; he might have called it "the synagogue."

12. No explanation is given for this exception. Some infer that the violence was directed only to the Greek-speaking Jews in the movement. It is more likely that Luke is unwilling to disconnect the movement entirely from Jerusalem.

13. He is known in Christian lore as Simon Magus. Allusion in later literature (Justin Martyr, *Apology* I.26, and Irenaeus, *Against Heresies* I.23.1-2) suggest that he led his own movement as a messianic pretender. In later legend he becomes the arch-heretic and "anti-Christ."

14. The city, founded by Herod the Great, was Gentile, the headquarters of the Roman procurators.

15. See 1 Macc. 15.15 on this right of extradition.

16. It occurs five more times: 19.9, 23; 22.4; 24.14, 22.

17. In the first (9.7) the men with Paul hear the voice but see no one; in 22.9 they see the light but do not hear the voice; in 26.13-14 all see the great light, but only Paul hears a voice. In the first account, Paul receives no commission; in the second account, the commission is

not given here but only later, in a trance and vision in the Temple, 22.17-21; in the third account the commission is given right here on the road, 26.16-18.

18. There has been no previous mention of missionary activity here.

19. There is no parallel in Luke to Mk. 7.1-23 (see also Mt. 15.1-20), which declares that no food, going into a man, defiles him, and that all foods are clean. This passage in Acts defers the nullification of Jewish food laws to after the lifetime of Jesus.

20. This greatly exaggerates and distorts; Jewish prohibitions were against possible food violations, and not against other associations; a Gentile was allowed to visit in a Jewish home; see, for example, Gen. Rabba 11.2.

21. The previous passage, 10.13-15, however, dealt with animals as food, not with men.

22. This is also sound Rabbinic doctrine. See Moore, I, pp. 278-79.

23. See 11.12, where these are mentioned as numbering six.

24. Unlike the account in ch. 2, here the people engage in ecstatic speech.

25. He is mentioned again in 21.10.

26. Roman historians confirm famines—though not world-wide ones—in the reign of Claudius. Josephus, Ant. XX (5.2), 101, mentions one in A.D. 46 which was very severe.

27. See Gal. 2.10; 1 Cor. 16.1-3; 2 Cor. 8.1-15.

28. See Gen. 48.16; Dan. 10.20-21; 12.1.

29. See Ant. XIX (8.2), 343-50. The angel of Acts does not appear at the death of Agrippa in Josephus; there are additional differences.

30. This title is that of the governor of a senatorial province, higher in rank than a procurator.

31. Why is not told. Apparently there has been a difference or even a quarrel. In 15.38, Paul is unwilling for John to go on an impending missionary journey because John has here withdrawn.

32. The entire region is also known as Galatia. Students of Paul's journeys are divided on what part of Galatia the Epistles speak of. See ch. 2, note 12.

33. See 2 Cor. 11.25.

34. Phoenicia and Samaria are mentioned; but there has been as yet no mention in Acts of the founded of churches in Phoenicia.

35. This latter phrase is missing from some early manuscripts.

36. Some scholars see a connection between these stipulations and the "seven laws of Noah," Gen. 9.1-7, which the Rabbis view as incumbent on all men, Sanhedrin 56b and JE, "Noachian Laws," VII, 648-650. But no direct connection should be inferred.

37. See above, note 31.

38. The child of a Jewish mother is deemed automatically Jewish, no matter who the father is. This is not the case where the mother is Gentile, even if the father is Jewish.

39. The issue turns on the word "full."

40. As if to be tried by a court.

41. Two names are mentioned, a man, Dionysius the Areopagite (who figures in later legends) and a woman, Damaris.

42. The edict, reported by Suetonius, came because Jews had created disturbances *impulsore Chresto*, "Chrestus instigating." Is Chrestus "Christ"? Or was there a Jew actually named Chrestus in Rome?

43. This is not mentioned in Paul's Epistles.

44. As in 10.2, someone attracted to Judaism, but not a convert.

45. His full name is Lucius Junius Gallio, the older brother of the famous Seneca. The date is A.D. 51.

46. See 21.24. In Num. 6.5, a Nazirite for the period of a vow does not cut his hair.

47. See IB, IX, pp. 283-84.

48. It is said, 21.28, that Paul has brought Gentiles into the Temple, defiling it.

49. In War, II (13.5), 261-62, there is an account of an Egyptian false prophet. He brought 30,000 "dupes" from the Wilderness to the Mount of Olives. The governor Felix slew or captured many, but the Egyptian escaped. Luke, if he has used Josephus here, is quite inexact.

50. In 9.29-30, however, the "brothers" in Jerusalem send him away.

51. See, for example, IDB, III, "Paul, the Apostle," p. 684. See also Part II, ch. 11, note 17.

52. Such purchase of citizenship is known from Roman sources.

53. In the passage it is said that the Sadducees deny resurrection, the existence of angels, and the spirit. Unless angels means demons, this is scarcely accurate, for angels are frequent in Scripture, and the Sadducees were literalists; spirit is also frequent in Scripture.

54. Antonius Felix was procurator from 52 until about 58. Felix is ascribed a bad character in Tacitus, *Histories*, V. 9. See War, II (13.2), 252-53, and Ant. XX (8.6-7), 167-78.

55. Ant. XX (7.1-2), 141-44.

56. Ant. XX (8.9), 182.

57. Allusion is made (27.9) to the "fast," probably the Day of Atonement, which, coming in September or October, signals the beginning of the stormy period. The mention is another touch that implies Jewish fidelity.

58. No information is available as to how Christians came to be in Rome. Acts is silent on the matter.

59. See especially Walter Bauer, *Orthodoxy and Heresy in Earliest Christianity* (Eng. trans.), Philadelphia, 1970.

BIBLIOGRAPHY

The books selected for listing herein are restricted to those available in English. The data on books in other languages, or technical works, mentioned in the Notes are presented there. Here the main purpose is to furnish material for further reading. Utility is the goal; a complete bibliography would be several times as long as this book. Reprints, especially in paperback form, have so multiplied in recent years as to have negated the relevance of date and place of publication; usually it is the original hardback that is here listed. The Jewish Encyclopedia (1901-1906) is in many ways outdated, but the recent Encyclopedia Judaica (1971) is both so uneven in the quality of individual articles and in the audience envisaged that it is often distressing; hence, The Jewish Encyclopedia is not superseded. The Interpreter's Bible Dictionary (1962) is eminently useable and is now amplified by a Supplement (1976). The projected Duke University–Doubleday Pseudepigrapha project will make these texts available in the future, but until then the edition of R. H. Charles, Vol. 2, The Pseudepigrapha (1913), can be used, though it is quite outdated. The recurrent problem in Charles, as in some other scholarly literature, is the intrusion of a prepossession that the Jewish literature is viewed not in its own terms, as it should be, but as a preparation for Christianity, with the reading into the documents of meanings which ought not so enter in and judgments that are at times both untenable and condescending.

Still another bibliographical consideration is that of the level of certain books. Emil Schuerer, The History of the Jewish People in the Age of Jesus Christ, revised and edited by Geza Vermes and Fergus Millar, of which volume I appeared in 1973, and volume II likely in 1977, is a scholar's tool of the very highest order; it is, however, a reference book, not one for the commuter reader. Other works, quite likely beyond the perspectives of all but advanced students, have needed to be listed. Periodical literature is here deliberately limited. The Loeb Classical Library is most admirable for the Greek and Roman historians, as well as for Josephus and Philo.

The Oxford Annotated Bible, using the Revised Standard Version, or the Oxford Study Edition of the New English Bible, are useful for the Apocrypha. *The Oxford Bible Atlas* (second edition, 1974) is available in paperback. For commentaries on New Testament writings, *The Interpreter's Bible* (12 vols., 1952) should meet the usual needs; it contains understandable guidance for those seeking more technical information.

The Soncino editions of the Babylonian Talmud, plus the two volumes of minor tractates, and the Soncino Midrash are superb.

Certain parallels to the Gospels often cited from Jewish sources need to be assessed with caution and reservations; see my "Parallelomania," *Two Living Traditions*, 1972, pp. 291-304. That earliest Christianity was a Judaism means that much was common, but Christianity also had its individuality. Some apparently common motifs turn out to be significantly different in context.

PART I

Alon, Gedaliah. *History of the Jews in the Land of Israel in the Period of the Mishnah and the Talmud.* Hebrew, 1952.

Askowith, Dora. *The Toleration and Persecution of the Jews in the Roman Empire under Caesar and Augustus.* 1915.

Bentwich, Norman. *Josephus.* 1914.

Bickerman, Elias. *From Ezra to the Last of the Maccabees: Foundations of Post-Biblical Judaism.* 1962.

———. *The Maccabees.* 1947.

Dodd, Charles Harold. *The Bible and the Greeks.* 1935.

Farmer, William R. *Maccabees, Zealots, and Josephus: An Inquiry into Jewish Nationalism in the Greco-Roman Period.* 1956.

Foakes-Jackson, Frederick John. *Josephus and the Jews.* 1930.

Foerster, Werner. *From the Exile to Christ: A Historical Introduction to Palestinian Judaism.* 1962.

Goodenough, Erwin R. *Jewish Symbols in the Greco-Roman Period.* 3 vols., 1953-58.

Hengel, Martin. *Judaism and Hellenism.* Tr. John Bowden, 2 vols., 1974.

Jones, Arnold Hugh Martin. *The Herods of Judaea.* 1938.

Lieberman, Saul. *Greek in Jewish Palestine.* 1942.

———. *Hellenism in Jewish Palestine.* 1950.

Momigliano, Arnaldo. "Herod of Judea," pp. 316-39, *Cambridge Ancient History.* Vol. X, 1934.

Oesterley, Wm. O. E. *The Jews and Judaism During the Greek Period.* 1941.

Reicke, Bo. *The New Testament Era: The World of the Bible from 500 B.C. to A.D. 100.* Tr. D. E. Green, 1974.

Rost, Leonhard. *Judaism Outside the Hebrew Canon.* Tr. D. E. Green, Nashville, 1976.

Rostovtzeff, Mikhail Ivanovich. *A History of the Ancient World.* 2 vols., 1945.

———. *The Social and Economic History of the Hellenistic World.* 1941.

Rowley, Harold Henry. *The Relevance of Apocalyptic.* 1964.

Sandmel, Samuel. *Herod: Profile of a Tyrant.* 1967.

Tarn, W. W. *Hellenistic Civilization.*[3] 1961.

Tcherikover, Victor A. *Hellenistic Civilization and the Jews.* Tr. S. Applebaum, 1959.

Vermès, Géza. *The Dead Sea Scrolls in English.*[2] 1975.

Welch, Adam Cleghorn. *Post-Exilic Judaism.* 1935.

Yadin, Y. *Masada: Herod's Fortress and the Zealot's Last Stand.* Tr. M. Pearlman, 1966.

———. *Finds from the Bar-Kokhba Period in the Cave of Letters.* 1963.

Zeitlin, Solomon. *The Rise and Fall of the Judean State.* Vol. 1: 332-37 B.C.E., 1962. Vol. 2: 37 B.C.E.–66 C.E., 1967.

PART II

Bowker, John. *The Targums and Rabbinic Literature.* 1969.

Büchler, Adolf. *Studies in Sin and Atonement.* 1928.

Burkitt, Francis Crawford. *Jewish and Christian Apocalypses.* 1914.

Cohen, Abraham. *Everyman's Talmud*. 1975.

Corré, Alan (ed.). *Understanding the Talmud*. 1975.

Danby, Herbert. *The Mishnah*. 1950.

Epstein, Isidore (ed.). *The Babylonian Talmud*. 34 vols., 1935-1948.

Etheridge, John Wesley. *The Targums of Onkelos and Jonathan ben Uzziel on the Pentateuch*. 2 vols., 1862-65.

Freedman, H. and Maurice Simon (eds.). *The Soncino Midrash*. 10 vols., 1961.

Ginzberg, L. *The Legends of the Jews*. 6 vols., 1913-1928.

Guttmann, Alexander. *Rabbinic Judaism in the Making: The Halakhah from Ezra to Judah I*. 1970.

Herford, Robert Travers. *Talmud and Apocrypha*. 1933.

Kadushin, Max. *The Rabbinic Mind*. 1965.

Lauterbach, Jacob Zallel. *Midrash and Mishnah*. 1915.

Mann, Jacob. *The Bible as Read and Preached in the Old Synagogue*. Vol. 1, 1940.

Mantel, Hugo. *Studies in the History of the Sanhedrin*. 1961.

McNamara, Martin. *Targum and Testament*. 1972.

Mielziner, Moses. *Introduction to the Talmud*. 1925.

Montefiore, Claude Goldschmid and H. Loewe. *A Rabbinic Anthology*. 1938.

Moore, George Foot. *Judaism in the First Centuries of the Christian Era*. 3 vols., 1924.

Neusner, Jacob (ed.). *The Formation of the Babylonian Talmud*. 1970.

———. *From Politics to Piety*. 1973.

———. *A Life of Yohanan ben Zakkai*. 1970.

Schechter, Solomon. *Some Aspects of Rabbinic Theology*. 1909.

Strack, Hermann Leberecht. *Introduction to the Talmud and the Midrash*. English trans., 1945.

Thackeray, Henry St. John. *Josephus the Man and the Historian*. 1968.

Van Goudoever, J. Biblical Calendars.[2] 1961.

Vermès, Géza. *Scripture and Tradition in Judaism: Haggadic Studies*.[2] 1973.

PART III

Bell, Harold Idris. *Cults and Creeds in Graeco-Roman Egypt*. 1957.

Kennedy, Harry Angus Alexander. *Philo's Contribution to Religion.* 1919.

Nilsson, Martin Persson. *Greek Piety.* 1948.

Sandmel, Samuel. *Philo's Place in Judaism.*[2] 1971.

Sevenster, Jan Nicolaas. *The Roots of Pagan Anti-Semitism in the Ancient World.* 1975.

Wolfson, Harry Austyn. *Philo.* 1949.

PART IV

Brandon, Samuel George Frederick. *The Fall of Jerusalem and the Christian Church,* 1957.

————. *Jesus and the Zealots.* 1967.

Bultmann, Rudolf. *The History of the Synoptic Tradition.* 1963.

————. *Primitive Christianity in its Contemporary Setting.* 1956.

Cadbury, Henry Joel. *The Making of Luke-Acts.* 1927.

————. *The Peril of Modernizing Jesus.* 1962.

Daube, David. *The New Testament and Rabbinic Judaism.* 1956.

Davies, William David. *Paul and Rabbinic Judaism.* 1955.

Dodd, Charles Harold. *The Apostolic Preaching and Its Developments.* 1936.

Enslin, Morton Scott. *Christian Beginnings,* 1938.

Grant, Frederick Clifton. *Roman Hellenism and the New Testament.* 1962.

Hengel, Martin. *Was Jesus a Revolutionist?* 1971.

Jeremias, Joachim. *The Problem of the Historical Jesus.* 1964.

Jonas, Hans. *The Gnostic Religion: The Message of the Alien God and the Beginnings of Christianity.* 1963.

Klausner, Joseph. *From Jesus to Paul.* 1943.

————. *Jesus of Nazareth: His Life, Times, and Teaching.* Tr. H. Danby, 1949.

Kümmel, W. G., P. Feine, and J. Behm. *Introduction to the New Testament.* Tr. A. J. Mattel, 1966.

Marxsen, Willi. *Introduction to the New Testament.* Tr. G. Buswell, 1968.

Montefiore, Claude Goldschmid. *Judaism and St. Paul.* 1973.

————. *Rabbinic Literature and Gospel Teachings.* 1930.

Redlich, Edwin Basel. *Form Criticism.* 1939.

Sandmel, Samuel. *The Genius of Paul.*[2] 1970.

————. *We Jews and Jesus.*[3] 1973.

Schweitzer, Albert. *The Quest of the Historical Jesus.*[4] 1966.

Smith, Morton. *Tannaitic Parallels to the Gospels*. 1951.

Stendahl, Krister (ed.). *The Scrolls and the New Testament*. 1958.

Vermès, Géza. *Jesus the Jew*. 1973.

Walker, Thomas. *Jewish Views on Jesus*. 1931.

Whiteley, D. E. H. *The Theology of St. Paul*. 1966.

Wilson, Robert McLachlan. *Gnosis and the New Testament*. 1968.

Winter, Paul. *On the Trial of Jesus*. 1961.

APPENDIX I
THE BEST KNOWN
PSEUDEPIGRAPHA*

Apocalypse of Baruch
Ascension of Isaiah
Assumption of Moses
III Baruch
I Enoch
II Enoch (Slavonic)
Letter of Aristeas
Jubilees
Life of Adam and Eve
Lives of the Prophets
III Maccabees
IV Maccabees
Psalms of Solomon
Rest of the Words of Baruch
Rest of the Words of Jeremiah
Sibylline Oracles
Story of Asenath
Testament of Abraham
Testament of Job
Testaments of the Twelve Patriarchs

* For additional titles, see James H. Charlesworth, *The Pseudepigrapha and Modern Research*, 1976, pp. 17-25.

APPENDIX II

THE BABYLONIAN

TALMUD

ORDER I: ZERʿAIM* ("SEEDS")

1. Berachót ("Blessings")
2. Peʾáh ("[Ungleaned] Corner of a Field")
3. Demaí ("Doubtful status," whether or not tithe has been taken from produce)
4. Kiláyim ("Mixture of two"; See Lev. 19.19 and Deut. 32.9-11.
5. Shebiít ("Sabbatical year")
6. Terumót ("Heave offerings," from priests, Num. 18.8-20)
7. Maʿaserót ("Tithes," for Levites, Num. 18.21-24)
8. Maʿasēr Sheni ("Second Tithe," Deut. 14.22-26)
9. Hallá ("Dough," an offering for priests, Num. 15.18-21)
10. ʿOrlā ("Uncircumcision," yield of immature fruit trees, Lev. 19.23-25)
11. Bikkurím ("First fruits," Exod. 23.19 and Deut. 26.1-15)

ORDER II: MOʿED ("FESTIVALS")

1. Shabbát* ("Sabbath")
2. ʿErubīn* ("Coalescences" of Sabbath boundaries)
3. Pesaḥím* ("Passover festivals," Temple and home)
4. Shekalím ("Shekels," the tax for the support of the Temple)
5. Yomá* ("The Day" [of Atonement])
6. Sukkót* ("Booths"; also known as Sukkah, "booth")
7. Betzá* ("Egg"; also known as Yom Tob, "Feast Day")

488

8. Rōsh Hashanā* ("New Year")
9. Ta'anīt* ("Fasting")
10. Megillā* ("[Esther] Scroll")
11. Mo'ēd Katan ("Minor Feast Days," intermediate days within Sukkot and Pesah)
12. Ḥagigā* ("The Feasting," rules for the festivals)

ORDER III: NASHIM ("WOMEN")

1. Yebamōt* ("Levirate marriages," Deut. 25.5-10)
2. Ketubōt* ("Marriage contracts")
3. Nedarīm* ("Vows")
4. Nazīr* ("[The vow of] the Nazirite," Num. 6.1-21)
5. Gittīn* ("Documents" of divorce)
6. Sōtā* ("The women suspected of adultery," Num. 5.11-31)
7. Kiddushīn* ("Betrothal")

ORDER IV: NEZIKIN ("INJURIES")

1. Babā Kammā* ("First Gate," compensation for damages)
2. Babā Metziā* ("Middle Gate," sales and ownership)
3. Babā Batrā* ("Final Gate," sales and ownership of real estate)
4. Sanhedrīn* ("Lawcourt," judicial procedures and criminal law)
5. Makkōt* ("Punitive lashes," Deut. 25:1-3)
6. Shebu'ōt* ("[Rash] oaths," Lev. 5.4-13)
7. 'Eduyōt ("Testimonial statements")
8. 'Abōdā Zarā* ("Idolatry")
9. Abōt ("[The Chapters of] the Fathers")
10. Hōrayōt* ("Legal decisions" made in error)

ORDER V: KODASHIM ("SANCTITIES")

1. Zebahīn* ("Sacrifices" at the Temple)
2. Menahōt* ("Flour offerings")
3. Hullīn* ("non-ritual slaughter")
4. Bekorōt* ("First-born of men and animals")
5. 'Arakīn* ("Estimates," the values involved in dedications, Lev. 27.2-33)

6. Temurá* ("Exchange" of dedicated animals, Lev. 27.10,33)
7. Keritót* ("The punishments of excision")
8. Me'ilá* ("Trespass" of a dedicated object, Num. 5.6-8)
9. Tamíd* ("Continual offering," morning and evening sacrifices)
10. Middót ("Measures," on the dimensions in the Temple complex)
11. Kinním ("Nests," on the offering of doves, Lev. 1.14-17; 5.7-10)

ORDER VI: TOHOROT ("PURIFICATIONS")

1. Kēlím ("Utensils")
2. Oholót ("Tents")
3. Nega'ím ("Leprosies")
4. Pará ("[Red] heifer," Num. 14.1-10)
5. Tohorót ("Purities," but euphemistic for minor defilements. Note that the Order is also called Tohorot)
6. Mikva'ót ("Ritual baths," Lev. 14.8; 15.5-27)
7. Niddá* ("Menstruous woman")
8. Makshirín ("Predisposings," defilement through a liquid conductor)
9. Zabín ("Those with bodily discharges," Lev. 15.1-30)
10. Tebúl Yōm ("Immersed for a day," Lev. 15.5)
11. Yadáim ("Hands," defilement and purification)
12. 'Uktzín ("Stalks" of fruit trees as conveying defilement)

* An asterisk here means that the tractate has a Gemara.

TRACTATES ARRANGED ALPHABETICALLY

Roman numeral means the Order, Arabic the usual place in that Order.

Bikkurim	I, 11	Niddah	VI, 7
Demai	I, 3	Oholot	VI, 2
		Orla	I, 10
Eduyot	IV, 7		
Erubin	II, 2	Para	VI, 4
		Peah	I, 2
Gittin	III, 5	Pesahim	II, 3
Hagiga	II, 12	Rosh Hashana	II, 8
Halla	I, 9		
Horayot	IV, 10	Sanhedrin	IV, 4
Hullin	V, 3	Sotah	III, 6
		Sukka	II, 6
Kelim	VI, 1	Shabbat	II, 1
Keritot	V, 7	Shebiit	I, 5
Ketubot	III, 2	Shebuot	IV, 6
Kiddushin	III, 7	Shekalim	II, 4
Kinnim	V, 11		
		Tamid	V, 9
Maaserot	I, 7	Taanit	II, 9
Maaser Sheni	I, 8	Tebul Yom	VI, 10
Makkot	IV, 5	Temura	V, 6
Makshirin	VI, 8	Terumot	I, 6
Mashkin	II, 11	Tohorot	VI, 5
Megilla	II, 10		
Meila	V, 8	Uktzin	VI, 12
Menahot	V, 2		
Middot	V, 10	Yebamot	III, 1
Mikvaot	VI, 6	Yadaim	VI, 11
Moed Katan	II, 11	Yoma	II, 5
Nazir	III, 4		
Nedarim	III, 3	Zebahim	V, 1
Negaim	VI, 3	Zabin	VI, 9

INDEX